THE PERSIAN WAR

If you go to the Hot Gates take some historical knowledge
and your imagination with you.
William Golding, 1965

The interest of Grecian history is unexhausted and inexhaustible.
As a mere story, hardly any other portion of authentic
history can compete with it.
Its characters, its situations, the very march of its incidents, are epic.
It is an heroic poem, of which the personages are peoples.
It is also, of all histories of which we know so much,
the most abounding in consequences to us who now live.
The true ancestors of the European nations (it has been well said)
are not those from whose blood they are sprung,
but those from whom they derive the richest portion of
their inheritance.
John Stuart Mill, 1846

THE PERSIAN WAR

in Herodotus and Other Ancient Voices

WILLIAM SHEPHERD

OSPREY PUBLISHING
Bloomsbury Publishing Plc
PO Box 883, Oxford, OX1 9PL, UK
1385 Broadway, 5th Floor, New York, NY 10018, USA
E-mail: info@ospreypublishing.com
www.ospreypublishing.com

OSPREY is a trademark of Osprey Publishing Ltd

First published in Great Britain in 2019

ISBN: HB 978-1-4728-0863-9; eBook 978-1-4728-0865-3; ePDF 978-1-4728-0864-6;
XML 978-1-4728-2219-2

19 20 21 22 23   10 9 8 7 6 5 4 3 2 1

Maps by www.bounford.com
Index by Zoe Ross

Typeset by Deanta Global Publishing Services, Chennai, India
Printed and bound in Great Britain by CPI (Group) UK Ltd, Croydon CR0 4YY

Front cover: 5th-century sculpture in the Sparta Museum, sometimes identified as Leonidas.
Back cover and spine: Persian Daric coin. (Granger/Bridgeman Images)

Osprey Publishing supports the Woodland Trust, the UK's leading woodland conservation charity.

Editor's note: All dates are BC unless otherwise specified. All images, unless otherwise attributed, are from
the author's personal collection.

To find out more about our authors and books visit www.ospreypublishing.com. Here you will find
extracts, author interviews, details of forthcoming events and the option to sign up for our newsletter.

Contents

Maps

THE PERSIAN EMPIRE

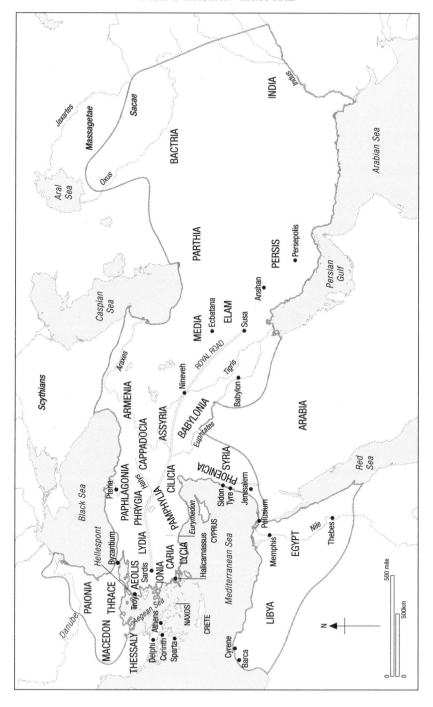

Greece, the Aegean and Western Asia

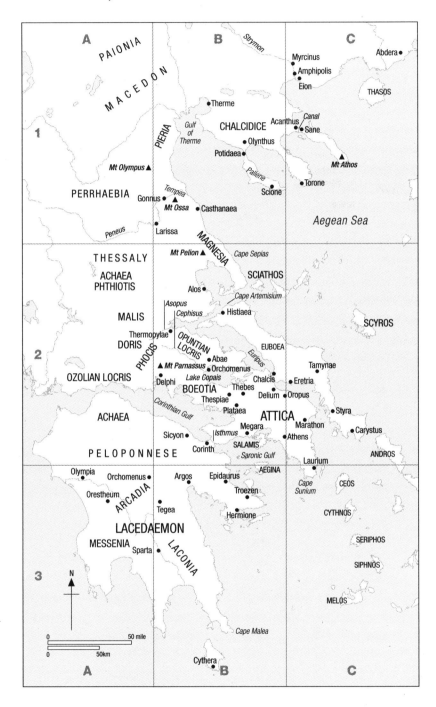

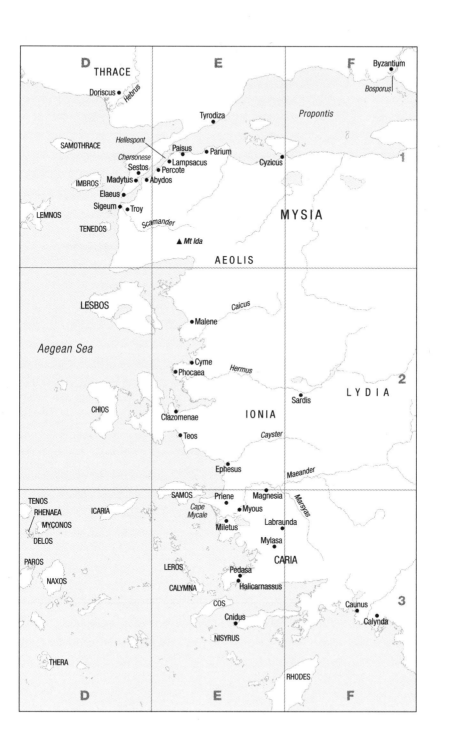

D THRACE **E** **F** Byzantium

Doriscus ● ●Hebrus

Bosporus

Tyrodiza ● *Propontis* **1**

SAMOTHRACE *Hellespont* Paisus ● ●Parium

Chersonese ●Lampsacus Cyzicus ●

Sestos ●Percote

IMBROS Madytus● ●Abydos

Elaeus ● **MYSIA**

Sigeum ● ●Troy

LEMNOS *Scamander*

TENEDOS ▲ *Mt Ida*

AEOLIS

LESBOS *Caicus*

●Malene

Aegean Sea

●Cyme

●Phocaea *Hermus*

●Sardis **LYDIA** **2**

CHIOS

Clazomenae● **IONIA**

●Teos *Cayster*

Ephesus● *Maeander*

TENOS SAMOS ●Priene ●Magnesia

RHENAEA ICARIA *Cape* ●Myous

MYCONOS *Mycale* ●Labraunda

DELOS Miletus● ●Mylasa

PAROS ●Mylasa

NAXOS **CARIA**

LEROS ●Pedasa

CALYMNA ●Halicarnassus

COS Caunus● **3**

Cnidus● Calynda●

NISYRUS

THERA

RHODES

D **E** **F**

GREECE, THE AEGEAN AND WESTERN ASIA
LIST OF LOCATIONS

Abae	2B	Chalcis	2B	LACEDAEMON	3A
Abdera	1C	CHERSONESE	1D	LACONIA	3B
Abydos	1D	CHIOS	2D	*Lake Copais*	2C
Acanthus	1C	Clazomenae	2E	Lampsacus	1E
ACHAEA	2A	Cnidus	3E	Larissa	1B
ACHAEA		Corinth	2B	Laurium	3C
PHTHIOTIS	2A	*Corinthian Gulf*	2B	LEMNOS	1D
Aegean Sea	2D	COS	3E	LEROS	3E
Aegina	3B	Cyme	2E	LESBOS	2D
AEOLIS	1E	Cythera	3B	LOCRIS,	
Alos	2B	CYTHNOS	3C	OPUNTIAN	2B
Amphipolis	1C	Cyzicus	1E	LOCRIS,	
ANDROS	2C	Delium	2B	OZOLIAN	2A
ARCADIA	3A	DELOS	3D	LYDIA	2F
Argos	3B	Delphi	2B	MACEDON	1A
Cape		DORIS	2A	Madytus	1D
Artemisium	2B	Doriscus	1D	MAGNESIA	2B
Athens	2B	Eion	1C	Magnesia	3E
ATTICA	2B	Elaeus	1D	Malene	2E
BOEOTIA	2B	Ephesus	2E	MALIS	2A
Bosporus	1F	Epidaurus	3B	Marathon	2C
Byzantium	1F	Eretria	2C	Megara	2B
CALYMNA	3E	EUBOEA	2B	MELOS	3C
Calynda	3F	*Euripus*	2B	MESSENIA	3A
Canal	1C	Gonnus	1B	Miletus	3E
Cape Malea	3B	*Gulf of Therme*	1B	*Mount Athos*	1C
Cape Mycale	3E	Halicarnassus	3E	*Mount Ida*	1E
Cape Sepias	2B	*Hellespont*	1E	*Mount Olympus*	1A
Cape Sunium	3C	Hermione	2C	*Mount Ossa*	1B
CARIA	3E	Histiaea	2B	*Mount*	
Carystus	2C	ICARIA	3D	*Parnassus*	2B
Casthanaea	1B	IMBROS	1D	*Mount Pelion*	2B
Caunus	3F	IONIA	2E	MYCONOS	3D
CEOS	3C	*Isthmus*	2B	Mylasa	3E
CHALCIDICE	1B	Labraunda	3E	Myous	3E

CARTHAGE, SICILY AND SOUTHERN ITALY

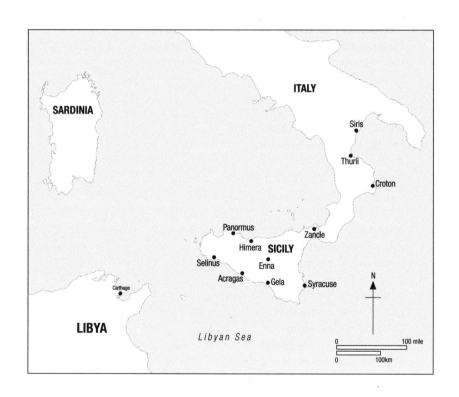

List of Illustrations

Preface

The Persian War is the name generally given to the first two decades of the period of conflict between the Greeks and the Persians that began in 499 BC and ended around 450. However, in 480 and 479, a massive Persian invasion force was defeated and driven out of mainland Greece and Europe, never to return.

> When they had gathered together all the spoils, the Greeks put one tenth aside for dedication to the god at Delphi. With this they set up the golden tripod resting on a bronze triple-headed serpent that is to be found very close to the altar. (*Historia* 9.81[1])

This 'Serpent Column' was 7m or 8m tall and crowned with a golden dish for sacrificial offerings to Apollo, its dedicatee. On its shaft were engraved the names of 31 city-states (*poleis*, singular *polis*) or peoples that had fought the Persians, one of the very few contemporary inscriptions to have survived as evidence of the war. The golden dish survived until only half-way through the following century, but, in the 4th century AD, Constantine the Great, Roman Emperor of the West and East, brought the column to Byzantium, the crossing point between Europe and Asia. The serpents (actually three of them, not one with three heads) were decapitated, allegedly by a drunken Mameluk soldier during the Ottoman era, but the twisted column still stands in the Hippodrome of Constantine, now Istanbul's Sultanahmet Square. Beyond, reliefs at

---

[1] From now on, references are assumed to be from Herodotus' *Historia* unless otherwise stated.

the base of a commemorative column show Theodosius I in his pomp as Emperor of the East in the late 4th century. The great basilica of Agia Sophia with its four minarets behind, and the Sultanahmet 'Blue' Mosque is close by. These are massive symbols of the glories of Greece, Rome, Christianity and Islam.

'Alternate history' is often little more than an entertaining game, but here the what-if questions are profound. If the Persian War had been lost in 479, would there have been the same golden flowering of Athenian culture and institutions in the decades that followed? If Greece had become part of a Persian empire with southern Italy now on its frontier, would Rome (which had turned republican at about the same time as the Athenians were taking their first steps towards democracy) have been allowed to grow into the world power that Constantine ruled? If not, what of Christianity? Without the bloodstream of the Roman Empire's communications network to sustain its growth, Christianity might never have spread to become a world religion and the catalyst that brought another, Islam, into being. A Persian victory would have changed much more than the scenery at the centre of the site of ancient Byzantium. It could have profoundly redirected the subsequent evolution of the cultural, intellectual, political and religious landscapes of Europe and the Middle East.

The many modern accounts of the Persian War generally include numerous references to what the ancient authors wrote about it, but directly quote from them only a little. Herodotus is by far the most substantial and important source to have survived and this book is built around his entire narrative of the conflict with extracts interwoven from the other ancient sources. It brings together translations of the original texts that tell us almost all that can be known about this immense clash of arms and the events that led up to it.

These ancient voices speak for themselves and powerfully communicate the intensity and epic drama of 'the great and marvellous deeds' that culminated gloriously in Greek victory on land and sea. But they do raise questions in the minds of 21st-century readers who come to the text with knowledge and expectations very different from those brought to it by the writers' contemporary audiences, who would mostly have been unconcerned by issues of omission, incompleteness, vagueness, bias or exaggeration that may exercise us now.

I address such issues as these as they arise in my commentary on the ancient texts and make the case where necessary for my preferred interpretations. Any interpretation or amplification must take the written evidence that is gathered together in this book as its baseline; there is little else.

The translations are my own, and translation and interpretation go hand in hand. My aim has been to produce versions that are readable and also linguistically accurate (which all translations, as opposed to adaptations, need to be) with a consistent focus on the military-historical content and the language in which it is presented. At the same time, I hope I have succeeded in conveying something of the character and style of the more extensively quoted authors. They have a glorious story to tell and retell, and the process of mining their texts for military history should not be allowed to prevent us from enjoying them at this level.

The successful defence of Greece by a few city-states against the vast Persian Empire was an extraordinary military feat and it is the earliest war about which enough is known to attract the serious attention of military historians. However, the historical study of armed conflict is a relatively modern discipline, mostly concerned with much more recent times. At an overarching level, it addresses the causes, effects and consequences of war, and its political, social, economic and cultural impact; closer focus is brought to bear on topics such as strategy, tactics, logistics, technology, and leadership and other human factors; at the discipline's most granular level, the subject matter embraces the specifics of campaigns, battles and battlefields, weapons and other equipment, and the study of individual combatants' roles. However, for a researcher at any of these levels, the evidence that has survived from the ancient past is sparse. To quote Philip Sabin, Professor of Strategic Studies at King's College, London:

> Hence, whereas the mass of secondary writing on more recent conflicts like the Second World War is based on an even larger mass of primary material such as archives and personal accounts, the situation for ancient military historians is exactly the reverse – an inverted pyramid in which modern knowledge teeters unsteadily above a narrow and unsatisfactory evidentiary base. (*Lost Battles* p.xi)

The Persian War has its own and constantly growing 'mass of secondary writing' and, in my own efforts to contribute to this, I have become quite familiar with the queasiness this top-heavy teetering can cause. The only antidote is to return regularly to the body of textual evidence on which the point of that pyramid rests, valuing the solid information contained in it, but accepting and attempting to negotiate its limitations. All modern accounts of the Persian War refer to, summarize and paraphrase this body of material but quote from it only selectively, and it is often not clear at what point and how far the author is travelling beyond the ancient texts, as is necessary, to create a more rounded and coherent narrative. This book offers a narrative of the Persian War that has at its heart the most significant writing on the subject to be found in the ancient sources.

The foremost of these is Herodotus. But this is not to say that other ancient voices are less worth listening to, although nearly all of them were first heard decades or centuries later. Their differing versions of events may be reconstructions based on shared evidence or tap into other strands of a broader tradition, or they may be partly or wholly speculative and formed by the writer's particular agenda or literary purpose. But most deserve to be taken as seriously as modern-day reconstructions and to be valued over them for the authenticity that is rooted in experience of a world much closer to Herodotus' than our own. The extracts included from other ancient writers add value to Herodotus' narrative in various ways: some offer fresh analysis and credible extra detail; some contradict him interestingly; some provide background illumination, sometimes in accounts of different wars; and some add drama and colour, probably imagined in most cases, but seen through the lens of the writer's own experience, knowledge and beliefs.

For the rest of the evidentiary base, archaeology has turned up very few finds on the battlefields themselves, and the physical landscapes are known to have changed significantly over the millennia. Even if Herodotus had been much more systematic and precise in his identification of landmarks and measurement of distances, it would not be possible to pinpoint the armies' positions and plot their movements with any greater degree of certainty. Doing the same for the opposing fleets on the waters off Artemisium and Salamis is an even more speculative process. There are the same problems of vagueness with Herodotus' timing and dating of events as with his topography. But these would not, of course, generally have been regarded as problems in a world in which the necessary disciplines, techniques and instruments did not exist.

Herodotus provides the central narrative strand of this book and takes centre stage. Other ancient writers appear in supporting roles and are introduced when they make their first entrance. In linking sections I offer comment and interpretation and background information where I feel it is needed, in full awareness that, in this process of speculative reconstruction, Professor Sabin's 'inverted pyramid' can quite legitimately be built up in a range of differing architectures. But my main purpose is to present the story of the Persian War as it was told by Herodotus and in other ancient voices, the textual base upon which that pyramid must rest, however constructed. This is indeed 'narrow and unsatisfactory' by the standards of modern military history. Nonetheless, it is possible to pick out many of the main building blocks from Herodotus and discern their positions in the structure, and to draw on other evidence to reinforce it in some places, and to add plausible detail in others where it is lacking.

Text references are given in the normal fashion so that passages can easily be found in other versions or the original language. I use footnotes to offer short answers to questions as they arise such as: who was Cynegirus son of Thrasyleus, where was Croton, what distance was a *stade* ... ? I also use them to comment briefly on points of narrative or linguistic detail where I think they are worth highlighting or clarifying. Spellings of Greek and Persian names are generally in their more comfortable latinized forms as found in *The Oxford Classical Dictionary*.

'The fighting went on a long time' is an elastic stock phrase that recurs several times in Herodotus' battle descriptions. In the case of this book, the writing certainly went on a long time and I am very grateful to Marcus Cowper and other friends and former colleagues at Osprey Publishing for their patience and support. I owe special thanks to Paul Cartledge and Jeremy Mynott for generously agreeing to be distracted periodically from their own writing projects to give me so much invaluable advice on the manuscript at various stages in its long gestation; my thanks too to Hans van Wees for the help he gave me in my earlier work on the battle of Plataea, for his insights on 'the hoplite question', and for sharing with me his most recent work on Thermopylae ahead of publication; and to my son, Henry, for shrewd comments and sustained encouragement.

Finally, I dedicate this book with love to Netta, my wife, my children and my grandchildren.

Introduction

As our foremost and actually most reliable source for the Persian War, Herodotus clearly recognized the significance of the conflict. His great work begins:

> Herodotus of Halicarnassus presents this *Historia* to ensure that the events of mankind should not fade in memory over time and that the great and marvellous deeds performed by Hellenes and Barbarians alike should not go unsung, and, additionally, to explain the cause of the war that they fought against each other. (1.1)

Historia is most accurately translated as 'enquiry', 'research' or 'investigation', not as 'history', the word's later evolution. It was a word used for the activities and writings of the thinkers known as the Presocratics who flourished in the 6th and 5th centuries in the Greek cities on the west coast of Asia. In the words of one of them, Heraclitus of Ephesus, they were 'enquirers into many things', which included the nature of the world and its origins, and the causes of natural phenomena. They created the intellectual climate in which Herodotus grew up and his declared mission to explain the cause of the Persian War is characteristic of it. In this and in his chronicling of 'events ... and great and marvellous deeds', Herodotus' main purpose is clearly historical, as the term is understood today, setting him apart from the *philosophoi*, 'lovers of wisdom', of his time and earlier generations, but, in common with them, he also recognizably explored fields such as geography, geology, ethnography and anthropology. Herodotus stood between the archaic oral tradition as faithfully preserved by Homer, and the classical, more recognizably 'modern' history-writing of Thucydides (*c*.460–400) and later Greek and Roman writers.

The phrase 'great and marvellous deeds' also evokes the spirit and content of epic narrative, the way previous generations did history, and Herodotus was an expert collector and teller of tales. He was as interested in the mythical and legendary past as in more recent times and living memory, and always looking for causal relationships between the former and the latter. He sees himself, like Homer, singing of heroic deeds and of the men who performed them, but in prose. The same intellectual movement that gave birth to the Presocratics had brought Greek prose writing into being. A succession of *logopoioi*, 'makers of accounts', some of them contemporaries of Herodotus, specialized in creating genealogies and chronologies of important events reaching back from recent times to the ancient pasts of gods and heroes as if they were seamlessly linked. The fragmentary evidence suggests that most of their creations were little more than lists of names and dates or locations, chronologies or itineraries with no literary pretensions. Herodotus most probably made use of some of them but there is no hint of acknowledgement in his text of any such source apart from one reference to the works of Hecataeus (6.137), thought to be the most significant of his prose-writing predecessors. There were almost certainly no written historical narratives in any way comparable to his own to refer to.

In Herodotus' precise words the great war was between '*Hellenes* and *Barbarians*'. The names 'Greece' and the 'Greeks' (Latin *Graecia* and *Graeci*) as we understand them, were coined by the conquering Romans, imposing on Hellas and the Hellenes the name of an obscure ethnic group they encountered in the north-west corner of mainland Greece. In this book, 'Greece' is used only to mean the mainland landmass and 'Greek' to mean the language. Hellenes occupied not only mainland Greece, but also many settlements spread out to the north, south, east and west of it. These 1,000 or so independent city-states that called themselves Hellene had a distinct view of themselves that differentiated them from the rest of their world. Herodotus expresses this concisely in his version of a speech in which the Athenians declare their unshakeable commitment to the Hellene Alliance and the idea of Hellas:

Then, there are the things that make us Hellenes, our shared origins and our language, the shrines of our gods and the sacrificial rites that we have in common, and our very way of life. It would be a terrible thing for Athens to betray all of that. (8.144)

It is worth noting that no claim is made here to a common political system: democracy was not a necessary qualification; at that time most Hellene city-states were not democracies. The four great religious centres of Delphi, Olympia, the Isthmus and Nemea with their regular *panhellenic* (all-Hellene) athletic festivals provided the only consistent focus for universal Hellene unity. But wars between Hellenes, suspended for the celebration of these festivals, were often resumed afterwards, and historic or mythological differences between communities or regions were frequently manipulated to justify Hellene-on-Hellene aggression. Armed conflict between 'blood relations' was a significant facet of the Hellene way of life, together with their special way of war, which was profoundly different from that of the Barbarians.

In the era of Classical Greece, 'Barbarian' (*barbaros*) did not generally carry the sense of 'barbaric', 'uncivilized' or 'wild'. The term was simply applied to any non-Hellene, including the Persians and the other races that belonged to their empire and did not speak Greek. The war was between an alliance of Hellenes and the Barbarian Achaemenid Empire, named after the dynasty of Persian kings that established it and ruled over it. Much of the first half of the *Historia* is devoted to the history of Persia and the only other known contemporary source on the subject was the *Persica*, written by Ctesias of Cnidus, a Hellene physician in the Persian court, and, judged on surviving fragments, he was an ill-informed lightweight. There are no comparable Persian historical sources so the narrative that has come down through the centuries is inevitably written from a Hellene perspective. However, the image Herodotus builds of Hellas' greatest enemy is far from negative. He tells us that the Persians valued a man most highly for his courage in battle and, next, for the number of sons he fathered, and that 'from the age of five to the age of 20 they teach their sons just three things: to ride, to shoot with the bow and to tell the truth' (1.136). They loved and were known to venerate trees, gardens and rivers. The immense luxury which the Hellenes saw as softness and excess was enjoyed by only a very small, privileged elite. By the standards of the time, the Persians were generally just and tolerant as imperial rulers, even liberal, so long as the absolute power of the Great King, exercised directly or through his representatives, was unequivocally accepted.

Their religion was more highly developed than the Hellenes' and Herodotus hints at the contrast:

> These are the Persian customs I know of: it is not their custom to create and dedicate statues, temples or altars and they actually take the view that it is folly to do so. It seems to me that they do not think, as the Hellenes do, of their gods as taking human form. Their way is to climb to the peaks of mountains and perform sacrifices to Zeus and they call the whole circle of heaven Zeus.[1] But they also sacrifice to sun, moon, earth, fire, water and wind. (1.131)

The influence of the faith named after its prophet Zarathustra (Zoroaster in Greek) has been traced in the development of other religions of the Near and Middle East, such as Judaism, and in the philosophical movements that were important precursors of Socrates, Plato and Aristotle. The basis of Zoroastrianism was belief in one supreme god, Ahura Mazda, standing for goodness and truth and opposed to a supreme evil being, Ahriman. A good person was one who had freely made the choice to follow the former rather than the latter and lived a life of goodness and truth.

Herodotus' course through the first four of his work's nine books is quite sinuous as he charts the rise of Persia and the Great Kings, and makes fascinating excursions into lands on the fringes of their fast-growing empire, notably Egypt and Scythia. All this is informative and entertaining, and clearly important to Herodotus as a backdrop to the main narrative of the war, but not part of it. Nonetheless, the first mention of contact between Hellenes and Barbarians comes early in Book 1, and a sequence of episodes spread across the next three books records the Barbarian subjection of the Hellenes of Asia and leads up to their revolt against Persian rule in 499. Along the way Herodotus offers many valuable insights into the most significant differences between Barbarians and Hellenes, their ways of life and worldviews and their ways of fighting wars. The six years of the 'Ionian Revolt' take up much of Book 5 and the opening chapters of Book 6, which climaxes with the Marathon campaign. Book 7 covers the ten

---

[1] Herodotus equates their principal deity Ahura Mazda with Zeus, the god who headed the Hellene pantheon.

years between Marathon and Xerxes' invasion of Greece and concludes with the battle of Thermopylae, Hellas' Maginot Line moment. Book 8 opens with the sea-battle of Artemisium, actually the other half of the Hellene strategy for the defence of central Greece and fought at the same time as Thermopylae, but it is mostly devoted to Salamis. Book 9 covers the final Hellene victories at Plataea and, on Asian soil, at Mycale.

Hans Delbrück, the 19th-century pioneer of military history, wrote, somewhat patronisingly, that 'certain portions of Herodotus' account correspond so closely, it is true, to the nature of the matter (Salamis), that we can well accept them.' Arnold Gomme (1886–1959), Professor of Ancient Greek at Glasgow University, protested that 'everyone knows that Herodotus' narrative of Marathon will not do'. John Lazenby, Professor of Ancient History at the University of Newcastle upon Tyne, responds to Delbrück, Gomme and all-comers:

> This implies that the truth is somehow recoverable without reference to Herodotus, and that we can then compare his account with it. But even though this is impossible, it is of some comfort that Herodotus is as good a source as he is. He was evidently so nearly contemporary with the Persian invasion of Greece that he was able to talk to people who had taken part; he evidently checked their stories against what little other evidence existed, his own observations and each other; and he was evidently a man of wide knowledge, broad sympathies, sound common sense and considerable humour. (*The Defence of Greece* p.13)

A large part of 'the nature of the matter' is authoritatively laid out for us by Herodotus. He was probably born between 490 and 480 in the decade that separated the battles of Marathon and Salamis. The Carian city of Halicarnassus (modern Bodrum) was on the west coast of Asia and the western fringe of the Persian Empire. Little is known about Herodotus' life but there is reasonable consensus about the bare bones of it. He was involved in his city's politics, ending up on the wrong side and being driven into exile on two occasions. His first period of exile was spent on the nearby island of Samos. In the second period from the mid 450s and for the rest of his life, he travelled widely, ranging across the Hellene world and also visiting parts of the Persian Empire. He spent time in Athens and seems to have been well connected there. In the late 440s he became a founder-citizen of Thurii, a Hellene settlement on the southern shore of Italy, and he died there early in the 420s.

Herodotus' investigative method was to travel widely and seek first-hand recollections by talking to veterans who had been involved in the war as young adults and also to the children or grandchildren or other family connections of older participants. This brought him closer to the events he was setting out to record than any other surviving source except for the tragic playwright Aeschylus. But there were limitations to the scope of the information he could gather. First, there is the inevitable unreliability of eyewitness accounts of battle. Thucydides, who, unlike Herodotus, had experienced combat at first hand, was certainly aware of this, as is clear from his description of a battle fought at night by the doomed Athenians in Sicily in 413:

> The Athenians became so disordered and confused that it was difficult to find out exactly what happened. By day, those involved can certainly see things more clearly, but this is far from the full picture and they scarcely know what is going on right alongside them. At night, how could anyone know anything for sure? (*History of the Peloponnesian War* 7.44)

Secondly, none of the senior Hellene commanders who survived the war would have been alive by the time Herodotus began his research. Pausanias, in his early 20s when commander-in-chief of Hellene land forces in 479, could have been the exception, but he came to his sad, bad end as an enemy of the Spartan people in 470 or a little later. So most of Herodotus' informants would inevitably have presented much narrower views of events experienced at a less senior level, seen from a local or family perspective, and often coloured by contemporary inter-state rivalry, especially the growing inevitability of collision between Athens and Sparta. Herodotus was clearly aware of the limitations he had to accommodate and is open about the way he handles them in these two general statements:

> My principle throughout this work (*logos*) is that I write down what everyone tells me just as I hear it ... As for me, I have an obligation

to pass on what I am told, but I am under absolutely no obligation
to believe it all, and this statement applies to my whole work.
(2.123, 7.152)

When he has collected differing accounts of events and feels unable
to decide which of them is true, he presents the conflicting versions
alongside each other, sometimes offering an opinion, sometimes
indicating doubt more subtly, and sometimes leaving it to his audience
to make up their own mind or accept that the issue cannot be resolved.
There is often a sense that Herodotus attached as much value to what
people believed and said as to what actually happened, even if the
reality was known or strongly suspected to differ from their report.
This blurring of what perhaps was not yet seen as a cut and dried
distinction can be understood in the context of a society in which
spoken word was still the predominant mode of communication.
Literature of all kinds was written down and published in a limited
fashion, but probably only a minority of the male population was
sufficiently literate to read it (illiteracy is thought to have been even
more widespread amongst females) and manuscripts could be produced
only laboriously and in small quantities. Plays and poetry reached a
significantly wider audience in performance and recitation, often before
a paying public and in competitions. Works like Herodotus' *Historia*
and the philosophical and scientific writings of the Presocratics were
disseminated in the same way and the authors could make a living from
it. Two 3rd-century sources mention that Herodotus was rewarded by
the Athenian Council 'for reading his books to them' and the second
states that the gift was worth ten talents. One talent of silver would
pay one day's wage for approximately 6,000 skilled craftsmen, so the
amount is somewhat implausible, but the anecdote gives a sense of
Herodotus' standing in Athens.

Herodotus' narrative was written primarily for oral delivery, and
for entertainment as much as for education. His analyses of political,
strategic and tactical issues are usually to be found in the form of
speeches put into the mouths of major characters at key moments in
his narrative. The exposition of abstract concepts in non-narrative text
was then in its infancy (when Plato was not yet born) but Herodotus'
contemporary audiences were accustomed to the communication of
complex issues and arguments through the medium of speeches and

dialogues in epic poems, in comic and tragic drama, in political and legal rhetoric, and in the presentation of scientific and philosophical theories. The speeches in the *Historia* may be complete inventions or based on only the finest wisp of handed-down memory, but the issues and arguments are often relevant and credible and show deep insight.

The 6th- or 7th-century AD Greek writer Marcellinus tells a nice story of an encounter between the two greatest historians of ancient Greece:

> Thucydides was in the audience when Herodotus was giving a public reading of his *Historia* and burst into tears as he listened to it. We are told that Herodotus noticed this and remarked to Thucydides' father, 'Olorus, your son has a natural disposition for learning'. (*Life of Thucydides* 54)

Marcellinus is not regarded as a serious historical source but the anecdote may be a true echo of his subject's admiration for and undoubted indebtedness to Herodotus, and it may reflect his ambition to surpass him. Thucydides was, indeed, superior both in his historical judgement and in his narrative and analytical writing technique; he was more focused and, for him, information took precedence over entertainment. Approximately 25 years younger, he bracketed his predecessors with 'poets who embellish the past in their chanting' and 'those prose chroniclers (*logographoi*, 'writers of accounts') who compose with more concern for attracting an audience than for truth'. He could not have thought of Herodotus as in the former category, but he may have been unjustly dismissing him as a mercenary 'chronicler'. He does anyway pay him the compliment of beginning his own history at precisely the point Herodotus brings his to an end.

Later generations, even up to the present, have been dismissive of Herodotus for, in their perception, his naivety, his lack of political, strategic and tactical understanding, his bias, his gossipy discursiveness and his uncritical delight in tall tales. These flaws are eminently forgivable in the intellectual and literary context of the middle decades of the 5th century BC, and when fair consideration is given to the quality of so much of the evidence he collected. Inevitably the different identifiable strands of this colossal work, created in a period when genres and academic disciplines were not formally distinguished, are often blurred and entangled. But as source material they are substantial and rich, meriting the writer's admiration as 'the father of history' by Cicero, and certainly much more reliable than implied in his dismissal by Plutarch as 'the father of lies'. As a historian, Thucydides stood on Herodotus' shoulders. Herodotus had no comparable support.

Unfortunately, in his accounts of 'the great and marvellous deeds performed by Hellenes and Barbarians', Herodotus does not supply a great deal of the 'granular' detail needed for a reconstruction of the campaigns and battles that would satisfy a modern military historian. This is largely due to the limitations of the information available to him. A further consideration is that his purpose was as much to celebrate and commemorate as to reconstruct. Moreover, he was addressing audiences in which the great majority had served in an army or fleet, and often done both; they knew far better than he did what it was like to fight as a hoplite on land, or to experience action at sea in a trireme, the oar-driven capital ship that projected Hellene and Barbarian sea-power in the Aegean and Mediterranean. There is no evidence that Herodotus had done either, but he could comfortably rely on his listeners or readers to supply their own detail, probably fully aware of the combat tunnel-vision identified by Thucydides. As for precise questions of topography, manoeuvre and chronology, there were no maps, no instruments for measuring direction or distance, and no clocks. That order of information would not have been available because it never existed. In a paper, first presented in 1920 but still essential reading, *On the Possibility of Reconstructing Marathon and Other Ancient Battles*, Noah Whatley writes:

> I am afraid that the more I study the subject the more sceptical I become about the possibility of reconstructing the details of these battles and campaigns with any certainty and of discovering what was in the minds of the admirals and generals who conducted them. (*Journal of Hellenic Studies* 84)

However, he goes on to acknowledge the value of the exercise, which clearly fascinated him, and sets out five sound principles that all engaged in it should apply. These 'Aids' include advice on the use of geographical and topographical evidence, a warning against dependence on *a priori* argument and an endorsement of the process of *Sachkritik*, of which 'reality check' seems a fair translation in this context. Whatley then introduces 'what I think I may call the Sherlock Holmes method ... a combined use of the three Aids I have previously mentioned together with an ingenious selection of statements from ancient authors of different periods and a subtle interpretation of them'. I prefer to think in terms of a Distressed Jigsaw Puzzle method. It is one of those 1,000-piece monsters, perhaps a detailed old-master landscape, but the cat has been comprehensively sick on the lid of the box and, inside, there are only about 100 random pieces, some of them just bits of sea or sky. One or two of them may possibly fit together, but there is an awful lot of space unfilled in between. Whatley gives excellent advice on the core activity of filling this space, for example, to guard against letting a particular theory govern the selection or rejection of pieces of evidence, and to avoid 'excessive ingenuity'.

Whatley's final principle 'consists in making the most thorough study from all sources of the armies engaged, their strategy and tactics, their weapons and method of using them, their system of recruiting and organization, their officers and staff'. Maybe a statement of the obvious with a hint of anachronism at the end, but if it is accepted that hoplite warfare followed an evolutionary path out of the Archaic period (defined as ending in 480/79), through the 5th century and into the 4th, it is necessary if undertaking 'this most thorough study' to approach Herodotus and the other sources with some sense of the stage it had reached in that process at the time of the Persian invasions.

The notes that follow are intended to supply some of the knowledge that Herodotus' audiences and readers would have brought to the *Historia* and also to explain some of the assumptions that underlie my interpretation of what the ancient voices are telling us. They may be read now as preparation for the narrative that begins in the next chapter or be dipped into as questions arise, and some readers may not feel the need for them and the granular detail they provide.

HOPLITE WARFARE

The heavy-armed infantryman had been the main element of the armies of Hellas for generations. The archetypal hoplite wore a bronze helmet, body armour (*thorax*) and greaves, and carried a large round shield (*aspis*), a long thrusting spear (*doru*) and a short sword as a secondary weapon. He is conventionally represented as fighting in a tight, closely ordered *phalanx* formation that was several ranks deep, eight being most usual, with each man occupying about 1m of space. However, the precise mechanics and techniques of hoplite combat have been and will continue to be energetically debated (see, for example: van Wees, 2004; Schwartz, 2010; Krentz, 2010; Matthew, 2012; and Kagan & Viggiano, 2013). Moreover, a large proportion of the more detailed written evidence that can be cited on the subject of the phalanx, and hoplite tactics and combat techniques dates from the closing decades of the 5th century or later, after decades of evolution in fighting methods brought on by the Peloponnesian War, which took place between Athens and Sparta in the second half of the 5th century, and by Theban and Macedonian innovation in the 4th century. The word *phalanx* occurs quite often in Homer's *Iliad*, in the poet's descriptions of more ancient methods of war, either of his time, the 7th century, or with some faint reflection of the 13th or 12th century, when the war which was his inspiration probably took place. But the word is used in the general sense of 'throng', 'ranks' or 'battle line' without any connotation of the later more structured hoplite formation. In the context of the first two decades of the 5th century, Herodotus uses the word *phalanx* only once and then not in its military sense but meaning 'log' (of ebony), and he never quantifies the depth of a Hellene battle line. Thucydides does not use the word at all, although he notes various file depths in descriptions of Peloponnesian War battles fought from 427 onwards.

In the literature, mostly Thucydides and Xenophon, covering warfare 50 years and onwards from that time, eight is the depth most frequently recorded, occurring in eight out of the 19 references to file depth, so it is not unreasonable to regard this as fairly common practice in the later decades of the Classical period. But the reappearance of the word *phalanx* in its precise tactical usage in 4th-century writing should be seen as marking the culmination of a long evolutionary process that was in an earlier stage at the time of the Persian War, a process at times influenced as much by social and political as by strategic and tactical developments. The more detailed image of hoplite warfare presented by sources later than Herodotus cannot be safely back-projected over half a century and more to fill out his sketchier accounts of the battles of the Persian War. Aspects of these accounts are actually at odds with what has been termed the 'orthodox' view, although this may be reasonably accurate when applied to combat between two very similar, disciplined, tight formations in the hoplite-against-hoplite battles of parochial Hellene border war. In some of these, a conclusion might be reached and honour satisfied with little bloodshed in a contest that might have seemed to modern eyes to bear more resemblance to a sporting event than warfare. But if this was all the Hellenes were used to and capable of, the Persian army, with its superior mobility and logistical capability, the vast numbers it could muster, and its alien integration of archers and cavalry with all types of close-combat infantry, presented a rather different set of challenges.

The rich contemporary artistic record in vase paintings and sculptural depictions of warriors and battle provides extensive visual information about both sides' arms and armour, but this too is open to widely differing interpretations. Representations of men in battle give clues about how individual warriors fought, but very rarely any sense of the tactical formations that might have been employed or, indeed, of engagement in mass combat on any scale. Both the nature of the media and convention and limitations of technique restricted the breadth and depth of the artists' fields of vision. Surviving fragments or whole items of arms and armour complement this evidence. However, in statistical terms, these remains represent a very small sample of what was worn and carried by the tens of thousands of hoplites who fought to turn back the Barbarian invasion, and are almost exclusively restricted to bronze and iron items. Of the wood, fabric and leather, the non-metallic material that was also widely used, there is hardly a trace.

The shield and the spear (*aspis* and *doru*) were the defining defensive and offensive weapons of the hoplite for the several centuries of his existence. It seems that part-time citizen soldiers did not require a high level of drill or training to use these weapons effectively in massed ranks at close quarters. In general, physical fitness from manual labour or exercise in the gymnasium, and readiness to stand by one's kinsmen and neighbours as a matter of honour and civic duty counted for rather more than skill at arms, and the skills of fighting at close quarters with shield, spear and sword were generally regarded as learned by natural instinct and experience. Formation and manoeuvre do not appear to have been drilled or practised in peacetime by any armies, with the probable exception of the Spartans. However, Herodotus does identify individuals who were formally or informally voted to have shown most bravery and been most effective (the verb is *aristeuein*, 'to be the bravest and best') and this suggests that there were phases of combat in which there were opportunities for especially skilled and brave fighters to stand out from the throng, literally as well as metaphorically, like the heroes of the *Iliad*. So, at the time of the Persian War, massed hoplite combat was a common-sense way of making war. Depth of file would have been mainly determined by length of front, to keep it at least equal to the enemy's. There seem to have been traditional formulae to settle allied contingents' stations from right to left, and, generally, the best soldiers, the fittest and best armed, also probably the foremost socially and including the army's commanders, occupied the front ranks. Within units, individuals probably then found their positions according to family, local and tribal hierarchy and relationships. Once in action, men simply had to follow a few basic rules to keep ranks and files in alignment and to support their comrades to their front and to right and left. There was usually little else in the way of tactical activity, beyond choosing the place to fight, and battlefield communication was minimal, limited almost entirely to simple trumpet calls signalling advance or retreat.

In a conventional hoplite battle, when the sacrificial omens confirmed that the time had come to fight, the two opposing lines generally advanced at a walk to maintain cohesion and alignment. The two lines came together, first at spear's length and then shield against shield, and fought until one or the other broke under the pressure of the other side's 'shoving' (*othismos*). What this meant precisely in practical terms is much debated. One interpretation has the front ranks pressed against each other with each man occupying a square metre or so of space with those behind pushing their shields into the backs of the men in front. Another takes a less literal view, interpreting the word more along the lines of 'thrust' or 'big push' in our contemporary military language. This would allow a more open formation and greater scope for individual spear- and sword-play, but without excluding a lot of pressing together of front-rank shields at the climax of the battle. With everyone very closely jammed together, the spear (pointed at both ends) could only be used with any freedom in overarm thrusts, and striking power with spear or sword would have been greatly reduced by the near-impossibility of moving the feet or pivoting the upper body. And, unless the pressure and resistance between the opposing lines were completely uniform across their length and depth, the formation would seem likely to have quickly become fatally unstable, like a collapsing rugby scrum. However, in some local Hellene border clashes, combat might even have been limited to a 'push-of-war', shields against shields, to minimize casualties. In either model, if the broken enemy did not immediately turn and run or call for a truce, the ensuing melee would generally quickly become a bloody rout. In broken formation and in flight, hoplites became much more vulnerable and this was the point where the losers' casualties tended to be most severe, as in all ancient and medieval warfare. Later in the *Historia* Herodotus represents Mardonius as ridiculing the limitations and simplicity of the hoplite method of war and as questioning the Hellenes' ability to adapt to meet the Persian challenge. But, while it was from this simplicity that Hellas drew the strength to resist and finally defeat the world-conquering Barbarian invader on land, there was plenty of evidence from past wars that Hellene armies were not actually so shackled by narrow tactical doctrine. And, as will be seen, they displayed a good deal of flexibility in the face of the challenges presented by the Great King's armies.

ARMS AND ARMOUR

Alongside physical fitness, tactical code, such as it was, and the straightforward norms of group behaviour, the heavy shield and spear were the only other constants throughout the hoplite era. Up to about half-way through the 5th century a hoplite's weapons were generally his personal possessions, not state-issued; they were his qualification for the role, as was the level of personal wealth they represented. Shields, body armour, helmets and swords, if inherited, were part of a man's wealth. Otherwise he needed to be able to pay the equivalent of many weeks of a craftsman's wage to acquire his kit. Off-the-peg equipment was at the low end of the price range. Made-to-measure helmet, shield and body armour distinguished the richest and most influential from the rest whilst the lowliest might muster with no more than shield and spear, perhaps an agricultural knife or cleaver, and a felt or leather cap to provide some head protection. Service was a civic duty and unpaid and, according to references in Thucydides and Aristophanes, each hoplite was required to set off on campaign with rations for three days and thereafter was responsible for procuring further supplies for himself, normally paid for in friendly territory. Servants or slaves would generally have done the purchasing or foraging and looting, when required.

The classic shield (*aspis*) was constructed by gluing a number of wooden planks together to form a disk and shaping this into its shallow bowl-shape by turning it on a rudimentary lathe. Willow or poplar (salicaceous varieties) seem to have been favoured for their capacity to absorb impact without splitting, and sheet bronze was used to add resilience around the rim or over the whole surface, and for decorative effect. Unfortunately, very few examples of the woodwork have survived, but the best shields were probably laminated with the grain running at different angles in successive layers for greater strength. Earlier shields had a central handgrip. The larger kind was supported by a baldric; smaller, lighter shields were held out at arm's length. The hoplite shield is thought to have weighed in the region of 7kg. It was carried on the left arm by means of a central armband and a leather or cord grip on the inside rim, and was also supported by resting the upper rim on the left shoulder in a side-on fighting stance similar to the present-day boxer's 'orthodox' position. Hoplites therefore did not fight 'shoulder to shoulder' in a literal sense, and for the hand-to-hand tactics of the early 5th century it may have been generally less important for shields to touch, let alone interlock, than for the arcs covered by each man's spear to overlap with those covered by his two immediate neighbours.

The hoplite spear (*doru*) was 1.8–2.4m long and weighed 1.0–1.5kg. Ash and cornel (a type of dogwood) were preferred for the shaft, which was approximately 2.5cm in diameter but tapered a little from the butt. Some spares were probably taken on campaign and later sources mention that spokeshaves were carried to shape replacements made from foraged timber. The leaf-shaped head was made of iron, sometimes bronze, and 20–30cm in length. The butt was tipped with a metal spike, generally square in section, known as the 'lizard killer' (*sauroter*). Its name and the square punctures found in some cuirass remains may support speculation that it was used as a secondary weapon when the head broke off or the shaft fractured, or for conveniently stabbing down on fallen enemies as the battle line rolled forward. Less dramatically, this spike reinforced the shaft against splitting down its length, counterbalanced the head and added to the weapon's mass; and it was useful for sticking the spear upright in the ground. The point of balance, where the spear was held in the right hand for action, was nearer the butt than the tip and bindings of twine or leather to improve grip are depicted in vase paintings. Practical experiments have demonstrated that both overarm and underarm thrusts could pierce a shield or body armour but this is undoubtedly easier to achieve in laboratory conditions than in battle and perhaps the extensive literature on this topic places too much emphasis on the possible nature of the 'kill shot'. Wounding, even if it was not immediately disabling, throwing one's opponent off-balance or simply forcing him back could all disrupt the enemy formation and, cumulatively, bring on a rout. The ability to drive the spear-point into any area of flesh unprotected by shield or armour may have been more highly valued than the strength and technique required to penetrate a shield or armour with a thrust.

The iconic closed 'Corinthian' helmet is the type most associated with the Persian War. This was impressively crafted from a single beaten and burnished sheet of bronze. The metal, ranging from about 1mm in thickness to 3mm over the brow and nose, and its elegant curvature gave good protection to the face and skull at the expense of restricted all-round vision, muffled hearing and minimal ventilation. It is often depicted as pushed back on top of the head to improve vision and hearing, and to provide ventilation when not in close combat. The artistic record strongly suggests that a new generation of lighter, more open helmets had been widely adopted in place of the Corinthian helmet by the early 5th century. The 'Chalcidian' type, frequently depicted in vase paintings and sculptures of the period, generally retained the nose-guard of the Corinthian type but exposed more of the face and had openings for the ears with cheek-pieces that were often hinged. A loose parallel can be seen in the way the medieval European 'great helm' was superseded by the lighter bascinet.

It is natural to visualise ancient Greece in the smooth tones and textures of marble and bronze, or the limited red-white-black palette of the vase painters. But analysis of traces of pigments and advanced imaging have revealed that marble sculptures were brightly painted to represent a much more colourful world. Helmets, for example, were highly decorated. The decoration may have been applied to a cover of fabric or leather, surfaces more receptive to paint than bronze, or leather or wood could have been used in the helmet's construction to create a composite alternative. This may explain why very few examples of the Chalcidian type have been found in Greece in contrast to its frequent depiction and the relative profusion of surviving solid-bronze Corinthian helmets.

If wearing body armour, the hoplite's chest and back were protected by the traditional bronze 'muscle' *thorax* or the more recently developed composite corslet, sometimes referred to as the *linothorax* (linen corslet). The former was more expensive in terms both of materials and of the craftsmanship involved in working the metal and tailoring it exactly to its owner's measurement. It is clear from the evidence of vase paintings and sculpture that the composite corslet was widely used in the Persian War and that it had begun to supersede the bronze cuirass a few decades earlier in the 6th century. The base material is thought to have been hardened leather or layers of fabric glued together or a combination of both. Linen was one of the fabrics used but Herodotus' four references to armour made of it suggest that, as far as the Hellenes were concerned, it was costly and exotic and therefore not for the rank and file. In addition to its relative cheapness, if linen was not used, and ease of manufacture, the composite corslet had other important advantages: at 4–7kg it probably weighed significantly less than the most solid bronze examples; it was cooler to fight in and more comfortable than all but the best-fitting bronze armour; and its flexibility and design probably allowed one size to be adjusted to fit a reasonable range of body measurements. Some illustrations appear to show reinforcement in the form of small metal scales or plates, riveted or sewn on, or sandwiched between layers of leather or fabric as in the medieval brigandine coat. Practical experiments using pre-industrial materials have shown that linen alone, glued in layers, is as resistant to pointed and edged weapons as 2mm bronze plate, and that hardened leather also stands up well. However, although the composite corslet could be as resilient as the best bronze cuirass and could have been significantly lighter and less costly to manufacture, body armour was largely phased out in Hellene armies as the 5th century progressed, along with the closed or semi-closed types of helmet, in an evolution comparable to that in 20th-century tank design with its trade-offs between mobility, protection and striking power.

In his account of the battle of Plataea, Herodotus states more than once that each hoplite was accompanied by one light-armed soldier (*psilos machimos*; literally 'bare fighter'), the Spartans by seven. But he hardly mentions the *psiloi* in his narrative and uses words for the same personnel which can be translated as 'attendant', 'servant' or 'baggage-carrier', reflecting their other support functions, which would have included carrying rations and procuring them. Nevertheless they undoubtedly had a combat role. Helots, the serf underclass of Lacedaemon, who died at Plataea were buried in a tomb that was separately identified and the Helot dead at Thermopylae were said to be mistaken for Spartans by the Persians. In his *Guide to Greece*, Pausanias, the 2nd-century AD travel-writer, mentions a tomb for the Athenian 'slaves' who fought at Marathon, presumably amongst the *psiloi*, just as some slaves rowed alongside citizens and resident aliens in the Athenian navy. Earlier sources (Homer, Tyrtaeus, Archilochus) picture light-armed mingled with heavy-armed and sheltering under their shields in the battle line. They were most likely used as skirmishers, screening flanks and out in front of the hoplites before the opposing lines engaged. They then fell back to the rear or took shelter in the line to support the hoplites by throwing missiles, perhaps bringing forward replacements for broken spears, carrying back the dead and wounded and even plugging gaps with spear and shield. Their mobility was an asset in the pursuit of a broken enemy and Herodotus mentions that Helots were given the task of gathering up the spoils and stripping the bodies when the battle of Plataea was over. Some of the *psiloi* may have had light shields of wickerwork or hide, others wrapped cloaks or hides around their left arms. Some had swords or knives, but many probably wielded farm implements or crude cudgels, and there were always stones lying around. Missile 'specialists' probably used hunting weapons for the most part. However, by the time of the Peloponnesian War, it appears that light-armed tactics had become more organized and effective with hoplite equipment becoming lighter and less elaborate for greater mobility as a consequence. Thucydides records several instances in which light-armed units, in support of hoplites or on their own, carried out ambushes, flank attacks or assaults on positions, and defeated hoplite units. Herodotus says very little about their contribution, which was probably lesser at this time, just as he underplays the very significant contribution of the same social classes and, at least in 480, the same men as oarsmen. These slaves and serfs were probably almost as well motivated as the poor free citizens they fought or rowed alongside to defend the way of life which they shared.

PERSIAN ARMS AND ARMOUR

Herodotus describes the Persians in his comprehensive survey of the troops available to Xerxes:

> They were equipped in this way: on their heads they wore floppy caps called *tiaras* and, on their bodies, colourful sleeved tunics plated with small pieces of iron that looked like fish-scales. They had trousers on their legs. Instead of *aspides* they had wickerwork shields from which their quivers hung; they carried short spears and great bows[1] with cane[2] arrows, and on their right thighs daggers hung from their belts ... The Persian cavalry were equipped like their infantry, except that some of them wore bronze or iron headgear. (7.61, 84)

The *tiara* (or *kurbasa*) was a sort of flapped hood or turban which could be worn open or tied across the face to cover the nose and mouth. Herodotus also uses the word *pilos* and, again, *tiara* for another type of Persian headgear, looking rather like that worn by Greek or Russian Orthodox priests. *Pilos* is also the word for the conical felt, leather or bronze cap worn by hoplites later in the 5th century, and some elite barbarian troops wore plain bronze helmets, less conical in shape. The fish-scale tunics may have been worn by officers or elite troops only, and the scales may have been more decorative than functional. Some vase paintings depict a kind of quilting which may have incorporated metal plates and others show something similar to the hoplite composite corslet, but the artists may never have seen a Persian warrior and have used their imagination and first-hand knowledge of Hellene equipment to interpret eyewitness descriptions. Elsewhere Herodotus emphasizes the Persians' lack of armour and, very probably, the majority wore no body armour of any kind. But there were two types of shield, the large rectangular *spara*, similar to the medieval pavise, which could be planted in the ground or held up by shield-bearers as protection for the ranks of archers, and the smaller, more portable variety, crescent, oval or scalloped in shape. Both were generally made of wicker interwoven with hide strips.

---

[1] *Toxa megala*, which could also be translated as 'long'.
[2] Often translated as 'reed'.

Light shields amply met the Persians' defensive needs in most of the
wars they fought in Asia.

The bow was the Persians' primary weapon (like trousers, considered
effeminate and dishonourable by traditionally minded Hellenes) and all
three types were probably used. The 'great bow' identified by Herodotus
was probably of the 'simple' variety, made from a single piece of wood,
and basic issue for the infantry. Mounted archers required a shorter bow
which would have been of either the 'compound' or the 'composite'
variety. The former was constructed from two pieces of wood, glued
and bound together in a double-convex 'cupid's bow' shape. The latter,
shorter still but similar in shape, was constructed by shaping and
laminating wood, horn and ox-tendons and its cost probably restricted
it to the aristocratic elite. It was more powerful and accurate than the
other two types but more skill and strength were needed to handle it.
The simple bow was effective against massed troop concentrations at
ranges of up to about 150m, especially if they were lightly armed, which
was generally the case in Asian wars. A skilled archer with a composite
bow could pick off individuals at up to 60m and hit formations at up
to about 250m. Bows with their arrows were carried in a distinctive
case called the *gorytos* and for composite bows this seems to have been
essential to protect them from weather and other damage. In his *Persae*,
the tragedy celebrating Athens' glorious victory at Salamis, Aeschylus
repeatedly contrasts the bow and the spear. The bow's symbolic
importance in Persian culture is reflected in the depiction of Darius as
an archer on the imperial gold coin and in Herodotus' description of
his ritualistic shooting of an arrow in the air as he prayed to the gods
for vengeance on the Athenians for their part in the attack on Sardis.

Herodotus states that Persian and Median cavalry were equipped in
the same way as the infantry, but that they would not have carried
shields when fighting as horse-archers. They were generally sent in to
attack first, repeatedly charging up into bowshot and javelin range,
harassing, wheeling and retiring. They then made way for the infantry,
who continued to shower the enemy with arrows and then attacked or
defended themselves with spears, and swords or light axes as secondary
weapons; their iron- or bronze-tipped spears were shorter than the
hoplite *doru*. The cavalry came in again when enemy formations were
broken and in flight, riding them down with spears and swords. They
were accomplished horsemen, riding without stirrups or saddles of any

kind, but they could operate effectively only in level, open country on ground that was reasonably kind to unshod hooves.

The Persian army was highly organized and, on the Hellene side, only the Spartan army seems to have been as formally structured. The largest operational unit appears to have had a 'paper strength' of 10,000 and this was subdivided into ten units of 1,000, which, in turn, were broken down into 100s and tens (*balvarabam*, *hazarabam*, *satabam* and *dathabam*) with a hierarchy of officers for each level. This organizational principle is documented in later 4th-century sources, but it is likely it was well established by the beginning of the 5th century, though, in practice, probably only the 10,000 royal guards known as 'the Immortals' maintained the arithmetic exactly. Persians and Medes were highly skilled soldiers, having learned archery and horsemanship from childhood, and they operated within what was, for their times, a sophisticated command structure. They could more appropriately be described as 'professionals' than any of the Hellenes except for the Spartans and the small elite units maintained by some other cities.

The Persian invasion forces included contingents from Hellene subject states, some of them substantial and surprisingly loyal to the Great King, with exactly the same arms and equipment as the defenders of Hellas and sharing their basic tactical doctrine.

TRIREME WARFARE

At sea, both sides went into battle in capital ships, triremes, that were very similar, if not identical, and therefore presented the same tactical options. The trireme had evolved over the centuries from the 30- or 50-oared longship which had been the norm. Shipbuilders had first increased the longship's power and manoeuvrability by introducing a two-tier oar arrangement and had then pushed this development to its technological limit by lengthening the hull and adding a third tier, more than trebling the oar power available but without increasing the size or weight of the vessel proportionately. The longship's primary function was to carry troops with a large proportion of them doubling as rowers, and to deliver them in expeditions to fight on land. A sea-battle was a matter of boarding or repelling boarders. Thucydides describes this as 'the old fashioned way ... victory depended more on the hoplites on board, standing and fighting on their stationary ships'. Herodotus first mentions the trireme in a reference to the shipbuilding programme of the Egyptian pharaoh Nechos at the end of the 7th century but Thucydides dates its appearance in Hellene navies somewhat earlier:

> As the Hellenes grew stronger and became more active in acquiring wealth ... they began to equip themselves with navies and took to the ocean. The Corinthians are said to have been the first to start building ships the way we do now, so the first Hellene trireme was constructed in Corinth ... This was about 300 years before the end of this war.[1] The earliest sea-battle we know of was between the Corinthians and the Corcyreans and took place about 260 years before the end of the war. (*History of the Peloponnesian War* 1.13)

Corinth, a significant power with its isthmus location giving access to the sea to the east and west, was very likely to have been a pioneer. The western island of Corcyra (Corfu), originally a Corinthian settlement, was an important staging post for commerce between Greece and Italy and clearly another early adopter. The context may imply that the battle between Corinth and Corcyra was a 'modern' engagement and Thucydides fully understood what he was writing about, having himself commanded triremes. However, he does go on to say that Corcyra did not have many of the new capital ships until early in the 5th century and this is therefore unlikely to have been an all-trireme battle. A number of the leading Hellene cities of the west coast of Asia became major naval powers during the reigns of Cyrus and Cambyses, though, according to Thucydides, even these fleets had only a few triremes 'and were instead equipped with penteconters[2] [50 oars] and longships, just like earlier fleets' (1.13). A little earlier Thucydides states that the longships of the heroic past, in which warriors doubled as oarsmen, 'had no decking, but were fitted out more in the old style of pirate ships' (1.10). The penteconter was the predecessor of the trireme in evolutionary terms. However, around the turn of the century it seems that some of these cities greatly enlarged the trireme element of their

---

[1] The Peloponnesian War; Thucydides' account ends in 411, when the war had seven more years to run and he is thought to have died in 404. He may therefore be counting back from 421, the year of the fairly short-lived Peace of Nicias.

[2] In terms of evolution, mid-way between the longship and the trireme.

fleets with the support of Persian funding, adding to the Great King's naval power. On the western side of the Aegean, the conflict between Athens and Aegina is put into perspective in the same passage by Thucydides' observation that Athens and Aegina then had small fleets which mainly consisted of penteconters, albeit probably of relatively modern design with two-tier oar systems. Only the wealthiest states could build a significant number of triremes over a short period of time, and man and maintain them, and an enterprise of such scale also called for a high level of leadership, political commitment and control. But by the end of the 6th century the strategic value of a trireme fleet must have been widely recognized across the Mediterranean world, because the smaller warships that the trireme was in the process of superseding were no match for it in battle. Thucydides credits the Corinthians with building the first trireme in Hellas, but this does not rule out the possibility that two- and three-tier oar systems may have been a Barbarian development originally. There is evidence that vessels with a second tier of oars had made their appearance at the eastern end of the Mediterranean earlier than the 7th century. A relief from the palace of Sennacherib dated to 701 could depict a Phoenician warship with a three-tier oar system. But, whoever initiated the evolutionary process, what followed probably took the form of a closely contested arms race between East and West, and competing European sea powers. The trireme with its ram was the weapon that dominated the Aegean, the waters off western Greece, southern Italy and Sicily, and the eastern Mediterranean until the end of the 4th century. It was then superseded by larger, heavier vessels carrying ship-to-ship artillery and serving as platforms for greater numbers of troops. Tactics had reverted to the 'old fashioned way' of boarding and deck-fighting with artillery missiles as an added ingredient. There was no longer much call for the highly skilled oarsmen who powered the trireme and made its agile manoeuvres possible. They had, in any case, become more difficult to recruit.

Up to the 1980s the range of fragmentary evidence for the nature and workings of the trireme, references in ancient texts, depictions in sculpture and vase paintings and on coins, and from other archaeological finds, provoked a wide variety of interpretations and seemingly endless argument. But, in 1987, the Hellenic Navy's *Olympias*, a full-scale, fully working reconstruction was launched and the sea trials carried out over the following seven years conclusively demonstrated that the team of classical scholars, oarsmen and sailors, boatbuilders, archaeologists and naval architects that had collaborated in this extraordinary experimental archaeology project had comprehensively resolved the 'Trireme Controversy'. *Olympias* probably most closely resembles an Athenian trireme of the second half of the 5th century and the time of the Peloponnesian War. It is likely that there had been some evolution in design and construction techniques, but earlier and sparser pieces of evidence suggest that the trireme of the Persian War did not differ from this in any major way.

A fully fitted-out and manned trireme weighed 40–50 tonnes. It was approximately 6m wide, including the outriggers for the top tier of its three tiers of oars, and approximately 40m long. It measured about 4m from deck to keel, which was a little less than 1m below the waterline. The deck superstructure accounted for about one third of the height above the waterline. The trireme was as light and durable, and as streamlined as materials, craftsmanship and techniques could permit. These qualities gave it the speed and manoeuvrability required for combat, and a working life that could exceed 20 years. Its shallow draft made it easy to beach and launch, and suited it to the enclosed or inshore waters on which it generally fought. But it was a fair-weather ship. In waves larger than 1m from crest to trough it risked taking in water through the bottom-tier oar-ports and planks could be sprung as a result of sagging in the middle as bow and stern were lifted by the swell.

The trireme's hull was built as a shell from the keel up, with the planks flush, and mortised and tenoned together at the edges. Thucydides comments that the triremes built by the Athenians in the 480s 'were not yet fully decked'. In a fully decked trireme, planking ran from bow to stern, forming a protective canopy over the oarsmen and providing a fighting platform; part-decking presumably covered areas at bow and stern. It is clear from other references in Thucydides that the navies of the Peloponnesian War included both part-decked and fully decked triremes, and this may have been generally true of Hellene navies in the Persian War. The former were lighter, speedier and more nimble, better suited to the demands of ramming tactics, but they could carry fewer deck-fighting troops. The latter were more suited to fighting battles in what Thucydides describes as 'the old-fashioned way', deciding the issue in hand-to-hand combat on their own decks or the enemy's. In both types, a companionway ran up the centre line of the ship below deck level. This gave access to the rowing positions and allowed movement and communication between the crew stations at each end. Also, importantly, commands and encouragement were relayed along it from the helmsman to the oarsmen.

A 5th-century Athenian trireme snugly accommodated 170 oarsmen in three tiers and it is possible this was accepted as an optimum arrangement at the end of the centuries of its evolution from the ancient longship. Athenian rowers were recruited mainly from citizens in the lowest property class, below hoplite status. Manual labour would have given most of them the stamina and upper-body strength necessary to pull an oar effectively for hours at a time, and the *Olympias* experiment revealed that a complete beginner could master the necessary basic rowing skill surprisingly quickly. It is known that Athenian oarsmen were paid a daily wage and required to supply nothing except perhaps for the sheepskin pad they sat on. Their personal kit probably consisted of a cloak and tunic and, for at least some, a personal weapon. There was not space to accommodate much more, and water in skins and jars would have taken up most of what storage there was. On *Olympias* the rowers consumed water at the rate of more than a litre per hour, so each trireme would have started the day with hundreds of litres on board and, on campaign, it was vital to have access to beaches with a good supply of fresh water. In addition to the rowers, the part-decked trireme could carry 16 officers and crewmen, and a basic fighting strength of ten hoplites and four archers. A fully decked trireme could accommodate an additional 20–30 deck crew, but the extra loading affected speed and manoeuvrability. On both types, stability was affected if the men were not spread out evenly over the available space.

On campaign, waiting for action or pausing on voyages for food and drink or rest, triremes were beached with their sterns ashore and their rams facing out to sea, and with ladders on each side of the stern for boarding and disembarking. It was found to be possible with good organization to embark or disembark the entire complement of *Olympias* in a matter of minutes. Some manpower was needed on the beach to push off, but with most of the oars immediately in action and the bows and the weight of the ram out to sea, the process would generally have been straightforward and quick. Anchoring offshore was a less desirable alternative; boarding and disembarkation were laborious processes and, on board, there was not enough space for whole crews to sleep, and no scope for catering. Normally, therefore, crews camped on the shore close by their ships, and shared feeding arrangements. Barley porridge, perhaps spiced up with a little salted fish or meat, was regularly, if not permanently, on the menu. This would have been supplemented by whatever could be foraged, purchased, stolen or looted on shore.

Ancient evidence for the time taken over various voyages indicates that a Greek trireme could sustain a cruising speed of 6–7 knots (11.1–13.0km/h) over a period of several hours and the *Olympias* project confirmed 10 knots (18.5km/h) to be a reasonable estimate of its top speed, produced in short bursts. The current Olympic record for an eight, the fastest type of oared boat ever built, was set at an average speed of 12.5 knots (23.1km/h). With one side rowing and the other with oars out of the water, *Olympias* could make a 360° turn in a circle less than two ship-lengths in diameter. With both sides rowing, she could turn in a circle 3.4 ship-lengths in diameter. A 90° change of direction could be made in seconds in half a length, and in less than a length under full oar power. *Olympias* could also zig-zag with precision and showed potential for sharp acceleration and deceleration. On this evidence the historic trireme with a good helmsman, rowing master and oarsmen could feint and weave and dart with even greater agility, essential capabilities for ramming combat. The trireme was also an efficient sailing ship, and the *Olympias* sea trials demonstrated that, in good sailing conditions, as fast a cruising speed could be achieved under sail as under oar. She performed best with the wind at around 15 knots (27.8km/h) and 30–40° abaft her beam and, for a boat of such shallow draft, could sail surprisingly close to the wind. The sails were easily handled by a small number of deck hands and steering was straightforward. However, under sail, the trireme could never achieve the manoeuvrability necessary for battle.

On the Persian side, the Hellene ships from Ionia and the northern Aegean would have been very similar to the Athenian trireme described above. However, the ships from further east, for example Phoenicia, were different in a number of ways: cedar, rather than fir or pine, was used for planking; their rams were pointed and longer; and their decks were surrounded by gunwales or by rails with shields hung over them.

These ships were designed to ride the larger waves generally encountered in the more open waters of the eastern Mediterranean and it is likely they were built with a slightly broader beam without outriggers for the top tier, the rowers sitting fully inboard rather than perched over the gunwales. The resulting larger deck area with its enclosing gunwales and, possibly, a fully or partly covered central companionway gave greater troop-carrying capacity. Their poop decks may have been higher to give the commander and helmsman a better view over the gunwales and more crowded deck. Finally, Barbarian ships would probably have been more extensively and colourfully decorated. At several points Herodotus describes the ships in the Persian fleet as 'better sailing' when compared to the Hellene fleet that faced them in 480. This may be attributable to a combination of factors including lightness of materials and structure, performance in heavier seas, superior build quality and maintenance, and, collectively, a higher level of training, better seamanship and more extensive naval experience.

Herodotus' few detailed references to the philosophy and practicalities of trireme warfare assume first-hand knowledge on the part of the reader and Thucydides, with his substantial personal experience, is not much more explicit. However, basic principles emerge clearly enough from these authors' and other accounts of battles and naval campaigns, and Herodotus' short description of the training given to the Ionian fleet before the battle of Lade by Dionysius the Phocaean offers some useful insight (6.11–12). First there is his call for hard work and discipline, which, as it turned out, was asking too much of his multi-national and amateurish command. Secondly, he introduces the *diekplous* tactic, 'sailing through and out', a manoeuvre involving breaking through the enemy line and turning quickly to ram one of the ships in the stern quarter or side-on, the objective being to disable it, either by puncturing its hull, or by shattering its oars without losing one's own. As a fleet or squadron manoeuvre this might be executed with a well-timed switch from line-abreast to line-ahead. For an individual ship, it would probably always have been an opportunistic move with the commander seeing an opening between enemy ships and driving his own through it. In the case of larger units, it was probably signalled by trumpet calls or perhaps flags, or simply by following the command ship's lead. Having punched through the opposing line, the column could then fan out in sharp turns to attack from the rear or sides, exploiting loss of cohesion in the manoeuvring that preceded contact. Whether or not such manoeuvring was planned or spontaneous, the actual fighting was mainly characterized by dogfight-like duels between individual ships with formations quickly breaking up after first contact. *Periplous*, 'sailing round' to enable attacks on the flanks or rear, was the other major tactic.

Hellenes and Barbarians were set on a collision course from a little over half-way through the 6th century. The Persian Empire was to grow rapidly to dwarf its European neighbours and its resources and manpower gave it ample capacity to engulf them. However, when the collision took place, the Hellenes opposed the Barbarians with a resilience that was ultimately decisive. One critical factor was the Hellene allies' robust self-belief as individuals and as independent peoples, and their iron determination to counter the doubly existential threat of brutal conquest by a distant foreign power and the imposition of autocratic rule. Their resilience was also founded on tactical and strategic superiority at sea and the effective deployment of massed hoplite formations on land, and without the triremes of Athens and the hoplites of Sparta, Hellas would not have survived.

King of kings, ruler of the lands

The Rise of Persia

CYRUS THE GREAT

Nothing if not thorough in his investigation, Herodotus goes deep into the mythical past to identify the original cause of this conflict between Hellenes and Barbarians, tracing it back to the war with Troy. In fact, at the time of the Trojan War, the forebears of the 5th-century Persians were a nomadic people occupying an expanse of territory to the southwest of the Caspian Sea, a long way from the shores of the Aegean. If the Hellene invasion of the Troad offended any superpower, it would have been the Hittites, whose empire was then on the verge of collapse. A few generations on, the people who became known as Persians had settled to the south in Persis, to the east of the territory of Elam, a civilization that had been in existence for nearly three millennia. In 550, Cyrus, a Persian of the Achaemenid clan and fourth in a line of kings of Anshan, an Elamite state, launched a rebellion against Persia and Elam's northern neighbours and overlords, the Medes. Successfully exploiting internal unrest and an alliance with the Median general Harpagus, he won two easy victories and the throne of Media from his brother-in-law Astyages. This was the first stage in the creation of the Achaemenid Empire, which was to last until its destruction by Alexander the Great in 331.

The Median province of Cappadocia bordered the militarily powerful, and wealthy and economically advanced kingdom of Lydia:

> The Lydians and the Hellenes have very similar customs. Also, the Lydians were the first people in human knowledge to mint gold and silver coinage, and the first to become retailers of goods. (1.94)

At the peak of its power Lydia controlled a large area of western Asia roughly equivalent to the western half of present-day Turkey. This included the many Hellene city-states spread along the western coastline. These had been founded centuries before by Hellene migrants and had mostly flourished individually and quite independently, whilst retaining ties of varying strength with their mother cities in Greece. Some, especially in the territory called Ionia, outshone these as powerful centres of wealth and culture. Lydia's relationships, significance and location had produced a culture that combined European and Asian features. In 547/6, Croesus, its king, crossed the River Halys and invaded Cappadocia. The strategic logic of a pre-emptive strike against the Persians may have seemed compelling, and 'he longed to acquire more territory'(1.73). He had consulted the Delphic oracle and been encouraged by the prediction, for which he had paid with lavish offerings, that 'he would destroy a great empire if he went to war with the Persians' (1.53). He had also acted on the oracle's advice 'to find out who were the most powerful of the Hellenes and to make friends with them' (1.53); Croesus had previously formed alliances with the Egyptians and the Babylonians. The Spartans were already well disposed towards Croesus because of an earlier act of generosity, very probably calculated to build credit to be accessed on some future occasion, and they were the dominant power in the Peloponnese. Croesus made overtures to them and a treaty was sworn joining Lydia and Sparta in a diplomatic and military alliance. Croesus' army already included Hellene mercenaries or levies, and he now had a potent ally in mainland Greece. So conflict between Hellenes and Barbarians had its beginnings more than half a century before the battle of Marathon.

Herodotus' brief account of Croesus' war gives us a first glimpse of Persia's military might in action. The Lydians had taken the Cappadocian city of Pteria on the River Halys, not far from the Black Sea coast:

Cyrus mustered his army and marched against Croesus, raising more troops from the lands he passed through. Before setting off he had sent heralds into Ionia, attempting to persuade the Ionians to defect from Croesus, but the Ionians would not agree to this. Anyway, he confronted Croesus with what forces he had and the two sides tried each other's strength in the country outside Pteria. It was a tough fight with many falling on each side and neither gaining victory, and nightfall brought it to an end. Croesus blamed the size of his army, having gone into battle with a much smaller force than Cyrus. So, next day, when Cyrus did not come out to fight, he ordered a retreat to Sardis.[1] He intended to spend the winter there and then to march against the Persians in the spring. With this in mind, once he was back in Sardis, he sent heralds to his allies summoning them to join him in Sardis in four months' time. In the meantime, he disbanded the entire army that had fought the Persians including the mercenary element of it. He could not imagine that Cyrus would march on Sardis after such an evenly matched contest. (1.76–77)

Cyrus anticipated this strategy and marched on Sardis long before it could be implemented, paying no respect to the convention of campaigning seasons:

He moved so fast that he himself was the messenger of his own arrival. Croesus was now in a desperate situation. Things had turned out quite otherwise than he had expected. However, he led the Lydians out to do battle and, at that time, there was no race in Asia more manly or valiant than the Lydians;[2] they were excellent horsemen and fought on horseback with long spears. The two armies met on the wide, bare plain before Sardis. Cyrus was most worried by the Lydians' cavalry when he saw them forming up for battle and, on the advice of Harpagus[3] the Mede, this is what he did. He gathered together all the camels carrying food and equipment in his baggage train, took their loads off and had men mount them in full cavalry kit. Having prepared the camels in this way, he positioned them in front of his army to lead the attack on Croesus' cavalry, ordered the infantry to follow the camels and sent all his own cavalry to the rear. He lined the camels up to face the cavalry because horses are afraid of them and unable to stand the sight or smell of them. His objective was to neutralize Lydia's finest asset, and, when battle was joined, the horses turned tail as soon as they smelled or had sight of the camels, dashing Croesus' hopes of victory. But the Lydians were not cowards, and they worked out what was happening, dismounted and took on the Persians on foot. After a time, when many had fallen on each

---

[1] The capital city of Lydia.

[2] A century later the Lydians were considered by Hellenes to be effeminate.

[3] A relative of Astyages, former King of the Medes, who became a trusted lieutenant of Cyrus.

side, the Lydians were beaten back and driven inside their walls. The Persians then laid siege to the city. (1.79–81)

Croesus, expecting the siege to last a long time, sent further messages to his allies, now calling for immediate assistance. The Spartans had just fought a border war with their neighbour, Argos, but decided to honour their treaty obligation:

> However, just when they had completed their preparations and their ships were ready to sail, a second message came in reporting that the Lydian stronghold had fallen and that Croesus had been taken captive and, on receiving this disastrous news, they called the expedition off. I'll now tell you how Sardis fell. When the siege was into its third week, Cyrus sent horsemen round the camp proclaiming that he would give a reward to the first man to scale the city-walls. The whole army launched an assault, but without success. However, when this attack was broken off, a Persian called Hyroades from the Mardian tribe managed to get up onto the acropolis at a point that was unguarded because it was thought that the sheer cliff there was unscalable; this is on the side of the city facing Mount Tmolus. Just here, the day before, this Mardian had spotted one of the Lydian defenders climbing down to fetch a helmet that had tumbled down from the top. He watched carefully and memorized what he saw, and so was able to climb up that way himself with some other Persians. They scaled the acropolis in sufficient force to take it, and the whole city of Sardis was sacked. (1.83–84)

Croesus had destroyed an empire as prophesied, but it was his own, not Cyrus'.

For the Persians, this may have been the first of several encounters with the type of troops that they were to face when they invaded Greece decades later. The mercenaries fighting for Croesus at Pteria would almost certainly have included Hellene hoplites, and Herodotus later describes the Lydians as 'armed very much the same as the Hellenes' (7.74). Croesus' cavalry probably fought at a distance throwing javelins, except when operating against broken infantry formations, but clearly they also fought on foot. This versatility might have seemed unusual in the 5th century. The role of cavalry as missile troops, and as shock troops in the right circumstances, would have been familiar, but the role of the mounted hoplite in which an elite, better armed than the rest, used horses as a means of getting around the battlefield but dismounted to fight, was a throwback to more ancient times. The Lydian cavalry arm was probably also exceptional for its size. The tactic of countering this threat by creating a camel corps and placing it in front of the rest was impressive, though not unique in military history. Camels were used both for cavalry and for transport in ancient warfare, but we are not told whether the riders here were expected to fight like cavalrymen or simply to control their mounts for as long as it took to scare off the enemy horses. In fact, horses are not chronically allergic to camels and training and familiarity can overcome the aversion Herodotus describes. But Croesus' cavalry was successfully spooked by what must have been a shocking first encounter with the beasts, some distance to the north of the regions in which their appearance on the battlefield would have been unexceptional.

The speed and unconventional timing of Cyrus' march on Sardis and rapid capture of western Asia's largest city were the most remarkable features of this campaign. It was a brilliant demonstration of Cyrus' qualities as leader and commander-in-chief of a highly flexible, motivated and effective army of Medes and Persians augmented by less regular conscripts. The campaign also marked out potential future enemies, or targets for Persia in the shape of Croesus' nominal allies, Egypt and Babylon, and the Hellenes of Sparta and the unco-operative cities of Ionia. Since the 580s the Ionians had been uneasy, fairly autonomous and certainly independent-minded subjects of Lydia. As soon as Cyrus had taken control of Sardis, they informed him of their wish to continue as his subjects on the same long rein and on the same terms as those under which they had been ruled by Croesus. This was not well received by the Great King, who had been irritated by their recent lack of co-operation. So, the Ionians set about fortifying their cities and strengthening their loose regional confederation. They also asked the Spartans to send military help, but this was not forthcoming:

Instead the Lacedaemonians[1] sent a herald to Cyrus to proclaim that if he did harm to any part of Hellas, the Lacedaemonians would not

---

[1] Lacedaemon was the name of the Spartan state that comprised Laconia and Messenia. Herodotus also uses it when he means Sparta, Lacedaemon's leading city. Spartans are sometimes referred to as Laconians and more often as Lacedaemonians.

tolerate it. They say Cyrus asked some other Hellenes attending on him, 'Who are these Lacedaemonian people and how great is their population that they should issue such a proclamation?'. When he was told, he said to the Lacedaemonian, 'I have never been afraid of people who set aside a place in the middle of their city where they gather together, swear false oaths and swindle each other. As I live, they will have troubles of their own to chatter about in place of the Ionians' troubles.' (1.153)

Napoleon Bonaparte allegedly ridiculed the British in rather similar terms. In this compact episode, very early in the *Historia*, Herodotus is setting up the Persians for their great failure, which is still decades in the future. Cyrus is shown as fatally underestimating the Spartans and scorning the way of life, alien to him, that they and other Hellenes would fight to the last to protect.

A rebellion in Sardis was quickly suppressed, and then Cyrus put the task of subduing Ionia into the capable hands of Harpagus. Very early in its existence, as early as 545 BC, the Persian Empire was directly at war with Hellas:

Harpagus went to Ionia and used earthworks to capture the cities; after driving the defenders inside their walls he would build mounds up against them and then storm them.[1] The Phocaeans were the only Ionians who would not accept slavery[2] and they abandoned the land of their birth. The rest (except for the Milesians) faced Harpagus in battle and each fought courageously for their homes, but they were ground down and defeated, and, staying in their lands, submitted to Persian rule. However, the Milesians had already pledged allegiance to Cyrus and were left in peace. So, Ionia was enslaved a second time.[3] Harpagus' conquest of the Ionians on the mainland frightened the Ionian islanders into submission to Cyrus. (1.162, 169)

However, Herodotus writes a little earlier, 'There was no threat to the islanders because the Phoenicians were not yet Persian subjects, and

[1] The Persians were applying techniques of siege warfare learned from the Assyrians, who had developed them two centuries or so before.
[2] The Hellene perception of Persian imperial rule.
[3] By Croesus the first time.

the Persians were not seafarers' (1.143). Lydia was not a naval power either and the islands had remained independent while the mainland was subject to Croesus. The Phoenicians, who had the most powerful navy in the Mediterranean, became part of the Persian Empire later so the islands probably kept their independence for several more years.

In one interpretation of the hazy chronology of this part of his reign, Cyrus then campaigned far to the east, subduing and bringing into his empire the wide plains and rugged highlands that lay between the River Oxus and the Hindu Kush. The highly mobile and fierce armies of the Sacae and Bactrians who had dominated that region were a powerful new asset, also forming a strong buffer against the constant threat of the Scythian nomads who ranged the steppes to the north. During this period Harpagus extended the empire south and then east, conquering Caria (Herodotus' country of birth) and Lycia. Then, in 539, Cyrus concentrated his empire-building energies closer to home:

> When he had control of all of Asia, he turned his attention to the Assyrians. Now there are many other great cities in Assyria, but the most famous and powerful was Babylon: the royal palace was established there after the destruction of Nineveh. (1.178)

Cyrus invaded the land of Babylonia, won what seems to have been an easy victory outside the great city and then laid siege to it. In Herodotus' account the quality of Cyrus' generalship and Persian excellence at siege engineering are again highlighted. According to Herodotus' source, the Babylonians had carefully prepared for this siege as they observed Cyrus' succession of conquests and confidently awaited him with a vast stockpile of food behind their moat and massive double ring of ramparts. The Euphrates flowed through the centre of the city, passing through the circle of walls. The two openings in the walls were secured by the depth of the channel and the strength of the current. However, the Persians lowered the water level by diverting the river upstream and took the city in a devastating surprise attack by wading in through each opening under cover of night. The bronze gates that sealed off the streets of the city from the riverbanks had been left open and the outer city was overrun while those in the centre, oblivious and too confident in their security, 'happened to be celebrating a festival, dancing, singing and revelling' (1.191). The fall of Babylon brought about the liberation of the people of Israel from exile and captivity in Babylonia, and Cyrus was acclaimed as Messiah. However, the prophet Isaiah took this opportunity to assert the superiority of his one god:

> Thus saith the Lord to his anointed, to Cyrus, whose right hand I have holden, to subdue nations before him; and I will loose the loins of kings, to open before him the two leaved gates; and the gates shall not be shut;
> I will go before thee, and make the crooked places straight: I will break in pieces the gates of brass, and cut in sunder the bars of iron:
> And I will give thee the treasures of darkness, and hidden riches of secret places, that thou mayest know that I, the Lord, which call thee by thy name, am the God of Israel. (*Isaiah* 45.1–3)

The conquest of Babylonia brought into the empire Syria and Palestine and, most important for its superb navy, Phoenicia, submitting of its own free will, Herodotus later notes. With the acquisition of significant sea-power, Persia was to become a direct threat to the offshore islands of the eastern Aegean. The strategically important sea-lanes from the Black Sea and the prosperous islands further west would then be in easy reach, and sea-borne attacks on the western shores of the Aegean and further afield throughout the eastern Mediterranean would be a new option. Sea-power increased Persia's capacity for imperial expansion.

In geopolitical terms, after Egypt, Europe was the next logical target. However, in 530 BC Cyrus launched a campaign in the opposite direction, against a nomadic tribe called the Massagetae, led by Tomyris, a warrior queen. Cyrus' purpose was probably to secure the north-eastern frontier of his empire by pushing it further out to the east of the Aral Sea:

> Here, a boundless plain flows towards the rising sun as far as the eye can see. The Massagetae control a substantial part of this mighty plain and Cyrus had a great desire to go to war with these people. He felt inspired and driven to do this for a number of reasons. Above all, there was his birth and the sense that he was somehow superhuman. Then there was the good fortune he had enjoyed in all the wars he had fought, for no nation he had launched a campaign against had been

able to stand against him. So, he advanced to the Araxes, leaving the Massagetae in no doubt of his intention to invade. He had bridges constructed to take the army over the river and turrets built onto the boats that were to carry men across.[1] (1.204–05)

There is a sense of the doomed tragic hero (appropriate in view of the outcome) in Herodotus' brief consideration of Cyrus' motivation here, and it is a theme he returns to when writing about the decisions made by his successors Darius and Xerxes. Herodotus names the river incorrectly; the Araxes actually runs into the Caspian and from the west and is backed by the mountains of the Caucasus rather than the 'boundless plain' of the steppes. The river in question would have been either the Oxus or the Jaxartes, both of which flow into the Aral Sea from the east. Herodotus makes up for this geographical error by correctly describing the Caspian as an inland sea at a time when others thought it was somehow connected with the Mediterranean.

After meeting with some initial success, Cyrus was drawn into a full-scale confrontation with Tomyris' army:

I consider this to have been the most violent battle ever fought between Barbarians, and this is what I found out about it: I was told that, first, they stood back and shot arrows at each other; then, when the arrows ran out, they charged together and set to work with their spears and swords. The fighting went on for a long time and neither side would give way, but finally the Massagetae won the day. Most of the Persian army was wiped out and Cyrus, too, met his end. He had been Great King for 29 years. (1.214)

This disaster may have been a consequence of overextension and fatal underestimation of the strength of the opposition, or simply bad luck, the loss of an extraordinary leader in a frontier skirmish which the Persians would otherwise have routinely won. The narrative of negotiations, stratagems and dreams that Herodotus wraps around the bare details of the campaign and final battle reads like epic and is Herodotus' storytelling at its best. A few lines later, after a gruesome

---

[1] Probably 'bridges of boats' with turrets added to the pontoons to protect them, or perhaps the turreted boats were for use as assault craft.

description of Tomyris' treatment of Cyrus' corpse, he remarks 'of the many stories told about his death, this was the most credible account I came across' (1.215), and it would be surprising if the episode had not swiftly acquired mythic status. However, the single sentence describing the river-crossing is a further glimpse of the Persian army's combat-engineering capabilities and the short paragraph on the final battle accurately outlines the fundamental principle of Persian tactics, massed archers wearing down the enemy from a distance and then, ideally when the enemy formation showed signs of collapsing, sheathing their bows and charging in to break it up and rout it with spears and swords.

CAMBYSES

Cyrus' successor, Cambyses, was his elder son and his nominated heir. In 525, spurned in his attempt to marry into the Egyptian royal family and bring Egypt and Persia together by peaceful means, he carried on his father's mission by going to war against the country with a mixed army, including subject Hellene levies from Ionia and Aeolis (north of Ionia), and, from an important voluntary newcomer to the empire, Cyprus, previously subject to Egypt. He won a decisive victory at Pelusium on the eastern edge of the Nile delta over an Egyptian army that included Hellene and Carian mercenaries and fielded its own hoplite-style troops. Sadly, Herodotus has little to say about the large army's march from Phoenicia to the delta through 'very arid country' (3.5) in Palestine and along the Mediterranean fringe of Arabia, and nothing to say about the battle or the subsequent, successful siege of Memphis. However, he does tell us about the part played by Phanes, a Halicarnassian mercenary commander in the service of the Egyptians. Phanes changed sides and brokered a deal with the king of Arabia under which Cambyses was allowed to take his army through his territory. The logistical preparations for this included transporting drinking water into the desert in camel skins and stockpiling it at intervals.

The two armies met in battle near Memphis and Herodotus gives rather more space to the vengeance his compatriot suffered for his desertion than to the fighting. Phanes had unwisely left his two sons with the Egyptian army and, just before the battle, he had to watch his former comrades cut their throats and mix their blood with wine and water:

> All the mercenaries drank this, then went into battle. The fighting was fierce, a large number fell on each side and the Egyptians were routed. They fled in disorder and took shelter in Memphis, and, after being under siege for a while, surrendered. (3.13)

So, some 2,500 years and 26 dynasties after its establishment, the kingdom of Egypt became a Persian province. To the west, Libya and the important Hellene settlement of Cyrene and its neighbours quickly submitted.

The Achaemenid Empire now extended along the north coast of Africa as far west as Sicily, and Cambyses next planned a sea campaign against Carthage. The addition of this important maritime power to the empire would have been a very serious strategic threat to Hellas, opening the way for expansion into Sicily and Italy and threatening the western shores of Greece. Carthage had quite recently already clashed with Hellene settlers over control of trade in the western Mediterranean and also had a significant presence in Sicily, where there were many Hellene settlements. But the Phoenician navy refused to take part because, according to tradition, the city had been founded by settlers from the Phoenician city of Tyre sometime in the 8th century:

> So, the Carthaginians escaped being made subjects, because Cambyses thought it would not be right to force the Phoenicians to go to war with Carthage, both because they had submitted to Persia of their own free will, and because the Persian navy was so dependent on the Phoenicians. (3.19)

In 522, Cambyses, now under threat of a coup and possibly insane, died what may have been an accidental death.

DARIUS

Cambyses had left no heir and, after some months of civil war, was succeeded by Darius. He had been one of Cambyses' commanders and was strongly supported by the Persian nucleus of the army.

He needed their support in the early months of his reign to suppress opposition in Media, Babylonia and even Persia, and also further afield, including Armenia and Bactria. Imperial expansion was ruled out for the time being, but, around 518, now confident that his position was secure, he pushed out east to add the valuable province of India, a large part of the Indus basin, not the whole subcontinent. However, Darius' main preoccupation at this time was to build on the work of his two predecessors to create the extraordinary administrative, financial and governmental infrastructure by means of which he and his successors were to maintain and run their empire for the next two centuries. Important elements were to survive Alexander the Great's conquest and remain in place for the three centuries of the Seleucid era that followed.

About ten years into his reign Darius launched the first Persian invasion of Europe. His objective was to subdue the Scythian-occupied territory to the north-west of the Black Sea. Its inhabitants were a nomadic people bracketed by the Persian term *Saka* with the Sacae conquered by Cyrus on the empire's north-eastern frontier and sharing the same origins in the steppes further north. Darius' strategic purpose was most likely the same as Cyrus', to strengthen and push back a similarly vulnerable frontier, in this case to his north-west, to win access to levies that would add substantially to the mounted-archer forces at his disposal, and generally to secure more territory and new sources of tribute.

> In preparation, Darius sent out messengers to his subjects commanding some to muster land forces, some to produce ships and some to build a bridge across the Thracian Bosporus. His brother, Artabanus son of Hystaspes, was strongly opposed to the idea of going to war with the Scythians and spelled out the difficulties the campaign would encounter. This was sound advice, but he could not make the King change his mind and gave up trying. So, Darius completed his preparations and led his army out of Susa.[1] After having gone to the shore of the Black Sea and gazed upon it, Darius sailed back to the

---

[1] The former capital of Elam: Darius built a great palace there and established it as the winter capital of the Achaemenid Empire.

bridge (its construction had been directed by Mandrocles of Samos[1]), and when he had also gazed upon the Bosporus, he set up there two pillars of white marble inscribed, one in Assyrian and the other in Greek, with the names of all the nations under his command, which were actually all the nations he ruled. The total, not counting the fleet but including the cavalry, was 700,000 men; 600 ships were assembled in total. By my reckoning, the point at which King Darius bridged the Bosporus was mid-way between Byzantium and the temple[2] built at the mouth of the straits.

Darius was well pleased with the bridge of boats and rewarded Mandrocles most richly.[3] He now crossed over into Europe, having already sent orders to the Ionians to sail into the Black Sea up to the Danube and, as soon as they got there, to build a bridge across it and await his arrival. The Ionians, Aeolians and Hellespontians were the main elements of the fleet and they sailed directly to the Danube. They then took two days to get upstream to the point where the river narrows at the head of the estuary, which is where the bridge was built. After crossing the Bosporus by this bridge of boats, Darius marched through Thrace and, on his way to the Danube, made the first conquest of the campaign of a people called the Getae,[4] who think themselves immortal. Other Thracians submitted without a fight but the Getae, the most courageous and most civilized of the Thracians, resisted stubbornly and were enslaved. (4.80–93)

The round numbers simply tell us that Darius mustered a very large force for this campaign. In reality, the land army would have been significantly less than 100,000 strong and far fewer than 600 ships would have been needed for the engineering and logistical role they were called upon to perform; no naval combat was anticipated. But, in his description of this combination of land and sea forces, comprising native troops and subject levies, and the efficient execution

---

[1] The word Herodotus uses for Mandrocles' role is *architekton*.
[2] There were known to be temples on both sides of the Bosporus where it opens out into the Black Sea and Herodotus is most likely referring to the temple of Zeus on the Asiatic side.
[3] Literally 'giving him ten of everything'.
[4] A Thracian tribe associated in some way with the Dacians, distinctive for their belief in an afterlife.

of large-scale engineering and logistical operations with Hellene support, Herodotus artfully pre-echoes the much larger campaign that Xerxes was to launch into Europe three decades later. However, in Book 4, he gives much more space to the geography of the region and the anthropology of the Scythians than to the narrative of the expedition.

So far, all was going to plan. Herodotus briefly describes a massive sweep to the north and eastward across the top of the Black Sea, even into the land of the mysterious Black Cloaks and Maneaters, and 'the Uninhabited Area', with the Persians constantly drawn onwards by the Scythians retreating over scorched earth. Then the Scythians changed their tactics:

> They sent part of their force to the Danube with orders to negotiate with the Ionians guarding the bridge and decided that the rest should stop leading the Persians all over the place and instead attack them whenever they came out foraging. So, they watched out for Darius' foraging parties and adopted this tactic, and the Scythian cavalry always put the Persian cavalry to flight. But when the cavalry fell back on the infantry, the infantry gave them protection and the pursuing Scythians wheeled round for fear of them. The Scythians even launched attacks like these at night. (4.128)

The Scythian cavalry, also mounted archers, clearly outnumbered the Persian cavalry and may have been of superior quality as well; Scythians lived their lives on horseback and saddles may have given them an edge in combat. But it seems that massed Persian infantry, out in the field or manning the camp's ramparts, were able to hold them off. However, with foraging impossible and supplies running low, Darius finally had to accept that his campaign had failed, and that retreat was the only option:

> This was the plan he carried out under cover of night. He left in the camp the men who were most exhausted, those he cared least about losing, and all the asses tethered there. He left the asses behind for their braying and he abandoned the men because they were weak, although he told them that their task was to protect

the camp while he went off to tackle the Scythians with the men from the army who were fully fit. After giving this order to the men to be left behind, Darius had the campfires lit and set off on a forced march to the Danube. The asses brayed even more than usual because they had been deprived of so much human company and the Scythians, hearing the asses, assumed that the Persians were all still there. (4.135)

The feeble rearguard surrendered next morning and the Scythians immediately set off after the Persians but, according to Herodotus' account, reached the Danube crossing ahead of them without making contact:

Since the Persians were mostly infantry and did not know the roads, which in any case were poorly marked, and since the Scythians were mounted and familiar with all the shortcuts, the Scythians missed the Persians and arrived at the crossing long before them. (4.136)

The Scythians then tried to persuade the Ionians to destroy the bridge and abandon Darius on the north side of the river:

The Ionians conferred. Miltiades,[1] the Athenian now ruling over the Hellespontine Chersonese as tyrant, took the view that they should do what the Scythians proposed and liberate Ionia. But Histiaeus of Miletus took the opposite view, arguing that it was through Darius that each of them ruled as tyrants in their cities. If Darius' power was overthrown, he would certainly not be able to carry on ruling the Milesians, and none of the others would be able to hold onto power either because their cities would all want democratic[2] rather than tyrannical government. When Histiaeus presented this argument, the rest came round to his way of thinking, although they had agreed with Miltiades' proposal at first. (4.137)

---

[1] Miltiades was an aristocrat who had held high office in Athens early in his career and then been sent out to the Chersonese to govern the Athenian settlements there. It is probable he was acting independently in that capacity rather than representing Athens' interests.
[2] 'People power' could be a threat to tyranny but had not yet evolved to the form that Herodotus' vocabulary implies here.

'Tyrant', *tyrannos*, was the term applied to autocratic rulers who secured and maintained autocratic power by unconstitutional means and often by the use or threat of force. Tyranny had tended to emerge across Hellas in earlier centuries as a resolution of conflict between aristocratic factions, or simply through the usurpation of traditional monarchy. From early in the 5th century, tyrannies evolved that could be described more precisely as military dictatorships. It was a form of rule that was not necessarily evil or violent, and there were tyrants who ruled with the full consent of the citizen body, some exercising power indirectly through existing political structures. However, the emergence of democracy and the concepts of personal and political liberty tended to harden opposition to tyranny. This was paralleled by the aversion to the absolute monarchical rule of the Great King that was to be a strong motivator of Hellene resistance to his imperial ambitions and a recurrent motif of Herodotus' narrative.

On this occasion, purely for selfish reasons in Herodotus' view, the Ionian tyrants decided to keep faith with Darius, which they would continue to do for the next decade or so. However, they did not inform the Scythians of this and dismantled only the northern end of the bridge up to a bowshot's distance from the riverbank. Herodotus' account has the Scythians turning back to look for the Persians but again failing to find them, allowing Darius to complete his withdrawal and make the crossing unopposed. However, with their greater mobility and knowledge of the country it should have been easy for the Scythians to track down and harass and even destroy the slower-moving Persian column, if that had been the intention. It is more likely that Darius had no option but to agree terms with the Scythians and Herodotus' version may be based on an official public account of this episode which showed the abandonment of the expedition in the most favourable possible light. In any case, it is clear that Darius had underestimated his enemy and the challenge of the inhospitable spaces to be covered, and Herodotus gives a strong hint that he did not take enough cavalry with him.

The Great King had overreached and met with failure, and close observers and potential opponents could now be less in awe of him. He returned to Persia leaving Megabazus, one of his most trusted generals, in the Chersonese to complete the subjugation of this threshold of Europe. The expedition across the Danube had been a failure, but the campaign had opened a corridor along the north shore of the Aegean for any future advance into the west, now the only realistic strategic option for imperial expansion. Also, closer to home, control of both shores of the Hellespont was a significant prize in itself.

Libya, including the Hellene cities of Barca and Cyrene, had submitted to Cambyses without a fight at the time of his conquest of Egypt in 525, so in North Africa the Persian Empire already extended further west than Athens. The Hellenes of Libya appear to have achieved an unacceptable degree of independence and at about the same time as the Scythian campaign an expedition was launched from Egypt to regain control of Barca and Cyrene. The expeditionary force was recalled before it could make a serious attempt on Cyrene, but Barca was taken. Persian expertise in siege-warfare proved inadequate in the face of ingenious countermeasures and a solid defence, but the city was finally tricked into surrender:

> The Persians laid siege to the city for nine months, digging tunnels to mine under the walls and also attempting to take it by storm. However, a metal-worker discovered a way of locating the tunnels by using a copper shield, taking it round inside the city walls and striking the ground with it. It gave a dull sound everywhere except where there was tunnelling going on, and there the metal would give a hollow ring. Then the Barcaeans would dig a countermine and kill the Persians tunnelling towards them. So, the tunnels were discovered, and the defenders beat off all attacks. This went on for a long time and many fell with no fewer casualties on the Persian side than amongst the defenders. So Amasis, their commander, made a new plan, having concluded that Barca could not be taken by force but that it might be taken by deception. And that is what he did ...[1]
> (4.200–01)

At the north-west corner of the empire, Megabazus went on to campaign as far as Paionia, extending the Great King's reach to the

---

[1] Herodotus goes on in 4.201–02 to describe the unsubtle deception which enabled the Persians to agree a treaty which they could immediately break, and the gruesome reprisals that ensued.

borders of Macedon. The Macedonians acknowledged his supremacy over them by making the traditional offering of 'earth and water' demanded by the Persians, but they were not actually invaded until 492 in what was to be the third Barbarian campaign into the west. However, the mainland of Greece now lay between the gaping jaws of a monster with its nose thrust into Europe, its body spanning the Middle East and its tail in the Indian subcontinent.

The best by far

The Rise of Athens

From 546 Athens had been ruled continuously by tyrants, first Pisistratus and then his son Hippias. Pisistratus had held supreme power for two earlier periods and been ousted twice. He finally secured his position with financial support from Thebes and other cities, and with military support in the shape of mercenaries from Argos and the powerful island of Naxos. With this force, he crossed from Eretria in Euboea where he had been living in exile with his family and supporters and landed at Marathon on the north-eastern coast of Attica. He was joined there by supporters from Athens and the rest of Attica; Herodotus remarks that 'these were people who found tyranny a more welcome prospect than freedom' (1.62). The best part of 40 years was to pass before Athens evolved into a democratic state and it is worth noting that Herodotus commends Pisistratus for the manner in which he exercised his autocratic power. 'He did not meddle with positions of authority or change laws that already existed, but governed the city fairly and well by means of its established institutions' (1.59). Herodotus writes with approval about other tyrants as well and it would be several decades before tyranny was condemned as the worst possible model of governance by Plato and Aristotle. But views of specific regimes were, of course, coloured in the Hellene mind by the ways in which tyrannical power might be secured or wielded, especially if external backing, Hellene or, worst of all, Barbarian, underpinned it.

Pisistratus marched on Athens with the army he had assembled and the Athenians took up position at Pallene about half-way between Athens and Marathon. But Pisistratus gave them no opportunity to form up and face him in battle. In any case, it seems they were poorly led and somewhat lacking in commitment: 'the Athenians from the city had just finished their lunch and some were playing dice, others were having a sleep when Pisistratus' men attacked them and routed them' (1.63). Taking control of Athens for a third time, Pisistratus ruled until his death in 527. He was succeeded by his son Hippias, who ruled with similar moderation. Athens seems to have prospered and Hipparchus, his younger brother and deputy, was responsible for substantial architectural works and other cultural projects. However, Hipparchus was assassinated in 514. The motivation appears to have been more dynastic rivalry or sexual passion than politics, but the killers, Harmodius and Aristogiton, were later elevated to heroic status as tyrannicides. Hippias' rule subsequently became harsh and the Alcmaeonids, powerful aristocratic rivals of the Pisistratid clan, began to plot his overthrow:

> According to the Athenians, these Alcmaeonids installed themselves as suppliants at Delphi and bribed the Pythia[1] to instruct any Spartans who came to consult her to set Athens free, whether their mission was private or public. So, the Lacedaemonians, having received this instruction again and again, sent Anchimolius son of Aster, a citizen of some distinction, with an army to drive the Pisistratids out of Athens. There were strong ties of friendship between them, but they respected the god's will more than the will of man. And so they loaded these troops onto ships and sent them by sea, and they put in at Phalerum and disembarked there. However, the Pisistratids had found out about the plan and called on the Thessalians to help them, which they could do because they had an alliance with them. The Thessalians' collective response was to send 1,000 cavalry and, when their allies had arrived, this is the strategy the Pisistratids adopted. First, they prepared the battlefield by clearing[2] the whole plain of Phalerum so that it could be easily ridden over, and then they sent the cavalry in against the enemy. They charged and cut down many of the Lacedaemonians including Anchimolius himself and drove

---

[1] The Pythia was the title of the priestess who uttered the oracles at Delphi.
[2] The Greek word *keirantes* means 'shaving' in its literal sense. Here it means cutting down trees and shrubbery and removing other obstacles to the manoeuvrability of cavalry. It is also used in the sense of 'laying waste'.

those that were left back to the ships. So, this first Lacedaemonian expeditionary force made its exit.

After this the Lacedaemonians sent a larger force to attack Athens and put their king, Cleomenes son of Anaxandridas, in command of it. This time they went by land rather than sea. When they entered Attica, the Thessalian cavalry were the first troops to engage them, but they were quickly beaten off and routed. More than 40 were killed and those who were left made off for Thessaly by the most direct route possible. Then Cleomenes came into the city and, with the help of the Athenians who desired freedom, drove the tyrant and his men into the Pelasgian fort[1] and laid siege to it. But the Lacedaemonians would never actually have taken the fort. First of all, they were only planning to stay in Attica for a short while[2] and, secondly, the Pisistratids were well supplied with food and drink. The Lacedaemonians would have besieged the place for only a few days and then taken off back to Sparta. However, by a stroke of luck that was bad for one side but convenient for the other, the Pisistratids' children fell into their hands while being escorted out of the country and this was the Pisistratids' undoing. In return for their children and on terms set out by the Athenians, they had to leave Attica within five days. That is how the Athenians got rid of their tyrants and so, after ruling in Athens for 36 years, the Pisistratids withdrew to Sigeum[3] on the River Scamander. (5.63–66)

Herodotus has little detail to offer on this episode, which took place in 510 or 509. However, it includes a useful insight into the influence that the Delphic and other oracles could exert on internal and inter-state Hellene affairs. It must have been widely understood that the oracle could be manipulated by bribery or sheer persistence, yet the 'god-sent' advice or command might still be acted upon out of respect for divine will. As far as the fighting is concerned, the battlefield preparation

[1] An ancient part of the Acropolis fortifications that did not survive the Persian invasion in 480/79.

[2] The Spartans were reputed to have little enthusiasm for sieges or much expertise in this branch of warfare.

[3] Sigeum was an Athenian settlement on the edge of Asia close to Troy and ruled by a Pisistratid tyrant, Hippias' brother Hegesistratus.

carried out by the Pisistratids suggests a degree of tactical sophistication (as does the surprise attack mounted by Pisistratus on his advance into Attica decades previously). In their initial setback, it is possible that the Lacedaemonians were caught by a rapid charge before they could form up properly after disembarkation and they may have sent only a modest force in anticipation of local support which did not reach them in time, perhaps cut off by the freely manoeuvring cavalry. They committed more to their second attempt in terms of both manpower and leadership, and this time they were clearly ready for the Thessalians. But the low casualty figure of 40 suggests that the force they routed with such ease was less than 1,000 strong on this occasion. The remark that 'the Lacedaemonians would have besieged the place for only a few days and then taken off back to Sparta' and the implication of ineffectualness in siege warfare would have played well with an Athenian audience in the years from 431 in which Sparta invaded Attica four times without penetrating the fortifications of Athens.

All this took place around the beginning of the final decade of the 6th century. The subsequent contest for political leadership was won by the Alcmaeonid Cleisthenes:

> Cleisthenes brought over to his side the common people (*demos*), who had previously been completely excluded ... Once Cleisthenes had won over the people, he was far more powerful than his rivals. (5.69)

He initiated the constitutional reforms that underpinned 5th-century Athenian democracy and the values that Athenian leaders would invoke in the conflicts that lay ahead. In 507, his main rival, Isagoras, turned to Sparta for support and managed a counter-coup, but this very quickly unravelled in the face of opposition from almost the entire citizen body. Sparta had sent its king Cleomenes with only a small force, presumably again expecting strong local support. This force became trapped on the Acropolis and had no option but to leave the city ignominiously under truce. Cleisthenes and his supporters were recalled from exile, Isagoras was banished and his closest supporters were executed.

> I will now tell you about the remarkable things the Athenians went on to do once they had gained their freedom and the remarkable things they achieved in the period up to Ionia's rebellion against Darius and

Aristagoras the Milesian's visit to Athens[1] requesting their support in this. Athens had been great before but became even greater, once rid of her tyrants.

With Cleisthenes restored, the Athenians, well aware that they had made enemies of the Lacedaemonians and Cleomenes, despatched envoys to Sardis with the objective of forming an alliance with Persia. When these envoys arrived in Sardis and delivered their message, Artaphernes son of Hystaspes,[2] governor of Sardis, asked who these people were, requesting an alliance with Persia, and where on earth had they come from.[3] When he had found out all he wanted to know from the envoys, his answer was short and to the point. If the Athenians agreed to offer King Darius earth and water, he would form an alliance with them, but if they did not wish to do so, he commanded them to leave. The envoys, in their desire to form this alliance, consented on their own initiative and faced serious charges on their return home. (5.65–66, 73)

The Athenian envoys may not have fully appreciated the significance of their symbolic act of submission. In any case, the Persians would have taken it at face value and noted the public repudiation implied by the 'serious charges' laid against them on their return to Athens.

Cleomenes, smarting at the humiliation inflicted on him by the Athenians' words and actions, raised an army from the whole of the Peloponnese. He did not state his specific purpose, which was to have his revenge on the Athenian people and install Isagoras, who had been ejected from the Acropolis with him, as tyrant. Cleomenes marched to Eleusis with a large force, and the Boeotians, in a co-ordinated attack, captured Oenoe and Hysiae, two districts (demes) on the borders of Attica, while the Chalcidians[4] delivered a separate thrust into Attic territory. The Athenians, under attack on

---

[1] This was at the turn of the century.
[2] Making him a half-brother of Darius.
[3] The same questions that Cyrus asked about the Spartans, attributed by Herodotus to Artaphernes here with the same intent.
[4] From Chalcis on the island of Euboea.

two fronts,[1] decided to take on the Peloponnesians at once, while they were at Eleusis, and to deal with the Boeotians and Chalcidians later. However, when the two armies were about to engage, the Corinthians decided amongst themselves that this was an unjust act and they were the first to about face and take themselves off. Then Demaratus son of Ariston, the other Spartan king,[2] followed suit even though he had brought the army from Lacedaemon, sharing command of it with Cleomenes and agreeing with him on everything up to this point. When the rest of the allies at Eleusis saw that the Lacedaemonian kings were at odds with each other and that the Corinthians were abandoning their position in the line, they also departed.

After this invasion force had fallen apart so ignominiously, the Athenians marched on Chalcis wanting to get revenge there first. The Boeotians marched to the Euripus[3] to help the Chalcidians and as soon as the Athenians knew of this, they decided to tackle them first. They fought the Boeotians and won a crushing victory killing a great many of them and taking 700 prisoners. And on the very same day[4] the Athenians crossed over to Euboea and fought the Chalcidians and defeated them as well. Afterwards they settled 400 colonists[5] in this horse-breeding country.

So the power of Athens grew at this time, fully demonstrating the value of giving every citizen the right to political equality (*isegoria*, literally 'equal voice'). While under tyrannical rule the Athenians were no more of a force in warfare than any of their neighbours, yet when they had got rid of the tyrants, they became the best by far. They were plainly half-hearted in the service of a despot, but, once liberated, every one of them was eager to achieve great things for himself. (5.74–75, 77–78)

---

[1] The Peloponnesians coming from the south-west and the Boeotians and Chalcidians coming from the north and north-east.

[2] In Sparta's unique constitution two kings reigned simultaneously.

[3] The channel separating Chalcis from the mainland.

[4] They probably did not move quite as fast as this. The channel is very narrow at this point but regrouping after the battle and then shipping the troops across would have been demanding and time-consuming.

[5] Known as *cleruchs*, this type of colonist remained an Athenian citizen with obligations to provide military or naval service and to hold land occupied by military action.

The Thebans wanted vengeance for the humiliating defeat they and their allies had suffered at the Euripus and, in 505/4, formed an alliance for this purpose with Aegina, a close neighbour (an island in the Saronic Gulf, visible from the Acropolis) and long-standing enemy of Athens. Thebes was the most powerful city in Boeotia and Aegina was a significant sea-power by local standards. The Athenians beat off the Theban attack easily, but, while they were engaged in this, the Aeginetans raided Phalerum and other coastal districts of Attica in 'an unheralded war ... and did the Athenians a lot of harm' (5.81). Athens had demonstrated new strength on land, but was still weak as a naval power.

This newly released energy was not restricted to making war. It was also evident in public works of sculpture and architecture, both sacred and secular, in commerce and in citizens' enthusiastic participation in government at every level. But meanwhile, Hippias still hoped to bring about his restoration as tyrant of Athens and Herodotus describes an attempt by Sparta to assemble an alliance to achieve this. If Sparta did make such an attempt, it seems that the rest of the Peloponnesians would not have anything to do with it and Herodotus may simply be recording some anti-Spartan propaganda put about around the middle of the 5th century. But the Spartans might have welcomed the opportunity this would have presented to neutralize a growing challenge to their own predominance in Hellas, while the Corinthians, who were, according to Herodotus, the most vociferous and influential critics of Sparta's plan, would have opposed it because they were in favour of the emergence of a significant counterweight to Sparta in Hellas' balance of power. Herodotus describes a conference, which he may or may not have invented, in which the Spartans attempt to persuade their Peloponnesian allies to join them in this campaign. The long speech Herodotus puts in the mouth of the Corinthian representative lifts the debate to a higher level in its opening lines. They are spiced with some irony in view of Sparta's recent involvement in Isagoras' abortive coup-attempt.

'To be sure, the heavens will sink beneath the earth and the earth will be raised up above the heavens, and mankind will dwell beneath the sea, and fish will dwell where men dwelt before, if you Lacedaemonians ever contrive to throw out the principle of equally shared power (*isocratia*) and bring back tyranny to the city-state. There is no greater injustice, nothing on earth more blood-spattered than tyranny.' (5.92)

Equal sharing of power and equal entitlement to a voice in decision-making were two defining principles of this newly emerged form of government 'by the people, for the people', *demokratia*. This was perceived as freedom in direct contrast to the slavery of tyrannical rule. Earlier in the *Historia* Herodotus introduces a third 'equality principle' and briefly describes some of the workings of the Athenian system in a lengthy reflection on the competing merits of monarchy, oligarchy and democracy that would not have been out of place in one of Plato's dialogues. But, surprisingly, it is framed as a debate involving seven leading Persians, one of them Darius, about the future governance of their nation after the death of Cambyses:

> Otanes, speaking first, argued that they should allow all the people of Persia to participate in government. 'How can monarchy be a harmonious system when an individual who is accountable to nobody can do whatever he wishes? But rule by the many has the most beautiful name of all, *isonomia* (equality under the law). It works in a completely different way from monarchy. In this system positions of authority are allocated by lot, authority is held accountable and policy-making is open to public scrutiny. So, in my opinion, we should set aside monarchy and empower the people, for the will of the many is paramount.'[1] (3.80)

At the end of the debate, 'the will of the many' receives one vote, oligarchy two and monarchy four. Darius successfully argues that 'there is nothing better than the rule of one man who is the best, flawlessly governing the people in his excellent wisdom' (3.82). Assisted by some trickery and 'thunder and lightning out of a clear sky', he secures the group's nomination and, after defeating a number of rivals, begins his 35-year reign as Great King. A third of the way through the *Historia* and 30 years before Persia and Athens meet in battle at Marathon, Herodotus is highlighting what he clearly sees as the most telling

---

[1] Literally 'for in the many is everything'.

difference between the two ways of life, and as an ideological driver of the conflict between east and west that his narrative is building towards. The democratic principles of *isegoria* and *isonomia* powerfully harnessed individual and collective political freedom (*eleutheria*) and were in direct opposition to the alternative forms of government: hereditary monarchy and specifically the rule of the Great King, tyranny and oligarchy. In Herodotus' view, democracy was superior to all other systems for the way in which it generated and channelled the energies of individual citizens to the greatest benefit of the city-state. In practical terms, of course, this grand vision of universal direct participation in government was limited by the exclusion of the majority of the population from full rights of citizenship. In Athens in the early 5th century these were the preserve of an adult male elite that was qualified by Athenian parentage and possession of sufficient wealth. Lowlier male citizens, however, were entitled to attend and cast votes in the Assembly though not to hold political, judicial or military office. Tyrannical rule sustained by external power, especially if that power flowed directly from a towering throne that was three months' march away, was a double contradiction of the democratic concepts of freedom in the sense of self-rule with no external constraints, and *autonomia*, a state's ability to make, implement and be governed by its own laws.

> When Hippias had made his way back from Lacedaemon into Asia, he took any opportunity to badmouth Athens with Artaphernes and made every effort to gain control of the city for himself, and Darius. When the Athenians found out what Hippias was doing, they despatched envoys to Sardis to urge the Persians to take no notice of Athenian exiles. However, Artaphernes commanded them to restore Hippias, if they valued their safety, and when that message was delivered to the Athenians, they rejected it. And this rejection amounted to an open declaration of war on Persia. (5.96)

Herodotus may be overdramatizing the significance of this diplomatic exchange, but the Athenians were already compromised by their public repudiation two or three years before of their earlier delegation's unauthorized, if unwitting, act of submission. However, events in Ionia would soon lead to an open act of war.

Individual Ionians and other Hellenes had gained great power and wealth in Darius' western empire and some of them served the Great King well. However, Histiaeus, tyrant of Miletus, had now become so powerful and influential that he was seen as a threat, a potential leader of Hellene insurrection. Herodotus represents his part in the rescue of Darius from Scythia as motivated by self-interest rather than loyalty, and there were probably other good reasons for distrusting the man. So Histiaeus was stood down as tyrant of Miletus and also of Myrcinus, an important Thracian city with which he had been rewarded for his services on the Danube, and given an invitation he could not refuse. He was summoned to Susa and granted the great honour of joining the imperial court as a 'dining companion and counsellor' to the Great King. His cousin and son-in-law, Aristagoras, took over Miletus as his deputy. Miletus was one of the foremost cities of Ionia and was on particularly good terms with its Persian overlords.

Around the turn of the century 'certain men of substance [literally 'stout'] had been driven out of Naxos by the people and took refuge in Miletus, and these cities were to become the source of great troubles for Ionia (5.30). The Naxian exiles asked Aristagoras for military support and he persuaded Artaphernes to fund an invasion of their large, rich island. With the approval of the Great King Artaphernes provided 200 triremes and 'a veritable multitude of Persians and other allies' (5.32). The trireme was the capital ship used by all the significant navies of the Mediterranean in the 6th and 5th centuries and this was a more formidable fleet than any Hellene city could muster at the time. In itself a fat prize, Naxos could also serve the Persians as a strategic stepping stone for a seaborne campaign against the heart of Hellas; Athens was only three days' easy sailing beyond. Darius gave his approval, but the expedition was abandoned after an unsuccessful four-month siege of the city, and the exiles were left on the island to fend for themselves. Aristagoras, fully responsible and impossibly in debt to his paymasters, was fearful of their retribution. Defection and insurrection seemed the only option and he began plotting. Coincidentally, so the story went, Histiaeus in his golden cage sent Aristagoras a secret message tattooed on the scalp of a slave, ordering him to start a revolt against the Persians.

Hellenes who lived in Ionia on the west coast of Asia (modern Turkey) had been Persian subjects since the middle of the 6th century, from the time Cyrus had pushed the western boundaries of his new empire to the eastern shores of the Aegean. They had prospered and were the source of cultural and intellectual developments that were to influence the 5th-century golden age of mainland Greece, and of Athens particularly. By the standards of the time, the Persians were generally just and tolerant as rulers, even liberal, so long as the absolute power of the Great King, exercised directly or through his satraps (regional governors), was unequivocally accepted and taxes, tribute and military service rendered. Persian rule allowed subjects to retain their local religious practices and, below the level of head-of-state, their political, legal and governmental institutions. So it was not regarded as a terrible fate by all Hellenes. However, obligations to their ultimate master, the Great King, in the shape of tribute and conscripted military service, and, in many cases, the imposition of autocratic rule by a tyrant had the potential to erode acceptance of a status that their western cousins who had recently discovered democracy would emotively describe as slavery.

Histiaeus and Aristagoras had their personal agendas but many of the numerous and widely dispersed Hellene communities of the eastern Aegean and the west coast of Asia were now ready to respond to their call to arms to rise up in a war of liberation from tyranny and Persian rule, although some of these communities' leaders may have quietly favoured the less radical step from tyranny to oligarchy. In any case there were other considerations. Whether or not Persian domination was to blame for a decline in commerce and prosperity, the tribute demanded of the subject cities was a drain on their resources, and there was also the burden of supplying levies of ships and men to support the policing and expansion of the Great King's empire.

The origins of great troubles

The Ionian Revolt

Aristagoras stood down, nominally, as tyrant of Miletus and introduced democratic institutions (*isonomia* is used again here), which was what the Milesians wanted; he also persuaded the other cities of Ionia to follow suit. Only the geographer and historian Hecataeus, one of several ground-breaking intellectuals active in Ionia at that time, advised against taking on the might of Persia. Presciently, he argued that only control of the sea would give Aristagoras any chance of success. Aristagoras did know that he was in need of strong allies and Sparta was his first port of call:

> Cleomenes was still king when Aristagoras, tyrant of Miletus, came to Sparta. When he went to speak with the king, the Lacedaemonians tell me that he had with him a bronze plate engraved with a map of the whole earth including all the seas and rivers.[1] Aristagoras began the conversation, saying, 'Do not let my eagerness to come here surprise you, Cleomenes, for look at what has come to pass! The sons of Ionia are slaves rather than free men, and this shames us and causes us great sorrow. And it must be the same for you, surely, above all the rest of the Hellenes, because you are the leading power of Hellas. Now, in the

---

[1] This is thought to have been Hecataeus' improved edition of the map of the world, the first known of in the western tradition, created by Anaximander, the 6th-century Milesian 'natural philosopher'. It would have been a novel and impressive visual aid in Aristagoras' presentations in Sparta and Athens, although it seems from an earlier comment that Herodotus himself found it unimpressive.

name of Hellas' gods, I call upon you to deliver your Ionian kinsmen[1] from slavery. This is a thing you can easily achieve, for your fighting qualities are superlative and the Barbarians are not brave at all. They go into battle with bows and short spears, wearing trousers and with soft bonnets on their heads, so they can be easily beaten. Also, the people who live in those lands possess more in the way of assets than the entire population of the rest of the world: gold, for a start, and silver and bronze, the finest clothing, and beasts of burden and slaves. All this can be yours if you wish. Let me show you where these peoples live in the order you would encounter them. Next to the Ionians are the Lydians, very wealthy and dwelling in a fair land.'

And, as he spoke he pointed to the map of the world he had brought with him, engraved on a bronze plate. 'Look here to the east of the Lydians. Here are the Phrygians with more livestock and better crops than any people I know of. Next to them are the Cappadocians, whom we call Syrians, and their neighbours the Cilicians, whose land stretches to the ocean here, where the island of Cyprus lies; the yearly tribute the Cilicians pay to the King is 500 talents.[2] After the Cilicians come the Armenians, another people rich in livestock, and then the Matieni, whose country you can see here. Next, we have the land of Cissia and, here, Susa on the banks of the River Choaspes where the Great King has his residence.[3] The treasure-houses of his wealth are there and, if you take that city, you can be assured that your wealth will rival the riches of Zeus.

'Now surely the time has come for you to cease fighting for small patches of valueless land with narrow borders, to cease fighting with the Messenians,[4] who are a match for you in battle, and with the

---

[1] Much is made elsewhere of the difference between Ionians and Dorians; Aristagoras the Ionian is here appealing to the Dorian Lacedaemonians as Hellenes.

[2] A talent was worth 6,000 drachmas and a drachma was roughly a day's wage for a skilled worker.

[3] The Great King had other palace-cities but Susa was the principal one and his principal treasury was there.

[4] The Spartans had conquered the Messenians by the end of the 8th century and successfully subdued them when they rebelled around the middle of the 7th. The Third Messenian War was to come some time after these events in the shape of the Helot Revolt of 465. The Messenians could hardly be described as 'an equal match' historically, and either Herodotus had his facts wrong, or felt the need to show Aristagoras up.

Arcadians and the Argives. These people possess neither gold nor silver, none of that treasure for which men are driven by desire to fight and die. Given this opportunity to become master of all of Asia with ease, what other choice do you have?'

That is what Aristagoras said, and Cleomenes replied, 'Milesian guest-friend,[1] I will put off answering you till the day after tomorrow,' and that was as far as they took things. On the day set for Cleomenes to give his answer they met as agreed and Cleomenes asked Aristagoras how many days' march it was from the Ionian Sea[2] to where the Great King lived. So far, Aristagoras had been clever and misled Cleomenes completely, but at this point he slipped up. He should never have answered with the truth if he wanted to bring the Spartans into Asia, but he did, and said that it was three months' march inland. At that Cleomenes cut off Aristagoras before he could start his detailed description of the journey, saying, 'Leave Sparta before sunset, Milesian guest-friend. You may wish to lead the Lacedaemonians off on a three-month march[3] from the sea, but there is nothing you can say that will persuade them to follow you.' (5.49–50)

Aristagoras made a final attempt to persuade Cleomenes, approaching him as a supplicant to be on the safe side and offering larger and larger bribes. According to Herodotus the king's eight-year-old daughter was with him and brought the discussion to an end:

'Father!' she exclaimed, 'Your guest-friend is going to corrupt you if you don't get away from him.' Cleomenes liked the child's advice and went off into another room, and Aristagoras left Sparta there and then. (5.51)

He went to Athens next:

The Athenians were already on bad terms with Persia when Aristagoras the Milesian arrived in their city after being ejected from Sparta by

---

[1] 'Guest-friendship' (*xenia*) was the ancient term for the respected bond which could be established between individuals from separate nations or states and of different ethnicity.
[2] The eastern side of the Aegean.
[3] Herodotus' figure of '90 days', arrived at after a detailed and not always accurate break-down of the probable route into its main stages, is a reasonable estimate for the 2,500km journey from the Aegean coastline to Susa.

Cleomenes the Lacedaemonian. He had come there because Athens was the next most powerful city after Sparta. He stood before the people[1] and gave the same speech as he had given in Sparta, describing the riches of Asia and declaring that the Persians could be easily defeated because they did not fight with the hoplite shield or spear. He said all this and also pointed out that the Milesians had been settlers from Athens,[2] and that it was right and proper for the Athenians to come to their aid with their great power. In his desperation there was nothing he did not offer, and he finally convinced the Athenians. It really does seem to be easier to deceive a crowd than a single man. Aristagoras could not deceive Cleomenes of Lacedaemon, one single individual, but he succeeded with 30,000[3] Athenians. So led astray, the Athenians voted to send 20 ships to support the Ionians and put Melanthius, a citizen of excellent reputation,[4] in command. Those ships were the origin of the great troubles that were to affect Hellenes and Barbarians alike. (5.97)

This episode is coloured by Herodotus' wish to lay responsibility for 'the great troubles' that were now in store on Aristagoras, and by his low opinion of the man's character. He shows him deviously underplaying Persian military might, making only a passing reference to their archery and no mention of their cavalry, vast manpower or immense navy. However, Hellenes did generally consider the bow an unmanly weapon, and trousers effeminate, and Aristagoras does correctly present the Barbarian spear as inferior to the longer hoplite weapon. But Persia's almost unbroken run of military success over the preceding half-century should have conveyed a more intimidating message and this could have been reinforced by the experiences of the many Hellenes who had fought as mercenaries or levies alongside or against Persians in the Great Kings' various campaigns.

In any case, Aristagoras' geography lecture and alleged attempt to bribe Cleomenes backfired as far as the Spartan king was concerned. But, as Herodotus drily observes, the Athenians, flexing their democratic

---

[1] A meeting of the Assembly, at which all citizens were entitled to speak and vote.
[2] This was probably true to the extent that there were influential Athenians amongst the migrants from mainland Greece that had settled in Ionia in previous centuries.
[3] The number of citizens eligible to vote was nearer 20,000 at that time.
[4] Otherwise unheard of.

rights in their quite recently instituted Assembly, were easily gulled. On the other hand, it could be reasonably argued that their decision, misguided as it was in strategic terms, was a principled one, to join kindred Ionians in a fight against an enemy of freedom that had already reached out half-way across the Aegean in its attempt on Naxos. Their commitment of a little more than 4,000 men, including a few hundred hoplites, was not a massive proportion of their total manpower, but the 20 ships probably represented close to half of their navy. The manpower commitment would have been smaller if some or all of the ships were smaller than triremes with their complement of 200–230 oarsmen, sailors, hoplites and archers.

The Athenians arrived at Miletus with their 20 ships and with them came five triremes[1] from Eretria. The Eretrians were not campaigning with the Athenians out of goodwill towards them but to repay the Milesians for being their allies in an earlier war that they had fought against Chalcis,[2] when the Samians sided with the Chalcidians against the Eretrians and Milesians. So, when they and the rest of his allies had arrived, Aristagoras launched his attack on Sardis. However, he did not go off to fight himself but stayed behind and appointed two other Milesians as generals, his own brother Charopinus and a fellow citizen named Hermophantus. On reaching Ephesus with this force, the Ionians left their ships at Coresus in Ephesian territory and marched inland with a large body of men, enlisting Ephesians to be their guides. They followed the River Cayster, crossed Mount Tmolus and came to Sardis. They captured the city without any opposition, all of it except for its acropolis, which was occupied by Artaphernes himself with a substantial garrison. But the Hellenes were unable to plunder the city they had taken. A lot of the houses in Sardis were built entirely of reeds and those that were built of bricks had thatched roofs. A soldier set one of these buildings on fire and the blaze went from house to house until it had

---

[1] Herodotus' use of the word *trieres* for the Eretrians' contingent but the generic *naus* (ship) for the Athenians' may indicate that the latter comprised or included smaller warships or even transport vessels.

[2] A war fought in about 700, probably over sea-trading interests. But the Eretrians may have felt some indebtedness to the Athenians for their defeat of the Chalcidians in 506.

spread over the whole city. With the city burning and its outskirts all ablaze, the Lydians and those of the Persians who were with them had no way of escape. So they all streamed down to the marketplace and the banks of the Pactolus. (This river carries gold dust[1] from Mount Tmolus and flows through the marketplace, eventually joining the Hermus, which runs down to the sea.) The Lydians and Persians, now massed in the marketplace, had no option but to stand and fight and when the Ionians saw that the enemy was going to put up a fight, and that many more were coming up in support, they took fright and fell back on Mount Tmolus. Then they set off back to their ships under cover of night. So, Sardis was burned and in it the temple of Cybele,[2] the mother-goddess worshipped there, an act which was to become the Persians' justification for destroying the holy places they later burned in Greece.

When the Persians who lived to the west of the River Halys heard what was happening, they gathered together and marched to support the Lydians. Finding the Ionians gone from Sardis they followed their trail and caught up with them at Ephesus. The Ionians formed up and faced them but suffered a severe defeat in the battle that followed and the Persians killed many of them, some of them famous, including Eualcides, commander of the Eretrians, a prizewinning athlete much praised by Simonides of Ceos.[3] Those who managed to escape from the battlefield scattered, each to their own city, and that was the end of the fighting there. Afterwards the Athenians completely abandoned the Ionians and refused to help them in any way, although Aristagoras sent many pleading messages. However, despite the loss of their alliance with the Athenians, the Ionians did not draw back from war with the Great King because they had already gone so far in their actions against him. They sailed to the Hellespont and took control of Byzantium and all the other cities in that region and then went on from the Hellespont and brought most of Caria over to their side.

[1] A source of the legendary wealth of Lydia under the 6th-century King Croesus.
[2] Cybele was the mother-goddess of non-Hellene Asia and shared attributes with the Hellene goddess Demeter.
[3] One of the leading Hellene poets of his time, active from about 515 until his death in Sicily 20 years after the Persian War.

Even the city of Caunus,[1] which had previously refused to be part of the alliance, now joined it after the burning of Sardis. (5.97–103)

The bold, even foolhardy Hellene attack on Sardis seems to have taken Artaphernes completely by surprise. His 'substantial garrison' was clearly strong enough to see off the Hellenes when it actually confronted them, and the most appropriate course of action would have been to meet them outside the city, rather than to wait for them to lay siege to the acropolis. The unplanned fire may have been more of an immediate problem for the attackers than the defenders, who would presumably have been safe inside the citadel walls on the heights above the city. The spreading blaze forced the Hellenes to gather in the open spaces by the river, enabling the Persians and Lydians to assess their strength and concentrate their forces to attack them en masse. When the Hellenes withdrew, the Persians and Lydians, reinforced from further inland, regrouped and caught up with the rebels before they could board their ships. They now clearly outnumbered the Hellenes and the speed of their pursuit suggests there was a strong cavalry element. Herodotus' only quantification of the forces involved is the 25 ships from Athens and Eretria. Their withdrawal probably did not significantly weaken the rebels, who were able to muster over 350 triremes four years later. But the early loss of their only support from the heartland must have been a blow to morale. There could have been a swift change of political mood in Athens with a desire to appease rather than provoke the Great King, but that was no longer possible.

When word came to Darius that Sardis had been taken and burnt by the Athenians and Ionians, and that Aristagoras the Milesian had led the conspirators who had hatched the plot, it is said that he was unconcerned about the Ionians because he knew they would not escape punishment for this rebellion. But he asked who these Athenians were, and, when he had been told, called for his bow. He took it, put an arrow to the string and shot it into the sky, and, as it soared up, he said this prayer: 'O Zeus, grant me vengeance on the Athenians.' And after doing this he gave orders that one of his servants should say to him three times whenever his dinner was set before him, 'Master, remember the Athenians.' (5.105)

[1] An important centre of trade and agriculture in the south-east corner of Caria.

It is unlikely that Darius needed to be told who the Athenians were, pleasing as the echo is of Cyrus' reaction to his decades-earlier encounter with the Spartans. He probably already knew that they had reneged on their offer of earth and water to Artaphernes, and very likely knew about their subsequent refusal to reinstate Hippias, even if the ex-tyrant had less access to him than Herodotus suggests. The King's dramatic oath has a ring of truth to it, however. He is calling on Ahura Mazda, the principal god of the Persians, regarded by the Hellenes as one and the same as Zeus. Ahura Mazda was actually an altogether more sophisticated divine being than the head of the Hellenes' chaotic pantheon, but the two shared roots in the ancient Indo-European tradition of a supreme sky-god. The bow, symbolic of Persian military might, was an important piece of the Great King's regalia and shooting an arrow into the sky sealed the oath powerfully.

In spite of their early setback the Ionians had quickly spread insurrection north to the Bosporus and south throughout Caria. Then all but one of the ten major cities of Cyprus rebelled, and Cyprus had been a rich and important imperial asset since the reign of Cambyses. The Ionian Revolt was no longer purely an Ionian affair, if it ever was. Since both the Carians and the Cypriots were as Asian as they were Hellene, it had become rather more than an irritating disturbance in a cluster of subject cities on one limited frontier. So Cyprus and the strategically important Hellespont region became higher priorities than Ionia. In the meantime, Histiaeus managed to persuade Darius to allow him to return home on the pretext that he would restore order. He disingenuously undertook to deliver Aristagoras for punishment, if it proved to be the case that he and the Milesians were responsible for the rebellion, and into the bargain he made a ridiculous promise to bring Sardinia, recently annexed by Carthage, into the Persian Empire.

Operations to put down the rebellion took place simultaneously in more than one theatre from 498 onwards. Herodotus does not give any precise chronology, but he deals with the suppression of Cyprus first. The Cypriots called on the Ionians for support and they sent a fleet, but declined to join in any fighting on land. The Persians had shipped a large army over from Cilicia supported by a Phoenician fleet and the two sides faced each other on the south side of the island by the city of Salamis on land and offshore:

> When the Persian army arrived on the plain of Salamis, the Cypriot kings[1] formed up their battle line. They placed the best of the Salaminians and Solians[2] opposite the Persians with the remaining Cypriots facing the rest of the enemy. Onesilus, the Cypriot commander-in-chief, took up position opposite Artybius, the Persian commander. Now, Artybius was mounted on a horse that was trained to rear up when facing a hoplite on foot. Onesilus knew about this and said to his attendant,[3] a Carian by birth and a famous warrior of great courage, 'I understand that Artybius' horse rears up and uses his hoofs and teeth to kill any man he comes up against. With this in mind, tell me which of the two you would prefer to take on, the horse or Artybius himself.' His attendant replied, 'I am ready to take on either or both, as your majesty wishes, but I will tell you what I think is most appropriate from your point of view. I say that it is right for a king and commander to fight a king and commander. For if the man you strike down is a commander, you do a great deed, and if, on the other hand, that man strikes you down (let this not be so!), your misfortune is halved because your death is at the hands of a worthy opponent. And it is right for a servant to fight a servant, or a horse. So don't worry about this horse's tricks. I guarantee he will never again rear up over any man!' This was his response, and immediately afterwards the opposing forces engaged on land and sea.
>
> The Ionian fleet was superb that day and defeated the Phoenicians, and the Samians fought best of all, and while this fight was going on, the two armies on shore swept together in battle. As for the two commanders, when Artybius the Persian astride his horse charged at Onesilus, the Cypriot followed the plan he had agreed with his

---

[1] Elsewhere termed 'tyrants'.

[2] Soli in the north-west was one of the ten or so major 'city kingdoms' of Cyprus.

[3] Herodotus (a native of Halicarnassus in Caria) uses the word *hypaspist* here, its only occurrence in the *Historia*. It is generally translated as 'shieldbearer' though this man's combat role is clearly more active. In Alexander the Great's army *hypaspist* was the term for medium infantry often deployed alongside cavalry.

attendant and aimed a thrust at him. The horse reared up and kicked out at Onesilus' shield and the Carian sliced off its hindlegs with one stroke of his billhook.[1] That is how Artybius the Persian commander met his end, he and his horse. While the rest were still fighting, Stesenor the ruler of Curium, which is said to be an Argive settlement, deserted with the substantial force under his command and, when the Curians deserted, the war-chariots of Salamis did the same. And so the Persians gained the upper hand over the Cypriots, and their army was routed with many slain. Onesilus son of Chersis, who had instigated the rebellion in Cyprus, and the king of the Solians, Aristocyprus son of Philocyprus, were among the dead. (5.112–13)

Herodotus' tantalizingly brief account of this significant land-battle and the single combat between the two commanders has an exotic and epic flavour. However, the cities of Cyprus were capable of mustering a large army, many thousands strong. Herodotus tells us that their infantry equipment was Hellene in style except for the headgear: 'the kings wrapped turbans round their heads, the rest wore felt caps' (7.90). This could be counted as another victory for Asian cavalry, and medium and light infantry, over western-style heavy troops, and the Persians could reasonably consider it a better test than the battle outside Ephesus. It is the only battle in which Herodotus mentions the involvement of chariots, though elsewhere he notes that the Libyan element of the imperial Persian army included them in place of cavalry. At this time the chariot was used as an archery platform rather than as a shock weapon. That appears to have come later when the Persians developed the scythed chariot towards the end of the 5th century.

It is disappointing that Herodotus has so little to say about the simultaneous sea-battle. Two years later the rebels faced the Persians with over 350 triremes, 60 of them from Samos, but there is no indication of their strength on this occasion. It is possible that the Phoenicians,

---

[1] *Drepanon*, sometimes translated as 'scimitar' or 'scythe', and compared to a medieval falchion. The context here suggests some form of long-handled weapon which Herodotus identifies elsewhere as carried exclusively by the Carians and the neighbouring Lycians. It may have been similar to the fearsome two-handed *falx*, wielded by the Dacians and Thracians in their wars with Rome a few centuries later.

from the Mediterranean's finest navy, were simply outnumbered here. However, with the Cypriots defeated on land, the Ionians could not exploit their victory, whatever its scale, and so sailed home. Nonetheless, it is surprising that Herodotus, with his liking for coincidences and portents, makes so little of this earlier Hellene naval victory near a place called Salamis.

All the cities of Cyprus that had rebelled were subsequently besieged and taken:

> Soli held out the longest but the Persians tunnelled under its outer wall and took it after five months. And so the Cypriots, after one year of freedom, were made slaves again. (5.115–16)

At this point Herodotus jumps back to operations on the mainland immediately after the burning of Sardis:

> The Persian generals Daurises, Hymaees, and Otanes, all of them married to daughters of Darius, pursued the Ionians who had marched on Sardis and drove them back to their ships. After this victory they divided the rebel cities between them and sacked them. Daurises set off for the cities of the Hellespont and took Dardanus, Abydos, Percote, Lampsacus, and Paisus, each in a single day. Then, as he marched from Paisus against Parium, word came to him that the Carians had joined up with the Ionians and risen against the Persians. So he turned back from the Hellespont and marched his army to Caria. (5.116–17)

It seems that the Persians had quickly regained full control of the Bosporus and Hellespont sea-lanes allowing Daurises to abandon operations to suppress the rebels on the Asian shore and to make the march of several hundred kilometres to the south to deal with Caria, presumably linking up with his brothers-in-law:

> The Carians managed to find out about Daurises' approach ahead of his arrival, and when they had this information, they gathered at a place called White Pillars[1] on the River Marsyas which flows

[1] Exact location unknown.

from the land around Idrias and joins the Maeander. When they had mustered there, many and various plans were proposed. The best of these, in my judgement, was suggested by Pixodarus of Cindye, the son of Mausolus[1] and husband of the daughter of Syennesis, king of Cilicia. His idea was that the Carians should cross the Maeander and fight with the river at their backs so that with retreat impossible they would have no option but to stand their ground and fight even more bravely than it was in their nature to do. But this idea was rejected and the decision was taken that the Persians, not the Carians, should fight with the Maeander at their backs, the purpose being that if the Persians were defeated and put to flight, they would be hurled into the river, never to return home.

When the Persians had come up and crossed the Maeander, the Carians engaged them by the River Marsyas and fought long and hard, but in the end they were overcome by superior numbers. About 2,000 Persians fell, but close on 10,000 Carians. The Carians who got away were penned into a large sacred grove of plane trees, the sanctuary of Zeus at Labraunda. Trapped as they were, they discussed what action might give them the best prospect of saving themselves, whether they would be better off surrendering to the Persians, or simply abandoning Asia. But whilst this debate was going on, the Milesians and their allies arrived to reinforce them and the Carians immediately set these thoughts aside and prepared to do battle all over again. They charged the Persians, engaged with them, fought a second time and were more severely beaten than before. The whole army sustained many casualties and the Milesians suffered most of all. However, the Carians recovered from this setback and carried on the fight. For example, having discovered that the Persians were launching a campaign against their cities, they set an ambush on the Pedasus road and the Persians fell into the trap and were wiped out with all their generals, including Daurises, in a night attack. The ambush force was commanded by Heraclides from Mylasa. (5.118–21)

---

[1] Of particular interest to Herodotus as a citizen of Halicarnassus, a long-established Hellene settlement assimilated into the Persian Empire along with the surrounding Asian region of Carià; Herodotus was a Hellene but probably had Carian family connections. The family name was to live on in the Mausoleum of Halicarnassus, one of the Seven Wonders of the ancient world, the tomb of Mausolus who governed Caria for the Persians in the mid 4th century.

Two of Caria's most important cities, Cnidus and Halicarnassus, had been founded as Hellene settlements centuries before, and Herodotus associates his ancient compatriots with the evolution of hoplite equipment. He credits them with teaching the Greeks how to fix plumes on their helmets and paint blazons on their shields, and with the invention of the revolutionary hoplite shield-grip system. He also tells of the impression hoplites made when they raided Egypt in the 7th century: 'an Egyptian who had never seen men in bronze armour before reported that "men of bronze" had arrived from the sea and were plundering the land' (2.152). In the early 5th century 'the Carians' equipment was Hellene except for their billhooks and daggers' (7.93). The Milesians, who joined them at Labraunda, were probably conventionally equipped hoplites. There would have been light-armed support alongside the hoplites but, it seems, no cavalry. Herodotus' generously rounded and most likely inflated casualty figure of 10,000 suggests a substantial force, which Caria and Miletus together were capable of mustering. Apart from stating that the Persians outnumbered them in the initial clash, Herodotus offers even less information about the force the rebels faced in these two battles. It probably outnumbered them quite significantly and consisted of a core of Persian and Median infantry and cavalry with levies from Lydia and other adjacent territories that had remained loyal. The Lydians, 'armed very much like the Hellenes', would have been a better match for the rebel hoplites in close quarter-fighting than the less heavily armed Persians and Medes. The Carians appear to have been led by committee without a formally or informally recognized commander-in-chief, and their decision to let the Persians make an unopposed crossing of the Maeander was as poor tactically as the suggestion that they fight with the river at their backs. As it turned out, the Marsyas probably complicated their retreat after the first battle, which was fought between the two rivers. The Milesian reinforcements were clearly not sufficient to give the Carian survivors a better chance in the second battle.

Caria may have held out for two or three more years till 493, and this final episode recorded by Herodotus suggests that the conflict became 'asymmetric' after Labraunda. However, the defeat at Pedasa, the Persians' only defeat on land in the whole of the Ionian Revolt, must have set counter-insurgency operations back for a while. The fact that the Carian commander was from the leading non-Hellene city in the region may indicate that the forces involved were significant, but it is equally possible that the Persian generals were caught travelling with only a modest escort.

At this point Artaphernes became directly involved and, with the general Otanes, campaigned west from Sardis and retook the important coastal cities of Clazomenae and Cyme. Herodotus brings Aristagoras into his narrative for the last time, making his opinion of him very clear:

> With these cities fallen, the Milesian demonstrated what a feeble character he was. For, seeing the great chaos and upheaval he had brought upon Ionia, he now began to plan his own escape, realising that he could not possibly get the better of Darius. (5.124)

He offered to take his followers to Myrcinus, the Thracian city that Darius had given to Histiaeus as a reward for his services in the Danube campaign, or to Sardinia, where he proposed to found a colony. However, it is unlikely that the Carthaginians would have made him welcome in Sardinia. The wise Hecataeus recommended retreating to the nearby island of Leros, fortifying it and waiting there for better times in Miletus:

> That was Hecataeus' advice, but Aristagoras thought it best to take himself off to Myrcinus. So, he accordingly entrusted Miletus to an eminent citizen called Pythagoras[1] and sailed to Thrace taking along any who would join him, and set himself up in that place as he had planned. But campaigning out of Myrcinus, he and his whole army were wiped out by the Thracians while laying siege to a town, even though the Thracians inside were willing to agree a truce and give it up. (5.126)

Aristagoras' co-conspirator, Histiaeus, still trusted by Darius and sent from Susa to assist in the resolution of the Ionian conflict, found it rather harder to deceive Artaphernes in Sardis:

[1] Not *the* Pythagoras, who was from nearby Samos but spent the latter part of his life in southern Italy and died early in the 5th century.

Artaphernes, who had accurate information about the insurrection, saw through his fabrications and said, 'This is how things are, Histiaeus: you cobbled the sandals and Aristagoras strapped them on.' (6.1)

Histiaeus slipped out of Sardis that night and was able to secure enough support amongst the Ionians to pursue his personal goal of reinstatement as tyrant of Miletus. But the Milesians had no desire for this and beat off his attempt to take the city back in a night attack. He was in communication with various Persians with whom he had already plotted, but Artaphernes intercepted the messages and had the conspirators executed. Now Histiaeus had lost most of the support he had built up in the region, but he was able to persuade the Mytileneans of Lesbos to give him eight triremes. He took these to Byzantium and used them for piracy in the Hellespont.

Dealing with Histiaeus was not Artaphernes' highest priority:

A large Barbarian army and fleet were now bearing down on Miletus. The Persian generals had consolidated all their resources into a single task force and were leading this against that city; the rest of the rebel strongholds were a lower priority. In the fleet, the Phoenicians were the most highly motivated, but the recently subdued Cypriots and the Cilicians and the Egyptians were deployed with them. This assault on Miletus was, in effect, an attack on the whole of Ionia, and when the Ionians learned of this, each city sent delegates to the Panionium.[1] They gathered there and conferred, and they resolved that they should not assemble an army to confront the Persians on land, but that the Milesians should defend themselves from inside their city walls while the rest of them manned all their ships, not leaving a single one in port. They were to assemble as soon as possible at Lade, a small island lying just off Miletus, and mount a seaborne defence of the city from there. And so the Ionians, including the Aeolians who lived on Lesbos,[2] manned their ships and came to Lade.

[1] The ancient sacred meeting place of the generally loose confederacy of the cities of Ionia. It was near the coast about half-way between Ephesus and Miletus.
[2] The Aeolian cities on the mainland were already back under Persian control.

The Hellene battle order was as follows: the Milesians brought 80 ships and were positioned on the right wing; next to them were the Prieneans with 12 ships, and the Myesians with three; next to the Myesians were the Teans with 17 ships and, next to them, the Chians with 100; then came the Erythraeans, who brought eight ships, and the Phocaeans with three; then there were the 70 ships from Lesbos and finally the Samians, positioned on the left wing with 60. In total there were 353 triremes. So that was the Ionian fleet. The Barbarians had 600 ships. When they reached Miletus and the land army had also arrived, the Persian commanders found out how many Ionian ships there were and became worried that they were not there in enough strength to defeat the Hellenes. They knew that if they did not have control of the sea, they would not be able to take Miletus,[1] and would then face the threat of punishment by Darius. With this in mind, they gathered together the Ionian tyrants who had been removed from their positions by Aristagoras of Miletus and had taken refuge with the Medes, and had, as it happened, joined them on campaign against Miletus. The Persians summoned them all and said, 'Men of Ionia, now is the time for you to show how you can be of good service to the House of the Great King by endeavouring to detach your countrymen from the rebel alliance. Make them this promise: if they are so persuaded by you, they shall not suffer punishment for their rebellion: their holy places and property shall not be burnt; nor shall they be treated any more strictly than before. But if they do not comply and are set on fighting, then deliver this threat: when they have been defeated, they shall be taken into captivity as slaves; we will make their sons eunuchs and carry off their maiden daughters to Bactria; and we will give their lands to others.' This is what they said, and the Ionian tyrants passed on the message that night, each to his compatriots. But the Ionians who received the message were stubborn and none of them would contemplate such treachery, each thinking that the Persians were making this offer to him alone. This is what happened immediately after the Persians' arrival at Miletus. (6.6–10)

[1] The Persians probably could have taken Miletus without defeating the Ionians at sea, but it would have been more difficult and taken longer.

Miletus occupied the tip of a promontory on the southern side of the opening of the Latmian Gulf. The city was strongly fortified on its southern landward side with two substantial natural harbours on its western side, facing the Aegean. Lade was about 4km to the west and the Hellene fleet was well placed there to command the approaches. In spite of their recent losses in Caria, the Milesians were clearly still capable of defending their city walls and manning the second-largest element of the rebel fleet; they probably operated out of their home port, which was not large enough to accommodate the rest. The Hellenes' naval strategy, to focus on protecting the city from seaborne attack and to keep its approaches and harbours open for the delivery of supplies and reinforcements, was sound enough. But they were presumably dependent on a steady shuttle of food and drink from the mainland, and unable to close off the 16km span of the gulf to prevent the Persian fleet occupying the beaches immediately to the south and east of the city in close contact with the besieging army. In any case, this was to be a fight to the finish that the Persians could not allow the Hellenes to win.

The ousted Hellene tyrants were not with the Persians by chance but would have been enlisted by the Persians as advisers and for use as envoys or covert negotiators in their customary strategy of combining the display and application of force with diplomacy and subversion. Reinstatement to their former positions, serving the Persians as compliant vassals, would be the tyrants' reward. Herodotus' use of the Greek word *agnomosune*, 'obstinacy' or 'stubbornness', to describe the rebels' seemingly honourable rejection of the Persian offer can be seen as criticism of their unwillingness to bow to the inevitable and makes sense as the opinion of the 'medizing' Hellene who may have been his source for this story; medizing was the term used for collaboration with Persia (the Medes) and could be applied to individuals or states. On the face of it 'disdainful' might fit the context better than 'stubborn'. But there is a general sense that Herodotus did not think very highly of the Ionians or their conduct of this war.

The Ionian fleet's battle order can be taken at face value. The 600 total given for the Persian fleet is a familiar stock figure. If the fleet had been that large, comprising, as it did, contingents from the four main sources of Persian seapower, its commanders would have had little cause for concern, even when bearing in mind their defeat off Cyprus. But, perhaps, their fleet was smaller or was a mix of triremes and less potent warships, and they had not anticipated how big the rebel fleet would be. It was actually almost as large as the fleet mustered by the Hellene Alliance in 480 and consisted entirely of triremes. On land the contest had for the most part been between two distinctly different methods of war, the close-quarter, close-formation shock fighting of the heavy-armed hoplite and the more fluid, long-range fighting of the lighter-armed Barbarian missile warrior, on foot or mounted. At sea, there would be little difference between the opposing forces, both consisting of triremes and with the same repertoire of tactics. The troops on board the Barbarian ships would have been a good match for the Hellenes when it came to deck-fighting. The Cypriots were very similarly equipped, and the Phoenicians and Egyptians also wore helmets and armour; the Cilicians, on the other hand, were less heavily armed:

> The Egyptians carried hollow shields with broad rims, naval pikes and great battle-axes, and most of them also had body armour and long dirks ... The Cilicians had their own type of helmet[1] and their shields were not hoplite shields but made of oxhide, and they wore woollen tunics. They each carried two javelins and a short sword very similar to the Egyptian dirk. (7.89, 91)

After they had all gathered at Lade, the Ionians held meetings[2] and amongst the several individuals that, I am sure, had their say at them, was Dionysius, the leader of the Phocaeans, and this is what he said: 'Ionians, we are now on the razor's edge. Are we to be free men or slaves, runaway slaves at that? If you are willing to face hardship and put in the effort now, you will be able to overcome your enemies and go on living as free men. But if you are feeble and undisciplined, I can hold out no hope that you will be saved from paying the Great King the price of your rebellion. So, put your trust in me and I promise

---

[1] Either this type of helmet was well enough known not to require description, or Herodotus did not know how it differed from other types.

[2] Herodotus uses the word *agora* here, literally 'marketplace' as scorned by Cyrus as 'a place set aside (by Hellenes) in the middle of their city in which they gather together, swear false oaths and swindle each other' (1.153). There is a suggestion here that the Ionians did not have a proper command structure or procedures.

you our enemies will not take us on in battle, or, if they do, that they shall be soundly beaten, if the gods treat us fairly.' The Ionians heard Dionysius out and put their trust in him, so every day he took them out to sea, lined them up and had the oarsmen practise the *diekplous* manoeuvre on the other ships, and he also had the deck crews train and equip themselves for action. Then for the rest of the day he kept the ships at anchor and made the men carry on training. (6.11–12)

Dionysius was in command of only three ships, but Phocaea had been a leading maritime power amongst the cities of Ionia until around 540 when most of its population had migrated to southern Italy to escape Persian rule. Their new settlement, Elea, thrived and was the birthplace of an influential early 5th-century philosophical school, but the home city never recovered. Dionysius' apparent reputation as an expert naval commander may have been acquired through privateering and mercenary activities in the Aegean and eastern Mediterranean, and perhaps he had distinguished himself in the Ionians' victory off Cyprus. Herodotus pointedly contrasts his professionalism and dedication with the softness of most of the other Ionians and this episode allows him to present some of the reasons he assembles for the failure of their rebellion. Leaving aside the underlying weaknesses of the alliance and the faultlines that ran through it, and the prejudices of Herodotus and his sources, the beaches of the small island of Lade would have been very crowded and the sickness that broke out probably had more to do with living conditions than unaccustomed exertion. The Persians could afford to watch and wait:

> For seven days the Ionians were obedient to Dionysius and carried out his orders.[1] But they were not accustomed to such hard work and were worn out by their efforts and the heat of the sun, and this is what they began to say to each to other, 'Which of the gods have we so offended that they force us to do this? We are out of our minds, taking leave of our senses to put our trust in this Phocaean tramp[2] who is contributing

---

[1] Dionysius most probably carried out his training programme before the enemy arrived off Miletus because the manoeuvring involved would have invited an attack.

[2] The word *alazon* may also be translated as 'charlatan' in later texts, but 'tramp' or 'vagrant' fits perceptions of Dionysius as a stateless buccaneer.

just three ships! He has completely taken over and is inflicting terrible suffering on us. Many of us are sick already, and many more are likely to fall ill as well. We'll surely be better off with any kind of suffering in place of our present hardship, even enduring the slavery that may be in store for us. Whatever form that suffering takes, it will not be as terrible as the burden that now weighs down on us. Come on, let's stop obeying this man's orders!' That's what they said and, from then on, no one obeyed Dionysius' orders, and they pitched tents on the island as if they were soldiers and lay around in the shade, refusing to get on board their ships and do any more training.

When the Samian commanders became aware of what was happening in the Ionian ranks, they thought again about the message that Aeaces son of Syloson[1] had been ordered to send to them from the Persians, calling upon them to desert the Ionian alliance. Now, having observed the total lack of discipline amongst the Ionians, they welcomed the invitation. In any case, they thought the Great King's power was irresistible and were certain that even if they defeated the fleet currently facing them, another one five times the size of it would come along.[2] So, when they saw that the Ionians were not prepared to do their duty, they had their excuse, and they could also see how they would benefit by keeping their temples and homes safe. Aeaces, from whom they received the message, was tyrant of Samos until he was deposed by Aristagoras of Miletus along with the rest of the Ionian tyrants.

When at last the Phoenicians put to sea, the Hellenes went out to meet them in line-ahead. The two sides bore down on each other and engaged, but I cannot say with any accuracy which of the Hellenes fought with gallantry in this sea-battle and which did not, because they now all blame each other. However, it is said that right at the start the Samians, having agreed terms with Aeaces, hoisted their sails,[3] abandoned their positions in the

---

[1] The ousted tyrant of Samos, acting as an intermediary for the Persians.
[2] The multiple is excessive, but the Persian navy certainly had the resources to regroup and return in greater force, if defeated.
[3] Battles were fought under oar power alone for greater manoeuvrability. There is evidence that the mainsails and masts were left on shore before battle, so it may have been only the smaller foresails that were hoisted when running away.

line and set course for Samos, all of them except for 11 ships whose captains ignored their commanders and stayed and fought. (Afterwards the people of Samos honoured these men by setting up a column inscribed with their names and a proclamation that they had proved their gallantry, and that column is still there in the marketplace.) Seeing the ships next to them deserting, the Lesbians did the same, and so did most of the Ionians. Of those who stayed to fight, the Chians did not behave like cowards but did glorious deeds, and so had the roughest time of all. They had provided 100 ships, as already mentioned, with 40 picked men on the deck of each. When they saw the majority of their allies betraying the alliance, they were not prepared to display such cowardice. Abandoned by the rest, they fought on with the support of just a few of the allies, breaking the enemy line and taking a large number of ships, but also losing most of their own; those in the ships that survived finally made their escape and returned home.

The crews of the Chian triremes that were crippled by battle damage escaped their pursuers by making for Mycale. They beached their ships and abandoned them there and set off across the mainland on foot, and their march took them onto Ephesian soil. It was night when they reached it and the women were celebrating the Thesmophoria.[1] The Ephesians had not yet heard what had happened to the Chians and were convinced that this was a robber band invading their territory and coming after their women. So, they came out in full force and slaughtered the Chians. As for Dionysius, when he saw that all was lost for the Ionians, he sailed off with the three enemy ships he had captured. But he did not immediately make for Phocaea because he knew very well that the city would be enslaved along with the rest of Ionia. Instead he sailed directly to Phoenicia, where he captured three merchant ships, and then on to Sicily with a load of booty. He made his base there and operated as a pirate, but only preying on Carthaginians and Etruscans, not on Hellenes. (6.12–17)

---

[1] This was an annual festival honouring the fertility goddess Demeter; it was held all over the Hellene world in early autumn.

The Persians most likely had good intelligence of the condition and state of mind of a large proportion of the more than 70,000 Hellenes they were about to face and went into battle confident that their subversion had worked. They probably came out from the beaches on either side of Miletus in line-ahead and then formed into line abreast to bear down on Lade and simultaneously threaten the two harbours of Miletus. The Hellenes had no option but to come out and meet them as they would have been unable to mount any kind of defence with their ships beached or at anchor. Herodotus, for the first time in any of his dealings with sea-battles, provides some tactical information. He has already mentioned the training that Dionysius had given to the fleet. The Hellenes moved out in line-ahead, presumably led by Dionysius' flagship, with the aim of using the *diekplous* manoeuvre. This tactic principally involved ramming. The Chians, with 40 hoplites on each of their ships, were also ready to fight in 'the old-fashioned way'. After the Samians, Lesbians and 'most of the Ionians' had turned and run, Dionysius was probably left with considerably fewer than 200 ships, but it seems he was still able to put up a good fight, suggesting that the Persians even then did not outnumber the Hellenes by a large margin.

In the absence of any reference to its part in the fighting, it seems probable that the substantial Milesian fleet fought its way home to the city's harbour when it became clear that the battle was lost. The explanation of the Chian survivors' cruel fate may have been invented, although interruption of the Thesmophoria, from which men were strictly excluded, would have been an act of great sacrilege. Ephesus was one of Ionia's foremost cities but did not have a fleet and is not mentioned as taking any part in the land warfare of the Ionian Revolt. The Ephesians may have been more sympathetically inclined towards Persia than the other Hellene cities of Asia, and the story told by Herodotus could have been created to cover up a shameful act of treachery. Dionysius' retirement to, or resumption of a life of patriotic piracy ends the account of the battle of Lade on a happier note.

> After defeating the Ionian fleet, the Persians were able to blockade Miletus by land and sea, and they undermined the walls using all kinds of siege machinery. And they took the city, town and acropolis,

five years after Aristagoras' rebellion and enslaved its people. This disaster came about as prophesied by the oracle at Delphi:

> 'O Miletus, contriver of troubles![1]
> Many shall feast upon you.
> You shall become a glittering gift-offering.
> Your women shall wash the feet of long-haired men
> And other hands shall tend our holy place at Didyma.'[2]

And this is indeed what happened to Miletus. Most of the men were killed by Persians, who wear their hair long, the women and children were reduced to slavery, and the holy place at Didyma, the temple and the seat of the oracle were looted and torched. I have told of the wealth of this holy place at other points in my narrative. The Milesian men who had been taken prisoner were brought to Susa and Darius the King did no more harm to them but settled them in Ampe on the Erythraean Sea[3] close to where the Tigris flows into it.

After the sea-battle off Miletus, the Phoenicians reinstated Aeaces in Samos as directed by the Persians in recognition of the great and valuable service he had done them. The Samians were the only people who had rebelled against Darius who did not have their cities and temples burned down, and this was because of their desertion with their ships in the battle. Once Miletus had been dealt with, the Persians went on to take control of Caria, some cities submitting voluntarily, others being forcibly subdued. So that was the end of it.
(6.18–20, 25)

But not quite ... Histiaeus, still ambitious to regain his former power, came south with his Lesbian fleet and conquered Chios, exploiting the island's weakness after its fleet's mauling at the battle of Lade. He then raised a larger force from Ionia and Aeolis and mounted an attack on Thasos but abandoned this when he heard that the Phoenician fleet was sailing up the Ionian coast from Miletus. He brought his fleet back to Lesbos, but food was in short supply so he took it over

---

[1] The powerful priesthood of Delphi was clearly advising against rebellion at the time Aristagoras was in the Peloponnese seeking support for it.
[2] An important shrine of Apollo about 10km to the south of Miletus.
[3] The Red Sea.

to the mainland to plunder the grain harvest on the plains along the River Caicus.

A Persian general called Harpagus[1] happened to be in the area with a substantial force and attacked the Hellene landing party. He killed most of them but took Histiaeus alive and this is how it came about. The Hellenes fought the Persians at Malene and held out until the cavalry was sent in and charged them. This was decisive, and the Greeks turned and ran. But Histiaeus, confident that the King would not have him executed for his latest transgression, displayed his instinct for survival in this way: when a Persian seized him as he fled and was about to skewer him, he came out with a few words of Persian to let him know that he was Histiaeus the Milesian. (6.28)

So Histiaeus survived, but Harpagus and Artaphernes had no intention of allowing him to charm the Great King yet again. So, they took him back to Sardis and had him impaled and decapitated, then delivered his embalmed head to Darius. The King was not pleased and ordered them to give the head a proper burial because he still thought that Histiaeus had served him and Persia very well. Herodotus ends this episode with a dismissive 'So that's what became of Histiaeus.' The final suppression of the Hellenes of the eastern Aegean took a little more time:

The Persian fleet wintered at Miletus and campaigned again the following year, easily conquering the islands lying off the western coast, Chios, Lesbos and Tenedos. When they had occupied an island the barbarians 'netted' the men on it. This is how it is done: each man joins hands with the next forming a chain from north shore to south and they work their way along the whole length of the island, flushing the male islanders out. The Persians also took back the Ionian cities on the mainland, though netting was not practicable there. And now the Persian commanders did not shy away from carrying out what they had threatened to do to the Ionians who had gone to war against them. They picked out the best-looking boys and made them eunuchs and transported the most beautiful

[1] Not related to Cyrus' formidable lieutenant, a Mede of the same name.

young women from the coast to the King, and when they had done this they burned down the Ionians' cities and their holy places too. And this is how Ionia came to be enslaved three times over, first by the Lydians then twice in succession by the Persians. Afterwards the Persian fleet sailed north and took back everything on the western side of the Hellespont. Everything on the eastern side was already under Persian control.

In the year that followed[1] the Persians brought all hostilities against the Ionians to an end and, in fact, did some things which were very much to their benefit. Artaphernes, the governor of Sardis, summoned representatives from all the cities and, through them, required the Ionians to draw up treaties amongst themselves under which they would settle disputes through litigation rather than by rape and pillage. This is what he made them do, and he also had their land measured in parasangs (the Persian term for a distance of 30 *stades*[2]). Artaphernes set the amount of tribute to be paid by each city according to this assessment of the Ionians' property and the amounts remained much the same in living memory;[3] they were actually not much different from what they had been before. So, there was peace.

Then, the following spring, Mardonius, son of Gobryas, came down to the coast in command of a very large land army and fleet. He was a young man who had recently married the King's daughter, Artozostre. He arrived in Cilicia at the head of this army and there went on board one of the ships and sailed with the fleet. Other commanders led the army on to the Hellespont. Sailing along the shores of Asia, Mardonius reached Ionia and there, I tell you, he did something that will come as a great surprise to Hellenes who find it impossible to believe that Otanes, one of the seven Persians who chose Darius as King, suggested that democracy might be the best form of government for Persia. Mardonius deposed all the tyrants in Ionia and introduced democracy in place of tyranny. (6.31–33, 42–43)

---

[1] 493/2.

[2] The *stade* was a measure of distance representing the length of a running track (*stadion*), a measurement that was not precisely standardized; 185m is a fair equivalent.

[3] By the middle of the century, with Persia's grip on the western edge of the empire loosened, tribute payments were no longer flowing east but to Athens.

In fact, tyrannies were not universally replaced with democracies and, in any case, the political systems adopted did not affect the cities' subject status. The Persians' priority was compliance, stability and internal order at both local and regional level, and, of course, revenue. But they appear to have made genuine efforts to address grievances and frictions that had fuelled the dissatisfaction and unrest which Histiaeus and Anaxagoras had so successfully exploited. A later, 1st-century BC source, Diodorus Siculus, involves the wise Hecataeus in this episode:

> Hecataeus the Milesian, who had been sent as an envoy by the Ionians, asked Artaphernes why he did not trust them. When Artaphernes replied that he feared that they would feel bitter resentment because of the pain they had suffered in defeat, Hecataeus responded, 'Well, if ill treatment breeds bad faith, fair treatment will surely cause our cities to be well disposed toward the Persians.' Artaphernes agreed with this and gave the cities back their laws and assessed their tributes according to their ability to pay. (*Library of History* 10.25.4)

This policy was in line with present-day counter-insurgency doctrine, recognizing that lasting success is achieved not by military force but through political and social measures. However, it was clearly still thought necessary to project military power beyond the western frontiers of the empire to reinforce this newly established stability.

> Mardonius pressed on to the Hellespont where a massive fleet and land army were now assembled. They sailed across the Hellespont and advanced into Europe. Their destination was Eretria and Athens, or that was the declared purpose of the expedition. In fact, the Persians' intention was to subdue as many Hellene cities as they could. This is what they did to Thasos with their fleet and the Thasians did not lift a finger to resist, and, with their army, the Persians added the Macedonians to their stock of slaves.[1] All

---

[1] Macedonia had submitted earth and water two decades earlier but the relationship clearly required reinforcement.

the peoples closer than Macedon were already in their power. The fleet crossed over to the mainland coast from Thasos and sailed along to Acanthus, and set out from there to round the Athos peninsula. As it was on the way round, a gale struck it from the north and it was very roughly tossed about. The ships could not ride the storm out and many of them were hurled onto the coast of Athos. It is said that 300 ships were lost and more than 20,000 men. The sea around Athos is full of man-eating fish[1] and some were snatched and killed by these, some were smashed against the rocks, some died of cold and some perished because they could not swim. So that's what happened to the fleet. As for Mardonius and his army, the Brygoi, a Thracian tribe, killed many of them in a night attack on their encampment in Macedonia and Mardonius himself was wounded. However, the Brygoi were not to escape slavery, for Mardonius did not leave their territory until he had made them Persian subjects. After subduing Macedon, he led his command back because it had been so badly battered, the land force at the hands of the Brygoi and the fleet by the ocean off Athos. His mission had been a disgraceful failure and he withdrew into Asia. (6.42–44)

If Herodotus is right about the broad scope of this mission, Mardonius had indeed fallen short in failing to drive deep into the heartland of Hellas and, specifically, to reach and punish Athens and Eretria. However, he had re-established or at least reinforced the empire's control of Thrace and Macedonia, securing the land route for any future thrust into Europe, and the rich island of Thasos was a substantial prize. His losses at sea may be somewhat over-dramatized, and the clash with the Brygoi did not affect the successful outcome of that piece of the campaign, so the expedition had not been a total failure. Nevertheless, Darius did not put him in command of his next thrust into Europe. Still, by the middle of the following decade, Mardonius 'had more influence with the Great King than any other Persian' and was to be a central figure in the campaign of 480/79.

---

[1] Shark attacks are documented in other ancient sources and still occur in the Mediterranean; drowning would have been the main cause of death, however.

The destruction of Miletus and the inevitable collapse of the Ionian Revolt shook Hellas:

The Athenians displayed their profound grief at the fate of Miletus in many different ways, most notably when Phrynichus put on his play *The Fall of Miletus*,[1] and the entire audience was reduced to tears. Phrynichus was fined 1,000 drachmas[2] for reminding the Athenians of a disaster that was so close to home, and the play was banned. (6.21)

Through this decade, the Hellenes had continued to fight their internal wars and the Persians would have looked on with interest. For example, at Sepeia in 494, the Spartans wiped out their neighbours and old enemy, the Argives, as a serious military force for a generation and consolidated their leadership of the Hellenes of the Peloponnese. However, the deposition and exile of Demaratus, one of their two kings, and the subsequent disgrace and strange and gruesome end of Cleomenes, the other, would have been seen as encouraging evidence of instability within one of the leading nations of Hellas. Darius made Demaratus welcome at court and he became an adviser to Xerxes, his successor. In the meantime, the Athenians were constantly at war with Aegina. The Persians continued to cultivate subversive links with reactionary factions in Athens through Hippias, like Demaratus a welcome Hellene exile, and his diminishing but influential body of supporters. For their part, the Athenians had been looking east, uncomfortably aware of the threat that grew as their eastern cousins, the Ionians, were progressively subdued. As in Britain in the run-up to World War II, there was a polarizing split between the forces of appeasement, spearheaded by a reactionary rearguard, who wanted to turn the political clock back, and the forces of resistance and active opposition. The latter were reinforced by the emergence of two strong war-leaders, Miltiades and Themistocles:

[1] This may have been the first tragedy to address a historical rather than mythical or legendary event.

[2] As one drachma was a skilled worker's daily wage, this was a very heavy fine.

Miltiades had recently returned to Athens from the Chersonese and had escaped death twice before becoming an Athenian general. First, the Phoenicians had chased him as far as Imbros, making great efforts to capture him and deliver him to the Great King, but he got away from them and reached home. He thought he was safe, but then his rivals brought him to trial on a charge of ruling as a tyrant in the Chersonese.[1] He survived this as well, and afterwards he was elected general by the choice of the people. (6.103–04)

Ironically, the aristocratic Miltiades owed his many lucrative years as an autocratic colonial governor to Hippias and had served the Great King, albeit with selective loyalty, for some of that time. Themistocles had risen from a less gilded background and was to become, in all but name, supreme commander of the Hellene fleet at one of the most critical wartime moments in the history of the western world. The war with Aegina enabled him to focus on the development of Athenian seapower, which at the end of the next decade was to lie at the core of the strategy for the defence of Hellas. Herodotus introduces him only when his narrative reaches the events of the first half of 480:

> There was a certain Athenian who had recently taken his place amongst the most prominent citizens. His name was Themistocles and he was called the son of Neocles. (7.143)

This is more of a put-down than a fanfare; he is more generous in his appreciation of him later in the *Historia*, but Thucydides supplies important detail about Themistocles' earlier career and neatly summarizes his strategic vision:

> Themistocles persuaded the Athenians to complete the fortification of Piraeus, a project he had initiated in the year he held the office of archon.[2] He saw that the place was excellently situated with its

---

[1] Implying that he could have been sentenced to death if found guilty of this emotively defined 'crime'.
[2] In 493/2 the archon was the civilian head-of-state selected to serve for one year with eight other archons. The nine archons shared various duties of government, administrative, military and religious. Miltiades had held this position in 524/3.

three natural harbours and reckoned that it would strongly support the efforts of the Athenian people to build the power of their city, now they had become seamen. Themistocles was the first to venture to suggest that they make the sea their own, planting the seeds of empire at that very moment ... He made seapower his priority because, I think, he had noted that the Great King's invasion force had come much closer to Athens by sea than by land.[1] So, Themistocles considered Piraeus to be of much greater value than the upper city[2] and he frequently gave the Athenians this advice, that if they were ever struggling to defend themselves on land, they should go down to Piraeus and their ships and then could take on the whole world. (*History of the Peloponnesian War* 1.93)

Persia increased the pressure on Hellas in 491. Herodotus continues:

Darius wished to find out if the Hellenes would put up a fight or surrender. So he sent heralds all over Hellas with his personal demand for offerings of earth and water. He also sent heralds to his subject cities on the coast of Asia, ordering them to build warships and horse-transports, and those cities set to work. The heralds who went to Hellas collected what the King had demanded from many of the cities of the mainland and from all the islands they visited. Aegina was one of the islands that offered earth and water to Darius and the Athenians strongly objected to this. They saw it as an act of hostility signifying their intention to side with the Persians in making war on Athens. Pleased to have this justification, the Athenians took the matter up with the Spartans and accused the Aeginetans of betraying Hellas. (6.48–49)

On the evidence of what happened at the time of Xerxes' invasion ten years later, it is likely that most of the cities of Boeotia and Thessaly offered submission. The islands of the eastern Aegean were already under Persian control, but earth and water may have been collected from some of the Cyclades. Later in the *Historia* Herodotus tells the

---

[1] In 490 in the Marathon campaign.
[2] The Acropolis and the inland conurbation that surrounded it.

story of the Athenians' and Spartans' emphatic rejection of Darius the King's command:

> Xerxes sent no heralds to Athens or Sparta to demand earth and water for this reason. Ten years earlier, when Darius had sent heralds with the same purpose, the Athenians had thrown them into the Pit[1] and the Spartans had thrown them down a well, telling them to get their earth and water for the Great King from there. But I cannot say what disaster the Athenians suffered for treating heralds like this. Certainly, their city and lands were laid waste, but I think that was for a different reason. (7.133)

Herodotus may be signalling a degree of scepticism here. Mistreatment of heralds was regarded as extreme sacrilege and laid the guilty open to the avenging curse of the hero Talthybius, King Agamemnon's herald in the Trojan War. Herodotus is rather weakly arguing that, if the Athenians did suffer from a curse, it was laid on them for a different reason, perhaps their part in the destruction of the temple of Cybele in Sardis. Because of what had already passed between Athens and Persia, it could be argued that a state of war existed between them, so Darius would have had no great reason to include them in his diplomatic offensive; Marathon would give Xerxes even less reason. Retribution had to be delivered and to be seen to be delivered, but, on the other hand, it was Persian policy always to keep open the option of diplomatic resolution. However, the invitation to collect earth and water from the bottom of a well has a salty Spartan flavour to it and the sense of solidarity shared between two leading Hellene cities rings true. Whatever dealings there may have been, Herodotus does give a feel for the internal political manoeuvring of the time. A later source links Miltiades with the Athenians' execution of the heralds. Members of the 'war party', including Themistocles, probably sponsored Phrynichus' *Fall of Miletus*. Sparta supported Athens in the conflict with Aegina, and Corinth, another major power, also became involved. Athens, given the opportunity to exploit a planned coup on the island, took a fleet of 70 ships, 20 of them on loan from Corinth for a nominal fee, but arrived a day too late. Nonetheless, the Athenians won a sea-battle

[1] A ravine into which condemned criminals were thrown.

and also defeated the Aeginetans on land before losing four ships in a subsequent skirmish. This episode seems to have been inconclusive but it usefully flexed Athens' muscles on land and sea, and affirmed the strategic stance that Miltiades and Themistocles and their supporters were promoting.

On nearly all the evidence of its campaigning over the past six decades of its existence, the Persian Empire had proved itself invincible. However, its first invasion of Europe had met with failure north of the Danube. Its second thrust to the west, the attack on Naxos in 500, had been unsuccessful and its third and most recent campaign led by Mardonius had fallen short of its objectives in mainland Hellas. The Ionian Revolt had been suppressed but operations had been stretched out over five or six years. Hellenes motivated to protect their homeland and freedoms could demonstrate that the Great King's mighty war machine was both fallible and resistible. Some could support this belief with plausible strategic and tactical insights based on first- or close second-hand experience of the way the Barbarians waged war. They could also suggest that geography and the gods of wind and ocean would be on their side. For his part, the Great King had already established that Hellas, even mainland Hellas, would not unite against him when he launched his next attack and he could be confident that any smaller alliances that might be formed would be fragile. On the evidence of several victories won on land in the suppression of the Ionian Revolt, he could also be confident of success in any future confrontation with Hellene armies, especially as he was now able to reinforce his Asian troops with Hellene levies. Herodotus makes no comment on the apparent trust in the latter to fight kindred Hellenes with commitment and some may have been token contingents taken along as hostages, in effect, to insure against insurrection in their home cities. More value may have been attached to Hippias, now in his 80s, and presumably other Pisistratid exiles who were to sail with the invasion force to connect with the small like-minded minority that still existed in Athens and would be willing to accept Persian rule as the price of rolling back the democratic reforms of still quite recent years; they would also be restored to power as puppet rulers with Hippias, tyrant of Athens once again, as their leader, or so the old man wished. At sea, the Hellene fleets that had defeated his Phoenicians off Cyprus and posed a significant threat in the early stages of the siege of Miletus would be fighting for him or sidelined. Moreover, through the 490s and well into the 480s, even if the Hellenes of mainland Greece who had not submitted to him had combined all their fleet, it would have been only about half the size of the fleet assembled by the Ionian alliance at Lade. The Persians' fourth campaign into Europe was to be seaborne and aimed directly at Eretria and Athens, delivering retribution for these cities' part in the burning of Sardis, but it had the larger goal of establishing a strategic foothold in mainland Greece. The Athenians, at least, were ready.

Grant me vengeance on the Athenians

Marathon

While Athens and Aegina were warring with each other, the Persian King, Darius, was preoccupied on his own account, with a servant repeatedly reminding him to remember the Athenians and with the Pisistratids at his side continually badmouthing them. At the same time, he wished to take this opportunity to make subjects of all the Hellenes who had not submitted earth and water.

Mardonius' expedition had been a dismal failure. So, the Great King relieved him of his command and appointed new generals to campaign against Athens and Eretria, Datis, who was of Median descent, and his nephew, Artaphernes son of Artaphernes. They were despatched with orders to reduce the Athenians and Eretrians to slavery and to bring them captive into his presence. So, the newly appointed generals set off on the Great King's mission and took a large and well-equipped force to the plain of Alae in Cilicia. They camped there and were joined by all the ships that had been assigned to the expedition including the horse-transports that Darius had ordered his tribute-paying subjects to prepare in the previous year. They loaded up the horses and got all the troops on board and sailed round to Ionia with 600 triremes. (6.94–95)

Of Mardonius' two replacements, Datis is known to have served at senior level in the suppression of the Ionian Revolt and Artaphernes had most probably gained experience campaigning with his father in Ionia and elsewhere. Unfortunately, Herodotus gives little detail on the make-up and even less on the size of the 'large and well-equipped force' that was assigned to this mission. He tells us later that it included Persians and Sacae:

> The Sacae, who are Scythians, had tall caps on their heads, which were stiff and tapered to a point, and they wore trousers; they carried their native bows,[1] and also daggers and axes which they call *sagaris*. (7.64)

Datis' force probably also included Medes, who were equipped in the same way as the Persians. These troops were the backbone of the armies that had expanded the Persian Empire and kept it secure; they were well organized, disciplined and battle-hardened. They had accumulated decades of experience of the distinctive Hellene way of war, fighting alongside hoplites, when they served the Great King as mercenaries or subject levies, and winning against them in the Ionian Revolt. Herodotus also mentions that Datis and Artaphernes set off from Asia with contingents of subject Hellenes from Aeolis and Ionia.

Until he gets to the casualty figures, Herodotus includes only one piece of numerical information, that the Persians sailed with 600 triremes but this is a standard figure which he uses earlier for two other large-scale naval deployments, Darius' Scythian expedition and the battle of Lade. However, assuming a fighting complement of 40–50 on each as recorded at Salamis, this number of ships could have transported a ground force of 20,000–30,000, which happens to match a reasonable consensus amongst modern historians. The poet Simonides, Herodotus' contemporary, records 90,000 and Plato, writing two generations later, gives half a million, though his estimate of 300 triremes seems closer to reality. Justin, in his 3rd-century AD abridgement of Pompeius Trogus' lost 1st-century BC history, settles for 600,000.

The figure of 600 triremes, probably about half the Persian Empire's total strength, is by no means an impossibility. But such a large and costly battlefleet was not actually necessary. In the unlikely event of the Hellenes uniting to combine all their fleets to oppose the invasion

---

[1] Probably of the shorter, composite type associated with the Scythians.

at sea, they could not have mustered more than about 150 triremes of variable quality.

The invasion fleet must have been entirely oar-driven. Regular merchant freight-carriers were sail-driven and, except with favourable winds, could not keep pace with oared warships. It is known from Thucydides' account of the Peloponnesian War that triremes, usually at the end of their serviceable life, were modified to transport cavalry, though he does say this was an innovation. In any case, 30 horses is a feasible cargo for a vessel of this type. Persian resources would not have been greatly strained by the inclusion of 1,000 cavalry in the invasion force. As for troop-carrying, the Athenians converted triremes into troop carriers for their landing on the island of Sphacteria in 425 by the simple process of dispensing with the top tier of oarsmen to provide seating for 62 passengers in addition to the 40 or so infantrymen that could be accommodated on deck. Similar arrangements could be made for the carriage of stores and equipment. In the event of a sea-battle the required number of triremes up to, say, 250 (starting with the most battleworthy) could be cleared for action and manned with full complements of rowers and regular complements of deck-fighters. The 70–80 ships left unmanned could be beached or towed until they were needed again. Calculated on this basis, a fleet of approximately 300 triremes and 30 horse-transports is quite plausible, although, on the evidence for Xerxes' invasion in 480, there would also have been some smaller oared warships and it is likely that sail-driven supply ships would have arrived later.

From Ionia the Persians did not follow the coast up to the Hellespont and Thrace, but put out from Samos and sailed past Icaria and then on a course that took them from island to island. In my opinion they were afraid to sail round Athos, because the previous attempt to take that route had met with such disaster.[1] Besides, they were drawn to Naxos by their earlier failure to conquer the island.[2] When the Persians had crossed over from Icaria and appeared off Naxos, the first place they intended to attack, the Naxians, with earlier events

[1] Mardonius' expedition in 492.
[2] Artaphernes (the elder) and Aristagoras' attempt in 499.

very much in mind,[1] did not stand and fight but took flight into the mountains. The Persians made prisoners of any they were able to capture and burnt down their holy places and city. Then they set course for the other islands.

While this was happening, the Delians abandoned their island and fled to Tenos. While the Persians were on the way, Datis sailed ahead having ordered his fleet not to anchor off Delos, but off Rhenaea, the island close by. When he found out where the Delians had gone, he sent a herald with this message: 'Holy men, why have you decided that my intentions are hostile and taken flight? I have no desire to do any harm in the birthplace of the two gods,[2] neither to the land itself nor to its people, nor is it the King's command that I do so. Return to your homes and carry on living on this island.' That was Datis' proclamation to the Delians, and he then heaped 300 talents[3] of frankincense on the altar and made a burnt offering of it.

When he had done this, Datis sailed on with his army towards Eretria, his next destination, and he had Ionians and Aeolians with him. After he had put to sea from Delos, the Delians say that the island was shaken by an earthquake, the first and last before my day. This was, maybe, a divine portent of the evil events that were now coming upon mankind. For, in the times of Darius son of Hystaspes, Xerxes son of Darius and Artaxerxes son of Xerxes, a period of three generations,[4] more evil befell Hellas than in the 20 generations before the time of Darius. Some was brought about by the Persians and some by the wars for supremacy fought between the leading nations of Hellas itself.[5] So, it was not at all strange that there should be an earthquake on Delos when there had

---

[1] The retribution suffered by cities that had resisted Persia in the Ionian Revolt rather than their successful resistance earlier.

[2] Apollo and his sister Artemis were born on Delos according to ancient tradition and worshipped there.

[3] Approximately 8 tonnes of this precious aromatic resin.

[4] 100 years from the beginning of Darius' reign in 522. Xerxes succeeded Darius in 486 and was assassinated in 465. Artaxerxes died in 424, probably in the same decade as Herodotus and during the Peloponnesian War.

[5] A reference to the rivalry between Sparta and Athens and their allies which escalated into the Peloponnesian War in 431.

never been one before. Also, there was an oracle that referred to this island stating: 'I will shake Delos, which has never yet been shaken.'[1] (6.95–98)

Samos, subject to Persia once again after deserting from the Ionian Alliance at Lade, would have contributed ships and men to the Persian expeditionary force but neighbouring Icaria, also a subject state, probably had little or nothing to offer. Naxos, the largest and most powerful and prosperous island of the Cyclades, had successfully withstood the Persians and Aristagoras a decade before, but Herodotus implies the Naxians did not wish to repeat the experience. In any case, it is likely that the force that threatened them on this occasion was much larger, and they would have known about the Persians' treatment of many of the cities they had recaptured in the closing stages of the Ionian Revolt, Miletus in particular. The Delians reacted in the same way as the Naxians, but Datis was at pains to treat them and their small sacred island with pious respect. This was an important and influential cult centre for the large community of Hellenes on the mainland and islands, as well as in Asia, who called themselves Ionian. If he sincerely intended to placate the local gods, he also had an eye to the hearts and minds of the Hellenes whose compliance was such a feature of Persian strategy. The treatment of Delos was in pointed contrast to the Hellene rebels' destruction of the temple of Cybele in Sardis eight years before, though less important holy places on other islands were not spared. The immensity of Datis' burnt offering was most probably inflated by propaganda and would have been regarded by some as extravagant flaunting of the Great King's wealth. In logistical and tactical terms, the transport of 40 horses (about the equivalent weight) would have been a much better use of freight capacity. But Darius was certainly well supplied with this very valuable commodity; according to Herodotus, the Arabians contributed 1,000 talents of it annually as part of their tribute.

Moving on from Delos, the Barbarians put in at other islands gathering troops as they went and taking the sons of the islanders hostage, and this cruise around the islands brought them to Carystus

---

[1] Poseidon, 'earth-shaker' as well as god of the ocean, speaking most likely.

on Euboea. The Carystians did not hand over any hostages and declared that they would not take part in a war against cities that were their neighbours, by which they meant Eretria and Athens. But then the Persians laid siege to their city and ravaged their land, and the Carystians submitted to their will.

When the Eretrians found out that the Persian fleet was now sailing to attack them, they called for help from the Athenians. The Athenians did not deny them support and offered 4,000 men from their colony in the horse-breeding country of Chalcis.[1] However, although they had called on the Athenians for help, the Eretrians had not come to a firm decision on their policy and there were two conflicting views on what action to take. There were some who thought it best to abandon the city and make for the highlands of Euboea, and others who were planning to betray it in hope of winning favour with the Persian King. Aeschines son of Nothon, one of the leading citizens of Eretria, found out about both plans and explained the situation to the Athenians who had now arrived, urging them to save themselves by leaving the city and going home, and they followed Aeschines' advice.

So those Athenians crossed over to Oropus and safety while the Persians sailed up and made landings at Tamynae, Choereae and Aegilea,[2] all in Eretrian territory. On landing at these places, they immediately disembarked their horses and prepared to engage the enemy, but the Eretrians had no intention of coming out to fight. Their plan was to defend their walls as best they could since the opinion that now prevailed was that they should not abandon the city. And their walls were fiercely attacked and in six days of fighting many fell on both sides. However, on the seventh day, two notable[3] Eretrians, Euphorbus son of Alcimachus and Philagrus son of Cineas, betrayed the city and the Persians came in and looted its holy places and burnt them down, avenging the burning of the temple in Sardis.

---

[1] This is an improbably large force for a young colony, even if it included light-armed troops as well as hoplites, and perhaps 4,000 was a round figure for its total population. There is no record of these *cleruch* troops taking any further part in the war but it is unlikely they did not, suggesting that there were far fewer of them than Herodotus states.

[2] The locations of Choereae and Aegilea are not known.

[3] The word *dokimos* can also mean 'trustworthy' and Herodotus no doubt intended the irony.

However, and here they were obeying Darius' orders,[1] they made all the inhabitants prisoners of war. The Persians waited a few days after dealing with Eretria then made the crossing to Attica, pressing on with their campaign and expecting to do to the Athenians exactly what they had done to the Eretrians. They headed for Marathon as this was a part of Attica very suitable for cavalry action and closest to Eretria, and it was Hippias son of Pisistratus who guided them to this place. (6.99–102)

The campaign was going well. The Aegean islands in the Persians' path had all given up without a fight. When the fleet reached Euboea, the Carystians had been a little stubborn but succumbed quickly to a show of force. Until they were betrayed by their two fellow-citizens, the Eretrians had actively resisted from behind their city walls for a few days, though the siege was probably not on the epic scale that Herodotus' stock phrase suggests. No attempt had been made to confront the three cavalry-led landing forces. Datis and Artaphernes had now secured the east–west sea route from Ionia to Euboea and acquired more Hellene troops from the Aegean islands to fight alongside the Aeolians and Ionians conscripted before leaving the Asian mainland. They were ready to launch their attack on Attica and Athens in mainland Greece, and had chosen the area of Marathon as their entry point. It was the corner of Attica closest to Euboea and offered space and appropriate terrain for cavalry, as Herodotus points out. The long sandy shore was ideal for beaching a large fleet and its distance from Athens assured an unopposed landing. Though much closer to Athens, the extensive beach at Phalerum and the plain behind were ruled out by their proximity to the city, and the Athenian fleet, which was based there, though heavily outnumbered, could have further complicated an opposed landing. The choice of Marathon, whether or not Hippias truly influenced it, would have been pleasing to him because of its association with his father's final successful counter-coup in 546. The Persians probably intended to reinstall Hippias as tyrant, this time to rule on behalf of the Great King, and were hopeful that the now small minority that would have

---

[1] Herodotus seems to imply that the looting and destruction of holy places was contrary to Darius' orders and that his wish was that all holy places and their presiding gods should be treated with the same respect as shown to Delos.

welcomed him back would cause division in the defenders' ranks and within the city with the same good result as at Eretria.

> As soon as they found out what the Persians were doing, the Athenians marched to Marathon in full force led by all ten of their generals.[1] Miltiades was the tenth of these. (6.103)

'Tenth' here has the force of 'first among equals'. Plutarch (*c.*50–120 AD) in his *Life of Aristides* puts it more plainly, and has a clear view of the full extent of Datis' mission.

> When Datis was sent by Darius, ostensibly to punish the Athenians for the burning of Sardis, but actually to crush all of the Hellenes, he landed at Marathon with his entire force and set about laying waste the countryside. Miltiades was then the most highly esteemed of the ten generals appointed by the Athenians to lead them to war, but Aristides was second to him in reputation and influence. (*Aristides* 5.1)

Miltiades undoubtedly had strong popular support in Athens. Aristocratic glamour and, no doubt, personal qualities, and an adventurous reputation more than compensated for the taint of association with tyranny and collaboration with the Barbarians. His acquittal from the very serious charge of ruling in the Chersonese as a tyrant sponsored by the Great King is evidence of his political and, very probably, financial clout. However, his record of expulsion from the Chersonese twice over, first by marauding Scythians and later by the Phoenicians, and involvement with the losing side in the Ionian Revolt were not obvious qualifications for high command. It may be that Miltiades' story, as told by Herodotus, was gilded by the greater achievements of Cimon, his son, in the three decades that followed the victories of 479. However, a general's responsibilities were as much political and administrative as military and it is possible that none of his nine colleagues at Marathon was much better qualified by applicable expertise or experience.

Up to the Peloponnesian War, the Athenians' preference was to meet an invader in the field rather than submit to the potentially long

---

[1] *Strategos* ordinarily meant 'military commander' but in Athens it was an important political office as well. From the end of the 6th century a panel of ten generals was elected each year, one from each of the ten 'tribal' voting groups, to serve from mid-summer to mid-summer.

drawn-out discomforts and uncertainties of a siege. This strategy could also limit the enemy's ability to live off the land. By 490 Athens may anyway have sprawled too far outside its original perimeter to be defensible. So they marched to Marathon to meet the Persians. They probably had some idea from reports received from Euboea of the size and make-up of the force they would be facing and were setting out in reasonable confidence of at least containing the Persians at their beachhead whilst awaiting reinforcements from other Hellene cities, Sparta in particular.

Herodotus does not give a number for the force that assembled at Marathon but other ancient sources point to a full mobilization of 9,000–10,000 hoplites, though some may have been left behind to keep the city secure or to man ships. It is likely that known supporters of Hippias were given no option but to march with the army, if they were not too old to fight. The military-age citizen body at that time, probably numbering about 25,000, was large enough to furnish 9,000–10,000 hoplites, and this is supported by Herodotus' figure of 8,000 at Plataea in 479, when 1,000 or so were with the Hellene fleet campaigning on the Asian side of the Aegean. Although Herodotus makes no mention of them in his account of Marathon, hoplites would normally be accompanied by 'attendants', combining the roles of soldier-servant, armour-bearer and baggage-carrier, and capable of fighting as light-armed troops (*psiloi*). These were either citizens too poor to equip themselves as hoplites, or slaves. Able-bodied male slaves offered an additional pool of potential recruits that generally outnumbered the citizen population eligible for military service. The conscription of slaves as attendants or as rowers, and even to serve as hoplites, seems to have been quite a normal measure in 5th-century Hellas, and they were sometimes given the incentive of a grant of freedom in return for their military service, if they survived. The thousands of *psiloi* would have significantly shortened the numerical odds against the Athenians, but with considerably less tactical impact.

The Athenians, overall, were considerably less battle-hardened than the Barbarian troops they were to face. Their last large-scale mobilization had been 15 years earlier, to fight the Boeotians and Chalcidians, and veterans of that campaign would have been in a minority. Amongst the younger troops, some would have been in the small contingent sent to support the Ionian rebels' fateful attack on Sardis in 498 and may have acquired some uncomfortable direct experience of Persian tactics in the subsequent retreat. In the ranks there would also have been a few who had served as mercenaries on one side or the other in the Great King's wars. Then a reasonable number would have seen action in the on-off conflict with Aegina, which even flared up in the year of Marathon, though occasional sea-battles and skirmishes in coastal raids were not ideal preparation for the challenge they were about to face. However, there were compensating strengths, such as a shared understanding of the basic rules of traditional hoplite warfare and universal subscription to its ethos, and, on the part of the majority, self-belief as individuals and as a people, and the determination to defend themselves from invasion by a distant foreign power and the re-imposition of tyranny. In any case, the words of the Old Testament prophecy predicting the destruction of Jerusalem by the Babylonians in the previous century would have rung equally true in Hellene ears:

> Lo, I will bring a nation upon you from far, O house of Israel, saith the LORD: it is a mighty nation, it is an ancient nation, a nation whose language thou knowest not, neither understandest what they say. Their quiver is as an open sepulchre, they are all mighty men. (*Jeremiah* 5)

There would have been no shortage of battle experience in the Persian ranks, which would have included veterans of the Ionian Revolt and Mardonius' campaign into Europe in 492. The subject Hellene troops in the invasion force were hoplites equipped in exactly the same way as the Hellenes they were about to face, and followed the same tactical doctrine. However, their morale and motivation are likely to have been less robust.

The Athenians were still hoping for Spartan support:

> Before they left the city the generals had sent a herald to Sparta. He was a professional long-distance runner,[1] an Athenian called Philippides, and he claimed that he had an encounter with Pan

---

[1] *Hemerodromos*, according to the 1st-century Roman historian Livy, 'what the Greeks call these men who can cover an enormous distance in a single day's running' (*History of Rome* 31.24); literally 'a day runner'.

while crossing Mount Parthenion above Tegea. He reported that the god had shouted out his name and commanded him to ask the Athenians why they were neglectful of him when he looked so kindly on them, and had served them well in the past and would continue to do so. The Athenians believed all of this and, when things were more settled, established a shrine for Pan at the foot of the Acropolis and honoured him there with annual sacrifices and torch races.[1] Carrying out the generals' mission on which he said Pan had appeared to him, Philippides arrived in Sparta the day after he had left Athens. He went before the leading citizens and said, 'Lacedaemonians, the Athenians urge you to send help, not to stand by while a most ancient city of Hellas falls, enslaved by a Barbarian people. Even now the Eretrians have been taken into captivity and Hellas has already been weakened by the loss of one important city.' So, he delivered his message as instructed and the Lacedaemonians resolved to send help, but they were unable to do this immediately. It was the ninth day of the month and they did not wish to break with custom, which, they stated, prevented them going to war on the ninth day of that month if the moon was not yet full. (6.106)

Philippides was probably sent to Sparta as soon as news came through that Eretria had fallen. Modern athletes have covered the same 240km in less than 24 hours so his arrival 'the day after he had left Athens' is entirely credible. It seems that runners were more reliable as message-carriers over the stony tracks of Greece than unshod horses. His vision of Pan may have been a hallucination resulting from dehydration or extreme fatigue, but the Athenians treated it as a divine message. For sincere religious reasons the Spartans refused to act immediately because they were celebrating the Carnea, an important annual festival in honour of Apollo; this took place in late August in the modern calendar, and lasted for nine days. However, ten years later the Spartans were to overcome the same scruples to the extent of sending Leonidas

---

[1] Pan was primarily worshipped as the guardian of flocks and herds but later evidence associates him with panic in battle. The shrine mentioned here dates from just a few years after Marathon and may reflect the belief that the god contributed to the victory by causing panic in the Persian ranks, and by protecting the Athenians from it.

and a small advance guard to join the other Hellenes preparing to halt the Great King at Thermopylae.

So, the Spartans waited for the full moon while the Persians were guided to Marathon by Hippias son of Pisistratus. The night before, he had seen a vision in which he appeared to be sleeping with his own mother. His interpretation of this dream was that he was going to return to Athens, regain power and end his days an old man in his native land. This was how he interpreted the vision, so he carried on supervising operations, the shipping of the captives from Eretria to an island off Euboea that belonged to Styra, the beaching of the fleet on the Marathon shore and the positioning of the Barbarian troops when they had disembarked. While he was busy with all this he had one of his sneezing and coughing fits, and this was unusually severe.

MARATHON, 490

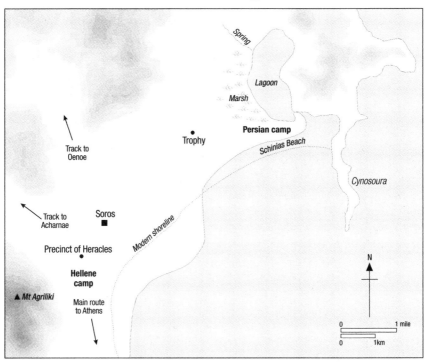

He was so old[1] that most of his teeth were loose and one flew out because he was coughing so violently. The tooth fell into the sand and he searched for it desperately, but could not find it. He groaned and said to the people around him, 'This land is not our land and we will not be able to make it subject to us. Whatever my share was to be, my tooth has it all.' Now Hippias understood how his vision would be fulfilled.

The Athenians were positioned on ground dedicated to Heracles and the Plataeans joined them there in full force.[2] They had placed themselves under the protection of Athens in the past and the Athenians had done a great deal to support them.[3] The Athenian generals were divided in their view of what action to take: some were against attacking, thinking they were too few to take on the Median army, others, including Miltiades, were strongly in favour of it. So, they were divided and the worse of the two arguments seemed to be prevailing. But there was an 11th vote, that of the polemarch,[4] who was appointed to the position by lot, though in the past the Athenians gave the polemarch an equal vote with the generals. Callimachus of Aphidnae[5] was polemarch at the time of Marathon. Miltiades went up to him and said, 'Now, Callimachus, the choice is yours, between enslaving Athens or securing her freedom and leaving a memorial for all generations such as not even Harmodius and Aristogiton have left. For Athens is now facing the greatest danger since her foundation. If the people bow down before the Medes they will be put under Hippias again, and we know what that will mean. But if the city survives, she is capable of becoming the leading city of Hellas.

[1] At least in his late 70s. Herodotus paints a comical picture of him bustling around, self-importantly but surely not in charge of establishing the beachhead. He would have been very much a puppet-ruler, and not for very long, if the Persian plan had succeeded.

[2] Later sources give 1,000 for the Plataean force, not specifying how many may have been hoplites; 500 is a more likely figure. According to Herodotus there were 600 at the battle of Plataea but, according to Thucydides, 400 to defend their small city when the Peloponnesians laid siege to it in 429.

[3] Forty years before, the Athenians had intervened at their request to protect them from Theban aggression.

[4] The polemarch ('war leader'), commander-in-chief of the city's army and navy, was one of the nine archons.

[5] A deme in the north of Attica, adjacent to Marathon.

'I will explain how this can be brought about, and why it is that you are in a position to decide the issue. We ten generals are divided, half in favour of fighting, half against. If we do not fight there is real danger that a change of opinion will undermine the resolution of the Athenian people so that they medize. But if we fight before the rot takes hold of certain citizens, and if the gods are kind to us, we can win this battle. This is your moment, it all depends on you. Vote with me and your homeland will be free and become the leading city in Hellas. But if you support those who are arguing falsely against giving battle, you will achieve the exact opposite of the good result I have been describing to you.'

Miltiades' words won Callimachus over and, with the polemarch's vote cast in favour, the decision was taken to give battle. Now, presidency[1] rotated among the generals, each taking it for a day in turn, and the generals who were in favour of fighting offered their days to Miltiades. He accepted but would not give battle until his day came round to preside. (6.107–10)

There is no more detailed information in any source about the timing or order of events at this point. It seems clear that the Athenians did not take any action to oppose the Persians' landing and that the Persians did not take any action to prevent the Athenians establishing a position facing them, but nothing can be safely deduced from this. However, the location of the 'ground dedicated to Heracles' has been established beyond reasonable doubt. It was at the south-west end of the plain where it narrowed to less than 1km in width between the shoreline and the flank of Mount Agriliki. The main land route to Athens passed through this gap, running south along the coast beneath Mount Pentelicon and then due west over the saddle between the south side of Pentelicon and Hymettus. The sacred grove, probably a dense cluster of mature olive trees, surrounding the shrine, and other trees and an area of marshland, and possibly some buildings, even the ancient settlement

---

[1] *Prytaneia*: in government the 50 tribal-group representatives that made up the 500-strong Council (*Boule*) took it in turns to act as *prytaneis* for a period of five weeks and take responsibility for day-to-day business. They did not have additional powers, such as a casting vote. It appears that the presiding general had similar administrative responsibilities as chairman of the board of ten.

of Marathon, made this a strong blocking position. It also covered the more direct route west which led to the deme of Acharnae by a steep mountain track around the north side of Pentelicon and then south-west to Athens. It would have been a slow and difficult alternative for a large infantry force and probably impossible for cavalry, but could be used by messengers running to and from Athens. Drinking water was available close to the Athenian camp from the mountain springs that fed into the marsh.

At its south-western end the plain was wider than it is today, bulging out at the widest point about 1,000m beyond the present shoreline. At the north-eastern end, in the area of the Persian camp, it was a little narrower. The widest part of the plain was closer to the Athenian camp than the Persian. It then narrowed to meet the present shoreline, a 3,000m stretch of sandy beach curving gently round to the east and sheltered by the natural breakwater of a narrow promontory (Cynosoura, 'dog's tail') jutting out approximately 2,000m to the south. The Persian beachhead and encampment were at this end of the bay protected on its inland side by marsh and probably by some field fortification at its western end. There was ample space for over a hundred ships with their sterns pulled up onto the sand, and a similar number could have been moored or beached along the western side of Cynosoura. Geological research has established that a small lake at the eastern end of this beach was, very probably, a larger lagoon with an entrance channel wide and deep enough to make it a natural harbour. Any ships that could not be beached or accommodated in the lagoon would have been roped at the stern to the bows of beached ships and anchored from the bows. Springs fed into the marsh on its north side and directly into the lagoon so the Persian camp was close to a good supply of drinking water, which was needed in large amounts for the horses. Until the early 20th century the plain probably changed little in character or appearance, remaining an open expanse of pasture and cereal fields with scattered trees and a few buildings. Now much of it is planted with fruit orchards and cross-hatched with roads, farm tracks and irrigation channels, or built over. The marshland at the eastern end is mostly drained, except for the large area taken up by the 2004 Olympic Rowing and Canoeing Centre, but Schinias beach must still be much as it was when the Persians occupied it, and the crescent of mountains rising steeply inland from the plain still walls it in. The distant views on the approach over Mount

Pentelicon from the south-west are more rewarding than exploration on the ground (by car or on foot), but in the clear grassy space around the *Soros* mound, the Tomb of the Athenians, which is actually at the edge of the battlefield itself, there is a moving sense of place in the sunlight of a quiet afternoon in late summer.

The Athenians appear to have debated what action to take at great length and probably repeatedly as information came in, first about the Persians' plans and preparations, and then about their progress through the islands. Whether or not surrender without a fight was publicly presented as an option, it does seem that there was a minority in favour of this amongst the aristocratic families who could expect to prosper under Hippias, restored as tyrant and backed by Persia. However, as far as the majority was concerned, this would be opting for slavery. It is probable that the decision to march out and meet the enemy in full force rather than prepare for a siege was taken some weeks before the Persians arrived at Marathon. The decision to seek assistance from Sparta and probably from other cities in addition to Plataea, would have been taken at this time too, if not earlier. If Philippides was despatched on his epic run as late in the day as Herodotus implies, his message was likely to have been a final urgent cry for help, following up on an earlier request, which Sparta may already have agreed to.

For dramatic effect Herodotus weaves rhetoric appropriate to those earlier debates into Miltiades' speech, neatly adding a reference to the destiny which Athens was to fulfil in the six decades that were to follow up to the time of writing. The decision that had to be taken in the field was clear-cut, however, between staying on the defensive and letting the Persians make the first move, or taking the initiative and attacking. If retreat was considered by the Athenians, it was not actually an option. On the move they would have been highly vulnerable to the missile firepower of the more mobile Persian infantry and cavalry, and, even if they held together in a fighting retreat, it would give the Persians time to ship a strong force round to Athens ahead of them. The Persians' goal was to destroy the defending force and move on to their final objective, Athens. If Hippias' faction could undermine Athenian resistance, Athens, like Chalcis and Eretria, would be taken with little or no effort. This was not going to happen, but references in Herodotus and other sources strongly indicate that subversive forces were at work or in danger of surfacing. It was a reasonable strategy for the Persians to wait for this 'rot' to take effect, rather than attempt to dislodge the Athenians from a strong defensive position. If the supplies which they had brought with them ran low, they could be resupplied from Euboea or further east, and they would not run out of drinking water. Autumn and rougher weather were still several weeks away so there was no immediate pressure to make preparations for sailing back to Asia. But it made better sense for the Athenians to give battle sooner rather than later to avert the risk of resolution crumbling in the ranks as a result of subversion, the discomforts of campaigning or plain boredom. On the other hand, it was worth waiting for reinforcements to arrive from Sparta, or anywhere, and with Athens and most of Attica to their rear, supplies would not be a problem. It is probable that neither side gave consideration to the threat of disease, which would have grown as the days passed. First, the marshy areas of the plain of Marathon were renowned for their mosquitoes and, secondly, dense occupation of the same area of land by thousands of men must have made conditions increasingly foul.

According to *The Constitution of Athens*, attributed to Aristotle and drawing on public records, the archons, including the polemarch, were still elected officials at the time of Marathon, being appointed by lot for the first time three years after the battle, so Callimachus may have been one of the last to have held this position on his merits as a soldier rather than chosen by lot as Herodotus states. It subsequently became a political-figurehead role because military expertise and experience could not be guaranteed amongst randomly selected citizens. Whether or not the generals who voted with Miltiades handed over their presidencies to him, it is very unlikely that the attack was postponed until his official day for that reason alone. In any case, Herodotus clearly presents Callimachus, not Miltiades, as commander-in-chief, delivering his crucial casting vote and taking the command position of honour on the right of the line.

Herodotus describes the fighting in less than 400 words of Greek:

When Miltiades' turn came around, this is how the Athenians were formed up for battle. Callimachus the polemarch was in command of the right wing,[1] it being customary in those days for the polemarch to

[1] *Keras*, also meaning the horn of an animal; the Zulu warrior term for their flank formations, *izimpondo*, uses similar imagery.

lead the Athenian right. The rest of the tribal regiments[1] were lined up in order alongside, finishing with the Plataeans, who were positioned on the left, and ever since this battle, when the Athenians gather for the great festivals which are held every four years and make their sacrifices, the herald prays that the Athenians and Plataeans may be equally blessed.[2] The Athenians' formation was extended to make it equal in width to the Medes' with the result that the line was a few ranks deep in the centre and weakest there while each wing was up to strength. When the men were all in position and the sacrificial omens were good, the starting signal was given and the Athenians advanced on the barbarians at the double. The distance between the two armies was about 8 *stades* [1500m]. As the Persians were making ready to meet the attack they saw that the Athenians were coming at them at the double.[3] They thought they were in the grip of a suicidal frenzy, seeing so few of them charging at the double without any support from archers or cavalry.[4] This is what the Barbarians thought, but when they had engaged with them at close quarters, the Athenians fought remarkably well. To everyone's knowledge, they were the first Hellenes to charge the enemy at the double and the first to stand firm at the sight of Median clothing and the men who wore it. Until that day the Greeks were terrified even to hear the name of the Medes spoken.

The fighting went on for a long time at Marathon. The Barbarians were winning in the centre where the Sacae and the Persians themselves were positioned. They were winning here and broke the Greek centre and drove it inland.[5] But on each flank the Athenians and the Plataeans were winning. They let the routed Barbarians run

---

[1] It is generally best in translation not to apply modern terminology anachronistically to ancient units of different shapes and sizes, but in this case 'regiment' is a good fit. The Athenian *phylai* (generally the term for 'tribe', here used for the unit in question) comprised the hoplite membership of each of the ten tribal voting groups with a nominal strength of 1,000 and each commanded by its elected general.

[2] In 427 Plataea fell to the Spartans and Thebans after a long siege and its defenders, including a number of Athenians, were executed.

[3] Literally translated, the Greek reads 'The Persians seeing them coming on at the double were preparing to receive them'.

[4] The Persians knew that the Athenians had few archers and no cavalry, but they were not used to being attacked without the preliminaries of cavalry harassment and archery bombardment.

[5] *Mesogaia*, generally meaning 'interior', was also the name Athenians gave to the central area of Attica which lay beyond the south-western end of the plain.

and wheeled each wing inwards to attack those who had broken through in the centre, and then the Athenians were victorious. The Persians turned and ran and the Athenians came after them, cutting them down until they reached the shore. Then they called for fire and tried to prevent the ships being launched. At this point in the action, Callimachus the polemarch was killed after fighting with great gallantry. One of the generals, Stesilaus son of Thrasyleus, died there too. Many other notable Athenians fell, including Cynegirus[1] son of Euphorion, his hand chopped off by an axe as he clung to a ship's sternpost. The Athenians managed to capture seven ships but the Barbarians got the rest away out to sea. (6.111–15)

'The fighting went on for a long time' but Herodotus covers it in just a few hundred words, fewer than in his accounts of any of the battles fought in 480 and 479, and a tiny fraction of the thousands of words written about Marathon by historians and commentators up to the present day. Three books were published in 2010/11 alone to mark the 2,500th anniversary of the battle, together adding a further 750 pages to the mountainous bibliography (Billows, 2010; Krentz, 2010; Lacey, 2011). The scope for speculative reconstruction is immense, and the more detail the reconstruction offers, the greater the speculation. This is the least informative of Herodotus' battle narratives.

If, as it is reasonable to argue, the decision to attack was not solely driven by Miltiades' 'presidency', Herodotus offers no other explanation. He tells us the distance between the two battle lines when the Hellenes began their rapid advance but gives no indication of its starting point or direction. He tells us that the line was extended to match the length of the enemy line and consequently weaker in the centre, but does not quantify the difference in terms of file depth. He clearly considers the speed of the advance to have been exceptional (the word translated as 'at the double' appears three times in quick succession) but does not put this in any tactical context. The pivotal moment when the victorious Hellene flanks wheeled to attack the Barbarian centre could not be described more economically; and the same has to be said of the running fight that ensued or the closing struggle at the ships. There is little that can be added from other sources.

---

[1] The brother of the tragedian Aeschylus, who also fought at Marathon.

However, Marathon was celebrated in a large painting displayed very publicly from the 450s in the Painted Stoa, a colonnaded space in the Agora of Athens. It was created when the battle was still in living memory and Herodotus would have been familiar with it. It was still a treasured exhibit when Pausanias, the travel-writer, visited the city in the 2nd century AD and wrote in his guide to Attica:

> Here you see the men who fought at Marathon. The Boeotians of Plataea and part of the Athenian force are fighting the Barbarians at close quarters and neither side is winning. Further into the battle the Barbarians are in flight and pushing one another into the marsh. The Phoenician ships are at the far end of the painting and there the Hellenes are killing Barbarians as they scramble on board. (*Guide to Greece* 1.15.4)

The three-part narrative of this painting corroborates Herodotus' sparse outline and also fills it out a little. First, it suggests that the fight between the Persians and Sacae and the flanking Athenians and Plataeans was closely contested for a time, and secondly it supplies the graphic detail that Barbarians were driven into the marsh and presumably drowned as they fell back on their camp and ships. Pausanias includes the marsh in his description of the battlefield:

> There is a lake at Marathon which is mostly marsh. The fleeing Barbarians fell into this because they did not know the paths through it, and it is said that they suffered their greatest losses there. (*Guide to Greece* 1.32)

In this final stage, the battlefield would have been very crowded as the retreating troops were funnelled into a relatively narrow corridor between the southern edge of the marsh and the sea. Some would have been trapped with the marsh at their backs and the carnage could have been terrible, and here the *psiloi* would have been as actively engaged as the hoplites.

The Roman writer Cornelius Nepos, writing in the 1st century BC, supplies a little more detail in his very brief account of the battle in his short biography of Miltiades:

His leadership inspired the Athenians to lead out their forces from the city and to set up their camp in an advantageous position. The next day, they formed their battle line at the foot of the mountain on ground that was not fully open because there were trees scattered here and there. Their battle plan was to use the mountain slopes as cover and the spread of trees as an obstacle to the cavalry to protect themselves from being surrounded by the enemy's superior numbers. Datis could see that the ground did not favour his men. However, trusting in the numerical superiority of his army, he was eager to engage the enemy, the more so because he thought it would be a good thing to give battle before the Lacedaemonians came to their aid. So, he formed up his 100,000 infantry and 10,000 cavalry and sent them into battle. In this fight, the Athenians were so much more valorous that they overwhelmed ten times their number of the enemy and filled them with such terror that they fled, not to their camp but even to their ships. There has been no battle more glorious than this one, ever. For never has so small a band of men overcome such a mighty host. (*Outstanding Foreign Leaders: Miltiades* 5)

Cornelius Nepos has never been highly thought of as a historian, and was dismissed as 'an intellectual pygmy' by one eminent classical scholar, but his mention of the trees, if it has any basis in fact, may help explain the Persians' reluctance to initiate the fighting, whether the description applies to rising ground and trees protecting the Hellene camp at the south-western end of the plain, or their chosen defensive position somewhere out in front of the camp. *Tractu arborum*, 'the spread of trees', can be translated as 'dragging up trees', to create a simple barricade or abbatis, an interpretation which has some appeal. But *tractus* also means 'area', and this makes better sense in the context of 'trees scattered here and there' in the previous sentence. However, after this promising start to the only other surviving ancient text which sets out to describe the battle in its entirety, however briefly, Nepos defies Herodotus and the whole tradition by having Datis take the initiative rather than the Athenian generals and polemarch; though it would indeed have made sense to take the Hellenes on before the Lacedaemonians joined them.

Herodotus tells us that the two armies faced each other for several days without any contact. They probably marched out each morning and took up position on the ground on which they chose to fight, the Hellenes staying quite close to their camp, drawn up in sufficient depth to withstand a frontal attack with their flanks secured by the sea to the right and the mountain spurs and perhaps Nepos' trees to the left. The camp itself was probably not fortified and, in any case, the Athenians' preference was to mount their defence in the open field rather than from within walls, and the Persians were known to be expert in siege warfare. With *psiloi* intermixed or positioned on each flank, the Hellenes could cover a front of up to 4,000m in sufficient depth to block the approaches to the main road to Athens exiting the plain at its south-west corner. The Persians may have done some tree-felling at their end of the plain to clear the battlefield and to acquire trees to build into a stockade as they did at Plataea and Mycale. They had to go further from their camp than the Athenians in order to take up a position roughly in the centre of the plain and, at least on the day of the battle, about 1500m from the Athenians. Here they could exploit their greater mobility and make their numerical superiority count, and, in particular, their cavalry could manoeuvre freely with good prospects of working round the enemy's flanks. However, each side was depending on the other to take the initiative and mount an attack. Sacrifices were routinely performed by each at the start of the day, supporting the commanders' tactical judgement and possibly manipulated on occasion to do so, until, for whatever reason, the decision was taken to give battle, sacrificial omens permitting. This was a pattern seen very often in ancient battles and was to be replicated in the course of the final, decisive confrontation at Plataea.

At Marathon, several days passed between the Hellenes' decision to take the initiative and give battle, and the battle itself. Leaving aside the significance of Miltiades' presidency, Herodotus may be hinting at a more specific reason for the timing of this decision. His text suggests that it was the speed of the advance that caught the Persians by surprise. In the days of waiting it had perhaps become apparent to the Athenian commanders that early each morning they had their men all formed up and ready for action before the Persians were fully in position, probably because the latter had to cover more ground to get out onto the wider part of the plain, and because their greater numbers took longer to manoeuvre. Perhaps the panel of generals benefited from Miltiades' experience of campaigning in a Persian army.

The *Suda,* a Byzantine historical encyclopaedia and dictionary of quotations, written in Greek in the 10th century AD, is more specific: it states that the Persians were not simply unprepared, but were in the process of dividing their force with the presumed intention of shipping the cavalry round to Athens:

> *The cavalry's not there!* When Datis invaded Attica, they say that, as he was embarking, the Ionians went up into the trees to inform the Athenians that the cavalry were departing, and that, when Miltiades had established that this was so, he gave battle and was victorious: hence this well-known saying applied to men who break up their order of battle. (*Suda* chi.444)

The *Suda* could be dismissed as an unreliable source because of its late date, but it is known to have been compiled from much earlier authoritative texts, although none have been found to connect with this particular entry. It presents Datis as 'embarking', presumably with part of his infantry as well as the cavalry, and it would have made sense to break the impasse by shipping a force round to Athens, which would have been lightly defended, if at all. There would have been Ionians, pressed into the service of Persia, who wanted to help their brother Hellenes (though it is quite possible this part of the story was created by the Ionians after the event). The mention of the trees echoes Nepos' description of the Hellene position and could be evidence of a shared earlier source. However, both the 5th-century frieze from the temple of Athena Nike on the Acropolis, which may include scenes from Marathon, and a relief carved on a 3rd-century AD Roman sarcophagus from Brescia, which is thought to have been based on the painting in the Stoa, include cavalry. Also, according to Pausanias:

> Every night at Marathon the sound can be heard of horses neighing and men fighting. No good has come to anyone who has gone there with the express purpose of experiencing this, but the spirits are not angered by those who encounter them unintentionally ... Above the lake there are some stone mangers used by Artaphernes' cavalry with markings made by tents in the rock. A stream flows out of the lake and here the water is suitable for livestock, but near its mouth it becomes salt and full of sea fish. (*Guide to Greece* 1.32)

Clearly, according to folk memory at least, the Persian cavalry did play a part in the battle. The 'mangers', presumably natural rock features that looked like mangers, could preserve eyewitness evidence for the location of the cavalry encampment, some distance from the shore and separated from the plain by the lake and marsh, but close to ample fresh water. In any case, it seems the cavalry was off the scene for at least long enough not to be a threat to the Athenians as they advanced across the widest stretch of the plain that separated them from the Persians. Once the two lines were locked together fighting hand to hand the cavalry could not be closely involved because their arrows and javelins would be as much a threat to their own side as to the enemy. They would have held back waiting, either to run the routed enemy down or to cover their own side's retreat. Whether it was because some or all of the horses were already loaded onto the transport ships when the Hellenes began their advance, or simply because they were deployed too late to attack the enemy formation when its flanks were exposed out in the widest part of the plain, the part the Persian cavalry played in the battle seems not to have been significant.

Apart from the hint in the *Suda* there is only one other piece of evidence that might suggest the Persian force was divided. Nepos states that Datis took the initiative and sent into battle 100,000 infantry, half of the 200,000 he landed with, but none of the 10,000 cavalry. Leaving aside the inflated numbers, if Datis was embarking half his infantry and all of his cavalry to ship it round to Phalerum, the Athenians had a compelling opportunity to attack on much improved terms and a pressing need to remove any potential obstacle to a rapid march to defend their city from impending direct attack. If this victory was won over a significantly smaller force than history went on to relate, it suited the Athenians not to correct the error.

There is no contemporary record of the order in which the ten tribal regiments would have been drawn up. Nor does Herodotus indicate how many regiments made up each wing and how many the centre, and there may have been no formal distinction between these three divisions. Command and control could be exercised only at the basic level of deciding where and when to fight, of communicating a simple battle plan in council with the next level of command and inspiring as many of the troops as could be in earshot with a rousing speech, and, finally, of leading from the front. Once battle was joined, however

distinctively plumed his helmet or blazoned his shield, Callimachus
would not have been visible to most of his army, but each regiment
had its own general, leading from the front and following what was
happening to his right to maintain cohesion. Then, individuals did
their best to stay close to their comrades on either side with the ranks
behind following as closely as possible. Trumpets were used to sound the
advance and to raise the spirits, but there was no system of bugle calls
or indeed any form of battlefield communication. Herodotus' language
suggests that the reduction of the Athenian centre to 'a few ranks' was
something that just happened, not a conscious tactical decision. In a
hoplite battle each side tried to keep its line the same length as the
enemy's to avoid envelopment, even at the expense of sacrificing depth
of file. At Marathon this process may have been carried out hastily just
before the off, or even when the advance was actually under way, and
weakened the centre because there was not time to adjust files uniformly.
Applying what is known from later sources describing battles that were
fought 60 years or more after Marathon, it could be assumed that this
stretching of the line would have left the wings eight-deep and reduced
the centre to around half this depth. But the formation that bore down
on the Persians was probably considerably less tidy than this, with
the hoplites followed closely or flanked by a completely unstructured
swarm of light-armed troops.

The Persians' first sight of the Hellene battle line would have been,
as on previous days, a long thin smudge spanning the south-western
end of the plain. There may have been occasional glints as the early
morning sun caught polished metal, but no detail would have been
visible. It is likely that mounted scouts brought the first information
that the Hellenes were on the move, but this would soon have become
apparent from the dust cloud that thousands of feet would have raised
from the dry farmland. Then, as the distance began to narrow, the
Persians started to take in the speed of the advance. The Greek word
which Herodotus uses is *dromos*, literally 'running', but, 'at the double'
is a more plausible translation; this can be justified by usage in military
contexts elsewhere in contrast to the term *baden*, 'at marching pace'.
Whatever assumptions may be made about hoplite battle-gear and the
typical physical capacity of the men burdened with it, a running charge
over a distance of 1,500m would have left the Hellenes completely out
of formation and in no condition to engage the enemy effectively, let

alone to win a hand-to-hand battle contested over a number of hours and a further 4,000m. The everyday equivalent of double pace is a jog trot, a speed of 7–8km/h, which would have enabled the Hellenes to cover the full distance comfortably inside ten minutes. Quite possibly they did run the final *stade* flat out, having paused briefly just out of bowshot to get their breath back and regroup.

The final charge would then have taken around a couple of minutes to drive home. Now shields were swung forward from the left side and raised and angled to protect against the volleys of arrows arcing up from the Persian line, 'indirect fire' at a rate of five to ten shots per minute from thousands of archers massed ten-deep behind their palisade of wicker. Shields, helmets and body armour and a rapid dash across the 'beaten ground' kept Hellene casualties to a minimum and then the hand-to-hand fighting began. If the massed hoplites began the final charge in good formation, it must have been impossible to maintain cohesion over the full 200m and this would have made the stretched centre more vulnerable to the fighting quality and superior numbers of the Persians and Sacae they engaged with. But it also gave opportunities for individual moments of glory all along the Hellene front line. It is a reasonable assumption that the Hellene troops on the Persian side were positioned on the wings, possibly along with inferior Asian troops not mentioned in any source. So, it was probably quite early in the fighting that the Athenian centre began to give way as the enemy flanks were pushed back and broken.

Some reconstructions of the battle treat the 'double envelopment' that immediately followed as a planned manoeuvre, even as a stroke of tactical genius which is quite often attributed to Miltiades. Appealing as this is, it assumes a degree of precision and co-ordination beyond the capabilities of an 'amateur' hoplite militia, and it is very unlikely that even the uniquely trained, drilled and disciplined Spartans could have overcome the problem of communication between the two wings over the hundreds of metres of noisy, dust-clouded, swirling battlefield that separated them; and at command level it assumes an improbable degree of tactical sophistication and an even less likely acceptance of the grave risk that the weakened centre would not simply bend but break, the battle then most likely to end in bloody rout.

The centre did break but what happened next was spontaneous and much less tidy than any tactical diagram would suggest. The Athenians and Plataeans on the wings were probably no more motivated to fight fellow Hellenes than the Ionians and Aeolians, and Aegean islanders facing them, and secret deals may even have been done before the battle. There could have been no hoplite clash, and any more lightly armed conscripts from other parts of the empire, if they stood their ground at all, would have been swept aside and could easily outrun their hoplite pursuers. With opposition melted away and the sudden advantage of a significant overlap on each flank, it would have been almost a reflex movement for the Athenians and Plataeans to wheel inward and attack their real enemy, the Barbarians, in both flanks and save their own collapsed centre in the narrow window of time before the rout became irreversible. If any individual is to be credited with initiating the manoeuvre, Callimachus is the strongest candidate, conspicuous as he would have been as polemarch and commander of the right wing. The action at this point, with individual leaders darting inward and random groups following, would have more resembled the behaviour of columns of ants than a drill refined on the parade ground. The Hellenes' longer spears and heavier shields then did their work.

The Persians' success in extracting nearly all of their ships suggests that they managed to make an effective stand at their camp's western entrance, which was probably stockaded. The seven ships that they lost may have been beached nearest to this point. It is unlikely that any was immediately available, but the Hellenes' 'call for fire' would have put audiences in mind of Homer's hero Hector launching his attack on the Hellene ships on the shore before Troy, giving orders to his men 'with a mighty shout':

'When I am there amidst the hollow ships,
Then be sure to bring me all-consuming fire,
Fire, that I may burn the ships and slay the men of Argos
Beside their ships, thrown into utter confusion by the smoke!'
(*Iliad* 8.180–83)

For the Athenians, the victory of Marathon seems to have been viewed at least in part as a throwback to the heroic past, sung of by Homer, and Herodotus may well be acknowledging this here. The depiction of the battle in the Stoa alongside paintings of the siege of Troy and Theseus' mythical battle with the Amazons is one of the earliest of many demonstrations of the significance Athenians attached to this historic victory. It had almost immediately generated its own mythology, with which Herodotus would undoubtedly have been familiar; but he clearly restrained himself in his narration. The artist of the Painted Stoa interwove the divine, the heroic and the mortal in his depiction:

> The hero called Marathon, after whom the plain is named, is depicted and Theseus is shown rising out of the earth, and Athena and Heracles may be seen as well (the people of Marathon say they were the first to regard Heracles as a god). Of the men who fought in the battle the most prominent figures in the painting are Callimachus, whom the Athenians had chosen to be polemarch, and Miltiades, one of the generals, and also a hero called Echetlus. They say this man, a countryman from his dress and appearance, fought in the battle and slew many Barbarians with a plough,[1] but then disappeared when it was over. (*Guide to Greece* 1.15.4, 32.4)

Herodotus concludes his account of the battle with an extraordinary story of the experience of one ordinary soldier:

> An astonishing thing happened to one Athenian. Epizelos son of Cuphagoras was fighting at close quarters with great gallantry and lost his sight without being wounded or hit by a missile in any part of his body. He was blind from that moment for the rest of his life. The story that I have heard he told was this. An enormous hoplite with a beard that covered the whole of his shield appeared directly opposite him but then stepped to one side and killed the man next to him. Well, I did hear that Epizelos used to say this. (6.117)

The nucleus of the story could have been a case of acute combat stress suffered by one of the Athenians who faced Hellene troops fighting for Persia. The *Suda* has an entry on the same topic that brings Pan back into the Marathon legend, fulfilling the promise he made to the Athenians on his encounter with Philippides:

> Polyzelos, after being blinded by the sight of an apparition with a beard that covered his shield (this was thought to be Pan, present as

---

[1] Presumably a hand-plough, or perhaps a heavy hoe or mattock. *Psiloi* were as likely to go into battle with agricultural or household implements as with conventional weapons.

their ally), fought on as if he could still see, distinguishing enemies from friends by their voices. (*Suda* iota.545)

Herodotus names only two of the Athenian generals, Miltiades and Stesilaus. Plutarch (*c.*50–120 AD) in his *Life of Aristides* identifies two more, Aristides and, by implication, Themistocles:

> In the battle, the Athenian centre had the hardest fight and the Barbarians facing the two tribes Leontis and Antiochis there held out the longest. Themistocles and Aristides fought brilliantly in their positions alongside each other, one being a Leontid and the other an Antiochid. (5.1, 3)

This may or may not be historical fact, though it suits the writer's biographical purpose. Themistocles had already served as archon and both he and Aristides were prominent politically and would be keen rivals in the decade that was to follow, so it is possible they were both elected generals in 490. Plutarch describes Themistocles as a young man at the time of Marathon (he was actually in his mid 30s), consumed by ambition and so preoccupied by Miltiades' fame that he could not sleep. However, he adds more convincingly, 'while others thought the defeat of the Barbarians at Marathon had put an end to the war, Themistocles saw it as just the beginning of a greater conflict … and trained the city up for it.' (*Themistocles* 3)

Other later sources, some much later, offer a little extra detail. For example, there was a more elaborate story of Callimachus' death, preserved by Aelius Aristides, a celebrated orator of the 2nd century AD:

> Though slain and bristling with Barbarian missiles, yet he remained standing as if he was immortal, terrifying what was left of the foe. (*Panathenaic* 88.202)

His comrade Cynegirus' death was more imaginatively described in the 3rd century by Justin:

> After killing a great many in the battle and chasing the fleeing enemy to their ships, he seized a fully manned trireme with his right hand, and would not let it go till he had lost the hand. Even then, with his

right hand cut off, he held onto the ship with his left. When he lost that as well, he finally hung onto the ship with his teeth. He had such fighting spirit that, unwearied by so much killing or by the loss of both his hands, defeated and dismembered, he fought with his teeth to the last like a wild beast.[1] (*Epitome of Trogus' Philippic Histories* 2.9)

Datis and Artaphernes had not yet accepted defeat.

The Persians collected their Eretrian prisoners from the island where they had left them[2] and sailed towards Sunium, aiming to get to Athens before the Athenians did. Some Athenians accused the Alcmaeonids of conspiring to bring this about and of having agreed to hold up a shield to signal to the Persians when they were back on board their ships.[3] So, the Persians sailed round Sunium, but the Athenians marched back to the city as fast as their feet would carry them and reached it ahead of the Barbarians, coming from one piece of ground dedicated to Heracles at Marathon to another at Cynosarges.[4] The Barbarian fleet lay at anchor for a while off Phalerum, Athens' naval base at that time, and then sailed back to Asia. (6.115–16)

Later tradition has the Athenians racing back to Athens immediately after the battle and taking up position facing the sea at Phalerum on the same day, an astonishing feat after several hours of heavy fighting, and not actually necessary, unless the Persian landing force had set off in the morning of the day before the battle. The distance by sea from Marathon to Phalerum is about 110km. A trireme with all oars

[1] Surely the inspiration for the heroics of the Black Knight in *Monty Python and the Holy Grail*.
[2] This was presumably done by a detachment of a few ships whilst the rest of the fleet went ahead to Phalerum.
[3] Herodotus discusses this at some length, firm in the belief that someone did signal with a shield at some crucial moment but unable to accept that the 'tyrant-hating' Alcmaeonids could have had anything to do with it. He may be protesting too much: from a long aristocratic line, the Alcmaeonids had been on good terms with the Pisistratids in the past. It is a pity he did not apply his curious mind to the questions of who was to receive the signal and where it was sent from.
[4] Its precise location is not known.

manned could cover this in ten to eleven hours of non-stop rowing but a substantial fleet, transporting troops and moving more slowly to preserve cohesion, would have taken significantly longer, even with the assistance of a following wind on the run down to Sunium, as mentioned by Plutarch. On top of the rowing, there would probably have been one or two breaks for eating and drinking and the time taken to launch (the last ships doing so under attack) and to get into formation on departure; then the manoeuvring that would have preceded a landing at Phalerum, possibly under attack from the small Athenian fleet, would have delayed things further. Additionally, movement during the hours of darkness was probably ruled out as too risky. The Athenians, on the other hand, were faced with a seven- or eight-hour route march with time to rest before setting off and attendants to carry their weapons and armour.

Herodotus gives a very precise and low figure for Athenian fatalities in contrast to a round and very high figure for the Persians, producing a remarkably tidy ratio of 1:33.333 – 'In the battle of Marathon about 6,400 Barbarians died and 192 Athenians; that was the number that fell on each side.' (6.116). It is hard not to accept the 192 because the fallen were all named and presumably meticulously counted as a very important matter of public record, but for a battle that went on 'for a long time', in which the Athenian centre was broken and 'many ... notable Athenians fell', it is a surprisingly small number, even for a winning side with superior defensive equipment. However, being 'notable' had its obligations, which included fighting in the front rank and therefore greater risk of dying a heroic death. There would also have been deaths amongst the Plataean hoplites and possibly a larger number amongst the *psiloi,* who would have received less respectful attention. And it is not inconceivable that an earlier error was faithfully transcribed into all the surviving manuscripts of the *Historia.*

Herodotus' numbers may not have included casualties who died of their wounds later. Flesh wounds missing major arteries or veins were treated with various, mostly simple remedies, wine being probably the most effective. These were generally survivable as long as bleeding was controlled and infection avoided, causes of morbidity that were partially understood. Larger wounds were sutured. The extraction of arrows, especially those with barbed heads, and other missiles called for particular expertise and appropriate instruments. There is evidence of reasonable proficiency in the treatment of simple fractures and dislocations. However, wounds penetrating the chest or abdomen and skull fractures were most likely to be fatal. Hippocratic texts from as early as the 5th century deal with wound management in some detail, but there appears to have been no organized system of medical care in the armies of the Persian War. Some doctors may have taken their place in the ranks and fought alongside fellow citizens until their skills were needed; others may have joined the armies as camp followers. Hoplites' attendants would also have served as paramedics and there were probably slaves amongst them with more refined medical skills.

The figure of 6,400 Persian dead, though rather more credible than Justin's 200,000 lost 'in the battle or in shipwrecks', seems very high. In ancient and medieval times such disparity was not extraordinary when a battle ended with the losing side cornered in a total rout, but perhaps Marathon did not end in this way. We are told that Datis and Artaphernes managed to extract all but seven of their ships, which suggests that the rout was finally contained around the entrance to the encampment, and it is hard to believe that they would have contemplated an attempt on Athens if they had lost 40–60 per cent of their men (assuming an original strength of 20,000–30,000 and roughly the same number incapacitated by wounds as killed in action).

By the time of the Peloponnesian War, if not earlier, it was the Athenians' custom to bring home the cremated bones of their war-dead and bury them publicly, but, according to Thucydides:

> They made an exception for those who fell at Marathon,[1] judging their service so outstanding that they performed the funeral rites for them on the battlefield. (*History of the Peloponnesian War* 2.34)

Pausanias describes the burial arrangements at Marathon:

> There is a deme called Marathon, about the same distance from Athens as from Carystus in Euboea. It was here in Attica that the Barbarians landed, were defeated in battle and lost some ships as they

---

[1] The Athenians also buried their dead on the battlefield at Plataea in 479.

were putting out to sea. The Athenians have a grave on the plain, and on it are tablets giving the names of the fallen according to their tribes. There is another grave for the Plataeans and also one for the slaves; this was the first time slaves fought in battle.[1] A trophy[2] of white marble was set up on the battlefield. The Athenians say that they buried the Persians because religion universally requires that corpses should be covered by the earth, but I could not find any grave and there was no mound, nor any other marker to be seen. They just carried the bodies to a trench and tossed them in. (*Guide to Greece* 1.32)

Pausanias' choice of the word *taphos*, simply meaning 'grave', is rather inadequate as a description of the burial mound known as the *Soros* (literally 'funerary urn'). Alluviation over the centuries has raised the level of the ground on which it stands by about 3m and erosion and destructive excavation from the 17th century to the 19th have reduced its height over time; when Pausanias saw it, it could have been 5m taller than its present height of 10m. Some of the pottery found in it may be evidence that there was an earlier, less spectacular burial mound on the site. But whatever its size and appearance immediately after the battle, it was built up to a greater height 20–30 years later, a project that Miltiades' son Cimon was closely involved with, and which included the erection of a memorial to his father. The mound may not actually have been brought to its full height till the 2nd century AD in works directed and funded by Herodes Atticus, the Athenian plutocrat. Excavations at the end of the 19th century, much more scientifically carried out than any before, finally uncovered a brick hearth near the centre of the mound and 1m below the ancient ground level, together with ashes and charred bones and pottery that could be firmly dated as not later than the early 5th century. This is almost universally accepted as confirmation that the *Soros* marks the cremation and burial site of the Athenian dead. Previous evidence had consisted of finds of dubious provenance such

---

[1] This is probably not correct.

[2] In battles between Hellenes it was customary for the winning side to take possession of the battlefield and strip the enemy dead, then to give permission to the losers to retrieve the bodies. The winners would construct a trophy displaying a sample of the armour and weapons they had collected.

as the quantities of arrowheads displayed in major museums and, for a period in the 18th and 19th centuries, the mound was identified as the Persians' grave. The ten marble tablets, which would confirm the Athenian casualty list, are lost, except for what may be a substantial fragment of one of them that quite recently came to light. The grave of the Plataeans and the 'one for the slaves' have not been found. There was presumably also a tomb for *psiloi*, who may or may not have been citizens, if they were not included with the slaves. On the evidence of other known battlefield sites, mass burials were not generally located where the winning side sustained the most losses as has been suggested in the case of Marathon. This battle, in any case, involved a lot of movement and was fought over a wide area, and it is likely that there were significant clusters of casualties at several points, including, furthest from the *Soros*, the beach.

The location of the *Soros* towards the south-western end of the plain and about 1,000m forward of the Hellene camp probably does not bear any relation to a particular phase of the battle, although it has been suggested that it marks the spot where the flight of the broken Athenian centre was halted, or that possibly it sits on the line of the defensive position occupied by the Hellenes up to the day of the battle. However, a trophy was traditionally set up by the victors at the place where the battle turned in their favour as indicated by the etymology of the Greek word for it, *tropaion*. The marble structure described by Pausanias has not survived but pieces of it have been identified. They were found built into the ancient church of Panaghia Mesosporitisa, which is mid-way between the seashore and the rising ground to the north, and about 1,000m from the western edge of the marsh. Here the fighting may have been particularly intense immediately before the rout. Recent archaeology has not turned up any Persian remains but towards the end of the 19th century a German researcher reported finding a mass of bones in a vineyard that lay between the church and the marsh, and more would have sunk into the marsh itself. The Persian bodies were probably put into shallow graves wherever they lay rather than more laboriously interred in a single mass-grave.

The heroic messenger's run which inspired the creation of the modern-era Olympic long-distance running event in 1896 is not mentioned in any surviving source earlier than Plutarch, who wrote about six centuries after the battle:

Heraclides Ponticus[1] relates that it was Thersippus of Eroeadae[2] who brought the news of the battle of Marathon. But most historians tell us that it was Eucles who made the run, still armed and hot from the battle, and that he burst in through the doors on the leaders of the state and could only say, 'Rejoice! We are victorious!', and then immediately breathed his last. (*Moralia* 347C/*De Gloria Atheniensium* 3)

The essayist Lucian (active a few decades later than Plutarch), associates it with an already familiar name in a discussion of the usage of the Greek word *chaire*, translated here as 'rejoice':

The word is said to have first been used in this way by Philippides, the long-distance runner. Bringing the news of victory to the archons, who were gathered together anxiously waiting to learn the outcome of the battle, his message was 'Rejoice, we are victorious!' and then he died with his last breath forming the words. (*Pro Lapsu Inter Salutandum* 3[3])

The story certainly inflamed the poetic imagination of Robert Browning, who preferred the alternative spelling of the long-distance runner named by Herodotus, also preserved in the street in central Athens called after him:

Unforeseeing one! Yes, he fought on the Marathon day:
So, when Persia was dust, all cried 'To Akropolis!
Run, Pheidippides, one race more! the meed is thy due!
"Athens is saved, thank Pan," go shout!' He flung down his shield,
Ran like fire once more: and the space 'twixt the Fennel-field[4]
And Athens was stubble again, a field which a fire runs through,
Till in he broke: 'Rejoice, we conquer!' Like wine thro' clay,
Joy in his blood bursting his heart, he died, the bliss!
(From *Pheidippides*, 1879)

---

[1] A 4th-century philosopher and student of Aristotle at his Lyceum in Athens.
[2] A deme of Attica.
[3] Literally 'In defence of a slip of the tongue in the exchange of greetings'.
[4] *Marathos* is the Greek word for fennel and the wild variety still grows on the battlefield.

Runners and perhaps horsemen probably carried messages between the army and the city quite regularly and Callimachus may well have despatched more than one on the day of the battle, first with the information that he was engaging the enemy and later with word of the outcome and the movements of the Persian fleet, and of his imminent march back to meet it. It was important that all of this was known as soon as possible by whatever government officials were left in Athens, but it is most unlikely that the message was entrusted to a runner 'still armed and hot from battle' or, indeed, that this was thought to be a proper assignment for anyone of hoplite status.

The Spartans kept their word and sent help as soon as their religious festival was over:

> Two thousand Lacedaemonians arrived in Athens, moving with such urgency, once the moon was full, that they were there two days after leaving Sparta. They were too late for the battle, but they were still eager to have sight of the Medes, so they went to Marathon and inspected them. After this they went back home full of praise for the Athenians and their achievement. (6.116, 120)

This was probably an advance guard, to be followed by a further 3,000 Spartans, if marching in full force, and contingents from the rest of Lacedaemon. They missed the battle by only a day or two, seemingly. Herodotus' purpose in this brief aside seems to have been chiefly to record that the Spartans were admiring witnesses to this Athenian triumph. If, as is likely, the Athenians knew that the Spartans would not march until the moon was full, this strengthens the argument that there was more to the decision to attack when they did, with only two or three days to wait for Spartan support, than settling on the day that Miltiades' 'presidency' came around.

In his own testimony to the Athenians' veneration of the battle Pausanias names one footsoldier of great fame:

> Marathon is the victory of which I believe the Athenians were most proud. Indeed, Aeschylus, when approaching death, wanted to be remembered for nothing else although he had also won so much honour for his poetry and for his part in the naval battles of Artemisium and Salamis. He simply gave his own name and his

father's, and the name of his city, and wrote that the hallowed ground of Marathon and the Medes who had landed there bore witness to his courage. (*Guide to Greece* 1.14.5)

This is confirmed by the simple epitaph inscribed on the great tragedian's gravestone, which was found in Sicily where he died about 30 years after the battle:

Aeschylus of Athens the son of Euphorion
Lies beneath this memorial.
He died in the rich wheat-country of Gela.
The hallowed ground of Marathon proclaims his famous bravery
And the long-haired Mede knows about it too.
(*Anthologiae Graecae Appendix*, vol. 3)

Aeschylus wanted to be remembered above all as one of the *marathonomachai*, 'those who fought at Marathon', the Athenian equivalent to the United States' 'Greatest Generation' of World War II. In his comedy *Acharnians*, Aristophanes introduces them as 'tough old men, hard as oak or maple' (180–81). In *Wasps*, performed in 422 during the fragile truce that followed Athens' defeat at Delium in the Peloponnesian War, Aristophanes celebrates the military achievements of these admired upholders of traditional values and standards, and also pokes some fun at them. In lines spoken by his chorus of improbably preserved veterans in wasp costume, he makes Marathon the epicentre of the whole war in defence of Greece. He transplants the occupation and burning of Athens ('they blew smoke') in 480 and 479 back to 490 and makes literary references to Thermopylae ('the rain of arrows') and Salamis ('harpooning'), but the main focus is Marathon, which was, conveniently forgetting the Plataeans, exclusively an Athenian, hoplite victory:

We alone are true sons of this soil, the true men of Attica.
We are the manliest of all races.
We gave our greatest service fighting for our country.
When the Barbarians came, they blew smoke over our city
And set it ablaze, desperate to seize our nests.
We swarmed out immediately with spear and shield

And gave them battle. We were drunk with the sharp wine of anger,
Man standing by man, each biting his lip[1] in the stress of battle.
Under the rain of arrows, we could not see the sky,
But towards evening we beat the enemy back with the gods' help;
Before the battle an owl had flown across our army.
So then we chased after the Barbarians
And harpooned them through their pantaloons.
They ran for it, already stung around the jaws and eyebrows.[2]
And even now the Barbarians tell each other
There is nothing in the world manlier than the Attic wasp.
(*Wasps* 1076–90)

This was a victory in which Athenians could justifiably take great pride and see as a crowning moment in the evolution which Herodotus saw them as setting in train by liberating themselves from tyrannical rule. It was a resounding demonstration of military prowess and collective resolve, but also very significant in terms of Athens' political identity. They had not only beaten off the invading army of a distant and immense foreign power but, doing so, also preserved the treasured democratic freedoms which they had won only half a generation before. Lord Byron caught the mood early in Greece's struggle for independence from the Ottoman Empire, but it was the freedom of Athens, not of Hellas, and their personal, individual freedoms that the *marathonomachai* were fighting for:

The mountains look on Marathon –
And Marathon looks on the sea;
And musing there an hour alone,
I dreamed that Greece might still be free;
For standing on the Persians' grave,[3]
I could not deem myself a slave.
(*Don Juan*, unfinished on Byron's death in 1824)

---

[1] Recalling well-known lines of Sparta's 7th-century poet Tyrtaeus and claiming Spartan warlike qualities for themselves.

[2] From the overarm thrusts of the longer hoplite spear aimed at their unprotected heads and faces.

[3] He was presumably standing on top of the *Soros*.

After this victory Athens could claim to share the status of 'leading power of Hellas' with Sparta. Aeschylus compresses all of this, much of it echoed by Herodotus in his writing, into a few lines of his tragedy, the *Persae*. Here Atossa, Darius' widow, is waiting for news of her son Xerxes' campaign in Greece and asks the Chorus to tell her about Athens:

Atossa	Where upon this earth do they say these Athenians live?[1]
Chorus	Far away towards the sinking rays of Lord Helios
Atossa	So why does my son desire their city for his prey?
Chorus	Because all Hellas will then be subject to the King.
Atossa	What power can they muster for their army?
Chorus	An army strong enough to do the Medes great harm.
Atossa	And what else have they? Are their treasure houses full?
Chorus	There is a fountain of silver, treasure from the earth.[2]
Atossa	Do they fight with sharp arrows and tight-strung bows?
Chorus	No! They fight close-in with spears and shields.
Atossa	Who shepherds them, who is master over their army?
Chorus	No mortal calls them slave or subject.
Atossa	Then how can they stand and fight invading enemies?
Chorus	Just as they destroyed Darius' fine great army.
Atossa	Parents of sons over there will think upon these words with dread!

(*Persae* 231–45)

According to Herodotus:

When news of the battle that had been fought at Marathon reached King Darius son of Hystaspes, he was still very angry with the Athenians for their attack on Sardis. His anger now became even more terrible and his desire to make war on Hellas even keener. (7.1)

---

[1] The same question as asked by Darius, according to Herodotus.
[2] The silver mines of Laurium in Attica.

However, for the Persians, this could be presented less dramatically as a modest if embarrassing setback, not a major disaster. Datis and Artaphernes had achieved all but one of their expedition's goals. Their failure to punish Athens and to secure a base from which the Great King could subsequently reach out and conquer the entire Greek mainland had merely delayed the fulfilment of his strategic purpose, to stabilize the central segment of the western frontier of the Persian Empire by extending it to include mainland Greece, if not all of Hellas. Pausanias managed to make Marathon sound quite unremarkable in his few words of summary, 'the Barbarians landed, were defeated in battle and lost some ships as they were putting out to sea', and an anecdote of Dio Cocceianus Chrysostomos, a 1st-century AD Greek rhetorician and philosopher, has a ring of credibility to it:

> I heard a Mede declare that the Persians agree with none of the claims made by the Hellenes, but tell it like this. Darius dispatched Datis and Artaphernes against Naxos and Eretria and, after capturing these cities they returned to the King. However, while they were lying off Euboea, a few, not more than 20 of their ships were driven onto the Attic shore and there was some fighting between the crews and the people who lived in the place ... Now this is clearly not a true account of what happened, but a likely explanation is that the King commanded that it be spread among the peoples of mainland Asia in order to keep them subdued. (*Orationes* 11.148–49)

Robert Graves, poet, classical scholar, novelist and soldier, created his own 'Persian version':

> Truth-loving Persians do not dwell upon
> The trivial skirmish fought near Marathon.
> As for the Greek theatrical tradition
> Which represents that summer's expedition
> Not as a mere reconnaissance in force
> By three brigades of foot and one of horse
> (Their left flank covered by some obsolete

Light craft detached from the main Persian fleet)
But as a grandiose, ill-starred attempt
To conquer Greece – they treat it with contempt;
And only incidentally refute
Major Greek claims, by stressing what repute
The Persian monarch and the Persian nation
Won by this salutary demonstration:
Despite a strong defence and adverse weather
All arms combined magnificently together.
The Persian Version (*c.*1940)

Professor Gomme sighed in exasperation, 'Everyone knows that Herodotus' narrative of Marathon will not do', and it is frustrating that this, our earliest and fullest ancient account of the battle, should be so brief and sketchy. But as far as Herodotus' audiences were concerned, it seems to have done well enough. Viewed from the generation of the Peloponnesian War, and through the lens of the preceding 50 years and the much larger events of 480–479, this battle was not of great significance to non-Athenians. To the Athenians, it was immensely important, not for the detail of what happened on that day, though every family had its own treasured stories, but for what it quickly came to stand for. It was central to their image of their city as the historic saviour of Hellas which, in turn, was their justification for the imperialism which had brought them into conflict with their brother Hellenes. The oral tradition that prevailed in Athens in Herodotus' time celebrated Marathon over and above the battles of 480–479. For Cimon and others, it was an inconvenient truth that much of the glory for the salvation of Athens and Hellas belonged to the *thetes*, citizens from the lowliest property class, who had served as oarsmen and crew in the Athenian fleet at Artemisium and Salamis, and continued to do so the decades that followed. Marathon was a hoplite victory and *thetes* could not serve as hoplites, but they were the power base of Cimon's political rivals, including Themistocles and Pericles.

Herodotus does not appear to buy into the full mythology of Marathon and later he properly recognizes the greater importance of Athens' central role in the naval campaigning of 480. However, he touches on facets of the victory that he felt to be more immediately significant:

> To everyone's knowledge, the Athenians were the first to stand firm at the sight of Median clothing and the men who wore it. Until that day the Hellenes were terrified even to hear the name of the Medes spoken. (6.112)

The Athenians were not 'the first to stand firm ...' The Hellenes of Ionia had sustained their attempt to shake off Persian rule and resist Persian military might in Asia for five or six years from 499. They had faced Barbarians in several pitched battles on land and sea and not always been the losers, though they had lost in the end, and failure and defeat were not unknown to Barbarians. But the Athenians, and the Plataeans, had won a resounding victory very close to home and set an example of collective and individual resolution and fighting spirit, and tactical adaptability which were an inspiration for just enough of their mainland and island neighbours when the Barbarians returned, as they inevitably would. Marathon did not have as decisive consequences as the battles of Salamis and Plataea, so has less of a claim to have 'changed history' or, more accurately, to have set European history on the course it took from the early 5th century. A Persian victory in 490 could have brought the Persian War to an early and different end, but not necessarily. A concerted and rapid response on the part of the Spartans and their Peloponnesian allies might have dislodged Datis and Artaphernes from their newly won foothold in Athens and Attica, though this would have bought only the same ten years' respite that was won at Marathon. If not dislodged, however, the invaders would have been reinforced the following spring and ready to execute Darius' larger plan. This was not abandoned, and planning was soon in train for a more powerfully resourced invasion of Europe:

> The orders Darius sent out had Asia buzzing for three years. But in the fourth year the Egyptians, whom Cambyses had conquered, revolted against Persian rule. Then Darius was even more eager to go to war against both the Hellenes and the Egyptians. Darius named Xerxes

as his successor[1] and gave all his attention to preparation for war. But in the following year he died in the midst of these preparations and, with Egypt in revolt, he could not take his vengeance upon the rebel Egyptians or the Athenians. He had reigned for 36 years, and, on his death, Xerxes succeeded him as Great King. (7.1, 4–5)

Xerxes had to deal with Egypt first, giving the Greeks six more years' breathing space.

[1] Darius had three elder sons but they were born before he was king and Xerxes took precedence as the eldest of the next three.

I will make all lands one land

The Return of the Great King

Herodotus begins his account of Xerxes' invasion of Europe with a dramatized reconstruction of the discussions that preceded Xerxes' commitment to this, the fifth and by far the largest of the Persian expeditions into Europe. Here, as elsewhere, he uses the medium of invented debate, in this case between Xerxes and his leading courtiers, to provide intelligent and valuable insights into the motivation and rationale for decisions taken; Thucydides and the tragedians and philosophers of his time used broadly the same literary technique to address the larger and universal questions they grappled with in their work. In the process, Herodotus adds telling brushstrokes to the steadily emerging portraits of two leading characters in the drama he is presenting, Mardonius and the Great King himself. The words are almost exclusively Herodotus' own creation since there were no transcripts available to him, and he would have needed translations in any case. But in his research and on his travels he would have talked to Persians and to Hellenes who had had direct or indirect contact with the Persian court and with participants in the deliberations that took place at that time. His better sources might even have been able to recall actual phrases and the main arguments, and to give reasonable summaries of the most important contributions or subsequent communications of decisions taken.

It had always been Xerxes' intention to launch a campaign against Athens after he had subdued Egypt, and so he summoned a special council of the leading Persians. His purpose was to sound out their opinions and to tell them all directly what he wished to do. When they were all assembled, this is the speech he gave. 'Men of Persia, I am not about to introduce new policy but am executing policy that has already been established. For, as I have learned from our elders, we have never relaxed our efforts from the day we won sovereignty from the Medes when Cyrus overthrew Astyages. It is God who leads us, and our fortunes grow as we follow his lead in our many enterprises. You know well what lands Cyrus, Cambyses and Darius, my father, conquered and added to our empire and there is no need to remind you of them. Since coming to this throne, I have been thinking of ways to ensure I do not fall short of my predecessors in the honours I gain or the power I add to the Persian Empire. And now I have worked out how we shall win glory and as much land as good and as fertile as we now possess, and, at the same time, how we will take our revenge and deliver retribution. This is why I have gathered you here, so that I can set out to you what I plan to do.

'My intention is to lay a yoke[1] across the Hellespont and march an army through Europe into Greece to take my vengeance upon the Athenians for the things that they have done to Persia and to my father. As you know, Darius, my father, was determined to go to war against these people, but died and could not take his vengeance. Now, for Darius and for all of Persia, I shall not rest until I have taken the city of Athens and burned it to the ground, for it was the Athenians who began this wrongdoing against me, as well as against my father. First, they came to Sardis with our Milesian servant,[2] Aristagoras, and burned the sacred groves and holy places. And then you all know what they did to our invasion force when it landed on their soil under the command of Datis and Artaphernes. That is reason enough for me to go to war with the Athenians, but when I think about this enterprise, I can see a number of benefits flowing from it. For, if we

---

[1] A metaphor for 'put a bridge across' with dangerous connotations of subjugation and enslavement.

[2] Herodotus uses the word *doulos,* which is generally translated as 'slave'. However, here, this may be a loose translation of the Persian *bandaka,* which applied to the more nuanced relationship between the Great King and vassal rulers under him (albeit seen as slavery by independent-minded Hellenes). In his account of the beginning of the Ionian Revolt, Herodotus states that Aristagoras ordered the attack on Sardis but did not actually take part in it, but there was no question of his responsibility for the uprising.

conquer the Athenians and their neighbours who live in the land of Phrygian Pelops,[1] we shall extend the territory of Persia to the very edge of the earth, even where it joins with God's heaven. When I have passed through Europe, there will be no lands under the sun that lie outside our borders, because with you I will make all lands one land. This I have established: there will remain no city of men, no nation of humankind capable of facing up to us in battle, once we have cleared out of our path those people I have named. Then those who have wronged us will bear the yoke of slavery, along with the innocent.

'When I have announced the time to muster, I should be greatly obliged if every one of you presents himself eager for action, and I shall reward with gifts of the kind we hold most honourable in our land[2] whomsoever I judge to have brought with him the contingent that is best equipped and best trained. So it shall be done. But, lest you think I have made a decision on this matter without any consultation,[3] I now lay it before you for open discussion, and command whoever wishes to declare his opinion to do so.' And so Xerxes brought his speech to a close. (7.8)

Herodotus comprehensively catalogues Xerxes' possible motivations: ancestral precedent; divine will; personal duty as Great King and as the Great King's son; personal glory; land and power; retribution and vengeance; and world domination, the establishment of an empire on which the sun never sets under the rule of one 'Great King, King of Kings, Ruler of the Lands'. But, to the Hellene mind, the offence against natural justice in his pledge to enslave not only 'those who have wronged us', but those who have done Persia no harm, and his 'vaulting ambition' tempted fate.

Mardonius spoke after the Great King: 'My Lord, you are the greatest Persian there has ever been, and ever will be. You have spoken

---

[1] Pelops was a hero associated with Olympia and a mythical king in the Peloponnese. His cult had roots in Asia as far east as Phrygia giving him subject status in Persian eyes.

[2] Such royal gifts might include a fine horse with golden trappings, gold jewellery, a golden sword and luxurious robes.

[3] Herodotus makes unique use of the word *idiobouleuein*, 'to make up one's mind on one's own', which is, of course, exactly what Herodotus represents Xerxes as having done.

excellently and everything you say is absolutely true. You will not permit those Ionian[1] nobodies who live in Europe to mock us so despicably. We have made ourselves conquerors and masters of the Sacae, the Indians, the Ethiopians, the Assyrians and of many other great nations. This was in order to extend our might, not because these people had done us wrong, so it would be a disgrace to let the Hellenes go unpunished for their offences against us.

'And what is there for us to fear? The size of the army they can put in the field? Their wealth? We know the way they fight, and we know their resources are feeble. We conquered their descendants[2] and hold in our power the peoples known as Ionian, Aeolian and Dorian who live in the lands that belong to us. And I have myself tested the Hellenes when, on your father's orders, I campaigned as far as Macedon, which is not far from Athens itself. No Hellene would come out to meet me in battle. Yet I have discovered that the Hellenes are not unaccustomed to warfare, but they do no planning and go about fighting in a dumb and senseless way. When war has been declared the two sides pick a nice level patch of ground, make their way to it and fight their battle. The result is that the winners leave the field in very bad shape, and I can't begin to describe the condition of the losers; they are totally wiped out. Yet these are people who speak the same language, and it should be normal practice for them to settle their disputes by using ambassadors and heralds, or by any means other than a pitched battle. If they must go to war, each should look for ground that is most advantageous to them and offer battle to the other there. The Hellene way of making war is no good and that is why they did not even think of putting up a fight as I approached Macedonian territory. So, who is going to put up a fight against you, Great King, as you lead your great host from Asia and all your ships against them? I do not think the Hellenes will have the stomach for it. But, if I'm mistaken and these people are fool enough to take us on in battle, they will find out that we are the best warriors in the world. In any case, we must be prepared to take risks. Things do not happen of their own accord, but risk-takers can achieve all sorts of things.' So Mardonius added his own gloss to Xerxes' proposal and ended his speech. (7.9)

---

[1] The term often used by Asian Barbarians for Hellenes in general.
[2] Meaning the Hellenes from previous generations settled in Asia.

Hellene audiences would have enjoyed the irony of the King's cocksure favourite's dismissal of the Hellene way of war. But the Persians would have had knowledge of the formalized hoplite contests by which the Hellenes settled local disputes.

Polybius, the 2nd-century BC Greek historian and soldier, echoes some of Mardonius' critique in a reflection on warfare in the latter part of the 3rd century:

> The ancients would not even employ deception to secure victory over their enemies and did not regard a victory as glorious or secure if it was not won in open combat by breaking the spirit of the enemy in set-piece combat. So, there was a mutual understanding that neither hidden weapons nor missiles would be used, and that matters could be decisively settled only by hand-to-hand fighting at close quarters. And for this reason they take that risk, and would identify the place where they intended to take up position and form up in battle array. But now it is said to be poor generalship to conduct operations openly like this. However, the Romans retain a slight trace of the ancient system of war, because they too give advance notice when they are going to war and make sparing use of surprise attacks, and they fight hand-to-hand at close quarters. There's no more to be said about today's leaders' enthusiasm for dirty tricks in the conduct of politics and warfare ... (*Histories* 13.3)

However, on many occasions, Hellenes had proved themselves capable of rather more strategic and tactical creativity than suggested here, and it is unlikely that the Persians were ignorant of this. Cleomenes, the Spartan king, had certainly resorted to 'dirty tricks' in his crushing defeat of the Argives at Sepeia in 494:

> The Argives had taken up position opposite the Lacedaemonians at a place called Sepeia near Tiryns and the two armies were close to each other. The Argives were not afraid of a fair fight but feared they might be tricked in some way, and this had been predicted by the Delphic oracle. So, they decided to protect themselves by executing whatever commands the enemy's herald signalled: whatever the Lacedaemonians did in response to their herald's signal, the Argives did the same. Cleomenes noticed this and ordered his men to arm

themselves and attack the Argives when the herald gave the command to take breakfast and this is what the Lacedaemonians did. They attacked and caught the Argives obediently eating their breakfast, and they killed a lot of them. But a larger number escaped and took refuge in a sacred grove, and the Lacedaemonians surrounded it and imprisoned the Argives there. And this is what Cleomenes did next. He had some Argive deserters with him and he collected a list of names from them. Then he sent a herald to call out the names of individuals trapped in the sacred precinct and bid them come out, saying that their ransoms had been paid (200 drachmas is the rate set by the Peloponnesians for the ransom of a prisoner of war). In this way Cleomenes persuaded about 50 Argives to come out, one after another, and he had them killed. The rest of the men in the precinct were unaware of this because the grove was dense and they could not see what was going on, but then somebody climbed a tree and saw what was happening, and nobody would leave the grove after that. So Cleomenes ordered the Helots to pile wood around the grove, and this they did. And then he set the grove on fire. (6.78–80)

The deceit and sacrilegious atrocities perpetrated around the sacred grove may be later embroidery added to blacken Cleomenes' name or to give the Argives some excuse for the crippling defeat they had suffered. But the surprise attack was evidence that the Hellenes were not necessarily as tactically hidebound as Mardonius might have suggested. In a later digression Herodotus gives another example:

Now, a few years before the Great King's expedition, the Thessalians and their allies had invaded Phocis with their whole army but were roughly handled and defeated in this way.[1] They had the Phocians surrounded on Parnassus, but the seer (*mantis*) Tellias of Elis who was with the Phocians worked out a plan for them. He had 600 of the bravest of them cover themselves all over with chalk, including their armour. Then he led them in a night attack on the Thessalians, ordering them to kill anyone they came across who was not all white. The Thessalian outposts were the first to see them and fled in terror under the illusion that their attackers were supernatural,

---

[1] This war was probably fought in the final decade of the 6th century.

and after that the whole army fled as well. The Phocians were left in possession of 4,000 corpses and they dedicated half of their shields at Abae[1] and the rest at Delphi. That was how the Phocians dealt with the Thessalian infantry when they were besieging them. And again, when the Thessalians invaded with their cavalry, they struck them a mortal blow. The Phocians dug a great trench in the pass near Hyampolis, filled it with empty wine jars and covered them with soil to match the rest of the ground. Then they waited for the Thessalians to attack. They charged the Phocian position expecting to sweep over it, but were brought down by the jars, which broke their horses' legs. (8.27–28)

Back in Susa, the debate continued:

The rest of the Persians said nothing, not daring to express disagreement.[2] But then Artabanus son of Hystaspes responded. He was Xerxes' uncle and this gave him the confidence to speak out. 'Great King, if an opposing opinion is not expressed, it is not possible to decide which is the better argument, and the sole argument that has been presented will inevitably prevail. If both arguments are presented, then it is possible to determine which is the better of the two. It is the same with gold; the purity of one piece cannot be determined on its own, but, when it is compared to another by rubbing on a touchstone,[3] we can then determine its quality. Now, I advised Darius, your father and my brother, not to launch his campaign against the Scythians, a people who live in a land without a single city in it, but he thought he could overcome these nomads. He would not listen to me and went off on the expedition, and he came back after losing many of his finest soldiers.[4] And you, O King, are set on launching a campaign against men who are far better than the Scythians, and who are said to be excellent fighters on sea as well as land. It is my duty to tell you how dangerous they are. You say you are going to lay a yoke across the Hellespont and take your army through Europe

[1] Like Delphi, a temple sacred to Apollo and also in central Greece.
[2] In contrast to the free and open debate expected amongst democratic Hellenes.
[3] Touchstone (dark stone of the slate type) had already been in use for millennia to assay gold.
[4] In 513.

into Greece. What if it turns out that you are defeated on land or sea, or on both? These Hellenes are famous for their valour and we already have evidence of this because the Athenians, on their own,[1] destroyed the great army that Datis and Artaphernes led to Attica. Even if they were not victorious on both land and sea, but won a naval engagement, the Hellenes could sail to the Hellespont and destroy the bridge. Then, Great King, you would be in grave danger.

'You know how God blasts creatures that have grown mighty with his thunderbolts and stops their boasting, while the lowly are of no concern to him. You know how he always strikes the loftiest buildings and trees. It is God's way to put down the mighty. So, a large army can be destroyed by a small one when God turns against it and strikes it with panic or the roar of thunder,[2] however undeserved the army's destruction. For God allows no one to call himself great, but God himself. Now, in all things, haste begets error, and great are the penalties. But restraint brings rewards and, though these may not be immediately apparent, they are, in time, revealed.' (7.10)

Artabanus has taken centre stage for a second time as the counsellor of caution. He speaks with the voice of the enlightenment of 5th-century Hellas (echoing the dialectic of the philosophers of the time and tragic choruses' regular warnings against overmightiness) and caps Mardonius' closing platitude with one of his own. After giving this advice to Xerxes, he turns on Mardonius, accusing him of belittling the Hellenes in order to induce the King to make up his mind to go ahead with the invasion. He then proposes that, if the King is persuaded, he, Mardonius, should lead the expedition and Xerxes stay behind in Persia. He also proposes that he and Mardonius stake their own and their children's lives on the outcome, death for Artabanus and his family if the expedition is successful, but death for the other's family if it fails, and for Mardonius himself if he survives and returns home. The speech closes with a dark prediction:

'If you are unwilling to accept this challenge and are absolutely determined to lead your army to Greece, then I tell you that those

---

[1] As here, Plataea's contribution is often overlooked.
[2] A reference forward to the violent storms encountered in the course of the invasion.

who are left at home will hear that Mardonius has brought great evil upon Persia, and is being ripped apart by dogs and birds somewhere on Athenian or Lacedaemonian soil, or maybe at some point on the march there. Then you will have found out what kind of men you are trying to persuade the King to wage war on.'

Angered by these words, Xerxes replied, 'Artabanus, you are my father's brother. That is all that saves you from the punishment your feeble speech merits. However, for this cowardly faintheartedness, I shall not allow you to march with me and my army against Hellas but will leave you behind in disgrace here with the women. I shall accomplish all that I say I will without your help. I am no son of Darius, no descendant of Cyrus and Achaemenes, if I do not take my revenge on the Athenians. I know for sure that if we remain at peace, these people will not. They will invade our land. This is clear from what they have already done when they marched into Asia and burned Sardis. There can be no turning back for either side. It is a question of taking action or becoming a victim, of determining whether all that is ours is to belong to the Hellenes, or whether all that is theirs is to belong to the Persians. There is no middle way out of this conflict. It is a matter of honour that we take revenge for the harm already done to us and when I carry this out, I shall see what "grave danger" I shall be facing when I launch my attack on these people, men whom even Pelops the Phrygian, my forefathers' slave, was able to subdue so effectively that they and their land[1] are named after their conqueror even now.' (7.10–11)

Hellene audiences would have enjoyed Herodotus' depiction of Xerxes' burst of rage and insulting, if controlled response to Artabanus' wise counsel. They would also have relished the idea of the threat Hellas posed to the entire Persian Empire, somewhat exaggerated even considering the great Hellene victory won on Persian soil at the battle of the Eurymedon in the mid 460s. Macedon, at this time a satellite subject state ruled by its first King Alexander, did not come into the reckoning. But there was no question that the Ionian Revolt had been responsible for five years of local instability over a significant area at the edge of

---

[1] Excluding the Athenians and Athens: Herodotus' shift of focus away from them onto the Peloponnesians and the Peloponnese adds another layer of irony to his version of this debate.

the empire and there was a case to be made for guarding against future instability by pushing the frontier further west. Even so, the Great King changed his mind and decided not to invade, but he had a recurrent dream that told him that the expedition must go ahead and would succeed. Dreams were an important means of divination in the ancient world, especially for the Persians. Artabanus, clearly still accepted as a close adviser, was rationally sceptical at first: 'the dreams that come to us tend for the most part to reflect what we have been thinking about during the day' (7.16). But he too was finally persuaded, having dreamed the dream himself, and helped Xerxes to make up his mind.

Herodotus begins his account of the preparations for the invasion, and then of the march into Europe and, finally, Greece with a long preamble on the unprecedented scale of the operation, a topic he will return to more than once:

> After Egypt had been reconquered, it took four years[1] to assemble the army and equip it, and in the course of the fifth year the Great King began his march at the head of this immense force. This was by far the largest army of invasion ever known. The army Darius led against the Scythians was nothing in comparison. The same can be said of the Scythian army that burst into Median territory in pursuit of the Cimmerians[2] and conquered and settled in most of the upper part of Asia;[3] it was for this that Darius set out to punish them. Xerxes' army was also far greater than the one that, so it is told, the sons of Atreus led against Troy,[4] and greater than the army of Mysians and Teucrians that crossed the Bosporus into Europe before the Trojan War was fought, conquering all of Thrace and reaching as far south on the shore of the Aegean as the River Peneus.[5] All these armies together, even with others added on,

[1] Probably a dramatic exaggeration: the troops were stationed in different parts of the empire but it would have taken months not years to move the more distant units to their assembly point in the west. However, it is quite possible that detailed planning began far in advance.

[2] The Cimmerians, originally from the steppes, went on to occupy Lydia in the 7th century but were either assimilated or wiped out by the Lydians and Syrians.

[3] This took place during the 7th century.

[4] The war of Homer's *Iliad* which is thought to have been loosely based on historical events that took place in or around the 12th century.

[5] Referring to population movements in the dimmer and more distant past.

would not have matched Xerxes' expeditionary force. What nation of Asia did Xerxes not lead against Hellas? Only the largest rivers could supply water for his men without running dry. Some of his subjects provided warships, some foot soldiers, some cavalry; some of those who marched with him also provided horse transports; some supplied longships[1] for the bridges and some supplied food and the ships to carry it.

Since the previous attempt to sail around the Athos peninsula had ended in shipwreck,[2] preparations for the invasion were begun there about three years in advance. A base was set up with triremes stationed at Elaeus in the Chersonese and detachments from every unit in the army were put to work on a canal, digging in relays under the lash; and the local people did some digging as well. Two Persians, Boubares son of Megabazus and Artachaees son of Artaeus,[3] supervised operations. The high and well-known peak of Athos juts out into the sea to form a peninsula which narrows at the landward end to an isthmus about 12 *stades* [2,200m] wide. The ground is flat here with some low hills and sea on either side and the Great King wanted to make island cities of five of the six settlements on Athos.

And this is how the Barbarians dug the canal. They laid out a straight line from a point not far from the city of Sane and divided up the work along its length between the different nations. When the trench had reached some depth, men stood at the bottom and carried on digging. Others took the spoil and passed it to men on scaffolding higher up who passed it up to others as they received it until it came to those at the top, and they carried it off and disposed of it. Except for in the Phoenicians' section, the steep sides of the canal kept caving in, doubling the work. This was bound to happen when the top was dug out to the same width as the bottom. But the Phoenicians demonstrated the same practical skill here as in

---

[1] Meaning warships rather than merchant ships.

[2] Mardonius' expedition in 492.

[3] Two commanders from just below the top tier of Xerxes' generals. Boubares was son of one of Darius' senior generals and Artachaees 'an Achaemenid and very well regarded by Xerxes; he was the tallest man in Persia, close to three metres in height, and had the loudest voice' (7.117). Xerxes mourned him deeply when he died of disease in 480.

whatever else they do. Setting to work on their allotted section, they initially dug a trench twice as wide as the canal was going to be and narrowed it as they dug down until they reached the bottom, when it was the same width as everyone else's section.[1] A marketplace was set up in a meadow nearby for the buying and selling of provisions, including large amounts of flour transported from Asia.

It is my opinion that Xerxes had this canal built out of arrogant pride, wishing to display his power and leave behind a memorial to himself. The Persians could have hauled their ships across the isthmus without difficulty, but Xerxes ordered a channel to be dug from shore to shore and it was to be wide enough for two warships to row through side by side.[2] The men who dug the canal[3] had a further task assigned to them which was to put a bridge across the River Strymon. (7.24)

Herodotus' dismissal of the Athos canal as a personal display of vanity on Xerxes' part does not significantly undermine the overall impression of a large-scale and well-planned and executed engineering project. However, his father's involvement with a rather more impressive feat of canal building, connecting the Nile with the Red Sea, may have been part of the motivation. In any case, a display of power on this scale would have had some strategic value in its impact on the morale of enemies or potential enemies. But, in practical terms, a careful watch on the weather could have been a more straightforward and economical way of eliminating the risk of rounding this cape and, as the Persians were quite soon to discover, there were more dangerous lee shores than Athos ahead of them. Nevertheless, in the longer term, the canal may have assisted the steady flow of transport ships following the invasion force and would have been of value to the local cities in their trade with each other and ports to the east. Herodotus mentions that local cities

---

[1] The Phoenicians were probably the most expert at building harbours and docks but it is very unlikely that the rest of the army was so much less competent in the basic task of digging the canal. Anecdotes of the sides collapsing at one point were perhaps blown up in the telling, maybe even by Phoenicians.

[2] Approximately 30m. Archaeologists have excavated conclusive evidence of this major feat of engineering.

[3] This may suggest that these were special engineering or 'pioneer' units.

provided some labour and this may have been done in some spirit of joint ownership rather than purely under compulsion.

Hauling the fleet across the isthmus might have been considered. For example, since the 6th century ships as well as their cargoes had been regularly hauled over the 6km that separated the Saronic Gulf from the Gulf of Corinth cutting out several days of sailing round the Peloponnese. In 411, during the Peloponnesian War, the Spartans took 21 triremes into the Saronic Gulf by this route and in 425 they hauled 60 over the narrower isthmus at Leucas to evade an Athenian fleet. The *diolkos* (literally 'through-haul') at Corinth was a paved trackway and deep wheel ruts indicate that trolleys were used, most likely as well as rollers. Paving a similar trackway across the narrower and flatter Athos peninsula would have been less of a labour than digging the canal but it would have taken several days, even weeks, to haul the far larger Persian battlefleet across, and fully laden transport ships were too heavy to haul and required unloading onto trolleys, which would have taken even more time.

> Xerxes gave the Egyptians and Phoenicians the task of making cables for the bridges out of papyrus and esparto grass,[1] and he gave orders for supplies to be stockpiled on the route the army was to take so neither man nor beast would go hungry as they marched on Hellas. Having already identified the most appropriate locations, he had these supplies shipped over from all parts of Asia in merchant ships and ferry boats. They brought most of them to the White Cape[2] (as it is called) in Thrace, but some were taken to Tyrodiza in Perinthian territory, to Doriscus, to Eion on the Strymon and to Macedon. While these things were being done, the entire land force had been mustered and was on the march with Xerxes to Sardis. It set off from Critalla[3] in Cappadocia, which was the place where the whole army that was to march overland

---

[1] Not 'white flax' (the definition of the word used by Herodotus) but the stronger esparto used by the Phoenicians for their rope and discovered in their historic trading contact with Spain.

[2] Location unknown.

[3] This place has not been identified but it is unlikely that the whole army mustered in Cappadocia. It is more likely that units converged from different parts of the empire to assemble at Sardis or perhaps even at Abydos.

with Xerxes had been commanded to assemble. However, I cannot say which of the generals received the prizes offered by the King to the one who brought the best-equipped contingent, and, actually, I don't know if any such award was ever made. (7.25–26)

There is a double criticism of Xerxes' and by extension Barbarian values in Herodotus' aside about the Great King's promise of material reward for good performance and his strong suspicion that he failed to keep that promise. But two other anecdotes from Xerxes' progress from Susa to Sardis add favourable detail to Herodotus' character portrait of the Great King. In gratitude for his exceptionally generous hospitality and the offer of an immense cash donation towards the cost of the invasion, Xerxes rewards Pythius, a grandson of the fabulously wealthy Croesus. He honours him by making him his personal guest-friend and, graciously declining the donation, makes him a gift of 7,000 Darics (a gold coin weighing 8.4g) to round up the 3,993,000 he already possesses. Then, just before reaching Sardis, Xerxes comes across a plane tree and he so admires its beauty that he has it garlanded with gold and given a royal guard (the inspiration for one of Handel's greatest tunes, *Ombra mai fù*).

> When Xerxes reached Sardis, the capital of Lydia, the first thing he did was to send heralds into Greece with demands for earth and water and promises of hospitality[1] for the King, but he sent no such demand to Athens or Sparta.[2] He had these demands for earth and water sent out a second time because he was confident that those who had not given earth and water to Darius the first time[3] would now agree to it out of fear. He sent his heralds to verify that this was indeed the case. (7.32)

The Hellenes who were prepared to fight had begun to meet and confer in 481, or perhaps even earlier. According to Pausanias, they met in

---

[1] Literally 'meals' (*deipna*): lavish entertainment for the Great King and his entourage could be demanded of any state that had submitted earth and water if they had the misfortune to be anywhere along his route.

[2] Because of their treatment of the Great King's heralds in 491.

[3] In 491.

Sparta at a place known as the Hellenion and it is possible they did gather there initially, but Herodotus names the Isthmus as the venue for later meetings:

> The Hellenes who were prepared to go to war with the Barbarians swore a solemn oath that, if things turned out well for them, they would make an offering to the god at Delphi of a tenth of all the possessions of the Hellenes who had submitted to Persia without being forced to. This was the oath these Hellenes swore. (7.132)

A 4th-century inscription known as 'the 'Oath of Plataea', discovered on the site of the deme of Acharnae in Attica, is a version of the oath sworn by the Hellene allies in 479 as they mustered to face the Persians in Boeotia. The inscription was probably set up with the purpose of raising morale and inspiring citizens to do their patriotic duty after the Athenians' terrible defeat at the hands of the Macedonians in the battle of Chaeronea in 338, and it is not a verbatim transcription of the original. But a lot of the wording and all of the spirit of the text may have been preserved in the folk memory of the war and something like it could have been used to swear in each member of the alliance on first joining, or by all at the start of each of the series of councils of war that took place as the crisis developed:

> The oath which the Athenians swore
> when they were about to fight against the Barbarians:
> 'I shall fight so long as I am alive,
> and I will not value my life more highly than liberty.
> I will not abandon my taxiarch[1] nor my enomotarch[2]
> whether he be alive or dead,
> I will not leave the field unless my commanders lead me from it,
> and I will do whatever the generals order me to do.

[1] The commander of a *taxis*, the widely used term for the largest subunits of Hellene armies. In the Athenian army it was the term for a tribal regiment, of which there were ten. Acharnae probably contributed more men to its regiment than any other deme (Thucydides records that this was the case in 431).

[2] An *enomotia*, roughly equivalent to a present-day platoon, was about 30 strong. 'Enomotarch' was an exclusively Spartan term at the time of the Persian War. This line may have been included in a version sworn by the Spartans.

I shall bury any of my allies who have died beside me
and shall leave none behind unburied.
Having won victory over the Barbarians,
I shall tithe the city of the Thebans[1]
and I shall not destroy Athens, Sparta or Plataea,[2]
nor any city that has been our ally.
Neither shall I allow any of them to go hungry
nor shall I deprive them of running water,
whether they be our friends or hostile to us.
And, if I abide by the terms of this oath:
may my city be free of disease,
but, if I do not, let it be diseased;
may my city never be sacked,
but, if I do not, let it be sacked;
may my city prosper,
but, if I do not, let it wither;
and may my city's women bring forth children like their parents,
but, if I do not, let them bear monsters;
and may my city's cattle bring forth offspring like their parents,
but, if I do not abide by the terms of this oath,
let the cattle bear monsters.'

This is the oath they swore, and covering the sacrificial offerings with their shields at the trumpet's sound, they uttered a curse, declaring that in the event of any breach of the oath's terms or any failure wholly to abide by it as it had been written, pollution would befall those who had taken it.

(*Oath of Plataea*, 4th-century inscription from ancient Acharnae)

All the Hellenes who cared about the good of Hellas gathered together for talks and to exchange pledges of trust. Their first resolution was to put aside all current disputes or armed conflict between any of them; there were several going on at this time but the most significant was the war between Athens and Aegina.

---

[1] 'Tithing' in this context meant dedicating a tenth of the booty to one of the gods. Thebes actually escaped being plundered, probably for pragmatic reasons, after surrendering to the allies after a short siege immediately after the battle of Plataea.

[2] Plataea was destroyed by the Thebans in 426.

Then, having found out that Xerxes was at Sardis with his army, they agreed to send spies into Asia to observe what the Great King was doing. They also decided to send delegations to Argos to seek an alliance with them against the Persians, to Gelon in Sicily, to Corcyra and to Crete, calling on them all to come and support Hellas. Their thinking was that with all of Hellas under this terrible threat, all Hellenes should unite and act in concert to deal with it. Gelon was said to have been especially powerful, more powerful than any of the other Hellenes.

The Hellenes made these decisions and, first, settled all their disputes. Then they sent three men into Asia to spy. These men reached Sardis and closely observed the Great King's army, but they were caught and, after being questioned under torture, were taken off for execution. They were sentenced to death, but when Xerxes heard of it he rebuked the generals for making this decision and sent some of his personal bodyguard with orders to bring the spies before him, if they still lived. They were still alive and were brought into the Great King's presence, and Xerxes found out the purpose of their mission for himself. He then ordered his guards to take them round and show them the whole army, infantry and cavalry, and, when the spies had gazed their fill, to send them off unharmed wherever they wanted to go. The Great King's explanation for this was that if the spies had been put to death, which would have been an insignificant loss to the enemy, the Hellenes would not have so quickly learned of the measureless might of his power. So, they should be allowed to make their way home to Greece. Then the Hellenes would hear of his might and surrender the freedom which was so special to them before the expedition was launched, and there would be no need even to lead an army against them. (7.145–47)

This is a nice story and illustrates a strategic view that Xerxes, or at any rate his high command, could plausibly have held. But Herodotus does not name the three spies nor give their nationality, information that would have added credibility; its absence may indicate his personal disbelief. More generally, the Hellenes probably had little need of spies to find out all they wanted to know about the forces the Great King was amassing and the other preparations he was making. These things were being done very openly and good intelligence would have travelled west through the network of communication that linked the Hellenes of Europe with their cousins in Asia and other trading partners. As the story illustrates, the Persians wanted the scale of the impending attack to be very visible in order to terrify their enemies into submission, ideally without having to strike a blow.

The diplomatic missions to Argos, Sicily, Corcyra and Crete were probably sent in 481 or even earlier. The Argives, old enemies of Sparta, opted to remain neutral. They had suffered very heavy losses at the battle of Sepeia in 494 and more recently, in 490, lost the best part of 1,000 men in that instalment of the war between Athens and Aegina; they had also fallen out with the Aeginetans at the time. Herodotus offers various reasons for their refusal to join the alliance, including advice from Delphi and their militarily weakened state, and a degree of ambivalence would seem to have been justified by their recent dealings with three of its leading powers. However, the outcome may not have been seen as entirely negative. The Argives, though suspected of favouring Persia over Hellas in their neutrality, did not do anything to disrupt communications in 480 or 479 between Sparta and central Greece, which they were well placed to do.

Sicily, which at that time meant Syracuse, the dominant power on the eastern part of the island, had a great deal more to offer. The mission was led by a Spartan called Syagros and Herodotus presents its message to Gelon, tyrant of Syracuse, in an exchange of speeches that Syagros opens:

'You wield great power, and as ruler of Sicily[1] you are master of a very substantial portion of Hellas, so we call on you to send help to those who wish to keep Hellas free and support them in this cause. If all the people of Hellas unite, a mighty force can be assembled which will be a match for the invaders when we meet them in battle. But if some betray the cause and others refuse to get involved, and only a small portion of Hellas stands firm, there is real danger that Hellas will fall. But do not imagine that the Great King will spare you if he has defeated us in battle and conquered us. You must give thought

[1] Gelon certainly wielded more influence and military power than any other Sicilian leader at this time, but he was some way short of ruling the whole island.

to your own defence before that day comes. Give us your support and you will be helping yourselves. It is generally the case that proper planning leads to a good outcome.' (7.157)

Gelon robustly protests that the Hellenes of Greece had not come to Sicily's aid in a former conflict with the Carthaginians and reminds the delegation that Sicily protected the trade interests of all Hellenes in the central and western Mediterranean by keeping the Carthaginians and their allies in check:

> 'But you are the ones actually confronted by war, and all of a sudden you think of Gelon! Well, even though you slighted me, I will not behave in the same way. I am prepared to support you by sending 200 triremes, 20,000 hoplites, 2,000 cavalry, 2,000 archers, 2,000 slingers, and 2,000 light-armed troops to support the cavalry.[1] I also undertake to supply grain for the whole Hellene army for the duration of the war. But I pledge all of this on one condition, that I lead the Hellenes against the Barbarians as commander-in-chief. I will not join you in person, or send anyone at all on any other terms.' (7.158)

The Hellenes were to muster an exceptional 38,700 hoplites for the battle of Plataea in 479 and no participating state fielded more than Lacedaemon's 10,000. The fleet at Salamis totalled 365 triremes, 200 of them Athenian. They had no cavalry and only a few hundred archers and possibly a handful of slingers, and their light-armed troops, though potentially numerous, generally could not match the quality or professionalism of the Sicilians' non-hoplite troops, who were very probably mercenaries. The extremely generous offer to supply grain for the whole Hellene defence force is an unlikely detail. An undertaking that the Sicilians would feed themselves would have been appreciated, indeed assumed, but as far as the rest of the Hellenes were concerned a guarantee that the grain supply from Sicily would be maintained was likely to have been the extent of it. Sicilian grain was important to most

---

[1] *Hippodromoi psiloi*, literally 'light-armed runners with the horses', which makes them sound like precursors of the *hamippoi* widely deployed alongside Hellene and Macedonian cavalry in the 4th century.

of the cities in mainland Greece as a supplement to local harvests, as were imports from the Black Sea, and Persian control of the Hellespont was a clear threat to the latter. The manpower figures may have been quite generously rounded but there is little doubt that Gelon could have assembled a force of such a scale. Reinforced by this, the defence of Hellas would probably have been a much less close-run affair in 480–479. If Gelon had been brought formally into a Hellene alliance a few years earlier, the Persians might even have decided against any immediate invasion of Greece.

Gelon's condition that he be made commander-in-chief of the entire operation does not seem unreasonable but Syagros finds it totally unacceptable:

> 'Agamemnon son of Pelops would cry out in pain on hearing that the Spartans were to be robbed of the leadership of Hellas by Gelon and the Syracusans!' (7.159)

The issue of the leadership of Hellas was to arise a number of times in the course of the war. On this occasion the Syracusan's moderate response, after pointing out that he commands a force substantially larger than Sparta's, is to propose a compromise, that Syracuse and Sparta split the command, one taking the fleet and the other the land force, whichever Sparta prefers. The Athenian delegate, anticipating Sparta's opting for command on land, steps in before Syagros can respond and declares that the Athenians will not give up command of the fleet, which they consider their entitlement, to anyone but the Spartans:

> Gelon replied, 'My friend, it appears that you Athenians are not short of leaders but that none of you is willing to be led. So, since you will concede nothing and want to have everything, the sooner you take yourselves off the better. Tell Hellas that spring has been cancelled this year.'[1] But the people of Sicily say that Gelon would have given the Hellenes his support, even under a Lacedaemonian commander-in-chief. They say he did not do this because Terillus

---

[1] Gelon was renowned for his wit and it is possible his words were noted down on this occasion, as on others, and reached Herodotus through a first-hand or close second-hand source.

son of Crinippus, the tyrant of Himera, who had been driven out of Himera by Theron son of Aenesidemus, ruler of Acragas, had brought an army of 300,000 men against him, consisting of Phoenicians,[1] Libyans, Iberians, Ligurians, Sardinians, and Corsicans; Hamilcar son of Annon, the king of the Carthaginians,[2] was in command. They also say it so happened that Gelon and Theron defeated Hamilcar in Sicily on the same day that the Hellenes defeated the Persians at Salamis. (7.162–66)

The figure of 300,000 for Hamilcar's army of invasion should not be taken literally but simply as the usual shorthand for 'a very large force'. But the specific detail of its make-up of troops conscripted or hired from all round the Mediterranean is credible. Diodorus Siculus adds the information that the Great King was behind the Carthaginian invasion of Sicily.

Xerxes, won over by Mardonius' arguments, was determined to lay waste all of Greece. So he sent an embassy to the Carthaginians to request them to join him in this undertaking, and it was agreed that he would go to war with the Hellenes who lived in Greece, and that the Carthaginians would at the same time assemble a great force to overcome the Hellenes who lived in Sicily and Italy. (*Library of History* 11.1)

This is plausible. Kinship between the Carthaginians and the Phoenicians, willing subjects of Persia since the time of Cambyses, was a bond. Success could win the Carthaginians, who had a power base in the Phoenician territories at the western end of the island, eventual control of the whole of Sicily. And the isolation of Syracuse, the strongest military power in Hellas, would greatly enhance the Persians' prospects of success on the mainland of Greece. In fact, local rivalries were sufficient cause and the Carthaginians were comprehensively defeated.

---

[1] Meaning Carthaginians here. Settlers from Phoenician Tyre founded the city as a trading outpost in the 8th century and it grew to dominate the western Mediterranean until its empire was finally contained and crushed by Rome in the 2nd century.

[2] Actually one of the two heads of state elected annually from amongst the Carthaginian elite.

However, as a consequence, the Hellenes of Sicily and southern Italy were represented at Salamis only by a solitary trireme from Croton and by no land forces whatsoever, surely an excellent outcome from the Great King's point of view, whether he had engineered it or not. In any case, according to Herodotus, Gelon decided to take out some insurance against Persian victory in Greece.

> On hearing that Xerxes had crossed the Hellespont, Gelon sent Cadmus son of Scythes[1] to Delphi with three penteconters, bearing a large sum of money and a message of friendship. He was to wait and see how the fighting ended and, if the Barbarian was victorious, his instructions were to present him with the money and to submit earth and water on behalf of Gelon and his subjects. However, if the Hellenes were victorious, he was to bring it all back. (7.183)

In Herodotus' view, there was no prospect that he might come to the rescue of Hellas at some later date in the event that the Carthaginians were defeated. And perhaps this was as would have been expected of a tyrant.

Corcyra (modern Corfu) was an important staging post on the trade routes to the central and western Mediterranean and a significant maritime power. According to Herodotus, the Corcyreans agreed to join the alliance and committed 60 triremes, but then decided 'like others, to wait and see how the war would go', fearful that the Hellenes would be defeated and hoping to be better treated by the Persians if they took no part. He adds a note of scorn when he repeats the excuse the Corcyreans made for missing the battle of Salamis, claiming that adverse winds prevented them rounding Cape Malea, the south-eastern point of the Peloponnese. This could have been a genuine excuse because the wind in late summer tended to blow from the north-east and could hold up sail- and oar-driven craft heading into it. But if this did happen to the Corcyreans, they could at least be criticized for leaving their departure on the mission so late. Most of the Hellene fleet had assembled in July or early August and was ready for action at Artemisium weeks before Salamis.

---

[1] Cadmus was well connected, if as is probable, his father was the Scythes who spent the final years of his life as a highly respected Hellene exile in the Great King's court after being deposed as tyrant of Zancle, an important city in north-east Sicily.

Considering the island's size, its former glories and its position on
the sea routes that joined Asia, North Africa and Europe, Crete was
puzzlingly insignificant in the Classical era. It could well be that its 40
or so unfederated cities had very little to offer in the way of hoplites and
triremes and, in any case, pleading advice from Delphi, they declined
the allies' invitation to become involved. But Crete was an established
source of mercenary archers and slingers in the 5th century and one
source mentions deployment of Cretan archers by the Athenians on the
island of Salamis. The alliance's delegation may at least have hired some
archers to serve on their triremes, and Athens with 200 of them to man
had the greatest need; and, on the Hellene side, Athens alone fielded a
unit of archers at Plataea.

In the two or three years leading up to the start of hostilities there
was undoubtedly a great deal more diplomatic activity of this kind than
Herodotus specifically records. There were approximately 1,000 city-
states or peoples that could be classified as Hellene. Those that were
already under Persian rule in Asia, or located along the land route the
Great King was preparing to take from the Hellespont to the northern
borders of Greece, could not reasonably be expected to take an active
part in the defence of Hellas; indeed, some were to fight on the Persian
side, as at Marathon. But there were hundreds of cities that did not
have this valid excuse in Greece itself, on the islands of the Aegean
and out to the west. The nucleus that conferred on strategy at the
Isthmus and sent out these diplomatic missions was probably formed
by fewer than 20 cities that had pledged themselves to the alliance.
Herodotus names 12 participants at Thermopylae, 17 at Salamis and
23 at Plataea, overall mentioning 44 once or more. There are 32 names
on the commemorative 'Serpent Column' that the Hellenes collectively
dedicated at Delphi immediately after the war. All of these names are
mentioned at least once in Herodotus' narrative. A case could be made
for the inclusion of two or three others (Croton, for one) and Sparta
is not individually named there but subsumed under Lacedaemon. On
the other hand, some of Herodotus' mentions may be due to fairly
immediate rewritings of history.

Whatever the actual number, which was certainly much closer to
30 than 44, the truth was a long way from the romantic image of all
Hellenes uniting in the heroic defence of their collective liberty. But it
was fortunate that the very small minority that was prepared to fight

included Sparta, Athens and Corinth: after Syracuse, three of the most powerful of all the Hellene city-states. Herodotus gives a good sense of the mix of naivety, fear, defeatism, self-interest and pragmatism that motivated so many of the others not to participate. And the deeply ingrained character trait that Gelon identified in the Athenians, an aversion to being led, was no doubt also a factor. Some may even have sensed where Spartan or Athenian hegemony might ultimately lead. In any case, the issue of leadership was to arise repeatedly within the Hellene Alliance, and to seriously endanger it at critical moments.

Herodotus continues:

> As Xerxes prepared for the march to Abydos, some of his men had been yoking the Hellespont between Asia and Europe. There is a broad headland opposite Abydos between the towns of Sestos and Madytus on the Chersonese and the two bridges were built out to this headland from Abydos. The Phoenicians used esparto grass cables on one bridge while the Egyptians used papyrus cables on the other and the distance from Abydos to the other side is 7 *stades* [1,300m].[1] So, the bridges were built across the channel, but then a great storm blew up and smashed them to pieces. When Xerxes got word of this, he was very angry. He commanded that the Hellespont be given 300 lashes and that fetters be lowered into the water, and I have even heard that he sent men to brand it with red hot irons. He ordered the men lashing the sea to chant these presumptuous Barbarian words: 'Hateful waters! Your master, who has done you no wrong, punishes you thus for the pain you have caused him without justification. Xerxes, the Great King, will pass over whether it is your will or not. For good reason no man offers you sacrifices, thou foul and brackish stream!' In this way Xerxes had the sea punished, and he also had the men in charge of the bridging operation beheaded. These dismal tasks were carried out as the Great King instructed. (7.33–35)

The total destruction of the two bridges may be myth, although bad weather would have caused some setbacks. However, it neatly sets up the scene of the Great King's response to what Hellenes saw as a clear warning that he was overreaching himself by challenging the elements

---

[1] Erosion over the millennia has widened the channel to about 2,000m at this point.

and the gods who controlled them. The physical punishment of animals or inanimate objects that were considered guilty of some offence was actually quite commonplace in the ancient world, but here it is by implication inflicted on Poseidon, and the 'un-Hellene' curse amplifies the impiety of this act in which the Hellespont, itself considered to be divine by the Hellenes, is being treated like a disobedient slave. Herodotus seems doubtful about the branding. The idea of this and of the shackles being lowered into the sea may have grown out of eyewitness accounts of the bridge-building process, which probably included large-scale forging of the metal links and brackets needed to secure the cables and a lot of red-hot metal, smoke and steam.

> Fresh engineers started work on the bridges, and this is the way they built them. They put together penteconters and triremes until there were 360 ships for the upper bridge nearer to the Black Sea and 314 for the lower one. The hulls lay at an angle to the Black Sea but in line with the flow of the current down the Hellespont to minimize the drag on the cables. When the ships were all lined up, they put down anchors on long ropes to make them secure against the winds that blow down from the Black Sea, and against the south and west winds that blow up from the Aegean. They left a narrow opening in each bridge so that small craft could continue to sail to and from the Black Sea. When all this had been done, they pulled the cables across, stretching them tight with wooden windlasses. This time they did not use only one kind of rope on each bridge, but two cables of esparto and four of papyrus. However, each kind was of the same thickness and fine appearance, but the esparto rope was heavier (a cubit's length of it weighed one talent[1]). Next, wooden planks were cut to equal widths and fitted together over the taut cables, and when this decking was fixed in place it was covered with brushwood. This in turn was covered with earth, which was trodden down firmly. Finally, screens were put up on each side to prevent the transport animals being spooked by the sight of the sea below them. (7.36)

[1] There was no precise 'international standard' but a cubit was the distance from elbow to fingertip, say 45cm; a talent was about 26kg as a measure of the weight of precious metal, or 38kg when used in the trading of commercial goods.

Herodotus' brief account gives a fair sense of this remarkable feat of engineering, though the two bridges might be better termed 'floating causeways' than 'bridges of boats'. But it only partially explains the process by which the hundreds of ships were 'put together'. However, Arrian, writing in the 2nd century AD, supplies some plausible detail in his account of the career of Alexander the Great. It is unlikely that this process had changed in any significant way over the six centuries that had elapsed and Arrian may even have had some direct experience of it in his years of military service under the emperor Hadrian.

> I cannot make up my mind whether Alexander bridged the Indus with boats, as Xerxes bridged the Hellespont and Darius the Danube and the Bosporus, or whether he built a regular bridge over the river.[1] But I think it is more likely that he bridged it with boats. It would not have been possible to build a regular bridge in that depth of water, nor could a construction project on such a scale have been completed so quickly. However, if it is indeed the case that he bridged this river with boats, I have not been able to decide whether it was sufficient for this purpose to lash ships together and moor them in a row in the same way as Herodotus says the Hellespont was bridged, or whether the Romans' method was used, as for their bridges across the Danube and the Rhine, and the Tigris and the Euphrates whenever the need arose. I know that the Romans found that they could make a bridge most quickly with boats, so I shall now explain their method to you because it is well worth describing. When the signal is given, the ships are floated downstream, not bow first, but astern. The current carries them along, as you would expect, but they are under the control of smaller boats[2] which guide them into their set places. Then pyramid-shaped wicker baskets[3] filled with stones are lowered from the bows of each ship to hold it against the current. Once a ship is anchored, the next one is placed alongside, prow pointing

---

[1] The width of the Indus here was about 500m.

[2] The vocabulary used here is generally taken to mean a light craft with a single bank of oars, which would exclude the trireme but include the penteconter and triaconter.

[3] Either the baskets were simply made this way, or they were designed to sink into the riverbed for greater effectiveness. An advantage of this kind of anchor is that it could be created on the spot and would have been considered disposable, unlike regular anchors made out of metal or a single large piece of stone.

upstream and at a distance calculated according to the load to be carried. Pointed timbers are fixed at right angles to the two hulls and planks are laid across them to tie them together. This is repeated with each ship until the river is spanned. Ramps are placed at each end and firmly fixed for the safety of the horses and pack animals, and to secure the bridge. This is all done in a very short space of time ...

Well, this is how the Romans have been doing it since the olden days. I cannot tell you for sure that this is how Alexander bridged the Indus because the men who were on the campaign with him have not told us how it was done, but I think the method he used was very like this. If he contrived it some other way, then so be it![1] (*Anabasis of Alexander* 5.7–8)

Triremes and penteconters were used in preference to merchant ships for their more streamlined hulls, but are likely to have been warships approaching the end of their useful life. The commitment of 674 front-line vessels, even if they were largely less effective penteconters or even triaconters, would have dangerously reduced the Persian navy's overall power and reach for a period of months, and there is no suggestion that they were drawn from the invasion fleet, whatever its size. If these ships were not brought to the Hellespont under tow, most of their crews were probably shipped home since accommodating and feeding tens of thousands of idle oarsmen would have been an impossible drain on resources. If the numbers of ships for each bridge are correct, and Herodotus' figure of 7 *stades* for the width of the Hellespont is reasonably accurate, it can be assumed that the hulls (triremes were about 5m wide) were lashed together without any spacing between. Their 'angle to the Black Sea' is topographically vague but their alignment with the current, which, as now, runs obliquely down the channel, makes good sense; indeed, ships at anchor would swing naturally into line with the current. Neither bridge, then, would have covered the shortest distance between shores. It is possible to envisage each hull being towed into position at the end of the growing line with only a skeleton crew on board to steer, handle anchors and cables, and to lash it to the next in line. The 'tugs' would have been

---

[1] And the same could be said over and over again in the process of 'speculative reconstruction', whether engaged in decades, centuries or millennia after the events.

fully manned and pentenconters or triaconters were best suited to this task with sufficient oar power to overcome current and wind but greater nimbleness than triremes; they were also more economical in terms of manpower. These boats would also have been used to place the anchors 'on long ropes' up- and down-stream, possibly at intervals rather than for each ship, and to ship the skeleton crews back to shore to man the next ship to be towed out. It is likely that there were four units at work at the same time, two building out to the centre from each shore.

The use of one kind of rope for each bridge first time around and then a combination of the two is a strange detail; both bridges had failed first time, so both kinds of rope had failed. However, the two kinds may have had complementary qualities which were found to give more resilience in combination. The weight given for the esparto cable is impossible and may be a transcription error. One talent per cubit equals approximately 58kg per metre or 84kg if, as is likely, the heavier 'trading' talent is intended. The bulkiest modern cable generally used for mooring large ships is 25cm in diameter and weighs about 7.5kg per metre. This implies a diameter very roughly ten times greater for the Persian cable, which would have made it impossibly difficult to handle, and indeed to manufacture with pre-industrial resources, leaving aside the challenge of transporting hundreds of tonnes of it to the Hellespont from wherever it was made. But thousands of metres of very stout cable will have been used, and massive windlasses would have been needed not only to tighten each length, but to draw it from one end of the bridge to the other, probably attached to lighter 'leader' ropes. The cables would have been manufactured and transported in more manageable lengths to be spliced together as each was fed out along the line of hulls and passed through ringbolts or something similar on each boat in the bridge. Laying the decking over the cables would have smoothed out height differences between adjacent hulls and given some flexibility as they rose and fell with the waves. Larger and smaller hulls were most likely not mixed randomly and perhaps the smaller ones were massed at each end of the bridges with the triremes placed in the central sections.

Herodotus is unable to answer the questions of how long the bridges were left in place after the crossing into Europe, or whether they were taken apart by the Persians or destroyed by stormy weather. However, if it was indeed the case that larger craft could not pass through the single 'narrow opening in each bridge', they were temporarily blocking a major sea-trade artery which was as important to the Persian Empire and its current war effort as to the rest of the population of the eastern Mediterranean and Black Sea regions. An anecdote which Herodotus includes later in his narrative highlights the grain traffic, and some nice strategic pragmatism on Xerxes' part:

> While he was at Abydos he saw ships laden with grain[1] sailing down from the Pontus[2] through the Hellespont and on their way to Aegina and the Peloponnese. His staff saw that they were enemy ships and were all set to capture them. They looked to the Great King for his command, but Xerxes asked where the ships were headed. They replied, 'To your enemies, Lord, carrying grain,' and Xerxes answered, 'Well, aren't we sailing in the same direction as they are, loaded up with all kinds of provisions including grain? What harm are they doing by transporting food for us?' (7.147)

In any case, the structures were vulnerable to extremes of weather if not to the cumulative background stress of normal winds, waves and current. There was also danger of attack from the sea, growing as the invasion force travelled further west. A single ship could have slipped in under cover of darkness to cut the cables and anchor ropes without much difficulty. Finally, even in the best of conditions, old hulls would have steadily taken in water causing the bridges to sag and adding to the stresses on them. So, it seems more likely that the bridges were disassembled soon after the army had crossed into Europe, with the component ships beached along the facing shores, many of them perhaps ultimately left to rot, and the cables stored nearby. There may have been no set plan to rebuild the bridges for the victorious troops' return march. An army of occupation would have stayed in Greece and returning units could be ferried back into Asia as and when they reached the Hellespont, as was to happen towards the end of the year in different circumstances.

Meanwhile, the canal at Athos had been finished off with breakwaters at each end to prevent the waves of the sea silting them up,[3] and word

---

[1] Unlikely to have been 'small craft'.

[2] A word generally used for any open sea but here meaning the Black Sea.

[3] Phoenician expertise may have been prominent in this part of the operation.

was brought that the canal was ready for use. So, having wintered in
Sardis and with all preparations completed, the army started out for
Abydos in early spring. But as it moved off the sun left its place in the sky
and vanished. The air was clear and there were no clouds, but day turned
into night. This caused Xerxes some anxiety as he watched it and took it
in, and he asked the Magi[1] what the phenomenon might portend. They
said that God's message was the eclipse[2] of the cities of Greece, telling
him that the sun foretold the future for the Hellenes but that the moon
foretold the future for the Persians. Xerxes was well pleased with this
interpretation and he pressed on with the expedition. (7.37)

Pythius the Lydian, terrified by the alternative interpretation that the
moon represented Hellas, begged Xerxes to release the eldest of his five
sons from service in the army to ensure his survival. Xerxes was enraged
by his so recently acquired guest-friend's request:

The Great King ordered his executioners[3] to find the eldest of Pythius'
sons and cut him in half, and to place one half of his body on the right
of the road and the other on the left so that the army could march out
between them.[4] This was done and the army marched out between
them. The baggage carriers and pack animals went first. They were
followed by over half of the units from all the different nations in the
army, not organized into divisions but all massed together. When these
had passed, a gap was left to keep them apart from the Great King.
Then came a thousand cavalry, hand-picked from all the Persians, and
next a thousand spearmen, also hand-picked, carrying their spears
pointing down. After them came ten horses of the Nisaean breed with
splendid trappings; these great horses are called Nisaean because they
are bred in Media on a wide plain of that name. Behind them, eight
white horses drew the sacred chariot of Zeus.[5] The charioteer followed

[1] Priestly experts on ritual and in the interpretation of dreams and other portents, often
influential as advisers in the Great King's court.
[2] The word *ekleipsis* can also be translated as 'abandonment'.
[3] Literally 'the men whose job it was to do these things'.
[4] There is evidence in the Old Testament of the practice of cutting sacrificial victims (animals
anyway) in two, and some record of a Persian custom of walking between the two halves to
guard against misfortune.
[5] Here meaning Ahura Mazda, the Persian supreme god.

on foot holding the reins, for no mortal man may ride in it. After this came Xerxes himself in a chariot drawn by Nisaean horses[1] with his charioteer beside him; his name was Patiramphes, son of Otanes, a Persian.[2] So, Xerxes rode out from Sardis, though whenever he felt like it, he would move over from the chariot into a carriage.[3] Behind him marched a thousand spearmen of the best and noblest blood of Persia, carrying their spears in the normal manner. After them came 1,000 picked Persian cavalry and then 10,000 footsoldiers, picked out of the rest of the Persians. One thousand of these had golden pomegranates on their spear-butts instead of a spike, and were formed up around the other 9,000, who had silver pomegranates on their spear-butts. Those who held their spears points downward also had golden pomegranates, and those nearest to Xerxes had golden apples. After the 10,000 infantry there was a formation of 10,000 Persian cavalry. The remaining contingents, all massed together, followed them 2 *stades* (about 400m) behind. (7.39–41)

Astronomical calculations give dates for two solar eclipses which would have been visible in the region around this time but neither of them occurred in the spring of 480. The portentous association of one of them with Xerxes' departure from Sardis probably evolved amongst Herodotus' Hellene sources. In the anecdote, the Magi give Xerxes an interpretation that he finds pleasing, but which would have been equally pleasing to Herodotus and his audiences for its wrongness; Hellas was not eclipsed, and, in any case, it was the lesser heavenly body that snuffed out the greater. If the story of the savage execution of Pythius' son is true, the events took place at a different time, but placing them at what Herodotus clearly sees as the formal start of the Great King's expedition adds to the drama, whilst, once again, highlighting extreme tyrannical behaviour.

The broad-brush depiction of the Great King's march out of Sardis could have been painted without the help of any eyewitnesses to

---

[1] Nisaea was somewhere in the plains of Media. The breed that originated there is extinct but was sought after and valued highly for its strength, speed and beauty. In Persia pure Nisaeans were the preserve of kings and nobles.

[2] Otanes was Xerxes' brother-in-law.

[3] Transport generally reserved for women.

the actual event and would have been replicated many times on the road to Sardis and then onward to Abydos. The baggage train could safely lead because at this stage the march was to be through friendly country. Sandwiching elite troops and the royal bodyguard between massed subject levies reflects the way lighter-armed auxiliary troops might be formed up on the flanks of a battle formation, or to lead and cover the rear of a march into hostile territory. The nice details of the reversed spears and the decorative apples and pomegranates might have been picked up from sculptural reliefs or other artefacts. Herodotus does not, and probably could not say what other nations were represented here and Xerxes may have been marching with only part of the invasion force at this stage. But there is a telling contrast between the tight organization of the Persian elite units and the massed levies from other nations.

After leaving Lydia, the army marched north, crossed the River Caicus, and headed for the Troad:

> They halted for the night at the foot of Mount Ida and a great storm of thunder and lightning fell upon them and many died. When the army reached the Scamander, which was the first river on their march from Sardis that failed to meet all the needs of the army's men and beasts, Xerxes went up to Priam's citadel as he had a great desire to see it. After he had looked around and asked questions about everything that had happened there, he made a sacrifice of a thousand cattle to Athena of Ilium,[1] and the Magi poured drink-offerings to the heroes of Troy. The night after they did this, panic fell upon the army, but at daybreak the march continued. (7.42–43)

Ida was a holy mountain in Hellene eyes, the grandstand from which the gods watched and manipulated the siege of Troy, and the mythical scene of other events such as the judgement of Paris and the rape of Ganymede. The violent storm would have been seen by Hellenes as a warning, a sign of the anger of their gods which should have been heeded. But the mountain was also sacred to the Asian goddess Cybele so there was a warning there for Barbarians as well. Xerxes behaves like a cultured tourist on the citadel of Troy but the lavish sacrifice to Athena,

---

[1] The name of the Hellene city founded on the site of ancient Troy in the 7th century.

guardian goddess of Troy as well as Athens, and the drink-offerings to the heroes of the *Iliad* were, like Datis' extravagant offering to Apollo at Delos, probably calculated to impress the Hellenes in his army as much as higher divine authority. The panic that broke out in the ranks (the same *phobos* that Pan was said to have sent to the Athenians' aid at Marathon) could be seen as a second warning. Both Hellene and Asian troops may have been unsettled by the storm sent down from Ida, and also by fear of the ghosts of the Trojan War. But the Persians carried on, and the fleet, or more probably a detachment of it, and army now converged on Abydos.

Meanwhile the Hellenes were debating what action to take. The further north they could form a first line of defence the better, but this could not be viable without the full commitment of the peoples of central and northern Greece, the Thessalians in particular:

The Thessalians had medized initially, but they had been forced to do this against their will as they now demonstrated. They were unhappy with the policies of the Aleuadae,[1] so, as soon as they heard that the Persians were about to cross into Europe, they sent representatives to the Isthmus, where special delegates from the cities that cared about the future of Hellas had gathered to consider possible courses of action. These Thessalians came before the council and said, 'Men of Hellas, the pass over Olympus must be held to protect Thessaly and all of Greece from this attack. We are prepared to share in its defence with you, but you will have to send a substantial force. If you do not, be assured that we will agree terms with the Persians, because it is not right that we should be left alone to die for the sake of the rest of you. If you are not willing to come to our aid, there is nothing you can do to prevent us agreeing terms because there is no force that can give power to the powerless. We will have to find some other way of protecting our interests.' This is what the men of Thessaly said.

The Hellenes' response was a resolution to send an army to Thessaly by sea to hold the pass. When this force was assembled, it

---

[1] Descendants of Aleuas the Red who headed the Thessalian confederacy in the 6th century; they held oligarchic power and were the main movers of Thessaly's medism, actively encouraging Xerxes to attack Hellas.

was shipped up the Euripus and on to Alos[1] in Achaea Phthiotis where it disembarked and marched to Thessaly, leaving the ships at the landing point. It arrived in the Tempea[2] and the pass which runs from lower Macedonia into Thessaly along the River Peneus between the mountain ranges of Olympus and Ossa, and here the Hellenes pitched camp. There were about 10,000 hoplites altogether and the Thessalian cavalry joined them. Evenetus son of Carenus was in command of the Lacedaemonians; he had been chosen from among the polemarchs[3] and was not of royal blood. Themistocles son of Neocles[4] was in command of the Athenians. However, the Hellene force stayed for only a few days. This was because messengers arrived from Alexander son of Amyntas, king of Macedon, advising them to withdraw rather than sit and wait to be trampled over in the pass, and informing them of the vastness of the Barbarian army and fleet. The Hellenes thought this was sound advice and it seemed to them that the Macedonian king was looking after their interests, so they did as he suggested. But it is my opinion that they took this decision because they were alarmed to discover that there was another pass[5] leading into Thessaly from upper Macedonia through Perrhaebia near the town of Gonnus, and this was in fact the way Xerxes' army entered Thessaly. So the Hellenes went back down to their ships and returned to the Isthmus. This expedition to Thessaly took place when the Great King had reached Abydos and was about to cross into Europe from Asia.

Now the Thessalians, abandoned by their allies, committed themselves fully to the Persian cause, medizing without hesitation. In the business that followed they proved themselves excellent servants of the Great King. (7.172–74)

Clearly, as far as Herodotus' sources were concerned, the details and true purpose of this expedition were fogged by the much larger

---

[1] It is puzzling that they did not shorten their march north by disembarking at Pagasae.

[2] *Tempea*, the word for the area containing a number of passes that gave access to Thessaly and linked its plains internally. The pass the River Peneus ran through was the best known of these and, confusingly, was also called the Vale of Tempe.

[3] The five regimental commanders in the Spartan army.

[4] Herodotus includes this episode as a flashback at a later point in his narrative, after introducing Themistocles as the architect of the defensive strategy that was to save Hellas.

[5] More than one, in fact.

events that were to follow in a matter of months. First, if the Persian army was still at Abydos, it was the best part of 800km away, several weeks' march, so it made little sense to take up a defensive position immediately. Secondly, although the pass in which the Hellenes were said to have taken up position was eminently defensible, there were good alternative routes leading south; the Peneus ravine was not the single gateway implied, as Herodotus goes on to tell us. Thirdly, with their ships so far back the Hellenes would have been fatally exposed to seaborne attacks in their flank and rear. An effective defence could only have been mounted across a much broader front, combining static positions with more fluid action in the wooded uplands and on the plains. Full Thessalian involvement would have been essential, bringing local knowledge of terrain, and mountain paths and tracks, and significant additional manpower; their strong cavalry arm would have been particularly valuable in any battles fought in open country.

It is disappointing, and perhaps revealing of the mission's true nature, that Herodotus gives no details of the logistics of shipping such a force to Alos. A troop of 10,000 hoplites, presumably each with an 'attendant', was a substantial cargo and oar power, rather than sail, was necessary to guarantee efficient delivery, so triremes would have been used. Assuming each one carried a maximum of 40 soldiers with its full complement of oarsmen and sailors, the operation would have called for 500 ships, 134 more than the Hellenes, according to Herodotus, were able to muster at Salamis. However, capacity could have been more than doubled by dispensing with the 62 top-tier oarsmen and seating passengers on their benches. Some, perhaps many, of the hoplites' attendants could also have rowed (in the 5th century hoplites appear to have taken oars only in exceptional circumstances) further reducing the number of triremes needed, perhaps to 200. But when the army marched north, it would have left behind not much more than half the number of rowers needed to fully man them for battle. One hundred triremes would have been quickly overwhelmed or bypassed by the much larger Persian fleet.

It is more likely that this expedition's purpose was not to take up position as a premature advance guard but to affirm the Hellene Alliance's commitment to making a stand in northern Greece and to secure the commitment of the Thessalians and of the cities of central Greece, many of which were known to be wavering, if they had not already medized. There was probably also some hope that Macedon, under its slippery king, Alexander 'the Philhellene', could be persuaded to come over to the Hellene side to harass the invaders from the rear, and the Thessalians may have been counting on this. So perhaps the Hellenes sent a much smaller party which, given the timing, needed no close naval support. The advance guard that marched to Thermopylae just a few days ahead of the Persians' arrival comprised a little over 6,000 hoplites. The Tempe mission could have displayed the alliance's commitment and created the necessary diplomatic atmosphere with a more modest investment of resources. In any case, neither Macedon nor Thessaly proved willing to join the fight.

> Meanwhile, it was Xerxes' wish to review his entire invasion force when he reached Abydos. The people of the city, obedient to the Great King's command, had already built him a throne of white stone on a hill well positioned for this. He was seated upon it with a view of the seashore and his army and fleet assembled there. And, as he looked them over, he desired to see his ships race. The Phoenicians of Sidon were the winners and Xerxes was well pleased with the racing and with his whole expeditionary force. But when he saw all of the Hellespont covered with his ships and the plains and shoreline of Abydos filled with his troops, Xerxes first thought himself the happiest of men, but then he wept. His uncle Artabanus, who at first had spoken out in advising Xerxes not to march against Hellas, saw that Xerxes was weeping and said, 'Great King, how quickly your mood has changed: a short time ago you thought yourself the happiest of men, and now you are weeping!' Xerxes replied, 'Indeed, I found myself reflecting upon the brevity of human life and was moved by the thought that one hundred years from now not one of those men before us will be alive.' (7.44–46)

Herodotus then has Artabanus, clearly now fully back in favour, philosophizing gloomily about life and the grief it brings to all. Xerxes waves this aside and asks him if he would have changed his mind, 'now we have such good things in our grasp' (7.47), if he had not already been persuaded to in the dreams they had shared.

> Artabanus replied, 'Great King, I pray that the vision I saw in my dream turns out to be true; we both wish this. But great dread fills

my mind. I can give many reasons for this, but most of all it is because I see that you are about to take on the two forces that are the most hostile of all, the sea and the land. First, the sea: it is my understanding that there is no harbour anywhere along our route large enough to accommodate our fleet and keep it safe if a storm gets up, but it is not just one harbour you need. You will need harbours all along the coast you will be sailing down, and there is not a single one that has the necessary capacity. And do remember that disaster has control over men, men do not have control over disasters. So, now let me tell you about the land, the second of these two enemies facing you. If you meet with no opposition but are forever drawn into the unknown, the further you advance, the greater an enemy the land will become. And remember, there is not a man who is ever fully satisfied by success. So, even if no man stands against you and you win more and more territory as time passes, this will lead to starvation. In circumstances such as these the best feel great anxiety as they do their thinking and consider all the possible outcomes, but are bold when they take action.'

Xerxes answered him, 'Great prizes are won by taking great risks and we will do as the Great Kings who came before us did. We are launching our campaign at the best time of year and we shall return home conquerors of all Europe. We shall not suffer starvation nor any other difficulties for we are marching with plentiful supplies, and we shall also possess ourselves of the produce of whatever lands or nations we set foot upon. These are farmers we are going to war with, not nomads.'[1] (7.49–50)

Artabanus attempts to give Xerxes one more piece of advice, not to trust the Ionian Hellenes he is about to lead against their kinsmen, and delivers a final cautionary aphorism, which Athenians at least would have easily recognized as a saying of the 6th-century lawgiver Solon: 'at the beginning we cannot see how anything will end' (7.51). Before finally appointing Artabanus regent in his absence, the Great King brushes this aside, citing the Ionians' (actually fragile) loyalty in Darius' Scythian expedition and adding his own chilling guarantee: 'They have

---

[1] A reference to the Scythians and the failure of Darius' expedition in 513.

left their wives and families and possessions in our land so they cannot contemplate turning against us' (7.52).

Next, after dispatching Artabanus to Susa, Xerxes summoned the Persians of greatest distinction into his presence. When they had gathered before him, he addressed them in these words: 'Persians, I have called you here to tell you what I require of you. You must prove yourselves valiant men and do nothing to discredit Persia's former great and glorious achievements. Let us strive, each and every one of us, for this shared goal. I urge you to engage in this war with all your might. I hear the men we will be fighting are valiant, but if we defeat them, no other mortal army will ever stand against us. So now let us pray to the gods who watch over Persia, and then let us cross.'

All that day the Persians made ready for the crossing. Next day they waited to see the sun rise and burned all kinds of incense on the bridges and spread branches of myrtle on the road. At sunrise Xerxes poured an offering into the sea from a golden bowl and, facing the sun, prayed that no misfortune would prevent him conquering Europe or set him back before he reached its furthest boundaries. After he had made this prayer, he threw the bowl into the Hellespont with a golden vase and a Persian short sword (their word for this is *akinakes*) – I have not been able to determine if he threw these things into the sea as an offering to the sun, or as gifts to the Hellespont in an act of penitence for having had the ocean whipped. This done, the crossing began. The foot soldiers and all of the cavalry crossed by the bridge nearer to the Black Sea; the baggage train and camp-followers used the bridge nearer to the Aegean. The Persian Ten Thousand were the first to cross, all wearing garlands, and they were followed by the mixed force of troops from every nation. This took all that first day. Next day, the cavalry crossed first including the contingent of Persians who carried their spears reversed; they too were wearing garlands. Then came the sacred horses and chariot and then Xerxes himself with a thousand horsemen and a thousand spearmen. The rest of the army followed and at the same time the fleet rowed to the opposite shore. However I have also been told that the King crossed over last of all. Anyway, Xerxes watched his army making the crossing under the lash and this took seven days and seven nights without a moment's halt. And there is a story that, after the Great King had crossed the Hellespont, a local man exclaimed, 'O Zeus, why have you taken on the likeness of a Persian mortal and changed your name to Xerxes? You wish to take the whole of mankind with you to uproot Hellas, but could you not do that on your own!' (7.53–56)

The final exhortation from Xerxes, and his prayers and offerings ring true. There were already bridgeheads on the western shore and there was no threat of any opposition, but it made sense to send a spearhead force across by the northern bridge and for the baggage train to cross by the southern one to be positioned to the rear of the combat troops when the march over European soil began. The organization for the crossing on the initial two days is then broadly similar to that for the march out of Sardis. Well organized, which at least the Persian and Median units would have been, it should have been possible to get several thousand men (marching four abreast for the sake of argument) across the bridge in an hour. A substantial army could have made the crossing in two days, in the daylight hours alone. Seven days, day and night, would certainly have begun to look like 'the whole of mankind', and Herodotus does not seem much concerned about the evident conflict between his sources. But it must have been an extraordinary sight, tens of thousands of men and animals filing across the long curves of the bridges, the glint of sun on metal against the sparkle of the water, and great dust clouds on each shore as the troops were marshalled on one side and dispersed on the other. Elements of the fleet including the elite Sidonians were probably patrolling the Hellespont south of the bridges but are unlikely to have been formally part of the crossing at any point. Two more portents were reported at that time (a horse giving birth to a hare, and a donkey producing a foal with female and male genitals) but the Great King 'did not give a thought to them' (7.58) and set off with the army for Doriscus, where the fleet was to wait for them.

Doriscus, part of Thrace, is a wide coastal plain and a great river, the Hebrus, flows through it. A fort, also called Doriscus, had been established here and garrisoned by the Persians from as long ago as Darius' Scythian expedition. This seemed to Xerxes a good place to sort the army into units and count it, so that is what he did. All the ships had now arrived at Doriscus, and, following Xerxes' orders, the

1. Herodotus of Halicarnassus, *c.*485–425. Without 'the father of history' and his *Historia* we would know very little indeed about the war between the Greeks and the Persians. Other portraits are immediately recognisable from the loosely parted beard. This one is a 2nd-century AD Roman copy of a 4th-century Greek bronze, which has not survived. That was unlikely to have been based on any likeness made in the subject's lifetime, but this marble copy does portray an intense and far from gullible questioner and listener. Metropolitan Museum of Art, New York.

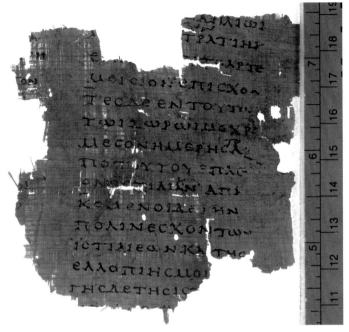

2. Fragment of a 2nd-century AD manuscript of Book 8 of the *Historia* (*P.Oxy 2009*) excavated a century ago with an immense quantity of other papyri from the rubbish dump of an ancient Graeco-Egyptian village called Oxyrinchus. It reads, '… to Artemisium. They paused there until noon and then sailed on to Histiaea, occupied the city and (overran) …' (8.23). (Courtesy of The Egypt Exploration Society and the University of Oxford Imaging Papyri Project)

3. The 'phalanx' concept of heavy infantry warfare was not new when developed in 7th-century Hellas, and the sculptor clearly grasped the principle but let his imagination run away with him when he carved the spears. Grave relief from Lagash in Lower Mesopotamia dated to *c.*2450. Louvre, Paris.

4. A fine Corinthian helmet from the first half of the 5th century, dedicated as a war trophy by the Messenians. Olympia Museum.

5. A young hoplite is almost ready for combat. The patterning on his composite corslet may depict reinforcing metal scales or decoration. He is wearing a Chalcidian helmet. His parents do not appear to share his optimism and the vase may commemorate the loss of their son in battle. Metropolitan Museum of Art, New York

6. This cast is coloured as it would have been when it first appeared on a pediment of the temple of the mother goddess Aphaea on the island of Aegina. The classification of helmets as 'Chalcidian', 'Corinthian' etc is an archaeological convention to do with a type's initial provenance and publication, and does not mean that this kind of helmet was worn especially or exclusively by hoplites from Chalcis or Corinth. Vinzenz Brinkmann's 'Gods in Colour' exhibition, Ashmolean Museum, Oxford.

7. The distinctive 'double grip' shield system is clearly shown in this depiction of single combat between Achilles and Hector. For technical or compositional reasons, shields were commonly painted edge-on to the enemy, exposing the warrior's torso. (© Trustees of the British Museum)

8. Unusually, this artist introduces some perspective to give a sense of two opposing battle lines, and the background figures are shown in an 'orthodox' fighting stance with their shields face-on to the enemy and resting on their left shoulders. National Archaeological Museum, Athens.

9. This *psilos* is using a cloak as a shield and his weapon is a cudgel. Athenians from the lowest citizen class and non-citizens served as troops of this kind as well as serving as rowers in the fleet. British Museum.

10. The Athenian corps of archers, an asset unmatched by any other city state in mainland Greece or the Aegean area, was made up of citizens, resident aliens, mercenaries and, probably, slaves. They served in both navy and army and also as police and, as here, are usually depicted in Barbarian dress. Vinzenz Brinkmann's 'Gods in Colour' exhibition, Ashmolean Museum, Oxford.

11. The Great King enthroned, borne up by the peoples of his empire. Cast of relief from Persepolis. (© Trustees of the British Museum)

Left 12. Persian gold was a powerful lever of imperial power. Hellenes were both fascinated and appalled by Barbarian treasure and often bought by it. The golden 'daric' was the imperial currency introduced by Darius, shown here with his bow and spear. (Tamashagah-e Pool (Money Museum), Tehran, Iran/ Bridgeman Images)

Below 13. The ruins of Darius and Xerxes' ceremonial capital, Persepolis. The tents in the background were part of the hospitality arrangements for the 1971 celebration of the 2,500th anniversary of the Persian Empire. (Carlo Bavagnoli/The LIFE Picture Collection/Getty Images)

14. Achaemenid treasure: this superbly crafted,
winged ibex dates from the mid 5th century.
Louvre, Paris.

15. 'Immortals' from the elite Great King's Guard in ceremonial dress carrying their bows and large quivers, and spears which were outreached by up to a metre by the hoplite's *doru*. Glazed-brick relief from the palace at Susa, Louvre, Paris.

16. The Persians did not go in for portraits, but this profile seems to reflect the qualities they would expect from their leaders, and which were evidently admired in Mardonius by Herodotus. Fragment of relief from Persepolis, Louvre, Paris.

17. An early 7th-century Phoenician warship with two tiers of oars and a pointed ram. Bulwarks and suspended shields protect the deck fighters. Pointed rams, enclosed decks and higher freeboard distinguished Phoenician triremes from Greek in the Persian Wars. Relief from Senacherib. (© Trustees of the British Museum)

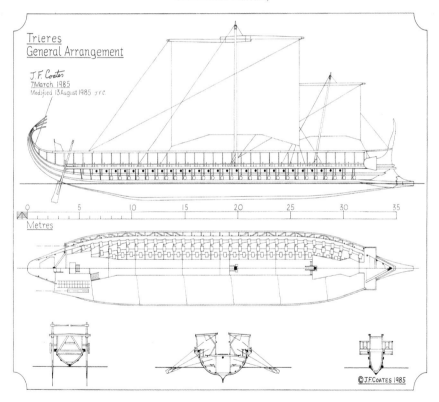

18. 'The builder of a *trires* in ancient times … would have been [therefore] perfectly clear about what he was to produce. His concepts and methods handed down and guarded by generations of master shipwrights before him are almost certainly lost for ever and probably impossible to reconstruct. As a modern but very incomplete substitute we can do no better than to offer a drawing of the general arrangement of the reconstructed ship' (Morrison, 2000). (J.F. Coates & the Trireme Trust Archive at Wolfson College, Cambridge)

19. *Olympias*, 'the restored ship', in the bay of Phalerum. The cruiser *Giorgios Averov*, flagship of the Hellenic Navy in Greece's wars with the Ottoman Turks, veteran of two World Wars and now a floating museum, provides an appropriate backdrop. (George Atsametakis, Alamy)

20. Achaemenid armies were skilled in siege warfare and similar equipment and techniques in their suppression of the Ionian Revolt. However, taking a siege train into Greece was not practicable. 8th-century relief from the Assyrian palace at Nimrud. (© Trustees of the British Museum)

21. Landlocked remains of the harbour at Miletus. The relief of the Triton holding a steering oar is part of a monument to Pompey the Great, celebrating his successful campaign against the pirates of the Aegean in the 1st century. The ridge in the background is Cape Mycale.

22. The bay and plain of Marathon seen from a spur of Mount Pentelicon just off the road up from Rafina.

23. Watercolour by the English artist John Varley in 1834. It is captioned on the back, 'Tumulus of the Persions [*sic*] who fell at Marathon'. The *Soros* was not conclusively identified as the Athenian war grave until the end of the 19th century. (Yale Center for British Art, Paul Mellon Fund)

24. The running track (*stadion*) at Olympia. The start line can be seen on the right-hand side. The distance was standardised as a *stade*, 212.54 metres in the case of Olympia, but varying at different venues.

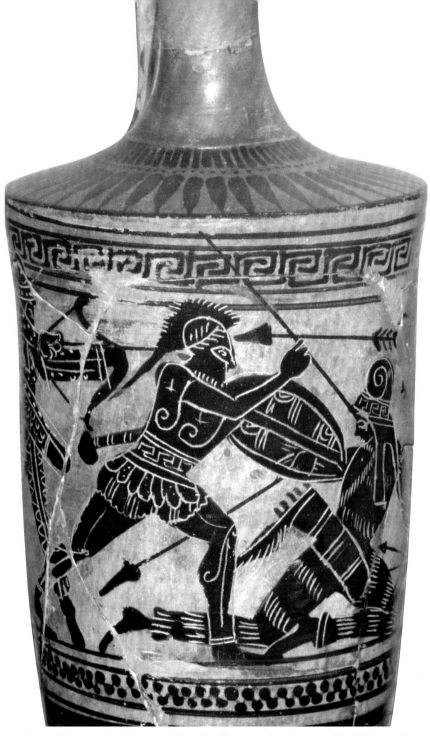

25. A crudely energetic white-ground olive oil jar illustrating the advantages of the Hellene hoplite over the Barbarian infantryman. His body armour, probably bronze, has brought him safely through the arrow storm, and his heavy spear is driving into his opponent's unprotected head. National Archaeological Museum, Athens. (© C.M. Dixon/Heritage Images)

26. The carving on this 3rd-century AD Roman sarcophagus could have been inspired by the painting in the Painted Stoa in Athens, as described by Pausanias in his 2nd-century AD *Guide to Greece*. Intriguingly, cavalry appears in the background. (Mary Evans/Iberfoto)

27. The *Soros* is still an imposing presence against the backdrop of the encircling mountains. Originally over 12 metres in height, and surrounded by fewer trees, it would have been even more imposing. Cimon, son of Miltiades, had it constructed 20–30 years after the battle to support his nationalistic political agenda.

29. The Hellespont around the point bridged by the Persians in 480.

28. This helmet was allegedly excavated with the skull inside by George, 2nd Baron Nugent of Carlanstown, at Marathon in 1834 (coincidentally the year John Varley painted the scene). The Baron also 'excavated' helmets at Thermopylae and Plataea. Royal Ontario Museum, Toronto.

30. The Hellenes thought Xerxes had offended Poseidon by presuming to 'yoke' the Hellespont with his bridges of boats and by punishing the sea for breaking his bridges. The storms that damaged his invasion fleet were seen as retribution. Late 6th-century 'austere-style' bronze, National Archaeological Museum, Athens.

31. This 2nd-century AD portrait of Themistocles is thought to be copied from a Greek original. It is so full of natural individuality and character, even in the copy, that it is hard to believe that the original was not sculpted from life. Ostia Museum, Rome.

32. A section of the beaches on the north shore of Euboea occupied by the Hellene fleet in defence of the Thermopylae–Artemisium line. The mountains to the west which temporarily blocked the Barbarians' advance can be seen through the distant haze.

commanders brought them to shore near the fort and beached them to dry out,[1] and meanwhile Xerxes counted his troops. I cannot tell you precisely how many men there were in each unit. Nobody has recorded that information, but, evidently, the infantry totalled 1,700,000. This is how they were counted: 10,000 men were marshalled into one place and packed together as closely as possible. A circle was drawn around them and the men were dismissed. A drystone wall was built to about waist height following the perimeter that had been drawn. Then the rest of the troops were marched through this enclosure until the whole army had been counted.[2] When the counters had counted them, they were formed up again into their national units. (7.59–60)

Doriscus was an important staging post. Supplies had been stockpiled there and much of the fleet may have been waiting for some time while the army took its dog-leg route from the Hellespont, drying out hulls and carrying out general maintenance. But when the army had arrived it is unlikely that time was spent counting the troops. The process Herodotus describes would have been very laborious and time consuming. Indeed, it provoked the commentator Reginald Walter Macan to exclaim in one of his occasional acerbic outbursts that 'the historian or critic who maintains the literal credibility of this Herodotean absurdity is past praying for!'. Herodotus' source (whom he probably did not believe) may simply have been fantasizing, or had actually observed a process faintly resembling this, perhaps setting out the perimeter for a camp or marshalling much smaller numbers of prisoners of war, and made a leap of imagination. The descriptions of Xerxes counting and, elsewhere, reviewing, interviewing and inspecting his troops build a nice image of a controlling autocrat. But the counting process, as described, would have been unnecessary; unit commanders with sufficiently accurate knowledge of the numbers of men under them could have passed their figures up the chain of command for aggregation by the King's scribes to produce a total, if a count was called for. While not exact, this would

---

[1] This could involve not only emptying the bilges but attending to leaks, recaulking seams, scraping off marine growths and applying a fresh coat of pitch. Time out of the water also allowed soaked timbers to dry, lightening the hull. Newly built or recently dried-out triremes performed significantly better than comparable ships that had been at sea for long periods.
[2] After repeating the process 170 times.

have been precise enough for planning and logistical purposes, and to satisfy general curiosity.

Herodotus revisits the question of the total size of Xerxes' invasion force later in Book 7. The initial total of 1,700,000 infantry turns out to have been just a starting point for the land force:

> There were the 1,207 ships from Asia, and the native crews from the different nations totalled 241,400 men, assuming 200 for each crew. However, in addition to the native crews, each ship had on board 30 extra fighting men, Persians, Medes or Sacae, amounting to an additional 36,210. To these two numbers I have to add the crews of the penteconters, assuming an average of 80 on each. As previously stated,[1] the fleet included 3,000 vessels of this type so that would have made another 240,000. The ships' companies from Asia therefore totalled 517,610. Then there were the 1,700,000 infantry and 80,000 cavalry, and I have to add the camel-troops from Arabia and the charioteers from Libya, reckoning that there were 20,000 of them, and so the grand total of the naval and land forces combined was actually 2,317,610. However, this is so far just a tally of the expeditionary force which was launched out of Asia, not counting the train of camp followers and the crews of the transport ships.[2] I also need to add to it the manpower gathered in Europe and here I can offer no more than my best estimate. The Hellenes of Thrace and the islands off its shores supplied 120 ships with 24,000 men on board.[3] In the land force, the European contingents totalled 300,000 by my reckoning,[4] including Thracians, Paionians, Chalcidicians, Brygoi, Macedonians, Magnesians and Achaeans who lived in those parts. With these added to the number from Asia, the absolute total of fighting men comes to 2,642,610. So that was how many combatants there were.

And then there were the camp followers and the crews of the transport ships and, of course, the other vessels sailing with them, and

---

[1] He actually wrote, 'The total number of triaconters [30-oared], penteconters [50-oared], lighter vessels and horse-transports came to 3,000' (7.97). The average crew would have been somewhat less than 80, Herodotus' figure for a penteconter.

[2] Specifically 'grain-bearing'. These would have had much smaller crews, being predominantly sail-powered.

[3] Their deck crews were evidently not strengthened by the addition of 30 Barbarian troops.

[4] Reckoned to be a massive over-estimate.

they would have been, in my belief, not fewer but more numerous than the combatants.[1] However, let us say they were equal in number, neither more nor fewer: if they were equal to the combatant element, there were as many myriads of them. Therefore, Xerxes son of Darius led a total of 5,283, 220 men to Cape Sepias headland and Thermopylae.

So that was the grand total of Xerxes' invasion force. But then again, who can say exactly how many cooks, concubines and eunuchs there were, or give a number for the draught animals, beasts of burden and Indian dogs that travelled with them? This was indeed a multitude that no man could number and so it does not surprise me at all that rivers ran dry. However, it does surprise me that there was enough food for so many myriads, for, by my reckoning, if each man received a ration of one *choenix* of wheat a day, and no more, 110,340 *medimni* would be required every day to feed them,[2] and in this calculation I am not including women, eunuchs or draught animals, or dogs ... Anyway, amongst all those myriads of men there was none worthier by reason of his fine looks or impressive stature than Xerxes himself to hold such a command. (7.184–87)

If there is an impression that Herodotus believes in the numbers he initially presents, this is steadily diluted by his progressive inflation of them, uncritical as it seems. Uncritical until he arrives at the Indian dogs and the big 'However ...' That comes a couple of sentences later; and there is the bogus precision of numbers like 517,610. Through his sources Herodotus may have had access to some official figures, and the 1,207 for Xerxes' triremes is a credible number for the entire front-line capital-ship strength of the empire at that time. Aeschylus gives the same number in the *Persae*. Documented figures for the empire's full potential military strength may also lie at the base of his calculation of the size of the land force, and it must have seemed fully appropriate

---

[1] Herodotus tells us later that each hoplite in the Hellene army was accompanied by an attendant and may be assuming this was the case throughout Xerxes' army. It is very unlikely to have been so beyond the elite royal guard.

[2] One *choenix* was a little over a litre and there were 48 of them in a *medimnos* so Herodotus' arithmetic is not quite correct. But he is close enough to the total, which equates to approximately 4,300 tonnes per day.

for Xerxes to take his entire army and navy with him to Greece (regardless of practicality and the needs of the rest of the empire). Besides, the tradition of tens of thousands of Hellenes heroically resisting myriad upon myriad of Barbarians was sacred and it was Herodotus' duty to celebrate this, not to challenge it openly. However, his reflection on the impossible amount of basic food that such a vast force would require to sustain it is as convincing as Hans Delbrück's application of *Sachkritik* to show that, if Xerxes' army had been that vast, the tail of the column of marching millions would have been just about leaving Sardis as its head arrived at Thermopylae. Herodotus' calculation, which significantly excludes fodder for horses and pack animals, gives a daily rate of consumption that would have been about 50 times that of the entire population of Athens. More strikingly, it has been calculated that in years of good harvest the granaries of the Mediterranean, Corsica and Sicily, could feed a mere 250,000 in a year. The Persians had imperial access to the fields of Egypt and North Africa and unparalleled buying power beyond their empire's frontiers, but even with a succession of surpluses everywhere from bumper harvests in the years of preparation, there could surely not have been enough grain available for stockpiling to feed such a monster, even if there was the logistical capability to move that tonnage to where it was needed as the campaign progressed. Herodotus' accounts of the battles fought in 480 and 479 place the manpower issue in a less theoretical context. Best estimates of the combatant strength of Xerxes' land force seem to point to a figure somewhere between 100,000 and 200,000 and a proportion of this total was most likely strung out to the rear protecting lines of communication and supply, and policing recently surrendered territory.

After the army had been counted and drawn up into its units, it was Xerxes' wish to ride through it and review it. And this he did, and as he rode in a chariot past each national contingent, he asked questions while his scribes took notes, until he had been driven the whole length of the line of cavalry and infantry. After this, the ships were hauled down to the sea and launched. Xerxes stepped down from his chariot and, now seated on a Sidonian trireme under a golden canopy, was rowed along the line of ships' prows, asking questions as he did with the army and having the answers written down.

The captains had taken their ships out about 120m from the shore and held them there in line with their prows towards the land and their marines armed and battle-ready. (7.100)

Doriscus, with the campaign now fully under way on European soil, was neither the place nor the time for this ceremonial review of land forces and fleet and it would have been a massive and lengthy exercise if the heroic tradition's vast numbers had actually been present. This colourful vignette comes immediately after a long section (7.61–99) listing and briefly describing all the national contingents in the army and fleet and naming their commanders. It reads like a glorious pageant with the army led by the Persians and Medes and featuring 43 other Asian nations of the Great King's empire. It is an exotic catalogue of costume and arms and armour, for example: 'helmets made of plaited bronze to some Barbarian design' worn by the Assyrians; the 'bright clothing and knee-high boots' of the Sarangae; 'Ethiopians dressed in the skins of leopards and lions, half their bodies painted with chalk and half with ochre before going into battle'; 'bronze helmets decorated with ox's ears and horns, also made of bronze, and a crest' worn by a tribe whose name is lost, but probably from the Black Sea area; the 'wooden helmets' of the Moschians and Colchians; the 'leather helmets' of the Milyans; and all manner of shields, spears, swords, daggers, axes and bows and arrows. However, just 12 of these contingents, including the Persians and Medes, appear again in the narrative of the land war and some of these get only the briefest of mentions. The listing is well organized geographically, suggesting that Herodotus had direct or indirect access to some kind of formal document, but no numbers are attached to any of the units. His navy-list (7.89–95), on the other hand, breaks the 1,207 triremes down into 12 national contingents ranging from 300 Phoenicians to 17 'islanders', the latter probably Hellenes from the Cyclades, who actually joined the fleet after the battle of Artemisium. Eight out of the 12 contingents named here also feature in one or both of the sea-battles of 480.

After his survey of the Barbarian invasion force, Herodotus focuses once more on the fighting qualities of their Hellene opponents:

Back on shore after he had reviewed the fleet, Xerxes sent for Demaratus son of Ariston, summoned him into his presence and said, 'Now, there is a question I would very much like to ask you. You are a Hellene and, so you yourself and other Hellenes I have spoken with tell me, come from a city which is certainly neither weak nor insignificant.[1] Now, tell me this: will the Hellenes stand and lift a hand against me? Speaking for myself, I think not, not even if all the Hellene people including those who live in the lands to the west join forces. They would be no match for me if they faced me in battle and, anyway, they are not united.[2] However, I wish to know your opinion of them.'

Demaratus' first response was to ask the King if he wanted a true answer or one that would be pleasing to him. Xerxes commanded him to speak the truth, assuring him that he would not lose favour by doing so. On hearing this Demaratus said, 'Great King, since you have commanded me to speak the whole truth, and not to say anything that you might later find out to be false, I will say this: in Hellas poverty has always come naturally, but *arete*[3] is nurtured, wrought out of wisdom and the strength of *nomos*.[4] This quality is Hellas' protection against despotism and the effects of poverty. I am referring here to all of the Hellenes who live on Dorian land.[5] However, I am not going to tell you about all of these people but will speak of the Lacedaemonians only. First, it is inconceivable that the Lacedaemonians will agree to any terms you might offer that would result in the enslavement of Hellas. Secondly, the Lacedaemonians will take you on in battle even if all the rest of the Hellenes submit to you. As to numbers, don't ask me how many men might stand against you. If 1,000 Lacedaemonians take the field, and there may be more, there may be fewer, they will fight.'

Xerxes laughed and replied, 'What a thing to say! If they were under the rule of one man, which is the Persian way, they would

[1] Sparta.

[2] Herodotus may be ironically suggesting some recognition on Xerxes' part that a fully united Hellas might be capable of mounting a successful defence.

[3] *Arete* used here in the sense of the quality of valour displayed by men judged to be 'bravest and best'. 'Valour', as celebrated in the inscription on the Victoria Cross, is perhaps the best one-word translation.

[4] *Nomos*: the broad sense of the word is 'law' in the statutory sense but it also embraces 'code' and 'custom', 'obligation' and 'duty'.

[5] The Peloponnese for the most part, thus excluding the 'Ionian' Athenians, amongst others. Halicarnassus, Herodotus' city of birth, was founded by Dorian settlers from Troezen in the Peloponnese, although it had become more Asian in character by the 5th century.

try their best for fear of that man. Driven by the lash they might fight on, though outnumbered, but given this freedom, I say that your Spartans would not do either of these things. How could 1,000, 10,000 or even 50,000 men stand up to an army as great as mine, if they are all equally free rather than under the rule of one man? If there were 5,000, say, we would outnumber them by 1,000 to one. It is true that under a single ruler, which is our way, their fear of him might make them better men than they are by nature, and under the lash they might be driven to attack a force stronger than their own. But if they were allowed freedom, neither of these things would happen. You are showing your ignorance by talking complete nonsense.'

Demaratus answered, 'Great King, I knew from the start that you would not be pleased to hear the truth, but you insisted on the absolute truth so I am telling you what it is to be a Spartan. In single combat Lacedaemonians are as good as any man, but fighting as a unit they are the best on earth. They are free men, though not free in all respects. *Nomos* is their ruler and they are in much greater awe of this than your men are in awe of you. They do what custom demands and one thing it always dictates is never to run away in battle, whatever the odds, but to keep one's place in the battle line and win victory or die. If you think this is nonsense I am talking, there is nothing else I am prepared to say. I spoke out because you compelled me to. Nevertheless, I wish you good fortune with your enterprise, Great King.' This was his response, and Xerxes was amused by it and not at all annoyed, but graciously dismissed Demaratus from his presence. (7.101–05)

Demaratus, one of Sparta's two joint kings until unjustly deposed in 491, had since then, surprising as it may seem, been living in exile as an honoured guest-friend at the Persian court. Like Hippias on Datis' Marathon expedition, he accompanied Xerxes as an adviser and there may have been plans for him to rule again in Sparta under the Persians once Greece was conquered. Herodotus does not seem to consider him a traitor, indeed Book 7 concludes rather abruptly with an anecdote of a secret message that he sent from Susa to Sparta, which ensured that 'the Lacedaemonians were the first to know that the Great King was making preparations to invade Greece' (7.239);

this recalls Histiaeus' communication with Aristagoras, stirring up the Ionian Revolt, but Demaratus' text was hidden under the wax of a blank writing tablet rather than tattooed onto a slave's scalp. Herodotus uses invented conversations between Demaratus and Xerxes to comment pointedly and effectively on the main narrative at more than one point. Here, he contrasts Hellene and Barbarian values, anticipating the heroic but doomed defence of Thermopylae and the ultimate Hellene victory at Plataea.

The inscribed text of the 'Oath of Plataea' is preceded by a version of the 'Oath of the Ephebes', a fuller Athenian expression of what most Hellenes would have recognized as *nomos*. This is thought to be an authentic text dating from 340–330 when the inscription was carved. In Athens, ephebes were citizens aged 18–19, making them eligible to take on civic and military duties. The formalities of this transition are well documented for the mid 4th century, including, for example, a period of military conscription. It is thought to have been more of a symbolic rite of passage at the time of the Persian War but there would have been some form of ceremony and an oath would have been sworn similar to the one inscribed at Acharnae:

> I will not disgrace the hallowed arms and armour we bear
> nor abandon my comrade in the battle line,
> wherever I am placed in it.
> I will stand my ground and fight for what we value,
> As ordained by god or man.
> I will not leave our fatherland diminished
> but, as far as I myself am able and with the help of all,
> I will hand it on greater and better.
> And I will be obedient
> to whoever is exercising command,
> so long as it is with good sense,
> and will be obedient to whatever ordinances are in effect
> or set out with the same good sense in the future.
> But if anyone overturns these, I shall resist him
> as far as I myself am able and with the help of all,
> And I will always honour our sacred ancestral customs.
> (*Oath of the Ephebes*)

The unique military code of Sparta had deep roots in the nation's 7th-century war with neighbouring Messenia and was celebrated at the time in the treasured poetry of Tyrtaeus:

No man proves himself to be a good man in war
Unless he can endure the sight of bloody slaughter,
And step up close to reach out and slay.
This is *arete*, prized above all things by humankind,
The fairest trophy that any young man can win.
And it is a noble thing for the common good of city and people
That a man will go forward and stand his ground in the front rank,
Giving no thought to craven flight.
He has learned endurance and steadfastness of heart
And his words inspire the comrade beside him in the line.
Here is a man who proves himself to be valiant in war.
(*Fragments* 12 10–20)

Three centuries on, Aristotle's *Nicomachean Ethics* expands on the idea of fighting both for personal honour and for the common good as the philosopher reflects on the qualities of the ideal citizen:

The good[1] citizen does much for the sake of his friends and his people, and he will lay down his life for them if need be. He will disregard wealth or high office, all those benefits that men strive for, in order to secure his own honour. He prefers to enjoy one hour of intense satisfaction to a long period of routine, a single year lived well to many years of drifting, and one great and glorious achievement to many small ones. This is how it is with those who lay down their lives for others, and so they win glory for themselves. (*Nicomachean Ethics* 1169)

Reaching back generations before Tyrtaeus, for Homer's heroes the motivation was more straightforwardly personal, as expressed by this character Odysseus has invented for himself:

I got myself a wife from a family of great property,
Winning her by reason of my *arete*,

---

[1] Aristotle's word here is *spoudaios*, which also has connotations of keenness and commitment.

For I was not a braggart who shrank from war ...
Ares and Athena gave me courage
And the might to break the battle line.[1]
When I picked the best men to join my band
Sowing seeds of evil for the enemy,
Thoughts of death never troubled my proud spirit.
I was always first to leap out with my spear
And slay the foemen taking to their heels before me.
I was such a man in war. Labour was never to my liking,
Nor home-life and the rearing of fine children.
Oared ships were precious to me,
And wars and smooth-shafted spears and arrows,
Causes of shuddering grief for other folk,
But not for me. This is my god-given passion,
For different men take delight in different pursuits.
Even before the sons of the Achaeans set foot on Trojan soil,
Nine times I commanded warriors and swift-sailing ships
In wars in foreign lands and won great spoils.
From all of this I picked what pleased me most
And won much more when lots were drawn for it.
So my family prospered,
And I was held in awe and respect amongst the Cretans.
(*Odyssey* 17.210–34)

Herodotus' narrative continues:

On his way towards Greece from Doriscus, Xerxes drafted every nation he encountered into his army; as I have already explained, the whole region as far as Thessaly had been made subject by the conquests of Megabazus and Mardonius after him and paid tribute to the Great King[2]... For the stage from Doriscus to Acanthus, Xerxes divided the land force into three columns. He ordered one

---

[1] In the *Iliad* Achilles is described as 'breaker of battle lines'.

[2] Megabazus stayed in Europe to take control of the Chersonese after the abandonment of Darius' Scythian expedition; Mardonius subdued the Thracian Brygoi after the disastrous end to his attempted invasion of Greece in 492. It was perhaps an exaggeration to credit them with conquering the whole region.

to march along the coast, keeping pace with the fleet. Mardonius and Masistes were in command of this division. A second division was ordered to take an inland route under the command of Tritantaechmes and Gergis. The third, in which Xerxes himself travelled, marched between the two, and its generals were Smerdomenes and Megabyzus. (7.108, 121)

It is unlikely that the Persians had a very tight grip on this region by 480, if they ever did, and the formation described was suited to an advance through potentially hostile territory. The centre column probably included the baggage train as well as the Great King and his entourage. The division that took the inland route screened them against attack from mountain tribes like the Satraians, 'who had never become anyone's subject' (7.110). The fleet screened the advancing army from any seaborne interference, and the column that followed the coast, tracking the fleet, could be there to support it, securing the beaches that the fleet would be fighting off, if attacked. Herodotus has previously introduced the six divisional generals as jointly commanding the whole land force. Mardonius is, after Xerxes, the most prominent Persian figure in Herodotus' narrative of the campaign. Masistes is mentioned once more for his involvement in the battle of Mycale. Soon afterwards he dies at Persian hands, one of the casualties of a sordid affair in which Xerxes attempted to seduce his wife. The other four do not feature in the accounts of any of the battles that are to come, but, 25 years later, Megabyzus was to destroy a large Athenian force that had been sent to Egypt to support a revolt against Persian rule under Xerxes' successor, Artaxerxes. Mardonius, Tritantaechmes and Smerdomenes were cousins of Xerxes; Masistes was his brother.

Herodotus names many of the places the army would have passed through or by, but it is impossible to work out what the separate routes taken by the two inland columns actually were and they probably converged at some points. At least one river and one lake were, allegedly, drunk dry. Herodotus tells of the suffering of Xerxes' 'hosts' along the way as they met his massive demands for food and accommodation. The advancing troops would also have lived off the land ruthlessly, and their organization into separated columns would have spread the impact over a very wide area. The River Strymon and possibly others were crossed by bridges built in advance. The troops conscripted on the way, and ships and their crews collected by the fleet, were taken along as hostages as much as to swell the ranks.

When they had reached Acanthus, fleet and army separated for the next stage, which was to take them to Therme. The army marched overland across the base of the Chalcidice peninsula by as direct a route as possible whilst the fleet passed through the canal at Athos, rounded the central and western prongs and sailed up the gulf to Therme to wait for the land force. Additional troops and ships were conscripted from many of the Hellene cities they passed. Herodotus adds little to the detailed itinerary he gives for both elements of the invasion force but is intrigued by reports of attacks on the baggage trains by lions of the African variety, which are known to have inhabited this part of Europe in the 5th century; 'they killed camels only and did not touch any other baggage animals or humans' (7.125). In a longer digression (7.128–30) he describes a cruise taken by Xerxes from Therme with the whole fleet in attendance to admire the dramatic scenery around the mouth of the Peneus and speculate on the possibility of flooding the lowlands of Thessaly by building a dam. This unlikely story may have grown out of sightings of a Persian reconnaissance of the strong defensive position the Hellenes might still have been planning to occupy, though there is no reason to doubt that the Great King enjoyed the views of Mounts Olympus and Ossa and the Vale of Tempe as he journeyed south. The Persians probably did not consider flooding Thessaly at any point, but this might have been imagined by Thessalians or Macedonians, awe-struck by Barbarian feats of engineering, and so entered the mythology of the war. Herodotus includes an impressive observation on the physical geography of the area and its formation by earthquakes:

> The Thessalians say Poseidon formed the channel through which the Peneus flows. And this is a reasonable explanation for those who believe that Poseidon is the Earthshaker and that the rifts made by earthquakes are the works of his hand, so they would recognize that this one was created by him. For it seems to me that it is the force of earthquakes that splits mountains. (7.129)

Herodotus moves Xerxes quickly on from Therme to the Macedonian coastal territory of Pieria:

Xerxes spent several days in Pieria whilst one of the three divisions cleared a route over the mountains of Macedonia for the whole army to take into the country of the Perrhaebians.[1] It was then that the heralds who had been sent through Greece to demand earth and water returned, some empty-handed, some bearing it. The peoples who gave earth and water included the Thessalians, the Dolopes, the Enienes, the Perrhaebians, the Locrians,[2] the Magnesians, the Melians, the Achaeans of Phthiotis, the Thebans, and all the Boeotians except for the Thespians and the Plataeans. (7.131–32)

It is likely that a smaller unit than one of the three divisions described earlier did the pioneering work and that the army marched into Thessaly by more than one of the available routes. The medizers, selectively named, span northern and central Greece from the Macedonian border to the mountains on the northern edge of Attica. The inclusion of Thebes in the list may be evidence of an ambivalent view of this ritual of submission, shared by some other Hellene cities; Thebes was to send a contingent to Thermopylae. Herodotus' timing of these submissions is dramatically effective, but they must have been spread out over a longer period of time. He has little else to say about the army's progress through the northern half of Greece apart from later mentioning one interlude in it:

> While in Thessaly, the Great King organized horseraces between his own cavalry and the Thessalians', having heard that their horses were the fastest in Greece. The Hellene horses were well beaten. (7.196)

Like the ship races at Abydos, these horseraces were probably not staged purely for Xerxes' entertainment, but had practical value for training purposes. Alos on the Gulf of Pagasae is the next stopping place named by Herodotus; here, as all along the way, guides give the King all the information they can about the area, and he shows respect for a

---

[1] This was one of the northernmost regions of Thessaly. The Persians had entered Greece.
[2] The Locrians occupied two regions. The Opuntian (and Epicnemidian) Locrians occupied the coastal strip running south from Thermopylae, the Ozolian Locrians an area on the north shore of the Corinthian Gulf to the west of Delphi. Herodotus later tells us there were Locrians on the Hellene side at Artemisium and Thermopylae, but on the Barbarian side at Plataea.

local sanctuary. Elements of the fleet and army had most likely secured Alos ahead of the King's arrival there.

Leaving his narrative of the Barbarians' march into Greece, Herodotus brings the heroes of Marathon back to centre stage. His wary introduction of the topic reflects the fact that at the time of writing about half the Hellene world was hostile to Athens or had even fallen victim to the might of the Athenian Empire:

> The declared purpose of the Great King's expedition was to mount an attack on Athens but, in fact, the whole of Greece was his objective. The Hellenes had known about this for a long time, but the knowledge did not affect them all in the same way. Those who had submitted earth and water to the Persians were confident that they would suffer no harm at the hands of the Barbarians. But those who had not submitted were very afraid, since there were not enough ships in Hellas capable of taking on the invader; indeed, most of them had no wish to get involved in the war and were now enthusiastically medizing.
>
> Now, at this point, I feel I must express an opinion which a majority may find offensive. However, since it is what I consider to be the truth, I shall not keep it to myself. If the Athenians had abandoned their country for fear of the approaching danger, or if they had not abandoned it but remained and submitted to Xerxes, there would have been no attempt to resist the Great King at sea, and with no resistance at sea I will tell you what would have happened on land. Even if the Peloponnesians had curtained the Isthmus with many walls,[1] the Lacedaemonians would have been deserted by their allies, forced into submission against their will as their cities were picked off one by one by the Persian fleet. The Spartans would finally have been isolated and, standing alone, would have done great deeds and died splendid deaths. Or, seeing the rest of Greece going over to the Persians, they would have come to an agreement with Xerxes.[2] Either way, Hellas would have come under Persian rule. I cannot see that the fortification of the Isthmus would have served any useful

---

[1] Literally, and vividly, 'if many tunics (*chitones*) of walls had been thrown across ...'.
[2] The Spartans were known to be seeking Persian support in the Peloponnesian War during Herodotus' lifetime, and the Athenians were doing the same.

purpose if the Great King had control of the sea. Anyone who says that the Athenians were the saviours of Hellas, then, is absolutely right. The Athenians were going to tip the balance, whichever choice they made, and their choice was that Hellas should remain free. It was the Athenians who fired up the Hellenes who had not yet medized. It was the Athenians, after the gods, who beat back the Great King.

Alarming prophecies had come out of Delphi that frightened the Athenians, but rather than desert Hellas, they stood fast and faced up to the invader of their land. They had sent special ambassadors[1] to Delphi and when they were ready to consult the prophet and had performed the usual rites, they entered the inner chamber and took up their positions as suppliants. The Pythia, whose name was Aristonice, delivered this oracle:

'Why are you here, poor wretches?
Fly to the ends of the earth.
Leave your homes; leave your city,
Its high citadel and its circling walls.
Neither head nor body
Nor feet nor hands will stand fast.
Nothing will remain, only disaster.
Fire and fierce Ares[2] driving a Syrian chariot
Will wreck your city, and other strongholds too.
Fierce flames will devour your holy temples.
Even now they stream with sweat
They quake with fear;
Dark blood runs from the roof tiles.
They foresee calamity inescapable.
Go, therefore, leave! Face your doom with courage.'

When the Athenian delegates heard this prophecy of doom, they were plunged into despair and gave up all hope. But then Timon son of Androbulus, one of the foremost Delphians, advised them to take olive branches and approach the oracle a second time as suppliants. The Athenians took this advice and said, 'Pythian master, give us

[1] *Theopropoi*: these seem to have been public servants who were sent to consult oracles and carry out other priestly functions, at the Olympic Games for example, on behalf of the city.
[2] The god of war.

a better prophecy concerning our fatherland's fate and look kindly upon the suppliant boughs which we have brought before you. Otherwise we will not leave your sanctuary, but stay here till we die.' The priestess responded with this second oracle:

'Pallas Athene cannot sway the will of Zeus
With words of prayer or clever argument.
But a second answer I will give you, firm as adamant.
All of the land held within Cecrops' borders[1]
And embraced by the slopes of holy Cithaeron
Shall be seized by the enemy.
But, Trito-born[2] one, far-seeing Zeus grants you this:
Only a wooden wall will keep you safe,
A safe keep for you and your children.
Do not wait for this mighty army coming overland,
Nor stand in the way of its horsemen and footsoldiers.
Retreat, turn your backs! Yet you will meet in battle –
Salamis divine, you will be the death of mothers' sons
At the time of Demeter's scattering or her gathering.'[3]

This response gave them more comfort than the previous one, and rightly so. The ambassadors wrote it out and left for Athens and, on their return, gave their report to the Assembly. Various interpretations of the prophecy were offered, but two of them were distinctly different. Some of the older men were of the opinion that the god was giving assurance that the Acropolis would survive. Their argument was that the Athenians of old had fortified it with a stockade[4] and that 'wooden wall' referred to this. But others said the god was talking

---

[1] Meaning Athens and Attica. Cecrops was a mythical king of Athens and an important figure in the story of the city's origins.

[2] One of the names given to the goddess Athene and an obscure reference to her mythical birth.

[3] Demeter and the cultivation of grain were closely associated. The oracle may mean that the deaths would take place earlier or later in the year, at seed-time or harvest; or it may be, more accurately, an allusion to the annual festival at the shrine of Demeter in Eleusis with which the battle of Salamis would have coincided, if the festival was held in 480. These last two lines may be too good to be true and have been added after the event to boost Delphi's reputation.

[4] The word used here (*rekos*) may also be translated as 'thorn hedge', which would have been of some use defensively, until set on fire.

about their ships and they insisted on dropping everything else to concentrate on fitting them out in readiness. But those who argued that ships would be their wooden wall could not make sense of the final two lines of The Pythia's utterance:

'Salamis divine, you will be the death of mothers' sons
At the time of Demeter's scattering or her gathering.'

These words seemed to contradict their claim that ships would be their wooden wall. Indeed, the oracle-readers[1] took them to mean that preparations to give battle off Salamis would lead to certain defeat. (7.138–42)

Oracles were written down and many Athenians would have witnessed the debate about the meaning of the characteristically riddling words, so Herodotus' evidence would seem to be at its most solid here. Neither response countenances surrender but the first foretells the destruction of Athens and the Acropolis and favours evacuation, while the second offers a case for resistance in some form. Both show awareness of the options the Athenians were wrestling with and the second may be the result of some priming by interested parties, Athenian or elsewhere in the Hellene Alliance. The delegation was probably sent to Delphi rather earlier than Herodotus' chronology suggests, but this suits his dramatic purpose, as does the timing of his introduction of a very important new character to his cast of leading players.

There was a certain Athenian who had recently taken his place amongst the most prominent citizens. His name was Themistocles son of Neocles. This man declared that the oracle-readers' interpretation was incorrect, arguing that if it was the case that those lines referred to the Athenians, the language would have been harsher, for example 'merciless Salamis' rather than 'Salamis divine', if it was the people who lived thereabouts who were to perish. The correct interpretation was that the god's message was not directed at the Athenians but at their enemies, and Themistocles proposed that they make

---

[1] *Chresmologoi*: these interpreters of oracles were specialists similar to the *theopropoi*, but freelance rather than public servants, and sometimes held up as charlatans. On this occasion they may have been in the pocket of the faction that was opposed to resistance.

preparations to fight at sea, trusting in their ships as their wooden wall. The Athenians thought Themistocles was giving them better advice than the oracle-readers. They were against preparing for war at sea and, in fact, against putting up any resistance whatsoever, instead favouring the abandonment of Attica and migration to some other country.

On a previous occasion Themistocles' judgment had prevailed at a critical moment. This was when the treasury had received substantially increased revenue from the silver mines at Laurium and the intention had been to distribute a share to all the citizens of Athens, each of them to receive ten drachmas. Themistocles persuaded the Athenians not to go ahead with this but instead to use the money to build 200 ships for the war, by which he meant the war with Aegina. Engagement in that war was the salvation of Hellas because it compelled the Athenians to become seamen.[1] Those ships were not actually used for the purpose for which they were built, but they were there in Hellas' hour of need and the Athenians had them constructed and ready, though it was necessary to build more as well. So, after debating the oracle's message, the Athenians decided to meet the Barbarian invaders of Greece in their ships with every man they could muster[2] and alongside all the Hellenes who were willing to join them. (7.143–44)

Themistocles had actually risen to high office in the 490s and held the elected position of archon for 493/2, when he had begun to lay out Athens' naval strategy and initiated the creation of the fortified naval base at Piraeus that was to be essential to it. Herodotus' low-key introduction is in tune with the ambivalence he or his sources display towards the man's character from time to time. In the eyes of more conservative politicians, Themistocles was a dangerous radical who had allowed the lower citizen classes, empowered by their vital service as oarsmen, to gain too much political influence. His father seems to have been wealthy, and perhaps involved in silver mining, but not to have been a man of influence politically. However, his name

---

[1] In Thucydides' approving words, Themistocles had already persuaded the Athenians 'to make the sea their own'.
[2] *Pandemei*, full mobilization of 'all the people', not limited to citizens.

(*neo-cles*, 'new-fame') suggests his family had achieved some degree of prominence. Themistocles' mother was not Athenian, but possibly Thracian, so Themistocles' climb to reach the top of the political tree when he was just into his 30s was a remarkable achievement. Herodotus and later writers portray a great leader and strategist who was a consummate political operator, gifted in rhetoric and repartee, and skilled in diplomacy, patronage and the manipulation of public opinion. But his reputation had also suffered decades of blackening by the time Herodotus had come to write about him. Moreover, seen through the lens of the Peloponnesian War, for which Athens now carried the blame, it was undiplomatic to speak too well of the city and her empire. But Herodotus goes on to show clearly that Themistocles was the architect of Athenian sea-power which was at the heart of the Hellenes' winning strategy in 480. Themistocles almost certainly fought at Marathon and probably as one of the ten generals. He was certainly elected to that important position in 480 and most likely held it in earlier years, a period of energetic political activity in which he saw off a series of better-connected rivals from the aristocratic and conservative end of the political spectrum, and from the significant faction that still favoured appeasement with the Great King. He would have learned about naval tactics and trireme design serving as a commander against the Aeginetans. The extraordinary strategic and tactical vision, and political and leadership skills that he displayed in the year of Salamis were forged over the 20–30 years during which he clambered from his fairly obscure origins to become, in effect if not in name, wartime commander-in-chief at one of the most critical moments in the history of the western world.

The citizen body of Athens totalled about 30,000 in the 480s so the sum to be distributed, probably an exceptional surplus in the year's mining revenues, would have been in the region of 50 talents, enough to fund the building of approximately 50 triremes. Another 80–100 were required to bring the fleet up to its strength of 200 at Salamis, to be funded out of reserves and regular income. 'The 'fountain of silver' that boosted the city's fortunes has been dated to 483 so the shipbuilding programme was highly intensive. It is likely that the construction work was done not only at Piraeus and Phalerum but also shared by boatbuilders around the rest of the coastline of Attica, and also on Salamis. Northern Greece, Macedonia and Thrace were the main source of fir, and it is probable that the Athenians had to use heavier pine extensively as supply became restricted under increasing Persian dominance of those regions. Timber supplies from the highlands of central Greece and Euboea could also have been augmented by imports from Sicily and southern Italy.

Details of the implementation of the strategy developed and proposed by Themistocles are preserved in an inscription similar in character to the Oath of Plataea, known as 'the Decree of Themistocles'. Set up in Troezen somewhat later than the former, it was probably a similar response to the conflict between Macedon and Athens that had continued into the 3rd century. Its purpose was to inspire citizens by celebrating Troezen's contribution on land and sea to the historic victory over the Persians. Troezen also provided generous accommodation for women and children evacuated from Athens and Attica. The inscription is more likely a compilation of a number of decrees enacted over the weeks and months leading up to the battles of Artemisium and Salamis than a transcription of a single decree enacted in a single day.

Pausanias on his travels describes what was most likely to have been the site of the inscription:

> Under a portico in the market-place there are stone statues of women and their children. These are the women and children the Athenians entrusted to the protection of the Troezenians when they took the decision to evacuate their city rather than to stay there to be attacked by the Persians on land. I was told that the Troezenians did not set up portraits of all of the women (indeed there are not that many statues) but only of those who were foremost socially. (*Guide to Greece* 2.31.7)

The resolutions would not have been recorded on stone at the time and it is questionable whether any transcripts that existed, which would have been on wooden tablets or parchment, survived the occupation and widespread destruction of Athens in 480 and 479. But, as with the Oath of Plataea, a lot of the wording and even more of its spirit would have been well preserved in the folk memory of the war.

Gods![1]

Resolved by the Council and the People[2]

as proposed by Themistocles son of Neocles of Phrearrhoi.[3]

The city shall be entrusted to Athena, Protector of Athens, and to all the other gods for its safe-keeping and for the protection of the land against the Barbarian.

The citizens of Athens and the non-citizens who are resident in Athens shall send their children and their women to Troezen, under the protection of Theseus the founding father of that land.[4] The elderly and all property of value shall be transported to Salamis. The guardians of the sacred treasures and the priestesses shall remain on the Acropolis and guard what belongs to the gods.

All the rest of the Athenians and non-citizens who are of age shall go on board the 200 ships that stand ready and shall drive off the Barbarian to preserve their own liberty and the liberty of all Hellenes, fighting alongside the Lacedaemonians, the Corinthians and the Aeginetans,[5] and any others willing to be a part of this enterprise.

The generals, starting from tomorrow, shall appoint 200 trireme commanders, one for each ship, selected from citizens up to the age of 50 with family property in Athens and legitimate children. Lots will be drawn to allocate their ships to them. The generals shall also enlist ten marines between the ages of 20 and 30, and four archers for each ship.[6] They shall allocate the crewmen to each ship at the same time as drawing lots for their captains. The generals shall post up the full ship's companies on the public notice boards, selecting Athenians from the registers of citizens and non-citizens from the lists held by the polemarch. They shall set the names out in 200 columns and

---

[1] The simple invocation 'theoi', called to witness the decree and to punish transgression from it.

[2] The Assembly.

[3] Themistocles' deme, close to the silver mines of Laurium, which were probably the source of his family's wealth.

[4] Theseus, the hero and legendary king of Athens, was born in Troezen.

[5] Remarkably, according to Plutarch, Athens' old enemy Aegina also took in Athenian refugees.

[6] This was the fighting complement of the part-decked trireme. Perhaps up to 30 more hoplites were allocated to triremes with the capacity to carry them.

they shall write the names of the trireme, commander and crewmen as allocated at the head of each column so that the men know which ship they are to embark upon.

When all the crews have been selected and allocated to triremes, all 200 shall be manned by order of the Council and the generals after offering sacrifices to propitiate Zeus the All-powerful, Athena Nike[1] and Poseidon the Protector. And when the ships are all manned, 100 of them are to take up position at Artemisium on Euboea, while the other 100 shall take station around Salamis and the rest of Attica to guard our land.[2]

And, in order that all Athenians may be of one mind in their resistance of the Barbarian, those who have been banished for ten years[3] are to go separately to Salamis and remain there until the Assembly comes to a decision about them, and those who have been publicly disgraced ... [the rest is broken off and lost] (*The Decree of Themistocles* from Troezen)

There is much more than a glimpse here of the range of skills and qualities Themistocles applied to the anticipation and resolution of the acute crises that Athens faced, starting with the evaporation of any prospect of resistance in northern Greece, soon followed by the collapse of the Thermopylae–Artemisium line and the realization that Attica and the city of Athens could not be saved. A vignette in Plutarch's short biography of Cimon, golden-boy son of Miltiades, highlights the unity that Themistocles forged in persuading the Athenian people with very few exceptions to abandon hearth and home to play their part in the implementation of the boldest of strategies to turn back the might of the Great King. Cimon and his wealthy and aristocratic comrades were representatives, albeit from the younger generation, of the political

---

[1] Victory, either as an attribute of Athena or invoked as a separate goddess.

[2] This does not agree with Herodotus' account of the actual dispositions of the Hellene fleet at Artemisium.

[3] These were victims of *ostracism*, a poll that could be conducted once a year to bring about the banishment of any public figure that a sufficient number of the electorate considered too powerful or disruptive for the good of the democratic state. Aristides, for one, was allowed to play a full part in the fighting. An amnesty was probably also applied in the case of some of those who had been 'publicly disgraced', and been deprived of citizen rights and banished by the courts.

group that had favoured appeasement or worse, in the years before and after Marathon.

> When the Medes were bearing down on Athens and Themistocles was trying to persuade the people to abandon their city and leave their land to make a fight of it with their fleet off Salamis to decide the issue at sea, most were horrified by the audacity of the plan. But Cimon son of Miltiades stepped forward and with great spirit[1] led a procession of his cavalry comrades through the Ceramicus[2] and up to the Acropolis. He was carrying a bridle and there he dedicated it to the Goddess, giving out the message that it was not horsemanship that the city needed in the present emergency but men to fight at sea. After dedicating the bridle, he took down one of the shields hanging on the walls of the temple, said a prayer to the Goddess, and went on down to the sea, giving courage to many of the people who had been fearful. (*Cimon* 5)

Athens was ready, and over the same period the Hellene strategy, which was to be so dependent on the Athenian fleet, was decided upon. Themistocles' was undoubtedly one of the most influential voices in the discussions that led to this decision, as much in the Hellene war council as at home.

> The Hellenes in council at the Isthmus debated how and where they should make their stand, considering the information Alexander of Macedon had given them. The proposal that was finally carried was to defend the pass at Thermopylae, seeing that it was narrower than the pass into Thessaly, and also nearer to home territory. Until the Hellenes arrived there and heard about it from the Trachinians, they knew nothing about the track by which the men at Thermopylae were cut off and trapped. Their plan was to prevent the Barbarians coming further into Greece by blocking the pass. The fleet was to sail

---

[1] The word used here, *phaidros*, can be applied to horses with their ears pricked up, which make it especially appropriate in this context.

[2] A large district to the north-west of the Acropolis; the procession would also have gone through the Agora, making it very public.

to Artemisium in the territory of Histiaea and the two forces would be close enough to each other to exchange information as things developed. (7.175)

Herodotus does not do justice to the Hellene strategy here. There was nothing fresh about Alexander's information on the size of the Great King's invasion force or the geography of northern Greece. The narrower width of the pass at Thermopylae compared to whichever 'pass (or passes) into Thessaly' he intended was not a key factor. Whether or not it was planned before the army marched, measures were taken to block the fatal 'track'. And it was to be a fully combined operation with the fleet actively engaged, not simply watching and waiting.

When they heard that the Persians had reached Pieria, the council adjourned and the Hellenes left the Isthmus, some of them marching to Thermopylae with their troops and others going by sea to Artemisium. So, the Hellenes went to their positions to face the enemy and, at the same time, the people of Delphi, full of fear for themselves and for all of Hellas, sought a prophecy from the god. They were advised to pray to the winds, who would be strong allies for Hellas. As soon as they had received this message the Delphians passed it on to all the Hellenes who wished to remain free, and they were forever grateful for this in their mighty dread of the Barbarian. (7.177–78)

Pray to the winds

Artemisium and Thermopylae

Herodotus' description of the straits of Artemisium is brief and unhelpful:

> Looking first at Artemisium, the open sea off Thrace narrows into a channel between the island of Sciathos and the mainland of Magnesia. Artemisium is on the Euboean shore directly opposite this channel and there is a shrine dedicated to Artemis above it. (7.176)

The straits form a spacious rectangle approximately 10km wide and 20km long. The modern ferry to Sciathos from Agios Constantinos on the mainland (just off the E75 a few kilometres east of Thermopylae) passes the opening of the Gulf of Malis and swings into the Oreos channel to sail a little north of east across the entire battlefield. This crossing gives an excellent sense of the relationship between the two Hellene positions on land and sea, and the space and distances involved, although Thermopylae itself is never in view. The narrower Oreos channel at its south-western corner, 5km wide at its eastern end and 3km wide at its narrowest towards the south-west, was actually the key to the naval defence of the Artemisium–Thermopylae line and the gateway to the Euripus, giving direct access to the shorelines of Boeotia and Attica; but the Oreos channel could not be held without also defending the beaches on the north shore of Euboea. Otherwise the Persians could have quickly delivered troops there to mount land attacks on Hellene-held beaches and harbours on the west coast of the island. The Hellenes also needed to be positioned to watch for any moves to send a force south by the longer, open-sea route down the east coast of Euboea. Both sides clearly needed ships afloat and closer to the opposite side of the Oreos channel than their own to observe activity on the beaches. The Hellenes needed to be able to spot and counter any Barbarian thrust towards the channel. The Persians were probably expecting the Hellenes to stay on the defensive and would have been looking out for any indications of withdrawal. There were, and still are, thousands of metres of shoreline suitable for beaching trireme fleets on both sides of the straits. The modern Pevki Bay is thought to have accommodated a large part of the Hellene fleet. The temple of Artemis stood on the headland above it, somewhere near the modern village of Potaki.

It was now August and northern Greece had fallen to the Great King without a blow being struck. But the waiting was over:

As Xerxes' fleet put to sea from the city of Therme a squadron of ten of his best ships was sent ahead on a direct course to Sciathos. Three Hellene ships were on patrol there, one from Troezen, one from Aegina and one from Athens, and when they spotted the Barbarian ships approaching they tried to get away. The Barbarians caught up with the Troezenian ship first and captured it immediately; Prexinos was its commander. They took the best-looking of the hoplites on board up to the prow and cut his throat, sacrificing the fairest of their first prisoners for good fortune. Their victim was called Leon[1] and perhaps his name had something to do with his fate. They had some difficulty with the Aeginetan ship, which was commanded by Asonides, and one of the hoplites, Pytheas son of Ischenous, fought with great distinction that day, carrying on after the ship had been taken until he was terribly hacked about. He was not dead when he fell but scarcely breathing, and, because of his valour, the Persians serving as marines did everything they could to save his life, treating his wounds with myrrh and binding them up with fine linen bandages.[2] They showed him off to the whole army when they rejoined the main force, and in their great admiration

---

[1] Lion: perhaps Herodotus is suggesting that this grand name brought his fate upon him. In any case he does not appear to consider this act of human sacrifice as anything out of the ordinary, and it was possibly a practice which the Persians were known for.

[2] Implying a better quality of battlefield medicine than was usual on the Hellene side.

of this man, they cared for him well, but treated the rest of the prisoners taken on the ship as slaves. So, two of the ships were boarded and taken, but the third, commanded by the Athenian Phormos, got away and was beached at the mouth of the River Peneus. There the Barbarians captured the ship itself but not the men on board. They had quickly disembarked the moment they ran it ashore and made their way through Thessaly back to Athens on foot.

The Hellenes who were in the process of establishing their base at Artemisium found out what had happened by fire signals from Sciathos. They were frightened and sailed back to Chalcis to mount their defence of the Euripus channel from there, but they left lookouts on the heights of Euboea. Then three of the ten Barbarian ships ran themselves aground on the shoal called 'the Ant' that lies between Sciathos and Magnesia and set up a stone marker which they had brought with them; it was Pammon of Scyros[1] who showed them where the shoal lay in the channel. (7.179–83)

The ten Barbarian ships involved in this first encounter were most likely Phoenician and probably from the elite Sidonian squadron. The task of the three Hellene ships was to keep watch and perhaps patrol to the north for the first sighting of the Persian fleet, which could have reached central Greece some days ahead of the army. Herodotus seems to have packed together a number of different anecdotes about this minor action into his brief account, and some of the sources appear to have been less than detailed or reliable. The direction of the Athenian ship's escape suggests that the Barbarians surprised the Hellenes by rounding the eastern side of the island, perhaps under cover of darkness, and entering the channel from the south to catch them putting to sea at dawn. However, it is unlikely that the escaping Athenians beached their ship as far north as the Peneus. This would have been a very long chase and taken them close to or even into the midst of the main Persian land and sea forces now on their way south. It may have been a tale that grew in the telling and from some confusion of an estuary further to

---

[1] Scyros out in the centre of the Aegean was well positioned on the main trade route from the Black Sea and Pammon, otherwise unknown, possibly had strong business ties with Asian merchants.

the south with the Peneus. But it was an achievement to outrun these particular pursuers over any distance.

The fire signals could have delivered only a simple, pre-arranged message and it may initially have been thought that the Persians were arriving in full force. However, reasonably detailed first-hand accounts of the skirmish probably followed quite quickly on a small boat. Recollections of an immediate withdrawal down the Euripus to Chalcis must have been incorrect. With the Persian fleet still not sighted and possibly days away from their position, the Hellenes were under no immediate threat and, in any case, they would not have been able to counter any seaborne move to get behind Leonidas' position at Thermopylae from so far south. Nonetheless the story could be a reflection of the desire of Peloponnesians other than Spartans to fall back on any excuse. However, the placing of the marker on the Ant (almost certainly the same shoal as the one now called Leftari in the middle of the channel off the south-west point of Sciathos) is credible and an impressive glimpse of the intelligence-gathering and reconnaissance which preceded the invasion.

With the way cleared at sea, and 11 days after the King had marched out of Therme, the whole fleet sailed south. A day's sailing brought the Barbarians to Magnesian territory and the coastline between the city of Casthanaea and Cape Sepias.[1] Up to this point and on land as far as Thermopylae, the invasion force had suffered no loss. It was possible to pull the first ships to arrive up the beach but because this is not very wide the rest had to lie at anchor off-shore, eight rows deep, and that was how they spent the night. But just before dawn, when the weather had been clear and still, a heavy sea boiled up and a great storm hit them with a gale from the east, which the people who live in those parts call a Hellesponter.[2] Those who noticed that the wind was getting up and were in a position to do something about it, beached their ships ahead of it and they and their ships

---

[1] A single trireme or small flotilla could have covered this distance (approximately 150km direct, 190km sticking to coastal waters) in a day, but a very large fleet which included supply ships would have been considerably slower. It is more likely to have paused for the night than to have sailed on in darkness.

[2] This was the local name for a wind blowing from the east or north-east.

survived. But the storm overwhelmed the ships that were caught out at sea. It drove some onto the rocks called the Ovens on the coast below Pelion and some onto the shore; some were dashed against Cape Sepias and some were wrecked off the city of Casthanaea. This storm was, indeed, an overwhelming disaster.

The story goes that the Athenians summoned up Boreas,[1] the north wind, in response to an oracle.[2] I cannot say whether or not Boreas attacked the Barbarians as a result of this, but the Athenians say that Boreas had come to their aid before and was responsible for what happened on this occasion. Indeed, on returning home they dedicated a shrine to Boreas by the Ilissus river. They say that at least 400 warships, countless lives and immense quantities of equipment came to grief in this storm, and there was no record of the number of grain-ships and other types of vessel destroyed. Fearful in their shattered state that they would be attacked by the Thessalians, the fleet commanders had a high stockade built out of the wreckage. That storm raged for three days but the Magi finally brought it to an end on the fourth by making sacrifices and chanting incantations to the wind, and they also sent up burnt offerings to Thetis and the Nereids. But maybe the wind stopped of its own accord.

On the second day of the storm the lookouts ran down from the heights of Euboea and gave a full report on the wrecking of the fleet.[3] The Hellenes, after praying to their saviour Poseidon and pouring drink-offerings, quickly rowed back to Artemisium expecting there would be only a few ships left to oppose them. So, they lay in wait at Artemisium a second time and from that day to this they honour Poseidon as Saviour.

When the wind had dropped and the sea had calmed, the Barbarians launched their ships and, following the coast, rounded the headland of Magnesia and sailed directly into the Gulf of Pagasae. Aphetae was to be the harbour for Xerxes' fleet. It happened that 15 of their ships

---

[1] Strictly speaking, the Hellesponter was a different wind, a possible reason for the doubt Herodotus expresses here.

[2] The Delphic message, 'pray to the winds'.

[3] The lookouts could not actually have seen anything beyond the southern end of Sciathos and the mainland but the Hellenes would have known about the storm, some probably shifting their position to shelter from it, and they would, in any case, have received news of its effect on the Barbarians inside a day or two.

had put to sea much later than the rest. They saw the Hellene ships off Artemisium, thought they were Barbarian and sailed in amongst them. Sandoces, the governor of Aeolis, was in command. He was one of the King's judges and in former times he had been sentenced to crucifixion by Darius because he had taken a bribe to give an unjust judgement. But when he had been strung up, Darius decided, on reflection, that Sandoces' good service to the royal house outweighed his wrongdoing and, realizing that he had acted with more haste than wisdom, had him released. So, having escaped death at the hands of Darius, he was not to make his escape a second time when he sailed in amongst the Hellenes. When the Hellenes saw his ships mistakenly sailing towards them, they came out and captured them all without difficulty. In one of these ships they took Aridolis, the tyrant of Alabanda in Caria, and in another the Paphian commander, Penthylus son of Demonous.[1] After questioning their prisoners and finding out all they wanted to know about Xerxes' invasion force, they sent them off to the Isthmus in chains. (7.183–84, 188–95)

If the slower-moving army was sent south some days ahead of the fleet, it displayed confidence that the Hellenes would not attempt a seaborne attack before the fleet caught up. There is no indication how far ten days' march (ancient convention included Day 1 in the count) took the army, but detachments may have secured the shore between Sepias and Casthanaea before the fleet arrived. The main force presumably headed directly to Trachis with the intention of linking up with the fleet when it reached the Malian Gulf.

The arrangement of a row of ships beached stern-first with further rows moored together at bow and stern lying at anchor out to sea is easy to envisage, as is its vulnerability to rough weather. Losses as crippling as described are improbable, but the arithmetic helps towards a more credible number for the fleet that actually faced the Hellenes in battle.

To escape the worst of the weather driving into the straits from the east it is likely that at least a part of the Hellene fleet shifted west into the Oreos channel, returning to the north shore as soon as conditions improved. The story of the panic withdrawal to Chalcis may have

---

[1] A Cypriot said to have already lost 11 of his 12 ships in the storm.

grown out of this more calculated movement. In any case, whatever the Hellenes knew of the effect of the storm on the Barbarian fleet, the capture of the unfortunate Sandoces' small, mixed squadron would have improved morale, if it had been affected by the skirmish off Sciathos.

In his description of the invasion fleet as reviewed by Xerxes at Doriscus, Herodotus itemizes the weaponry of the fighting complements of each ethnic group that the Hellenes were to face:

The Phoenicians with the Syrians of Palestine brought 300 ships. They were equipped with helmets very similar to those worn by the Hellenes, wore linen body armour and carried javelins and shields without rims.[1] The Egyptians supplied 200 triremes. They wore woven helmets and carried hollow shields with broad rims, naval pikes and big axes.[2] Most of them wore body armour and had long swords. The Cypriots brought 150 ships. Their princes had turbans on their heads and the ordinary people had felt caps, but in every other respect they were equipped like the Hellenes. The Cilicians came with 100 ships, wearing their own kind of helmet and woollen tunics and carrying shields made of uncured oxhide; they each had two javelins and a sword very similar to those carried by the Egyptians. The Pamphylians supplied 100 ships and were armed like the Hellenes. The Lycians brought 50 ships. They wore body armour and greaves and carried javelins and cornel-wood bows with unfeathered cane arrows. Goat-skins swung from their shoulders, and on their heads were feathered caps, and they also had daggers and billhooks.[3] The Dorians of Asia came with 30 ships and, being of Peloponnesian descent, their weapons were Hellene. The Carians supplied 70 ships and had billhooks and daggers, but the rest of their equipment was Hellene. The Ionians brought 100 ships and; their equipment was Hellene too, likewise the Islanders[4] who provided 17

---

[1] This could mean that their shields were smaller than the regular hoplite type, lacking the reinforcing bronze rim which was commonly part of it. Their linen armour may not have been as elaborate as the kind Herodotus occasionally mentions elsewhere.

[2] Their helmets may have been made of metal decorated in a particular way, or actually woven out of leather strips or strong cords. The standard hoplite shield could be described as 'hollow', simply meaning convex, and the Egyptian shield was likely to have been similar.

[3] *Drepanon.*

[4] From medizing or press-ganged Aegean islands, or from those subjected nine years before in the Marathon campaign.

ships and the Aeolians with their 60. A fleet of 100 ships came from the Pontus and the Hellespont (this included none from Abydos because the King had ordered the people to stay at home to guard the bridges). The original settlers were Ionian and Dorian so these men too were armed in Hellene style.

Persians, Medes and Sacae also served as marines on all the ships. The best[1] of these were supplied by the Phoenicians, and of these the Sidonians' were best of all. All of the ships, as for each unit in the army, had their native leaders but I have not recorded their names since that would be beyond the scope of my research. The leaders of each nation are not worth mentioning, and then every city of each nation had a leader of its own. These were not there as generals but as slaves, like the rest of the expeditionary force. I have already named the generals who were in supreme command and, also, the Persians who were in command of each national contingent. (7.95–96)

This enormous total of 1,207 triremes, crews totalling more than 250,000, may have been derived from contemporary levy lists and could therefore fairly represent the entire naval power of the Persian Empire early in the 5th century. Aeschylus, writing decades before Herodotus, also gives 1,207, a curiously unround number for a poet to invent. However, he could be interpreted as meaning '1,000, *including* 207 fast ones', 1,000 being a conventional approximation for an even larger force than 600. Shortly before his account of the disaster off Cape Sepias, Herodotus increases the Persian strength by an estimated 120 triremes raised from 'the Hellenes of Thrace and the islands off the coast of Thrace' (7.185). However, the storm enables him to scale the numbers down dramatically. A more plausible starting figure for the invasion fleet is 700–800 triremes, as discussed earlier. It is likely that some of these were detached to protect supply routes and harbours in the rear as the advance progressed, and the storm off Magnesia would have reduced this number further. So perhaps 500–600 faced the Hellenes at Artemisium. Herodotus also notes that 3,000 'triaconters, pentekonters, lighter vessels and horse transports' (7.97) sailed with the triremes. There would certainly have been a good number of smaller warships for reconnaissance and

[1] 'Best-sailing' literally, embracing build quality, general condition and effectiveness of command and crew.

communication, and a support fleet carrying food and water and other supplies that could not be stored on the triremes in sufficient quantities, but 3,000 must be epic exaggeration. In any case, the smaller warships could not be pitted against triremes, so were of little or no use when battle was actually joined.

The ethnic mix of a more realistically sized Persian fleet was most likely not in the same proportions as detailed by Herodotus. However, it is possible that all maritime subject states were represented, some only in token contingents taken along as in the land force for display and as insurance against insurrection at home. It is likely that the Phoenicians and Ionians made up the bulk of the fleet. Of the rest named by Herodotus, four are specifically mentioned in the Artemisium narrative, the Egyptians, the Cypriots, the Cilicians and the Carians. Apart from the Cilicians, these had on board troops that were heavily armed enough to be a match for the Hellene marines in deck-fighting, and for the Egyptians deck-fighting seem to have been a speciality. However, the detachments of Persians, Medes or Sacae, 30 strong on every ship as Herodotus states elsewhere, would have significantly outnumbered the native troops, 40 being generally accepted as the maximum marine complement that a fully decked trireme could carry; the broader-beamed ships from the eastern Mediterranean may have had greater capacity. The Barbarian fleet had a significant advantage in archery firepower but in any hand-to-hand fighting after a boarding they would have been less effective than many of their subject comrades in the face of hoplite spears and shields. It is thought that these Asian troops may have been put on board as much to 'encourage' subject levies as to fight the enemy, in which case they probably were not deployed across the whole fleet but only in the less trustworthy contingents. These might have included Hellenes and perhaps the recently suppressed Egyptians, diluting elements that were best equipped to tackle hoplites. A further drawback was that these inland warriors could not swim and, in their princely but landlubber high command, were very ill-qualified to serve as admirals.

Herodotus is dealing with more plausible, 'public-record' figures when he details the strength of the Hellene fleet facing the Persians across the straits of Artemisium:

It was made up of the following contingents in order of size: the Athenians contributed 127 triremes (the Plataeans with no naval expertise but courageously devoted to the cause helped man some

of them); the Corinthians contributed 40 and the Megarians 20;
the Chalcidians manned 20 ships supplied by Athens; there were 18
triremes from Aegina, 12 from Sicyon and ten from Lacedaemon;
then eight from Epidaurus, seven from Eretria, five from Troezen
and two triremes and two penteconters from Ceos; finally the
Opuntian Locrians added their support with seven penteconters.
Not counting the penteconters, the total assembled at Artemisium
was 271. The commander-in-chief was the Spartan Eurybiades. This
was because the allies had declared that, if a Spartan was not in
command, they would refuse to accept Athenian leadership and
abandon the operation that was being planned. From the start,
even before the attempt to bring Sicily into the alliance, there had
been talk of entrusting the Athenians with command of the fleet,
but, when allies opposed this, the Athenians, in their great concern
for the survival of Hellas, conceded, recognizing that conflict over
leadership would bring about its destruction. And they were quite
right: for internecine conflict is as great an evil in comparison to a
united war-effort as war is to peace. Accepting this, the Athenians
did not press their claim but held back, though for not a day
longer than they felt they needed to. They made this plain when
the alliance had driven the Persians out of Greece and carried the
war into their territory. Then, the Athenians took over leadership
from the Lacedaemonians giving Pausanias'[1] overbearing behaviour
as their reason. But that happened later. (8.1–3)

The Spartan fleet was only 16 strong at Salamis, and Sparta could not
be classed as a significant naval power for much of the 5th century, but,
as well recorded by Herodotus, there was substantial rejection of the
logic of giving supreme command to Athens with her 200-strong fleet,
which was by far the largest. However, Sparta claimed entitlement as
Greece's leading warrior nation and had the support of allies in the
Peloponnesian League, which she headed and which were to muster
over a quarter of the ships at Salamis. The Athenians pragmatically
accepted Spartan command but were, nevertheless, the true leaders in
the naval campaign. Each of the 17 contingents, from the Athenian

---

[1] Pausanias was the Spartan commander-in-chief of the Hellene Alliance's land forces in
479.

fleet to the single trireme from Cythnos, had its own commander and was a voluntary member of the Hellene Alliance. Unlike their counterparts in the Persian fleet, each had a voice in the councils that convened on a number of occasions to debate and advise upon strategy and tactics. However, Herodotus mentions only three cities' commanders by name, Eurybiades, Themistocles and Adeimantus of Corinth. Corinth contributed 40 ships to the fleet. Aegina's commander, leading 30 of the best ships in the fleet, must have been equally influential, but is not named.

The command structure was flat, with Eurybiades presiding over the alliance's naval war council, which comprised the 16 other national commanders and probably a number of other senior figures. It is likely that the larger fleets were divided into squadrons with their commanders taking some responsibility for training, supervision of fitting out and maintenance, and leadership in battle. As in a land-battle, generals led from the front, going to sea in command of their own ships. In the initial phases they could direct changes of formation or direction and other manoeuvres by means of trumpet calls and perhaps flag signals, or simply by giving a lead. But, once the fleets had engaged, in head-on collision or after breakthrough or flanking movements, the battle was mainly carried on between individual ships rather than larger formations. Higher-level command and control ceased to be practicable. The outcome was then chiefly decided by individual ships' captains and their helmsmen, and the quality and performance of their oarsmen and deck crew.

Nothing is known about Eurybiades outside his involvement in the naval campaign of 480, his only recorded command. He was not a king. There was now a law to prevent both kings being out of the country on campaign at the same time, and Leonidas was leading the defence of Greece on land. Herodotus points out that Eurybiades was not even a member of either of the royal families. However, he had probably risen on merit in a lifetime's soldiering in the supreme military system of Hellas. His main, even entire expertise and experience would have been in land warfare, but his apparent acceptance and understanding of Themistocles' strategic and tactical vision, and the part he played in its communication, together with his evident powers of leadership, contributed very significantly to the Hellene victory. If Eurybiades had given in to strong Peloponnesian League pressure to retreat, with or without the Athenians, to the defensive line prepared at the Isthmus, the war would have been lost.

When the Hellenes arrived back at Artemisium and saw so many ships harboured at Aphetae and the fleet filling the whole expanse of water, they were alarmed because the Barbarians were in much better shape than they had expected[1] and they decided to withdraw down the Greek coast. When they found out about this, the Euboeans tried to persuade Eurybiades to delay for a short time to enable them to evacuate their children and households. They were unsuccessful in this but then approached Themistocles, the Athenian commander, offering to pay him 300 talents[2] if he could make the Hellenes stay where they were and give battle off Euboea. Themistocles managed this by passing on five talents out of the cash he received to Eurybiades as if it was a gift from his personal funds. Then, with Eurybiades persuaded, Adeimantus, the Corinthian commander, still resisting, declared that he was going to sail away from Artemisium straightaway. So, Themistocles gave him this pledge, 'You are not going to desert us because I will personally reward you more generously than the King of the Medes would if you deserted the alliance.' This said, he delivered three talents of silver to Adeimantus' ship. Everyone was brought round by his bribery, the Euboeans were well pleased and Themistocles made an excellent profit. Nobody knew he kept the rest of the money and those who had a share of it were convinced that it had been provided by Athens for the purpose.

So, the Hellenes stood firm in Euboea and fought a sea-battle and this is how it was. The Barbarians reached Aphetae early in the afternoon and already knew that just a few ships were lying at Artemisium. When they saw them with their own eyes, they were eager to take them on and defeat them. But they decided not to sail straight for them there and then in case the Hellenes, seeing them coming, put to sea and made their escape as night was falling.[3]

---

[1] Perhaps a gentle hint that neither the starting number nor the losses in the storm were credible.

[2] A fantastically large sum.

[3] Night-time manoeuvres were difficult enough; fighting a battle by night was out of the question.

The Barbarians felt sure they would try to get away, but their aim was not to allow even a single fire-keeper to escape with his life.[1] They planned to bring this about by detaching 200 of their ships and sending them up past Sciathos so that they could then sail round Euboea unseen by the enemy and into the Euripus channel. They would then have the Hellenes trapped with their line of retreat cut off, and the rest of the fleet would launch a frontal attack. This was the plan, and they sent off the squadron they had detached with no intention of engaging the Hellenes that day or subsequently until the signal had been given to confirm that it was in position. After sending this squadron off they reorganized the ships that remained at Aphetae.

At this time there was a diver from Scione[2] in the Persian camp, a splendid character called Scyllias. He had salvaged a lot of valuable things for the Persians when their ships were wrecked off Pelion, and had helped himself to a lot as well. Scyllias had been contemplating deserting for some time but no opportunity had presented itself as yet. I cannot tell you with certainty how he came over to the Hellene side, but the story is an amazing one, if it is true. The story goes that he dived into the sea at Aphetae and did not surface again until he had reached Artemisium, having swum a distance of about 80 *stades* [15km] underwater. Now there are other tall tales about this man and some have a ring of truth about them, but I must tell you that in my opinion he made this crossing to Artemisium by boat. Anyway, when he got there he immediately informed the commanders about the damage done by the storm, and also about the encircling squadron. (8.4–8)

Eurybiades would not have considered abandoning the position and leaving his king exposed to a seaborne attack from the rear, and the bribery story is almost certainly a malicious piece of the mythology that built up in later years around Themistocles' extraordinary career.

---

[1] This meant total annihilation but the origins of the proverbial expression are obscure: the *purphoros*, who kept alight a flame taken from the sacred fire from home for use in sacrifices made on campaign, was thought to have had the same inviolable status as a herald. If the saying was current in the 5th century, it is very unlikely that the Persians were familiar with it.

[2] On the south-western tip of the promontory of Chalcidice.

ARTEMISIUM, 480

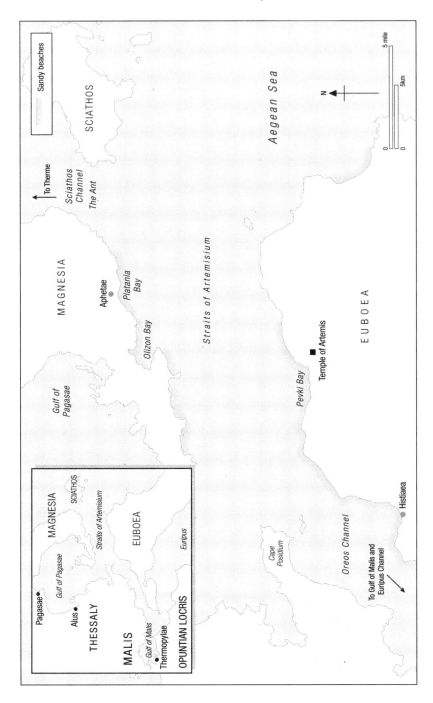

Themistocles did not need to be bribed to follow his own strategy and it can be reasonably argued that Adeimantus did not need to be either. However, this is one of the several points in his narrative where Herodotus dramatically highlights the very real fragility of the Hellene Alliance.

The account of the despatch of a large squadron to sail round Euboea and attack the Hellenes from the south is equally unconvincing. It would have taken around two days of non-stop rowing and three to four days with necessary pauses for food, water and rest to make the circuit, a long time for such a large element of the fleet to be out of touch. Then, the narrows at Chalcis could be easily blocked. There were also the risks of encountering units of the Hellene fleet not yet committed at Artemisium and of cruising along a hostile shore where beaches and harbours might still be defended. Additionally, off the inhospitable east coast of Euboea, the squadron would have been exposed to any rough weather that might brew up in the open sea. Finally, Herodotus later highlights reluctance on the part of the Persians to divide their fleet in different circumstances when there were stronger arguments in favour of doing so. Herodotus closes this section with the tall tale of Scyllias' epic swim and takes the opportunity to remind us that he does not believe everything he was told.

By now, Xerxes and his land force were encamped in the territory of Trachis in Malis. The Hellenes were in the pass. This place is generally known as Thermopylae, 'Hot Gates', though the people who live in it or nearby just call it Pylae, 'Gates'. So, this was each side's position, one controlling all the land from Trachis northward in the direction of Boreas, the other controlling the mainland to the south in the direction of Notos.[1]

The pass from Trachinian territory onward into Greece narrows to about half a *plethron*[2] but it is even narrower at other points, and at Alpeni and by the River Phoenix near the city of Anthela it is only wide enough for a single wagon. To the west of Thermopylae, the mountainside rears up, impassable, sheer and lofty, towards the

---

[1] Herodotus allows himself an epic flourish in naming the gods of the north and south winds here and this is a fair statement of the situation in territorial terms.

[2] A *plethron* was one sixth of a *stade*, or about 30m.

heights of the Oetaean range.[1] To the east of the road lie mudflats and
the sea.[2] There are hot bathing pools in the pass, known as Chutroi,
'Cooking Pots', by the locals and, close to them, an altar dedicated
to Heracles.[3] A long time ago the Phocians had built a wall with
gates in it across the pass. They did this for fear of the Thessalians
who were in the process of migrating from Thesprotia[4] in order to
settle in Aeolis, land which now belongs to them. The Thessalians
threatened to overrun the Phocians and they protected themselves in
various ways to prevent the Thessalians invading their land, including
diverting the hot springs into the pass to carve gullies in the ground.[5]
This ancient wall was mostly in ruins and the Hellenes now decided
to rebuild it to block the Barbarians' entry into Greece. Also, the
village called Alpeni is close to the road here and this was to be their
supply depot.[6] These places seemed ideal to the Hellenes. They had
reconnoitred the area and concluded that the Barbarians would not
be able to exploit their weight of numbers or their cavalry in the pass,
so this is where they resolved to make their stand against the invaders
of Greece. (7.201, 176–77)

Thermopylae is used interchangeably to name both the point at which
the Hellenes made their stand at the 'Middle Gate' on the 8km of road
between Anthela to the east and Alpeni to the west, and the narrow
strip of coast that the road runs through. This was the main land route
from the north into central and southern Greece and an important
strategic corridor. It had been fought over previously and it was to be
fought over again in later centuries, most resonantly in 279 BC during

---

[1] Thermopylae is at the foot of the Callidromus range. The Oetaean range is next to
Callidromus.

[2] The mountainside is actually to the south of the road and the Malian Gulf to the north.

[3] The altar is lost but it is still possible to take a sulphurous hot bath (about 40°C) in the springs
a short distance to the west of the battlefield.

[4] An area of north-west Greece. The Thesprotians are mentioned by Homer and there is
archaeological evidence of Mycenaean occupation.

[5] Centuries before, according to their mythology, Thessalians had migrated eastward, some
settling eventually on the west coast of Asia, but the ancient wall was probably built and rebuilt
a number of times by Phocians, Locrians or others to defend or control this important strategic
corridor. The gullies, on the other hand, were most likely a result of natural erosion.

[6] Supplies may have been brought in by sea; the village was close to the shore.

Brennus the Gaul's invasion, in 1821 in the War of Independence, and in 1941 in World War II. Herodotus' description is quite accurate, as far as it goes (apart from his orientation of the pass from north to south rather than west to east), and his naming of so many places and features suggests personal knowledge of the area. However, the landscape today is of little or no help in any attempt to build on this information to construct a more detailed description of the battlefield or the three days' fighting. Herodotus' wording is vague, but he is presumably referring to the Middle Gate when he states that the pass 'narrows to about half a *plethron* (15m)' so the Hellenes were defending a very narrow front. Herodotus later indicates that there was a wider area of open ground immediately to the west of the position. Leonidas' right, on the north side of the road, rested on 'mudflats and the sea' and a mention of Persians falling in and drowning during the final day's fighting suggests that it gave his flank secure protection, perhaps with a sheer drop into deep water at this point. However, silt carried down into the Gulf by rivers and streams over the millennia has caused this shoreline to recede several kilometres and significantly raised the level of the ground at the foot of the northern flanks of the 1,000m Callidromus range. The exact line of the road is not known. Seen from the north, the mountains certainly look impenetrable, rising in a vertical wall from the plain at the west end of the Malian Gulf. However, close up, there seems to be no point now where Leonidas' left would have been secured by 'impassable' cliffs, though the escarpment does rise at a sharp angle from its base, approaching the vertical higher up. Finally, there were the ruins of the 'ancient wall' which had included a gateway. There are some remains of stonework of the right vintage and excavations in the mid 20th century revealed foundations extending approximately 200m along the line of the pass, not across it. It is now thought that this was built later than 480, possibly by the Trachinians, incorporating parts of the older structure and recycling its distinctive archaic masonry. No physical evidence has been found of any 6th-century or early 5th-century 'wall with gates in it across the pass', but this was undoubtedly the centrepiece of the Hellenes' defensive arrangements, built from scratch if there was nothing already in place to block the road or access, if any, across the lower slopes of Callidromus.

Clearly, the combination of natural and man-made features gave the position excellent protection against frontal attack. However, as the combatants in 480, and in earlier and later wars discovered, these mountains were far from impassable; Thermopylae could be turned by substantial bodies of men using relatively easy mountain tracks. Herodotus pointed out earlier that the Hellene commanders from further south did not find out about the position's fatal weakness before they got to Trachis, but it is unlikely that anyone was under the illusion that there was no way round it. The corridor that the Gates controlled was, and still is, the main arterial link between northern and central Greece but there was another option, inferior as a main highway but rather more adequate than the mountain tracks. This was (and is now) a road that runs south-west past Trachis up the gorge of the River Asopus, climbs to a saddle between the Callidromus and Oetaea ridges and then swings south-east to follow the River Cephisus down to Lake Copais (a significant physical feature, drained in the 19th century) and into Boeotia. This may have been rejected by the Persians as their main line of advance for more than one reason: it would have entailed a significant degree of separation from the fleet; the city of Trachis overlooking the road and, garrisoned by its citizens and quite probably the Opuntian Locrians, might present a significant obstacle; there were several points at which small numbers could block it; and, finally, the long narrow column snaking slowly through the mountain terrain would be vulnerable to guerrilla-style harassment by day and night. On the other hand, it undoubtedly merited aggressive reconnaissance, if not a full-scale attempt to force it. Herodotus mentions no consideration of this route in the Barbarians' planning, but records later in his narrative that they made full use of it immediately after the battle, brushing aside Phocian resistance. It is unlikely that the Hellenes' strategy failed to take account of this and other options, but Thermopylae lay on the fastest route into central Greece and blocking that route was an immediate priority; the establishment of a supply base at Alpeni suggests that the intention was to hold the position for an extended period. Herodotus goes into no detail on the rebuilding of the decayed Phocian wall, though it would clearly have been less of a field-engineering challenge than the rapid fortification of the Isthmus defence-line that was carried out shortly afterwards. However, it is a reasonable assumption that the ancient remains were turned into a substantial bastion.

Herodotus details the hoplite element of Leonidas' command precisely and, as with his other listings of Hellene forces, the numbers

Thermopylae, 480

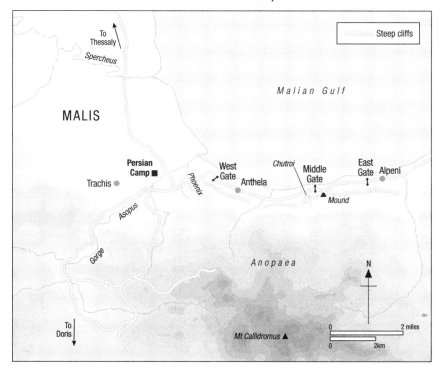

can be relied upon, if mostly rounded to the nearest 100, as reasonably reflecting the records and public knowledge of his time:

> The Hellene force awaiting the Persians was made up of 300[1] Spartan hoplites, 1,000 Tegeans and Mantineans (500 of each), 120 from Orchomenus with 1,000 from the rest of Arcadia, 400 from Corinth, 200 from Phlious and 80 from Mycenae. That was the Peloponnesian contingent. Then, from Boeotia, there were 700 Thespians and 400 Thebans. In addition, the Opuntian Locrians' entire army[2] and 1,000

---

[1] This is perhaps the one unchallengeable round number. Three hundred was the traditional complement of the Spartan royal bodyguard, and of elite units in other Hellene cities around this time.

[2] Pausanias suggests a strength of 'not more than 6,000' which seems on the high side, even for all the cities in this mountainous and not very large region.

Phocians[1] had answered the call. The Hellenes had appealed to them directly. They had assured them that they had nothing to fear, telling them that the force posted to Thermopylae was an advance guard and the rest of the allies were expected to join it any day, and that they were protected at sea by the Athenians, Aeginetans[2] and other naval contingents assigned to this task. A further assurance they gave was that it was a man advancing into Greece, not a god, and that there was not, nor ever could there be any mortal man who did not meet with disaster at some point in his life, and, finally, that it was the greatest men who suffered the greatest disasters. Therefore, being mortal, the man bearing down on them was bound to fall short of achieving his goal.[3] The Opuntian Locrians and Phocians took all this in and marched to Trachis to assist in the defence.

Each of these contingents was under the command of a general from their own city, but the leader of the whole army was the most admired of all, Leonidas, the Lacedaemonian, son of Anaxandridas and descended from Heracles.[4] He came to Thermopylae with the customary 300 picked men, but these were selected from those with living sons.[5] He also brought with him the Thebans I mentioned when I gave the Hellene numbers. Leonidas had made a point of including the Thebans, singling them out from the rest of the Hellenes because it was strongly suspected that the city was about to medize. He summoned them to join in the war because he wanted to find out if they would send men or openly reject the Hellene Alliance. They did indeed send troops, but had other plans.[6]

The Spartans had despatched Leonidas and his men so that the rest of their allies would see them and take up arms rather than medize,

---

[1] This was probably not their full hoplite strength.

[2] Aegina had only contributed 18 triremes to the 271-strong fleet assembled initially at Artemisium but the island was a major sea power in the early 5th century, and, more significantly in the present context, had a long history of bitter enmity with Athens. Aegina had offered earth and water to Darius in 491.

[3] Echoes of the tragic concept of *nemesis* and general belief in the workings of fate.

[4] Herodotus lists all 20 ancestors in Leonidas' impressive genealogy.

[5] The Spartan royal bodyguard of 300 'knights' (*hippeis*) was not normally selected by one of the kings, and fatherhood was not a criterion for selection.

[6] Thebes medized, but after Thermopylae. The decision to do so appears not to have been taken at this point and the small contingent that was sent was probably representative of the faction that was committed to the defence of Hellas.

which indeed they might have done if they heard that the Spartans were hanging back. The rest of the Spartans were detained by the feast of Carnea but, as soon as they had celebrated it, they intended to mobilize their full strength and, leaving a small garrison in Sparta, to march to join them with all speed. The rest of the allies had similar intentions. In their case, it was the Olympic Festival that fell at the same time as these events and they were not expecting matters to come to a head so quickly at Thermopylae, so they too sent advance contingents only. This had been the plan, but when the Persians came closer to the entrance to the pass the Hellenes there became frightened and began to discuss how they might escape. The rest of the Peloponnesians were in favour of retreating to the Peloponnese and defending the Isthmus, but the Phocians and Locrians were greatly angered by the idea and Leonidas carried a vote in favour of staying where they were but sending messages urging every city to send reinforcements since their force was too small to hold the Persians off.[1] (7.201–07)

On Herodotus' count the Hellene 'advance guard' totalled 5,200 plus, possibly, a couple of thousand Locrians. By his count, there were 3,100 Peloponnesians, including the 300 Spartans (301 including Leonidas). The Peloponnesian allies that marched with Leonidas also sent relatively small contingents. None sent more than one third of the contingents they fielded at Plataea. Corinth was closest to Sparta, sending 400 to Thermopylae and, in the following year, 5,000 to Plataea; however it contributed 40 ships to the Hellene fleet, four times as many as Sparta at Artemisium.

According to Diodorus Siculus, there were 1,000 Lacedaemonians:

The leader of the entire expedition was Eurybiades, the Lacedaemonian, and in command of the troops sent to Thermopylae was Leonidas the Spartan king, a man who attached great importance to his courage and generalship. When Leonidas was given this assignment, he announced that only 1,000 men would be accompanying him on

---

[1] Herodotus almost certainly introduces this further round of debate for dramatic effect. The size of the force now facing them would not have come as a surprise to the Hellenes. Information had been coming into them for months as it rolled into Europe and it was Persian strategy to do nothing to impede the flow of this information.

the campaign. The ephors[1] declared that he was leading far too few against such a mighty force and instructed him to take more. He told them in confidence that they were few if their mission was to stop the Barbarians getting through the passes,[2] but actually many in terms of the mission they were setting out on. Baffled by this riddling response, the ephors asked him if he thought he was taking them to perform some task that was of little worth. His answer was that he was, in all appearance, leading them out to hold the passes, but the truth of it was that they were going to die for the freedom of all. So, if these 1,000 men marched, Sparta would win greater renown when they died, but if the Lacedaemonians marched out in full force, Lacedaemon would be wiped out, because not one of them would consider taking flight to save his life. There were, then, 1,000 Lacedaemonians, including 300 Spartans, and 3,000 other Hellenes[3] were sent with them to Thermopylae. (*Library of History* 11.4.2–5)

The 700 additional Lacedaemonians would have been *perioikoi*, 'neighbours', hoplites from cities of Laconia other than Sparta. It was normal for the *perioikoi* to supply levies for any Spartan mobilization and the presence of 1,000 Lacedaemonians is also attested by an earlier source, the 4th-century Athenian orator Isocrates. Diodorus introduces the idea that Leonidas was knowingly setting out on a suicide mission and, while he does not incorporate it in the *Historia*, Herodotus does seem to have been aware of this alternative narrative, which Diodorus and others go on to develop fully. Leonidas' selection of his 300 from 'those with living sons' would be as appropriate for a mission that was high-risk rather than suicidal, however.

Even after the detachment of the 1,000 Phocians and the unknown number of Locrians, and on the assumption that the actual numbers of effective combatants were 5–10 per cent lower than Herodotus' rounded figures, Leonidas had 4,000–5,000 hoplites at his disposal to

---

[1] 'Overseers': five senior officials elected annually for a term of one year only, wielding executive power alongside the two kings and able to override them in certain circumstances.

[2] Possibly noting that there was more than one pass to be defended, though Diodorus uses the plural at a later point referring to the pass at Thermopylae only.

[3] Context strongly suggests that Diodorus is referring exclusively to the troops sent from the Peloponnese here. Herodotus' figure of 3,100 for this component is close to Diodorus' 4,000 less the 700 extra Lacedaemonians.

hold a front which narrowed to about 15 m at the wall and was strongly protected on both flanks. When most tightly formed up, hoplites each occupied about 1 m, so 120 in files of eight, for the sake of argument, would have created a formidable human barrier in the space in front of the wall. And hoplites were not the only resource. Each would have come with his attendant, a Helot serf in the case of the Spartans and a lower-class citizen or slave for the rest. In addition to fulfilling the role of soldier-servant and baggage-carrier, these men would have provided the labour for rebuilding the wall and could also take on a light-armed combat role, potentially doubling Leonidas' combat manpower. Leonidas was more than amply resourced to hold the pass of Thermopylae, but a significantly larger force would have been needed for any attempt to defeat Xerxes and drive him out of Greece. If the Artemisium–Thermopylae line could be held for a couple of weeks, and if, as Herodotus states, there was the will to commit the full strength of the Peloponnese's land forces so far north of the Isthmus, 30,000–40,000 hoplites might then have faced the Barbarians with at least the same number of light-armed troops in support. This army would have been outnumbered, but by nothing like the factor Herodotus' figures would suggest and, at this stage of the campaign, the invasion force would not have included the significant hoplite contingents of the medizing cities of central Greece.

Xerxes' army of invasion, as already discussed, could not have been as monumentally vast as chronicled by Herodotus. The most plausible guesses at the combatant strength of Xerxes' land force point to a figure no greater than 200,000. A proportion of this total was probably strung out to the rear protecting lines of communication and supply and policing recently surrendered territory, and a further significant proportion was probably diverted to open up the alternative route over the mountains into Boeotia. In his account of the fighting at Thermopylae Herodotus mentions only three out of the 45 peoples named in his epic muster-list, the Medes, the Cissians and the Persians. It could have been a substantial spearhead group made up of elite troops rather than Xerxes' entire land force that arrived at Thermopylae. This would still have outnumbered the Hellenes by a factor of ten or more, but 'would not be able to exploit their weight of numbers or their cavalry in the pass'. Thermopylae could be held against frontal attack for any period of days or weeks.

The special appeal made to the Locrians and Phocians reflects concern that they might medize (earlier Herodotus states that the Locrians already had), undermining the defence before it could even be mounted by placing it in enemy territory. Herodotus describes them as marching 'to Trachis to assist in the defence'. Trachis here can be taken to mean the city of Trachis or the general area in which the Hellenes were gathering to meet the Barbarians. In favour of the former interpretation, the city of Trachis commanded the northern end of the alternative, inland route up the Asopus Valley and then over the mountains towards Boeotia, and the role of the Trachinians in the defensive plan must have been to block this. The position was as important strategically as the Middle Gate at Thermopylae, a detail not mentioned by Herodotus or any other source for this campaign, but supported by evidence that the city, later known as Heraclea, played a part in the defence of Thermopylae on a number of subsequent occasions, including Brennus' invasion. The Trachinians would have had as important a role here as the Thessalians and Macedonians in a defence of the Tempe line; Locris was a close neighbour and Phocis lay to the south on the inland route so there was a logic to their reinforcing the Trachinians.

The tradition of suspending warfare for the duration of major festivals like the Panhellene Olympic Games and Sparta's Carnea was generally respected but clearly not allowed to stand in the way of the mobilization of Leonidas' 'advance guard' or the much greater commitment represented by the simultaneous deployment of the entire allied fleet. The two festivals concluded at the full moon in the same month, the Olympic Games lasting five days, the Carnea seven (this was the full moon that the Spartans had to wait for in 490 before marching to Marathon); the Olympic festival was pan-Hellenic while the Carnea, Dorian in origin, was a strictly Peloponnesian affair. Herodotus tells us later that the fighting at Thermopylae had ended before the Olympic Games were over so Leonidas' call for urgent reinforcement was quite probably received in the Peloponnese after the Carnea had begun. Leonidas' message is unlikely to have been a cry for help with the defence of the Thermopylae position against the forces immediately facing it. He and the rest of the Hellene commanders may have more realistically reassessed the threat of outflanking by the western route, or even received intelligence that a major thrust was already under way. It is understandable that there would have been greater reluctance to abandon the festivals' rituals and celebrations once they had begun, and it was perhaps assumed that a couple of days' delay could be afforded. In the event, it is likely that even an immediate response would have been too late. The Hellenes had not been expecting 'matters to come to a head so quickly' and it seems they were caught out by the speed of the Barbarians' advance south from Macedon, a lightning strike in contrast to their ponderous march from the Hellespont to Therme.

Even for an advance guard, 300 hoplites, albeit commanded by a king, was a very small number to send if the Spartans' intention was to lead by example; a Lacedaemonian spearhead force of 1,000 would have made more sense. Three hundred was indeed the customary number for a royal bodyguard, but it was customary for recruits to be picked from Spartiates (full citizens of Sparta) who were between the ages of 20 and 30. A Spartan could not marry until he was approaching 30 so; exceptionally, Leonidas (and not the committee that selected the *hippeis*) picked his 300 from older Spartiates who had fathered sons. Spartiate status could be inherited only down an unbroken male line and, in this way, Leonidas was acknowledging the risk of the mission by sending men who would and could fight to the death without compromising their state's future military strength. Ironically, half a century on, at the time the *Historia* was first being heard and read, local wars, natural disaster and, above all, social change had significantly reduced the Spartan elite, a demographic trend that was to continue into the 4th century with inevitable consequences. This initial deployment of a fraction of Spartan hoplite strength, 300, perhaps plus 300–400 aboard their ten ships in the fleet at Artemisium, if marines were not supplied by the *perioikoi*, was very modest in comparison to the 5,000 to be committed at Plataea the following year. But it appears to have had the desired effect of cementing the Hellene Alliance at this crucial moment and of securing Spartan leadership on land and sea, recognition of Sparta's reputation as the supreme warrior nation of Hellas. In any case, as has been seen, Athenian leadership was unacceptable to the rest of the Peloponnesians.

Xerxes sent a mounted scout to see how many Hellenes there were and to observe what they were doing. While still in Thessaly he had heard that this small force was being assembled and that it was to be led by the Lacedaemonians and Leonidas of the house of Heracles.[1] When the scout rode up towards the enemy position he was able to take a good look at it. However, he could not see the whole of the defending force because part of it was out of sight to the rear of the wall that had been rebuilt. But he could see the men who were in front of it with their weapons laid out on the ground, and it happened to be the Spartans who were posted there at that moment. The scout was amazed to see that some of them were exercising while others were simply combing their hair. He counted them and closely observed all that he could. Then he rode back unchallenged, for there was no pursuit and in fact nobody took any notice of him at all.[2] So, he returned to Xerxes and reported everything he had seen. Xerxes listened to this but could not comprehend its meaning, which was that these men were making themselves ready to be killed and to kill to the best of their ability. Their behaviour seemed laughable to him and he sent for Demaratus who was in the camp and questioned him to find out why they were doing this.

Demaratus replied, 'I told you about these men before, when we were setting off for Greece. But you just laughed while I told you how I saw this business turning out. Yet it is very important to me that I set out the facts before you, O King. So listen to me now. These men are here to fight with us for the pass, and that is what they are preparing to do; it is their custom to dress their hair when they are about to risk their lives. You must understand that if you can overcome these men and those that have stayed behind in Sparta, no other race of mankind remaining will be able to lift a hand against you. For now, O King, you are taking on the fairest city-state, the fairest kingdom, and the finest men in all of Hellas.' Xerxes found it quite impossible to believe what he was hearing and asked a second time how such a small force could face his army in battle. Demaratus answered, 'Punish me as a liar, O King, if things do not turn out as I say they will.' But nothing he could say would convince Xerxes. So, the Great King waited for four days, confident that the Hellenes would sneak away. (7.207–10)

---

[1] Xerxes had good intelligence of the alliance's planning and preparations, and was well aware of its fragility and the tensions within it.

[2] Pursuit on foot would have been pointless and the scout would have kept out of range of sling- or bowshot, if there were any slingers or archers amongst the non-hoplite attendants.

Diodorus Siculus offers a briefer version of this conversation in which Demaratus makes a telling point:

> The Great King asked the Laconian, 'Will the Greeks fly more swiftly than my horses can gallop, or do they have the spirit to stand and fight this mighty force?' Demaratus, they say, replied, 'You have personal knowledge of Hellene bravery,[1] for you use Hellene troops to suppress Barbarians who rise against you. So, do not think that men who fight better than Persians to make your rule secure will place themselves in harm's way any less bravely when fighting against Persians for their own freedom.' With a scornful laugh, Xerxes commanded Demaratus to stay at his side and see the Lacedaemonians put to flight. (*Library of History* 11.6)

The wall was now high enough to conceal the men immediately behind it, and more of the defence force may have been further to the rear in Alpeni. It is likely that the rebuilt stonework had been extended upward with a timber palisade and head-cover, perhaps with hides as some protection against fire-arrows. It had probably been necessary to construct a new gate, timber reinforced with bronze, to block the 2–3m opening. This was wide enough for a single wagon or two or three hoplites standing side by side and, importantly, would serve as a sally-port. The Spartans now in front of the wall may not have been the entire 300 but would have been in sufficient numbers to form up in depth in the narrow space to hold attackers back to prevent them scaling the wall or getting their hands on it to break it down.

In the period of waiting it is likely that there was communication between the two camps, through heralds or less formal channels. Herodotus records several instances where the Persians attempt to parley or informally cajole entire armies, individual contingents or leaders into surrender before joining battle. Mardonius' critique of the Hellene way of war mentioned the Persian approach of 'settling differences by using heralds and messengers, or by any means other than battle'. At Thermopylae, Plutarch famously records a direct and blunt exchange between Xerxes and Leonidas:

[1] *Andreia*: also with the meaning of 'manhood'.

When Xerxes wrote a second time, 'Give up your weapons', Leonidas wrote back, 'Come and get them.' (*Moralia; Laconian Aphorisms* 51.11)

Leonidas' archetypally laconic response, '*molon labe*', may be literally translated as 'coming take' with the challenging implication 'first you have to get here'. But, sadly, this is almost certainly a later invention, and it is hard to imagine Herodotus omitting it in his account if he had come across it anywhere in his researches. In any case, the two sides would very probably not have communicated in writing.

THERMOPYLAE: FIRST DAY

After four days when the Hellenes had still not budged, Xerxes, now angered by the lack of respect he felt they were foolishly displaying, sent in the Medes and the Cissians,[1] commanding them to take the Hellenes alive and bring them into his presence. They swept down on the Hellene ranks. Many fell but others took their place and would not be driven back despite the great violence of the resistance. However, it was plain for all to see, and especially for the King, that in this great mass there were few real men.[2] The fighting went on all day and eventually the Medes were withdrawn, very badly mauled, and the Persians took over the assault. These were the men the King called his Immortals and Hydarnes was their commander, and they were expected to win the battle without difficulty. But, when they engaged with the Hellenes they did no better than the Median contingent.[3] This was because they were fighting in the pass on a narrow front and with shorter spears than the Hellenes, and they could not exploit their superior numbers. The Lacedaemonians fought most remarkably, demonstrating their

[1] The Cissians were close neighbours of the Persians and were armed like the Persians and Medes and, no doubt, fought in the same way.

[2] In successive sentences Herodotus highlights the Barbarians' commendable determination to press home their attack against immovable opposition and their lack of true-Hellene manliness. But he clearly has a higher opinion of them than projected by earlier comparisons of Hellene and Barbarian qualities and motivation.

[3] The Immortals were clearly intact enough to carry out the demanding mission they were to be sent on just 24 hours later.

combat skill in the face of men who lacked it. For example, they would all turn their backs and pretend to give way and the Barbarians, seeing this, chased shouting and clattering after them. When they had almost caught up with them, the Lacedaemonians wheeled round to face them again and killed Barbarians beyond counting, and there were just a few Spartan casualties. So, finally, the Persians fell back. They had made no progress into the pass although they had tried attacking in waves and in every other way. The King watched the battle from a throne, and it is said that during these assaults he leapt up three times in his deep concern for his troops.[1] (7.210–12)

Diodorus Siculus' account of the fighting is broadly similar but offers some extra colour and detail:

Xerxes gathered his army together and launched his attack on the Hellenes at Thermopylae. He positioned the Medes out in front of all the other peoples, either selecting them for their courage or because he wished to be rid of them all; for their spirit was still unbowed, having only recently lost the hegemony which their ancestors had enjoyed.[2] And he picked out the brothers and sons of men who had fallen at Marathon to stand by the Medes in the belief that they would take their revenge upon the Hellenes with the greatest fury.

So, the Medes, drawn up as I have described, attacked the defenders of Thermopylae. But Leonidas was ready for them with his Hellenes massed in the narrowest part of the pass. The fighting was ferocious. With the King present to observe how bravely the Barbarians fought, and the Hellenes focused on their liberty with Leonidas urging them on into the fray, an astounding struggle developed. They were fighting hand-to-hand at close quarters and the lines were densely packed together, so, for a long time, the battle was evenly balanced. But the Hellenes' valour was superior and their shields were larger, and the Medes gradually gave way, for many of them fell and not a

---

[1] 'It is said ...' can be interpreted as Herodotus' strong hint that this dramatic vignette may be pure invention.

[2] The Medes had actually had longer to get used to Persian rule than any other people in the empire.

few were wounded. Their place in the line was taken by Cissians and Sacae, chosen for their bravery. These were fresh troops taking on men who were already exhausted, but they could not stand the heat of battle for long. They were cut down and forced back by Leonidas' men, and they too gave way. The Barbarians were equipped with small round shields or *peltai*,[1] which gave them the advantage on open ground where there was space for movement. But in this tight space, they could not easily wound their opponents, formed up as they were in close order with large shields protecting their entire bodies, whereas the lightness of the Barbarians' protective gear was a disadvantage and they received numerous wounds.

At last, observing that the entire area of the pass was heaped with corpses and that the Barbarians could not withstand the valour of the Greeks, Xerxes sent in the picked band of Persians known as the Immortals, who were renowned as the bravest in his entire host. But when these too were put to flight after resisting only briefly, then finally, as night fell, the battle ended. Many Barbarians had been slain but only a few Hellenes had fallen. (*Library of History* 11.6–7)

This was the opening chapter of the story that the Spartans who did not go and the Hellenes who did not stay to die wanted told. Glorious legend swiftly cloaked what could be easily presented as tragic and embarrassing failure. The tactics described do not chime well with the glimpses Herodotus gives us of other Barbarian battles in the *Historia*. With or without cavalry (mounted archers and javelin-throwers), the Persians were primarily missile-fighters. Repeated and, even less, continuous efforts at shock-tactics with frontal attacks on a more heavily armed, static enemy secure on both flanks, do not ring true and are not recorded anywhere else. The Persians had fought alongside and against hoplites many times over previous decades and, as Diodorus' Demaratus points out to Xerxes, they knew what hoplites were capable of, and they were also well aware of their own capabilities, and, no doubt, limitations.

However, Herodotus does add the detail that the Persians 'tried attacking in waves *and in every other way*' and a clue to what may have been the true character of the fighting comes later in his account of

---

[1] Lightweight shields made predominantly of hide and often shown as crescent-shaped.

the third and final day of the battle: 'On the two previous days they had defended the line of the wall ...'. This sounds less like a pitched battle than a siege, with a succession of Barbarian attempts on the wall and Hellene sallies to drive them back from it. The assault groups would have carried light scaling ladders and tools for undermining and hacking at the stonework, but heavier siege gear, such as rams and wheeled towers, is not mentioned anywhere in Herodotus' account of the invasion and it would not have been practicable to transport it on the march to Greece. The Persian way of fighting a pitched battle was to begin with a sustained barrage of arrows delivered by massed footsoldiers and squadrons of horse-archers, the latter advancing and retiring in waves without coming into direct contact. Swords and spears were brought into play in close combat, ideally when enemy formations were broken or sufficiently weakened by missile attacks. Herodotus gives a brief description of these standard tactics in his very short account of Cyrus' last battle and describes it in more detail in his narrative of Plataea. There and in his shorter account of Marathon he also shows how hoplites could deal with these tactics.

Herodotus does not mention Persian archery at Thermopylae until the third day but, as groups approached the wall, they would have been supported from behind by massed archers, showering the defenders with arrows. However, it is a reasonable assumption that they were well protected, not only by their shields and helmets, but by frontal and overhead structures. The groups charging out to drive off assault teams would have presented only fleeting targets before they engaged, when arrows would be as likely to strike friends as enemies. The Lacedaemonian manoeuvre, so vividly described, could have been used in some of their sorties; if this is a true memory, probably the Spartans alone had the professionalism to execute it with such deadly efficiency. Nevertheless, the practice of darting out in front of the battle line individually or in small groups is, in any case, well documented in contemporary and near-contemporary accounts of hoplite warfare. Thucydides supplies a little more detail in his description of a battle fought in 423 between a force under the command of Brasidas, the great Spartan general, and a larger body of non-hoplite Barbarian troops, in this case Illyrian:

Seeing that the Illyrians were about to attack, he formed his hoplites into a square and placed his contingent of light-armed inside it and prepared to retreat. He positioned the youngest soldiers so that they could dash out to meet an attack from any direction and himself stood ready at the rear with 300 picked men to make a stand against the leading ranks of the enemy to screen the withdrawal. (*History of the Peloponnesian War* 4.125)

This was a fighting retreat, but Thucydides' description of the tactical use of hoplite skirmishers (*ekdromoi*, literally 'runners out') fits well with Herodotus' glimpse of the action. It also acknowledges the combat role of *psiloi*. The tactics here are proactive, and the mention of hoplite skirmishers, of light-armed deployed amongst hoplites, and of the special role for the elite 300 (*logades*), suggests a degree of flexibility that many later descriptions of the classic phalanx would not seem to allow.

ARTEMISIUM: FIRST DAY

In Herodotus' chronology, the fighting on land and sea took place on the same three consecutive days. He enjoyed symmetries of this kind, but the reality was probably less tidy, though it is very likely that the fighting came to an end on both fronts on the same day.

The Hellenes discussed the information Scyllias had brought and, after much talk, they concluded that they should stay put for all of that day, then, after midnight, move out to confront the squadron sailing round the island. However, when no attack came and they had waited till late in the afternoon, the Hellenes sailed out against the Barbarians facing them with the aim of testing them in battle and trying out their line-breaking manoeuvres (*diekplous*). When Xerxes' generals and soldiers saw the Hellenes bearing down on them in just a few ships, they thought this was madness and pulled towards them confident of an easy victory; and they were so confident because they could see that the Hellene ships were few whilst their own significantly outnumbered them and were more seaworthy. Underestimating them in this way, they manoeuvred to surround them. Those Ionians who were serving Persia unwillingly and looked upon the Hellenes as their friends thought they were witnessing a great disaster as they watched them being surrounded. They were certain that none of them would see their homes again so convinced they were of the Hellenes' frailty.

But there were other Ionians who were delighted to see what was happening and they competed with one another to be the first to capture an Athenian ship and win a reward from the King, for there had been a great deal of talk about the Athenians in their camps.

On the first signal, the Hellenes manoeuvred to face the enemy prow to prow with their sterns all turned towards a central point. On the second signal, tightly hemmed in as they were, they set to work head-on and took 30 Barbarian ships. They captured the brother of the king of Salamis in Cyprus, an important man in the Persian invasion force, and the first Hellene to take an enemy ship was an Athenian, Lycomedes son of Aeschraeus, and he won the prize for valour. The contest was still in the balance when night fell and separated the two sides. The Hellenes sailed back to Artemisium and the Persians, having done much less well than expected, sailed back to Aphetae. In this battle Antidorus of Lemnos was the only Hellene on the King's side to desert to the Hellene side and the Athenians rewarded him with land on the island of Salamis for this act. (8.9–11)

According to Herodotus' account, the Hellenes decide on a day of inactivity before leaving their position in the middle of the night to confront the encircling squadron in the Euripus channel. However, the narrows at Chalcis could have been blocked by a very small number of triremes and moving the whole fleet south would have left the Oreos channel open and the land position at Thermopylae exposed to seaborne attack from the rear, demolishing the whole defensive strategy. Sailing under cover of darkness might have given the Hellenes a head-start but the Persians would have discovered their absence soon after first light at the latest and immediately moved to exploit it. The Hellenes then change their minds when nothing has happened by late afternoon and, according to Herodotus' sources, proactively mount an attack, to all intents for training purposes. Both sides presumably had ships out on the straits throughout the day, keeping watch on the other's movements and testing their reactions. However, with the odds against them, it would have been unacceptably risky, if not suicidal, for the Hellenes to initiate a full-fleet engagement in the open water that lay between the two fleets, even if the enemy offered battle. It is more likely that they were content to stay on the defensive, ready to counter any thrust to the west with as many ships as necessary. Their priority was to hold the Oreos channel. The Barbarians may also have been content to wait in the hope that fear and disunity amongst the Hellenes would settle things in their favour, as at Lade, but now decided that the time had come to make their first move in the direction of the channel, or to provoke the Hellenes by sailing directly at them.

Herodotus' description of the Hellenes' response fits formation into a circle, or into a crescent with flanks dropped back. The former tactic is documented twice by Thucydides in his account of the Peloponnesian War, but only as executed by units of up to about 50 ships. It would seem impracticable to form a larger number of ships into a complete circle while under attack without creating openings for enemy *diekplous* as the manoeuvre was carried out. Assuming 6m of clear water between each trireme's oar blades, which would have been tight and would have required very precise co-ordination, the Hellene fleet would have formed an unwieldy circle well over 3km in circumference and approximately 1km in diameter. Ships would have been highly vulnerable as they manoeuvred into this formation from either line or column, and it would have been a lengthy process requiring parade-ground precision. A more likely interpretation is that the Hellenes re-formed their line into a crescent. This would have been demanding enough for such a recently formed multi-national fleet in its first action.

If Herodotus' sources were correct, the Hellenes, Athenians to the fore, can be envisaged as going into battle with a specific plan to fight in a tight formation to prevent the Persians exploiting their numerical advantage and the 'better sailing' quality of their ships. The risk was reduced by the timing of the engagement, late in the afternoon. The Persians had enough ships and sea-room to overlap both Greek flanks and began their envelopment. In response to a trumpet signal given by the command ship and repeated down the line, the Greeks drove forward or held position in the centre and backed water on the flanks, turning to keep their rams pointed at the enemy. Alternatively, the number of ships committed was small enough for a circle formation to be practicable and, possibly, this manoeuvre was carried out. On a second signal, they went at the Barbarian ships prow on prow or side-on if passing across their bow. The apparent initial success of this tactic may have come about because the Barbarian fleet was caught out of formation as it manoeuvred to respond. The result was undecided when darkness fell, but, as at Thermopylae, the Hellene defence had held.

THERMOPYLAE: SECOND DAY

The battle continued in the same way as before, and the Barbarians did no better in the contest. Because the enemy were so few the Barbarians hoped that they would be weakened by wounds and unable to hold out any longer. But the Hellenes each took their turn in the battle line organized into contingents, city by city, with the exception of the Phocians, who were tasked with guarding the track over the mountain.[1]

So, the Persians fell back yet again, having achieved no more than on the previous day. The King was struggling to think what action he could take to deal with this situation when Ephialtes son of Eurydemus, a Malian,[2] came to speak with him. Hoping to be richly rewarded by the King, he told him about the track that led over the mountain to Thermopylae and thus brought about the death of the Hellenes who made their stand there. Ephialtes is the man who showed the Barbarians how to get over the mountain on that track and here I record his guilt. Xerxes approved Ephialtes' proposal and, in much better spirits, gave his orders to Hydarnes and the unit he commanded,[3] and they started off from the camp at lamplighting time. The track was first used by the Malians who lived in the area when they guided the Thessalians into Phocis after the Phocians had built their wall to block the pass and protect themselves from attack. For all that time the Malians had known about the evil use the track could be put to. It begins by the River Asopus where it passes through its ravine, and the track and the mountain it crosses are both called Anopaea. It follows the mountain's spine and ends by the city of Alpeni,[4] which is in the part of Locris closest to Malis. It comes out by a rock

---

[1] This is Herodotus' first mention of any specific action to deal with the known threat on the position's southern flank. The Phocians' position, which cannot be precisely identified, would have been reached more easily from Trachis than the Middle Gate of Thermopylae.

[2] Later identified more precisely as from Trachis, the main city of Malis. *Ephialtes* means 'nightmare' in modern Greek.

[3] The Immortals.

[4] Previously referred to as a village. Quite substantial remains were identified at the end of the 19th century so it seems it was a fairly significant settlement.

known as Melampygon ('Black Buttock')[1] and the sanctuary of the Cercopes. It is very narrow here.[2] So, the Persians followed the track I have described after crossing the Asopus and marched through the night with the Oetaean mountains on their right and the Trachinian mountains on their left.[3] (7.212–17)

Whatever the nature of the fighting, the Hellenes would have been able to rotate the men in the narrow front line at regular intervals, giving the Persians little prospect of wearing them out. In fact, it may have been a quieter day. With the flanking march planned but possibly postponed because of the storm that hit the Persian naval encampment after the first day's fighting at Artemisium, the Persians may have been content to sit back and wait. But the Hellenes who were to abandon Thermopylae the next morning would have wanted to be remembered for taking a more active part in the fighting than they actually did, and perhaps created their own legends. It is unlikely, if they did not know already, that it had taken the Persian generals the best part of a week to discover that there was a way round the Hellene position that did not involve a long detour inland. However, finding a trustworthy guide to lead a night march over the peaks, ridges and valleys to the south of Thermopylae could have taken time. The Persians may also have wanted to wait until their fleet was ready to break through at Artemisium and move south in step with the army. In their initial confidence that the blocking force would simply fade away or could be quickly swept aside, the Persians may even have thought a flanking move would not be needed, until it became embarrassingly clear that neither of these things was going to happen. Ephialtes stands out from a number of Hellenes named in the

---

[1] This unidentified rock formation was named after Heracles' deeply suntanned buttocks and presumably looked like them, seen from certain angles. The Cercopes were two mischievous imps who lived in this place. According to a genteel footnote written a century or so ago, Heracles, in one of his adventures, 'carried off two on his back, hanging head downwards, in which position they had every opportunity of observing his title to the above epithet; until their jests on the subject moved him to release them'.

[2] Herodotus may mean the East Gate rather than the path.

[3] The Oetaean range lay to the south. 'Trachinian mountains' probably means the western end of the Callidromus range, which would have been on the Persians' left as they followed the Asopus. They may have crossed the river at the point they left it to strike out over the mountain; however, it is tempting to translate the word used (*diabantes*) as 'marching along' or 'following'.

sources as the traitor of Thermopylae. He was probably representative of a local faction that was in favour of medizing and perhaps hoped to be rewarded with a position of authority over his compatriots, as well as with Persian gold.

If Herodotus is correct that Hydarnes and his men initially took a road up the Asopus gorge, the inland route over the mountains to Boeotia was now open, and the Trachinians, and whoever else was with them, had clearly failed to play their part in the Hellene defensive plan. Ephialtes could have taken the Persians up onto Callidromus by one of the steeper and narrower tracks to the east of the Asopus gorge. However, this would have been a difficult climb for a large force, particularly at night. Pausanias includes some later history in his description of the area which includes the information that Brennus the Gaul took his considerably larger force along the same route as Hydarnes. Brennus' Thermopylae, as told by Pausanias, includes some other intriguing parallels:

There are two ways over the Oetaean mountains.[1] The one above Trachis is a severe climb and very steep; the other, passing through Aenian territory, is better for the movement of an army. It was by this route in former times that Hydarnes the Persian attacked Leonidas' Hellenes from the rear, and this was the way the Heracleans and the Aenians[2] offered to lead Brennus, not out of any ill-will towards the Hellene cause, but because they were intent on getting the Celts out of their land before they occupied and ruined it.[3] Brennus liked their offer and so he left Acichorius in charge of the main army with orders to launch his attack the moment they had the Hellenes surrounded, then he picked out a detachment of 40,000 men and set off along the track. That day it chanced that the mountain was covered in a thick fog that blocked out the sun and the Phocians who were keeping watch over the track had no idea that the Barbarians were approaching until

---

[1] Pausanias may have regarded the western end of Callidromus as part of the Oetaean range; otherwise he has the Gauls (and Persians) detouring an unnecessary distance away from Thermopylae at the beginning of their march.

[2] Later in the 5th century Trachis was renamed Heraclea when occupied by the Spartans. The Aenians came from north and west of the Asopus but may have had influence or been trying to establish it in the Trachis area at the time.

[3] The sort of pragmatism that caused many Hellene cities to medize in the 5th-century war.

they were right on top of them. The Gauls attacked immediately and
the Phocians put up a stout defence, but in the end they were forced
back off the track. However, runners managed to get down in time to
tell their comrades what had happened before the envelopment of the
Hellene army was quite complete and the Athenians arrived in their
triremes just in time to evacuate the Hellenes from Thermopylae.
(*Guide to Greece* 10.22.8–12)

Both Hydarnes and Brennus initially followed the road that ran alongside
the Asopus, eventually leading to Boeotia through Doris, then left it to
continue east and then north across Callidromus to descend from the
ridge above the East Gate and Alpeni. Whilst the first third or so of
this route can be traced with a degree of confidence, most of the rest
cannot. There were, and are, a number of tracks leading across Anopaea,
taken here as meaning the whole upland area not one particular path.
Some of these would have been more than footpaths and used for the
movement of livestock, and they were not unsuitable for the movement
of large bodies of troops. If Pausanias' statement that Brennus took
40,000 men this way in 279 is reasonably accurate, Hydarnes could
have comfortably taken all of his 10,000 and would have wanted to,
not knowing that more than half of the original defenders would be on
their way back to the Peloponnese before he arrived at the East Gate.

ARTEMISIUM: SECOND DAY

Although it was high summer there was torrential rain all through
the night with thunderclaps rolling off Mount Pelion, and the
wreckage and corpses driven into Aphetae became draped around
the prows of the ships and entangled with the oar-blades. With such
terrible things happening to them, the Barbarians were convinced
they were doomed. For as soon as they had recovered from shipwreck
in the tempest raging off Pelion, they found themselves caught up
in a sharp sea-battle, and after that they were hit by another terrible
storm with flash-floods streaming down to the sea and great claps of
thunder. This happened to the fleet at Aphetae that night, but the
ships detached to sail round Euboea suffered much more terribly.
They were caught out in the open sea and their fate was dire. The
tempest struck them while they were off a stretch of coast called the

Hollows and they were carried blindly before the wind and dashed against the rocky shore.[1] So, divine intervention brought it about that Hellene and Persian numbers would be more evenly matched. The force off the Hollows of Euboea was wiped out; the Barbarians at Aphetae were very glad to see the dawn. They made no move the next day, content to rest up after the suffering they had been through. However, the Hellenes were reinforced by the arrival of 53 more Athenian ships, and this and the report they now received that the Barbarian fleet sailing round Euboea had been completely destroyed gave them great encouragement. So, after staying on the defensive they sailed out at about the same time as the day before and attacked some Cilician ships. They sank them and sailed back to Artemisium as night fell. (8.12–14)

The overnight storm and its impact on the Barbarian fleets are graphically presented. A second Hellesponter could have blown up in the night in this period of unsettled weather, and would have had the same devastating effect off the east coast of Euboea. But, coming in from the north-east, it would have driven the wreckage and corpses from the previous afternoon's fighting towards the Hellene position, so perhaps it blew in from the south on this occasion. The echoes of the descriptions of the storm that came down on Xerxes' army from Mount Ida near Troy and of the one that did so much damage to his fleet off the coast of Magnesia might suggest later amplification of rather thin original source material. Herodotus' reference to 'divine intervention' could then be a hint that he saw the tale of the mission and destruction of the 200 ships as an invention, like Scyllias' epic swim. In any case, this disaster conveniently reduced the Great King's fleet to a size that more credibly matched the memories of those who actually faced it, or served in it at Artemisium and Salamis. But it can also be read as the writer's sincere acknowledgement that divine forces were at work; the weather in the Aegean at this time of year is generally more settled.

Herodotus' few lines on the action suggest that it was much like the previous day's, with the Persians standing off and the Hellenes watching

---

[1] The Hollows have been identified as a cluster of rocky promontories and inlets on the east coast towards the bottom end of Euboea.

and waiting, perhaps with some feinting and parrying, and one burst of real fighting. Herodotus lists the Cilicians as contributing 100 ships to the Persian fleet, so this action could have been more than an interception and minor skirmish. It may have been a second attempt on the Oreos channel successfully parried by the Hellenes. On the other hand, the Cilicians could have been late arrivals from the north caught by the Hellenes as they swung west into the straits, like the squadron of 15 stragglers taken earlier.

THERMOPYLAE: THIRD DAY

Dawn was breaking as the Barbarians reached the crest of the ridge. Here 1,000 Phocian hoplites were in a defensive position, as I have already explained, protecting their own territory and keeping watch over the track. The lower pass was defended as I have described; the Phocians had willingly agreed with Leonidas that they would take on the task of defending the track over the mountain.

This is how the Phocians discovered that the Persians had made the climb. At first they were unaware of their approach because the mountainside is covered with oak trees. But there was no wind and then they heard the rustling of many feet in the carpet of dry leaves.[1] So, the Phocians ran to their positions and began to arm themselves, and in a moment the Barbarians were there in front of them. They were surprised to see men arming, for they were not expecting any opposition but had come up against an army. Hydarnes was concerned that the Phocians might be Spartans and asked Ephialtes where these men were from. Much reassured that they were from Phocis, he drew his Persians up in battle formation. Under a hail of arrows, the Phocians hastily retreated to the top of the ridge ready to die, thinking that the Persians' primary objective was to attack them. So they thought, but the Persians with Hydarnes and Ephialtes paid no further attention to them and set off down the mountain, moving fast. (7.217–18)

---

[1] No one who was there could have forgotten the shock of hearing this sound, cutting through the stillness of the dawn.

There are some doubtful details in this account. Having dealt with any opposition around Trachis, or having encountered none, Hydarnes may not have expected to encounter any on the way, but 1,000 hoplites, even with as many light-armed attendants, would not have looked like an army to his 10,000, and the Persians quite probably knew what Spartans looked like from the previous days' fighting. In any case, the ineffectualness of the Hellene flank-guard needs explanation. If Hydarnes had his full 10,000 with him, the Phocians were significantly outnumbered and evidently not in a position where they could avoid being outflanked and surrounded. Perhaps it was felt necessary only to secure the south-western area of the Callidromus and the most likely route to the East Gate against the smaller force that might have been sent up a narrower, rougher track that led up from the plain to the east of Trachis. It seems the Phocians were positioned to block access to a well-trodden track that led east and then roughly north through Anopaea and across Callidromus to the eastern end of Thermopylae, and maybe near to an intersection with one or more other tracks leading up from the surrounding valleys and plain. To the extent that the Phocians did indeed meet the Barbarians, the plan was good. But it did not anticipate their arrival in such force and so early in the day, nor perhaps that the enemy would move on without any delay rather than form up and fight a pitched battle. Also, Herodotus hints at what may have been an ambiguity in the orders given to the Phocians when he describes them as 'protecting their own territory and keeping watch over the track'. Phocis lay roughly to their south whereas the route the Persians were to follow led east, along or alongside the southern ridge of Callidromus and then north.

In this interpretation, the Phocians, detached from the force based in the city of Trachis blocking the inland route to Boeotia, would have been positioned close to a point where the road from Trachis branched south towards Doris, Phocis and Boeotia, and east or north into Anopaea to become the path of that name. It was correctly predicted as in 279 that a Barbarian flanking force would pass this way. This south-western location is supported by two other details in Herodotus' narrative. There are plenty of oak trees on the lower slopes and in the valleys at the western end of Callidromus, but pines and firs take over higher up. Secondly, it is a reasonable assumption that the night part of the march, moving more slowly in the dark and mostly climbing, would have covered about one third of the 20–25km to the East Gate from the start point somewhere on the plain of Trachis.

If they made a choice, the Phocians may simply have decided to mount a defence of their home territory without realizing that the enemy force had no intention of heading in that direction; or, they may have prepared for battle in the hoplite manner in the best defensive position available to them, not thinking that the enemy might ignore them if they were not in their way. In any case, they were clearly unprepared for a dawn attack, and their rapid retreat to a position that was no obstacle to Hydarnes' flank march showed a lack of tactical vision or lack of clarity in the orders they had been given. A thousand hoplites in a good blocking position could have held up the Immortals for some time. However, such a position may not have been available to them, making it inevitable that they would be bypassed, whether there was any contact or not. Herodotus acknowledges the Phocian 1,000's responsibility but does not question their courage or commitment, nor does he blame anyone, from Leonidas downwards, for these failings. Conventional hoplite tactics and doctrine, better suited to symmetrical, formal clashes in the cultivated valleys and plains of Greece, less fit for more fluid and tactically complex warfare in rougher terrain, may have been partly to blame.

Unfortunately, Herodotus has nothing to say about the role of the Trachinians and Locrians in the disaster. However, he includes the Locrians, probably Opuntian rather than Ozolian, but maybe both, amongst the Hellenes who submitted earth and water around the time Xerxes entered Greece. Later, he mentions the Opuntian Locrians' contribution of seven penteconters to the Hellene fleet at Artemisium but lists the Ozolian Locrians amongst the Hellenes fighting on the Persian side at Plataea. The Trachinians are not mentioned again. It is possible they sat things out behind their city walls whilst the Locrians medized for a second time, perhaps as a consequence of the Trachinians' 'neutrality'.

The Hellenes at Thermopylae first found out what was in store for them from the seer Megistias. He could see from his sacrificial victims that death would come to them on the following day. Then deserters[1] came in during the night and told them about the Persians' flank march. Finally, after sunrise the lookouts came running down from the heights. The Hellenes held a council and opinions were divided. Some were against abandoning the position, some took the opposite view. Decisions were made, and some contingents pulled out and dispersed, returning to their cities, while others made their preparations to stay at Leonidas' side.

It is said that Leonidas personally dismissed the contingents that went home out of concern for their survival but that he thought it would be unseemly if he and the Spartans with him abandoned the position which they had set out to defend in the first place. There is another view, which I hold firmly myself, that Leonidas ordered the others to withdraw because he had observed their lack of enthusiasm and unwillingness to play their part in facing up to the danger. As far as he was concerned, retreat would be dishonourable but by staying behind he won great glory, and also secured the good fortune of Sparta. For the Spartans had consulted the Delphic oracle about the war when it first began and the Pythia[2] had prophesied either that Lacedaemon would be laid waste or that one of its kings would fall. Her response, given in verse, was worded as follows:

'Your doom, you who dwell in Sparta's wide lands:
Either your great, far-famed city will be sacked by the Persians,
Or else all of Lacedaemon shall lament a fallen king of Heracles' blood.
The might of bulls and lions[3] cannot resist the power you face.
It has the might of Zeus and, I tell you, cannot be resisted
Unless one or other of these prophecies is fulfilled.'

I think it was with this response in mind, and in his desire to win glory exclusively for the Spartans, that Leonidas dismissed his allies,

---

[1] These would have been from amongst the Hellenes drafted into Xerxes' army from the west coast of Asia, the north shore of the Aegean and northern Greece. They may be an invention: there is no mention in any source of Hellenes on the Barbarian side being involved in the fighting at Thermopylae, and it would have been very difficult to find a way through or round the narrow and closely contested front line.

[2] The title of the prophetess at the shrine of Apollo in Delphi whose inspired utterances were interpreted and transcribed, often ambiguously, for the enlightenment and often confusion of individuals or delegations seeking the god's advice.

[3] Perennial symbols of strength and courage, but also with a play on Leonidas' name.

but it also ensured that their withdrawal was orderly. In my view, an important piece of evidence for this is that, as is well known, Leonidas wanted to send home Megistias, the Acarnanian seer who had come along with the army. He was said to be descended from Melampous and had foreseen from his sacrificial offerings what was going to happen. However, though he had been dismissed, he would not leave and, in his place, sent home his son, his only son, who was serving with him in the army.[1]

So, the allies who had been dismissed went off, obedient to Leonidas, and the Theban and Thespian contingents were the only ones that stayed behind with the Lacedaemonians, the Thebans reluctantly and against their will because, in truth, Leonidas kept them there as hostages. But the Thespians were fully committed. They had refused to leave Leonidas and abandon his men and so stayed with them and shared their death. Their commander was Demophilus son of Diadromes. (7.206–22)

It was probably later in the day than Herodotus suggests when the Hellenes were informed that the Phocians had been outflanked, but runners, as in 279, could have arrived a couple of hours ahead of the Barbarians. In any case, there would have been little time for debate amongst the various commanders and this contingency may have already been planned for. The loss of Leonidas' entire force, dead or captive, would have left the alliance more critically outnumbered and, more seriously, would have undermined the resolve of its members. But a rearguard action had to be fought to buy as much time as possible for the retreating contingents to get beyond the reach of pursuit. They needed to set off as soon as possible and in an orderly fashion because their pursuers would be cavalry and Xerxes' faster-moving infantry. 'Concern for their survival' is a plausible reason for ordering them to leave promptly. However, there is nothing in Herodotus' account of the previous days' fighting to support the suggestion that he himself agrees with, that Leonidas had perceived a 'lack of enthusiasm' on the part of these men. If anything, their morale is likely to have been high

---

[1] Megistias, from north-west Greece, was distinguished for his descent from Melampous, a famous seer identified elsewhere by Herodotus as a major influence on the early evolution of the cult of Dionysus. Megistias' son presumably came along as his assistant.

after playing their part in mounting, so far, a successful defence, though it may have quickly plunged when word of the flank march came down the line. But if Leonidas had not stayed with his men, there could not have been a rearguard; in the warfare of ancient Greece, leadership in battle could only be by example and from the front. Herodotus must be correct, then, in his suggestion that thoughts of honour and duty, that is to say *nomos*, played an important part in his decision. Leonidas' desire for personal glory and his acceptance of fate and the will of the gods as communicated by the oracle reinforced it and linked his 'great and marvellous deeds' with the heroic past, as sung by Homer. Audiences and readers would have been reminded of Achilles' resolve to avenge the death of Patroclus in full knowledge that he would lose his own life:

My doom I will accept whatever time it is the will of Zeus
Or other immortal gods to bring it on.
Not even mighty Heracles escaped his doom.
Most dear he was to Zeus, Cronos' son, the king,
But fate and Hera's fierce anger broke him.
And so, I too will lay me down to sleep in death
If a like fate is wrought for me.
But for now, let me win high renown ...
For all your love for me, do not try to hold me back from battle
Or change my mind.
(*Iliad* 18.115–21, 126)

It is, of course, possible that the Delphic prophecy emerged and was even fabricated after the event, adding another facet to the legend created to vindicate the Spartan sacrifice, and to give credit to Delphi. Herodotus' omission of this detail earlier in his narrative, when he introduces Leonidas as the commander of the Hellene land force, may indicate his own scepticism. The story of Megistias is an interesting illustration of the importance attached in warfare to the rituals of divination and to the professionals who carried them out, but does not prove anything about Leonidas' dealings with the rest of his troops. Megistias' insistence on staying is remarkable because he was not a Spartan, not a soldier and not under Leonidas' command. As for the 400 Thebans, it is unlikely that they were pressed into service as unwilling hostages on that final day; as such they would have been worse than useless in the desperate fighting. More probably they were representatives of the democratic faction that was opposed to the city's oligarchic rulers' intention to medize, unequivocally demonstrating their commitment to the Hellene cause. According to Diodorus in his account of the battle:

> There were some 400 Thebans from the opposition[1] party, for the people of Thebes were divided against each other over the question of forming an alliance with the Persians. (*Library of History* 11.4.7)

Like the 300 Spartans, these Thebans represented a small fraction of their city's hoplite pool. On the other hand, it seems that the 700 from Thespiae were that small city's entire strength. Both Thespiae and Thebes were cities of Boeotia, much closer to the action and under more immediate threat than the Peloponnese, and that may have influenced their contingents' decision to remain with Leonidas. Whatever their motivation, Leonidas could buy more time with nearly 1,400 hoplites at his disposal according to Herodotus' count, or 2,000 adding on the 700 Lacedaemonian *perioikoi* from the alternative tradition.

In an anecdote preserved by Plutarch, Leonidas 'encouraged his men to eat up their breakfast because they would be dining in Hades' (*Laconic Sayings* 225d). If this was said, there were no Spartan survivors to pass it on and it is unlikely that a Theban overheard it, but the dark humour would have been appreciated because there would be nothing for their shades to eat in Hades and only blood to drink.

> At sunrise Xerxes poured offerings of wine to the gods then waited till about the time that the market fills[2] before ordering his men to attack. Ephialtes advised this timing because the route down from the mountain is more direct and much shorter than the path around and up it. So, the Barbarians under Xerxes launched their attack and the Hellenes under Leonidas, knowing that their mission was to end in death, now advanced into the wider section of the pass, much further forward than they had been before. On the two previous days, they had defended the line of the wall, moving forward to fight only in

---

[1] Literally 'other'.
[2] Around 10.00am.

the narrower space, but now they engaged the Barbarians outside this defile. A great number of the enemy fell. Behind them their commanders drove the ranks ever forward with whips, thrashing their men indiscriminately.[1] Many of them fell into the sea and drowned, even more were trampled to death by their comrades. The slaughter was indescribable.

The Hellenes fought with all their strength and with reckless fury, knowing very well that death was closing in on them, brought by the force that had come over the mountain. By this stage in the battle most of their spears were broken and they were killing the Persians with their swords. And, in the thick of this, Leonidas fell, his excellence proved, and with him fell many other famous Spartans: I found out the names of all the men of distinction, in fact I know the names of the whole 300. At the same time, many famous Persians died. Amongst them were two sons of Darius, Abrocomes and Hyperanthes, half-brothers of Xerxes, who fought and fell. There was a mighty struggle between the Persians and the Lacedaemonians[2] over Leonidas' body, and the Hellenes finally dragged it away after four times heroically driving the enemy back.

That was the situation until the Persians with Ephialtes came up and, as soon as they knew that they had arrived, the Hellenes changed their tactics. They fell back on the narrower section of the pass, retreated behind the wall and took up position on the mound, where the stone lion commemorating Leonidas now stands. They formed up tightly there, except for the Thebans, and in this place they fought on with their swords, those who still had them, and with their hands and with their teeth. The Barbarians, after demolishing the wall, showered them with arrows and javelins and pinned them down from the front whilst the flanking force encircled the rest of the position. (7.223–25)

Perhaps Xerxes launched his attack earlier than necessary, but it was important to keep the Hellenes fully occupied while the Immortals

---

[1] If it is Herodotus' intention here to shock, British troops, for example, in World War I and Russians in World War II were similarly 'encouraged' at gunpoint. To Hellene eyes this was the treatment of slaves.

[2] Meaning *perioikoi* as well as Spartans?

made their way down from the ridge and formed up at the eastern end of the pass. If it was necessary to negotiate a very narrow passageway, either the East Gate itself or at the point where the track came down to the road, this could have taken some time. Leonidas' proactive response may have been intended simply to take as many Barbarians with him as he could. In the circumstances, with no prospect of holding out for much longer, he could commit all his remaining hoplites to form a line at least 150m wide, even in files of eight. More gently rising ground on his left may have exposed that flank, but was probably too rough and overgrown for an extension of the hoplite line. Perhaps Thespians and Thebans and light-armed Helots were positioned there. If the water was deep enough for Barbarians to drown in, the right was naturally secured. In his account of the Hellene defence of the pass against Brennus and the Gauls in 279 Pausanias describes the Malian Gulf as a swamp, but navigable at this point. He also clearly indicates the advantage that close-in naval support would have given one side or the other:

> With difficulty and at some risk, the Athenians steered their ships through the mud-banks that stretch far out to sea and brought them as close to the Barbarians as possible. Then they raked their flank with arrows and every other kind of missile. (*Guide to Greece* 10.21)

Herodotus clearly contrasts the Hellenes' aggression in the opening phase of their last stand with the previous days' defensive tactics. They can be visualized advancing through the arrow storm in full force and in close order, probably not at the double, but at the steady pace preferred by the Spartans, and engaging hand to hand across the whole front. They were now fully committed for the first time with no reserves to the rear. The more lightly protected Persians with their shorter spears could not bring their weight of numbers to bear while the Hellenes' hedge of spears remained intact. The epic fight over Leonidas' body brings Homer to mind, and this short extract from the battle to recover the fallen Patroclus conjures up the scene and pre-echoes the discipline of hoplite combat:

> So they made a stand around Patroclus
> Their shields and thrust-out spears a palisade ...

The ground grew purple, soaked with gouts of blood.
Corpse was heaped on corpse,
Trojans and their mighty allies, and Hellenes too.
They too were bloodied in the fray, but fewer of them fell,
For each was ever mindful of his purpose in the press
To save his comrades from the precipice of death.
(*Iliad* 17. 354–55, 360–65)

But spears began to break and the line thinned as casualties mounted, and there were no replacement spears. Then the much shorter reach of the hoplite sword allowed the Persians to engage closer up, pushing shield against shield. The Hellene shield wall seems to have held as it was pushed back, and there may have been a brief rearguard stand at the wall whilst the rest fell back on the mound, perhaps with light-armed servants carrying Leonidas and any other casualties that could be recovered. The hand-to-hand fighting at this point probably lasted as long as the dwindling number of hoplites were able to charge out and take on the enemy. The final image of the Barbarians finishing off the last remnants of Leonidas' Spartans and Thespians and their servants with a deluge of arrows pouring in from all sides is starkly believable and was probably witnessed by the surviving Thebans.

The lion memorial is long lost (if it had been there in Pausanias' time, he would surely have included it in his guide to the site) but the hill on which the Hellenes made their last stand has been convincingly identified by the excavation of large numbers of Barbarian arrowheads, though it seems they were not lying where they fell, but gathered together and probably buried as an offering. This is the only battlefield of the Persian War on which any substantial archaeological evidence of this nature has been discovered. No human remains that can be conclusively dated have yet been found at any of them except, possibly, some charred bones under the *Soros* at Marathon.

Out of all the Lacedaemonians and Thespians who were so brave that day, it is said that the Spartan Dieneces was best of all. There is a story about what he said when a man from Trachis told him before the battle that there were so many Barbarians that when they shot their bows the great cloud of arrows covered the sun. Dieneces, unperturbed and unimpressed by the size of the Median army, replied, 'Our Trachinian friend brings excellent news. If the Medes are going to block out the sun, we shall be fighting them in the shade out of its heat.' They say Dieneces left not only this saying but others like it as his memorial. After him, two Lacedaemonian brothers, Alpheus and Maron, sons of Orsiphantus, were said to have won the greatest honour and, of the Thespians, Dithyrambus son of Harmatides is most highly spoken of. (7.226)

There can have been no Thespian or Spartan eyewitness accounts of the final day's fighting, though some memories could have been handed down by Theban survivors. Dieneces is famous only for what he is said to have said, though this particular saying is attributed to Leonidas by Plutarch, and is not very laconic as quoted. The heroic deeds of the Spartans Alpheus and Maron, and the Thespian Dithyrambus are, not surprisingly, unspecified.

Diodorus Siculus gives a dramatically different version of the battle's grand finale:

Leonidas, the king of the Lacedaemonians, in his desire to crown himself and the Spartans with the greatest glory, gave orders to the rest of the Hellenes to depart and save themselves to fight alongside fellow Hellenes in the battles that were still to come. But the Lacedaemonians, he declared, must stay behind and not abandon the defence of the pass, for it was most fitting that the leaders of Hellas should be ready to die as they strove to win the highest honour. So, all the rest immediately took themselves off, and Leonidas and his comrades stayed behind to do heroic and incredible deeds. Although the Lacedaemonians were few and he kept only the Thespians with him and had no more than 500 men altogether,[1] he was ready to embrace death for Hellas. After this, the Persians, having negotiated the difficult terrain with their Trachinian guide, soon had Leonidas trapped between the two forces. The Hellenes gave no thought to their own safety and chose glory in its place. With one voice they

[1] This implies a very high casualty rate sustained in the earlier fighting by the 300 Spartans, the 700 Lacedaemonians and the Thespians (Diodorus gives no number, but there were 700 according to Herodotus).

urged their commander to lead them out against the enemy before the Persians heard that their men had worked their way round to the rear. Leonidas was pleased with the spirit his men were showing and ordered them to eat up their breakfast as they would be eating next in Hades. He ate breakfast himself in obedience to his command to keep his own strength up for as long as possible to endure the stresses of battle.

When they were all ready after this quick meal, he ordered his soldiers to attack the Persian camp and make directly for the Great King's own tent, killing anyone in their path. Obedient to his command, they formed up in close order and launched a night attack[1] on the Persian camp, and Leonidas led the assault. The Barbarians were taken by surprise and unaware of the attack's objective, and so they rushed out of their tents and gathered together noisily and in great disorder. They thought that the troops who had set out with the Trachinian had been wiped out and that the entire Hellene force was in their midst, and they were terrified. So, many of them were killed by Leonidas and his men and even more died at the hands of their comrades, who mistakenly took them for enemies. The darkness of night made it impossible to work out what was really happening and the confusion that spread through the whole camp resulted in great slaughter, as one would expect.

The Barbarians kept on killing each other because the conditions made identification impossible, because no general was giving any orders, and because there was no password to be exchanged, and, generally, nobody was thinking rationally. In fact, if the King had stayed in the royal tent, he could easily have been killed by the Hellenes and the whole war would have been brought to a swift end. As it turned out, Xerxes had burst out of his tent into the midst of the tumult and the Hellenes fought their way into it and butchered almost everyone they caught there. Then, all night long they roamed throughout the camp looking for Xerxes, and this was the right thing to do. But, with the dawn, the situation became fully clear. Then the Persians saw how few the Hellenes were and became less concerned. However, they would not tackle them face to face but, fearful of their valour, took up positions

---

[1] Diodorus glosses over the period between breakfast and nightfall.

around their flanks and rear and shot arrows and hurled javelins from every direction, and killed them every one. And that is how the soldiers with Leonidas who held the pass of Thermopylae met their end. Who could not marvel at the valour they displayed? Without exception, they refused to abandon the post assigned to them by Hellas but gladly gave their lives to save all Hellenes. They preferred to die gloriously rather than to live on in shame. (*Library of History* 11.9–11)

Herodotus' and Diodorus' descriptions of two days of more or less continuous close-quarters fighting are highly implausible, but the final act of the drama, as told here by Diodorus, is far beyond belief. The reality was that the Persians had the Hellenes under siege, pinned down at their wall, and they would have kept a strong force within bowshot-range day and night, ruling out any possibility of mounting an attack on their camp. The Hellenes would have had to negotiate the even narrower West Gate first and then to cross the thousands of metres of more open country that lay between the pass and the Persian camp, which would in any case have been palisaded, gated and guarded. Plutarch offers a briefer version of this episode:

Herodotus, in his account of this battle, has blacked out Leonidas' greatest deed when he says that all fell in the narrow ground near the mound. It did not happen that way. For when they found out in the night about the Barbarians' flank-march, the Hellenes formed up, headed directly for the enemy camp, and came very close to the King's tent. They had resolved to kill him and die around him. So, they came close to his tent, killing or driving off anyone in their way. But they could not find Xerxes there so went ranging through that vast camp in search of him until, completely surrounded, they were, with some difficulty, cut down by the Barbarians. (*On the Malice of Herodotus* 32)

If, as is likely, this alternative narrative first came into being very soon after the battle, Herodotus would have known of it but clearly chose not to include it in the *Historia* and is taken to task for this by Plutarch. However, the epic, all-out confrontation forward of the wall with the Homeric struggle over Leonidas' body may well be his more modest concession to the glorious legend, putting a gloss on what may have been a less dramatic but brutal process of attrition once the Persians had the Hellenes surrounded. It was glorious enough that the Lacedaemonians and Thespians, and their attendants, resisted to the last man, but Spartan prestige required greater justification for the sacrifice.

ARTEMISIUM: THIRD DAY

Troubled at their humiliation by so few ships and fearful of Xerxes' reaction, the Barbarian commanders decided not to wait for the Hellenes to offer battle but advanced into the channel around midday, cheering each other on. It so happened that these sea-battles were fought over the same days as the land-battles at Thermopylae.[1] The Hellenes' objective was the same at sea as on land, for the fleet to cover the Euripus channel whilst the land army with Leonidas blocked the pass. The Hellenes were determined to stop the Barbarians advancing further into Greece; the Barbarians were equally determined to wipe out the Hellene defenders and clear the way. Anyway, Xerxes' ships sailed out but the Hellenes at first made no move forward from their position on the Artemisium side. But then the approaching Barbarians formed their ships into a crescent formation in order to envelop and surround the Hellenes, and they now moved out and engaged. Both sides had equal success, but Xerxes' fleet fell foul of its own mass and scale. His ships were thrown out of formation and collided with each other, but nonetheless they held firm and would not give way, thinking it disgraceful to be defeated by such a small number of ships. Many Hellene triremes and men were lost, but far more ships and men were lost by the Barbarians, and so the battle went until each side disengaged.[2] Out of Xerxes' navy, the Egyptians fought best and took five Hellene ships along with their

---

[1] Herodotus would have enjoyed the tidiness of this coincidence. The actual fighting may not have covered exactly the same three days, but continuing to hold the position at Artemisium was not an option once the defensive line at Thermopylae had been overwhelmed, so both land- and sea-battle ended on the same day.

[2] Possibly because night was falling, or because both sides accepted that their crews were too exhausted to continue.

crews.[1] On the Hellene side the Athenians excelled and Cleinias,[2] son of Alcibiades, was the best of them; he had contributed his own trireme with its 200 men to the fleet, all at his personal expense. (8.16–17)

Herodotus' opening sentence begs the question of the outcome and scale of the fighting on the previous days but, in his rapidly sketched outline of each side's objectives, he displays good understanding of the interlocking strategies on land and sea. For the Persian fleet, a breakthrough into the head of the Euripus would expose the rear and flank of the Hellene position at Thermopylae on the shore of the Malian Gulf to the west, and open the sheltered channel that led to the south. The task of the outnumbered Hellenes was to guard against such a breakthrough and it is unlikely that they would have taken the risk of sailing out into the wide space of the straits of Artemisium 'to offer battle' at any point during the confrontation. The account of the first day's engagement may have been the product of the same sort of legend-weaving that shaped 'the Spartan version' of the Thermopylae story. Here, though, it was to give matching glory to the Hellene fleet and, in particular, the Athenians, who supplied 200 of the 324 triremes that fought for Hellas at Artemisium. The fighting on the final day is likely to have been the only full-fleet action.

Herodotus goes into little detail, though he may be envisaging the two fleets sailing straight out and meeting somewhere in the middle of the channel to fight across it, each with a friendly shore to its rear. But a more plausible interpretation has the Persians, finally ready, making for the Oreos channel. They may have been waiting for orders to attack but it is unlikely that they were held back until progress had been made at Thermopylae because a breakthrough at Artemisium would have quickly made the Hellenes' land position untenable. The fleets swung west as they moved out from their beaches and moorings.

---

[1] With so many ships locked together there would have been a lot of deck-fighting and the Egyptians' success may be attributed to the fact that their marines were as heavily armed as Hellene hoplites.

[2] He was either the father or the great-uncle of the Alcibiades who won great fame and notoriety in the second half of the century. He too fitted out a trireme at his own expense, for the Peloponnesian War.

The Hellenes, on the look-out for this and with less water to cover, responded by forming a line across the channel's 5km-wide entrance. Allowing 15–20m for each, their 324 triremes, now including the 53 Athenian ships that had joined the fleet the day before, were sufficient to block this space in a single line, its left resting on unoccupied Cape Posidium and its right on the friendly shore of Euboea. But there may have been a phase in the manoeuvre when one, the left, or both of their flanks were exposed giving the advancing enemy an opportunity for *periplous*. Before the Persians could achieve this, the Hellenes may have fallen back into the narrower section of the channel, funnelling them into a situation where greater numbers and superior agility gave no advantage and a bow-to-bow slugging match ensued in the tighter space. Diodorus, in his description of a battle fought on the Hellespont towards the end of the Peloponnesian War, describes in a little more detail what happened when two fleets faced each other and engaged:

> As the fleets approached each other, they drew up their triremes in battle order. When they were ready, the commanders raised the signal for battle and at a single word of command the trumpeters sounded the attack. The rowers showed no lack of enthusiasm and the helmsmen handled their steering-oars with great skill, and an amazing contest ensued. For whenever a trireme drove forward, with perfect timing just before the moment of impact, the opposing helmsmen would cleverly change course so that the ships clashed ram to ram. As for the men on deck, whenever they saw the side of their trireme exposed to the enemy, they were terrified, fearful for their lives. But whenever their helmsman used his skill to parry the attack, they were cheered and felt much better about their prospects. (*Library of History* 13.45)

Herodotus continues:

> Each side was glad to return to base after breaking off, but at the end of the fighting the Hellenes were left in control of the corpses and the drifting hulls. However, they had been severely battered with the Athenians taking damage to half their ships, and indeed they were now planning to withdraw further into Greece. Themistocles believed

that the Hellenes might yet be able to get the upper hand over the
Barbarians, if the Ionians and Carians could be detached from them,
so he called all the commanders together to tell them that he had
devised a plan which he hoped would persuade the best of the King's
allies to desert, which was all he revealed of what he had in mind.
The Euboeans had driven their livestock down to the shore[1] and he
told the Hellenes that circumstances dictated they should sacrifice as
much of this as they wished, for it was much better that they should
have it than the enemy. He also urged each commander to order their
men to light fires. Finally, he assured them that he would take care of
the timing of their departure and their safe withdrawal into Greece.
This met with everyone's agreement and the Hellenes lit fires and set
to work on the livestock.

While this was being done, a scout[2] came in from Trachis. There
was also a scout at Artemisium, Polyas from Anticyra, stationed there
with a boat ready to row to bring word to Thermopylae if the fleet was
overwhelmed. The scout who came from Trachis was Abronichus son
of Lysicles, an Athenian, and he was with Leonidas and ready to carry
a message to Artemisium in his triaconter if there were developments
on land. Now Abronichus arrived with the news of Leonidas and his
army's fate and, so informed, the Hellenes delayed their withdrawal
no longer, moving off according their order of battle, the Corinthians
first and the Athenians bringing up the rear. (8.21)

When the fighting came to its inconclusive end, the Hellenes were 'left
in control' of the floating wreckage and corpses, maybe simply because
the battle was fought nearer to their beaches than to the Persians'.
But this would traditionally have signified victory in a Hellene land-
battle, and their fleet had fulfilled its mission that day. Themistocles,
not mentioned in the brief account of the fighting but surely in the
thick of it, orchestrating the execution of the plan that he had probably
crafted and leading from the front, was to pull this off for a second

---

[1] This was probably the daily process of bringing the flocks and herds down from pastures in the
hills rather than an emergency measure.
[2] *Kataskopos*, which might also be translated as 'observer' or 'look-out'. Polyas was a Malian.
Abronichus served alongside Themistocles in tricky diplomatic dealings with the Spartans
immediately after the war and was, it seems, assigned an important liaison role 'with Leonidas'.

time and decisively a few weeks later. The Hellenes had held the straits against the odds, but the cost in casualties and battle-damage had been so heavy that there was clearly little confidence that this could be repeated if the Persians, still numerically superior, attacked the next day. An earlier full-fleet battle would have had the same consequences and Thermopylae would very probably have fallen sooner. However, since the Hellenes were to confront the Persians in greater strength than at Artemisium just a few weeks later, much of the damage sustained cannot have been completely disabling. Some damage would have been reparable overnight or at sea but more of it would have required days or weeks of work on shore using dock facilities and timber and other materials stockpiled on Salamis or further south.

Herodotus' narrative becomes rather tangled in the next few sentences. If the commanders were planning withdrawal, they would already have been in council and Eurybiades, as fleet-commander, would have called them together. Sacrificing the Euboeans' livestock may have been his idea or Themistocles'. It would deprive the enemy of a useful supplement to their supplies and the customary distribution of meat after sacrifice would provide a welcome square meal before the Hellenes departed. In addition, the many fires would give the impression that they were not leaving, a tried and tested ruse, if they decided to sail that night. Herodotus was also interested in the episode because it appeared to fulfil an obscure prophecy.

Having received the bad news from Thermopylae, the Hellene commanders decided to abandon Artemisium and go south immediately without further debate:

> Themistocles selected the most seaworthy Athenian ships and put in at sources of drinking water along the coast. He had a message inscribed on the rocks to be read by the Ionians who would get to Artemisium the next day. This is what the message said: 'Men of Ionia, you do wrong to take up arms against your ancestors and enslave Hellas. Best you come over to our side, but, if you feel unable to do that, declare yourselves neutral and urge the Carians to do the same. But if neither of these things is possible and a greater power restrains you from deserting, then, when you go into action and we come together, hang back and remember that you are descended from us and that this conflict with the

Barbarians was brought about and brought upon us by you.' In my view Themistocles wrote this with two purposes in mind. The King might not find out about it, but it could persuade the Ionians to change sides and join up with the Hellenes; or, when it was reported to him, and this would be in the worst possible light, then he might become so distrustful of the Ionians that he would keep them away from the fighting. (8.22)

Themistocles' plan to detach Hellene elements from the Persian fleet, as described by Herodotus, did not amount to much and was to be almost completely ineffectual. It was a message that was undoubtedly communicated to the Hellenes on the Persian side at every opportunity before and during the invasion. But it is hard to imagine formally worded inscriptions being set up in these circumstances and Themistocles would have been content to leave an abbreviated version of it, and more crudely presented, on the rocks of the beaches that he was speedily abandoning.

Herodotus closes his account of the fighting at Thermopylae with anecdotes of the survival of one or two out of the Spartan 300:

It is said[1] that two of the 300, Eurytus and Aristodemus, were given a choice, upon which they had to be in agreement, between escaping to safety in Sparta or, if they did not wish to go home, dying with the rest. They had been granted sick leave by Leonidas and were in bed at Alpeni with serious eye infections. Either option was open to them, but they could not agree and made opposing choices. When Eurytus was told about the Persians' flank march, he called for his armour and put it on. Then he ordered his Helot to guide him into the thick of the fighting. This the Helot did but afterwards immediately took to his heels and Eurytus plunged into the fray and to his death. But Aristodemus was left behind, in a fainting fit.[2] Now if it was only Aristodemus that had been sick and returned home to Sparta, or if both men had returned together,

---

[1] Herodotus' signal that he is not convinced.

[2] The Greek word is *lipopsychia*, meaning unconsciousness caused by physical exhaustion or wounds. But *opthalmia* of itself would not have caused fainting and some scholars have suggested *philopsychia* as an alternative reading, meaning attachment to life or cowardice.

I don't think the wrath of the Spartans would have been directed at them at all. However, one of them was killed while the other, with no special excuse, chose not to meet his death. Inevitably, great was the Spartans' wrath with Aristodemus. However, while there are some who say that he survived the battle because he was sick, others say he was sent away from the camp to deliver a message and could have come back to take part in the fighting, but that he saved himself by loitering on the way whilst his fellow messenger returned and was killed. Anyway, back home in Lacedaemon, Aristodemus was shamed and dishonoured.[1] For example, no Spartan would give him a light for his fire or even speak to him, and, in his disgrace, he was known as Aristodemus the Runaway.[2] However, at the battle of Plataea he purged himself of all the guilt that had been laid upon him. Finally, it is said that there was another survivor from the 300 called Pantites, who had been sent to Thessaly[3] with a message, and he was so ashamed of the disgrace when he came home that he hanged himself. (7.229–32)

There were also Thebans who survived:

As for the Thebans under Leonidas' command, they had fought for a while for the Hellenes against the King's army because they were forced to. But when they saw that the Persians were getting the upper hand, at the moment when the Hellenes with Leonidas were rapidly falling back towards the mound, they peeled off towards the Barbarian lines. They stretched out their hands in supplication and declared, and they were indeed telling the truth, that they had medized and that Thebes had been amongst the first of the Hellenes to give the King earth and water,[4] and that they had been forced to come to Thermopylae and could not be blamed for any of the losses suffered by the King. They saved themselves in this way for

---

[1] *Atimia*: to be stripped of all honours, privileges and respect.
[2] A slightly different reading of the Greek *tresas*, preferred by most, gives the more graphic 'Trembler', but running away would seem more significant a breach of *nomos*.
[3] By now there would have been no point communicating with the Thessalians.
[4] Thebes is included with the Locrians in Herodotus' listing of the Hellenes who submitted earth and water around the time of Xerxes' arrival in northern Greece.

they also had the Thessalians to vouch for them. But this was not the best of outcomes because the Barbarians killed some of them as they were approaching and made the rest prisoners. They branded most of them with the royal mark on Xerxes' orders, beginning with their commander, Leontiades. This man's son, Eurymachus, was executed by the Plataeans sometime later after he had occupied their city in command of a force of 400 Thebans.[1]

So, that is how the Hellenes fought the battle of Thermopylae. (7.233)

The 'survivor' anecdotes leave a feeling of anti-climax. Aristodemus and Pantites were clearly seen as cowards whose behaviour was in breach of *nomos*. However, it is hard to see the logic in the deal that the two sick men were offered and Pantites' unavoidable absence does not seem so disgraceful as to justify suicide, although Herodotus expresses the view that Aristodemus, with the same affliction, had 'no special excuse'. Herodotus may have felt bound to include them because they were already embedded in collective memory. In Aristophanes' *Frogs* (first performed in 405), Charon, the ferryman of Hades, refuses to take the god Dionysus' slave on board if he has not served at Arginusae, a sea-battle fought towards the end of the Peloponnesian War. The slave says he did not 'because I happened to have an eye infection'. This may simply have been a well-known malingerer's excuse, but a few lines on, when Dionysus is trying to talk his way out of doing the rowing himself, he declares, 'I have no experience, I am a landlubber and I did not fight at Salamis'. So, in the dark days leading up to Athenian surrender in the Peloponnesian War, Aristophanes was reminding his audience of the glories of the Persian War.

Whatever the circumstances of the Thebans' surrender, and perhaps they were detached to secure the hill while the rest fell back on it, it is unlikely to have been as dishonourable as painted here. Herodotus' attitude to the Theban 400, who may have been as committed to the fight as any of the other Hellenes up to this point, can be explained by

---

[1] This was in 431 BC at the outbreak of the Peloponnesian War. According to Thucydides (*History of the Peloponnesian War* 2.3), Eurymachus was not actually in command of the Theban force that attempted to take the city with inside assistance, but he was one of the leaders of the operation. Plataea held out for best part of three years in the subsequent siege.

later events which took place in his lifetime. There was war between Athens and Thebes in the middle of the century and Thebans carried out the attack on Plataea, Athens' most loyal ally, which started the Peloponnesian War in 431. Throughout that war, Thebes was on the same side as Sparta, of course, but recognition of the latter's decisive contribution to final victory over the Persians appears to have outweighed any similar prejudice, even before an audience of Athenians.

> When the fighting was over, the Great King walked amongst the heaped-up corpses. Leonidas lay amongst them and when he was informed that this was the body of the Lacedaemonian king and commander, Xerxes ordered his men to cut off his head and impale it on a stake. It is plain to me from this piece of evidence, not the smallest of many, that Xerxes the King was more enraged by Leonidas while he lived than by any other man. Otherwise he would not have committed this outrage,[1] for I know very well that of all peoples the Persians customarily show the greatest respect and honour to brave warriors. Anyway, his men carried out the order that they had been given. (7.238)

Leonidas may have been identified by some feature of his insignia or equipment, for example a transverse crest on his helmet, and he was probably some years older than any of his comrades. But perhaps it was Demaratus who pointed out his body and he would have deeply regretted the consequence, regardless of the circumstances of his exile. Herodotus treats Xerxes more sympathetically elsewhere, but here he points up the savagery and arrogant folly of the alien autocrat that Hellas was resisting.

The Hellene strategy for the defence of the Artemisium–Thermopylae line can be summarized as follows. The fleet's mission was to keep the Oreos channel closed to the Barbarians. On land, the mission was to block the main route south via Thermopylae, and the alternative inland route through Doris. Leonidas was well dug in at the Middle Gate of Thermopylae with an advance guard that was more than adequate to

---

[1] Decapitation and mutilation in general were normal methods of punishment in the Persian world. In the Hellene world it was customary for the victor to treat the enemy dead with respect and return them under truce, having stripped the bodies.

hold off frontal assaults indefinitely, so long as the fleet could protect the rear and right of his position from seaborne attack. The inland route was to be blocked by the Trachinians, Locrians and Phocians, based in the city of Trachis; the Phocians were given the task of blocking the track that led to the upland area of Anopaea with its access to the East Gate to the rear of Leonidas' position. The defence to be mounted around Trachis was as critical to the overall plan as the blocking force at Thermopylae. With the reinforcements that were to come up as soon as the two festivals were over, the Hellenes presumably planned to give battle on the plain of Trachis to defeat the Barbarians and drive them out of Greece. But whatever the future intentions, only a fraction of available Hellene hoplite strength was committed at this point. On the other hand, most of the Hellene fleet was committed from the outset. Absolute defeat of the Persian fleet may have been the ultimate goal, but successfully blocking the way to the west and south was a more realistic aspiration. The long way around the eastern side of Euboea was left open, it seems, but maybe the reserve of 53 triremes that came up later was initially positioned to the south of the island to counter that possible threat.

The plan did not work. It seems that the invaders reached the Artemisium–Thermopylae line sooner than expected and in greater force. The Trachinians and Locrians gave up, probably without a fight. The Phocian blocking force failed, surprised and hopelessly outnumbered, to stop or even delay Hydarnes' flank march. The Hellene triremes held the straits for as long as the army held the pass, though it seems that the enemy could have broken through in a second day of full-fleet action. With the battle comprehensively lost on land, total disaster was only just avoided. The heroism and sacrifice of Leonidas and his rearguard were glorious and the extraordinary example of the 300 Spartiates (not to mention the 700 Thespians and 700 Lacedaemonians, if the latter were there) undoubtedly reinforced the morale and resolution of the Greek alliance. But this effect would have been limited in the depressing context of a disastrous failure of planning and battlefield command that allowed the Great King such an easy passage on land into Boeotia and Attica. Planning was a collective responsibility, but Sparta's voice had been the most influential in the debate; battlefield command had been Sparta's absolute responsibility. So, there was an urgent need to present the failed defence of Thermopylae in the best possible light.

In World War II, Dunkirk, presented convincingly as disaster turned to triumph even before the evacuation was complete, was the same sort of phenomenon, though Winston Churchill did feel the urgent need to introduce some balance by pointing out that 'wars are not won by evacuations'.

There would have been more clear-eyed views of Thermopylae. The Athenian Thucydides recreates a conference that took place in the Peloponnese in 432 to consider action to counter Athenian aggression and expansionism. His version of a Corinthian delegate's speech includes criticism of Spartan procrastination and apparent lack of commitment:

> You Lacedaemonians are unique amongst the Hellenes in the way you defend yourselves against an enemy without making a move or using any force, but simply by saying what you intend to do; and you are unique in the way you do nothing to curb an enemy's power when it first starts to grow and then deal with it when that power has doubled. Nevertheless, it was said that you could be relied upon, but this was bending the truth because, as we know, the Mede had to come all the way to the Peloponnese from the ends of the earth before you properly committed yourselves to facing him. (*History of the Peloponnesian War* 1.69.4–5)

That is to say, the Spartans only 'properly committed' themselves when they mobilized in force to fight at Plataea; what they did at Thermopylae was too little and too late, and the Athenians would have taken the same view of their late arrival at Marathon. If Leonidas had been able to hold out longer at Thermopylae, the Spartans could argue, the necessary commitment would have been demonstrated a year earlier, but who could know? The rapid failure of this defensive plan threatened to undermine Sparta's claim to battlefield leadership of the Hellene Alliance and, closer to home, Spartan hegemony in the Peloponnese. This effect was compounded by the victory that was to be won only weeks later at Salamis, nominally under Spartan leadership but undeniably an Athenian triumph. So, the myth was quickly spun of the glorious failure of a heroically suicidal mission launched with the objective of ending the war by killing the Great King. It helped that there were no surviving eyewitnesses of that last day or, rather, night's fighting on the Hellene side, and the Peloponnesians who had fought on the previous days would not have been inclined to play down the tale of, mostly imagined, close-quarters combat in which the Barbarian hordes were repeatedly beaten back. Herodotus subscribed to this element of the myth. The final scene in the Persian camp does not emerge in surviving sources earlier than Diodorus Siculus but his account is likely to have been based on his important source, Ephorus, whose 4th-century histories have not survived.

The Hellenes were buried where they fell[1] and an inscription, which was also for those who had died before the rest were sent home by Leonidas, was set up saying:

> 'From the Peloponnese four thousand battled here
> Against three hundred times ten thousand.'

This was for all of them.[2] The Spartiates have an epitaph of their own:

> 'Stranger, let the Lacedaemonians know
> That here we lie, obedient to their commands.'[3]

That was for the Lacedaemonians and there is also one for their seer:

> 'In memory of famed Megistias,
> Slain by the Medes when they crossed the River Spercheus,
> A seer who had clear sight of his approaching doom
> But scorned to forsake Sparta's leader.'

The first two inscriptions and memorial stones were commissioned by the Amphictyons.[4] Simonides, the poet, personally set up the epitaph for the seer Megistias because he was his friend.[5] (7.228)

---

[1] This is unlikely to have been precisely the case, taking account of what the Persians did with the bodies after the battle.
[2] Not all from the Peloponnese; there were also the Thespians, who fought and died to a man as gloriously as the Spartans, and the Thebans who fell.
[3] The Greek word *rhemata* has the more general meaning of 'words' or 'sayings' and may have intended connotations of *nomos*. *Rhetrai*, 'covenants', might have been a better choice of word but would not have produced the perfect cadence of the closing two words, *rhemasi peithomenoi*.
[4] Organizations made up of representatives from the various cities of Hellas with responsibility across Hellas to look after the interests of the great sanctuaries, Delphi, in particular.
[5] Simonides is thought to have written all three.

The first inscription is a commemoration of all the Peloponnesians who fought at Thermopylae, including those who died. Herodotus' figure for this element of Leonidas' force is 3,100, which might reasonably have been rounded to 3,000. However, the addition of the 700 Lacedaemonian *perioikoi* cited by Diodorus Siculus and Isocrates to Herodotus' count could justify the round figure of 4,000. If the 700 Lacedaemonians were present, Herodotus would have known about it but, if he did, he chose to follow a version that omitted them in order, presumably, to add more gloss to the noble sacrifice of the Spartan 300. But, if their closest allies had shared in that sacrifice, it is hard to believe that the Spartans would or could have written them out of the story. Perhaps they were part of Leonidas' original force but sent home at the same time as the rest.

The two lines for the Spartiates set an impossibly high standard for the epitaphs of all other wars and is simply inscribed in modern Greek on a plain granite slab on top of the hill, to be read facing the Persians' line of attack from the west:

Ω ΞΕΙΝ ΑΓΓΕΛΛΕΙΝ ΛΑΚΕΔΑΙΜΟΝΙΟΙΣ ΟΤΙ ΤΗΔΕ
ΚΕΙΜΕΘΑ ΤΟΙΣ ΚΕΙΝΩΝ ΡΗΜΑΣΙ ΠΕΙΘΟΜΕΝΟΙ

This is rather more moving and inspiring than the 'Leonidas Statue', set up in the 1950s alongside the car park on the other side of the road in a spot that would have been underwater in the 5th century. Herodotus states that the epitaph is for the Spartiates alone. 'Lacedaemonians' could be used to mean citizens of Sparta (the city) as well as members of the wider community of Laconia and Messenia, and the ambiguity is convenient here. The poet may also have preferred it to 'Spartiates' for metrical reasons.

The individual epitaph for Megistias, sponsored as well as written by one of the foremost poets of the time, is an indication of the seer's distinction. The omission of participants, apart from Megistias, who were not from the Peloponnese is not unusual in this sort of nationalistic context (the Athenians did not always include the Plataeans when remembering Marathon), but there were other memorials which Herodotus may not have seen, or simply did not include. A separate epitaph for the Thespians has been preserved:

These men once dwelt beneath the brow of Helicon.
Spacious Thespiae proudly hails their valour.
(*Palatine Anthology* App. 94)

It is possible that Simonides also created an epic-style elegy on the battle. He is known to have celebrated the battles of Artemisium and Plataea in this way and the occasional Homeric flourishes in Herodotus' narrative may echo these. Diodorus quotes a few lines which could have been part of the Thermopylae elegy:

The men who died at Thermopylae,
Glorious their deeds, beautiful their end.
Their grave an altar. Remembrance is theirs
In place of lamentation, praise-singing their reward.
Nor mould nor all-conquering time
Shall tarnish this burial-offering.
This sepulchre of the brave is made a home
For the fair renown of Hellas.
Leonidas, Spartan king, is witness.
He leaves behind a glorious crown of valour
And undying fame.
(*Library of History* 11.11)

The potent mythology of the land-battle rapidly inflated its importance in comparison to the simultaneous sea-battle, reducing the naval action to the status of a lesser sideshow. Thermopylae was a hoplite battle and the Hellenes were led by a Spartan king. Excelling with spear and shield alongside fellow-members of the hoplite class was far superior to pulling an oar in a trireme; this was work for lowlier citizens, resident aliens, Helots (in the Spartan fleet) or slaves. The commander of the Hellene fleet was a Spartan, probably an aristocrat but not a king. Themistocles, the Athenian man of the people, was truly in command, and 200 of the 324 triremes finally deployed were supplied and mostly manned by Athens, unpopular, even hated, towards the end of the century, now overshadowed by the Peloponnesian War. In terms of assets, the Hellene commitment was far greater at Artemisium than at Thermopylae. The triremes themselves represented massive capital investment and were irreplaceable within the probable timescale of the war, even supposing timber was immediately available. The figure of 70,000 is a reasonable estimate of the total manpower on board with at least 4,000 and as many as 10,000 drawn from the hoplite elite. Fewer than 6,000 hoplites were deployed on the first two days of fighting at Thermopylae, supported by about the same number of light-armed and support troops. Defeat at Thermopylae was as tragically disastrous as it was inevitable, and it was necessary to make a stand there if the Greeks were also to fight at Artemisium, but it was survivable, so long as the fleet held its position. Defeat at Artemisium, yielding control of the sea to the Persians, would have lost the war, which, of course, might have happened if the Hellene fleet had not withdrawn and the Persian fleet had attacked again. The naval alliance had held together and its triremes, seamanship and combat skill, albeit with many participants tested in action for the first time, had proved itself a match for the Great King's fleet. But, not surprisingly, in view of the mythology, Herodotus says rather less about Artemisium (8.6–23) than about Thermopylae (7.200–38), and later sources add very little.

However, Plutarch, writing half a millennium later in his largely unflattering *Life of Themistocles*, has the perspective right. He recognizes that Artemisium was inconclusive (a bruising draw would be a fair description) but eloquently summarizes what the Hellenes gained from the battle and quotes with approval a fragment of Pindar, who lived through the Persian War. Plutarch focuses on the positive psychological effect that needed no propaganda to boost it, but it is also possible to see hints of the tactics that were successfully used, and Pindar gives due credit to Athens:

The battle which was fought against the Barbarian fleet in the straits of Artemisium did not decide the outcome of the war, but the Hellenes benefited greatly from the experience they gained. From what they were able to achieve when severely tested, they learned that men who knew how to engage at close quarters and who had the courage to stand and fight had nothing to fear from overwhelming numbers of ships, from glittering ornamentation and insignia, nor from shrieked-out warcries and barbaric battle-hymns. They learned to treat such things with contempt. They learned that they must hurl themselves upon the enemy to grapple with him in a fight to the finish. Pindar showed his understanding of all this in words he wrote about the battle of Artemisium:

> 'Here the sons of Athens
> Set in place the corner-stone of freedom,
> Brightly shining.'

For fearlessness is truly the foundation of victory.
(*Themistocles* 8.1–2)

But the Persians were also entitled to a degree of confidence. It had taken them just a few days to open up the land routes into central Greece and they had achieved this with little loss. They had not won a decisive victory at sea, but the Hellene fleet had abandoned its position and was limping south and the sea route to the Saronic Gulf and the Isthmus was now open.

Fire and fierce Ares

The Fall of Athens

Herodotus' account of the Persians' resumed advance southward to Attica and Athens and into the Saronic Gulf is quite fragmented and not very extensive. However, between his descriptions of the battles of Thermopylae and Artemisium he provides some strategic context in a review of the options open to the invaders. He does this through the medium of discussions between the Great King and two of his closest advisers:

> Xerxes sent for Demaratus[1] to ask him some questions. He began, 'Demaratus, you are a man I can trust. I am persuaded of that by the way things have turned out, because everything has happened as you told me it would. So now answer me this. How many Lacedaemonians are there left? And of these warriors, how many are as good as those who fought here, or are they all as good?' Demaratus replied, 'Great King, the population of Lacedaemon is large and there are many cities[2] in it. But I will tell you what you really need to know. In Lacedaemon there is one city called Sparta. About 8,000 men live there who are all of them equals[3] of those who fought here. The rest of the Lacedaemonians are not their equals, but they are good men.'

[1] The former Spartan king's final appearance in this role.
[2] These were the cities of the *perioikoi*. The exact number is not known but there were perhaps 40–50 at this time, all smaller than Sparta itself.
[3] *Homoioi*, a term also applied to the Spartiates, full-citizen members of Sparta's warrior elite.

Xerxes then asked, 'How can we conquer these people with the least difficulty? Come on now, advise me! You were their king so you must understand the way they make their plans.' Demaratus answered him, 'Great King, if you really want advice from me, I must give you the best that I can. This is it. Send 300 ships from your fleet to the coast of Laconia. There is an island off it called Cythera. Chilon,[1] our wisest citizen, said this would be of greater benefit to the Spartans if it sank beneath the sea than if it stayed above its surface. He was concerned about the use to which it might be put, as I will now explain. He had no foreknowledge of your invasion; rather, he was fearful of any invasion. You must use this island as a base from which to harass the Lacedaemonians. With war brought so close to home, it is inconceivable that they would march to the aid of the rest of Hellas as it fell to your army. With the rest of Hellas enslaved, Laconia will be weakened and on its own, but if you do not do this thing, here is what you can expect. A narrow isthmus leads into the Peloponnese and there you can expect tougher fighting than any so far with all the Peloponnesians who are allied against you. However, if you do what I advise, that isthmus will be yours without a fight and the cities will agree terms with you.'

Achaemenes,[2] one of Xerxes' brothers and commander of the fleet, spoke next. He was involved in the discussion and was beginning to fear that the King might be persuaded to do what Demaratus suggested. 'Great King,' he said, 'I see you are being taken in by the words of a man who envies your success and may even be a traitor to your enterprise. And this is indeed something that Hellenes take great delight in, for they are jealous of good fortune and detest the superiority of others. In the present circumstances, with 400 of your ships destroyed, the enemy will be able to face you on level terms if you detach another 300 to cruise around the Peloponnese. But if you keep your whole fleet together, it will be very difficult for the enemy to make any impression on it; indeed, they will be unable to put up any kind of fight. The entire fleet will be there to support the army and

---

[1] An ephor in the mid 6th century BC renowned for his wisdom and wit, celebrated as one of the Seven Sages of Hellas and worshipped as a hero by the Spartans.
[2] Achaemenes was a full-brother of Xerxes and, as satrap of Egypt, commander of that contingent as well as the whole fleet.

the army will be there to support the fleet as both advance together. But, if you divide the fleet, it will not be a good use of your forces and they will not be able to serve you as you would wish. In my view, you should settle on the plan that works best for you and not concern yourself with questions of where and how the enemy will give battle or in what strength. They can be left to think things out for themselves, and the same applies to our side. However, if the Lacedaemonians do come out against us, the Persians, to give battle, they will find no cure for the mortal wound they have just suffered.' (7.234–36)

The advice put into Demaratus' mouth was good, and he would have known of Cythera's strategic value. It had been a Spartan possession since the mid 6th century. Herodotus would have known of the Athenian attack on the island in 456–455 during the period of conflict known as the First Peloponnesian War (460–445). He may have still been alive and writing when the Athenians occupied it in 424, to hold it for three or four years. On both occasions they were putting it to the strategic use recommended by Demaratus. A seaborne attack to its south would indeed have made the Isthmus indefensible, however well fortified. Achaemenes' words of caution are less solidly based. The risk, if significant, of swinging the odds in favour of the Hellene fleet would have been mitigated by the probable detachment of sufficient numbers in response to the Persian flanking move. The segment of the Persian fleet left with the army could still have been sufficient to provide substantial protection and support on the seaward flank of the advance. No reference is made to the fighting off Artemisium, which might have led to a re-assessment of the opposition that favoured a more cautious approach. But possibly this was a conscious omission on Herodotus' part since his account of the naval action was still to come. In any case, the closing suggestion that no attempt should be made to discover or anticipate what action the enemy may take is fatuous. Nevertheless, Xerxes decides to follow Achaemenes' advice but rejects his view of Demaratus' motivation, honouring him as a guest-friend. Herodotus re-examines Xerxes' options, framing them slightly differently, in a discussion that immediately precedes the decision to fight in the straits of Salamis. In both passages, he is setting the Great King up for disaster. In a brief digression Herodotus tells the story 'as it is told' of a secret message sent by Demaratus to Sparta warning them of the impending invasion. He leaves it to the reader to decide whether Demaratus did this out of spite towards the people who had exiled him or out of goodwill, having given his own view that it was out of spite. There would actually have been no great advantage in being the first to find out this piece of intelligence. The Persians would not have wanted to conceal it and it would quickly have become common knowledge throughout Hellas.

The Hellene fleet had successfully slipped away from the northern shores of Euboea under cover of darkness:

> A man from Histiaea sailed over and told the Barbarians about the Hellenes' withdrawal from Artemisium. They did not believe him and put him under guard while sending fast ships to investigate.[1] The ships came back and confirmed what he had reported and so, when the sun had spread its rays, the whole fleet crossed to Artemisium. They paused there until noon and then sailed on to Histiaea, occupied the city and overran all the coastal villages that lie in the part of Ellopia that belongs to Histiaea.
>
> While the fleet was at Histiaea Xerxes arranged the dead bodies for display at Thermopylae. Out of all the corpses from his army, and there were 20,000 of them, he retained just 1,000. He had trenches dug for the burial of the rest and these were covered with earth and leaves to conceal them from the men from the fleet. Xerxes had sent a herald over to Histiaea, and when he had made the crossing he called together the entire force and proclaimed, 'Allies, Xerxes the King gives permission to any of you who wish to leave their post to come and behold how he gives battle to people who mindlessly presume to take on the might of the Great King.' After this proclamation, boats were suddenly in very short supply because so many people wanted to view the battlefield. They crossed over and walked amongst the corpses, examining them and taking them all for Lacedaemonians and Thespians; but, in fact, they were looking at Helots as well. However, the men who had come over were not deceived by what Xerxes had done with his own casualties. It was truly laughable: they could see 1,000 corpses from their own side all laid out and the Hellene dead

---

[1] Their caution suggests both healthy suspicion and a view that the Hellene fleet might still be in a fit enough state to fight again.

piled up together in a heap, 4,000 of them. This sightseeing took all that day;[1] on the following day, they rejoined their ships at Histiaea or resumed the march with Xerxes. (8.24–25)

Herodotus relates that the 'sightseers' were not taken in by the Great King's window-dressing. However, it could have been that the Persians had lost as few as 1,000 men, or fewer if most of their fighting was done at a distance, and 20,000 sounds like epic exaggeration. As far as the Hellenes were concerned, even stripped naked, the Spartans dead with their long hair and beards should have been unmistakable, but dead Thespians and Thebans could have been confused with Helots and other non-hoplites, at least by Barbarian eyes. Any Hellenes that made the trip from Histiaea would have had a better understanding of what they were looking at.

The figure of 4,000 Hellene dead that Herodotus gives here agrees with the first of the three commemorative inscriptions he quotes, but the number there represents the Peloponnesian hoplites who fought at Thermopylae; it is not a casualty count. Assuming 5–10 per cent wounded or killed over the previous days, which could be on the high side for a successful defence of a fortified position, Leonidas began his last stand with around 1,300 Spartan, Thespian and Theban hoplites. It appears that most of the Thebans were taken prisoner leaving approximately 1,000 hoplites to fight to the death. Assuming again, first, that casualties from the previous days had already been removed by the retreating Hellenes, or buried or burnt, and, secondly, that there was one light-armed attendant for each hoplite, a count for the final day of a little over 2,000 Hellene dead seems plausible. If the Lacedaemonian *perioikoi* and attendants were with Leonidas on that final day, the body count would have been in excess of 3,000. Heaped up together, they would have been a gorily arresting sight. The contrast with the 1,000 Barbarian corpses, most likely laid out in a more dignified way, would have been striking.

At this time, a few Arcadian soldiers-of-fortune[2] had joined up with the Persian army, needing to earn a living and willing to be of service.

---

[1] Probably two or three days after the battle ended.
[2] This is more often translated as 'deserters' but Arcadia, a poor region of the Peloponnese, was a well-established source of mercenaries.

They were taken before the King by the Persians and one, speaking for all of them, asked what the rest of the Hellenes were now doing. The Arcadians replied that they were celebrating the Olympic Festival and watching athletic and equestrian contests. A Persian asked what was put up as a prize for the contestants and they told him that the winner was given an olive wreath. Then Tritantaechmes son of Artabanus[1] made a splendid remark, though the King called him a coward for it: 'Good heavens, Mardonius! What kind of men have you brought us to fight against? They do not compete for money, just for the honour of it.' These were Tritantaechmes' words. (8.26)

This anecdote is, first, a reminder that Hellenes were willing to volunteer to fight for Persia if it suited their individual interests. Secondly, it adds another facet to Herodotus' representation, building up all through the *Historia*, of the contrasting characters of the two civilizations in conflict. In fact, the rewards of Olympic success could be more than symbolic, and there is plenty of evidence in the *Historia* and elsewhere that gold and other material gain could motivate Hellenes as powerfully as the pursuit of honour and *arete*, and the observance of *nomos*.

After a digression on the historic enmity between the Phocians and the Thessalians, who had medized earlier in the year, Herodotus describes the next stage of the Persian advance deeper into Greece:

The Thessalians, angered by the Phocians' refusal to betray Hellas, guided the Barbarian on their march. From Trachis they thrust into Doris. A narrow neck of Dorian land, about 30 *stades* (5.5km) in width, lies between Malis and Phocis and this is the motherland of the Peloponnesian Dorians.[2] Anyway, the Barbarians did this land no harm as they passed through it because the Dorians who lived there had medized; also, the Thessalians wanted it left unharmed. When

---

[1] Tritantaechmes was one of Xerxes' senior generals. In the debate at Susa four years earlier, Herodotus has his father warning Xerxes against invading Greece and Mardonius giving the plan his fullest support; the Great King calls Artabanus' caution cowardice.

[2] The Dorians were, with the Ionians, identified by the Hellenes as one of the two largest ethnic subgroups of Hellas. They are thought to have settled in the Peloponnese around the beginning of the millennium and according to Spartan tradition paused for a period in Doris during their migration south and left a settlement there.

the Barbarians advanced out of Doris into Phocis they failed to make contact with any Phocians. Some of them had taken to the heights of Parnassus where there is space for a large number of people to gather. This area is called Tithorea and the city of Neon lies below it. The Phocians went up there taking their possessions to safety with them. More of them took refuge in Ozolian Locris and the city of Amphissa, which is situated above the plain of Crisaea. The Barbarians overran all the land of Phocis and the Thessalians led them on as they torched and laid waste all the ground they covered, burning down cities and holy places in their path. They carried on along the River Cephisus destroying everything and burning all these cities: Drymus, Charadra, Erochus, Teuthronium, Amphicaea, Neon, Pedieis, Tritaeae, Elatea, Hyampolis, Parapotamii and Abae.[1] There was a wealthy temple of Apollo at Abae, richly endowed with treasures and offerings, and, then as now, it was the seat of an oracle. The Barbarians looted this temple and burned it down, and they caught up with some Phocians heading for the mountains and killed some of their women in gang rapes.

They passed by Parapotamii and reached Panopeus. There the army was divided into two groups. Xerxes with the larger and more powerful group marched on towards Athens and entered Boeotia by way of the territory of Orchomenus.[2] The whole population of Boeotia had now medized and Macedonian troops sent by Alexander were distributed round the cities for their protection, the purpose being to make it clear to Xerxes that the Boeotians had indeed gone over to the Medes. (8.31–34)

Herodotus manages to weave a number of strands into this compact account of the next stage in the invasion of Greece, taking Xerxes from Trachis and the battlefield of Thermopylae into Boeotia. First, he clearly identifies the route Xerxes follows, ironically, the inland one, not mentioning the route that the Hellenes had failed to block at Thermopylae. However, it is likely that the Thermopylae route was

---

[1] Herodotus lists these cities on either side of the Cephisus, quite accurately in the order in which Xerxes' army would have come to them as it followed the river to Orchomenus. Orchomenus is known to have medized and was presumably spared destruction.

[2] Along the western shore of Lake Copais but then to swing east in the direction of Thebes.

used. Part of the army and a lot of the baggage train were probably sent that way, maintaining contact with the fleet before swinging inland to join up with the rest of the army in Boeotia. This was a better road beyond the Thermopylae choke-points, and the Locrians, whose territory it ran through, had now medized. But Xerxes could not risk going further south with Phocis unsubdued in his rear. Secondly, Herodotus highlights the Persians' exploitation of the enmity between the Phocians and Thessalians, a typical strategy. Then there is the clear contrast between the exemplary destruction of the cities and lands of peoples who will not submit and the gentle treatment of medizers. Acts of sacrilege and the implied inevitability of divine retribution are noted, and the atrocity of gang-rape is added to pillage and destruction in this catalogue of total war. Finally, Alexander I of Macedon, one of Herodotus' most interesting minor characters, makes one of his several appearances in the *Historia*, typically presented as doing the Boeotians and the Great King simultaneous favours.

Leaving Xerxes and the main land force to complete the final, unopposed and, evidently, uneventful stage of their march on Athens, Herodotus' narrative makes a dramatic detour.

But the real mission for which they were detached from the rest of the army was to loot the shrine at Delphi and present the treasures to King Xerxes. I have discovered that Xerxes knew more about all the most notable items in the shrine than about any he had left behind in his palaces; and he was especially interested in the offerings made by Croesus son of Alyattes,[1] which have always been the subject of much talk. When the people of Delphi heard about this they were terrified and in their great terror consulted the oracle, asking whether they should bury the sacred treasures in the ground or remove them to some other place. The god forbade them to remove anything and declared that he was, as ever, quite capable of looking after his own property. Having heard this, the men of Delphi took thought for their own safety. They shipped their women and children over to Achaea.[2] Most of the men took refuge on the heights of Parnassus, storing their property in the Corycian cave, but some made their

[1] The fabulously wealthy 6th-century king of Lydia.
[2] On the southern shore of the Gulf of Corinth.

escape to Amphissa in Locris. So, all the Delphians abandoned their city except for 60 men[1] and the priest who interpreted the oracles.

As the Barbarians approached the sanctuary and came into view, the priest, whose name was Aceratus, saw some weapons laid out in front of the temple. He realized they were the sacred weapons. It was sacrilege for any mortal man to touch them, but they had been transported out of the building. He went and reported this wonder to the Delphians who had stayed behind. But the Barbarians carried on and, when they came closer to the temple of Athena Pronaea, found that even greater wonders than the first were in store for them. It was a great marvel that those weapons of war should appear outside the temple, laid on the ground of their own accord.[2] But what happened next was as astounding as any supernatural event ever marvelled at. As the Barbarians pressed on and came up to the temple of Athena Pronaea, thunderbolts from heaven struck amongst them, two peaks broke away from Parnassus and thundered down, crushing many of them, and a great battle cry rang out from the sanctuary. All this combined to throw the Barbarians into a panic and the Delphians charged out when they saw them running away and killed quite a number.

The surviving Barbarians headed straight for Boeotia. Those who did get away, so I have learned, were witnesses to a further manifestation of the divine. Two hoplites of more than human stature came after them, killing as they gave chase. The people of Delphi say these two were local heroes called Phylacus and Autonous; they each had a plot dedicated near the temple, Phylacus by the road above the temple of Athena and Autonous close to the Castalian Spring at the base of the Hyampean Cliff. The rocks from Parnassus have lain undisturbed to this day, just where they came to rest in the precinct of the temple after crashing through the Barbarian ranks. This is how it came about that these men were expelled from the sacred precinct. (8.35–39)

Herodotus gives no indication that he doubted any of the information he had gathered about this episode, but he may have concealed his

---

[1] These may have been temple staff responsible for security or officials who were required to stay.

[2] *Automatos*, a word first encountered in Homer, applied to the automatic gates of Olympus and robotic wheeled tripods constructed by Hephaestus, the god of metalworkers.

scepticism out of respect for Delphi and Apollo. Diodorus Siculus gives a plainer account, putting the Persian setback down to nothing more supernatural than exceptionally bad weather, though this could, of course be regarded as heaven-sent, 'the god's handiwork':

> The King left a part of his army behind and ordered it to march on Delphi to burn the precinct of Apollo and plunder the treasures dedicated to the god. He went on into Boeotia with the rest of the Barbarians and encamped there. The force that had been dispatched to loot the oracle's shrine had got as far as the shrine of Athena Pronaea when an incredibly violent thunderstorm suddenly burst upon them from the sky. Bolts of lightning showered down on them and the storm broke off huge rocks and hurled them into the ranks of the Barbarians. This caused the death of a large number of the Persians and the rest of them fled the place, terrified by the god's handiwork. (*Library of History* 11.14.2–3)

There may have been no attack on Delphi, and the tale as passed on by Herodotus could be a myth of the Delphians' own creation to counter suspicion of double-dealing in their relationships with Hellas and Persia. The great shrine had hedged its bets on the future of Hellas in a number of important prophecies and came through the war unscathed, in spite of its proximity to Xerxes' line of march and the easy accessibility of the treasures it housed. The story of a Barbarian attack repelled with divine aid was much better for its reputation than talk of any sort of deal to secure the Great King's protection. Equally, this story may have grown out of Hellene demonization of Xerxes for his perceived acts of sacrilege and impiety. An attack on Delphi would have offended all Hellenes, not only those who were resisting, and Xerxes may have had the same, more than pragmatic respect for Delphi and the god Apollo, as had been shown on the sacred island of Delos by Datis on his way to Marathon in 490. However, Apollo's temple at Abae had been looted and burned only weeks before. Anyway, the despatch of a separate contingent to subdue and secure western Phocis made sense. If Delphi was the mission's final objective, maybe the intent was more diplomatic than hostile, perhaps to raise cash against Asian treasure held there, or to extort it. The storm and rockfall could have been actual events remembered from around that time, and might even have disrupted negotiations of some kind between the Delphians and Persians.

Leaving Xerxes in Boeotia with Athens now in easy reach, Herodotus switches attention back to the Hellenes:

> At the request of the Athenians the Hellene fleet had put in at Salamis on the way back from Artemisium. The Athenians had begged the rest of the Hellenes to join them there to enable them to evacuate their women and children from Attica, and also so that a decision could be made on what course of action to take next. The way things had turned out, they felt they had been misled and wanted to convene the war council. They had expected to find the Peloponnesians fully mobilized and confronting the Barbarians in Boeotia, but there was no sign of them. Instead they discovered that they were busy fortifying the Isthmus as if their priority was the survival of the Peloponnese, mounting their defence there and letting the rest go. It was this discovery that made the Athenians beg the Peloponnesians to put in at Salamis.
>
> While the rest of the Hellenes put in at Salamis, the Athenians sailed to the mainland. On their arrival, a decree went out that every Athenian should make the best possible arrangements for the safety of his children and household, and most of them shipped their households to Troezen, but some to Aegina and some to Salamis. They were eager to carry out the evacuation because they wanted to comply with the oracle,[1] also, not least, for the following reason. The Athenians say that a great serpent lives in the temple and is guardian of the Acropolis; this is what they say, and every month they put out an offering for it as if it actually existed. The offering is a honey-cake and it had always been eaten up in former times, but on this occasion it was left untouched. The priestess interpreted it as a sign that the goddess had abandoned the Acropolis, which made the Athenians all the more anxious to abandon Athens themselves. (8.41)

Herodotus clearly had his doubts about the story of the temple serpent. But it neatly parallels his injection of the supernatural into

---

[1] The Delphic advice, 'Only a wooden wall will keep you safe ... Retreat, turn your backs!', interpreted by Themistocles.

his account of the abortive attack on Delphi, both adding colour and dramatic tension to this compact prelude to the next and arguably most important battle of the war. Plutarch adds an appealing twist:

> When Themistocles found it impossible to persuade the people with rational argument, he brought on signs from heaven and prophecies to convince them in the same way as a tragedian uses stage machinery. One sign he used was the alleged disappearance of the serpent from the sacred precinct at this time. When the priests found that the daily offerings they made to it had been left untouched, they gave out a proclamation that the goddess had departed from her city and was showing the people the way to the sea, and it was Themistocles who told the priests what to say. (*Themistocles* 10.1)

The serpent (if it existed) may or may not have disappeared. The story may not have originated with Themistocles, but a convincing claim to the sanction of the city's patron goddess for the evacuation of Athens and his 'wooden wall' strategy could have provided him with the powerful argument he needed to carry the people with him. Herodotus would have agreed with Plutarch that this well-contrived *deus ex machina* was typical of the man.

When the decision was taken to retreat from Artemisium, the Hellene commanders were probably already aware that the main Peloponnesian land force had not made any move north of the Isthmus and that it was now very unlikely to do so after the collapse of the Thermopylae position. It should not then have surprised the Athenians to learn that there was no sign of their allies in Attica or Boeotia. In any case, if Boeotia had been considered earlier, it was not an option now that it was occupied by the Persians, and so much Hellene manpower was committed to the fleet. In the close-fought battle of Plataea the following year, it took a much larger Hellene army than could have been fielded at this point in 480 to defeat a reduced Persian force. But it suited Herodotus' dramatic purpose to remind his audiences of this potentially catastrophic fault-line running through the Hellene Alliance's strategy.

It would have taken a few days for the fleet to get back to Salamis from Artemisium and there was enough time to complete the evacuation of Athens and Attica before the Persian army arrived. However, it must have been recognized that the Persian fleet might arrive in the Saronic

Gulf close on the heels of Hellenes, in the event of withdrawal from Artemisium. From a logistical point of view, the preparation of the island of Salamis as a naval base and refuge for evacuees that could accommodate hundreds of ships and provide for their maintenance and repair, and shelter and feed many thousands of people must have taken months rather than weeks. So, it must be the case that this work and much or all of the evacuation was completed before the allies sailed for Artemisium. But Herodotus' timing adds further drama to his narrative and the event is vividly pictured by Plutarch:

> The entire city was putting to sea and this sight filled some with pity, but others marvelled at the bravery of it. For the men who were going to fight were sending off their families in one direction and, unmoved by the groaning and weeping of their parents, making the crossing to the island. There was sorrow for the many citizens who were left behind because of their age, and emotions were stirred by the affection shown by the domestic animals and by their distressed cries as they ran alongside their masters on the way to their ships. The story goes that one of these, a dog belonging to Xanthippus, Pericles' father, could not bear to be left behind. He dived into the sea, swam across alongside his master's trireme and just made it to Salamis. But then he immediately collapsed and died. To this day the locals point out the spot[1] and call it the Dog's Grave. (*Themistocles* 10.5–6)

Herodotus breaks the stride of his narrative to review the Hellene fleet, now gathered in its entirety on Salamis. This is a convention that audiences would have recognized from the *Iliad* and other epic literature, and Herodotus incorporates it before all the main actions of 480 and 479 with the literary purpose of adding epic flavour and dramatic tension, and the practical purpose of setting out detailed orders-of-battle.

> After the contingents from Artemisium had put in at Salamis, the rest of the Hellene fleet joined them from Troezen, when they had been informed of their arrival. Their original orders had been to assemble at Pogon, the port of Troezen. A much larger number of ships from

---

[1] Presumably on the Cynosoura ('Dog's Tail') promontory.

more cities than had fought at Artemisium were now assembled at Salamis. The fleet commander[1] was the same as at Artemisium, Eurybiades son of Euryclides, a Spartan but not of royal blood. Athens provided by far the largest contingent and its ships were also the best in the fleet.[2]

And this is how the fleet was made up. From the Peloponnese, Lacedaemon contributed 16 ships, Corinth the same number as at Artemisium [40], Sicyon 15, Epidaurus ten, Troezen five and Hermione three. Apart from Hermione, these were Dorian peoples. The contingents from the rest of mainland Greece were as follows – Athens provided 180 ships, more than anyone else, and they were crewed entirely by Athenians. The Plataeans did not supply any crews at Salamis[3] for the good reason that when the retreating Hellenes reached Chalcis they went ashore on the Boeotian side of the channel so that they could go and attend to the evacuation of their homes; they took no part in the battle because they were making their families safe. The Athenians were Pelasgians originally, when the Pelasgians occupied the land we now call Greece. When Cecrops was their king they were known as Cecropians and, when Erechtheus succeeded him, they took the name of Athenians. But then they called themselves Ionians after Ion, who was the commander of their army.[4] Megara was there in the same strength as at Artemisium [20], Ambracia joined the fleet with seven ships and Leucas with three.

Next, the islands – Aegina provided 30 ships. They had more, fully manned, which they kept back to protect their homeland, but the 30 that sailed to Salamis and fought there were their best. The Aeginetans are Dorians from Epidaurus. Chalcis sent 20 triremes and Eretria seven, the same numbers as at Artemisium. Naxos supplied four ships. In fact, the citizen body, acting in the same way as other islanders, had despatched them to fight for the Medes, but the crews disregarded their orders and joined the Hellene fleet. They were

[1] *Nauarch.*

[2] *Arista pleousas*, 'best sailing'.

[3] This small, landlocked city and devoted ally supplied crewmen to serve on Athenian triremes at Artemisium.

[4] This is a sketchy version of the city's foundation mythology focused on the tradition that the Athenians were the original Ionians, an indigenous people and not the descendants of migrants, such as the Dorians.

urged to do this by a highly regarded Naxian called Democritus, the commander of one of their triremes. The Naxians are Ionians who came from Athens. Styra sent the same number of ships as to Artemisium [two], and Cythnos one trireme and a penteconter. Finally, Seriphos, Siphnos and Melos joined the fleet, and they were the only islands that had not given earth and water to the Barbarians.[1]

All of these people mustering at Salamis lived to the south of Thesprotia and the River Acheron, for the Ambraciots and Leucadians share borders with Thesprotia and they had come from furthest away. The only people to come from further off to help Hellas in her great need were the Crotonians[2] with one ship commanded by Phayllus, three times a winner at the Pythian Games. All brought triremes except for the Melians, Siphnians and Seriphians, who came with penteconters, the first with two, the other two with one each. The total number of ships, not counting the penteconters, was 378. (8.42–48)

Herodotus' opening paragraph is a crisp reminder of Athens' central role in the defence of Hellas. The supreme commander of the allied fleet may have been a Spartan, but the Athenian fleet was by far the largest element, with the best ships. Elsewhere, however, Herodotus implies their triremes were not all of the highest quality. It is probable that some were less well made in the hurried building programme instigated by Themistocles in response to Xerxes' known plans and preparations to invade. And the term 'best sailing' could also apply to the quality of commanders and crew, and this too would have been variable. Veterans must have been significantly outnumbered by comrades who had experienced war at sea for the first time only days before at Artemisium.

It was an exaggeration to say that there was a much larger number of ships assembled at Salamis than fought at Artemisium. Herodotus gives a total of 378 against 324 at Artemisium (271 at the start plus the 53 Athenian triremes that joined them on the second day). The figure of 378 may be correct, even if the numbers Herodotus gives for the individual contingents at Salamis actually add up to 364; but Aeschylus'

---

[1] Herodotus later refers to this short list of islands that did not medize as five in number. Seriphos, which is not listed on the Serpent Column, may be included in error here.
[2] The sole representative of western Hellas.

figure is 310, which could be a reasonable argument for taking the arithmetically correct 364, or going even lower. The number of cities participating did increase more significantly to 21 from the low base of 13 at Artemisium less Plataea and Opuntian Locris, but between them the ten newcomers added only 19 triremes. Any net increase after replacing ships lost or irreparably damaged at Artemisium would have been an achievement, and the muster at Salamis, which included all the reserves from the Peloponnese, would seem to be good evidence of the allies' resolute commitment, at least as far as the fleet was concerned. Forming the next line of defence at the Isthmus need not necessarily be interpreted as any kind of betrayal of this. But there was evidently no lack of commitment here either:

> There were tens of thousands of men, every one of them working on the wall. It was close to completion as they piled on rocks, bricks, timber and baskets of sand, taking no break from their labour by day or night. (8.71)

The Athenians' contribution of just under half the triremes in the Hellene fleet dwarfed Lacedaemon's contribution of 17 and was more than twice the size of the entire Peloponnesian contingent. Herodotus' remarks about the origins of most of the participants not only add to the epic feel of the passage, but reminded audiences, at a time when the Peloponnesian 'Dorians' and the Athenians and other 'Ionians' were tearing Hellas apart, that they could be united in a common cause. The absence of the Plataeans is explained. Opuntian Locris had probably medized and, in any case, had been overrun immediately after Thermopylae. No blame is laid on the Aeginetans for holding back a large part of their fleet; their island, out in the Saronic Gulf, was going to be very exposed, and they would be protecting not only their own homes and families, but evacuees from their former enemy, Athens.

Herodotus takes up the narrative again:

> When the commanders from all the cities listed above had assembled at Salamis they met in council. Eurybiades suggested that anyone who wished to should give their views on the most suitable place to give battle at sea within the area which the Hellenes still controlled. Attica was already lost and he was talking about what remained. Most of the

speakers were in favour of sailing to the Isthmus and fighting with the Peloponnese at their backs. Their main argument was that if they stayed on Salamis and were defeated, they would be blockaded on an island with no prospect of escape, but if they sailed to the Isthmus, they would be able to get away into their own territory. This is what the commanders from the Peloponnese were arguing for, but then an Athenian came in and reported that the Barbarians had reached Attica and were setting it all ablaze. The Persian force with Xerxes at its head had marched through Boeotia and burned down Thespiae and Plataea, the inhabitants having already evacuated their cities and taken refuge in the Peloponnese. It had now reached Athens bringing total devastation. Thespiae and Plataea were burned because the Thebans had informed the Persians that these cities had not medized.

From beginning their march after crossing into Europe (the actual operation of bridging the Hellespont had lasted about a month), it took the Barbarians three months to get to Attica. Calliades was archon[1] for that year. (8.49–51)

It is unlikely that the entire Hellene fleet, reserves included, would have assembled at Salamis to confront the Persians in Attic waters and not further south if consensus had not already been reached. The sudden news of the Barbarian army's arrival is a dramatic touch, but the Hellene commanders would not have been surprised by it. They would have had regular reports of its progress, and the Barbarian fleet had probably been at Phalerum for days. But Herodotus goes on presenting this argument as unresolved until shortly before dawn on the day of the actual battle when there was no other option but to fight off Salamis. As elsewhere, he uses the medium of invented debate to examine the real strategic and tactical issues in some detail.

As in the earlier stages of its march into Europe, the Persian army was probably divided into two or three columns to enter Attica from Boeotia by separate routes. Three months' march from the Hellespont to Athens was reasonably good going for a force of this size. But the campaign had been well planned and prepared for, and Thermopylae was the only interruption of any significance. The month spent in crossing the Hellespont is at odds with Herodotus' earlier and grander-sounding

---

[1] The year would have been named after him as 'eponymous' archon.

'seven days and seven nights without a moment's halt'. In the former, his source might have included activity on either side of the Hellespont before the crossing itself. The latter was conjuring up the vision of an immense column flowing continuously over the bridges into Europe. 'Fire and fierce Ares' finally reached Athens:

The town was deserted when the Barbarians occupied it, but they found there were still a few Athenians who had stayed behind in the temple precinct. These were treasury officials and some poor folk, and they had barricaded the Acropolis with planks and timber to protect it from attack. It was not only because they lacked the means that they had not made the crossing to Salamis. They also thought they were the ones who had correctly worked out the meaning of the Pythian oracle's prophecy. They believed that their 'wooden wall' would be impregnable and that this, not the ships, would be their 'safe keep', according to the oracle.[1]

The Persians took up positions opposite the Acropolis on the hill which the Athenians call the Areopagus, and this is how they laid siege to them. They wrapped tow[2] round their arrows, set light to them and shot them at the barricade. The besieged Athenians held out although their barricade had played them false and their situation was now desperate. They rejected offers of terms conveyed to them by the Pisistratids and continued to find ways to defend themselves, for example by rolling boulders down onto the Barbarians as they advanced towards the gateway. So, for a long time Xerxes was quite at a loss and unable to take their position.

Eventually the Barbarians found a way out of this stalemate, for, according to the oracle, all of mainland Attica was destined to fall to the Persians. At the opposite end of the Acropolis from the gateway and the ramp, there is a place where no guard had been posted because it was thought that no mortal man could climb up. Some Persians climbed up at that very spot, by the shrine of Cecrops' daughter Aglaurus, although the cliff-face is vertical there. When the Athenian

---

[1] Charred beams quite recently excavated on this spot and identified as contemporary with the Persian assault on the Acropolis suggest that timber and stonework were combined in the gateway complex that was in the process of construction.
[2] Dipped in pitch or some other flammable material before lighting and shooting. .

defenders saw that the Acropolis had been scaled, some threw themselves off the walls to their death below and others ran into the inner chamber of the temple[1] for sanctuary. The Persian scaling party made straight for the doors, forced them open and slaughtered them, suppliants though they were, and, when they had all been cut down, looted the temple and set fire to the whole Acropolis. (8.51–53)

The temple staff that remained on the Acropolis were wealthy citizens who could easily have paid whatever was required to make the crossing to Salamis. They were doing their duty as detailed in Themistocles' decree: 'the guardians of the sacred treasures and the priestesses shall remain on the Acropolis and guard what belongs to the gods.' With the 'poor folk', there were probably other citizens who believed strongly enough in the alternative interpretation of the oracle to entrust themselves to the protection of the goddess Athena, and presumably of Apollo, and the temple officials could also hope that the sanctity of their status and respect for the holy precinct would keep them from harm. Dismissive as he is of this insignificant garrison, Herodotus describes a stout defence. Extensive building works, a great new temple of Athena on the future site of the Parthenon and the new grander gateway, supplied materials for their barricade which blocked the top of the ramp that led straight up to the only entrance to the citadel. It also supplied the defenders with missiles to hurl down into the Barbarian ranks. In reality, this was a very strong position, even if lightly manned, and little or no attempt may have been made to take it by frontal attack. The Pisistratid negotiators, travelling with the invasion army as Hippias did to Marathon, would have been sent in first, and reconnaissance to find a way of scaling the cliffs that protected the rest of the perimeter would have begun immediately. Any attack would have been preceded and covered by showers of arrows and the fire arrows would have been an effective additional distraction as the scaling party came up from the rear. The massacre of the Athenians seeking sanctuary in the holy precinct, and the burning and looting were an act of great sacrilege.

As far as Xerxes was concerned, the Athenians had been justly punished for their part in the burning of the city of Sardis and its temple of Cybele 18 years before, and Athens was the final Hellene city

---

[1] Most likely the 6th-century temple of Athena Polias.

to pay the price for this, and the defeat at Marathon had been avenged, though not yet in battle. Aeschylus tersely puts the capture of Athens, traumatic as it must have been for the Athenians, into perspective:

Messenger The gods protect the goddess Athena's city.
Atossa Then Athena's city is not yet destroyed?
Messenger No. While her men still live, her ramparts[1] stand intact.
(*Persae* 348–50)

Herodotus and his audience were well aware that Xerxes' 'Mission Accomplished' despatch was fatally premature and ironic emphasis could have been placed on 'up to this point'.

With Athens completely in his hands, Xerxes sent off a despatch rider to Susa to inform Artabanus of the success he had enjoyed up to this point. The messenger-system devised by the Persians is swifter than any on this earth. It is said that whatever the length of the journey in days, they have horses and riders positioned at intervals along the route so that there is a horse and rider for each daily stage. Snow, storms, heat, the darkness of night: nothing stops them completing their stage in the shortest possible time. The first rider hands the despatch over to the second, the second to the third, and so the message travels on, passed on from rider to rider; it is like the torch-race run by Hellenes in honour of Hephaestus. By the way, the Persian word for this chain of despatch-riders is *angareion*.[2] When the news that Xerxes had taken Athens reached Susa, the Persians who had stayed behind strewed myrtle branches in all the streets, burned incense, offered up sacrifices and made merry in their rejoicing. (8.54, 98–99)

The day after sending the messenger, the Great King summoned the Athenian exiles who had accompanied him[3] and commanded them to go up onto the Acropolis and offer sacrifices in their customary way. Either he was compelled to do this by a dream or he now regretted

[1] The Greek word *erkos* used here can also be translated as 'fence' or 'enclosure' and has strong connotations of a wooden wall.
[2] The Royal Road along which the message was carried from Sardis to Susa was 2,000km in length and had 111 staging posts on it.
[3] The Pisistratids.

burning down the temple. Anyway, the Athenian exiles did as they were told. I will tell you why I mention this. On the Acropolis there is a temple dedicated to Erechtheus, the Earth-Born[1] and, inside it, an olive tree and a salt-water pool. The story the Athenians tell is that Athena and Poseidon put them there once upon a time to stake their competing claims for supremacy over the land. Now it happened that this olive tree was burned by the Barbarians along with everything else in the precinct. But the day after the fire those Athenians who had been ordered to go up to the temple to offer sacrifices saw that a shoot had sprouted from the stump and was already about a cubit long, and they reported what they had seen. (8.54–55)

The olive was closely associated with the goddess Athena, 'protector of cities', above all Athens, and with victory in the Olympic and Panathenaic Games; it was also an important crop, and olive oil from Attica was of high quality. The new shoot allegedly sprouting from the charred stump was easily interpreted as a portent that Athens would rise again from the ashes beyond the city's former glory to imperial greatness, and clear assurance that the goddess had not deserted the Athenians.

[1] An important cult-figure at the centre of Athens' foundation mythology.

A wooden wall

Salamis

In the second half of September in the days before the battle, when the full Hellene fleet was assembled on Salamis, the beaches and bays on the western side of the straits were lined with triremes, organized in battle order contingent by contingent. Each required approximately 15m of shore front to allow sufficient space for launching with oars out, and there was space for all 380, and level or gently sloping ground immediately behind to accommodate the 80,000 crewmen. The island was also temporary home to most of the rest of the able-bodied male population of Athens. This included the balance of the city's hoplite force, maybe 2,000–4,000, and any archers and other light-armed troops not serving on the ships. Their role would be to guard the beaches, and it seems that this was sufficient to discourage any thought of an amphibious landing outside the straits. There were also thousands of non-citizen *metoikoi* (resident aliens) and slaves, both state- and privately owned, in addition to those serving as rowers alongside the citizen oarsmen. Their role would generally have been as on the mainland, to provide skilled and unskilled labour in the fields, shipyards and armouries, to do clerical work, and to distribute, cook and serve food. They were also servants to the wealthier citizens (and *metoikoi*) and their women and children, those, probably a minority, that had not been evacuated to Aegina or the Peloponnese.

Herodotus has already stated that the rest of the Hellenes who had fought at Artemisium put in at Salamis at the Athenians' request to support the sea-borne evacuation of Athens and Attica, 'but also so that they could discuss with them what to do next'. However, he says a little later that the rest of the fleet, which had been lying at Pogon, the port of Troezen, well to the south of the Isthmus, immediately sailed to join up with them at Salamis, which suggests that a collective, if fragile decision had already been taken to confront the Persians there. Herodotus represents it as being hotly debated right up to the night before the battle. This certainly adds dramatic tension to his narrative and allows him to set out the main strategic and tactical considerations in some detail. It also enables him to spotlight the three leading characters, Themistocles, Eurybiades and Adeimantus, representing the three leading powers in the fractious alliance.

Ending his account of the fall of the Acropolis, Herodotus switches back to Salamis where the Hellene commanders are, again, in conference and receiving a report on the latest developments:

> When the Hellenes on Salamis learned what had happened on the Athenian Acropolis, some of the Peloponnesian generals were so panic-stricken that they did not even wait for a collective decision to be made, but hastily boarded their ships, hoisting their sails for flight. Those that were left resolved to give battle off the Isthmus. So, as night fell, they left the meeting place and returned to their ships.
>
> When Themistocles got back to his ship, an Athenian called Mnesiphilus[1] asked him what had been decided. On being told that the decision was to withdraw the fleet to the Isthmus and fight in defence of the Peloponnese, he said, 'If the fleet withdraws from Salamis, you will no longer be fighting for a single Hellene people. Each contingent will go back home to its own city and it will be impossible for Eurybiades or anyone else to stop the fleet breaking up, bringing about the destruction of Hellas by their lack of judgement. If there is anything you can do to reverse this decision by persuading Eurybiades to change his mind and remain here, go and try it.' This advice was greatly to Themistocles' liking. He said nothing and went straight to Eurybiades' ship. Arriving there, he let Eurybiades know that there was a matter of mutual concern he

---

[1] Later sources identify Mnesiphilus as a mentor to Themistocles. His intervention is likely to have been a fiction introduced into the tradition by Themistocles' detractors. But there is evidence that an Athenian of this name was important enough to be nominated for ostracism in Themistocles' time.

wanted to discuss. Eurybiades asked him to come aboard[1] and tell
him whatever it was he wanted to say. So, Themistocles sat down
beside him and repeated exactly what Mnesiphilus had said to him,
presenting the advice as his own and making several additions to it.
And, in the end, his pleading persuaded Eurybiades to go back on
shore and call the commanders back to the meeting place.

As soon as they were all assembled and even before Eurybiades
could explain why he had summoned them, Themistocles spoke out
with an intensity that matched his sense of urgency. The Corinthian
commander, Adeimantus son of Ocytus, interrupted, 'Themistocles,
at the games a false start gets you a whipping.' Themistocles retorted,
'But if you are left on the starting line you get no crown';[2] he was
responding to the Corinthian mildly at this point. He then carried
on addressing Eurybiades. But he did not utter a word of what he
had said just before, that if the Hellenes left Salamis they would go
their different ways. It would not have been constructive to make this
accusation to the allies' faces. Instead he produced another argument:
'You can save Hellas if you listen to my advice and stay here and
fight. Ignore these others and their idea of taking the fleet down to
the Isthmus. Listen to me now and consider the arguments. If you
engage the enemy off the Isthmus you will be fighting in the open
sea, which will not favour our prospects at all because our ships are
heavier and we are outnumbered. Even if we are actually successful
there, you will have lost Salamis, Megara and Aegina. Additionally,
their army will follow behind their fleet on land and you will be
drawing them towards the Peloponnese and thus putting the whole of
Hellas in danger. But consider the benefit of doing what I am telling
you to do! First, by taking on their many ships in the narrows with
our few, we shall win a great victory. That is the likely outcome of a
battle in the narrows, which will be as much to our advantage as one
in the open sea will be to the enemy. Then, Salamis and the women
and children we brought to safety will be saved. And there is another
consideration, one of particular importance to you: if you make the

---

[1] The ships were beached rather than at anchor off-shore and the crews camped out on the shore,
but it does appear that commanders stayed on board, probably sleeping in the small cabin at
the stern; senior crew members may also have slept on deck or in the central companionway.
[2] Olive wreaths at the Olympic Festival.

right decision and stay and fight here rather than off the Isthmus, you will be defending the Peloponnese just as effectively. If things turn out as I expect them to and we are victorious with our ships, the Barbarians will not then face you at the Isthmus. They will not advance any further than Attica but withdraw in disorder and we shall get the benefit of the survival of Megara and Aegina, and also of Salamis, where it has been prophesied that we shall overcome our enemies. Men who make realistic plans generally meet with success. But if their planning is unrealistic, God is not inclined to back the judgement of mortal men.'

While Themistocles was saying this, Adeimantus the Corinthian renewed his attack, arguing that a man without a homeland should keep silent and demanding that Eurybiades deny this stateless person[1] the right to put forward any proposal. He told Themistocles he would be entitled to share his thoughts when he was in possession of a city, a pointed reminder that Athens had been taken and was now occupied. This time Themistocles responded vehemently and at length, attacking the Corinthians in general as well as Adeimantus personally. And he declared that while they had 200 ships fully manned, the Athenians had both a greater city and more territory than the Corinthians, and that there was not a city in Hellas that could withstand their attack, if they were to launch one.

After making these points, he turned back to Eurybiades and spoke to him with more vehemence than before. 'If you stay here, you will keep your reputation as a good and noble man. If you leave, you will be the ruin of Hellas. Without our fleet, we are nothing in this war. So, listen to me. If you do not do what I say, we Athenians will immediately gather up our households and ship them to safety in Siris in Italy. This is territory we have owned since ancient times, and there are prophecies that say we are to plant a settlement there.[2] You will remember my words when you find yourself abandoned by the allies who are so valuable to you.' It was with this speech that Themistocles made Eurybiades change his mind. But, in my view, he changed it mainly out of fear that the

---

[1] A stateless person might also be an outlaw, denied *isonomia*, 'equality under the law'.
[2] Athens appears to have had no historic claim to this city, but the general idea was not unrealistic and Themistocles had daughters named Italia and Sybaris, suggesting some connection.

Athenians would indeed sail away if he took the rest of the ships to the Isthmus. With the Athenians gone, what was left would be no match for the enemy, so he adopted Themistocles' plan, to stay where they were and give battle.

After this heavy exchange of verbal missiles, Eurybiades made his decision and the Hellenes at Salamis prepared to fight a sea-battle there. As the sun rose the following day, there was an earthquake on land and sea and it was agreed that the time had come to pray to the gods, and also to summon the descendants of Aeacus to their aid. And they acted on this resolution immediately, offering prayers to all the gods, calling up Ajax and Telamon from Salamis itself, and sending a ship to Aegina for Aeacus and his sons.[1] (8.56–64)

Themistocles had built a formidable case, overriding but still playing on first thoughts of local self-interest, backed by four potent arguments and a personal appeal to Eurybiades' honour. The credible scenario of a retreating Peloponnesian alliance breaking up without making a stand was for Eurybiades' private consumption. The other four arguments are addressed to Eurybiades but presented to all in the public arena of the Hellene 'meeting place'. The first of these is tactical: in the straits the Persians would not be able to exploit their superior numbers, manoeuvrability or seamanship, but these qualities would be overwhelmingly to their advantage in the open waters off the Isthmus. In fact, the Persians with their 'better-sailing' triremes would have been able to cut the Hellene fleet off in the open sea of the Saronic Gulf before they came close to the Isthmus. The second argument is more strategic: fighting a sea-battle at Salamis would be as good a defence of the Peloponnese as it would be at the Isthmus. In the event of the victory Themistocles was anticipating, the Hellenes would have control of the sea and be able to threaten the flank and rear of the Persian army if it advanced on the Isthmus, and guard against sea-borne Persian attacks on

[1] These were important preparations for imminent battle. Ajax, prominent in the *Iliad*, and Telamon, his father, were local heroes of Salamis. Aeacus, son of Zeus, the local hero of Aegina, was father of Telamon and Peleus, who were respectively fathers of two of Homer's greatest heroes, Ajax and Achilles. Telamon and Ajax were associated with the island of Salamis. Effigies of such heroes were believed to give support in battle, and fetching the Aeacidae was an important piece of the Hellenes' preparations.

the flank or to the rear of the Hellene defensive line. Saving Salamis was, of course, extremely important to the Athenians, and the Aeginetans and Megarians, both from outside the Peloponnese and contributing 50 triremes between them, would have had a significant voice in the debate. The confidence with which Themistocles spoke of victory could be justified by the good performance of the Hellene fleet at Artemisium when it had held its own against similar odds in much more open water.

The remark with which Herodotus has Themistocles closing his violent exchange with Adeimantus (commander of the second largest contingent at Salamis) would have resonated strongly with his contemporary audiences five decades on, when Athenian sea-power held sway over so much of Hellas and had for a period swung the balance of the Peloponnesian War in Athens' favour. Corinth was Sparta's chief naval ally in that war and had been involved in some humiliating defeats. Swinging back to Eurybiades, Themistocles delivered his killer punch: the Athenians would abandon the alliance and migrate to Italy if the decision were taken to fall back on the Isthmus. And, if all the other allies from outside the Peloponnese had decided to look after their own interests, Eurybiades would have led just 89 triremes from Salamis to the Isthmus. Of the rest, as advised by Mnesiphilus, 'each contingent will go home to its own city'. Although Eurybiades is represented as having definitively made up his mind to stay and fight at Salamis at this point, the matter is not yet finally settled in Herodotus' account. There is still more drama in store. His narrative compresses negotiation and debate that must have been spread out over a number of months and several different locations into about 48 hours, two beached ships and the Hellene meeting place on the island of Salamis. Against this dramatic, fictional backdrop, however, there are credible glimpses of the actual thought processes involved in the planning and the real tensions and internal conflicts that had to be navigated if Persia was to be resisted with any prospect of success.

Herodotus' brief mention of the natural portent of the earthquake and the Hellenes' invocation of divine and heroic support leads into a more detailed account of a significant supernatural event. As with other anecdotes of this nature, Herodotus leaves it to listeners or readers to decide whether to believe it or not. He rarely names individual sources, and Dicaeus, the Athenian, may have been a man of some importance, but he is otherwise unknown (which has not prevented some ingenious scholarly theorizing, even finding a family connection with Thucydides):

Dicaeus son of Theocydes, an Athenian exile who had acquired some status amongst the Medes, told how he was with Demaratus the Lacedaemonian on the Thriasian plain[1] at the time the countryside of Attica was being ravaged by Xerxes' army when the land had been abandoned by the Athenians. He said they saw a dust-cloud coming from the direction of Eleusis, as big as one that might be raised by 30,000 men. They were wondering in their amazement who these men could be, raising such a dust-cloud, and just then they heard a great shout. It was like the cry of 'Iacchus' at the mysteries. Demaratus knew nothing about the Eleusinian rites and asked Dicaeus what this shouting meant. Dicaeus explained, 'It is inconceivable that the King's forces are not about to meet with some great disaster. Attica is deserted so it is absolutely clear that this is a divine voice calling from Eleusis to bring the Athenians and their allies vengeance. If the omen turns towards the Peloponnese, the King himself and his army on land will be in danger. But if it turns towards the ships at Salamis, the King will be in danger of losing his fleet. Every year the Athenians keep this festival in honour of the Mother and the Maiden,[2] and any Athenian or other Hellene who wishes may be initiated. What you are hearing is the cry of 'Iacchus'[3] that they shout out at this festival.' Demaratus replied, 'Keep silent and do not give this explanation to anyone else. If these words of yours reach the King, you will lose your head. I shan't be able to protect you. Nobody could, so keep quiet about it! What happens to the King's forces is in the hands of the gods.' That was the firm advice Demaratus gave Dicaeus. And after the

[1] This plain was to the north-east of Eleusis and the north-west of Athens and crossed by one of the main roads Xerxes' army could have taken from Boeotia into Attica. It is likely that the two Hellene exiles were there because they had entered Attica that way with the army, or with a part of it. 'Ravaging' was as much to do with living off the land as laying waste to it.

[2] Demeter, the grain goddess, and Persephone, her daughter, were important deities of crops and vegetation.

[3] Iacchus was the patron of the initiates (Greek-speaking men only, excluding murderers). An effigy of the god was carried along the Sacred Way in an annual procession from Athens to Eleusis and repeatedly and loudly acclaimed by name.

dust-storm and the shouting a cloud rose high in the air and drifted over to Salamis and the Hellene camp, and they knew from this that Xerxes' fleet was going to be destroyed. This is what Dicaeus son of Theocydes used to say, calling upon Demaratus and others to be his witnesses. (8.65)

This event seems to have been a significant piece of the mythology of the Persian War. It is unlikely that Demaratus did not know about the 'Eleusinian Mysteries', a major festival in the Hellene religious calendar; Dicaeus' brief description is there for the benefit of Herodotus' wider, 'international' audience. The episode adds further dramatic tension, and is also one of several reminders that a divine plan was at work that would bring victory to the Hellenes and disaster to the Great King. In this context, the reference to Xerxes' autocratic power of life and death over his subjects is well timed. Hellene emotions would also have been struck by the story's implied message that the festival was celebrated, albeit supernaturally, in the absence of mortal participants and in the presence of the enemy that had kept them away from it, all this witnessed by two returning Hellene exiles.

But there could be a more prosaic explanation for the dust-cloud that was observed. A few chapters on Herodotus writes, almost as an aside, 'that very night the Barbarian army was on the march towards the Peloponnese' (8.70). A large force of cavalry might have been sent probing to the west as the first phase of a planned advance on the Isthmus by Xerxes' land force, or in a manoeuvre with more limited objectives like securing beaches on the mainland to the north of Salamis, or simply feinting an attack on the Isthmus line to increase the pressure on the Hellene Alliance. Herodotus does not place Dicaeus and Demaratus' experience on the Thriasian plain at any single point in his loose chronology, whereas 'the march towards the Peloponnese' is set the night before the sea-battle, but the two could have coincided at any point during the occupation of Attica. Fast-moving cavalry would have raised plenty of dust and alien commands and war-cries might easily have been imagined to be the festival acclamations. Also, the month was Boedromion, which quite closely coincided with the modern calendar's September, and it is likely that whatever gave rise to the story happened on the day, late in that month in 480, on which the procession would have taken place.

Xerxes' land forces may have been involved in another operation before the sea-battle. According to Herodotus, after the battle, Xerxes 'attempted to build a causeway over to Salamis, lashing together Phoenician cargo ships to form both a pontoon bridge and a boom' (8.97). He does not give a location and the timing has no logic. However, a fragment of Ctesias goes into a little more detail than Herodotus on this operation and brings it forward in time (he also brings Plataea forward in time, placing that battle before Salamis!):

> After this, Xerxes moved on to a narrow section of the Attica shoreline called the Heracleum, and constructed a causeway in the direction of Salamis, planning to make the crossing on foot. On the advice of the Athenians Themistocles and Aristides, Cretan archers were called for and came up in support. Then there was a sea-battle between the Persians and the Hellenes ... [which is then dispensed with in a hopelessly inaccurate passage of about 40 words]. (*Persica* 57)

The geographer Strabo, writing four centuries later and working his way east from Eleusis, supports Ctesias' timing of the operation:

> Next we come to the Thriasian plain and the coastline and community of the same name. Then we come to Cape Amphiale and the quarry above it and the channel across to Salamis, about 2 *stades* [around 400m] wide, over which Xerxes tried to build a causeway. But the naval battle and the flight of the Persians prevented him doing this. Here too are the Pharmakoussai (Enchantresses), two small islands; Circe's tomb may be seen on the larger one. (*Geographia* 9.1.13)

These passages have been rejected as evidence on the grounds that Herodotus is more reliable, but, on this occasion, it is tempting to override that generally sound principle. Strabo's '2 *stades*', equivalent to about 400m, is well short of the actual distance of 1,000m between the two shores, but it is not a bad guess at the 600m between the two Enchantress islands. And the shrine of Heracles, the Heracleum that Ctesias mentions, is thought to have been close to Perama, the small port on the Attic shore sheltered by the smaller Enchantress (Enchantress 2).

It would not have been very challenging for the Persian engineers and manpower that bridged the Hellespont, cut through the Athos Peninsula and drove roads through the mountain forests of Thessaly, and were renowned for spectacular siege-works, to span the 200m of shallow water between the mainland and Enchantress 2. Easy access to the island would have been tactically valuable. The next stage, crossing to the larger Enchantress (Enchantress 1), would require a bridge of boats and protection from the enemy fleet and would have been possible only after defeating the Hellenes in the straits. There would then be less than 300m of water, quite a lot of it possibly wadable, to cross over to Salamis at the narrowest point. With the Hellene fleet eliminated or at least contained, a concentration of triremes and transport ships could then quickly deliver a large force assembled on Enchantress 1 to the beaches of Paloukia Bay. If the Cretan archers were

SALAMIS, 480

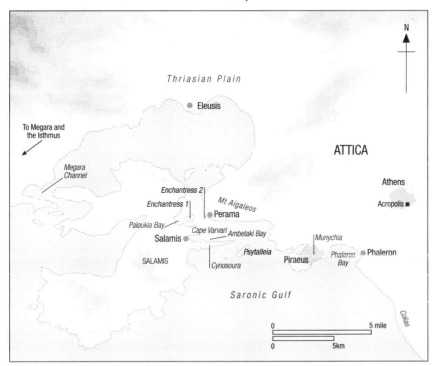

put onto Enchantress 1, their longest shot would not have reached even half-way to Enchantress 2, but they would have been well positioned to harass any Persian ships that came within range and, if accompanied by hoplites, to oppose a landing. Alternatively, this engineering work, which seems too well documented to be an invention, may have had the less ambitious purpose of creating a harbour from which to launch an amphibious attack on Salamis.

At this point Herodotus turns his attention to the Persian fleet again. Naval action was to be the next main phase of operations and Herodotus reviews Xerxes' options by giving an account of the consultations which may have taken place. Artemisia, tyrant queen of Halicarnassus, takes centre stage. Herodotus previously introduces her as one of the most notable of the smaller-unit commanders (*taxiarchoi*):

> I find it quite amazing that she, a woman, went to war against the Hellenes. On her husband's death she took over as tyrant and, although she had a son who was a young man, she had the fortitude, the masculine courage to go off on campaign when she did not have to.[1] Artemisia was her name, and she was the daughter of Lygdamis, of Halicarnassian stock on her father's side and Cretan on her mother's. She was in command of contingents from Halicarnassus, Cos, Nisyrus and Calymna, and contributed five ships, which were rated the best in the whole fleet after the triremes from Sidon. Out of all his allies, Artemisia gave the King the best advice. (7.99)

Herodotus was born in Halicarnassus. He clearly admired Artemisia and was proud of his kinship with her, even though he wrote the *Historia* as a political exile from his birthplace. It was then still subject to Persia and ruled by Artemisia's grandson, also called Lygdamis. Herodotus' account of Artemisia's part in the events of 480, disproportionate to her position in the Persian chain of command and to the scale of her contribution to Xerxes' armada, may be as much a bid for reconciliation

[1] Without dishonour she could have sent her son to lead her modest squadron and Xerxes would have put no pressure on her as a subject to join the campaign. It is not clear if the five ships were her entire command or only the Halicarnassian component of it.

with her descendants as an exercise in nostalgia and nationalistic pride. However, from a gender aspect, her story is a remarkable one. Tomyris, queen of the Massagetae and a shadowy historical figure from half a century earlier, is the only other female ruler and war-leader mentioned by Herodotus.

After viewing the scene of the Laconian disaster at Thermopylae, the Persians waited at Histiaea for three days, and then sailed down through the Euripus.[1] After three more days they reached Phalerum, the port of Athens. In my view, as great a number of Barbarians descended upon Athens by land and sea as came to Cape Sepias and Thermopylae. Against those lost in the storm, at Thermopylae and in the naval actions off Artemisium, I set those who at that time had not enlisted in the King's forces: I mean the Melians, Dorians and Locrians, the Boeotians, in full force except for the Thespians and Plataeans, and also the Carystians, Andrians and Tenians and all the rest of the people from the islands, except for the five cities whose names I have already mentioned.[2] The further into Hellas the King of the Persians advanced, the more peoples followed him. All of these went on to Athens except for the Parians, who were left behind on Cythnos and were waiting to see which way the war would go.[3] When the ships had all arrived at Phalerum, Xerxes went down in person, wishing to mingle with the men who sailed them and find out what they thought. He came down and was enthroned before them, and the tyrants of all the different national contingents and the senior commanders from the fleet, all had been summoned into his presence. They were seated in order of precedence reflecting their standing with the King, first the king of Sidon, next the king of Tyre[4]

---

[1] Time presumably spent repairing battle-damage and resting crews.

[2] Ceos, Naxos, Cythnos, Siphnos and Melos.

[3] Paros was a large and prosperous island in the Cyclades. After the war Paros escaped reprisals by paying reparations to the Hellenes, or, allegedly, by bribing Themistocles to let them off. It clearly suited them to be 'left behind' and perhaps they had been trustingly tasked with watching over the channel between Cythnos and Ceos, two of the islands which had not medized. This channel was at the western end of the most direct route from Ionia to the Saronic Gulf.

[4] Tyre and Sidon were the leading cities of Phoenicia. In Xerxes' navy 'the best of all the ships were supplied by the Phoenicians, and the best of these were from Sidon' (7.96).

and then the rest. When they were all settled in their rows, Xerxes sent Mardonius amongst them to sound each of them out by asking if he should give battle at sea. (8.66–67)

Herodotus has introduced a touch of satire here. Xerxes' idea of 'mingling' (the Greek word also has sexual connotations) is somewhat formal and he actually avoids direct contact with his naval commanders. This is left to Mardonius, his most trusted general:

Mardonius passed amongst them, commencing with the king of Sidon, and asked the question. They were all in agreement, strongly recommending giving battle at sea, all except for Artemisia ... She said, 'Mardonius, tell the King from me that I, who was not a coward but fought with distinction in the sea-battles off Euboea, have this to say: 'Master, it is right and proper that I should let you know my true opinion. This is what I personally think will be best for your cause. I say to you, for the sake of your fleet, do not give battle. At sea their men are as superior to your men as men are superior to women, so why do you feel such need to take the risk of fighting at sea? Have you not captured Athens, your goal when you embarked on this campaign? And now the rest of Hellas is in your hands: no one is standing in your way, and those who did stand against you received what they deserved.

'Let me tell you what I think your enemies will do. If you do not rush to give battle but keep your ships where they are, staying close to land, or even advance on the Peloponnese, then, Master, you will easily achieve what you planned to do when you came here. The Hellenes cannot hold out for long. You will scatter them, and they will make their escape, each to their own city. I have found out that they have no food on this island and, if you launch your land forces in a strike against the Peloponnese, it is unlikely that those contingents that came from there will either stay quietly where they are or be inclined to fight a sea-battle for the sake of Athens. But if you rush into battle straightaway, I have a foreboding that a defeat for the fleet will lead to the ruin of your army. Also ponder on this, Great King: it is generally the case that good masters have bad slaves and bad masters have good slaves. You are the best of all men, so your slaves are bad. They are reckoned to be your allies, those Egyptians, Cypriots, Cilicians and Pamphylians, but they are quite useless.'

As Artemisia was speaking to Mardonius, those who were well disposed towards her thought her words would bring disaster on her in the form of some terrible punishment from the King, because of her firmly delivered advice not to give battle at sea. But others, who were not admirers of Artemisia and who envied the way she was honoured as if she was one of the leading members of the alliance, were pleased to see this confrontation, thinking it suicidal. But when her views were reported to Xerxes, he was mightily pleased with her advice. Even before he had had an excellent opinion of her, and now he rated her even more highly. However, the order he gave was to follow the recommendations of the majority, for he believed that at Euboea his fleet had underperformed because he was not present. This time he made arrangements to watch the battle in person. (8.68–69)

Artemisia's advice in part mirrors the arguments Themistocles presented to Eurybiades and the irony of Herodotus' remark that 'she gave the King the best advice' is intentional. Xerxes did not take it. However, it is unlikely that there was a serious shortage of food on Salamis. It was as important to deprive the invaders as to stockpile provisions for the enlarged population of the island, and the evacuation ships probably transported at least as much tonnage of grain, oil, wine and livestock from Attica as people. But there is just a hint of the strategic option which could possibly have won the war for Xerxes. This was to split his fleet, retaining a force large enough to contain the Hellenes within the straits and sending the remainder to make landings to the rear of the Hellene defensive line in support of a frontal attack on the Isthmus by the army. Her illogical 'good masters–bad slaves' theory and closing strident dismissal of four of her allies, who together accounted for around 40 per cent of Xerxes' navy, rather undermine the wisdom of the rest of the speech. There was a hierarchy of slaves in the Hellene world from trusted and respected family staff and public servants to forced labourers in the Athenian silver mines, all termed '*douloi*' in Greek. In the Persian Empire the kings (and queen) and tyrants who served the Great Kings enjoyed autonomy, respect and power as rulers of subject nations infinitely beyond the highest status that might be achieved by any slave of the Hellenes. But, in the context of Herodotus' thematic highlighting of the fundamental differences between Persian autocracy and the recently emerged Hellene, and especially Athenian values and style of governance, the Hellene conference does not stand out as superior. It is chaotic, with Themistocles bulldozing his case through, Adeimantus interrupting aggressively and attempting to deny him *isegoria* (the equal right of all citizens to free speech) and Eurybiades, albeit wisely, apparently ruling against the majority. Xerxes' consultation is orderly; all are invited to give their views (though they might not dare to say what they think). Artemisia's frankly expressed minority-of-one opinion is listened to with respect and Xerxes, albeit unwisely, goes with the majority. However, if each of the 17 city-states represented at the Hellene meeting formally had a vote and the seven from the Peloponnese were the only ones to cast their vote against Themistocles, Eurybiades' mandate was clear. Dissenters were free to leave but, if any genuinely wished to do so, this was, in the end, not a practical option.

At Artemisium the two fleets had been facing each other across an 11km stretch of open water with a clear view of each other's movements. At the narrowest point, less than 1,600m separated the Hellenes on Salamis from Persian-occupied Attica, but the Persians were beached at Phalerum, an indirect 16km away. Each was conveniently placed for fighting on their battleground of choice, the Hellenes in the confined waters of the straits of Salamis, the Persians in the wider Saronic Gulf. The Hellenes were in a strong position. Reinforcements from the reserve held at Pogon had brought the strength of the fleet up to 380, a figure arrived at somewhat shakily by Herodotus. It may have been lower; Aeschylus in his tragedy *Persae* puts it at 300. According to Herodotus the Hellene fleet included just two deserters from the other side, contrary to Themistocles' hopes and best efforts. It probably also included a few ships captured at Artemisium and refurbished and crewed to replace losses. A plausible starting figure for Xerxes' invasion fleet is around 800 triremes rather than the 1,207 first cited by Aeschylus and repeated by Herodotus. It is then likely that some were detached to protect supply routes and harbours in the rear as the army and fleet advanced into Europe, and the storm off Magnesia would have reduced the number further. So perhaps 500–600 faced the Hellenes at Artemisium. The number may have been the same, or perhaps slightly smaller at Salamis, with captured ships with new crews, and the newly medized Hellenes

33. One of the international crews of oarsmen and oarswomen involved in the *Olympias* project pictured early in their stint. The top tier is functioning quite well but the lower tiers are clearly still learning. (George Atsametakis, Alamy)

34. The three tiers of oarsmen seen from the bows, from left to right, *thranitai*, *zygioi* and *thalamioi*. The central companionway is visible on the right. Only the *thranitai* could see their oar-blades in the water and the *thalamioi* could not see out at all. *Olympias* is shown here on a visit to London in 1993, part of the celebrations of 2,500 years of Greek democracy. (Thierry BOCCON-GIBOD/Gamma-Rapho via Getty Images)

35. The Hot Gates, looking west over the area in which Leonidas' defensive line was established. Any traces of the Middle Gate, as described by Herodotus, lie buried, but the 1,000-metre ramparts of Callidromus must be little changed.

36. An engraving from a sketch by R. Belle in *Le tour du monde; nouveau journal des voyages* (1877) gives some sense of the ancient landscape, perhaps, and the shoulder of Callidromus depicted reasonably matches that shown in the middle distance of the preceding photograph. (Mary Evans Picture Library)

37. This hero-figure, sometimes identified as Leonidas, was sculpted early in the 5th century when portraits were not made of living individuals in Sparta. However, the serene and unflinchingly resolute expression is an excellent reflection of the unique Spartan military spirit. His helmet is of the Attic type. Sparta Museum.

38. The crags of Parnassus looming over the remains of the precinct of Athena Pronaea at Delphi.

39. This heavily restored gold and ivory effigy identified as Apollo is quite different from the 'Greek god' of the Classical era. It is the sort of image the defenders of Hellas at the end of the Archaic era would have had in mind when invoking divine protection. Delphi Museum.

40. The Straits of Salamis from the east. Modern port installations have encroached on the north side and the road that runs behind them roughly marks the ancient shoreline. The smaller boats are roughly the size of triremes; with 800 or more engaged, the space between Cynosoura and the Enchantress Islands was very crowded.

41. The bluntness of the ram reduced the risk of getting locked into a fractured or pierced hull. The universal eye decoration may still be seen painted on the prows of Aegean fishing boats.

42. The Straits of Salamis from Paloukia at the west end. The island connected by a modern causeway is Enchantress 1. Paloukia Bay sweeps round to the tip of Cape Varvari. Beyond is the Bay of Salamis (Ambelaki) and then the long Cynosoura promontory.

43. Entering the straits through the channel at the north-east end of Psyttaleia with modern Perama and the Aigaleos range visible beyond.

44. *Olympias* from one of the best angles of attack with least risk of losing oars or becoming locked into the enemy hull when ramming. Helmsmen taking a tiller in each hand found the hefty twin rudders surprisingly easy to operate. (George Atsametakis, Alamy)

46. Boeotia, 'the dancing floor of Ares', from the skirts of Cithaeron above ancient Hysiae. The Asopus lies beyond the tactically important but gentle ridges in the middle distance, and the Persian fort was somewhere in the area below the grey warehouse buildings in the top right-hand corner.

45. Athena triumphant brandishing a torn-off Barbarian figurehead. Earlier in the *Historia* Herodotus mentions figureheads on Phoenician ships as 'representations of pygmies' (3.37) and this is perhaps what the painter had in mind. British Museum.

47. View from the area in which the Persians built their fort. The Asopus lies in the dip in the foreground. The notch in the wooded ridge to the right of the lamp post is where the main pass over Cithaeron emerges into the foothills above Hysiae.

48. No portrait of Pausanias survives, if one ever existed. This early 5th-century bronze statuette depicts a cloaked Spartan warrior with his carefully dressed long hair. The transverse crest depicts senior rank. (Allen Phillips/Wadsworth Atheneum)

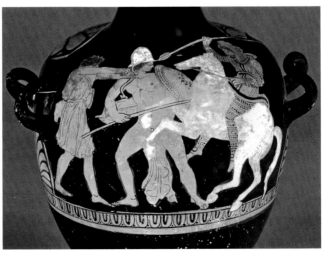

49. This mid 5th-century Athenian battlescene shows a hoplite wearing a *pilos* helmet and an archer in a Hellene tunic. However, the intention may be to recall the Athenians' successful action on the first day of fighting at Plataea. (© Trustees of the British Museum)

50. An early 5th-century depiction of archer and hoplite fighting side by side. The hoplite holds two spears, giving him the option to throw one before using the other in close combat, which may have been the norm for much of the Archaic period. Metropolitan Museum of Art, New York.

51. Part of the frieze of the Temple of Athena Nike (Victory) on the reconstructed Acropolis. Temples were more typically decorated with depictions of the wars of gods and heroes; the theme and the hoplite's nudity are heroic in style, but the Persian cavalryman is entirely realistic. The scene could recall the historic fighting over the body of Masistius at Plataea. (© Trustees of the British Museum)

52. Slave, Helot or lower-class citizen carrying water or wine, and in a hurry. The Greek defensive line may have been kept supplied with water from the spring of Gargaphia in this way. Agora Museum, Athens.

53. An early 4th-century Graeco-Persian sarcophagus with some of its original colouring preserved showing Barbarian cavalry, probably Phrygian, fighting Hellene *psiloi*. Archaeological Museum, Çannakale.

54. View to the east from above the site of ancient Plataea. The Hellenes' initial position ran along the base of Cithaeron. The Island was somewhere between Plataea and Hysiae, just beyond modern Erythres in the middle distance.

55. 'The Persians set aside their bows and faced up to the Hellenes, and at first the fighting was along the wall of shields ... (they) were not inferior in courage or physical strength' (9.62). The Persian's 'bonnet', *spara* shield, quilted body-armour and exotic trousers are clearly depicted. The 'Brygos painter' treats the Barbarian with the same respect as Herodotus does in his narrative. Ashmolean Museum, Oxford. (Nick Sekunda)

56. In the 5th century the shoreline at Mycale may have run along the line of greenery just beyond the telephone pole. The Persian camp can be envisaged below the hillock on the left of the picture.

57. This triumphal Attic 'Toby jug' from the mid 5th century is an extraordinary depiction of battlefield stress, and not unsympathetic. In the contrasting domestic scene above, a grand Athenian lady is attended by a Barbarian slave-girl, perhaps from the spoils of victory. (© Trustees of the British Museum)

58. Column drums from the wreckage of the great temple of Athena, the unfinished precursor of the Parthenon destroyed by the Persians in 480, were built into the ramparts of the Acropolis in the hasty reconstruction work done in the autumn of 479.

59. The quantities discovered of mass-produced *ostraka* (pottery fragments, in this case the bottoms of vases or cups) naming Themistocles are evidence of the opposition he had to surmount in the 480s to get his successful defensive strategy accepted. Agora Museum, Athens.

60. Athena, the complex patron goddess of Athens, Sparta and other *poleis*, equally associated with military prowess and the more civilized qualities of craft skill and wisdom. A miniature 3rd-century copy in marble of the massive figure made by Phidias, faced with ivory and gold and erected in the Parthenon in 438. National Archaeological Museum, Athens.

61. The remains of the Serpent Column in Istanbul. Minarets added to the 6th-century Christian basilica of Hagia Sophia in the 15th and 16th centuries can be seen to the right of the Obelisk of Theodosius, which was erected in the 4th century. (Wikimedia/Gryffindor/Public Domain)

Below 62. The Serpent Column was still intact in the late 16th century, as depicted in *Surname-i Vehbi*, a collection of Ottoman miniatures. (Wikimedia/Bilkent University/Public Domain)

63. Roman copy of a Greek portrait of Thucydides (455–395), part of a double bust, back to back with Herodotus. This artistic linking of the two greatest historians of the Classical Greek world shows how well their interdependence and their respective intellectual and cultural contributions were recognized in their own era. Naples Museum.

making up for battle losses. The Hellene fleet, 300–400 strong, was outnumbered but more than sufficient to mount a deep defence of the two entrances to the south-eastern end of the straits on either side of Psyttaleia and, simultaneously if necessary, to take care of any threat from the north-west by blocking the channels between the two Enchantress islands and, if navigable when sea level was lower, between Enchantress 1 and Salamis.

With crews mustered close to their ships, they would have sufficient time to put to sea and form up to counter any Persian thrust into the straits of Salamis. A single trireme, rowed at 6 knots (11.1km/h), following the course likely to be taken by an attacking column, entering the straits through the wider channel to the east of Psyttaleia and steering north-west, would take 15–20 minutes to reach a point off the Attic shore opposite the tip of Cynosoura. A mass of 300 or 400 ships, travelling more slowly to preserve cohesion, would take considerably longer to perform the same manoeuvre. To this must be added the time taken to advance a further 2,250m to the west to align with the Greek left wing, and to swing from column to line to face the enemy. Two hours seems a reasonable estimate. Depending on where it was beached, a Greek trireme could launch and reach the nearest point on the Attic shore in 10–20 minutes. A full-fleet manoeuvre, which would include straightening the line in the course of the crossing, might take an hour. The Greeks were not in danger of being caught at their moorings (certain disaster), and had a range of options for counter-manoeuvre. These included envelopment of the head of an attacking column as it entered the straits, punching into its flank in column at one or more points, delaying until more ships had entered and attacking in line before they were fully deployed, or simply waiting for them to advance and fighting a defensive action.

It is easy to cruise the battlefield. A ferry service runs quite frequently from Gate 8 of the main harbour of Piraeus to Paloukia at the northern end of the straits. It passes to the east of Psyttaleia and then quite close to the tip of the promontory of Cynosoura and the entrance to the deep bay of Ambelaki, the site of the ancient town of Salamis. It stops at modern Kamatero, then continues westward past the long bay where the Athenian fleet forming the Hellene left and most of their centre was beached, and ends close to the causeway that now joins the island of St George (Enchantress 1) to Salamis. The trip takes 30 minutes. Even allowing for the extensive 20th-century seaport infrastructure and the many large cargo and cruise ships lining the shores, it is very striking how tight the space would have been for this immense clash of several hundred triremes (and around 200,000 men and one woman), and how narrow the south-eastern and northern entrances to the straits were. This was the whole point of Themistocles' strategy and the measure of the Persians' misjudgement. It is what all the sources, maps, analyses and commentaries tell us, but none of them more vividly than the direct experience of chugging through those same waters at not much more than ramming speed in a ferryboat of about the same length and width as a trireme and its 170 oars. It is possible to take the same boat back to Piraeus after a few minutes wait, but it is well worth spending a little longer. There is a truly authentic *kapheneio-ouzeri*, 'To Perasma', just a few steps from the ferry station ready to fortify the researcher with beer and wine, sardines and octopus before or after (preferably after) the essential scramble up the hill behind. From this ridge there is a view across to the south and west of the island which demonstrates that watchers on those shores could easily communicate by simple smoke or fire signals with the Greek command on the north-eastern side. More important is the panoramic view over the island of St George down the straits to Cynosoura and Psyttaleia, with Piraeus beyond. This takes in the whole stretch of water that was fought over and, on its southern side, the beaches and bays of Salamis and, opposite, the steep flanks of Mount Aigaleos on the Attic shore from where on some vantage point, possibly inside the secure perimeter of the modern Greek naval base or amongst the unromantic apartment blocks of Perama, Xerxes on his golden throne watched his disaster unfold. The view from the ridge behind Paloukia is like looking down the length of a great stadium. Back on the mainland, the tram-route from central Athens to Piraeus takes in Flisvos Marina where *Olympias*, when in dry dock in the Maritime Museum, keeps a watchful eye on Salamis and the approaches to Piraeus.

In Herodotus' chronology, the Persians immediately obeyed Xerxes' order and put to sea:

> When the command to launch was given, the Barbarian fleet set course for Salamis and, under no pressure, formed up in line. However, by then it was too late in the day to fight a battle and night was coming on, but they were ready to fight next day. (8.70)

This can be plausibly explained as an unsuccessful attempt to draw the Hellenes out into the wider space of the Saronic Gulf, after which the Persians returned to Phalerum for the night when it was clear there would be no action. The timescale is telescoped here, as at other points, either for literary effect or because Herodotus' information was sparse. 'Next day' implies that the night-time manoeuvres that preceded the battle followed on immediately from that afternoon's manoeuvres. But it is unlikely that ships would have been sent out again immediately on a long night patrol with the expectation of combat the following morning. It could be that the Persians were hoping the Greeks would behave as they did at Artemisum and engage with them late in the day. Certainly, if the Persians were offering battle outside the straits, the Greeks were not tempted. The night operation that immediately preceded the battle is much more likely to have taken place a day or two later.

Fear and terror now gripped the Hellenes, especially those who had come from the Peloponnese. They were terrified because they had been posted to Salamis and were about to fight at sea to protect the Athenians' homeland, and knew that if they were defeated they would be trapped on an island and under siege, leaving their own land unguarded. In fact, that very night the Barbarian army was on the march towards the Peloponnese. And, indeed, all possible measures were being taken to prevent the Barbarians invading by land. As soon as the Peloponnesians had learned that Leonidas and his men had met their end at Thermopylae, they had hastily gathered at the Isthmus and taken up position there. Cleombrotus son of Anaxandridas, the brother of Leonidas, was in command. With the Isthmus established as their base, they demolished the Scironian road[1] and then built a wall right across the Isthmus as they had agreed to do when they were debating what action to take. Since there were tens of thousands of them all working together, they made excellent progress, bringing up stones, bricks, timber and baskets of sand. They worked at this together day and night without resting for a moment.

---

[1] On the coast road that linked Attica and the Isthmus. Just after Megara it ran along a ledge high above the sea. It may not have been made impassable (this never happened in the Peloponnesian War) but the Hellenes could certainly have made it more difficult for large numbers of cavalry or footsoldiers.

These were the Hellenes who mustered in full force at the Isthmus:
the Lacedaemonians, all of the Arcadians, the Eleans, the Corinthians,
the Sicyonians, the Epidaurians, the Phliasians,[1] the Troezenians and
the Hermioneans. They were the ones who marched out fearing for
Hellas in her time of peril. The rest of the Peloponnesians did not
care, even though the Olympian and Carnean festivals were now
over. All the remaining cities of the Peloponnese, except those I have
listed, stayed neutral. However, if I may put it bluntly, in staying
neutral they actually medized. (8.70–73)

The focus of Herodotus' narrative has switched briefly to land-based
operations. A large Persian force may actually have been on the march
towards the Isthmus in anticipation of victory off Salamis and the
elimination of any seaborne defence of the position. Alternatively,
this may simply have been a feint to put more pressure on the already
strained alliance, or troop movements to secure beaches around
the bay of Eleusis. Herodotus' brief digression on the fortification
works at the Isthmus, which he later states were not yet finished
in the early summer of 479, provides an opportunity to shame the
majority of the cities of the Peloponnese that took no part in the
defence of Hellas.

The Peloponnesians at the Isthmus were so engaged with their work
because they regarded their efforts as a race which had to be won at
all cost, and also because they did not expect their ships to win. Those
who were at Salamis knew what the Peloponnesians at the Isthmus
were doing, but they were still very anxious, though not so much afraid
for themselves as for the Peloponnese. For a while men only talked
quietly to their neighbours, sharing their dismay at Eurybiades' lack
of judgement. But then this blew up into open discussion and many
of the arguments were repeated. The Peloponnesians were for sailing
back to the Peloponnese and taking their chance in its defence, and
firmly against staying to fight for land that had already fallen under
the spear. The Athenians, Aeginetans and Megarians wanted to stay
where they were and defend that position.

---

[1] From Phleious, a little west of Corinth.

Themistocles was losing the argument with the Peloponnesians
so he slipped away from the meeting place and sent a man by boat
to the Median camp with instructions to deliver a message. The
man's name was Sicinnus, and he was a household slave and tutor to
Themistocles' children. Later, after these events, Themistocles made
him a rich man and enrolled him as a Thespian, when the Thespians
were taking on citizens.[1] He arrived in his boat and this is what he said
to the Barbarian commanders, 'The Athenian General has sent me to
you and the other Hellenes know nothing about it. He is actually a
supporter of the King and wishes you success, not the Hellenes. His
message which I bring to you is that the Hellenes are terrified and
plan to withdraw. You now have the opportunity to achieve the finest
of all results, as long as you do not hold back and let them make their
escape. The Hellenes are disunited and will not stand against you.
Instead, you will see them fighting amongst themselves, those who are
for you fighting those who are against.' (8.74–75)

Herodotus' wonderful story of Themistocles' brilliant stroke of double-
cross intelligence may well be part of the rapidly evolved mythology of
the Persian War. However, as already seen, it was a core Persian strategy
to maintain dialogue with their opponents, even up to the moment
of battle, attempting to bring about a bloodless victory through high-
level negotiation, or by undermining resistance with divisive bribery
and threats further down the chain of command. Whatever means
Themistocles used (and the Persian commanders would have been happy
to speak with him directly), it was in character for him to exploit this
channel to encourage Xerxes to order an attack without further delay.
And Themistocles' message that the fleet at Salamis was about to fall
apart was one Xerxes wanted to hear, and probably even anticipated.
He knew that only a tiny minority out of the 1,000 or so city-states that
called themselves Hellene was standing against him on the island. Of
this minority, some had until very recently been in dispute or at war
with each other, and there were long histories of rivalry and enmity.
Finally, it is likely that Xerxes had been kept well informed of the heated
and narrowly won debates in which the Hellene defensive strategy

[1] They badly needed to replace the 700 hoplites lost at Thermopylae, the core of their adult
male citizen-body.

had been forged, and of the stresses and frictions that jeopardized its implementation.

Sicinnus made himself scarce after delivering his message. It seemed genuine to the Persians, so they landed a substantial force on the island of Psyttaleia that lies between Salamis and the mainland, and then, in the middle of the night, they advanced their west wing in a circling movement towards Salamis, and the ships stationed around Ceos and Cynosoura also advanced so that they controlled the whole passage as far as Munychia. Their purpose in deploying their ships in this way was to prevent the Greeks escaping and to trap them on Salamis, and so pay them back for their success at Artemisium. Their purpose in landing men on the island called Psyttaleia was so that they could be there to give help to friends and kill enemies, for the island lay in the channel in which the fighting was about to take place and, when the battle took place, disabled ships and survivors would be carried onto it. They did all this in silence to prevent the enemy knowing about it, and they made these preparations overnight without any pause for sleep. (8.76)

As usual, Herodotus' topographical information is vague about direction and location (hardly surprising in an era long before compass bearings, map references and scientific measurement of distance) and is open to various interpretations. The occupation of Psyttaleia provided the Persians with a piece of friendly shore in the middle of the eastern section of the channel they would be contesting, but he does not necessarily mean that the fighting was going to take place exclusively around the island of Psyttaleia. 'The ships stationed around Ceos and Cynosoura' have not been previously mentioned and Herodotus gives no indication of the size of this detachment from the main fleet at Phalerum, or of its precise mission. If he is referring to the island of Ceos south-east of the southern tip of Attica, it is possible that the objective was to blockade a line from that point to the promontory of Cynosoura on Salamis, to prevent any ships escaping or reinforcements reaching the island; the Parians stationed on Cythnos may have had a role in this. Additionally, it could have covered Aegina, the closest potential source of Hellene reinforcements. However, a shorter line running north from Psyttaleia close to the tip of Cynosoura and up to the mainland would have served the first two purposes more efficiently. It has been suggested that Ceos is the forgotten name of a small island just to the west of Psyttaleia, but this would suggest too small a concentration to stretch diagonally from Psyttaleia to Munychia. A third suggestion is that it was the name of a beach or harbour somewhere to the north-east on the shore of Attica; this would imply two squadrons spreading out from their bases and joining up to control 'the whole passage as far as Munychia'. The advance of 'the west wing in a circling movement towards Salamis' makes best sense in the context of Herodotus' later statement that, at the start of the battle, 'the Phoenicians were facing the Athenians, positioned on the western flank, which was nearest to Eleusis' (8.85). So, Salamis is taken here to mean the town and surrounding area, not the whole island. It was not literally encircled but the Persian fleet can be visualized forming an arc from its left flank resting on Psyttaleia to its right, resting on Cape Amphiale.

This was all done as quietly as possible under the cover of darkness. Night manoeuvres, though difficult and risky, are documented and were certainly within the capability of the best navies, but night fighting with friends and enemies indistinguishable in a melee was impossible. So, the Persians would have been able to enter the straits unopposed keeping close to the north side of the straits with the Phoenicians leading to form the right wing when they turned to face the Hellenes. It is very likely that the Hellenes were aware of the Persian manoeuvres. In the stillness of the night a watcher on the tip of Cynosoura could not have failed to hear the movement of hundreds of ships and the beat of thousands of oars across only 1,500m of open water, however hard the crews were trying to work their ships in silence. With little moon or an overcast sky, it might not have been possible at sea level to pick out silhouettes against the land behind, but they would have been visible against the water from higher ground. With a gentle breeze in the right direction watchers could even smell the ships. But there was nothing the Hellenes could do except prepare to attack or be attacked at first light.

Aeschylus the tragedian (c.525–455) fought at Marathon. Judging from his epitaph, this was the achievement of which he was most proud. It was more important to him than his many victories in the drama contests at the annual festivals of Dionysus, or his prodigious output of at least 80 plays, or, according to Pausanias, than serving in the fleet at Artemisium and Salamis. At 45 he was too old to fight on deck as a hoplite so he may have pulled an oar, or even commanded a trireme, like his brother Ameinias. In his *Persae*, staged in Athens in the festival of 472, a messenger brings news of the battle to Xerxes' mother, Atossa. In a sense, this can be considered an eyewitness description, but Aeschylus' purpose, poetic and religious, in writing his tragedy was different from Herodotus' in writing his *Historia*. *Persae* was a triumphant yet pious celebration of a glorious, god-given climactic moment in the maturing of a city that was already deeply conscious of its present and future greatness. Aeschylus' primary purpose was not to present a historical record as Herodotus understood the term. The play was well received, winning first prize with its three accompanying plays in that year's contest. So, impressionistically, at least, it must have been an acceptable reflection of collective and personal memories of this very recent event in which most of the audience would have been directly involved. Many had also shared in the triumph of Marathon and lived through the tense decade that followed, and there would have been some older citizens in that cheering audience who had wept at Phrynichus' *Fall of Miletus* 21 years before. The universal tragic theme, which is also woven into Herodotus' narrative, of a great man who has offended the gods and will inevitably suffer for it, is at the heart of the play. But Aeschylus' dramatic and poetic account of the battle also includes detail that valuably complements the *Historia* by reason of its contemporaneity and eyewitness credibility:

> The whole disaster was set in train, O Queen,
> By some avenging power or evil spirit.
> A Hellene came from the Athenian fleet
> And this is what he told your son, Xerxes:
> 'When night's dark mantle falls,
> The Hellenes will wait no longer
> But spring to their rowing benches and scatter
> To save their lives and steal away.'
> Xerxes took heed, not sensing Hellene deception
> Nor the gods' displeasure with him.
> So, he gave these orders to his admirals:
> 'When Helios ceases to warm the earth with his rays

And night's mantle shrouds heaven's holy space,
Divide your massed ships into three squadrons
To guard the channels and the paths of the sounding sea,
And send the rest to encircle Ajax's isle.[1]
If any Hellene avoids his sorry fate
And finds some way to escape by stealth,
Execution will be the penalty for all.'
With confidence he made this declaration
In ignorance of the gods' plans for him.
With discipline and obedient to their orders
Our crews prepared their supper.
Next, each man took his oar
And looped its thong over the tholepin, ready to row.[2]
Then, as the sun's last radiance faded
And night came on, all had embarked,
Commanders of their oars or masters of their weapons.
The files of rowers cheered each other up and down the ships,
And so they put to sea, each captain following his orders.
All night long our ships kept station
And all the crews stayed at their oars.
But, when the night was almost over,
The Hellene fleet had made no attempt to steal away.
(*Persae* 353–85)

Themistocles' deception is alluded to; while it was not proper to mention a living mortal's name in tragedy, both his political supporters and his opponents would have relished the reference to him as 'an avenging demon'. The tasks given to the three squadrons into which Xerxes divides his fleet are described in one line: 'guard the channels and the paths of the sounding sea'. This can be interpreted in various ways but could be echoed in Herodotus' 'they advanced their west wing to envelop Salamis, and the ships stationed between Ceos and Cynosoura also advanced so that they controlled the whole passage as

---

[1] Salamis.
[2] This touch of practical experience would have resonated with men in the audience who had rowed in the fleet.

far as Munychia'. 'The rest' in Aeschylus' next line, not mentioned by Herodotus, may have been identified by Diodorus Siculus:

> Xerxes very much wanted to prevent the Greek naval forces linking up with their land forces, so he sent the Egyptian squadron with orders to seal off the straits between Salamis and Megara, and he sent the bulk of his fleet towards Salamis itself with orders to engage the enemy and settle the conflict in battle. (*Library of History* 11.17)

This puts the large and effective Egyptian fleet in position to cover the narrow Megara channel and pick off any Hellenes taking that route to the Isthmus. It could explain why Herodotus makes no mention of the Egyptians taking part in the battle. He later indicates that they were present at this point in the campaign, stating that Mardonius disembarked the heavy-armed Egyptian marines to be part of the army that was to stay behind in Greece to continue the war on land the following year.

> In the meantime, the Hellene commanders on Salamis remained locked in close combat in their debate.[1] They were not aware that they were now surrounded by the Barbarians' ships but expecting to see them deployed as they had been through the day.[2]
>
> While the generals were fighting it out, Aristides son of Lysimachus crossed over from Aegina. He was an Athenian who had been ostracized by the people and, having made a study of his character and conduct, I consider him the finest and most just man of his time in Athens. This man came to the meeting place and called Themistocles out of it, although he was no friend of his but, in fact, a bitter rival. Because of the scale of the present threat, he put all that out of his mind and called Themistocles out of the meeting because he wanted to discuss things with him. He had already heard that the contingents that had come from the Peloponnese were desperate to set sail for the Isthmus.

---

[1] Here Herodotus, dramatically sustaining his metaphorical treatment of this extended debate as a battle, uses the word *othismos*, 'shoving', which is often applied to the climax of a hoplite engagement when the two sides are locked together, shield against shield (see page 33).

[2] Perhaps all they could see during the day was the blockading force strung out between Psyttaleia and the mainland.

So, when Themistocles came out to him, he said, 'It is a good thing that we are in opposition to each other; competing to be the one who does most for our fatherland is a good thing in all circumstances, and especially now. But I can tell you that it now makes no difference how much or how little the Peloponnesians have to say about sailing away from here. I have seen with my own eyes that, however much even the Corinthians and Eurybiades himself want it, they will not be able to get out. We are surrounded by the enemy. Go back in there and spell this out to them.'

Themistocles replied, 'That is excellent advice and it is good news that you bring. You come here after seeing with your own eyes that what I wanted to happen has come about. You should know that it was I who made the Medes do this. Since the Hellenes have shown themselves unwilling to stand and fight when they could choose not to, it has become necessary to force them to do it whether they like it or not. Since you are the bearer of this good news, tell it to them yourself. If it were me telling them, they would think I was making it up and would not believe that the Barbarians have been taking this action. So, go in there yourself and make it clear to them how things stand. It will be best if they are convinced by you, but if they still cannot believe what they are being told, it is all the same to us. They will not be able to escape, if we are indeed completely surrounded as you say we are.' That is what Themistocles said.

So, Aristides went in and addressed the meeting. He reported that he had come from Aegina and only just managed to slip through the blockade to make the crossing, because the Hellene position was completely surrounded by Xerxes' ships, and he advised them to make ready to defend themselves. When he had finished speaking, he withdrew from the meeting and the arguing started all over again because most of the commanders did not believe what Aristides had told them. And these Hellenes were still not convinced, but then Tenian deserters arrived in a trireme commanded by a man called Panaetius, son of Sosimenes, and he confirmed that this was indeed the true situation. For that act, the Tenians[1] are included amongst the names of those who overcame the Barbarians inscribed on the column at Delphi. With this ship deserting at Salamis and the one

---

[1] Tenos is a small island on the eastern edge of the Cyclades.

from Lemnos that had previously joined it at Artemisium, the Hellene fleet was brought up to a total strength of 380 having previously fallen two short of that figure. (8.78–82)

Aristides' dramatic entrance and dialogue with Themistocles was spiced up for Herodotus' Athenian audience by the knowledge that this leading politician had been ostracized two or three years previously as a consequence of his rivalry with Themistocles. Themistocles' first appearance in the narrative is similarly stage managed. In fact, it is very unlikely that Aristides burst onto the scene in this fashion, because all ostracized citizens had been recalled from exile earlier in the year as one of the emergency measures taken to prepare the city for the anticipated invasion. The aristocratic Aristides, to be known later as 'the Just', was popularly contrasted with wily Themistocles, the man of the people. However, this collaboration in the national interest was to last for the next couple of years in which Athens established her leadership of the Delian League, the formal Hellene alliance that was to evolve into the Athenian Empire.

The Hellene commanders decided to believe what the Tenians told them and made their ships ready for battle. With the dawn they called their marines together and Themistocles' speech was the best, setting out all that is strong in human nature and the human condition in contrast to the lesser qualities. He urged the men to embrace the former and then gave the command to embark. The men went on board and, at that moment, the trireme which had been despatched to collect Aeacus and his sons[1] returned from Aegina.

The Hellenes put out to sea in full force, and, as they were putting out to sea, the Barbarians bore down on them. Some backed water and came near to beaching their ships, but then an Athenian, Ameinias of Pallene, darted forward and rammed an enemy ship. The two ships were locked together and could not separate, and others came to Ameinias' aid and joined the fight. This is how the Athenians say the battle began; but the Aeginetans say the ship that made the crossing

---

[1] These important relics may indeed have been shipped from Aegina to Salamis, but this is more likely to have been done before the Persians had blockaded the eastern entrances to the straits.

to Aegina to collect Aeacus and his sons started it. The story is also told that a female spectre appeared and shouted orders in a voice loud enough to be heard by the whole Greek fleet, beginning with this reproach, 'Madmen, how much further are you going to back off?' (8.83–84)

After their overnight manoeuvres the Persians were poised to attack at sunrise and the Hellenes were ready to meet them. Some reconstructions of the battle follow Diodorus Siculus, who states that the Hellenes 'occupied the passage between the Heracleum and Salamis' (*Library of History* 11.18), suggesting that initially their line ran across the straits around 2,000m from the eastern entrance, its right resting on Salamis and its left on the mainland shore. If the Hellenes had waited there and allowed the Persians to enter the straits in columns and manoeuvre into line, they would have left their beaches and encampments on Salamis to the east of their position completely exposed. Also, they would have had to keep 100m or more of clear water between their left flank and the shore to stay out of range of the thousands of archers that the Persians could mass at the water's edge; their oarsmen were protected but all on deck would have been lethally exposed. The Persians would then have had a good chance of streaming through this gap and carrying out a decisive *periplous*. Their left would not have been exposed to the same threat from the Salamis shore because supplying the standard complement of four archers for each trireme would have left only a modest number on land.

A more plausible reconstruction has the two sides following the tactical principle of fighting with a friendly shore at their backs and facing each other across the straits, the Persians formed into line after entering under cover of darkness and the Hellenes coming straight out from their beaches. Contact was almost immediate, as Herodotus indicates, because the fleets were only a few hundred metres apart by the time the Hellenes had launched and formed their line, which was probably two ships deep and approximately 3,000m long. On engagement, their left rested on the eastern edge of Enchantress 1 and their right on the tip of Cynosoura. Elements may have thrust further forward initially and then backed water to draw the enemy on as the gap between the two fleets narrowed. In any case commanders and helmsmen would have been adjusting their positions in the line, darting short distances forward and astern, feinting attack and probing for openings whilst avoiding creating opportunities for the enemy. The ideal manoeuvre was to break into the enemy line with a sudden sprint and then to turn sharply and ram their target in the side or the stern quarter. Thucydides, who commanded triremes in battle, makes the limitations of eyewitness accounts very clear in his description of the disastrous defeat of the Athenian fleet in the harbour of Syracuse in 413:

> The opposing armies on shore suffered the most agonizing and conflicting emotions whilst victory hung in the balance ... Their view of the battle from the shore was inevitably as variable as the fighting itself. Close up to the action and looking at different pieces of it, some who saw comrades winning and drew courage from this were moved to call upon the gods not to deny them salvation, while others who saw comrades losing shouted cries of despair, and suffered more stress as spectators than the actual combatants ... In that one Athenian army, while the outcome of the battle remained uncertain, you could hear, all at the same time, shrieks, cheers, cries of 'We're winning' or 'We're losing' and the whole range of reactions you would expect from a great army in mortal danger. And it was much the same for the men on the ships. (*History of the Peloponnesian War* 7.71)

The story of the female spectre reflects the emotions experienced by the Hellenes watching from the shores of Salamis or, even more specifically, the consternation felt by onlookers who did not understand what was going on tactically. Ships off Enchantress 1, the promontory on the north side of Ambelaki Bay and the eastern end of Cynosoura would have begun the battle close to shore and any tactical backwatering might have appeared suicidal; a beached ship was hopelessly vulnerable.

At this point, according to the later Athenian slander that Herodotus repeats, Adeimantus fled with his 40 Corinthian ships:

> The Athenians say that the Corinthian commander Adeimantus was in such a state of terror and panic at the start of the fighting when the first ships engaged that he unfurled his sails and turned and fled. Seeing their commander taking flight, the rest of the Corinthians followed suit. But when they had withdrawn as far along the shore

of Salamis as the temple of Athena Sciras,[1] they were met by a small craft. It must have been despatched by the gods, they say, because no mortal man appears to have sent it and because the Corinthians knew nothing about what was happening to the rest of the fleet when it approached them. That is why they think this was a case of divine intervention. When this boat had drawn closer to the Corinthian ships, the men on board hailed them. 'Adeimantus,' they shouted, 'by turning your ships to flight you are betraying the Hellenes. They are actually winning the battle and overcoming the enemy as they prayed they would.' Adeimantus would not believe this. Then they told him that they were willing to be taken hostage and killed if the Corinthians found that the Hellenes were not the victors. So then Adeimantus and the rest of them turned their ships round and rejoined the fleet when the fighting was all over. This is the story told by the Athenians, but the Corinthians contest it and argue that they played a leading part in the battle, and the rest of Hellas confirms that this was so. (8.94)

It is impossible to square this story with other evidence that the Corinthians, the second strongest element in the Hellene fleet, played a leading part in the fighting. If they did leave their position in the line somewhere to the right of the Athenians and sail between them and the advancing enemy and out of the straits between the Enchantresses, this must have been to reinforce Themistocles' disinformation that the Hellenic Alliance was falling apart. After pausing briefly then receiving a signal that the Persian right was fully engaged, they could have rowed back and launched an unexpected attack on its flank and rear. In his strange and vicious essay, *On the Malice of Herodotus*, Plutarch misses Herodotus' clear signals that he does not believe this story himself and, to refute it, quotes the inscription on a memorial to the Corinthians who died at Salamis:

When all of Hellas hung on a razor's edge,
We gave our lives to save her.
(*On the Malice of Herodotus* 39)

---

[1] The location is unknown but it may not have been far along the shore and was perhaps on a promontory which temporarily concealed the Corinthians whilst they paused before rejoining the battle.

Aeschylus paints a more glorious picture than Herodotus of the battle's opening phase:

> As soon as the white colts of daybreak,
> Brilliant to behold, covered the earth,
> A cry rang out from the Hellene ranks
> Like a triumph song, and a high echo
> Bounced back from the island rocks.
> Terror gripped the Barbarians,
> Terror and shattered hopes. This was not flight!
> The Hellenes were singing their sacred paean
> And surging into battle with spirits high.
> A trumpet call set them all afire.
> Straightway, on the command, they dipped their oars,
> All striking the ocean brine together.
> Swiftly the whole fleet came into view,
> The right wing leading in perfect order
> And then the whole host coming out against us.
> And we could hear a great shout,
> 'Sons of Hellas, forward to freedom!
> Freedom for the land of your fathers!
> Freedom for your children and wives!
> Freedom for the shrines of your ancestral gods,
> For the tombs of your forefathers!
> Now all is at stake!'
> From our side, a hubbub of Persian voices answered back.
> Now there could be no more delay.
> Straightway, ship struck ship with brazen prow.
> A Hellene ship was the first to strike,
> Breaking off the whole sternpost of a Phoenician.[1]
> Then all the rest picked targets for their spearing rams.[2]
> (*Persae* 386–411)

---

[1] A classic ramming manoeuvre, sweeping in to ram the enemy ship's stern and, here, with spectacular results.

[2] The metaphorical use of *doru*, 'spear' (but also 'timber'), is particularly powerful in the context of Aeschylus' description of Xerxes' invasion as 'victory for the Dorian spear'.

Aeschylus graphically captures the moment, under wispy cloud lit by the risen sun or with morning mist breaking up along the shoreline, when the Greek fleet gathered itself to advance. Trumpet call and paean were a long-established part of the ritual of hoplite war. Aeschylus may be quoting words from one of the speeches given before Salamis, even Themistocles'. Some reconstructions of the battle have been ingeniously based on a literal interpretation of the three lines describing the emergence of the Greek fleet, including one in which it appears in its entirety from either side of Enchantress 1, which would have been a dangerously cramped and unwieldy manoeuvre. But, as there is no indication of the position from which the Persian messenger was observing, there are a number of possibilities, and, given the nature of the source, it is fairly pointless to debate their merits. Ameinias and other participants named by Herodotus may well have been in the audience in 472. However, as with Themistocles, the conventions of tragedy would not allow any of them to be named and Aeschylus' focus on the clash of two civilizations, Hellene and Barbarian, ruled out parochial nationalism. But he and his fellow citizens knew who the real heroes were. Specific incidents mentioned by Aeschylus and Herodotus could have taken place more or less simultaneously at different points along the 3,000m line.

The battle would have entered its main phase with an increasing number of 'dogfights' flaring up with no major breakthrough. The Greeks probably had kept few ships back in reserve but the Persians will have sent in large numbers as soon as possible after sunrise, pressing in behind the assault squadrons. Herodotus gives about the same amount of space to the fighting at Salamis that he gives to the fighting at Thermopylae. However, here, he does not organize the narrative chronologically, but broadly divides it into two accounts of the battle, first from the Persian point of view and then from the Hellene, focusing on the performance and fortunes of the main contingents. He picks out the exploits of some individuals, giving most prominence to two central characters, Artemisia and Themistocles. Sadly, he gives only glimpses of the overall shape of the engagement. However, his placing of the Phoenicians opposite the Athenians 'on the western flank, which was nearest to Eleusis' and the Ionians 'on the eastern flank, which was nearest to Piraeus' clearly indicates that the battle commenced with the two fleets facing each other across the straits. Although Eleusis is actually some distance to the north of Salamis, the section of the straits (leading to Eleusis) in which the battle was fought runs from east to west.

The Phoenicians were facing the Athenians, positioned on the western flank, which was nearest to Eleusis. The Ionians were opposite the Lacedaemonians on the eastern flank which was nearest to Piraeus. Just a few of the Ionians followed Themistocles' instruction to hang back and most of them did not. I could recite a long list of the Ionian commanders who took Hellene ships, but I shall name just two, Theomestor son of Andromadas and Phylacus son of Histiaeus.[1] The reason I mention only these two is that Theomestor was installed as tyrant of Samos[2] for the service he had done, while Phylacus was publicly honoured as a King's benefactor and awarded a lot of land. The Persian word for King's benefactors is *orosangai*. So much for those Ionians. The majority of their ships at Salamis were sunk, some destroyed by the Athenians, some by the Aeginetans.

Because the Hellenes fought with discipline and held their formation, while the Barbarians allowed theirs to be broken up and did not seem to be following any plan, the outcome was inevitable. Yet the Barbarians conducted themselves much better that day than they did off Euboea, for they all fought hard out of fear of Xerxes, each one thinking that the King was watching him personally. As for the rest of the Barbarians and the Hellenes on their side, I cannot tell you in detail how any individuals fought, except for Artemisia. This is what happened, and it made the King think even more highly of her.

At the point when the King's fleet had been reduced to absolute confusion, Artemisia's ship was being chased by an Athenian. She could not get away from it, for friendly ships were in her way and she was close to the enemy. So, she decided on a course of action which proved most effective. With the Athenian ship on her tail, she bore down and rammed one of the friendly ships; it was manned by Calyndians and had Damasithymus, king of Calyndos,[3] on board.

---

[1] Not the tyrant of Miletus, but a Samian of the same name.

[2] For less than a year as Samos joined the Hellene Alliance in 479 and he was presumably ousted.

[3] Calyndos was an important city in the border country between Caria and Lycia so a close neighbour to Halicarnassus.

Maybe she had some quarrel with him while they were still at the Hellespont and did this intentionally, or maybe it was chance that put the Calyndian ship in her way: I can't say. But when Artemisia rammed and sank it, she had the good fortune to benefit twice over. When the Athenian commander saw her ram a Barbarian ship, he thought that Artemisia's ship was either Hellene or a deserter from the Barbarians fighting on his side, so he changed course to pursue other targets. And so it turned out that Artemisia managed to make her escape and save herself, and the trick she played won her high approval from Xerxes. For it is said that the King, as he watched the battle, saw her ship ram the other, and one of his attendants said, 'Master, do you see how well Artemisia has been fighting? She has just sunk an enemy ship.' The King asked if it was truly Artemisia who had done this and they confirmed it, because they clearly recognized her insignia on the ship and assumed it was an enemy ship that she had sunk. As I have said, all this was most fortunate for her, and additionally no one on the Calyndian ship survived to bear witness against her. It is said that Xerxes' response to this was, 'My men have become women, and my women men.' Well, this is what they say Xerxes said. (8.85–88)

This is a great story that would have been treasured by the Halicarnassians. Also, Xerxes' (alleged) exclamation neatly echoes Artemisia's earlier frank appraisal of his men's fighting qualities and chimes with Herodotus' more general, quite regular comparisons of Hellene manhood to the Barbarian variety. However, if Artemisia's ship was actually identifiable from Xerxes' vantage point, which is doubtful given the probable distance, it is unlikely that the Calyndian king's would not also have been recognizable. Earlier, Herodotus names Damasithymus as one of the leading commanders in the Persian fleet. This made him Artemisia's peer and his insignia would presumably have been equally distinctive. Finally, Herodotus says later that the Athenians had put an enormous price on Artemisia's head, 'appalled that a woman should go to war against Athens' (8.93). It does seem very unlikely that the Athenian commander, Ameinias, would have failed to identify her ship when he had it in his sights, when the Persian staff on shore hundreds of metres away could apparently pick it out in the melee.

In this struggle the general Ariabignes, son of Darius and brother of Xerxes, and many other famous Persians, Medes and allies fell. But only a few of the Hellenes died because they knew how to swim. When their ships were sunk, if they had not been killed in the hand-to-hand fighting, they swam over to Salamis.[1] Most of the Barbarian dead were drowned because they did not know how to swim. Most of their ships were sunk at the point in the battle when those in the front line turned to fall back and those behind, trying to push through to put up a good show for the King, fell foul of the ships on their own side that were trying to get away.

At the height of all this confusion it happened that some Phoenicians who had lost their ships approached the King and blamed the Ionians for their destruction, accusing them of treason. But it turned out that it was not the Ionian commanders who were executed, but their Phoenician accusers who were rewarded in this way. As they were speaking, a Samothracian ship rammed an Athenian. While the Athenian ship was foundering, an Aeginetan ship rammed the Samothracian. But the Samothracians are javelin fighters and they swept the deck of the ship that had rammed them with their javelins, charged aboard and captured it. This incident saved the Ionians' lives, for when Xerxes saw them performing this excellent feat he rounded on the Phoenicians and, laying the blame in every direction in his deep displeasure, gave orders that their heads be cut off to stop men who had revealed how base they were slandering their betters. Xerxes was seated at the foot of the mountain called Aigaleos that faces Salamis and whenever he saw one of his ships doing well in the battle, he asked who the commander was and the scribes wrote down his name, his father's name and the name of his city. Ariaramnes, a Persian who was a good friend to the Ionians, happened to be amongst those present and he had some part in the Phoenicians' evil fate. So Xerxes' men dealt with the Phoenicians as instructed. (8.89–90)

---

[1] It was not necessarily true that all Hellenes could swim but highly likely that very few of the Barbarian troops on board Xerxes' ships had this ability. If, as the context suggests, Herodotus is referring specifically to Hellenes on the Persian side, he is implying here that the fighting took place closer to Salamis than the Attica shore.

Both the incidents above, Artemisia's ruse and the Samothracian capture of the Athenian ship, took place in the latter part of the battle when the Athenians and the rest of the Hellenes were driving Xerxes' fleet out of the straits with the Aeginetans harrying its flank. Thucydides, in his description of the battle of Sybota (fought off Corcyra in 433), gives a convincing impression of the nature of the fighting in the earlier phase when the Hellene and Barbarian fleets were locked together with neither giving way. He is writing from the perspective of a 'modern', Peloponnesian War-era naval commander:

> When the signal flags had been hoisted, the two sides engaged and, in their inexperience, fought this sea-battle in the old-fashioned way with many hoplites on deck, and also archers and javelin men. It was a tough fight, not in terms of competing seamanship (*techne*), but more like a land-battle. For, when they rammed, it was difficult to pull back with the number of ships crowded together, and victory depended more on the hoplites on deck, who had to stand and fight on their stationary ships. There was no *diekplous*. It was a contest of guts and brute strength rather than tactical skill and there was a great deal of noise and muddle. (*History of the Peloponnesian War* 1.49)

It seems that the bulk of the fighting in this phase of the battle of Salamis was done in what Thucydides calls the 'old-fashioned way'. *Diekplous* and *periplous*, manoeuvres that characterized the modern way, had already become the part of the Hellenes' tactical vocabulary by the time of the battle of Lade in the first decade of the century. But Themistocles and his fellow-commanders do not appear to have attempted them in the fleet engagements of 480 because they could not match the skill and experience of their opponents with their 'better-sailing' ships. Instead they opted for the more static 'land-battle at sea' in the confined waters of the straits, to be fought out on deck by massed infantry as much as by manoeuvre and ramming. The battle of Sybota, a prelude to the Peloponnesian War, was fought between the Corcyreans, aided by Athenians, and the Corinthians and their allies. Thucydides points out that 270 ships were engaged there, making it a larger battle than any previously fought between Hellenes. At Salamis there were around three times that number locked in combat, with at least three times the 'noise and muddle'.

Plutarch, more interested in his subject's character than his greatest achievement, gives only a little space to the battle of Salamis in his *Life of Themistocles*. But he does add detail and colour to Herodotus' account:

Themistocles is thought to have selected the best time to fight with as much precision as he selected the place. This is because he was careful not to send his triremes into attack on the Barbarians until the hour of the day in which a fresh breeze blows in from the sea and drives a swell through the straits. This breeze was not a problem for the Hellene ships, as they were low in the water and relatively small. But it was disastrous for the Barbarian ships, with their towering sterns, lofty decks and heavy displacement. When it struck them, it swung them broadside-on to the Hellenes. Then they darted into the attack, following Themistocles' lead because they had confidence in his tactical understanding. They were up against Xerxes' admiral Ariamnes[1] on a huge ship, showering arrows and javelins off it as from a city wall. He was a brave man, the most powerful and just of the King's brothers. Two Athenians, Ameinias of Decelea[2] and Socles of Paeanea, rammed him head-on and the two ships were locked together by their bronze beaks. Ariamnes tried to board their trireme but the two Athenians held him off and hurled him into the sea with their spear thrusts. Artemisia recognized his body drifting amongst the other wreckage and recovered it for Xerxes. (*Themistocles* 14)

Themistocles' successful exploitation of local weather conditions as remarked on here has been incorporated in modern reconstructions of the battle, and local knowledge must have given the Hellenes some advantage. But Herodotus makes it clear that the Hellenes were in no position to delay contact when the enemy bore down on them at sunrise. Secondly, Xerxes' ships would have had no more difficulty than the Hellenes in coping with any breeze or the light swell that it blew up. The seagoing and fighting capabilities of the non-Hellene ships in

---

[1] Herodotus names an Ariamnes in the staff of Xerxes' army but does not identify him as one of his brothers. Plutarch may have confused him with Ariabignes, the foremost Persian casualty (8.89).

[2] This may be the same Ameinias as mentioned twice by Herodotus, but he gives Pallene as his deme.

the Persian fleet are discussed in the Introduction (from page 46). The clash Plutarch describes may well have been replicated many times over in the battle.

Herodotus continues and concludes his account of the battle:

The Athenians and the Aeginetans did the most damage to the Persian fleet. When the Barbarians were put to flight and trying to get out of the straits and back to Phalerum, the Aeginetans were lying in wait for them in the channel and did famous deeds. For while the Athenians were dealing with those ships that put up some resistance or were trying to make their escape in the confusion, the Aeginetans dealt with those that were trying to get out of the straits. So, any that escaped the Athenians ran straight into the Aeginetans.

Themistocles, in pursuit of an enemy ship, came alongside Polycritus son of Crius, an Aeginetan, who had just rammed a Sidonian ship. This was the one that had captured the Aeginetan ship that was patrolling off Sciathos with Pytheas son of Ischenous on board, the man whose courage had so amazed the Persians that they kept him on their ship after cutting him to ribbons. This Sidonian ship carrying him in the Persian fleet was now captured in turn, so Pytheas was brought back safe to Aegina. When Polycritus saw the Athenian ship, he identified it as the flagship from its pennant and called out to Themistocles, taunting him and reproaching him for the allegation that Aegina had medized, aiming these disparaging remarks at Themistocles as he rammed the enemy ship.

The surviving Barbarian ships escaped and got away to Phalerum and the protection of the land forces. In this sea-battle the Aeginetans were spoken of as the Hellenes who fought the best, and after them the Athenians, and individually named were Polycritus the Aeginetan and the Athenians Eumenes of Anagyrus and Ameinias of Pallene, the one who pursued Artemisia. If he had known that she was on board that ship, he would not have given up the chase until he had either captured her or been captured himself. These were the orders given to the Athenian commanders and a prize of 10,000 drachmas was also on offer for whoever took Artemisia alive, so appalled were they that a woman should go to war against Athens. But, as I have already said, she escaped with the rest of them, those whose ships had survived, to Phalerum. (8.91–93)

As there were only 30 Aeginetan ships in the battle, Herodotus may be exaggerating the scale of their contribution, but theirs was one of the most experienced naval contingents on the Hellene side, and it is possible to envisage it positioned as a reserve in Ambelaki Bay and darting out into the flank of the retreating Persians. Herodotus clearly relished the stories of the rescue of Pytheas and the sharp exchange between the former enemies, Polycritus and Themistocles.

Aeschylus moves in one line from the opening clash to a graphic description of the disastrous rout that closed the battle. He powerfully evokes the horror of the Persian defeat and accurately summarizes the main cause of it but, like Herodotus, he offers little in the way of descriptive detail on tactics or combat. Of course, their audiences could readily fill this out from personal experience of naval combat or from the shared memories of friends and relatives.

At first the great stream of Persian ships held its own,
But, when the mass of them crowded into the narrows,
Far from giving support, they crashed into each other
With their bronze-beaked prows shattering all their rowing gear.
The Hellenes systematically worked their way around them
And struck from all directions.
Capsized hulls covered the open water
Clogging it with wreckage and the dead.
The shores and reefs were draped with corpses.
Every ship was flying in chaos,
Every ship, that is, in the Barbarian fleet.
The Hellenes, like fishermen netting tuna or some other haul of fish,
Battered and skewered with broken timbers and splintered oars,
And screams and groans filled the salty air
Until black-eyed night brought the horror to an end.
(*Persae* 412–28)

Themistocles' plan had worked. He had drawn the enemy into a space in which their superior numbers and 'better-sailing' ships gave them no advantage, and met them on the Salamis side of the straits with his flanks protected by Enchantress 1 to the left and the tip of Cynosoura to the right. The Hellenes were probably lined up two-deep with some reserves held back in Ambelaki Bay and off Paloukia beach. The

Corinthians would have made their decoy run early enough for the gap left by their 40 triremes to be filled before the two fleets engaged. The Persian line, perhaps three-deep initially, became deeper as it compressed on its approach to the shorter Hellene line. Their helmsmen had very little room for manoeuvre; evasive action led to crippling collisions and the more freely moving Hellene triremes were able to exploit the mounting chaos 'systematically' like a wolf pack herding and picking off a large flock of sheep. A turning point may have been the moment when the Corinthians rejoined the battle and helped the Athenians roll up the Persians' left and start to drive them back down the straits. One of the Hellene trophies was set up on Enchantress 1; a second trophy on Cynosoura was perhaps intended to celebrate the ejection of the Barbarians from the straits. In the course of the fighting, the blockading squadrons may have entered the straits to join the battle and made the situation worse when they met the retreating assault squadrons.

Another *Persae*, a highly wrought solo ode (*nomos* in a different usage of the word) sung to the lyre and first performed about 70 years later, compresses the action into even fewer lines. Its writer, composer and performer, Timotheus was from Miletus, the most renowned *citharode* (lyre-player and singer) of his time and highly regarded as an innovative composer. Like many classical and romantic opera librettos, his verse, when divorced from its musical accompaniment, tends not to be of the highest literary quality. But what a word-picture he paints with his lurid palette! His audiences were Hellenes who would have been wearily familiar at first- or close second-hand with the realities of combat at sea in the grim closing years of the Peloponnesian War. In that period, ironically, Persian gold was to underwrite the Spartans' war effort leading to their ultimate success in 404. Timotheus' celebration of the great victory at Salamis in which Athens played such a decisive part would have been especially comforting and inspiring for citizens, still heavily bruised by the disastrous failure of their Sicilian campaign and knocked about by political upheaval, which even overturned democracy for a period:

Spray flying from the oars,
The fleets sweep together
Ploughing through the swell
Ram teeth bared.

They close, and curving prows
Rip through the fir-tree limbs.[1]
A strike on one side shatters oars
And throws the rowers all one way.
Then, on the other side, a second strike
Smashes more banks of oars and seafaring pine
And hurls the rowers back again.
Ships stripped of their limbs
Show their flax-girt hulls.[2]
Some overturn, blasted by thunderbolts of lead.[3]
Others founder as metal-capped rams
Sheer off their ornamented stern-posts.
Like an inferno spreading,
Thong-spun javelins leap from many hands
And find their mark in quivering flesh.
Flaming brands[4] like roasting spits shower down
And from the bowstrings arrows fly,
Winged, far-shooting darts of bronze
Heaping slaughter upon slaughter
Until the emerald tresses of the ocean
Turn crimson round the ships
And shouts and shrieks fill the air.
So, the Barbarian fleet was driven back
Over the shining fish-garlanded folds
Of Amphitrite's robe.[5]
(*Persae* 1–39)

[1] The oars.
[2] This may refer to the fibre used with pitch in caulking, or to reinforcing cables around or along the hull below the waterline.
[3] This is an anachronistic reference to a ship-to-ship weapon introduced later in the 5th century, a heavy weight suspended from the yardarm and dropped onto enemy ships from alongside.
[4] There is no earlier reference to the use of incendiary missiles in naval battles, but Herodotus does mention fire-arrows in his account of the Persians' attack on the Acropolis in 480. Here, context and vocabulary suggest, again anachronistically, more substantial missiles, perhaps fired from ship-borne artillery, of which there is no earlier record.
[5] Amphitrite was a sea-nymph.

A few lines further on, Timotheus piles on the metaphors to add yet more lurid detail:

The Barbarian fleet fell back in hasty flight
And the battle lines crashed together
Caught in the long neck of the straits.
The ships' mountain-feet[1] ripped from rowers' hands
Smashed their mouths' bright-shining offspring.[2]
The waters were strewn with constellations
Of breathless, lifeless bodies
And the beaches were heaped with corpses.
(*Persae* 86–97)

And his lines on a drowning landlubber Persian are equally graphic:

He was a man from the plains,
Lord of lands a day's journey wide.
With his feet and hands
He pounded the water,
A floating island battered by the ocean.
And each time the wind fell in one direction
It rose against him from another,
And Bacchus had no part
In the foaming floodtide
Surging through his gullet.[3]
Desperate and crazed, with chattering teeth
He spluttered curses at the ocean,
His mortal destruction.
(*Persae* 40–71)

Ineffectually, he reminds the sea that the Great King 'has yoked your turbulent neck with bonds of hemp' (meaning the 'neck' of the

---

[1] The oars, again (made of wood from fir trees grown in the mountains).
[2] Teeth.
[3] Likening the drowning man to a vomiting drunk.

Hellespont) and warns that 'his roving seamen will control his plains'. He ends with a curse, then dies:

'Your rage brings woe,
Hated from ancient times,
Fickle bosom-friend of the swift-drenching wind!'
Breathless, he cried out
And from his grimly frothing mouth
He spewed up deep-sea brine.
(*Persae* 79–85)

When the Persians had finally been driven out of the straits, the Hellenes could deal with the Barbarian force that had been landed on Psyttaleia during the night. Herodotus and Plutarch present this as a major operation involving hoplites. Pausanias in his *Guide to Greece* gives a more realistic idea of its scale:

I drew attention to the excellence of the Athenian Aristides son of Lysimachus a little earlier. This is what he did in the affair at Salamis. He gathered together a large force from the Athenian hoplites who were lined up along the beaches and led them in an assault on the island of Psyttaleia, and they slaughtered all the Persians who were on that small island. (Herodotus 8.95)

Aristides, observing that the small island of Psyttaleia that lies in the channel off Salamis was full of enemy troops, landed boatloads of the most committed and warlike citizens on the island, joined battle with the Barbarians and killed them all, except for the most notable amongst them, who were taken alive. (Plutarch *Aristides* 9)

Here they say that about 400 of the Persians landed, and when the fleet of Xerxes was defeated, these also were killed after the Greeks had crossed over to Psyttaleia. (*Guide to Greece* 1.36)

Aeschylus gives a fuller and grander account as the Messenger continues his report to Queen Atossa:

The scale of disaster that followed
Was twice as terrible as that which came before.

Men of Persia in the prime of life,
Finest spirits of most noble birth
And foremost in loyalty to the King
Have met an ugly death, inglorious fate!
There is an island just off Salamis,
Small and not a good place to drop anchor.
Pan, who loves to dance, haunts its shore.
The King despatched those men there with this charge
To kill enemy Hellenes who would be easy prey
When they abandoned ship and sought safety on the island,
And to rescue friends from the channels of the sea.
How badly he misread events!
For when some god had granted Hellas glory in their ships,
That same day, Hellenes, fully armed in bronze,
Leapt ashore and made a circle all around the isle.
There was nothing our men could do, nowhere to turn.
Many were struck down by stones flung at them,
Or by the arrows that showered from bowstrings.
And then they charged in one great rush
And hacked at the wretches' limbs and butchered them.
Xerxes wailed as he watched this great disaster,
For he was seated with a clear view of all his forces
On a lofty headland close by the sea.
He tore his garments with bitter groans
And gave immediate orders to his land force
Urging it to disorderly flight.
That is the second disaster you must lament.
(*Persae* 433–71)

Aeschylus does not depict a classic hoplite action, rather suggesting that a mixed force with a large, light-armed element dealt with the enemy force on Psyttaleia. With the Athenian triremes heavily manned for a 'land-battle at sea', as described by Thucydides, there may not have been a very large body of Athenian hoplites on Salamis to call upon for this operation. The later tradition may be a reflection of political rivalry between the property-owning classes, who filled the hoplite ranks, and their lowlier fellow citizens who rowed the triremes; Aristides was champion of the former, Themistocles of the latter. If, as is likely, there was a lot of fighting on deck, defending their own or attacking the enemy's, the contribution to victory of the hoplites did not actually require extra recognition. But their traditional role was in land-battles.

> When the engagement was broken off, the Hellenes towed all the disabled ships that were still in the straits back to Salamis in readiness to fight again because they expected the King to carry on with the ships that were still available to him. A west wind took hold of many of the disabled ships and carried them to the part of the coast of Attica that is called Colias. So, the prophecies about this battle which the oracles Bacis and Musaeus[1] had written were fulfilled, and also the prophecy many years earlier of Lysistratus, an Athenian soothsayer, concerning the wrecks that were carried to shore there. The Hellenes had previously been quite unable to interpret his words, 'The Colian women will cook with oars'. But this was to happen after the King had marched away. (8.96)

Neither Herodotus nor Aeschylus quantifies the losses on either side but a Roman source, possibly with access to some earlier record, states quite plausibly that the Greeks lost over 40 triremes and the Persians more than 200. The loss of life on the Persian side would have been proportionately higher because of their larger deck crews which included Persians, Medes and Sacae who mostly could not swim. On this arithmetic, Xerxes, with the uncommitted Egyptian squadron as a nucleus, still had numbers in his favour, but the crews that had escaped from the straits were demoralized and many of the ships would need work to make them battleworthy again. His reaction to the day's defeat would not have been as extreme as Queen Atossa's, as imagined by Aeschylus: '*Aiai*! A vast ocean of disasters has swamped the Persians and the entire Barbarian race' (*Persae* 433–34). He had taken and destroyed Athens and become master of central and northern Greece, and, though he had lost a battle at sea, his massive land army was intact and undefeated. However, he was a long way from home and the centre of empire, and the campaigning season was drawing to a close.

---

[1] Bacis and Musaeus were the authors of collections of prophecies which were widely consulted in the 5th century as an alternative to asking questions of the major oracles.

When Xerxes fully understood the scale of the calamity, he became afraid that one of the Ionians might advise the Hellenes to sail to the Hellespont and destroy the bridges, if they did not think of it themselves. He would then be cut off in Europe and in mortal danger. So, he began to plan his escape but wanted to conceal this from both the Hellenes and his own men. He attempted to build a causeway over to Salamis, lashing together Phoenician cargo ships to form both a pontoon bridge and a boom,[1] and he also prepared his fleet for action as if he was going to fight another battle. All who saw Xerxes doing these things did not doubt that he fully intended to stay and fight. But Mardonius, who knew very well from experience how the King's mind worked, was not taken in.

While doing all this, Xerxes sent a messenger to Persia to announce the disaster. This second messenger, coming in soon after the first, caused the Barbarians such distress that they all tore their clothing and cried out with endless wailing, and they put the blame on Mardonius. It was not the loss of their ships so much as fear for the safety of Xerxes himself that put them in this state. This was the feeling in Persia from the message's arrival until Xerxes' return.[2] (8.97–100).

Herodotus states earlier that Gelon of Syracuse won his victory over the Carthaginians at Himera on the same day as the battle of Salamis but offers no description of the campaign. The Sicilian Diodorus Siculus, placing it earlier in the year, concludes his account of it by rating it as highly as the two great Hellene victories in Greece:

Many writers compare the battle to the one the Hellenes fought at Plataea and compare Gelon's generalship to the ingenuity of Themistocles, and, because of each man's extraordinary merit, some rate one most highly and some the other. It turned out that Gelon won his victory on the same day that Leonidas and his men were coming to the end of their fight against Xerxes at Thermopylae, just

---

[1] As previously discussed, this could not have been built any distance out into the channel without protection and logistical support from the Persian fleet. If this had been viable before the battle, it was much less so afterwards.

[2] Herodotus later tells us that Xerxes did not hurry back to Susa but spent some time womanizing in Sardis after he had crossed over into Asia.

as if it had been divinely ordained that both the fairest victory[1] and
the most highly renowned defeat[2] should take place at the same time.
(*Library of History* 11.23)

A different result would have tipped the balance of power in Sicily
significantly in favour of the Carthaginians and Phoenicians and
their Hellene allies, and could have had damaging repercussions for
Hellas as a whole, whatever the outcome of Xerxes' invasion. In the
short term, Hamilcar's invasion made it impossible for Syracuse and
other potentially sympathetic Sicilian powers to assist in the defence
of Greece. So even if the scale of this particular clash is exaggerated by
Diodorus, and whether or not there was any Persian involvement, it
was more than a sideshow in the events of 480.

[1] A phrase Herodotus preserves for the battle of Plataea.
[2] Especially renowned in its most extreme mythology.

Razor's edge

Autumn 480 to Spring 479

Herodotus, clearly not oversupplied with detailed information by his sources, mainly uses his account of this six-month period to fill out his portraits of central characters and to offer reconstructions of the strategic deliberations and diplomatic manoeuvring that took place after the battle of Salamis:

> Mardonius could see that Xerxes thought the battle had been a complete disaster and suspected that the King had already decided on a speedy withdrawal from Athens. He reckoned it was likely he would have to pay the price for persuading the King to go to war with Hellas, so he decided that it would be best to take a gamble: to conquer, or to die a noble death in a great adventure. He was inclined to the view that he was going to conquer Hellas, so, with that in mind, he put a proposal to the King.
>
> 'Master, do not grieve for what has happened to us or think of it as a disaster. The success of our enterprise will not be decided by ship-timber, but by men and horses. These Hellenes think they have won total victory but not a single one of them is prepared to come ashore and face you, nor will any of those already on dry land stand against you. And those who did have paid the price. So, let us make an immediate attempt on the Peloponnese, if you so decide. On the other hand, if you choose to hold back, that is also an option. Do not be depressed by the present situation, because the Hellenes cannot possibly avoid being subjugated by you, nor can they escape paying

the penalty for the harm they have done you, just now and formerly. I urge you to do what I recommend.

'But, if you have already decided to march your army away, then I have a different plan. Great King, you must not allow Persia to become the laughing-stock of Hellas. If you have suffered harm, it is not the Persians' fault. You cannot say we Persians have shown ourselves to be cowards in any way. It was the Phoenicians, Egyptians, Cypriots and Cilicians who showed themselves to be cowards, so we Persians had nothing to do with what happened. Therefore, since we Persians are not the cause of the problem, take this advice from me. If you have decided not to stay here, you must head off home with most of your army. For my part, I will deliver Hellas to you as a subject nation after picking out 300,000[1] of your troops for this purpose.' (8.100)

Mardonius is presented as craftily steering the King towards approval of his personal agenda, to justify his earlier advice to invade Greece and to win glory for himself. Herodotus' audiences, fully aware of the fate that was soon to befall him, would have enjoyed this recurrent note of dramatic irony.

Xerxes took what comfort he could from this, considering the difficulty of his position, and told Mardonius that he would give him an answer after consultations to determine which of the two plans he should follow. After talking with his Persian advisers,[2] he decided to send for Artemisia because it was clear to him that previously she had been the only one to identify the right course of action. When she came in, Xerxes dismissed everyone, his advisers and his personal guard, and told her what Mardonius had said and asked her what she thought.

'Great King,' she replied, 'advising you on what to do for the best is a difficult task. But, as things now stand, I think you personally should head for home and leave Mardonius here with the men he

---

[1] A modest fraction of the immense headline figure that Herodotus cites for the army, but, of course, the customary shorthand for 'a very large force'. The reality was probably between a third and a quarter of this, still a very large army for the time.

[2] A group close to the King of the highest-ranking and most trusted courtiers, but clearly they were not involved in all his decision-making.

is asking for, if this is what he wishes. If he executes his plan and conquers Hellas as he says he will, the success will be yours, Master, since it will be your servants who have achieved it. On the other hand, if things turn out contrary to his expectations, it will not be so great a disaster, so long as you and your household are secure. For while you and your royal household live, the Hellenes will have to fight many battles for their survival. But, as for Mardonius, it will not matter much if he fails. And, if the Hellenes meet with some success, it will not be a true victory because they will have killed your servant only. But you will be marching home after burning Athens, your mission accomplished.'

Artemisia's advice pleased Xerxes greatly because she had put his own thoughts into words. However, in my opinion, he was in such a state of terror that, even if everyone, male or female, had advised him to stay, he would not have stayed. So the King commended Artemisia for her counsel and sent her off to escort his sons (the half-blood princes[1] who had accompanied him) to Ephesus. (8.102–03)

Artemisia is given the honour of a private audience and presents Xerxes with a cynical summary of the situation that conveniently matches his own conclusions. Her exit escorting the royal bastards home to Asia is one further indication of her standing in the Great King's court, at least as imagined by Herodotus or his Halicarnassian sources.

Next, the Great King summoned Mardonius and commanded him to select the men he wanted from the army, and then to do his best to perform deeds that matched the promises he had made. That concluded the day's activity, but that night[2] at the King's command, his generals put to sea from Phalerum and set sail with all speed for the Hellespont to protect the bridges for the King to cross over.[3] When the Barbarians were off Cape Zoster, they thought the small

[1] The sons of his concubines, princes but of lesser status than the sons born to the King's wives.

[2] It is very unlikely that the fleet sailed that night, having spent the previous night at sea and much of the day fighting and losing a battle.

[3] Herodotus tells us a little later that the bridges were no longer in place when Xerxes reached the Hellespont. As discussed earlier, they may have been dismantled quite soon after his army had crossed into Europe.

headlands which jut out from the mainland there were enemy
ships[1] and scattered over a wide area. But after a while they realized
that these were headlands not ships, regrouped and continued on
their way.

The morning after the battle, the Hellenes saw that the Barbarian
army was still in position[2] and assumed that the fleet was still at
Phalerum. Expecting to fight again, they made ready to defend
themselves. However, when they had established that the ships had
gone, they immediately decided to give chase and followed Xerxes'
fleet as far as Andros. When they had reached Andros without
sighting the enemy, they held a council. Themistocles proposed that
they should continue the pursuit on a course through the islands
and sail directly to the Hellespont to destroy the bridges. However,
Eurybiades spoke against this, arguing that the destruction of the
bridges could have very bad consequences for Hellas. He reasoned
that if the Great King was forced to stay in Europe, he would not
remain inactive because, if he did so, he could neither carry on with
his mission nor find a way to get home, and his army would die of
starvation. However, if he were to take things actively in hand before
it came to that, it was quite possible all of Europe, city by city, nation
by nation, would be brought over to his side, either by conquest or
by treaty. He would then be sustained by the fruits of the Hellenes'
yearly harvests. But in Eurybiades' view the King would not stay
in Europe after being defeated at sea, and so should be allowed to
make his escape and return to his own country. From then on, he
declared, the fighting should be over Barbarian territory. The other
Peloponnesian generals were in agreement with this.

When Themistocles saw that he could not obtain a majority in
favour of sailing to the Hellespont, he addressed the Athenians. They
were angry that the Persians had got away and were quite prepared to
sail for the Hellespont on their own, if the other Hellenes were not
willing to. 'It is something I have seen for myself on many occasions
and heard of even more often,' he said. 'Beaten men backed into a

---

[1] A somewhat unlikely error, but it is possible there were some panicky false sightings of
triremes moving out from the mainland, even though neither side would have contemplated
a night attack.
[2] Along the shore on the opposite side of the straits.

corner will fight back and recover from their former disaster. So I say to you, let us not pursue men who are already running away. We and Hellas have driven off a great swarm of enemies by an unexpected stroke of good fortune. We did not bring this about. It was the gods and heroes who would not allow Europe and Asia to be ruled by one man, one impious and arrogant man who destroyed our temples and our homes and burned and cast down the images of our gods, and even bound the ocean in chains and thrashed it with whips. At present, the right thing for us to do is to remain in Greece for the time being and take care of ourselves and our households. Let each of us rebuild his home and attend to his crops, now we have driven out every one of the Barbarians. But when spring comes, let us set sail for the Hellespont and Ionia.' He said this to put the Persians in his debt in case he ever needed a place of safety if the Athenians turned against him, and this did actually happen.

Themistocles was not being straight with the Athenians, but they were taken in. They had always thought he was wise, and now he was clearly demonstrating both wisdom and good judgement and they were ready to go along with whatever he said. Having brought them round, Themistocles immediately sent a delegation off in a boat. These were men he could trust not to reveal the message he had ordered them to give to the Great King, even under torture, and amongst them was his servant Sicinnus. When they reached Attica, the rest stayed in the boat and Sicinnus made his way into Xerxes' presence, and this is what he said. 'Themistocles son of Neocles, the Athenian commander who is the wisest and best in the entire Hellene Alliance, has sent me to tell you that he, Themistocles the Athenian, desiring to be of service to you, has restrained the Hellenes from giving chase to your ships and destroying the bridges over the Hellespont. You may make your way home without any hindrance.' With the message delivered, Themistocles' men sailed back in their boat. (8.107–10)

Herodotus implies here that the Persian fleet abandoned Phalerum overnight and headed home immediately the night after the battle. However, he tells us earlier that Xerxes 'prepared his fleet for action as if he was going to fight another battle' (8.97) and, if he is correct that work was started on a causeway across to Salamis after the battle, this could not have been attempted without naval support. In any case, even if the decision was taken immediately, some time would have been spent repairing battle damage and generally preparing for the return passage. If this activity was observed by the Hellenes, it could have led them to expect another attack and they were clearly not sure enough of the scale of their victory to go onto the offensive immediately. When they set off after the enemy, it is easier to imagine a shadowing operation than hot pursuit, but there is a ring of truth about Athenian advocacy of a more aggressive and vengeful strategy, championed by Themistocles, and opposition to this from the Spartan commander-in-chief and the more cautious Peloponnesians.

Herodotus draws on less flattering elements of Themistocles' personal legend to portray the smooth-talking political operator in action. But his fellow citizens would have been cheered by the idea of returning to the mainland to rebuild their homes and work their land, sowing the seed for the coming year's harvest. At this point it may have been generally assumed that Xerxes' entire invasion force had been seen off and there could have been 'back channel' exchanges between the two camps in which the Hellenes undertook not to impede the Barbarians' retreat on sea or land. But if Sicinnus had delivered Themistocles' first message, the disinformation that the alliance was collapsing just before the battle, he would have been the worst possible choice as bearer of this second message. It is, in any case, very unlikely that he would have been allowed to deliver it directly to the King. At least Plutarch names a different messenger in his version of the tale. Whether or not Themistocles was motivated by self-interest in his dealings with Persia in 480, the Athenians and Spartans turned against him about ten years later and he was ultimately made welcome at the Great King's court as a valued adviser. He became governor of Magnesia in Asia, a rich city inland from Miletus on the River Maeander, where he lived comfortably for the final years of his life.

Satisfied that the Persians were headed east but before dispersing the Hellene fleet, Themistocles and Eurybiades led a brief campaign to collect reparations from islands that were considered to have medized:

> The Hellenes now laid siege to the city of Andros. The Andrians were the first islanders to receive a demand for cash from Themistocles but would not pay. Themistocles declared that the Athenians had

the support of two powerful gods named Persuasion and Pressure and that the Andrians therefore had no option but to pay up. The Andrians replied that they could now understand why Athens was so great and prosperous, being blessed with the support of such useful gods. But they declared that for their part they were blessed with an extreme shortage of land and supported by two useless gods who loved living on the island and would never leave it, and they were called Penury and Powerlessness. Since they were in possession of these gods, they could give no money, and the power of Athens could never be stronger than their weakness. The Andrians were put under siege because they responded in this way and would not pay up.

There was no limit to Themistocles' greed. He sent the same representatives as he had sent to the King with threatening messages to the other islands, demanding money and saying that if they did not pay what he asked, he would bring the Hellene fleet and blockade them and take their cities. By means of these threats Themistocles collected large sums from the Carystians and Parians. They had heard that he was laying siege to Andros because the island had medized, and they knew of his reputation as the best of all the generals, so they were afraid of him and paid up. I cannot say if other islands sent money but I believe some did, not only these two. In any case, payment did not protect the Carystians from harm. However, the Parians bought Themistocles off and they avoided being attacked. So, without the other commanders knowing, Themistocles sailed out of Andros and collected cash from the islanders. (8.111–12)

Herodotus clearly has no inclination to challenge what were very probably slanders invented in later years to blacken Themistocles' character. Herodotus implies that he was acting on his own initiative to raise as much money as possible for himself, using the Hellene fleet as if it was his personal resource. But he was not in command of the fleet and, in any case, the alliance badly needed to raise funds to cover the costs of a very expensive campaign, and securing the approaches to mainland Greece through the Cyclades was an important strategic priority. However, this episode would also have resonated strongly with the Athenians' enemies at the time of the Peloponnesian War as a reminder of their increasingly aggressive raising of cash from former allies in pursuit of imperial power.

The land forces with Xerxes waited for a few days after the sea-battle and then set off to Boeotia by the same routes as they had come. Mardonius felt he should escort the King. He had, in any case, decided that it was too late in the year for campaigning and that it would be better to spend the winter in Thessaly and then mount an attack on the Peloponnese in the spring. On arrival in Thessaly, Mardonius selected as his first choice the whole of the Persian unit known as the Immortals, except for their commander, Hydarnes, who said that he would not leave the King's side. Next, from the rest of the Persians, he picked out all those who had body armour[1] and the elite unit of 1,000 cavalry, and also the Medes, Sacae, Bactrians and Indians, both their infantry and their cavalry. He chose these nations' entire contingents, but from the rest he selected just a few individuals, either for their imposing looks or because he knew they had already done good service. He chose more of the Persians with their torques and bracelets than of any other nation apart from the Medes. Actually, there were as many Medes as Persians, but the Medes were not as tough as the Persians. So, Mardonius mustered a total of 300,000 men, cavalry included.[2]

At this time, while Mardonius was picking his army and while Xerxes was still in Thessaly the Lacedaemonians had consulted the Delphic oracle and received a response that stated they should demand compensation from Xerxes for the death of Leonidas and accept whatever offer the King might make. So, the Spartans despatched a herald immediately and he caught up with the whole army while it was still in Thessaly. He came into Xerxes' presence, and said, 'King of the Medes,[3] the Lacedaemonians and the Heraclidae of Sparta demand

---

[1] Presumably meaning the Persians and Medes who wore 'fish-scale' body armour as mentioned earlier (7.61). But more than once Herodotus implies that Barbarian body armour, if worn at all, was inferior to hoplite body armour. However, the hoplite shield and spear were the most significant factors when it came to close combat.

[2] The true figure was probably in the region of 100,000 and a large proportion of the original invasion force.

[3] Not a conventional way of addressing the Great King and possibly indicating some lack of respect.

that you pay compensation for the death of their king, slain by you while he defended Hellas.' Xerxes burst out laughing and carried on laughing for a long time. Then he pointed to Mardonius, who happened to be standing next to him, and said, 'So be it: Mardonius here will pay those people the appropriate compensation.' The herald accepted this answer and withdrew. (8.113–14)

Herodotus lists the same main contingents when he sets out Mardonius' order of battle at Plataea, but adds an estimated 50,000 medizing Hellenes enlisted later and also names some of the other nations represented by small units. He does not mention the Immortals again and it seems unlikely that they would have been separated from their commander, let alone the Great King himself. It made sense to pick the most heavily armed Persian troops, but they were probably an elite minority and not much more of a match for hoplites in terms of defensive equipment than their more lightly armed colleagues. In his description of Xerxes' grand march out of Sardis, Herodotus includes two 1,000-strong elite cavalry units and it is more likely that Mardonius was allocated one of these than the 10,000 Immortals.

According to Herodotus, Xerxes laughed before Thermopylae when Demaratus warned him of the Spartans' supreme fighting quality. That battle, as described by Herodotus and in later versions, might have given the King cause to regret this, but, if the unembroidered version is accepted, he could have been justifiably well pleased with his victory. There would be no justification for laughter on this occasion; the Great King's response to the Spartan herald's demand was to come true, but not as intended.

Xerxes left Mardonius in Thessaly and made his way as quickly as he could to the Hellespont. He reached the bridgehead in 45 days, bringing with him not a fraction, as the saying goes, of his invasion force. Wherever they went, whatever people the land belonged to, they commandeered their food and devoured it. If they could find no food, they ate growing plants and peeled the bark and stripped the leaves off the trees, both cultivated and wild. They were starving and left the land bare. There was an outbreak of plague in the ranks and many died of dysentery on the march.

Xerxes left the sick behind, commanding each city he arrived at to care for them and feed them; these were cities in Thessaly, Siris of Paionia and Macedonia. He had left the sacred chariot of God in Siris on the way into Greece, but he did not recover it on the way back. The Paionians had given it to the Thracians, and when Xerxes demanded its return, they said its team had been put out to grass and then been stolen by some other Thracians who live upcountry by the source of the Strymon.

In fact, the Persians who had marched through Thrace to the Hellespont made a hurried crossing to Abydos by ship, because they found the bridge of boats had been broken up by a storm and was no longer there. They paused at this point and were issued with more rations than they had been given on the whole march. Then many of the army's survivors died from overeating and from the different water they were drinking. Those that were left finally arrived at Sardis with Xerxes. (8.115–17)

Herodotus gives a somewhat contradictory impression of Xerxes' march to the Hellespont. It took half the time of his whole army's advance to the west, but an average of about 12km a day could not be described as headlong, especially for a more compact force. The hardships described may have been suffered by some stragglers, perhaps, but the arrangements made for the sick suggest an orderly retreat rather than a panicked withdrawal. The loss of the ceremonial chariot and its beautiful team to Thracian horse-thieves was an embarrassment, but it was probably left behind in northern Greece because it would have been an encumbrance on a march through increasingly hostile territory. Finally, it is unlikely that the Persians did not know that the bridges were no longer in place before they reached the Hellespont.

Aeschylus gives no impression of order or control:

In a rush, the commanders of the ships that were left took flight,
Scattering without order before the wind.
The army that remained was wiped out in Boeotian territory.[1]
Some of us lay sick with thirst beside bright springs,

[1] At Plataea.

Others, lungs bursting, made it into the land of Phocis
And on to Phocian soil and then to the Malian gulf
Where the Spercheus river generously waters the plain.
And finally, running out of food, the country of Achaea
And the cities of Thessaly took us in.
By then very many had died,
Killed by our travelling companions, Starvation and Thirst.
We came to the land of Magnesia then onward to Macedonian soil,
Crossed the Axius river and the reedy marsh of Bolbe,
And reached Mount Pangaeus and the land of Edonia.
That very night God called up winter weather before its season
And froze hard the hallowed waters of the river Strymon.
Then men who formerly gave no thought to the gods
Prostrated themselves in prayer to Earth and Sky.
And, done with praying, set out across the frozen water.
Those of us who started before the sun-god spread his beams
Safely reached our goal. But then his bright orb
Played its burning rays across the ice and melted it,
And all the rest fell through.
Happy the man who earlier breathed his last!
Those who survived and reached safety,
Struggled through Thrace with great suffering.
They escaped, and they were few,
To return to hearth and homeland.
Now the Persian capital must mourn,
Yearning for the precious youth of its land.
This is all true, but in my telling of it
I have left out so much of the horror
Sent down upon the Persians by God.
(*Persae* 480–514)

The line mentioning that the army had been 'wiped out in Boeotian territory' is not Aeschylus' only reference to the battle of Plataea in the play and his telescoped chronology with the Messenger's allusion to the Persians' defeat on land could explain the contradictions in Herodotus' account of the retreat after Salamis. The hardships described by both writers are more likely to have been suffered on their homeward march by survivors from Plataea in the following year.

Herodotus collected a different and more detailed account of Xerxes' crossing into Asia:

There is another version of this story that I heard. When the Great King reached Eion on the Strymon in the retreat from Athens, he travelled no further by land, but put Hydarnes in command of the troops to lead them to the Hellespont. He himself went on board a Phoenician ship and was transported to Asia. In the course of this voyage he was caught in rough seas whipped up by a gale known as the Strymonian. The ship was wallowing dangerously in the storm because there were so many Persians crowded on deck to make the voyage with him. In a fit of terror, the King shouted out to the helmsman, asking him if there was any way they could survive. The man replied, 'Master, there isn't any way unless we can somehow get rid of the crowd of passengers we have on deck.' To continue the story, on hearing this Xerxes said, 'Men of Persia, now is your chance to demonstrate how much you care for your King. It would seem that my survival depends on you.' These were Xerxes' words and his men saluted him and jumped into the sea, and the ship, now lighter, came safely back to Asia. As soon as he was ashore, Xerxes did two things: for saving the King's life he rewarded the helmsman with a crown of gold, then he had him decapitated for losing so many Persians. So here we have a different tale about Xerxes' journey home, but I do not believe a word of it, especially the story of what happened to the Persians. If the helmsman had really given that advice to Xerxes, in my view, not one in 10,000 could think that the King would not have ordered the men on deck to go below. Remember, these were Persians and of the highest rank. However, the rowers were Phoenician and he would surely have thrown an equal number of them overboard. As I have already said, Xerxes made his way home to Asia with the rest of his army by the land route.

And the main evidence for this is that on his way home Xerxes came to Abdera and sealed a bond of friendship with its citizens, presenting them with a gilded *akinake* and a *tiara* shot with gold. The people of Abdera say it was here on his way back from Athens that Xerxes first felt secure enough to change his clothes, but I do not believe this story. However, Abdera lies nearer to the Hellespont than the River Strymon and Eion, where he was said to have boarded the ship. (8.118–20)

Herodotus makes it very clear that he does not believe this story, but evidently likes it too much as an illustration of Barbarian despotic behaviour and unquestioning obedience to feel able to omit it.

In a digression in the closing pages of the *Historia*, Herodotus gives one more indication that Xerxes' withdrawal was more measured than he implies elsewhere:

> It happened that the Great King stayed in Sardis from the day he had arrived there after his defeat in the sea-battle and his withdrawal from Athens.[1] While at Sardis he lusted after Masistes' wife, who was also there. But his messages of love could not win her over and, out of respect for his brother Masistes, he would not use force, and the woman was able to hold out because she knew that force would not be used. So, when he saw that this was not working, Xerxes arranged a marriage between Darius, one of his sons, and Masistes' daughter. This, he thought, would give him the best chance of winning over her mother. So, the couple were married with all the proper ceremonial and then Xerxes moved on to Susa. But when he had arrived there and had brought Darius' bride into his house, he gave up on Masistes' wife, switched his aim and successfully seduced Darius' wife, Masistes' daughter. Her name was Artaynte. (9.108)

There is no sense here of the distraught homecoming represented by Aeschylus; dalliance is a more appropriate description. The well-told story continues to a sordid and bloody end (at 9.113). The author's purpose is to add final touches to his kaleidoscopic portrait of Xerxes and to display further examples of Barbarian behaviour and the workings of despotism for his audience to contrast with Hellene values; but it also shows that the King was in no great hurry to get back to Susa. A little later Herodotus returns once more to the question of Xerxes' journey out of Europe:

> Artabazus son of Pharnaces was already a famous man in Persia and set to become even more famous after the battle of Plataea. In command of 60,000 men from the army that Mardonius had assembled, he escorted the King as far as the straits. (8.126)

---

[1] Xerxes would have arrived in Sardis well before the end of 480 and his attempted seduction must have taken up several weeks.

Leaving aside the exaggerated strength of Artabazus' command, this has a plausible feel to it and may have been the version Herodotus favoured above the rest. A strong force was required to escort the Great King through potentially hostile territory and keep the cities they passed through friendly. This does suggest that most of the invading army was left behind with Mardonius. If Hydarnes and the Immortals were also with Xerxes, as is likely, they would have carried on to Sardis and then finally to Susa while Artabazus and his troops marched back to rejoin the army of occupation in northern Greece.

Xerxes was now back in Asia. Artabazus had come as far as Pallene on his way to rejoining Mardonius, who was now in winter quarters in Thessaly and Macedonia and had not yet ordered him to rejoin the rest of the army. Finding Potidaea in a state of insurrection, Artabazus took the view that he should suppress it. In fact, the Potidaeans had openly rebelled against the Barbarians as soon as the Great King had passed by their city at the time of his fleet's withdrawal from Salamis, and the rest of Pallene[1] had risen as well. So Artabazus laid siege to Potidaea, and, suspecting that Olynthus was also plotting rebellion against the King, he laid siege to that city also. After taking it, he marched the defenders out to a nearby lake and slaughtered them all. They were Bottiaeans who had been driven from their land at the head of the Gulf of Therme by the Macedonians. Artabazus installed Critobulus of Torone, a Chalcidian by birth, as governor and that is how Olynthus became a Chalcidian possession.

After taking Olynthus, Artabazus focused his attention on Potidaea, and he had the support of an undertaking from Timoxenus, the general in command of the Scioneans,[2] to betray the city. I cannot say how this was arranged because there is nothing recorded, but this is what happened in the end. When Artabazus and Timoxenus wanted to communicate with each other, they would write a message and wrap it around the shaft of an arrow at the nock end, reattach the flights and shoot it to a prearranged spot. However, Timoxenus' plot to betray Potidaea was discovered when Artabazus shot an arrow

[1] The westernmost of the three peninsulas of Chalcidice.
[2] Scione, the southernmost city of the peninsula, was allied to Potidaea and had sent troops to assist in the defence.

that missed the agreed spot and hit a Potidaean in the shoulder. As happens in war, a crowd quickly gathered around the wounded man and, as soon as they had extracted the arrow, the message was found and taken to the generals, who included allies from the rest of Pallene. They all read the letter and identified the traitor Timoxenus, but they decided not to indict him for carrying out this act of betrayal for his city's sake[1] because they did not want the Scionean people to have an everlasting reputation for treachery. So that was how Timoxenus' treason was brought to light.

Three months into the siege of Potidaea there was a great ebb-tide which lasted for a long time. Seeing their opportunity, the Barbarians set off through the shallows for the shore of Pallene.[2] When they were about a third of the way to their objective, the sea flooded back; and the local people say that the surge was greater than on any of the many other previous occasions on which this had occurred. Some of the Barbarians, those who did not know how to swim, were drowned; the Potidaeans came out in boats and killed those who were able to swim. The people of Potidaea say that this tidal surge and the Persian losses in it came about because those same Persians who died in the sea had defiled the temple of Poseidon on the outskirts of the city and the image of the god in it, and I think this explanation is correct. So, Artabazus brought the survivors back to Mardonius in Thessaly, and that is what happened to the King's escort.

The surviving ships of Xerxes' fleet, after withdrawing from Salamis and reaching Asia, ferried the king and the troops with him over from the Chersonese to Abydos and then wintered at Cyme.[3] (8.126–30)

Potidaea, Olynthus, Torone and Scione, with other cities of Chalcidice, had previously submitted to the Great King and contributed men and ships to the invasion force. They had not interfered with the Persian

---

[1] A plea in mitigation that was not uncommon in Hellene criminal cases.

[2] Potidaea straddled the narrow neck of the peninsula and Artabazus was trying to exploit an exceptional tidal event, caused by local conditions or possibly seismic activity, to get troops round to the south side of the city.

[3] Cyme was an important seaport city of Aeolis on the west coast of Asia. It is unlikely that the whole fleet spent time ferrying the King and his men across the Hellespont before wintering at Cyme.

retreat after Salamis, but they posed a threat in Mardonius' rear on the flank of the land route to Asia, and Artabazus clearly had the capability to carry out a winter campaign to secure Chalcidice. Ruthlessly clearing the non-Hellene Bottiaeans out of Olynthus and handing the city over to Hellene Chalcidians may have been calculated to win support from the local Hellenes. The three-month siege of Potidaea was a failure but was probably not as catastrophic as Herodotus implies. However, Artabazus' efforts to win the city through treachery and his abortive attempt to launch an attack from the south are intriguing details. Poseidon, the earth-shaking god of the sea, may well have been credited with the tidal surge that thwarted the latter.

The Hellenes were unable to take Andros and went to Carystus next and laid waste its land.[1] They then returned to Salamis, and the first thing they did was to set aside the pick of the spoils as offerings to the gods. After dividing the spoils, they sailed on to the Isthmus and set about choosing the man who had shown himself most worthy of the award for excellence in the fighting that year. But when the commanders gathered together and cast their votes at the altar of Poseidon to determine who should be first choice and who second, each of them voted for himself, thinking he had performed the best. However, a majority gave second place to Themistocles. So, others received only a single vote for first place while Themistocles had far more votes than anyone else for second.

The Hellenes were too full of envy to make the award and so sailed off homeward without making a decision. All the same, Themistocles was praised to the skies throughout all of Hellas and rated the cleverest of the Greeks by far. But, because he had not received the honour owed him by those that fought at Salamis, he immediately went to Lacedaemon desiring to be honoured there. Indeed, the Lacedaemonians welcomed him warmly and bestowed great honours on him. They presented Eurybiades with an olive wreath as his reward for excellence and gave a similar wreath to Themistocles for his cleverness and quick-wittedness. They also presented him with the finest chariot in Sparta, and, with much

[1] This was hard on the Carystians if they had already paid up to Themistocles, but may be taken as evidence that his moneymaking enterprise, there at least, was a slanderous invention.

praise, sent him off home with the 300 picked Spartans who are known as the Knights to escort him as far as the Tegean border. Themistocles was the only man known to have ever been given such a send-off by Spartans.

When Themistocles returned to Athens, Timodemus of Aphidnae ranted and raged at him for visiting Lacedaemon. He was one of his political opponents, though otherwise of no distinction, and was insanely jealous of the man. He argued that the honours he had received from the Lacedaemonians were actually earned by the city of Athens, not by Themistocles personally. Timodemus carried on in this vein until Themistocles retorted, 'Absolutely right! If I came from Belbina,[1] I would not have been so honoured by the Spartans. But nor would you have been, dear sir, even though you are from Athens.' And that put an end to that. (8.121–25)

At this point Themistocles leaves Herodotus' stage, bowing out with a characteristic *bon mot* but on the sour note of the suggestion that he was behaving peevishly in seeking from the Spartans the honour he had not been granted at the Isthmus. He had no recorded involvement in the decisive campaigning of 479 and Diodorus offers an explanation for this:

After the battle of Salamis, all of Hellas credited the Athenians with the victory. They became puffed up with pride and it was plain to all that they intended to challenge the Lacedaemonians for command of the fleet. The Lacedaemonians anticipated this and were eager to deflate their arrogance. And so, when a vote was called to determine who should receive the awards for valour, they used their influence to secure the prize for Aegina out of all the cities, and the individual prize for Ameinias of Athens, the brother of the poet Aeschylus, because he was in command of the trireme that had been first to ram the Persian flagship, sinking it and killing the admiral. When the Athenians showed their anger at this unjustified slight, the Lacedaemonians were afraid that Themistocles, in his annoyance with what they had brought about, would plan some great evil against them and the rest of the Hellenes. So, they honoured him

[1] A small barren island some way off the southern tip of Attica, and probably uninhabited.

with twice the share of booty given to those who had been awarded the prize of valour. When Themistocles accepted this, the Athenian Assembly took away his generalship and gave it to Xanthippus. (*Library of History* 11.27)

It is more likely that Themistocles was simply not re-elected. He may have been pushing for a more aggressive naval strategy than there was popular appetite for in 479. Herodotus quotes him as saying after Salamis, 'when spring comes let us sail for the Hellespont and Ionia'(8.109), but he may not have been able to swing a majority in favour of committing the entire fleet to a second consecutive long season of campaigning. It is possible this would have been Sparta's preference, taking the war east with Athens doing the heavy lifting and a cynical explanation of their generosity to Themistocles. Anyway, in his version of a speech given by an Athenian delegation to the Spartans and their allies in the late 430s, Thucydides gives Themistocles the accolade he had undoubtedly earned:

> The outcome of the battle of Salamis clearly demonstrates that the issue was decided in the Hellenes' favour by their ships and that we Athenians made the three most valuable contributions: the largest number of ships; the wisest general; and the most steadfast courage. Towards the total of 400[1] ships Athens contributed a little less than two thirds. Themistocles was in command. He brought it about that the battle was fought in the narrows and nobody can deny that this was our salvation. And that is why you bestowed greater honours on him than on any other visitor that has ever come to your country. (*History of the Peloponnesian War* 1.74)

The Hellenes may have believed or at least hoped that the Persians' march north meant the entire invasion force was leaving Europe, but from early in the autumn they would have known that Mardonius was staying behind with a substantial army and would have been kept informed of Artabazus' operations. For the next few months the two sides were separated by the width of central Greece on land, and at sea by the Aegean. But confrontation was inevitable once the new campaigning

---

[1] Generously rounded up.

season arrived, and the outcome was very likely to be decisive, as it needed to be.

In the first flowering of spring Xerxes' fleet mustered at Samos, where some of the ships had spent the winter. Most of the deck-fighting crews were Persians and Medes. New commanders joined the fleet, Mardontes[1] son of Bagaeus and Artayntes son of Artachaees, and Artayntes brought in his nephew Ithamitres to be a commander alongside them. However, because of the major setback they had suffered, they did not advance further to the west and, indeed, were under no pressure to do so, but kept their station at Samos to guard against insurrection in Ionia. They had 300 ships in all, including some from Ionia. In fact, they did not expect the Hellenes to sail across to Ionia but reckoned that they would be content to defend their home territory. They arrived at this assessment on the basis that the Hellenes had not pursued them after they had sailed away from Salamis, and had been glad to be rid of them. Their confidence had been destroyed at sea, but the Persians expected Mardonius to win an easy victory on land. So, they stayed at Samos, pondering what damage they could do to the enemy and listening out for news of how things were turning out for Mardonius.

As for the Hellenes, they were roused to action by the arrival of spring and Mardonius' presence in Thessaly. The army was not yet mustered, but a fleet of 110 ships gathered at Aegina. Their commander and admiral was Leotychidas[2] son of Menares. He was descended from Heracles through several generations, and from the second of the two royal houses of Sparta. The Athenian commander was Xanthippus.

When all the ships had gathered at Aegina, an Ionian delegation arrived at the Hellene camp. They had been in Sparta a short while before, making an appeal to the Lacedaemonians to liberate Ionia.

---

[1] The previous year he had been in command of a contingent of 'islanders from the Erythraean Sea' (here taken to mean the Persian Gulf). These seem to have been Medians who had been settled there so these would have been high-quality troops, evidence of Mardontes' status.

[2] Successor to Demaratus after Cleomenes had engineered his deposition in 491. As for Leonidas before Thermopylae, Herodotus list his ancestors all the way to Heracles.

One of its members was called Herodotus,[1] son of Basilides. They
had been in a group of seven conspiring to assassinate Strattis, tyrant
of Chios,[2] but their plot was uncovered when one of the conspirators
gave their plan away. The remaining six managed to slip out of Chios
to Sparta, and then on to Aegina where they appealed to the Hellenes
to sail to Ionia. They persuaded them to go as far as Delos. They did
this with some difficulty because the Hellenes were afraid of whatever
lay beyond. They knew nothing about those parts and thought the
enemy was everywhere, and it seemed to them that Samos was as
far away as the Pillars of Heracles. So, it came about that in their
fearfulness the Barbarians did not dare sail further west than Samos,
while the Hellenes did not dare sail further east than Delos in
response to the Chians' pleading. Fear patrolled the space between
the two sides. (8.130–32)

Herodotus is probably correct that the priority for the Persian fleet
was to police Ionia, but it also represented a threat which the Hellenes
could not ignore to the sea-lanes from the Black Sea, to the islands of
the Aegean and even to the mainland. The immediate priority for the
Hellene fleet was probably to protect the more strategically important
Aegean islands and to guard against a landing on the east coast of
the Peloponnese behind their defensive line at the Isthmus or further
forward. It had reassembled in much less force than for the previous
year's naval campaign to retain sufficient manpower on land to oppose
Mardonius' occupying army when it came south. The placing of a
Spartan king in command of the allied fleet may reflect recognition of
the importance of its mission, and perhaps the intention or hope was
that it should be enlarged at some point.

Herodotus' remark that the Hellenes were afraid to venture further
outside their home waters may reflect the views of those, including
Themistocles, who were in favour of a more aggressive strategy. In any
case, the eastern waters of the Aegean would have been quite familiar to
regular Hellene seamen, but caution was justified whilst the Barbarian

---

[1] No family connection, but the author would have enjoyed the coincidence.
[2] Tyrant of Chios from at least the time of Darius' Scythian campaign. He was presumably
deposed at the beginning of the Ionian Revolt but reinstated after its suppression. The Chians
had put up the strongest resistance to the Persians at the battle of Lade in 494.

fleet included the Phoenicians, and outnumbered the Hellenes by such a factor. Delos was, in any case, a good point in the middle of the Aegean from which to parry any new seaborne attack on the Greek mainland and, no doubt, selected for its significance as a Hellene religious centre. The Hellenes did sail further east than Delos when the Ionians had convinced them that they planned to revolt a second time, but the Athenians were probably not prepared to move until they knew the Peloponnesians were marching north to join up with the Athenian army and the rest of the allies in central Greece.

The Greeks, then, sailed to Delos. Mardonius, while wintering in Thessaly, had sent a Carian called Mys to travel round and consult as many oracles as possible. I don't know what Mardonius wanted to find out from the oracles when he gave Mys this task because no one has been able to tell me, but I suppose he wanted to know what they had to say about his present business, and that was all. Mardonius read[1] whatever it was that the oracles had to say and then sent Alexander of Macedon as his envoy to Athens. He chose him partly because he had family connections with Persia and partly because he knew of his service to Athens as *proxenos* and benefactor.[2] He thought he could use Alexander to win the Athenians over, having heard that they were both numerous and valiant as a people. He also understood that they had been the chief architects of the disaster that had befallen the Persians at sea. He was confident that he could easily achieve superiority at sea if he succeeded in winning the Athenians over, and this would indeed have been the case. He thought he was much the stronger on land anyway. So, this was how he reckoned he could gain the upper hand over the Hellenes. Perhaps the oracles had foretold this and advised Mardonius to form an alliance with the Athenians, and perhaps it was in obedience to them that he sent Alexander as his envoy. (8.133, 136)

---

[1] Mardonius almost certainly could not understand Greek or read in any language (literacy and foreign languages were not amongst the accomplishments of most Persian nobles).

[2] Alexander's sister was married to Boubares, one of the Persians in charge of digging the Athos canal. The role of *proxenos* was similar to that of a consul, representing a foreign state's interests in his home country.

Herodotus is probably right that Mardonius was seeking support from the oracles for his strategy, if this was forthcoming, and favourable responses could be bought. But their shrines would also have been good sources of intelligence on the intentions and mood of the various cities they served, and there was advantage in being seen to show respect for the gods of Hellas by consulting them.

Alexander's speech before the Athenian Assembly is brilliantly crafted and staged by Herodotus, deftly contrasting the straightforwardness of Xerxes' gracious offer, Mardonius' hectoring threats and the Macedonian king's emollient advice. It is very unlikely that all these negotiations took place neatly on the same day or even in the same place. But Herodotus drew on many memories, some of them eyewitness, and perhaps also on contemporary written records, though none has survived, to distil the main mood, arguments and even some of the words that were spoken into his elegant dramatizations of pivotal dialogues between the main players. Herodotus adds power to the drama here by naming only one of the direct speakers, Alexander. Persia is distanced by the device of Xerxes and Mardonius' reported speech, and Sparta and Athens speak in their turn as nations:

So, Alexander came to Athens as Mardonius' envoy. This is the speech he gave. 'Men of Athens, Mardonius says, "I have a message from the Great King – I forgive the Athenians all the wrong they have done me. Mardonius, this is my command. Return their land to the Athenians and let them take for themselves more besides, whatever land they wish. Let them live under their own laws.[1] And, if indeed they wish to agree terms with me, you shall rebuild all their temples which I burnt down. These are the Great King's commands, which I must obey, so long as you do not make it impossible for me. And now hear what I, Mardonius, have to say. Why are you so insane as to wage war against the Great King? You cannot defeat him, and you cannot hold out against him forever. You saw the size of his army and what it is capable of. You know the power of the force I now

---

[1] This state of *autonomia* did not generally imply true independence and certainly would not in this instance. Athens would have been a subject state owing absolute loyalty to the Great King, supplying military levies whenever required, paying tribute and no longer a true *demokratia*.

command. Even if you defeat us and win victory (and if you think
you have a hope, you are out of your minds), another much larger
army will come along! So, don't even think of trying to measure up to
the Great King. You will lose your land and be running for your lives
forever. Make peace with the Great King instead. You can do this on
the best possible terms because he wills it so. Stay free and form an
alliance with us without trickery or deceit.""[1]

Alexander continued, 'Athenians, that was the message Mardonius
charged me with delivering to you. For my part, I will make no
mention of the goodwill I have shown you, which you would not be
hearing about for the first time anyway, but it is my earnest wish that
you accept what Mardonius proposes. I can see clearly that you will
not be able to go on fighting a war with Xerxes forever. If I had seen
that you were able to, I would never have come before you to make
such a speech. But the Great King's might is beyond human and
his arm is long. So, I fear for you if you do not immediately agree a
treaty while the terms offered to you are so excellent. Out of all the
Hellene allies, your land lies most directly in the path of invasion and
it never escapes devastation; the land you possess is marked out as a
battleground. Accept the Great King's offer, for it is a great thing for
you that he is ready to forgive you, only you out of all the peoples of
Hellas, your offences, and that he wishes to be your friend.' That was
the speech Alexander gave. (8.140)

The Athenians do not respond to Alexander immediately. The drama is
heightened by the revelation at this point that a Spartan delegation is
also present at the meeting:

Now, the Lacedaemonians had heard that Alexander had come to
Athens to talk the Athenians into agreeing terms with the Great
King. They recalled certain oracles[2] predicting that they and the rest
of the Dorians would be driven out of the Peloponnese by the Medes

---

[1] Similar formulaic declarations of good faith appear in the texts of 5th-century Hellene treaties
quoted by Thucydides.
[2] Whatever the origins of these oracles, true or invented, their message added credibility to
concerns that the Athenians might be persuaded to medize and was quite possibly manipulated
by the Athenians to strengthen their bargaining position in negotiations with the Spartans.

and the Athenians, and they were very afraid that the Athenians might indeed agree terms with the Persians. So, they immediately resolved to send envoys and it happened that these were present at the same session of the Council as Alexander. This was because the Athenians had waited until they arrived, delaying proceedings in full knowledge that the Lacedaemonians were going to find out that an envoy had been sent by the Persians to offer terms; they knew that the Lacedaemonians would send their own envoys as quickly as possible. This they did with the set purpose of making their intentions clear to the Lacedaemonians.

So, when Alexander had finished, the envoys from Sparta joined the debate. 'We have been sent by the Lacedaemonians to urge you not to do Hellas grievous harm by accepting the Great King's terms. That would be an unjust and disgraceful thing for any Hellene to do, but most of all for you Athenians. There are a number of reasons. It was you who stirred up this war, which we had no wish for.[1] From the start the fighting was over your land, and now all Hellas is involved. That apart, it is intolerable that, on top of it all, you Athenians, who have been known of old as liberators on many occasions, should become responsible for the enslavement of Hellas.[2] Nevertheless, we grieve with you in your sufferings, not least the loss of two harvests[3] and the ruination of your prosperity over such a length of time. By way of compensation, the Lacedaemonians and their allies formally announce that they will take into their care your women and all other non-combatant members of your households for as long as this war lasts.

'Do not let Alexander the Macedonian seduce you by adding his own polish to Mardonius' words. Isn't this how this tyrant would behave, conspiring with a tyrant?[4] But not you, if you are in your right minds! For you know that Barbarians cannot be trusted or believed.' That was the speech the Spartan envoys gave.

---

[1] Meaning Athens' involvement in the Ionian Revolt. The following sentence embraces Marathon and Salamis.

[2] Ironic in the context of Athens' later imperialism.

[3] Harvest time was still to come at this point in 479. This could be simply an anachronistic slip on Herodotus' part, or indicate that the Athenians decided not to sow once they knew that the Persians would be back with no certainty that they could be held in Boeotia.

[4] Both were actually hereditary monarchs, but tyranny was a more emotive term.

The Athenians responded to Alexander first. 'We do know that the power of the Mede is far greater than ours so there is no need to criticize us on that count. All the same, we will do our very best to defend ourselves to preserve our freedom. But do not attempt to mislead us into agreeing to the Barbarian's terms. We will not agree. So, go back now and tell Mardonius what the Athenians have to say. "As long as the sun holds his present course, we will never, ever agree terms with Xerxes. We will come out and fight him, putting our trust in our allies, the gods and the heroes to whom he showed no reverence when he burnt their shrines and their statues."

'As for you, do not ever again appear before the Athenians with such a proposal, and never again try to persuade us to do wrong under the pretext of granting us a favour. We would not want something untoward to happen to our *proxenos* and friend.'[1] That was the answer the Athenians gave to Alexander.

And now, this was the Athenians' reply to the Spartan envoys. 'The Lacedaemonians are only human to fear that we will agree terms with the Barbarian. But we think it shameful that you should think such a thing, familiar as you are with the spirit of the Athenians. There is no gift of any amount of gold, no gift of lands surpassing all others in fairness and richness anywhere on earth, that could persuade us to medize and condemn Hellas to slavery. There are many powerful considerations that stop us doing this, even if we wanted to. First and above all, we must fully avenge the burning and destruction of the images and shrines of our gods, and give no thought to any kind of treaty with the man who committed these crimes. Then, there are the things that make us Hellenes,[2] our shared origins and our language, the shrines of our gods and the sacrificial rites that we have in common, and our very way of life.[3] It would be a terrible thing for Athens to betray all of that.

'If by any chance you do not already know this, be assured that so long as there is one Athenian standing, we will agree no treaty with Xerxes. Nevertheless, we are deeply touched by your concern for

---

[1] This was not an empty warning. There was a real danger of mob violence, as events proved shortly afterwards on Salamis.

[2] *To Hellenikon*; 'Hellenism, Greekness'.

[3] *Ethos.*

us, your recognition of the ruination we are suffering and your offer to take our households into your care. That is extremely generous of you, but we shall continue to hold out as best we can without becoming a burden to you. However, with circumstances as they are, you must now send out your army with all speed. We reckon that it will not be long before Mardonius is here, bearing down upon us as soon as he receives our message that we will not do what he demands. Now it is time for us to march out together to meet him in Boeotia before he reaches Attica.' That was the Athenians' reply, and the envoys returned to Sparta. (8.141–44)

The Athenians' robust response to Persia's demands is in the form of an oath. The first half of their response to the Spartans is equally high-toned. It is their sacred duty to avenge the insults suffered by their gods and to keep faith with the values that bind all Hellenes together. As Herodotus repeatedly shows, this bond was fragile, and, at any level of detail, ethnic origins, language, religion and *ethos* showed broad diversity, and he was, of course, conscious as he wrote, that imperialistic Athens was casting a long shadow over Hellas. However, at 'razor's edge' moments such as this one in the war against the Barbarians, there was sufficient belief in Hellas, amongst the small minority of *poleis* that fought it, to hold them together. But self-interest, powered by 'love of freedom' in its many shades, was probably always more influential. It was fortunate that perceptions of self-interest and of the interests of Hellas coincided at these moments.

When Alexander had come back and told him what the Athenians had said, Mardonius led his army off towards Athens at a brisk pace. On the way he gathered troops from all the places he passed through. The leaders of Thessaly did not regret what they had already done and helped him on his way with even greater enthusiasm; Thorax of Larissa, who had helped Xerxes in his flight, now openly gave Mardonius safe passage into Greece. When the army reached Boeotia, the Thebans tried to keep Mardonius there, advising him that he could find no better country than theirs for his base. They insisted that he go no further, but stay where he was and find ways of conquering the whole of Hellas without having to fight a battle. They pointed out that it would be difficult even for the whole world to overcome the Hellenes by force of arms if those who were currently united stayed together. 'But, if you take our advice,' the Thebans argued, 'you will be able to find out their true states of mind with little difficulty. Send cash to the men in positions of influence in their cities, and by doing this you will split Hellas apart. After that, with the help of those who have come over to your side, you will easily defeat any who oppose you.'

That was the advice the Thebans offered, but Mardonius ignored it because it was his burning passion[1] to take Athens for a second time. This was partly fuelled by the arrogant folly of the man, and partly because he intended to use a chain of beacons across the islands to inform the Great King at Sardis that he had taken the city. However, when he reached Attica, he found no Athenians there, as in the previous year, and discovered that most of them were on Salamis or aboard their ships. So, he did capture the city, but it was deserted. Nine months had passed since the Great King's capture of Athens and Mardonius' occupation. (9.1–3)

Contrary to the impression Herodotus gives here and his treatment of this character elsewhere, Mardonius knew what he was doing. He did not need to be told that the co-operation of Hellene states could be bought and that the Hellene Alliance, such as it was, was far from robust. The chain of beacons across the Aegean and into Asia, whatever the source of the story, must have been an invention. Most of the islands of the Aegean had been back under Hellene control since the autumn of 480 and the Persian fleet had withdrawn to the western shores of Asia, so this option was not available to Mardonius. However, for most it would have brought to mind the opening scene of Aeschylus' *Agamemnon* (first performed in 458, 14 years after *Persae*) in which news of the fall of Troy reaches Mycenae by fire signals, a prelude to the bloody death of the victorious king. Nor was the second occupation of Athens the act of vanity that Herodotus suggests. It made perfect psychological sense to send the Athenians an ultimatum from their own city. The threat of further destruction of land and property, including any rebuilding that had been done since the Persians' last visit, could be left unspoken. Mardonius' foremost

---

[1] Herodotus is using the language of sexual desire here.

priority was to apply pressure to the fault-line that divided Athens
and Sparta.

> When Mardonius reached Athens, he sent a man from the Hellespont
> called Murychides[1] to Salamis bearing the same offer of terms that
> Alexander the Macedonian had presented to the Athenians. He
> made this offer for the second time because, though fully aware of
> the Athenians' hostile reaction to it on the first occasion, he was
> hopeful that they would relent from their obstinate folly now that
> Attica was under the power of his spear.[2] That was his purpose in
> sending Murychides over to Salamis. He came before the Council
> and delivered Mardonius' message and Lycides, one of its members,
> said that it seemed to him that the best course was to receive the
> offer brought to them by Murychides and lay it before the people.[3]
> He proposed this either because he had been bribed by Mardonius,
> or even because he liked the idea. However, it made the rest of the
> Athenians in the Council furiously angry and had the same effect on
> the crowd outside, when they got word of it. They gathered around
> Lycides and stoned him to death, though they did allow Murychides
> the Hellespontian to leave unharmed. Salamis was in uproar because
> of this business and, when the women of Athens heard what had
> happened, they passed the word to each other and went on their
> own initiative to Lycides' house, and stoned his wife and children to
> death. (9.4–5)

The shocking mob violence that led to the death of Lycides and his
family would not have been easily forgotten. The act would have been
regarded as *anathema*, 'accursed', and if Herodotus doubted the truth
of the story, he would surely have at least given a hint that he did, or
not have mentioned the episode at all for fear of offending his Athenian
audience. It can, in any case, be regarded as a graphic indication of the

---

[1] Like Mys, otherwise unknown, but also like Mys (a Carian) from the eastern edge of the
Hellene world. Both probably had some knowledge of Aramaic.
[2] Here Herodotus gives Mardonius some credit for strategic thinking.
[3] The functions of the 500-strong Council (*boule*) included preparing proposals for the Assembly
(all male citizens of voting age) to consider and vote upon.

tense and volatile mood of the Athenian evacuees, now aggravated by Mardonius' presence in Attica.

> Now, this is how the Athenians' second evacuation to Salamis came about. They stayed in Attica for as long as they had hopes that troops from the Peloponnese would come to their aid but, when the Peloponnesians continued to drag their feet and news came that the invader was now in Boeotia, then they shipped their possessions out and made the crossing to Salamis.
>
> At the same time, they sent envoys to Lacedaemon to rebuke the Lacedaemonians for standing back and watching while the Barbarians invaded Attica, and for not joining up with the Athenians to confront them in Boeotia. Additionally, the delegation was charged with reminding the Lacedaemonians of the great rewards the Persians had promised the Athenians if they changed sides, and with warning them that they would find some other way of protecting themselves, if the Lacedaemonians did not come to their defence. At this time, the Lacedaemonians were celebrating the festival of Hyacinthus and they attached great importance to the performance of the rites.[1] Also, they were in the process of adding the battlements to complete the wall they were building across the Isthmus. (9.6–7)

For all the talk of meeting the invaders in Boeotia, this second occupation of Athens may have been anticipated as a likely worst case. The second evacuation was very probably not as large-scale an operation as the first. With Mardonius and his substantial army wintering in northern Greece and doubtless making no secret of his intention to march south again in the coming year, it is possible that a significant proportion of the population of Athens and Attica did not return home from Salamis, Troezen and Aegina. A decision may have been taken not to sow seed to prevent the occupying army feeding itself from the harvest.

Spartan observance of religious festivals had caused similar delays at the times of Marathon and Thermopylae. Here it seems that the same pragmatism was applied as in the case of the Carnea festival and Leonidas' deployment at Thermopylae: while the rites were

---

[1] This festival, in honour of Apollo as well as the hero he accidentally killed, lasted three days and was celebrated in early June.

being performed, it seems there was no interruption to the work of fortifying the Isthmus, if there was much to be done; Herodotus tells us earlier that it was close to completion immediately after the disaster at Thermopylae.

When the Athenian envoys arrived in Lacedaemon, bringing with them envoys from Megara and Plataea,[1] they came before the ephors and said, 'the Athenians have sent us to tell you that the King of the Medes is ready to give us back our country, and wishes us to be his allies on fair and equal terms without trickery or deceit, and will grant us any land we may choose in addition to our own. But, because we respect Zeus, the god of Hellas, and would think it a dreadful crime to betray Hellas, we have not consented, even though the rest of the Hellenes are doing us wrong by betraying us utterly.

'We know that there will be more profit for us in agreeing terms with the King than in fighting a war with him. But no, we will not willingly agree terms with him! There is absolutely no deceit in our dealings with fellow Hellenes. But what of you? You were terrified that we might agree terms with the Great King, but now that you have a clear idea of our intentions and are assured that we will never betray Hellas, now that the wall which you are building across the Isthmus is well on the way to being finished, you do not care about us. You have abandoned us in spite of the promise you made that you would confront the Persians in Boeotia,[2] and you have permitted the Barbarians to march into Attica. The people of Athens are now incensed by your dishonourable behaviour and insist that you send an army to return with us with all speed to meet the Barbarians in Attica. Since Boeotia is lost, the most suitable place in our territory to give battle is the Thriasian plain.'

After listening to this, the ephors put off answering until the next day and then again until the day after. They did this for ten days, putting off answering from day to day. Meanwhile the Peloponnesians

---

[1] These two were the only other cities from north of the Isthmus which had not yet medized or been overrun but they do not otherwise feature in this episode. Plataea had been burnt by the Persians in 480 but the Plataeans kept the faith with the Athenians.

[2] This is the first and only mention of any such promise.

were all working frantically on the wall across the Isthmus, and it was nearly finished. I am unable to explain why it was that the Lacedaemonians were so frantically afraid that the Athenians might medize when Alexander the Macedonian came to Athens, but now they did not seem to care at all. It is possible that they thought they no longer needed the Athenians, now that the Isthmus was fortified, whereas, when Alexander came to Attica, the wall was unfinished and they were working at it in great fear of the Persians.

But, finally, the Spartans despatched their troops and gave their answer, and this is how it came about. On the day before what would have been the Athenian delegation's final hearing, Chileos, a Tegean, who had more influence with the Lacedaemonians than any other outsider,[1] asked the ephors exactly what the Athenians had been saying to them. When they told him, he promptly replied, 'Ephors, gentlemen, this is how it is. If the Athenians are not in league with us but join with the Barbarians in an alliance, wide gateways into the Peloponnese will swing open before the Persians, however strong a wall you throw across the Isthmus.[2] You must take heed of what they are asking you before they decide to do something that will bring about the fall of Hellas.'

This was the advice Chileos gave to the ephors, and they immediately took it to heart. They said nothing to the envoys who had come from Athens, Plataea and Megara, but they gave orders for 5,000 Spartans to march that night with seven Helots assigned to each of them.[3] They put Pausanias son of Cleombrotus[4] in command. Pleistarchus[5] son of Leonidas had the right to lead the army, but he was still a boy. Pausanias was his guardian and also a cousin. Cleombrotus son of Anaxandridas, Pausanias' father, had died in the previous year, shortly after leading the troops who had been building the wall back from the Isthmus. He brought the army back from

---

[1] The Spartans regarded even their closest Hellenic neighbours as 'foreigners', an equally good translation for the word *xenos* in this context.

[2] Herodotus has already made this point: 'I cannot see that the fortification of the Isthmus would have served any useful purpose if the Great King had control of the sea'.

[3] This total of 35,000 is clearly a significant exaggeration but indicates a much more extensive mobilization than usual of the Helot population of Laconia and Messenia.

[4] Leonidas' younger brother, very close to him in age, and regent for a few months.

[5] Leonidas' successor as king.

the Isthmus because the sun had grown dark in the sky[1] while he was offering a sacrifice to determine what action to take against the Persians. Pausanias chose a man from the same family, Euryanax[2] son of Dorieus, to share responsibility.

So, Pausanias and his men set off from Sparta and, at daybreak, the envoys came before the ephors, but they knew nothing of this and had actually decided to depart themselves and go back home. They came before the ephors and said, 'Now stay where you are, Lacedaemonians, keep your Hyacinthia, have fun in your celebrations,[3] and betray your allies utterly. Wronged by you and lacking allies, the Athenians will agree the best terms they possibly can with the Persians. It is plain to see that we will then become the Great King's allies and campaign on his side against any land, wherever Persia leads us. Then you will find out what you have brought upon yourselves.' The ephors' response was to tell them on oath that they believed their army was already at Orestheum[4] and on the march towards the 'foreigners' (this was what they called the Barbarians). The envoys were completely unaware of this and questioned the ephors until they had all the facts, which greatly surprised them. They set off after the army as quickly as they could and 5,000 Lacedaemonian hoplites, the pick of the *perioikoi*, left with them. So, they pressed on towards the Isthmus.

As soon as the Argives found out that Pausanias and his men were on the march from Sparta, they sent the fastest long-distance runner they could find as a herald[5] to Attica. They had previously promised

[1] 2 October, 480 is the date calculated for this partial eclipse. The large Peloponnesian force under Cleombrotus was presumably there to hold the Isthmus line if necessary as well as to build the wall. Eclipses were taken very seriously as omens and this may of itself have been sufficient justification for Cleombrotus' retreat. But Xerxes' withdrawal to the north may already have begun.

[2] It is possible that Euryanax was appointed to this position by the ephors in recognition of Pausanias' youth and inexperience (he was in his mid 20s). His father Dorieus, who died in Sicily in 510, was Leonidas' elder brother and it is not known why Euryanax did not succeed Cleomenes, Dorieus and Leonidas' senior half-brother, on his death in 490.

[3] The second of the three days of the festival was given over to singing and dancing.

[4] Not the most direct route to the Isthmus, but better suited to a large army with baggage train.

[5] As an ordinary messenger he probably would not have been allowed over the Isthmus line, but heralds were regarded as neutral and had special rights.

Mardonius that they would keep the Spartans out of the war, but on reaching Athens, this is what he had to say to Mardonius: 'The Argives have sent me to tell you that the youth of Lacedaemon[1] is on the march and that the Argives cannot stop them. Good luck with your plans for dealing with this!' The herald delivered this message and left, and Mardonius, on hearing it, no longer had any desire to stay in Attica. Before he had this information, he had restrained himself. He wanted to know how things stood with the Athenians and to discover their intentions, so he had not ravaged or pillaged the countryside of Attica because he had remained hopeful that the Athenians would agree to the terms. But when he learned the truth of the matter, that he was not going to persuade them to do this, he withdrew from Attica before Pausanias' army had reached the Isthmus. But first he set fire to Athens, demolishing any wall, house or shrine that was still standing. He led his army away because Attica was not good cavalry country, and because, if he gave battle there and met with defeat, there would be no escape route except a pass so narrow that a few men could block it. And so he decided to fall back on Thebes and give battle there on ground suitable for cavalry with a friendly city at his back. (9.7–13)

Herodotus builds dramatic tension by contrasting Athenian urgency, even desperation, with Spartan stolidity and procrastination. Audiences who had memories of this critical time would have recognized the moods, attitudes and thought processes of the main protagonists that underlay his reconstruction of speeches and events. The wall had probably been finished some months earlier and may have been defensible if not complete the previous autumn, but Herodotus' cliff-hanging timing adds to the drama. The Peloponnesians surely understood the importance of control of the sea in this defensive plan and did not need to be reminded of it by an 'outsider'; the argument had been well rehearsed in diplomatic activity prior to Salamis. A Persian fleet based on Samos was not such an immediate threat, and the mission of the Hellene fleet, now stationed at Delos, included keeping the Barbarian fleet away from the Isthmus and the

---

[1] Meaning 'of military age', between 20 and 45 in the case of Sparta. Perhaps 3,000 stayed behind for home defence.

shores of the Peloponnese. But the Hellene fleet was at not much more than a quarter of the strength mustered at Salamis and included only around 40 of the 200 triremes Athens had available, and Persia still had the capacity to outnumber the largest fleet the Hellenes could muster by a significant margin. Full commitment on the part of the Athenians would be essential if the Persians elected to sail west. Athenian manpower would also be a very important element in a land campaign; 8,000 of the 41,000 hoplites to be deployed in Boeotia were Athenian. However, the Athenians could not man their entire fleet and put 8,000 hoplites in the field at the same time. The Spartans would have understood this reality. Perhaps believing that the Athenians' resounding pledge to keep faith with the alliance was not actually conditional upon the Hellenes mounting a land campaign north of the Isthmus, they were hoping to be able to settle for a Peloponnesian-resourced land operation at the Isthmus, with flank and rear protected if necessary by the full Hellene navy.

Whether or not the Athenians formally delivered their unequivocal threat to medize, and it is significant that Herodotus places this after Pausanias had marched, the Spartans finally concluded that they had no option but to agree to their demands, perhaps also recognizing that giving battle was a better strategy than passive defence. Negotiations with other Peloponnesian states, including Chileos' Tegea, and concerns about potential threats from Messenia and Argos, may have contributed to the delay, probably with a measure of typical bloody-mindedness. It is likely that the Argives, still weakened by their massive losses at the battle of Sepeia 15 years before, would have been brushed aside by Pausanias' force if they had attempted to stop them and Herodotus reflects this and the hollowness of their promise in their 'herald's' perfunctory message.

It seems Athens was not completely destroyed, even this second time. There is archaeological and literary evidence that some major structures survived. According to Thucydides:

After the departure of the Barbarians from their country, the Athenian people immediately set about bringing back their children and wives and what possessions they had left from the places where they had sent them, and prepared to rebuild their city and their fortifications. Only isolated sections of the city wall had been left standing, and many of the houses were in ruins. The most important Persians had been quartered in the few that survived. (*History of the Peloponnesian War* 1.89)

Mardonius' reasons for abandoning Attica were sound. He had the option of meeting the Hellenes on the Thriasian plain, which would have given ample space for cavalry manoeuvre and the possibilities of opposing an Athenian landing from Salamis and attacking the Peloponnesians at the western end of the plain before they could fully deploy. However, though there was more than one route over the mountains out of western Attica, they were potentially dangerous choke points and the advantages of fighting in Boeotia tipped the balance. He would have friendly Thebes at his back and his supply lines would be shortened and the Hellenes' stretched. The coastal plain south of Athens might have been considered but ruled out on similar grounds. The Hellenes had to fight. Mardonius had the advantage of being able to choose the battleground.

The most glorious victory ever known

Plataea

The Persian plan for their campaign in Greece in 479 did not include naval force, but success was still a real possibility and would be guaranteed if the Hellene Alliance could be undermined. This remained a key element of Persian strategy. Overt diplomacy, both direct and through intermediaries such as Alexander of Macedon, open or covert bribery and subversion were the customary tools. Mardonius had stayed in Attica as long as he had hopes of detaching the Athenians from the alliance, and until the Spartans and their allies finally committed to a campaign north of the Isthmus. If the war could not be won by any other means, the intention was to conclude things by fighting on open, level ground where mobility and the reach of missile tactics, and his numerical advantage (which was probably not very great) could be exploited to best effect. Mardonius appreciated the resilience of a tight hoplite formation that maintained its cohesion when under missile attack or when engaging at close quarters with lighter Asian infantry, but he also knew that the advantages of the heavier Hellene weaponry evaporated when formations broke. There would, in any case, have been reasonable hope that in a prolonged stand-off, the Hellenes could simply be starved out at the end of their long and fragile supply chain and on land that had been stripped bare.

The Hellenes' strategic objective was to resist further penetration of mainland Greece and drive the Barbarians out by defeating them on land. However, there had been the same conflict as in 480 between the Spartan view that Greece should be abandoned north of the Isthmus and the Persians confronted at that narrow gateway to the Peloponnese, and Athenian insistence that they should be met forward of that line in Boeotia. As in 480, the conflict had reached crisis point and been resolved for the same fundamental reason: without Athens the alliance's strength would be fatally reduced on land and sea. It was well understood that victory on land would depend on maintaining cohesion in the face of remorseless missile attacks and on bringing about circumstances in which hoplites could engage in formation at close quarters and grind down the more numerous but 'softer' barbarian infantry. It was as desirable for the Hellenes as for the Persians that they fought on ground of their choosing. This was a common situation in ancient battles, which were often preceded by a long stand-off during which neither side was prepared to move from its chosen position. To mount a successful attack both sides at Plataea required level and open terrain; ample space for manoeuvre was a particularly important requirement for the Barbarian mounted troops; rising or broken ground, or other features on its flanks could significantly reinforce a static Hellene defensive position.

At sea, the Persians were still able to muster a larger fleet than the Hellenes, but demoralization after Salamis or priorities elsewhere, or both, seem to have narrowed their strategic vision. However, the reduced fleet that remained in the eastern Aegean, primarily to police Ionia and the Hellespont area, was capable of launching a diversionary attack on the islands or mainland Greece, and of disrupting the important shipping lanes which brought grain from the Black Sea to Greece. In any case, it indirectly supported Mardonius' land campaign by denying Pausanias the use of the 2,000–3,000 hoplites and much more numerous non-hoplite personnel, including a few hundred archers, required to man the Hellene triremes.

With the waiting almost over, Herodotus brings the opposing forces into Boeotia to face each other in two brisk paragraphs. These are divided by an intriguing episode involving the Phocians, whose country had been overrun by the Persians after their failed defence of Leonidas' flank at Thermopylae.

Mardonius began his withdrawal from Attica and, when he was on the march, a message came in that a detachment of 1,000 Lacedaemonians had reached Megara (this report was premature, in fact). When he was informed of it, he decided to destroy this force, and so he turned his army about and directed it towards Megara.

The cavalry went ahead and trampled over the city's farmland, and that was the closest to the setting sun that the Persian army came in Europe.[1] Mardonius then received information that the Hellenes were assembled at the Isthmus,[2] and so he marched on again through Decelea. The Boeotarchs[3] had sent people who lived beside the River Asopus to be his guides and they took him to Sphendale and then on to Tanagra. He camped for the night there and, next day, moved on to Scolus. He was now in Theban territory, but even though the Thebans had medized, he stripped the land of its trees. This was not an act of hostility but driven by the need to build a fort as a refuge for his men to fall back on if things did not turn out as he wished when they engaged the enemy.[4] His army was now spread out along the Asopus covering the ground from a point opposite Erythrae past Hysiae and as far as Plataea. This is not to say that his fort extended this far, because it measured about 10 *stades* (1,900m) on each side.

So, Mardonius had his army in position in Boeotia and all the Hellenes of the region who had medized had supplied troops and enthusiastically joined him in his occupation of Athens. This was with the exception of some of the Phocians who had come along under duress rather than of their own free will. It was a few days after the Persians had reached Thebes that these Phocian hoplites arrived. There were 1,000 of them and they were led by Harmocydes, a citizen of the highest esteem. When these men arrived in Thebes, Mardonius sent horsemen to order them to form up on the plain. As soon as they had done this, all of the Persian cavalry appeared on the scene and a rumour travelled through the entire Hellene contingent that was with the Medes that Mardonius was going to slaughter the Phocians with arrows and javelins. The Phocians heard it too, but their commander Harmocydes was able to rally them with these words: 'Men of Phocis, it is clear that these Barbarians have every intention of killing us, and

[1] The Persians had gone further west in the previous year when they attacked Delphi. But this was the furthest they got to the south-west, and their deepest penetration of Greece.
[2] The Athenians were still on Salamis. They could not safely cross to the mainland until the Persians had left Attica.
[3] Representatives of its member cities on the executive board of the Boeotian confederacy.
[4] This was also valuable as battlefield preparation.

I suspect Thessalian slander is behind this. Now is the moment for every one of you to prove his valour, for it is a far better thing to end our lives in action, fighting to defend ourselves, than simply to offer ourselves up and so suffer a shameful end. No, let them find out, every one of them, what it means for Barbarians to contrive the slaughter of men of Hellas.' This was how he rallied his men.

The cavalry surrounded the Phocians and then charged at them as if they were about to wipe them out. They raised their weapons ready to shoot, and perhaps one or two of them even let fly. But the Phocians stood firm, drawing their ranks together all round and making the files as deep as possible, and the cavalry wheeled and galloped away. Now I cannot say for certain that the Thessalians had requested the destruction of these Phocians and that the Persians, seeing them taking up defensive positions, backed off on Mardonius' orders for fear of suffering a setback themselves; or did Mardonius want to put the Phocians' fighting spirit to the test? Anyway, when the horsemen had ridden off, Mardonius sent a herald with this message: 'Fear not, men of Phocis, for you have proved your valour, which is not what I had been led to expect. Now, play your part in this war with zeal, for you will assuredly be more than amply rewarded by myself, and the Great King too, for your good services.' That was what happened with the Phocians.

Meanwhile, the Lacedaemonians had reached the Isthmus and encamped there. With them were the rest of the Peloponnesians who were inspired by the greater good, though some of them came round to thinking that it would be wrong to stay behind only when they had seen that the Spartans were on the march. And so, with omens favourable, they marched on together from the Isthmus and arrived at Eleusis. There they sacrificed once more and the omens remained favourable. So, they continued their march, and the Athenians were now with them, having joined them at Eleusis after crossing over from Salamis. When they came to Erythrae in Boeotia, they were immediately able to observe the Barbarians encamped by the Asopus and, taking note of this, they formed up on the foothills of Cithaeron facing the enemy. (9.14–15, 17–19)

The thrust towards Megara may have been no more than a reconnaissance mission to check that the Hellenes had not reached that point in any force. Later sources record a battle in which the Megarians comprehensively defeated the Barbarian cavalry, suggesting local mythmaking to inflate Megara's contribution to the defence of Greece. If Mardonius 'turned his army about', it may simply have been to prepare it for the attack that might materialize if the Hellenes had moved faster than anticipated. Evidently this diversion did not delay his exit from Attica for long. There were more direct routes into Boeotia, but the one taken by Mardonius' army was the most suitable for a large force. There was the option of using one or more of the passes over Cithaeron but there would then have been the risk of attacks on the tails of columns backed up in the passes' southern entrances. The information on the Hellene army's movements was presumably supplied by Hellenes, either hired agents or freelancers selling their services, and the Boeotians were acting as to be expected of hosts who were formally in the service of the Great King. There is a sense that Mardonius' withdrawal was measured and well organized.

It has been calculated on the basis of the dimensions of Roman forts that a square perimeter of the dimensions described and covering about 360 hectares could have accommodated 60,000–70,000 men including up to 10,000 cavalry. Mardonius' fort may not have been designed to hold the entire force under his command, and the city of Thebes was also available to him as an alternative refuge, but with only a fraction of the capacity of the fort. Nonetheless, this is a useful measure to set against the traditional figure of 300,000 offered by Herodotus. Herodotus gives a little more detail on the construction of the fort that was being built at much the same time to protect the Persian fleet beached in Ionia: 'they built a wall of timber and stones, and cut down fruit trees and set sharpened stakes into the ramparts' (9.97); stones would not have been as freely available on the banks of the Asopus as on the seashore at Mycale, but the Persians clearly had well-established procedures for the creation of field fortifications.

The Phocian episode both introduces a pause in Herodotus' fast-moving narrative and anticipates the much larger-scale confrontation which is about to take place. Paradoxically, it parades Hellene valour in the face of overwhelming odds but displayed by Hellenes who have medized, albeit 'under duress', and are about to face their compatriots in battle. Phocis is partly redeemed by Herodotus' later aside that 'not all the Phocians had medized; those that had taken refuge on Parnassus supported Hellas by mounting guerrilla attacks on Mardonius' army and on the Hellenes that had joined it.' (9.31) But he also expresses the opinion earlier that it was simply because they hated the Thessalians that these Phocians, alone of all the peoples in central Greece, did not medize. The Thessalians with Mardonius may have liked the idea of a massacre of their old enemies, though it seems unlikely that they had the influence to bring it about. But Mardonius may have been as interested in the Phocian hoplites' tactical response to the threat of envelopment by cavalry as in their motivation.

It is likely that the Hellene army took the most direct route over Cithaeron via the border fort of Oenoe. The present-day E962 connecting Elefsina and Thiva (Eleusis and Thebes) follows this quite closely. There are excellent views of the whole battlefield as the road winds down from the pass and approaches the modern village of Erythres, which is a little to the west of the likely site of ancient Hysiae; Erythres is confusingly named after ancient Erythrae but is some distance to the west of its probable site. At Erythres it is easy to pick up the minor road that runs east along the base of Cithaeron and roughly parallel to Pausanias' opening position, which extended 5–7km from somewhere between the site of the city of Plataea and modern Erythres, to modern Dafni and the probable site of ancient Erythrae. There are a number of spurs thrusting forward from the base of Cithaeron that could have anchored the Hellene left and right flanks. Grundy (1894) thought the landscape was little changed from the time of the battle and this was most likely true as far as the patches of cultivation – vineyards, olive groves, orchards and woodland – were concerned. However, the various streams running down from Cithaeron had probably brought about significant physical change over the centuries. Certainly, in more recent decades, modern agriculture and the abstraction of water flowing down from Cithaeron for agricultural, domestic and industrial use have smoothed out what would have been a more deeply etched landscape between the rocky base of Cithaeron and the river plain. But the broad outline of the terrain is probably much the same, not only along the base of Cithaeron but also in the succession of low ridges that stretch down to and along the River Asopus. These may not appear to have much tactical significance to modern eyes but, in ancient warfare and for many centuries beyond, anything more than a gentle incline, rising even just a couple of metres, could give significant advantage to a defender.

A car and at least one full day are essential to do this exceptionally large battlefield justice. Thiva (Thebes) makes a good base for an overnight stay, though sadly nearly all of its millennia of myth, legend and history are buried in layers under the modern town. However, its important museum, closed for a number of years for extensive refurbishment, is now open again. The city is 90km from Athens and most easily reached by the E75, which roughly follows the route taken by Mardonius when he withdrew from Attica.

After coming over Cithaeron the Hellenes had manoeuvred east towards Erythrae and west from Hysiae to form a defensive line facing north and extending 5,000–7,000m along the foothills. The rising ground gave them some frontal protection and each flank would have been protected by spurs, at the exit from the pass on the left and by one of the more pronounced features on the right; there may also have been reliance on screens of *psiloi*. The Hellenes clearly favoured a static defence in as strong a position as they could find. The Spartans would have led the march through the pass and then east along the foothills to take their place on the right of the line. The Hellene left deployed to the west with the Athenians probably straddling the western of the two roads running down from Cithaeron to Thebes. Herodotus does not set out the opposing sides' orders of battle at this stage but it is a safe assumption that the two strongest hoplite contingents, 10,000 Lacedaemonians and 8,000 Athenians, respectively formed the right and left flanks. Mardonius made no move to prevent the Greeks emerging from the pass and forming up to face him. This option, if actually considered, may have been rejected because it would have meant fighting on difficult terrain and in circumstances that might prevent a decisive outcome by allowing the Hellenes to fall back into the pass. They would then have been defending a narrow front in depth, at least as substantial an impasse as that encountered by the Persians at Thermopylae. It was now August. If Mardonius could have brought about this confrontation earlier in the year, he chose not to. There had been the not unreasonable expectation that diplomacy or subversion could break up the Hellene Alliance for an easier victory.

Even at this point, Mardonius appears not to have been eager to give battle. The two armies, now about 5,000m apart, may have faced each other for a few days before he finally took the initiative:

Plataea, 479

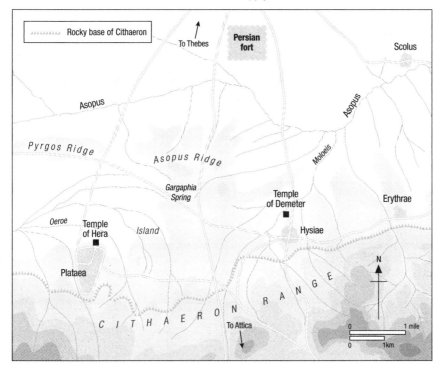

The Hellenes would not advance onto the plain, so Mardonius sent in all his cavalry. Their commander was Masistius, a man of great renown among the Persians; he rode a Nisaean horse with a golden bit and magnificent trappings. His horsemen charged up to the Hellene lines and attacked them in waves,[1] harassing them severely and calling them women. As luck would have it, the Megarians' place in the line was the most vulnerable in the whole Hellene position. The cavalry could come at them very easily and were putting them under great pressure, so they sent a messenger to the Hellene commanders. He made his way to them and said, 'I bring word from the Megarians, who say, "Allies, we cannot hold off the Persian cavalry by ourselves

---

[1] Charging up and riding from left to right along the Hellene front, showering it with arrows and javelins at close range.

in this position we have occupied from the start of the battle. Up to now, though hard-pressed, we have stood our ground with patience and courage. But now we have to tell you that we will abandon our position in the line[1] if you don't send men over to replace us.'" That is the message he delivered, and Pausanias called for volunteers to go to that part of the line and relieve the Megarians. The rest of the Hellenes were unwilling, but the Athenians agreed to take this on, sending 300 picked men under the command of Olympiodorus son of Lampon.[2]

These volunteers took up position out in front of the entire Hellene force and they brought their archers with them. The fighting went on for some time and this is how it finally ended. The cavalry continued to attack in waves but Masistius' horse, which stood out from the rest, was hit by an arrow in its chest. It reared up with the pain of it and unseated Masistius. When he was thrown, the Athenians caught his horse and crowded around Masistius as he tried to defend himself, and they could not finish him off at first because of his armour. Underneath his purple tunic he was wearing a cuirass with golden scales[3] and their blows had no effect when they struck it. Then someone realized what was happening and speared him in the eye, and finally he fell down and died. Surprisingly, the rest of the cavalry were unaware of this. They had not seen Masistius being thrown from his horse or meeting his death, and so were quite unaware of his fate as they wheeled and withdrew. But they missed him the moment they pulled up because there was no one to give them orders to regroup. Then, when they realized what had happened, they urged each other on in a mass charge to recover his body.

When the Athenians saw all the horsemen charging them at once, not in squadrons as before, they called for assistance from the rest of the army. The entire force rallied to help them and there was bitter

---

[1] Regarded as a shameful crime, and it would have been in breach of the opening lines of the Oath of Plataea specifically.

[2] Olympiodorus is otherwise unknown but it is possible that his son, Lampon, who, like Herodotus, is known to have emigrated to Thurii in Italy, was the main source for Herodotus' account of this episode.

[3] Presumably the scales were of iron or bronze and gilded.

fighting over the corpse. In the period they were on their own, the 300 were coming off much worse and were close to abandoning the corpse. But once the rest came up in support, the cavalry could no longer hold their ground. They had no chance of recovering the body, and began to sustain more losses. So, they fell back about 2 *stades* [around 400m] and discussed what to do next. Since there was no one to give them orders, they decided to withdraw and report back to Mardonius. (9.20–23)

Plutarch covers this episode more briefly in his typically selective account of the battle but adds a little extra detail:

Mardonius decided to use the assets which gave him the greatest edge over the Hellenes and sent in the full strength of his cavalry against them. The Hellenes were all in strong positions on rocky terrain along the spurs at the foot of Cithaeron except for the 3,000 Megarians, who were on more level ground. They were put under severe pressure by the cavalry surging at them and attacking from every angle, and quickly sent a message to Pausanias requesting he send support, because the Barbarians were too numerous for them to hold out on their own. Pausanias received the message and could see that the Megarian position was becoming swamped by the volume of javelins and arrows raining down, and that its defenders were now huddled together in a narrow space. But there was nothing he could do himself to protect them from the cavalry with his phalanx[1] of heavy-armed Spartans. So, he made an appeal to the honour and pride of the other Hellene generals and unit-commanders who were around him by asking for volunteers to make a sally and go to the help of the Megarians. They all hung back except for Aristides[2] who accepted the mission on behalf of the Athenians and sent off his most enthusiastic commander,

[1] This is a typical later use of the Greek word *phalanx*. It is never used by Herodotus, except in the completely different sense of a log of ebony, or by Thucydides.
[2] Herodotus also tells us that Aristides was the general in command of the Athenian contingent so Plutarch's specific reference to his involvement here can be taken at face value. Elsewhere Plutarch relies on sources later than Herodotus or his own imagination to suit his literary purpose to paint a picture of the very prominent part played by his subject in the Hellene victory.

Olympiodorus, with a combined force of his 300 picked men and the Athenian archers. Having quickly made their preparations they advanced to the attack at a run.[1] Masistius, the commander of the Barbarian cavalry, a man admired for his prowess and for his exceptional stature and looks, saw them coming, wheeled his horse in their direction and charged. Then there was a ferocious struggle between the men facing this charge and those who made it, both sides convinced that everything was at stake at this point. But then an arrow struck Masistius' horse and he was thrown and lay where he fell, immobilized by the weight of his armour. However, the Athenians could not kill him, though they crowded round and rained blows on him, for not only his chest and head, but also his arms and legs were plated with gold, bronze and iron. Eventually someone finished him off with a thrust of the butt-spike of a javelin through the eye-slit of his helmet[2] and the rest of the Persians abandoned his body and fled. (*Aristides* 14)

Herodotus is playing to Athenian audiences in his dramatic account of the part played by Athenian troops in this incident, and also by tainting the Megarians, enemies of Athens before and after this war, with the grossly dishonourable intention of abandoning their position in the line. However, he acknowledges that their position was the most exposed. As for the prominence of the Athenians' role, theirs was the only contingent that included a unit of archers at Plataea. Also, their position was conveniently close to the Megarians', if, as is likely, the Hellenes were lined up broadly as detailed by Herodotus slightly later in his narrative. It is to the Athenians' credit that they 'volunteered', but they happened to be best equipped and best placed to carry out the assignment. They can be envisaged as facing the Barbarians in a tight formation with the archers shooting from behind its wall of hoplite shields and spears. Their successful intervention came at a critical moment. If the Megarians had

---

[1] The word translated as 'made their preparations' is also used in the sense of disposing of things, and the men may have removed armour for greater mobility and to enable them to run to their new position.

[2] The magnificence of Masistius' physique and appearance, and of his suit of armour, including a closed helmet of some description, was probably amplified as the story of this important engagement was told and retold.

given way, Mardonius would have succeeded in opening a 400m gap between the Hellene left and the collection of smaller units to the right of the Megarians. His cavalry, followed in by some of his best Asian infantry, would have been able to exploit this with devastating effect, and standard Barbarian tactics could have won the battle on the first day of fighting. However, his infantry was clearly not close enough to become involved and perhaps the initial purpose of the cavalry action was harassment and reconnaissance rather than full-on assault.

When the cavalry returned to the camp, Mardonius and the whole army went into deep mourning for Masistius, shaving their heads and also the manes of their horses and pack-animals. Their lamentations resounded across all Boeotia because the dead man was, after Mardonius, the most highly esteemed by the Great King and all of Persia. So, the Barbarians paid their respects to the fallen Masistius in their own fashion. The Hellenes, on the other hand, were greatly encouraged by the way they had stood up to the cavalry's assault and beaten it off. They laid out Masistius' corpse on a wagon and wheeled it along their lines. It was a sight worth seeing because he was so handsome and well built. That is why they did this, and the men broke ranks to take a close look at him.

A decision was now taken to move down onto Plataean soil. It was felt that a position there was much more suitable than in the area of Erythrae, chiefly because it would be better supplied with water. So, the Hellenes decided to take up position in battle order there. The spring called Gargaphia was nearby. They gathered up their kit and made their way along the lower slopes of Cithaeron past Hysiae and onto Plataean land. On arrival they formed up again in their national contingents across the low hills and flat ground near the Gargaphia spring and the shrine of the hero Androcrates. (9.24–25)

Encouraged by their success, the Hellenes advanced north and a little to the west to a position on the undulating ground immediately to the south of the River Asopus; the accessibility of the spring was an important consideration. However, the previous position was probably at least as adequately supplied by streams running down from Cithaeron. More importantly the move was a provocative display of confidence and, in most respects, tactically sound. After the fighting

and the parading of Masistius' impressive corpse it is very unlikely that
this manoeuvre, which would have taken several hours, was carried out
on the same day. It would certainly have been observed by the Persians
and it presented an opportunity to attack the Greeks whilst they were
on the move with inevitable loss of cohesion. But Mardonius did not
try to exploit this. He may have been content to allow the Greeks to
move towards more open ground, which was where he wanted them,
and to stretch and expose their supply line, and, in any case, he probably
needed to give his cavalry some recovery time. However, even without
cavalry to spearhead it, a well-timed and concentrated infantry thrust
at a point in the Hellene centre, which was likely to be less resilient
because it included a dozen units that were less than a thousand strong,
could have significantly changed the course of the battle.

Herodotus' topography is, as always, vague and his naming of two
landmarks, a shrine dedicated to an obscure hero called Androcrates and
the strategically important spring, is not helpful because their locations
are now unknown, though both appear to have been some distance
back from the river. However, it is generally agreed that the Hellenes
were now spread out over about 7,000m from one of the north-eastern
'fingers' of the Asopus ridge directly north of Hysiae to the western end
of what is known today as Pyrgos Ridge. They now occupied rising
ground overlooking the river plain and blocking all three roads leading
south from Thebes; they had a clear view of the entire enemy line to the
north of the river and could observe activity around the Persian camp
and on the roads to Thebes. However, the new position had weaknesses
which were to become apparent in a few days' time. Whether or not
these were recognized and assessed by the Hellenes, the Persians could
have exploited them sooner than they did.

The few visible remains of the city of Plataea are 4km to the west
of Erythres. The battle gets its name because it was fought in Plataean
territory. The city had been evacuated and then burned down by the
Persians in 480 and no fighting took place within or immediately outside
its walls. A track leads up from behind the modern village (Kokla) to an
abandoned hang-gliding centre on the 600m contour. From here there is
an excellent view of the western half of the battlefield, diagonally across the
ridges to its north-eastern corner and along the base of Cithaeron. Roads
lead north-west and slightly east of north from Plataea to the opposite
ends of the low but well-defined Pyrgos Ridge overlooking the Asopus,

which was held on its forward slopes by the Greek left in this long central phase of the battle. Pyrgos means 'tower' and there is a building (only a couple of centuries old), which is a useful landmark. Even now the ridge falls away quite steeply to the west and was as defensible against attacks from the rear as from the front. Looking east from this ridge, the ground falls away quite gently and then rises to the crest of the broad Asopus ridge, which was held by the Hellene right. It is also worth crossing the river and driving the short distance up to the village of Melissochori for a view of the Hellene position from behind the Persian right.

The Hellene line can be envisaged as extending east to straddle the road linking Hysiae and Thebes with its right flank probably protected by one of the gullies carved into the landscape of the time by the north-flowing tributaries of the River Asopus. The Asopus cannot really be described as a river now, at least in summer, but most of its course can still be traced from a distance by following the strip of shrubs and trees growing along it. Today, the only significant water feature on the plain is a stretch of the 170km aqueduct that carries drinking water to Athens from the north-west, a more formidable tactical obstacle than the Asopus would have presented in the late summer of 479. But it would have been difficult, even impossible, for advancing hoplites to maintain their formation while negotiating its meandering channel and banks under heavy missile attack from the opposite side, and no attempt was made to do this. Equally, a determined hoplite defence of the south bank, which could have been quickly mounted by moving down from the ridges, would have effectively blocked a Barbarian crossing. During the long middle phase of the battle the Persians were able to prevent the Hellenes getting water from the river by shooting arrows at them from the north bank. But, eventually, unopposed crossings presented neither side with problems. The Persians stormed across it on the last morning of the battle after the Hellenes' tactical withdrawal, and the Hellenes crossed it in the opposite direction later that day during the final rout.

At this point Herodotus sets out the Greek order of battle. He prefaces this with an account of a dispute between the Tegeans and the Athenians, each claiming the left flank, the second most honourable position in the line (no one disputed the Spartans' claim to the right). The Athenians won the argument by trumping the Tegeans' boasted single achievement in the mythical past with five of their own, including victory over the Amazons and the part they played, 'second to none in the struggle for Troy'. More relevantly they point out that they alone of all the Hellenes had stood against the Barbarians and been victorious, temporarily 'forgetting' the Plataeans who had fought beside them at Marathon:

> 'Because of what we did at Marathon, we merit this honour, and more besides, because, alone of all the Hellenes Athens met Persia in single combat and not only survived in that great enterprise but won victory over 46 nations.[1] Surely that single achievement entitles us to the honour of this position? But it is not right to be quarrelling over a place in the battle line at a time like this. We say we are ready and willing to obey your orders, men of Lacedaemon, and to take up whatever position opposite whichever enemy contingent you decide makes most sense. Wherever you put us, we will do our best to prove our worth. So, give us our orders in confidence that they will be obeyed.' This was the Athenians' response and the entire Lacedaemonian contingent shouted out in assent[2] that they were more worthy of the flank position than the men from Arcadia. And that was how the Athenians prevailed in this battle of words and how the Tegeans were overcome. (9.25–27)

While, once again, blowing the Athenians' trumpet, Herodotus does not mention a powerful consideration, that the Athenians might have raised in their dispute with the Tegeans: their hoplite contingent was four times larger and, uniquely, reinforced by archers. As it turned out, the Tegeans, diplomatically stationed alongside the Spartans, were to play a critical part in the final phase of the battle. There probably was considerable debate, also involving other contingents, but it is likely that the battle order was settled before the army marched from Eleusis, and it is very unlikely to have been left as late as Herodotus records, to be done in the face of the enemy.

> After this all the Hellenes, those who had mustered at the start and the later arrivals, were assigned their positions. There were 10,000

---

[1] The Persians and the Sacae are the only Asian contingents mentioned in Herodotus' account of the battle of Marathon. There may have been token representatives of other nations, but this was, in any case, a gross exaggeration.

[2] This was the Spartan way of casting votes.

Lacedaemonians on the right flank. The Spartans, 5,000 strong, were supported by 35,000 light-armed Helots, seven allocated to each of them. The Spartans showed their respect for the courage of the Tegeans by selecting them for the position alongside them; 1,500 of them were hoplites. Next along the line were 5,000 Corinthian hoplites and Pausanias added to their ranks the 300 Potidaeans who had come from Pallene. Then came 600 men from Orchomenus in Arcadia,[1] 3,000 from Sicyon and after them 800 from Epidaurus. Next to them were placed 1,000 Troezenians, 200 from Lepreum, then 400 from Mycenae and Tiryns. Then there were 1,000 men from Phlious and, alongside them, 300 from Hermione. Next came 600 men from Eretria and Styra, then 400 from Chalcidice and 500 from Ambracia. After them there were 800 from Leucas and Anactorium then 200 from Pale in Cephallenia. 500 Aeginetans were placed next to them in the line, then 3,000 Megarians and 600 Plataeans. Finally, the Athenians, 8,000 strong, were in position to lead the march down and hold the left flank. Their commander was Aristides son of Lysimachus. All of these were hoplites, a total of 38,700; that was the number of hoplites assembled to face the Barbarians. The light-armed element was made up as follows: 35,000 were deployed with the Spartans, seven with each, and all equipped for combat; the light-armed troops assigned one per hoplite to the rest of the Lacedaemonians and the other Hellenes totalled 34,500. This brought the number of battle-ready light-armed troops up to 69,500. So, the grand total of the Hellene force that gathered at Plataea, hoplites and light-armed combined, was 1,800 short of 110,000. Add to this the 1,800 Thespian survivors[2] who had come along (but without hoplite equipment) and the total came to 110,000. This was the force that formed up for battle along the Asopus. (9.28–30)

Although Herodotus' individual-contingent numbers do not quite add up to his grand totals for hoplites and light-armed, they would have been drawn from reliable public records and, in the greatest crisis

---

[1] The distinction is important. Orchomenus in Boeotia had medized the year before.

[2] Refugees from the destruction of their city after Thermopylae, where 700 of their comrades had stayed to die with Leonidas. Some may have been loaned hoplite equipment, but they probably formed a rather hybrid unit.

ever faced by the Hellene world, mobilization was probably as near total as it ever would have been. But the numbers probably reflect total 'paper' strengths and may not properly account for the hoplites and rowers serving in the Hellene fleet, or for other unavoidable absences. Nonetheless, a figure in the region of 35,000 seems entirely plausible for the hoplite core of Pausanias' army. However, the unprecedented mustering of seven Helots per Spartan does not ring true. It has been suggested that these volatile serfs were considered less dangerous when armed and on campaign with their masters than left at home looking after their estates, but that would seem a very high-risk policy. In fact, 7:1 is a reasonable estimate of the ratio of adult male Helots to Spartans altogether and this figure may have been mistakenly drawn into the tradition of an exceptional level of mobilization. In these special circumstances extra Helots were probably drafted in and armed, and other contingents may have brought along additional non-hoplite troops (such as the several hundred archers with the Athenians). Some would have been strung out on the long supply route from the Peloponnese, though still 40,000–50,000 may have been deployed on the battlefield alongside their hoplite superiors or masters. Finally, late-arriving troops continued to swell the Hellene ranks in what seem to have been significant numbers, but it is not clear if these were whole new contingents or reinforcements joining contingents already there.

When the Barbarians with Mardonius had completed their mourning[1] for Masistius and observed that the Hellenes had moved onto Plataean land, they also moved to positions along the Asopus opposite them. This is how Mardonius arranged his troops. He placed the Persians opposite the Lacedaemonians. Because they outnumbered the Lacedaemonians by a significant margin, they were drawn up in greater depth with their front overlapping the Tegeans'. Mardonius picked out the strongest Persian units to face the Lacedaemonians, and positioned the weaker ones to face the Tegeans and he did this following the advice and direction of the Thebans. He placed the Medes next to the Persians facing the contingents from Corinth, Potidaea, Orchomenus, and Sicyon.

---

[1] Perhaps the intense mourning process was sufficient reason for taking no action whilst the Hellenes deployed into their new positions.

He positioned the Bactrians next to the Medes, facing the men from Epidaurus, Troezen, Lepreum, Tiryns, Mycenae, and Phlious. He placed the Indians alongside the Bactrians, opposite the contingents from Hermione, Eretria, Styra and Chalcis. Next came the Sacae, facing the men from Ambracia, Anactorium, Leucas, Pale and Aegina. Finally, alongside the Sacae, he positioned the Boeotians, Locrians, Malians, Thessalians and the 1,000 from Phocis to face the Athenians, Plataeans and Megarians (not all the Phocians had medized; those that had taken refuge on Parnassus supported Hellas by mounting guerrilla attacks on Mardonius' army and on the Hellenes that had joined it). He also placed the Macedonians and others who lived on the borders of Thessaly opposite the Athenians. Those named above were the greatest of the nations in Mardonius' order of battle. They were the most notable and renowned but there were also men of other nations mingled amongst them, Phrygians, Thracians, Mysians, Paionians and others, Ethiopians, for instance, and Egyptians, the swordsmen[1] known as the Hermotybians and Calasirians, the only Egyptians classed as fighting men.[2] These had actually been serving as marines but Mardonius ordered them to disembark before they left Phalerum. There was no Egyptian contingent in the land army that Xerxes led to Athens. There were 300,000 Barbarians in total, as already stated. No one knows how many Hellene allies Mardonius had with him because no one kept count, but I reckon there were, at a guess, in the region of 50,000. This was the battle order of the infantry; the cavalry was separately deployed. (9.31–32)

Herodotus gives his total of 350,000 for the Persian army. It is unclear whether he has included the cavalry in his count, and there is no indication as to how it was divided up between contingents, beyond his cautious guess at the total number of medizing Hellenes. However, he is specific about the positions of the main contingents of the Persian army

---

[1] They were members of the Egyptian warrior caste. They took no recorded part in the battle, though they could have been a formidable asset. The fighting complement from the 200 Egyptian ships in Xerxes' fleet is described earlier as armed with 'hollow shields with broad rims, and spears for sea-warfare, and great battle-axes. Most of them wore cuirasses and carried long swords' (7.89). They were hoplites in effect and there may have been 30–40 of them on each ship, if, of course, Herodotus' information was correct.

[2] Herodotus describes this warrior caste in his survey of Egyptian history and society (2.164–65).

in relation to the Hellenes opposite them, which gives some idea of their relative strengths. Mardonius probably did have some numerical advantage but his conduct of the battle strongly suggests that this was not nearly as great as tradition has it, suggesting a total in the region of 100,000 for all the types and races of troops under his command. With a significantly larger force he could have been expected to attempt a decisive move earlier in the confrontation. If his army had been closer in size to the Greek army, or smaller than it, then the Greeks could arguably have been more proactive after they had advanced to the south bank of the Asopus.

Pausanias' right-flank division comprised 11,500 hoplites supported by at least as many *psiloi*. This was also the most likely position in his battle line for the 1,800 Thespians, who were not fully armed as hoplites. According to Herodotus, Mardonius' Persians greatly outnumbered a substantial array of almost 55,000, but a figure in the region of 30,000 seems more plausible and makes better sense alongside the strength Herodotus gives for the Hellene left. So, Mardonius' Persians could be estimated as up to 40,000, or four *balvarabam*. Next in line, his Medes, perhaps 20,000 in two *balvarabam*, faced around 8,000 hoplites and supporting light-armed from the north-eastern Peloponnese, including the powerful cities of Corinth and Sicyon. Then came the Bactrians, Indians and Sacae, perhaps totalling 20,000, up against a number of mostly small contingents from the eastern Peloponnese and Euboea, perhaps 7,500 hoplites in all with an equal number of light-armed. Mardonius' large force of medizing Hellenes from Thebes and further north totalled 50,000, according to Herodotus' extravagant guess, but it is not clear whether this number includes light-armed or cavalry. The Hellene left was anchored by the 8,000 Athenian hoplites with the 600 faithful Plataeans and 3,000 Megarians to their right, a total of 24,000, allowing for an equal number of light-armed with 800 Athenian archers also in the line. Thebes and other Boeotian cities, and Locris, Malis and Macedon were capable of fielding a force that was equal to this, and were certainly present in enough strength to attack the Hellene left and put up a hard fight on the final day of the battle. So, it is likely that the two sides were fairly equally matched here.

The Sacae, Medes, Indians, Bactrians and medizing Hellenes also supplied cavalry and, with the 1,000 elite Persian horse that Mardonius

ORDERS OF BATTLE ACCORDING TO HERODOTUS

BARBARIANS *Various infantry* *and cavalry*	*HELLENES*	*Hoplite*	*Non-hoplite*
Persians	Spartans	5,000	35,000 armed Helots
	Lacedaemonians	5,000	5,000
	Tegeans	1,500	1,500
	Thespians		1,800 'survivors'
		11,500	**43,300**
Medes	Corinthians	5,000	5,000
	Potidaeans in Corinthian ranks	300	300
	Arcadians of Orchomenus	600	600
	Sicyonians	3,000	3,000
		8,900	**8,900**
Bactrians	Epidaurians	800	800
	Troezenians	1,000	1,000
	Lepreans	200	200
	Mycenae and Tiryns	400	400
	Phleiasians	1,000	1,000
		3,400	**3,400**
Indians	Hermionians 3,000	3,000	3,000
	Eretrians and Styrians 600	600	600
	Chalcidians 400	400	400
		4,000	**4,000**
Sacae	Ambraciots	500	500
	Anactorians and Leucadians	800	800
	Paleans	200	200
	Aeginetans	500	500
300,000		**2,000**	**2,000**
Medizing Hellenes: Hoplites and light-armed from Thebes and Boeotia, Locris, Malis, Macedonia, Thessaly and Phocis	Megarians	3,000	3,000
	Plataeans	600	600
	Athenians	8,000	8,800 including archers
50,000		**11,600**	**12,400**
350,000		**41,400**	**74,000**

retained in Greece at the end of the previous year's campaigning, this important arm would have been several thousand strong, certainly sufficient to press the Hellenes very hard at more than one stage of the battle. It still gave the Persians a potential edge in spite of the early setback. Persian infantry numbers may not have been greatly superior when averaged out along the line, but the Hellenes had no cavalry other than a few scouts and despatch-riders. The several hundred Athenian archers were the only substantial counter to the tens of thousands of Barbarian mounted and infantry bowmen. The rest of the Greek light-armed troops would have provided little comparable long-range fighting capability.

In the region of 200,000 men fought in this battle for the future of western civilization, about the same number as at Waterloo, alive and dead after Blücher had arrived, and rather more than fought at Gettysburg or were shipped over the Channel on D-Day.

So, both armies were formed up by nation and unit and, on the next day, both offered sacrifices. Tisamenus son of Antiochus, the seer attached to the army, performed the rituals for the Hellenes. He was an Elean by birth, a Clytiad of the Iamid clan but the Lacedaemonians had granted him Spartan citizenship. They did this because, when he was consulting the Delphic oracle about his prospects for fatherhood, the Pythia had prophesied that he would be the winner of five great victories. He misinterpreted the prophecy and went into training, thinking he was going to win at athletics. In fact, he competed in the pentathlon and missed Olympic victory by one fall in his wrestling bout with Hieronymus of Andros. However, the Lacedaemonians somehow worked out that the prophecy was about success in war, not in athletics, and they determined to hire Tisamenus to lead them in their wars alongside their Heraclid kings. When he saw how highly the Spartans valued his support, he raised the price of his services, making it clear that nothing would persuade him to agree to their request except for an offer of citizenship and all of the rights that came with it. The Spartans were at first outraged and immediately broke off negotiations. But then, under the looming menace of Persian invasion, they sought out Tisamenus once more and agreed to his terms. When he knew of their change of heart, he said that he was still not satisfied and demanded that his brother Hegias also be made a Spartan with the same rights as he would be granted himself. The Spartans were so desperate to hire Tisamenus that they agreed to all his demands. And under this agreement, Tisamenus of Elis, now made a Spartan, became their seer and indeed worked with them to win their five greatest victories.[1] No one else ever became a Spartan citizen in this way.

So, this man Tisamenus was brought to Plataea by the Spartans to be the Hellenes' seer. And the omens were favourable so long as they remained on the defensive, but unfavourable if they crossed the Asopus and started the fighting. The sacrificial omens were also unfavourable for Mardonius, if he were to take the initiative and start the fighting, but good if he stayed on the defensive. Mardonius actually carried out his sacrifices in the Hellene way and his seer was Hegesistratus, also of Elis, whom he had hired for a considerable fee. He enthusiastically performed the sacrifices for him out of hatred for the Lacedaemonians and his desire for personal gain.[2] (9.33–38)

Following normal practice before battles, each commander had his seer (*mantis*) sacrifice sheep, goats, lambs or calves and interpret the omens for success or failure from the appearance of the victims' internal organs, especially the liver. Herodotus' digression reveals what importance was attached to divination and the status that was attached to the most prominent seers. But he also displays a degree of ambivalence towards these individuals, though not the messages they conveyed from the gods. Both commanders were clearly satisfied with the divine guidance they were receiving and, no doubt with its endorsement of their own tactical assessments, and each army settled down to wait for the other to make the first significant move. Each

---

[1] Plataea, 480; Tegea, Dipaea and Ithome in the 460s; Tanagra, 458 or 457. Four out of the five were victories over other Hellenes; in the last the Athenians were on the losing side.

[2] In a balancing digression Herodotus tells the story of this equally distinguished soothsayer. Earlier the Spartans had imprisoned him for the great harm he had done them (possibly blaming him for misfortune that he had correctly foretold). One of his legs was shackled but he managed to escape torture and death by sawing off half his foot and tunnelling through a wall. When his foot had healed, he had it repaired with wood and publicly declared himself an enemy of the Spartans. He worked for their enemies for a number of years but sometime after 480 the Spartans captured and executed him.

was in position on ground on which they believed they could fight most effectively. The Hellenes were well placed for static defence, protected on much of their front by rising ground and by gullies or steeper inclines on their flanks. They were also well placed to respond to any attempt to cross the river in force. The Barbarians were drawn up on the level ground north of the river, more suitable for cavalry action and the more expansive manoeuvring that their lighter infantry was capable of, and improved by extensive tree-felling. The river was only a modest obstacle, but the commanders on both sides would have been aware that a large force attempting to cross it in formation would inevitably lose cohesion. Mardonius, with Thebes and subdued central and northern Greece at his back and his logistics well organized, was probably more comfortably placed than Pausanias and, in any case, his best troops were veterans of long campaigns far from home. Moreover, he could still reasonably hope that internal frictions, aggravated by hunger and fear, might cause the Hellene Alliance to collapse. While a bloodless victory was probably too much to expect, some contingents might yet medize and others might run, and perhaps only a few cities would ultimately be prepared to fight, Sparta for sure, Athens conceivably not. Then Mardonius would have an opportunity to exploit his superior mobility and missile firepower against a retreating and fragmented enemy.

Pausanias, on the other hand, was in country that had already been stripped bare by the Persians and there must have been very little left in the way of resources to draw on in Attica. Hellene armies normally carried just a few days' supply of food with them on campaign and otherwise expected to live off the land by plundering it, or in more civilized fashion if they were in friendly territory, and they mostly had little experience of long campaigns. This was the largest Hellene army ever to take the field and it was increasingly dependent as the days went by on a long supply line, a situation completely outside Pausanias' or any of his fellow generals' experience.

Neither the Persians nor the Hellenes who were on their side (with their own seer, Hippomachus of Leucas[1]) could obtain omens that

---

[1] Not known otherwise, but further evidence of the importance attached to divination in military decision-making.

favoured giving battle and the Hellenes continued to pour in, enlarging their army. Then Timagenides son of Herpys, a Theban, advised Mardonius to block the pass over Cithaeron, pointing out to him that Hellenes were streaming down it all the time and that he could intercept large numbers of them. The armies had sat facing each other for eight days when he gave this advice. Mardonius thought it was sound and at nightfall sent his cavalry to the pass over Cithaeron that leads into Plataean territory; the Boeotians call this pass Three Heads, the Athenians call it Oak's Heads. The horsemen were quite successful in their mission. They caught a column of 500 transports[1] and their attendants with supplies for the Hellene army from the Peloponnese as they emerged from the pass onto the Plataean plain. Falling on their prey, the Persians killed without mercy, sparing neither attendants nor beasts, and when they had had enough of slaughtering, they rounded up the remnants and drove them down to Mardonius and the Persian camp.

After this action the two sides let two more days go by, neither wishing to start a battle. Although the Barbarians came right up to the Asopus to challenge the Hellenes, neither army crossed over. However, Mardonius' cavalry kept the Hellenes under pressure and continually harassed them. The Thebans, enthusiastic medizers that they were, involved themselves in the war wholeheartedly and repeatedly guided the cavalry into contact with the enemy. But then the Persians and Medes took over and they were the ones who actually displayed any courage.

So that was all that happened in those ten days. The Hellenes had greatly increased their numbers and Mardonius was losing patience with this inactivity. (9.38–41)

The extended stand-off could be evidence that neither commander felt he had sufficient numbers to be confident of success in an all-out attack, but delay was now more likely to favour Mardonius than Pausanias. His supplies may have been dwindling, but he still had access to them whilst he had cut the flow of supplies and reinforcements to the Hellene position. In fact, Mardonius could have

[1] *Hypozugia*, lit. 'things under yokes', probably a mixture of ox-carts and pack animals of various kind.

sent troops round either flank and to the rear of the Hellenes at any time in the preceding week. Indeed, it is likely that his cavalry did cross the river on missions of probing and harassment, perhaps after taking a couple of days to recover from their setback in the first day's fighting. But incompetence or lack of spirit cannot be ruled out, and Herodotus' attribution of the overdue attack on the supply train to an otherwise unknown 'perfidious Theban' can be interpreted as thinly veiled criticism. However, a prolonged stand-off was consistent with a waiting strategy. When the time came to fight again, Mardonius would have the Hellenes in this more exposed position, weakened by days of uncertainty and diminishing supplies, and possibly attacking out of desperation or retreating in disorder. And the rewards for medizing, no doubt, remained on offer. In any case, the harassment that Herodotus describes as taking place after the attack on the supply column most probably began soon after the two armies had taken up their new positions on either side of the river. Certainly, the attack on the supply column, cutting off any subsequent replenishment, sharply increased the pressure.

Herodotus pauses the narrative at this point with a four-part interlude, which interweaves hearsay and perhaps some harder source material with his own dramatic imaginings, to explore the critical situation which, in his understanding, the main players were now having to deal with. It is worth remembering here Herodotus' earlier gentle disclaimer that, while he feels it is his duty to record everything he is told, belief is another matter and also that, nonetheless, 'his accounts ... are always worth examination since at least they represent what an intelligent and knowledgeable Greek, far closer to the events than we are, believed to be the truth' (Lazenby, 1993).

Mardonius son of Gobryas and Artabazus son of Pharnaces debated the situation (remember, Artabazus was one of the few men that Xerxes had a high opinion of), and these were the views expressed. Artabazus thought that they should abandon their position as soon as possible and move the whole army inside the walls of Thebes where there were large stocks of provisions for the men and fodder for the animals. They could then take their ease and achieve their goal in the following way. They had with them large amounts of gold, both coin and bullion, silver, and precious drinking vessels, and he proposed that these be distributed amongst the Hellenes, holding nothing back and picking out the leading men in their cities. Then the Hellenes would swiftly give up their freedom without the Persians having to risk going into battle. This was the same advice that the Thebans had given,[1] and Artabazus had an even better idea of what was in store. However, Mardonius' position was more strongly held, less rational and not open to any compromise. He thought that the Persian force was much stronger than the Hellene and that they should therefore give battle as soon as possible and not allow the Hellenes to build a larger force than they had already. As for Hegesistratus' sacrifices, they should ignore the omens and not try to make them come out right but rather give battle in Persian style. So Mardonius made his case. Nobody spoke up against it and he won the debate, such as it was. Anyway he, not Artabazus, was commander-in-chief by authority of the Great King.

Next, Mardonius called together his divisional commanders and the Hellene generals who were campaigning with him and asked them if they knew of any prophecy that foretold disaster for the Persians in Greece. The assembled company did not utter a word, either because they did not know of any prophecies or because they were afraid to say what they did know, so Mardonius did the talking: 'Clearly, you either know nothing or are afraid to tell me what you do know, so I am going to tell you what I have found out. There is a prophecy that states that any Persians who come to Hellas and plunder the holy place at Delphi will be doomed to die, every one of them, after committing this act.[2] Very well, since we know all about this, we will not go near that temple, we will not make any attempt to plunder it, and, as a consequence, no disaster will befall us. And so all of you who are on Persia's side can be of good cheer because this means we shall overcome the Hellenes.' So he spoke and then gave the command to put everything in place and form up to engage the enemy the following morning.

---

[1] They gave Mardonius the same advice when he arrived in Boeotia on his march south.
[2] Herodotus makes no reference to the dramatic failure of the Persian attempt on Delphi in the previous year but immediately follows up with a neat put-down.

I happen to know that this prophecy that Mardonius said was about the Persians was, in actual fact, about the Illyrians. But there is a prophecy of Bacis that refers to this particular battle:

'On the grass-grown banks of the Asopus
Hellenes will come together and Barbarians will shriek with pain.
When that fateful day arrives, there many a Median bowman
Will be struck down before his allotted time.'

Anyway, after Mardonius had made his enquiry about prophecies and delivered his speech, night fell and sentries were posted. In the middle of the night when all was quiet in the camps with the men sleeping soundly, just then, Alexander son of Amyntas, the Macedonian commander-in-chief and king, rode up to an Athenian outpost and requested a meeting with their generals. Most of the sentries stayed where they were, but some ran to their commanders and told them that a man had ridden over from the Persian lines and told them nothing except that he wished to speak with the generals, asking for them by name. On hearing this, the generals went to the outpost immediately. On their arrival, Alexander said, 'Men of Athens, I bring you information in good faith on the understanding that you will not disclose it to anyone except Pausanias, for you will be the ruin of me if you do. I actually would not be telling you this if I did not care so much about all of Hellas, being myself of Hellene ancestry from ancient times.[1] I have no desire to see Hellas exchange freedom for slavery, so I am here to inform you that the sacrificial omens are not turning out to the liking of Mardonius and his men. If they were, you would have been in battle long ago. But now, because, in my opinion, he is alarmed by the way your numbers are increasing, he has decided to ignore the omens and to launch his attack at the first glint of dawn. Be ready for this, but if Mardonius holds and does not attack, stand firm; he now has provisions for only a few days.[2] If this war ends as you purpose, then you must give thought to securing my freedom.

[1] It was accepted that Macedonian royalty was of Hellene descent but as a people the Macedonians were considered Barbarian.
[2] This is not a contradiction of Artabazus' assurance that Thebes was well stocked with provisions if his idea was that the Persians commandeer them to supplement their own.

I have taken a great risk for the sake of Hellas in my urgent desire to inform you of Mardonius' plans in case the Barbarians suddenly fall upon you when you are not expecting them. I am Alexander the Macedonian.' After saying this he rode back to his position in the Persian lines.

The Athenian generals went to the right of the line and told Pausanias everything that Alexander had told them. On hearing this, Pausanias became increasingly fearful of the Persians and said, 'Well then, if the battle is to begin at dawn, it is you Athenians who must face the Persians and we must face the Boeotians and other Hellenes who are positioned opposite you. You understand the Medes and their way of fighting because you fought with them at Marathon while we have no experience or knowledge of these men. Not a single Spartan has any experience of fighting the Medes, but we know all about the Boeotians and Thessalians.[1] So let's pick up our weapons and change places, you to this flank and we to the left.'

The Athenians replied, 'Right from the start, when we saw the Persians forming up opposite you, we had been thinking of suggesting what you have just proposed, but we were afraid that you would find the idea displeasing. Now you have put it into words, we are delighted to hear it from you and are ready and willing to do what you say.' This was approved all round and they changed places in the line at the first light of dawn, but the Boeotians spotted it and informed Mardonius. He immediately attempted to change position himself by moving the Persians so that they still faced the Lacedaemonians. When Pausanias found out what was happening, he knew that his movement had been observed and led the Spartans back to the right flank, and Mardonius did the same moving back to his left.

When they were all back where they had started, Mardonius sent a herald to the Lacedaemonians with this message: 'Men of Lacedaemon, the people around here say you are the finest of men

---

[1] There had actually been no known battle between Spartans and Boeotians. The only known encounter between Spartans and Thessalians was in the former's campaign to help drive the Pisistratids out of Athens in 511/10, in which they were initially defeated by Thessalian cavalry.

and they admire you greatly because you never shrink from combat or abandon your position, but stand your ground and either kill your enemies or get killed. But clearly there is not a word of truth in this! Even before we could engage with you at close quarters,[1] we saw you abandon your position. And we saw you positioning the Athenians so that they would test us out for you and positioning yourselves opposite our slaves.[2] Is this the action of brave men? Not at all! We have been terribly misinformed about you. Because of your reputation we expected you to send a herald over challenging the Persians and calling us alone out to fight with you. We were ready and willing to do that, but now we find you have no challenge to offer and instead are cringing before us. So, if you will not challenge us, we will take the initiative. What is to stop us taking each other on in equal numbers, you, who are reputed to be the best of them, fighting for the Hellenes and we for the Barbarians? If the others want to fight, let them fight after us, later. But if this does not appeal and it is felt that we alone will suffice, let's fight it out to the finish and whichever side is victorious shall decide victory for the whole army.' The herald delivered his message and waited for a while. Not a word was said in reply, so he made his way back to Mardonius and told him what had happened. (9.41–49)

The formal opening of Herodotus' brief account of the debate ('such as it was') between Mardonius and Artabazus is ironic. His purpose is to contrast the latter's wisdom and caution with the former's rashness, a characteristic which had not actually been displayed by Mardonius up to this point in the campaign of 479. However, Herodotus has already presented him as an enthusiastic and personally ambitious advocate of the conquest of Greece and later as persuading Xerxes to entrust him with the task of completing the mission in spite of the defeat at Salamis. Herodotus is, of course, setting Mardonius up for the inevitable fate of a tragic hero. Artabazus' specific advice that he withdraw inside the walls of Thebes was wrong-headed and impractical; withdrawal from the Asopus line would relieve the

---

[1] 'Rule of hands', *nomos cheiron*.
[2] A slighting reference to the medizing Boeotians.

Hellenes of pressure that was becoming more painful by the day and it would have been physically impossible to fit such a large army into the approximately 25-hectare space within Thebes' city walls. However, with so many Hellene states having already 'come round to their way of thinking', with others cynically neutral and with a number of them willingly providing contingents, it was not unreasonable to hope for further such gains through diplomacy and bribery. On the experience of the land-battle of Salamis in Cyprus in 496 and the sea-battle of Lade in 494 such investment could even pay off in the shape of large-scale desertions when the fighting was actually under way. But, on the other hand, diplomacy and bribery had made no impression on the hard core of the same alliance that had faced the Persians in 480.

Next, Mardonius, who has previously shown respect for, and even cultivated, oracles and prophecies and the gods of Hellas, is shown as digging an even deeper pit for himself by insisting they take no further notice of Hegesistratus' divination but go into battle. Pre-battle sacrifice and divination, so important to the Hellenes, does not appear to have been customary for the Persians but 'Persian style' may have a more general meaning here, reflecting the aggressive spirit of a world-conquering empire which Mardonius no longer wishes to suppress. But rather than ignoring oracles, Mardonius claims he has thoroughly researched them and has come up with none that foretell defeat for the Persians. Herodotus points out that he was wrong about the prophecy concerning Delphi in a crucial detail and supplies another which Mardonius might either have missed or kept to himself; Herodotus does not comment.

So the decision is taken to step up the previous days' harassment to full engagement. The Hellenes are likely to have quickly found out about this, either through contact with sympathetic compatriots in the Persian camp or by observation of new and increased activity across the river, but the story of Alexander's secret mission adds drama. It may have been invented by him soon after the war as a response to justified accusations of medism. In his two previous interventions, the second as Mardonius' ambassador, he advised the Athenians that resistance was pointless. Here he acknowledges that the Hellenes may win and that he now has 'no desire to see Hellas exchange freedom for slavery', but he also reveals concern for his own future in the event that the

Hellenes are victorious. We can sense Herodotus' enjoyment in writing this mischievous cameo.

The episode that follows is completely unbelievable. The switching of flank positions between the Athenians and the Spartans and subsequent reversal of the manoeuvre would have involved tens of thousands of troops in round trips of 10–15km and it is inconceivable that Mardonius would simply have shadowed the movement by switching his own flanks rather than immediately attacking to exploit the enemy's self-inflicted disruption. As in the dispute between the Tegeans and Athenians over the left-wing position, the debate Herodotus records may well be an echo of earlier discussion of the Hellene battle order. Weighed against the supreme effectiveness of the Spartan army, the Athenians' unique experience at Marathon was probably not of great significance, though the kudos was undeniable, and also the confidence that victory had given them. This story was probably an Athenian invention to put a better shine on their part in the great Hellene victory and the suggestion in it of Spartan exploitation of Athens would have resonated strongly with audiences during the Peloponnesian War. In any case, Herodotus thought it worth including in his record and it does neatly set up the final episode in which Mardonius once again takes centre stage.

His taunting challenge has an air of fantasy about it, except there was at least one precedent in Spartan history, the Battle of the Champions in 546, for such a formal attempt to settle things on the battlefield; and it was consistent with Mardonius' more general view of the Hellene way of war, as presented to the Great King at his planning meeting in Susa in 484. Here Herodotus is also echoing the taunts and challenges that Homer's heroes hurl at each other in the *Iliad*. If such a challenge was issued, Pausanias did not grace it with a response.

Encouraged by this hollow victory, Mardonius launched his cavalry against the Hellenes. His horsemen rode up and mauled the whole Hellene army with their javelins and arrows and, as they were mounted, it was impossible for the Hellenes to engage with them. They also fouled the spring of Gargaphia and blocked it up, and this was where the entire Hellene army had been getting its water. The Lacedaemonians were placed closest to this spring, but it was further away from the rest of the Hellenes in their various positions whilst the Asopus was within easy reach. But they had to go to the spring because they were kept away from the river and prevented from drawing water from it by the cavalry and their missiles. In this situation, with the army now cut off from its water supply and being severely harassed by the cavalry, the Hellene commanders gathered together with Pausanias on the right flank to discuss these and other problems, because they had an even greater worry. They were out of food and the support troops sent to the Peloponnese to fetch supplies had been completely cut off by the cavalry and could not rejoin the army. (9.49–50)

The attack's objective was to fracture the Hellene defensive line and create openings for the cavalry, to be followed in by the infantry, to break through and exploit; standard Persian tactics. Hellas was now closer to the 'razor's edge' than at any other moment in the war; Mardonius was winning the deciding battle. The earlier incident, when Mardonius put the Phocian hoplites to the test outside Thebes and they responded by 'drawing their ranks together all round and making the files as deep as possible' (9.18), gives an idea of the defensive tactics that would have been used by the Greeks, who were very probably now under attack from all sides. It is possible to visualize the entire Greek army in a formation similar to Brasidas' when fighting the Illyrians, or divided by main division into a number of squares or rough ellipses with light-armed sheltering inside, though skirmishers on foot would generally have been ineffectual against mounted attackers. The implied failure of the Lacedaemonians to defend the spring is surprising. However, the water would have been collected and carried by support troops rather than hoplites, maybe under cover of darkness and with a light-armed escort, if any. So, the Persians may only just have discovered the spring's existence and its importance to the Greeks, and then moved too quickly for any defence to be mounted. The spring was probably only temporarily blocked or fouled, but, as Herodotus reveals, the Greek command had a bigger problem. They had run out of food and could not be resupplied because the Persian cavalry had cut them off from the supplies accumulating at the foot of the pass over Cithaeron. Also, several days' dense occupation of the same area of land by tens of thousands of men within a tight perimeter must have made the conditions increasingly foul.

The outcome of the commanders' conference was a decision to fall back on 'the Island', if the Persians held off making an all-out attack for the rest of the day. This place is 10 *stades* [about 2,000m] from the Asopus and the same distance from the spring of Gargaphia and the area where the army was now positioned, and is in front of the city of Plataea.[1] It is a kind of landlocked island formed by the division of a river into two channels as it flows down from Cithaeron into the plain; the distance between the channels is about 3 *stades* [550m] before they join again. The river is called Oeroe and the locals call it 'Asopus' Daughter'. Their plan was to move to this place so that they would have a plentiful supply of water and protection from frontal attack by the cavalry. They decided to do this during the second watch of the night to prevent the Persians seeing them setting off and pursuing them with their cavalry and disrupting the manoeuvre. After reaching this area where the Oeroe, Asopus' Daughter, divides as it flows down from Cithaeron, the intention was then to send half the army up to Cithaeron in the course of that night to fetch the support troops who had gone for supplies and been cut off on the mountain. (9.51)

The Island's position cannot be identified from Herodotus' vague bearings, but it must have been rather more than 10 *stades* (better interpreted as meaning 'about 2,000m' than more precisely converted) from any point on the River Asopus itself, and even though this same round number seems a fair approximation of the distance from the spring, Gargaphia's exact location somewhere behind the Spartan position on the Asopus ridge is another unknown. And, in any case, the loops of 'Oeroe, Asopus' Daughter' can no longer be traced. Whatever the actual topography, Herodotus seems not to have been fully informed by his sources, or simply to have misunderstood the Hellene plan. The less vague dimension of 3 *stades* (500–600m) that Herodotus gives for the width of the Island suggests an area that would have been an impossibly tight fit for tens of thousands of men. If the surrounding river channels offered better protection from direct assault than the features they had previously occupied, the Hellenes would still have been very exposed to close-range bombardment from archers

---

[1] Interpreted below as not directly in front but to the north-east.

lining the opposite banks; and before or after the army divided it would have been easy for the Persians to surround the position completely. It is more likely that the Island was intended to form a central part of a shorter defensive line on the rising and higher ground between Plataea and Hysiae with its right covering the exit to the pass over Cithaeron and reconnected with the stranded supply train.

It has been suggested that this whole manoeuvre was a ruse to entrap Mardonius somehow, in the same way as the Persian fleet was lured into the straits of Salamis by Themistocles, but there is no evidence apart from a possible hint in Diodorus Siculus to support such a theory, and Herodotus would surely not have failed to tell us if he had come across any indication of it in his investigations. Equally, this was not the start of a retreat to the Isthmus, which would have caused an immediate break-up of the Greek alliance and almost certainly led to total defeat. Most likely, it was to be a forced regrouping, entirely defensive in purpose, and then the waiting was to continue, and the hoping that the Persians might themselves run out of food or commit themselves in some way that would finally allow the Greeks to fight back in favourable circumstances. Mardonius' plan was probably to resume the cavalry attacks the following morning in the reasonable expectation that his strategy of attrition would at last take effect and create an opening for a full-scale infantry assault. But, though he did not yet know it, the Hellenes were finally going to make a move, and the cohesion that they had so resolutely maintained was shortly to fracture:

> The Hellenes made their plan and the cavalry continued to press them hard, keeping them under remorseless pressure for the whole day until it drew to a close and the attacks came to an end. Night fell and, at the time agreed for making the move, a large proportion of the Hellene army set off from their positions. But these men had no intention of taking up the new position that had been agreed upon. Once they were on the move they were so happy to be making their escape from the Persian cavalry that they carried on in the direction of the city of Plataea, coming to a halt only when they reached the sanctuary of Hera, which is just outside the city and 20 *stades* [about 4,000m] from the spring of Gargaphia, and they grounded arms in front of it. (9.52)

The language here is less derogatory than implied by Plutarch's remark that Herodotus 'simultaneously accused them of disobedience, desertion and treachery' (*On the Malice of Herodotus* 42), though in similar instances where bias may be at work, such as the alleged flight of the Corinthians at Salamis, Herodotus does question the truth of what he has been told. In fact, in his account of the battle, Plutarch actually depicts a more chaotic scene which is even less to the credit of the troops involved:

> Night came on, and the generals led their contingents off to the new position that had been picked out for them. However, the men showed no inclination to follow them or to keep together. Instead, as soon as they had moved out of their original perimeters, most of them hurried towards the city of Plataea, and there was general confusion as they spread themselves out and pitched camp in disorder. (*Aristides* 17)

Herodotus does not identify which contingents were involved in this episode, but in his account of their actions in the next day's fighting he names the Corinthians and the Megarians. The former were originally positioned immediately to the left of the Tegeans and the Spartans and the rest of the Lacedaemonians, and the latter immediately to the right of the Plataeans and the Athenians; and he also mentions the Phleiasians, a smaller unit from the middle of the battle order. It is a reasonable assumption that all the contingents stationed between the Corinthians and the Megarians, over half Pausanias' hoplite strength, withdrew with them.

If Herodotus is exercising or transmitting some bias here, it would have been fuelled by the knowledge that almost all the cities represented in this centre division were to become enemies of Athens in the Peloponnesian War. By way of mitigation, if there was a degree of panic and chaos in the ranks, these troops did not carry on running over Cithaeron but halted on the higher ground in front of the ruins of the city, which may actually have been the new position intended for the Athenians and the Plataeans on the Hellene left. Secondly, the contingents which had been positioned on the level ground between the Asopus and Pyrgos ridges would have been under the greatest pressure from the harassing Barbarian cavalry and could be forgiven for being especially enthusiastic about the manoeuvre. It could also have been that orders had not been clearly communicated or fully understood, or simply that the majority moved off in slightly the wrong direction in the dark.

So, these men took up position around the shrine of Hera. When Pausanias saw that they had moved off, he ordered the Lacedaemonians to take up arms and follow suit, assuming that the others were on the way to their agreed position. All his commanders stood ready to carry out the order, except for Amompharetus son of Poliades, commander of the *lochos* (regiment) from Pitana.[1] He flatly refused to run away from 'those foreigners' and was not prepared to bring disgrace upon Sparta in this way. He had not been part of the earlier discussion and was astonished at the course of action that had been decided upon. Pausanias and Euryanax[2] were appalled by his disobedience and even more appalled that his refusal to move might cause them to leave the Pitana regiment behind. They were afraid that if they did what had been agreed with the rest of the Hellenes and left Amompharetus and his men behind, they would be abandoning them to be wiped out. So, with that in mind, they kept the rest of the Laconian contingent[3] where it was and carried on trying to persuade Amompharetus that he could not behave like this.

While this argument went on with the only man amongst the Lacedaemonians and the Tegeans who was not willing to move, the Athenians remained in their position, well aware of the Lacedaemonian tendency to say one thing but intend something quite different.[4] When the rest of the formation began to break up, they sent one

---

[1] One of five ancient villages that were combined to form the city of Sparta. It is thought that, at this time, each of them maintained a *lochos* of a roughly equal number of Spartiates.

[2] This is Euryanax's only appearance in the narrative of the battle but he is presented here as exercising command jointly with Pausanias.

[3] Meaning not only the Spartans, but also the Lacedaemonian *perioikoi* and the Tegeans, who were facing the Persians with them on the right of the line.

[4] This can be taken as a reference to the tricky behaviour of the ephors in the face of the Athenian delegation's pleas that the Spartans mobilize, as promised, to face the Persians in Boeotia, but it would also have resonated with the Spartans' enemies and victims, like the Plataeans, in the Peloponnesian War.

of their horsemen[1] to see whether the Spartans were starting to move off or actually intending to stay where they were, and to ask Pausanias what the Athenians were supposed to do. The messenger arrived to find the Lacedaemonians in their original position and their leaders arguing. Euryanax and Pausanias were trying to make Amompharetus see the danger of staying where he was, isolated from the rest of the Lacedaemonians. But they could not convince him, and the Athenian messenger rode up just as the argument was growing more heated. In the course of it Amompharetus picked up a boulder in both hands and threw it down at Pausanias' feet, saying that this pebble was his vote[2] against running away from 'those foreigners', by which he meant the Barbarians. Pausanias told him he was crazy, out of his mind, and then turned to the Athenian herald, who asked the questions he had been sent to ask. Pausanias instructed him to go back and report on the situation, and to request the Athenians to link up with the Spartans and follow whatever they did as they withdrew. (9.53–55)

Although Herodotus gives no sign of doubting any of this wonderful story, it is hard to take it at face value. However, looked at in the context of other information, it becomes more credible and illuminating in some respects. First, arguments of this kind, instances of disobedience and insubordination, even in the Spartan army, are documented elsewhere. Strategy and tactics were collectively discussed and vigorously debated as often as handed down from the top, and here Pausanias and Euryanax are shown as attempting to persuade their subordinate rather than give him a direct order. Secondly, the authority of the young and relatively inexperienced Pausanias probably did meet with challenges of this kind. It is not actually clear where Amompharetus fitted into the Spartan order of battle. Thucydides in a brisk aside, possibly a professional jab at Herodotus, even says 'there was no such thing' as the Pitana *lochos* (*History of the Peloponnesian War* 1.20). However, it was probably a substantial unit of around 1,000 (representing a fifth of the

---

[1] There were no cavalry units on the Hellene side and this is the one reference to any use of horsemen, which were clearly engaged only in despatch-riding and, probably, scouting.
[2] This is very likely to be embroidery. The Spartans, unlike the Athenians for instance, did not use pebbles as voting tokens; they shouted.

Spartan contingent) and more numerous Helot light-armed, and the story may be an echo of its deployment as a 'rock-like' rear-guard whilst the main body fell back towards the new line. Herodotus' account of the episode also has literary echoes, which he probably fabricated himself, in its similarity to the conflict between King Agamemnon and Achilles in the *Iliad*, and the character he paints of Amompharetus as a sturdy, probably veteran upholder of old-fashioned values may also be a literary creation.

Things may not have been as chaotic as Herodotus' narrative suggests, but the situation was now very serious. According to Herodotus' figures, 21,300 of Pausanias' total of 41,400 hoplites were now beyond his control and retreating, leaving a 4,000m void in the centre of his 8,000m defensive line. The 8,600 Athenian and Plataean hoplites of his left wing were isolated on Pyrgos Ridge, and he was isolated with his 11,500 hoplites 4,000m to the east of them on the Asopus ridge; and he was in danger of losing 1,000 Spartans if Amompharetus could not be shifted. It would seem that the Athenians were already under orders not to leave Pyrgos Ridge until they knew that the Spartans were on the move, otherwise they would have taken their cue from the Megarians immediately to their right. There could have been no visual contact in the darkness over the 4–5km of undulating ground that separated the two flanks, and trumpet calls, if practicable, would have alerted the enemy. Horsemen or runners were the only possible means of communication.

> The messenger went back to the Athenian position. Dawn found the argument still going on. Pausanias had not made any move from the position so far, but now he took the view that Amompharetus would not stay behind if the rest of the Lacedaemonians marched off, and that is how it turned out. So, Pausanias gave the command and led the rest of the Lacedaemonians back along the ridge, and the Tegeans came with them. The Athenians also moved off as ordered, but took a different path from the Lacedaemonians. The Lacedaemonians hugged the ridges on the lower slopes of Cithaeron in fear of the Persian cavalry while the Athenians wheeled down into the plain instead.
>
> At first Amompharetus would not believe that Pausanias could do such a thing as leave him and his men behind, and he was as

determined as ever to stand firm and not abandon the position. But, when the men with Pausanias had gone some distance, he knew for sure that they were leaving him behind. So, when his men had gathered up their weapons, he led his *lochos* at walking pace towards the main formation. The rest of the Lacedaemonians were now about 10 *stades* [about 2,000m] away, waiting for Amompharetus' *lochos* to catch up with them, and in an area called Argiopium by the River Moloeis where there is a shrine of Eleusinian Demeter. They had paused there so that they could get back and give support in case Amompharetus and his *lochos* did not move from their original position. In fact, the moment Amompharetus' unit rejoined the others, the Barbarian cavalry came up in full force and closed with them. They had followed normal practice and, seeing empty ground where the Hellenes had been positioned for days previously, kept on pushing forward and attacked them as soon as they had caught up with them. (9.56–57)

It would be interesting to have Herodotus' thoughts on what suddenly convinced Pausanias that Amompharetus would follow. In any case, it would have been suicidal to attempt to hold a position that was now generally considered to be too dangerously exposed for the whole flank division. In his mention of the nature of the ground each flank division crossed, Herodotus must have picked up on some Athenian prejudice. The Athenians actually had no choice but to come down off their ridge and cross the lower ground, whereas the Lacedaemonians' line of march led along the higher ground of the Asopus ridge; this was clearly not a choice driven by 'fear of the Persian cavalry'. However, from 431, Athenians would have enjoyed this slur in the context of their own cavalry's regular sorties in the course of successive Spartan invasions of Attica; although these actions were only modestly effective in tactical terms, they boosted morale inside the city walls.

Elements of Herodotus' narrative may support the idea of a less spontaneous chain of events, making it possible to envisage a planned rearguard action carried out by Amompharetus. If his *lochos* was approximately 1,000 strong with a larger number of Helots, he could have straddled Pausanias' line of march and covered a front of several hundred metres, and, moving slowly, maintained a tight formation ready to face attack from any direction. The '10 *stades*' covered by Pausanias before halting is a reasonable approximation in Herodotus' loose topography of the distance between the Asopus ridge position and Hysiae at the foot of the pass over Cithaeron. It may be that Pausanias halted here, not because he had changed his mind about Amompharetus once more, but because his division was now in its correct position at the right of the new defensive line, the only division to successfully execute the plan agreed by the Hellenes the previous day. The movement was probably carried out by dividing into columns and reforming into line on arrival, a drill of which the Spartans are known from later sources to have been masters, and it may not have taken much more than an hour. Amompharetus' task would have been to screen the rear of the main force whilst it was moving fast in open order and to rejoin it, if necessary after a fighting retreat, when it was formed up in line of battle again.

Unfortunately, the location of Argiopium is unknown and the River Moloeis cannot now be traced. However, Plutarch places the shrine of Demeter quite near to the ancient village of Hysiae, and archaeological evidence in the shape of some worked stone and two fragments of an inscription relating to the worship of the goddess supports this. Drawn up in close order, Pausanias' 11,500 hoplites (Spartans, Lacedaemonians and Tegeans) with substantial light-armed support, possibly including the Thespians, could have formed a solid front of 2,000–3,000m. His right may have rested on the Moloeis which would have run through a gully carved into the base of Cithaeron, or dropped back under the protection of one of the spurs further to the east. Terrain may have provided similar protection on the left, but this was perhaps where the Corinthians were supposed to have taken up position and therefore dangerously exposed. However, Pausanias was now closer to the main pass, an escape route if needed, and to the supplies that had been stranded there, and he had repositioned most of his division without any contact with the enemy. The simultaneous arrival of Amompharetus' *lochos* and the Barbarian cavalry may or may not have been a coincidence. This reconstruction does beg the question of timing, but a case could be made for delaying the withdrawal of the right-flank division until dawn. With its Spartan core it was most capable of all the divisions of executing the manoeuvre efficiently, even if it turned into a fighting retreat. The multi-national centre would need more time to move and regroup into its new position and activity at first light on the right flank could secure additional breathing space. On this logic the plan may also have kept the Athenians and Plataeans in position till dawn on Pyrgos Ridge.

When Mardonius had learned that the Hellenes had gone off under cover of night and saw that their position was abandoned, he summoned Thorax of Larissa and his brothers Eurypylus and Thrasydeus and said, 'What do you have to say now, Aleuadae,[1] now you see this position abandoned? You, their close neighbours, kept telling me that Lacedaemonians never retreat from battle and are masters of war above all other men. Yet you have already watched them switching places in the battle line and now we can all see that they have run away during the night that has just passed. Clearly, when they could no longer avoid being tested in combat with men who really are the bravest of all mortals, they showed themselves up as a bunch of nobodies in the company of Hellenes, who are all nobodies. As far as I'm concerned you can be absolutely forgiven for heaping praise upon people you know well when you had little experience of the Persians. But I was astonished by Artabazus' terror of the Lacedaemonians and his disgraceful proposal that we should strike camp and fall back on the city of Thebes and put ourselves under siege. The Great King will certainly hear of this from me. But that reckoning is for another time. Now our enemies must not be allowed to do this thing. They must be pursued until they are overtaken and made to pay the penalty for all that they have done to the Persians.' This is what he said.

So Mardonius then led the Persians at the double across the Asopus on the trail of the Hellenes, thinking they were running away. But it was only the Lacedaemonians and Tegeans he was following because the Athenians were crossing the low ground and were out of sight behind the ridges.[2] When they saw the Persians

---

[1] The Aleuadae, descendants of Aleuas the Red of Larissa, a 6th-century tyrant, were one of the ruling clans of Thessaly and enthusiastic medizers.

[2] The Athenians were probably raising some dust behind the ridges, but the contingents from the centre were right out of sight.

charging off in pursuit of the Hellenes, the commanders of the remaining Barbarian divisions all immediately raised their standards and joined in the chase as fast as their feet would carry them, out of formation and in total disorder. So, this mob shouted their war cries and swarmed up, fully confident that they would sweep the Hellenes away.

Pausanias, now under pressure from the cavalry, sent a horseman to the Athenians with this message: 'Athenians, we are facing the supreme contest to determine whether Hellas remains free or is enslaved, and we Lacedaemonians and you Athenians have been betrayed by the allies who ran away last night.[1] It is clear what we have to do. We must support each other and put up the best fight that we can. If the cavalry had attacked you first, it would have been our duty and the duty of the Tegeans, who have not betrayed Hellas and are still with us, to come to your aid. But now all of the cavalry is about to attack us, so the right thing for you to do is come up in support of that section of the army that is most hard-pressed. However, if circumstances now prevent you coming to our aid, we should be obliged if you would send your archers over. We are fully aware of the extraordinary commitment you have shown in the present conflict and know you will pay heed to this request.' When the Athenians received this message, they moved off quickly to reinforce the Lacedaemonians and give them their full support. But as soon as they had started to move, they were attacked by the Hellenes who had been positioned opposite them,[2] those who had gone over to the Great King, and they were unable to assist them in any way. (9.58–61)

Herodotus loads the final words he puts into Mardonius' mouth with heavy irony, amplifying his earlier, but not entirely consistent characterization of him as lacking in judgement, impetuous and arrogant, and once again signalling the 'reckoning' in store for him. The all-out charge he launches across the Asopus in impious defiance

---

[1] Their night-time withdrawal was part of the plan; finishing up in the wrong place did not constitute betrayal or running away.
[2] Medizing Thebans, other Boeotians, Locrians, Malians and Phocians, and, from further north, Thessalians and less Hellene Macedonians.

of the gods' warnings is sharply contrasted with the measured tread of Amompharetus' withdrawal. If Mardonius' cavalry and Pausanias' division were out of sight, he would have known where they were from messages sent back and probably from the dust cloud raised. Herodotus implies that Mardonius thought he was pursuing the whole of the Greek army, but it is more likely that he was seizing what he saw as an opportunity to overwhelm one significant part of it by concentrating his cavalry and best Asian infantry. But the rest of his Barbarian troops may have been under this illusion as they crossed the river and set off after the Persians.

Pausanias' message to the Athenians begins with a rallying cry that echoes Miltiades' before Marathon and Themistocles' before Salamis, but Plataea was to be the decisive battle, truly 'the supreme contest'. The call on Athens to stand alongside Sparta in a battle in defence of the freedom of Hellas would have had a painful resonance during the Peloponnesian War. The main target of the clumsy slur (probably of Athenian origin) on the rest of the Hellenes may have been the Corinthians, who, as represented by Thucydides, were the most energetic and effective advocates of that conflict amongst Sparta's allies. In the spirit of Hellene unity, the language of Pausanias' message is not that of a commander-in-chief giving orders to a subordinate. However, the Athenians were unable to 'oblige' because the medizing Greeks on the Persian right had tracked their movement off Pyrgos Ridge, crossed the river and probably passed through the gap between the two ridges. Herodotus picks up on this collision between two substantial hoplite forces at the end of his account of the decisive confrontation between Pausanias' right and Mardonius' left:

> The Hellenes on the Great King's side fought half-heartedly except for the Boeotians, who had a long battle with the Athenians. The Theban medizers fought with especial commitment and spirit and, as a result, 300 of their foremost and best died at the hands of the Athenians. But then they too turned and fled back to Thebes. (9.67)

Plutarch adds some embroidery:

> The Athenians calmly stayed in position waiting to follow the Lacedaemonians' lead. But then the shouts of battle fell upon their

ears and, so it is told, a messenger arrived from Pausanias and reported what was happening. So, the Athenians set off with all speed to give him support. However, as they were advancing across the plain to his aid, the medizing Hellenes bore down upon them. When he saw them, Aristides immediately stepped out far in front of the line and called on them in the name of the gods of Hellas to hold off from fighting and get out of the Athenians' way so as not to prevent them going to the assistance of men who were risking all for the sake of Hellas. But when he saw that they were paying no attention to him and were indeed forming up for battle, he abandoned his rescue mission and engaged with them; they were about 50,000 strong. Most of them[1] broke immediately and fell back when they saw that the Barbarians had also quit the field, and the battle is said to have been fought mainly with the Thebans. The foremost and most influential citizens were very enthusiastic medizers at that time and the majority of the people went along with them, not out of rational choice but directed by the few.[2] (*Aristides* 18.4–6)

This could have been a battle on the same scale as Tanagra in 457, Delium in 424 and Mantinea in 418, making it one of the largest hoplite vs hoplite engagements of the 5th century, and it is disappointing that Herodotus has so little to say about it. He earlier estimates that the Hellenes in Mardonius' right-flank division totalled 50,000, but this is not credible in demographic terms and would, in any case, have given Mardonius numerical superiority in hoplites alone, which could have significantly altered things. Judging from Herodotus' terse statement that the Thebans and other Boeotians, in his stock phrase, 'fought the Athenians for a long time', the two sides must have been quite evenly matched. There were 8,600 Athenian and Plataean hoplites on Herodotus' count, plus the Athenian archers and attendant *psiloi*. Before the Megarians fell back, the Hellene left totalled 11,600 hoplites and it is a reasonable assumption that the force facing them through the days of stalemate was roughly similar in size. It also included Theban and Thessalian cavalry, which could have swung the balance of this

---

[1] Presumably meaning the medizing troops from north of Boeotia, offsetting the impact on Hellene numbers of the Megarians' withdrawal from the line.
[2] Oligarchic behaviour, as Plutarch's language makes clear.

particular confrontation, for example, with a well-timed strike before the Athenians had been able to get into battle formation. However, at this point, they could have been elsewhere on the battlefield scouting for the Hellene centre. The 300 'foremost and best' Thebans may have been an elite unit similar to the Spartan *hippeis* and a precursor of Thebes' Sacred Band, established a century later in their war of liberation from Spartan rule. Alternatively, Herodotus may be referring in round numbers to the casualties amongst the leading citizens who would have fought in the front line and been the promoters of medism. The Athenians had possibly won a notable victory which was, unfortunately overshadowed by the more spectacular victory that was being won a short distance away, a cause of future resentment that coloured subsequent decades' historical writing, particularly Plutarch's. However, Salamis was the Athenians' battle, Plataea was about to become the Spartans'. Whatever happened, whether this was a skirmish or a full-on battle, the Boeotians held the Athenians up for long enough to prevent them giving Pausanias any assistance.

So, the Lacedaemonians and the Tegeans stood alone. In total, including light-armed troops, there were 50,000[1] from Lacedaemon and 3,000 from Tegea; the Tegeans were inseparable from the Lacedaemonians.[2] They performed the sacrifices required before they could join battle with Mardonius and his army, but the omens would not come out right for them and during this time many fell and many more were wounded. The Persians had made a palisade from their wicker shields and were showering them with arrows from behind it. Even the Spartans were struggling and still the sacrifices were unfavourable. So, Pausanias turned his face towards

[1] Arrived at as follows: 5,000 Spartan hoplites each attended by seven light-armed Helots and 5,000 *perioikoi* and 1,500 Tegean hoplites, each with one light-armed attendant. The hoplite totals can be accepted as reasonably accurate, if generously rounded numbers, and the original count would have been reduced by casualties sustained over the previous ten days. There may have been more than one Helot per Spartiate on the battlefield, filling out the ranks and giving light-armed support on the flanks, but 35,000 would have been an unmanageable liability and is, in any case, not credible.

[2] This alliance dated from the mid 6th century. Tegea was a useful buffer between Sparta and Argos and the alliance may originally have been forced on the Tegeans by the Spartans.

the sanctuary of Hera[1] at Plataea and called upon the goddess for assistance, begging her not to disappoint them in their hopes. As he prayed, the Tegeans got to their feet, stepped out in front of the rest and advanced towards the Barbarians. And, at that moment, just after Pausanias had made his plea, the omens from the sacrifices at last became favourable, and the Lacedaemonians advanced upon the Persians as well. (9.61–62)

Herodotus uses the same word, *echoreon* translated here as 'advanced', for the Tegeans as for the Spartans and its meaning better fits the typical measured advance of the Spartans than the Athenians' running charge at Marathon. Thucydides describes this in his account of the battle of Mantinea in 418, when, with the Tegeans again at their side, the Spartans faced the Athenians:

Then the armies came together. The Argives and their allies advanced with furious energy, the Lacedaemonians steadily to the music of many pipers spread out through their ranks, not for any religious purpose, but to make them go forward together stepping in time to the beat without breaking up their formation as large armies tend to do in the moments before they engage the enemy. (*History of the Peloponnesian War* 5.70)

Arguably, Herodotus would have remarked on it if Pausanias had launched a running charge. The Lacedaemonians may have had the nerve and confidence in their close formation and shields, helmets and armour to walk through the arrow storm when Pausanias gave the order to advance. The Persians may have started to run out of arrows, a consideration perhaps more powerful than favourable omens.

The Persians set aside their bows and faced up to the Hellenes, and at first the fighting was along the wall of shields but, when that went down, there was a hard struggle around the sanctuary of Demeter. It went on for such a long time that, for the Hellenes, it came down

---

[1] Looking over his left shoulder; the building may have been visible, picked out by the morning sun.

to *othismos* because the Barbarians kept seizing their spears and breaking them. The Persians were not inferior in courage or physical strength, but they were not armed like hoplites or trained in their way of fighting, and they did not have the tactical skill of their opponents. They were darting forward singly or in groups of ten, gathering together in larger or smaller groups and hurling themselves at the Spartans, and getting cut down.

Wherever Mardonius was fighting, mounted on his white charger with his picked band of a thousand, the flower of the Persians, there they pressed the enemy hardest. And while Mardonius still lived, they held their own and, fighting back, struck down many Lacedaemonians. But when Mardonius had fallen and when the men around him, the best in his army, had been slain, then the rest were put to flight and gave way before the Lacedaemonians. Their greatest disadvantage was the lack of armour in their equipment. They were, in effect, naked men[1] battling with hoplites. (9.62–63)

Plutarch adds some frills and his own spin to Herodotus' narrative:

At day-break Mardonius, who was well aware that the Hellenes had abandoned their position, formed his men up and launched his attack on the Lacedaemonians. The Barbarians came on with great clattering and shouting. They thought that there would be no battle and that they would pick the Hellenes off as they fled; it would just take a small push to tip the balance. Pausanias, seeing what was happening, halted his men and gave the order to take up battle positions. But, because he was either so angered by Amompharetus, or so confused by the speed of the enemy's advance, he failed to give any signal to the rest of the Hellenes. As a result, they did not rally to him immediately or all together, but joined him in small, scattered detachments when the fighting had already begun.[2]

---

[1] Herodotus uses *gymnetes*, a graphic synonym for *psiloi* here.
[2] It suits Plutarch's literary purpose to contrast Pausanias unfavourably with Aristides, the hero of this particular *Life*. There is no reason to believe that any other Hellenes came along at any point to take part in this particular confrontation (and to take a share of the Lacedaemonians' and Tegeans' glory); they were too far away, or otherwise engaged in the case of the Athenians.

The omens would not come out right from the sacrifices, so Pausanias commanded the Lacedaemonians to sit patiently behind their shields and to wait for orders, and to take no action to fight the enemy off whilst he offered more sacrifices. By now the charging cavalry was upon them, missiles were landing amongst them and they were taking casualties. They were suffering terribly, but the endurance the men displayed was wonderful. They made no attempt to retaliate against the enemy attacking them, but stayed at their posts, being shot at and dying while they waited for word of the critical moment from their god and their general. Then, despairing of the situation as the seer heaped sacrifice upon sacrifice, Pausanias turned toward the Heraeum and, lifting up his hands with his eyes full of tears, he begged Hera of Cithaeron and the other gods worshipped on Plataean soil that, if the Hellenes were not to be granted victory, they might at least do great deeds before they paid the price, and so prove to their enemies that they had gone to war with good men who knew how to fight a battle. And as Pausanias made this appeal to the gods, as he prayed, the omens were revealed, and the seer's interpretation was 'victory'.

The word was passed along the line to stand up and fight the enemy and the phalanx suddenly took on the appearance of a single ferocious beast, bristling and ready for a fight. Now the Barbarians knew that they were pitted against men who were going to fight with them to the finish, so they made a palisade of their wicker shields and shot their arrows into the Lacedaemonian ranks. But the Lacedaemonians took care to keep their shields tightly together[1] as they advanced and crashed into the enemy ranks, tearing through their shield wall. Then, spearing them in the face and chest, they killed many of the Persians. But the Barbarians fought with spirit before they fell, grabbing the Hellenes' spears with their bare hands, breaking many of them; and then they went to work with their blades, wielding their daggers and swords, wrenching aside their enemies' shields and wrestling with them.

---

[1] Plutarch uses the word *synaspismos,* which first appears in Diodorus Siculus and is associated by Arrian (2nd century AD) with the Roman *testudo* in which rectangular shields were locked together to a degree not possible with circular shields. It can also be translated in the more general sense of 'close order'.

They held out for a long time, but finally Mardonius was killed by a Spartan called Arimnestus, who hit him on the head with a rock.[1] (*Aristides* 17–19)

Mardonius had now brought about the decisive trial of military prowess that he had called for in his challenge, though that specified an equal number of footsoldiers, Persian and Spartan. After they had caught up with Pausanias' formation, his horsemen would have harassed it for an hour or more, the time it would have taken their infantry to cover the 3,000–4,000m from the north bank of the Asopus. The Hellenes did as the Phocians did when Mardonius tested them on joining his army earlier in Boeotia, 'drawing their ranks together all round' (9.18), and as Brasidas did half a century later, fighting the Illyrians, when he 'formed his hoplites into a square and placed his contingent of *psiloi* inside it' (Thucydides, *History of the Peloponnesian War* 4.125). The *psiloi* would have thrown stones at any rider who came within range and some may have had bows or slings, and the enemy's javelins could be returned. But it was mainly a matter of enduring the steady rain of missiles coming in from the circling squadrons intermittently and from all sides, probably including the rear. Skirmishers on foot, hoplite or light-armed, could make no effective contact with horsemen.

When the infantry had arrived and formed up behind their shield wall, the cavalry withdrew to breathe their horses and replenish javelins and arrows, waiting for the moment to attack again when the Hellene line broke. The massed archers now increased the pressure with a much steadier and heavier barrage of arrows. The range was probably about 40m; closer would have been in too easy reach of sorties. It seems that no attempt was made on foot to outflank or surround the Hellenes, possibly calculated avoidance of the risk of flanking columns themselves being attacked in the flank by their more heavily armed opponents. Mardonius was relying conventionally on a concentrated frontal bombardment of arrows to weaken and ultimately fracture the enemy formation, his men drawn up in

---

[1] Maybe, like his gloriously dead compatriots at Thermopylae, Arimnestus had already broken his spear and sword.

files of ten with the *sparabara* (shieldbearers) planting their *spara* (rectangular wicker shields) at the front.

Pausanias' formation was probably narrower and deeper than it had been on the Asopus ridge but could still have been 1,500–2,000m across, depending on file depth and the shape of the formation. This could have been a simple battle line several ranks deep with *psiloi* mingled or to the rear, or square or oblong with ranks of hoplites forming the perimeter and *psiloi* inside. The hoplites crouched, knelt or sat behind their shields (well visualized by Plutarch) as the arrows arced in. Their shields, body armour and helmets were generally proof against the light Asian arrows, but they could find their way through a helmet slit or a weak point in a *thorax*, or into an exposed neck, arm or leg; an incapacitating wound would serve the enemy just as well as a lethal hit. Herodotus describes one such casualty, Callicrates, 'who was wounded in the side by an arrow as he sat in his position while Pausanias was conducting the sacrifices' (9.72). Light-armed troops huddled close amongst the hoplites and did what they could to protect themselves with their hide or wicker shields, if they had them, but must have suffered more than their heavy-armed superiors.

Sacrifice before battle was taken particularly seriously by the Spartans, and the signs from successive victims' entrails were unfavourable, but Herodotus makes it clear that it was Pausanias' intention to counter-attack, not simply defend his new position. He and probably Tisamenus, his seer, were assessing the tactical situation as coolly as they interpreted the messages from the gods. Piety and prayer, command and rational decision-making were not mutually exclusive. The Tegeans may have been carrying out their own sacrifices with an earlier positive result, or perhaps they could no longer contain themselves. In any case, it was a happy coincidence that the signs changed for the Lacedaemonians as the Tegeans began their advance, and probably more than a coincidence that the delay ultimately worked in the Hellenes' favour by allowing time for the other Barbarian contingents to crowd in behind the Persians. Their involvement may not have been spontaneous. Mardonius may have wanted to bring all his available strength to bear in order to destroy Pausanias' division totally and as quickly as possible. But, fatally, the resulting congestion denied him the potential advantage of greater mobility and numerical superiority, mirroring the failure of the Persian fleet at Salamis.

It made tactical as well as religious sense for Pausanias to hold off attacking as he did. When that moment came, neither Herodotus' nor Plutarch's language suggests a running charge. There would have been a short period in which both Barbarians and Hellenes could skirmish forward out of the ranks. Some of the Hellenes named and honoured after the battle for their individual excellence may have distinguished themselves at this point as *promachoi*, fighting out in front of the battle line.

Aristophanes' lines for his chorus of Athenian 'wasps', veterans of Marathon, treat the decisive advantage of the Greeks over the Barbarians with dark humour:

> Then we chased after them, harpooning them through their pantaloons,
> And they ran for it, already stung around the jaws and eyebrows.
> (*Wasps* 1087–88)

Persians, standing up to hoplites without the protection of a helmet or heavy shield, would have sustained terrible facial, head and upper-body wounds from spear thrusts. And amongst the rank and file probably only the elite troops with Mardonius wore body armour of any kind. The word *thunnazontes* translated as 'harpooning' more literally means 'spearing tuna' and recalls Aeschylus' graphic description of the scene at the end of the battle of Salamis:

> The Greeks, like fishermen netting tuna or a haul of fish,
> Skewered and battered the Barbarians with broken timbers and
> splintered oars.
> (*Persae* 425–26)

Herodotus and Plutarch note with admiration that the Barbarians put up strong and courageous resistance, in spite of the disadvantages which Herodotus so clearly highlights. In the specific sense used here *othismos* was an exclusive component of hoplite-on-hoplite warfare, and its occurrence in this less symmetrical confrontation of different tactical doctrines is testimony to the Persians' toughness as opponents. Plutarch diminishes Mardonius' death somewhat by adding the extra detail of the weapon used, just as he does in the case of Masistius on the first day of the battle. But Herodotus, setting aside his earlier depictions of character flaws and misjudgements, sums up Mardonius' passing, leading from the front as all great ancient commanders did, and dying his hero's death, in a tone that is both epic and tragic:

> And on that day, in accordance with the oracle,[1] due compensation was fully paid by Mardonius to the Spartans for the killing of Leonidas, and the most glorious[2] victory ever known was secured by Pausanias son of Cleombrotus son of Anaxandridas (I already named Pausanias' more distant ancestors when I gave the lineage of Leonidas, which is the same). Mardonius was killed by Arimnestus, a famous man in Sparta. In a war long after the Median affair[3] he led 300 men into battle against the entire army of Messenia at Stenyclerus and died there along with his 300. (9.64)

Diodorus Siculus gives a brief, alternative account of the battle which perversely weaves distinct echoes of Herodotus into a reconstruction that is almost completely at odds with the tactical detail of his narrative:

> Discovering that the enemy army was heading for Boeotia, Mardonius advanced from Thebes and, when he reached the River Asopus he set up a camp, which he fortified with a deep ditch and a wooden palisade. The Hellenes totalled close to 100,000 men, the Barbarians some 500,000. The Barbarians were first to engage, swarming out against the Hellenes at night[4] and mounting an assault on their camp with all their cavalry. The Athenians quickly spotted this, formed themselves up and boldly confronted them, and there was

---

[1] This was the previous year's instruction from Delphi that the Spartans seek reparation for the killing of Leonidas and its mention here gives Herodotus a second chance to enjoy the irony of Xerxes' jeering response that Mardonius 'will pay the Spartans the compensation they are owed'.

[2] *Kalliste* (the superlative of *kalos*) could equally well be translated as the finest, fairest, most beautiful, most noble, most proper; most glorious seems to cover the range best.

[3] This was the Third Messenian War or Helot Revolt of 464–55. One can sense Herodotus' regret as he records the deaths of heroes of 'the Median affair' in parochial Hellene wars.

[4] Ephorus, Diodorus' main source, liked his battles fought at night.

a tremendous battle. Finally, the rest of the Hellenes drove off the Barbarians they were up against, except for the Megarians. They were facing the Persian cavalry commander and the best of their cavalry and were very hard-pressed, though they did not abandon their position. They sent messengers to the Athenians and Lacedaemonians calling on them to send support as quickly as possible. Aristides swiftly dispatched the picked Athenians who were with him. They fell upon the Barbarians in close formation and rescued the Megarians from the danger they were in, slaying the Persian commander and many more, and putting the rest to flight.

Having brilliantly displayed their superiority in the opening act of this drama, the Hellenes grew confident that they could win an outright victory, so, next, they moved their camp down from the foot-hills to a new position. This offered better prospects of total victory because they had a high hill to their right[1] and the River Asopus to their left, and their camp was in the space between, protected by the natural fortifications of the terrain. The Hellenes' tactics were clever. The narrowness of the space was very much to their advantage, since the Barbarians could not extend their battle line to its full breadth and so, as it turned out, were not able to exploit their many myriads of troops. This made the men with Pausanias and Aristides feel secure and they went forward, formed up in a way that made the best use of the terrain, and advanced upon the enemy.[2]

Mardonius was forced to increase the depth of his battle line. He put the men into the best formation possible, shouted out the command and led the advance on the Hellenes. He led the attack with his best soldiers around him, driving into the Lacedaemonians who faced him, and fought most gallantly, slaying many Hellenes. However, the Lacedaemonians resisted stoutly and faced up to the dangers of battle with great spirit so that many Barbarians were slaughtered.

[1] Presumably the Asopus ridge, if Diodorus had any feature specifically in mind. But he may have confused one of the tributaries running north with the Asopus itself, which runs from west to east.

[2] It would not have made sense to take up this position and then advance beyond the flank cover provided by the ridge. If Ephorus envisaged the Hellenes facing east with the Asopus on their left, the Persians could have crossed the river unopposed to the west and attacked their rear.

As long as Mardonius and his picked men were in the thick of the fighting, the Barbarians bore up under the pressure courageously, but when Mardonius fell, fighting hard, and a number of his picked men were killed or wounded, their courage failed them and they turned and ran. (*Library of History* 11.30–31)

Diodorus is offering an explanation of this unlikely victory in the face of odds of five-to-one (based on the false premise that these were the odds) and, more interestingly, he explicitly praises the Hellenes' and, by implication, Pausanias' clever planning to bring it about. Herodotus presents Pausanias' management of the decisive confrontation as spontaneous and opportunistic, but he is unequivocal in his praise for Pausanias' triumph as 'the most glorious victory ever known' and displays none of the caution with which he hedges his praise of Themistocles as the architect of the previous year's successful defence. He rightly credits Pausanias and the Spartans with winning the war at Plataea and does not allow the conflicts and enmities of the decades that followed to cloud this statement. Thucydides speaks of Pausanias as 'held in high honour by the Hellenes on account of his leadership at Plataea' and later refers to him as 'the Lacedaemonian, Pausanias son of Cleombrotus, who liberated Hellas from the Medes alongside those Hellenes who were willing to share in the risk of the battle that was fought near here [Plataea]' (2.71). The latter is from a speech put by Thucydides into the mouth of a Plataean envoy pleading with the Spartans not to attack their city in 429. The wording of the speech may have been invented, but this sentiment rings true.

Mardonius had indeed paid the price, but the battle was not yet over:

Back to the fighting: the Persians who had been routed by the Lacedaemonians fled in disorder to their camp and the shelter of the wooden wall[1] which they had built on Theban ground. By the way, I was astonished to discover that although the battle was fought next to the grove of Demeter, there was no sign that any

---

[1] The several repetitions of 'wooden wall' seem to be conscious echoes of the oracle on which Themistocles successfully based the previous year's naval strategy.

Persian had entered the sacred precinct or died within it, and most of them fell in the unconsecrated ground outside. In my view, if one may hold a view on the business of the divine, the goddess herself kept them from entering, because they had burnt down her shrine at Eleusis.[1] Anyway, this is what happened in that part of the battle.

Artabazus son of Pharnaces had been unhappy all along that Mardonius had been left behind by the King and that, for all the advice he had given up to this point, he had failed in his many attempts to stop him giving battle. This is what he did in his displeasure at Mardonius' actions. He was in command of a substantial force of nearly 40,000[2] men and as soon as the battle began he could clearly see what was going to happen. So, he led them off in good formation, ordering them to follow him no matter in which direction he led them and to keep up with the pace he set. He gave these orders as if he was leading them into battle. But when he was further up the road, he could see that the Persians had indeed been routed. Then, no longer keeping his men formed up, he wheeled around and ran flat out, not to the wooden fort or the walls of Thebes, but to Phocis with the aim of reaching the Hellespont as quickly as possible. So that is where those men went. Meanwhile the Boeotians who had been defeated by the Athenians fled to Thebes. The Persians, and the whole mob of the rest of their allies who had played no significant part in the battle and achieved nothing of any note, fled to their fort. All this makes it plain to me how totally dependent the Barbarians were on the Persians, because those who ran away before they had even engaged with the enemy did so when they saw that the Persians were falling back. So, they all fled except for the cavalry, the Boeotian cavalry in particular, who covered the withdrawal by keeping close to the enemy and shielding their comrades as they fled before the Hellenes. (9.65–68)

---

[1] This is not previously mentioned by Herodotus but could have taken place in 480 before Salamis or in 479 when Mardonius sent a force as far west as Megara before falling back into Boeotia after burning Athens.

[2] According to Herodotus, after Salamis he had taken 60,000 of the men selected by Mardonius and escorted Xerxes. If the 40,000 represent the same command, some may have continued with Xerxes or been left behind to keep Chalcidice subdued, and some may have been lost in action.

When the Persians gave way, the other Barbarian contingents followed suit. Herodotus' language suggests that some of these had been involved in the fighting, but that none had distinguished themselves. It was not an absolute rout, however. Herodotus records that the cavalry, Hellene with better effect than Barbarian, became involved again and screened the retreating infantry, and that Artabazus succeeded in extracting a significant contingent, most likely Persians or Medes. There were probably a good many fewer than 40,000 of them, but they could have represented a significant proportion of the actual strength that Mardonius began with. Herodotus tells an unlikely story that Artabazus led the march at such a pace that he kept ahead of news of the Hellene victory at least as far as Thessaly, where he was well received, though he may have made his hosts believe that Mardonius would be passing through soon with a larger force. He concludes the episode more plausibly:

He led his men swiftly through Thessaly and Macedonia taking the most direct inland route to Thrace, and so reached Byzantium.[1] He left many behind, cut down by the Thracians or laid low by hunger and exhaustion. He made the crossing from Byzantium by boat and this is how Artabazus made his way home to Asia. (9.89)

Artabazus, the wise and cautious veteran, presented previously as disapproving of Mardonius' more aggressive strategies, survived and it seems that his reputation did not suffer as a result of this action. He may actually have been credited with salvaging something from the disaster. It had not been fully played out when he made his exit:

The Hellenes now had the upper hand and were going after Xerxes' men, hunting them down and slaughtering them. As the rout gathered momentum word came to those who had taken up position by the sanctuary of Hera[2] and stayed away from the fighting that a battle was being fought and that Pausanias and his men were

---

[1] By the time he reached Thrace the Hellenes were besieging Sestos and well placed to prevent him crossing the Hellespont into Asia.
[2] This was outside the walls of Plataea, where the centre division had ended up during the night.

winning it. When they heard this, they set off without forming up in any order. The Corinthians and those who were alongside them kept to the foothills of the mountain and followed the road that led straight up to the shrine of Demeter; the Megarians and Phleiasians made their way over the flattest ground across the plain. However, as the Megarians and Phleiasians got closer to the enemy, the Theban cavalry under the command of Asopodorus son of Timander[1] saw that they were pressing forward in disorder and charged them, and in this action they rode down 600 of them and scattered the rest and drove them back to Cithaeron. So those men died with nothing to show for it. But when the Persians and the mob of the rest of them had made it inside their wooden wall, they got up into the towers before the Lacedaemonians arrived and did their best to strengthen their defences, and, when the Lacedaemonians did arrive, the contest was keenly fought. But, until the Athenians came up, the Barbarians mounted a strong defence and had much the better of the Lacedaemonians, who had no understanding of siege warfare.[2] However, when the Athenians had arrived, the fighting became heavier and went on that way for a long time. But, finally, the Athenians' bravery and perseverance prevailed and they scaled the wall and made a breach, which the Hellenes then streamed through. The Tegeans were first in and they were able to plunder Mardonius' tent, taking everything including his horses' manger, which was made entirely of bronze. The Tegeans set it up as a thank-offering in their temple of Athena Alea and it is well worth seeing; they handed over everything else to be shared out amongst all of the Hellenes. Anyway, when the stockade was breached, the Barbarians fell apart and lost any will to resist, such was the terror and despair that seized the tens of thousands of them that were squeezed into this tight place. (9.69–70)

Word of the action being fought to their right would have reached the contingents drawn up outside Plataea's walls before the rout began, and

[1] This may be the same Asopodorus, 'gift of the Asopus', celebrated by the poet Pindar for his victory in the chariot race at the Isthmian Games.

[2] In the course of their annual invasions of Attica in the Peloponnesian War the Spartans made no attempt to breach the walls of Athens.

the Corinthians and whichever other contingents went with them set off to the east in the right direction to join in; but, if they linked up with the Lacedaemonians and Tegeans at all, this seems to have been after the main work had been done. The Megarians and Phleiasians, and probably others, went north down onto the plain, perhaps aiming to pass through the gap between the Pyrgos and Asopus ridges and to follow the victorious Athenians over the river. In the original battle plan the Megarians were positioned just to the right of the Plataeans and Athenians, and the Phleiasians were close to the centre, confirming to some extent that these Hellenes advanced 'without forming up in any order'. The Theban cavalry killed 600 of them, a heavy casualty rate if only the 3,000 Megarians and 1,000 Phleiasians were involved, and an indication of the damage they could have done if they had been there in support of the Boeotian infantry, and been able to catch the Athenians on the move and in open order.

The 'wooden wall' of the Persian camp was clearly quite elaborate with look-out towers at intervals around the perimeter. However, there would have been little time to strengthen it before the Hellenes arrived beyond, perhaps, reinforcing gates with extra timbers and raising parapets by attaching shields to them. Herodotus credits the Athenians with finally scaling and breaching the wall but here he may again, for Athenian ears, be offsetting his unqualified praise of the Spartans' victory. In Herodotus' view, siege warfare was not of much interest to the Spartans. However, at this time, the Athenians could not claim superior expertise, though they were to acquire it in the decades that followed, albeit achieving their successes through long drawn-out blockades rather than assault. In any case, the first breach, or a simultaneous one, was made by the Tegeans, so honours were shared. But the Athenians' archers may well have made an important, if not decisive contribution by supporting the scaling and breaching parties with covering fire, and their several thousand hoplites and *psiloi* were a significant reinforcement, even if they did not supply the tactical expertise that was lacking. Aeschylus' description of the much more modest massacre on the island of Psyttaleia at the end of the battle of Salamis would have reminded many of this bloody final act at Plataea. The Hellenes had again been 'given glory', and for the Barbarians being trapped in a fort was much the same as being trapped on an island.

Herodotus sums up each side's casualties very briefly:

Such was the slaughter that the Hellenes left scarcely 3,000 alive out of the 260,000 that remained after Artabazus had escaped with his 40,000. Ninety-one Lacedaemonians, all Spartans, 17 Tegeans and 52 Athenians made up the total of Hellene dead in this engagement. (9.70)

Plutarch has a little more to say on the subject and on the issue of Herodotus' account of Hellene involvement generally:

Just 40,000 Barbarians out of the original 300,000 are said to have escaped with Artabazus. On the Hellene side a total of 1,360 fell. Fifty-two of these were Athenians and, according to Cleidemus,[1] they were all from Aeantis, the tribe that fought most bravely; 91 were Lacedaemonians, and 16 were Tegeans. I am astounded by Herodotus' statement that these were the only Hellene contingents that actually engaged the enemy and that none of the rest did. The multitude that fell and the monuments that were set up are clear evidence that this success was shared by all. Besides, if only three cities had done the fighting while the rest sat idly by, these words would not have been inscribed on the altar they built:

> In this place, the Hellenes, triumphing in Ares' toil,
> Routed the Persians and, for his deliverance of Hellas,
> Together dedicated this altar to Zeus Deliverer.
> (*Aristides* 19)

Three thousand may be a reasonably accurate number for the Barbarians who survived and were taken prisoner by the Hellenes on the final day. They were distributed as slaves and an important part of the spoils, and would have been counted. But 257,000 by Herodotus' arithmetic, even adjusted for casualties inflicted earlier in the day and throughout the battle, would have been an impossible feat of butchery. Perhaps several thousand were left to fall back on the fort but many probably kept on running, with the Hellenes at their heels and the choked gateways to

---

[1] A 4th-century Athenian historian.

the fort ahead of them. Some, including especially the intact Barbarian cavalry, could have joined up with Artabazus' contingent and this might have been the moment he organized his exit. Certainly, disorganized stragglers would have stood very little chance of making it back to Asia through expanses of now hostile territory and so would sooner or later have increased the body count or been captured. Even so, Persian losses inside the fort would have been very heavy; upward of 10,000 is conceivable, though nobody would have counted the corpses. These would have been thrown into a mass grave, as at Marathon, but, after so many centuries of alluvial and agricultural activity, no remains have been found to locate this.

Total Hellene casualties were undoubtedly much lighter but would have significantly exceeded Herodotus' modest yet meticulously itemized tally, and by 'this engagement' he may mean only the storming of the stockade. For a start, he excludes the round 600 he gives as the number from the central division cut down by the Theban cavalry. Plutarch repeats Herodotus' figures for the Athenian, Lacedaemonian and Tegean dead (one short in the case of the last) but offers an overall total of 1,360, which still seems low. The cost to the Hellenes of the heavy fighting between the Athenians and the Boeotians was surely greater than 52 and not from only one of the ten tribes, though Aeantis may have taken the most casualties, if they were at the point where the two columns collided and perhaps fought with the Theban elite unit. A possible explanation for this particularly low number is that Herodotus or his source counted only the Aeantis names inscribed on the gravestones on the battlefield. Again, a total of 107 or 108 Lacedaemonian and Tegean dead is not consistent with the intensity and duration of the fighting as described in the decisive confrontation or subsequently at the fort. Here, a separate count of fatalities amongst the *perioikoi* may also have been omitted, and dead *psiloi* were probably not counted at all.

Looking at the battle as a whole, there must have been Hellene casualties in the opening clash at the base of Cithaeron and during the days of attrition that followed. Subsequent deaths from wounds should be factored in as well. Non-hoplite casualties seem not to have been considered worthy of record. Barbarian javelins and arrows in the clashes on the first and last days, repeated harassment by mounted archers in between, and the successful Persian attack on the Greek supply train may have accounted for a significantly higher tally in the more vulnerable ranks of the Helots and other *psiloi* and support personnel than amongst the hoplites. A total Hellene body count in the low thousands is therefore probably a realistic estimate. Barbarian losses were probably between five and ten times greater.

Plutarch is over-sensitive on behalf of all the Hellenes he considers to have been slandered by Herodotus and is especially protective of the reputation of the Corinthians (and also of his ancestors the Boeotians, who sided with Persia) in *On the Malice of Herodotus*. However most of his charges can be dismissed by means of a less selective and biased reading of the *Historia* than Plutarch's against the backdrop of a much-changed Hellas torn by the Peloponnesian War and with Herodotus' own caveats in mind. Omissions that caused offence could generally be attributed to lack of information on the subject (not always an inhibition as far as Plutarch was concerned) or to editorial economy.

On the Barbarian side, the Persian infantry and the Sacae cavalry fought best and Mardonius was named[1] as the most outstanding individual fighter. For the Hellenes, the Tegeans and Athenians did very well, but the Lacedaemonians were best of all. I make this assertion, having considered all of the Hellenes who prevailed over the enemy that faced them, solely on the grounds that it was the Lacedaemonians who fought and overcame the strongest opposition.

In my opinion, the bravest individual Hellene by far was Aristodemus who had borne the shame and dishonour of being the sole survivor of the 300 at Thermopylae. Next best were Posidonius, Philocyon, and Amompharetus, all Spartans. However, the Spartans who took part in the general debate to determine who had been bravest of all were of the view that Aristodemus wished to die a spectacular death to free himself from the guilt laid upon him and so was actually berserk[2] when he charged out in front of the line and did

[1] By the Hellenes presumably.
[2] The word Herodotus uses here is used by Homer in the *Iliad* for the battle-frenzy that possessed Hector and Achilles, 'eager to win glory'.

his great deeds. But Posidonius also proved his worth and he had no wish to die, and that made him the better man. The Spartans may have just said this out of spite, but all the individuals I name who died in that battle were specially honoured, except for Aristodemus. He wished to die because of his guilt as I have described, so he was not honoured in this way. These were the men who won the highest renown of all who fought at Plataea. Callicrates, the most handsome man in the army, not only amongst the Lacedaemonians but amongst all of the Hellenes, died away from the fighting. He was sitting on the ground in his position while Pausanias was offering the sacrifices and was hit in the side by an arrow. The rest had gone into battle when he was carried from the field grappling with death, and he told Arimnestus, a Plataean,[1] that he had no regrets that he was dying for Hellas. But it grieved him that he had not been able to strike a blow or achieve anything worthy of his reputation, for all his eagerness to do so.

Sophanes from the deme of Decelea was said to be the Athenian who fought best and there are two different stories about him. In one he was armed with an iron anchor which was attached to the belt of his armour with a bronze chain. He would drop anchor whenever he closed with the enemy to prevent them dislodging him when they charged out from their line, and when they were beaten back his tactic was to lift anchor so that he could give chase, so that story has it. According to the other story, which contradicts the first, he had an anchor painted on his shield, which he constantly swung around and never held still; the anchor was not fastened to his armour. Sophanes was famous for another great deed he had done. When the Athenians were at war with Aegina,[2] he challenged and killed the Argive Eurybates, a pentathlon victor. Long after all this, he met his death at Datus where he served with distinction

---

[1] At this point the Plataeans were elsewhere on the battlefield, very probably with the Athenians, so Callicrates may have hung on for at least the rest of the day.

[2] This probably took place at some point between 490 and 480. Athens and Aegina were at war with each other, on and off, from about 505 for 50 years until Aegina was finally forced to join the Athenian Empire. The Aeginetans had submitted earth and water to Darius in 491, but they fought alongside the Athenians at Artemisium, Salamis and Plataea, and probably Mycale too.

sharing command of the Athenians with Leagrus son of Glaucon.
He was killed by the Edonians in a battle for the gold-mines there.[1]
(9.71–75)

Not surprisingly, Herodotus singles out the Lacedaemonians,
including the *perioikoi* presumably, as the Hellenes who fought
best. But perhaps his bracketing of the Tegeans with the Athenians
as second best and his omission of the Plataeans, if they fought
alongside the Athenians that day, are less than generous. And all
26 named contingents deserve great credit for their endurance of
increasingly difficult conditions and their solidarity over the ten-day
confrontation. On the Barbarian side, Herodotus' respect, even
admiration for the Persians who put up such a good fight is well
justified by the preceding narrative, but he does not mention any
action specifically involving the Sacae cavalry.

In Herodotus' more detailed review of individual *aristeia* (valour)
Mardonius, not surprisingly, is the only Barbarian named. For the
Hellenes, he names four Spartans, three of them picked out in
the semi-formal process by which these honours were collectively
agreed. He had already dealt with the disgrace and mentioned the
future redemption of Aristodemus, in his account of Thermopylae.
The choice of Amompharetus, 'mettlesome and daring' in Plutarch's
eyes, strongly suggests that there may have been a more orderly
explanation for his actions than blow-hard principles. Nothing
else is known of Posidonius and Philocyon. Herodotus adds the
information that all four died in the battle quite obliquely; their
aristeia is immortal.

There are suggestions here of a tactical code that allowed the most
capable hoplites to fight and excel individually out in front of the
battle line. Callicrates was clearly a warrior who was well known to
have distinguished himself in the past and had come to Plataea with
high expectations. His dying words of regret that 'he had not been
able to strike a blow or achieve anything worthy of his reputation'
are a succinct expression of the general ethos of warrior excellence
that the foremost hoplites aspired to. The double anecdote about the

---

[1] This took place in the 460s, if, as is probable, it was in the course of a disastrous attempt
referred to by Thucydides to establish an Athenian settlement on the River Strymon.

Athenian Sophanes depicts single combat and his shield-play, if not his mythical anchor-play, also indicates a high degree of skill. Aristodemus, who was evidently given a front-rank position despite his 'Trembler' or 'Runaway' status, was not faulted for charging out on his own but for the uncontrolled spirit in which he did it. John Milton, who knew his Thucydides, perfectly captures the code Aristodemus had breached in his visualization of Satan's angel phalanx, while giving a powerful sense of what it would have been like to face thousands of Spartan hoplites in battle:

> A forest huge of spears: and thronging helms
> Appeared, and serried shields in thick array
> Of depth immeasurable: Anon they move
> In perfect phalanx to the Dorian mood
> Of flutes and soft recorders;[1] such as raised
> To height of noblest temper heroes old
> Arming to battle, and in stead of rage
> Deliberate valour breathed, firm and unmoved
> With dread of death to flight or foul retreat,
> Nor wanting power to mitigate and swage
> With solemn touches, troubled thoughts, and chase
> Anguish and doubt and fear and sorrow and pain
> From mortal or immortal minds. Thus they
> Breathing united force with fixed thought
> Moved on in silence to soft pipes that charmed
> Their painful steps over the burnt soil; and now
> Advanced in view, they stand, a horrid front
> Of dreadful length and dazzling arms, in guise
> Of warriors old with ordered spear and shield,
> Awaiting what command their mighty chief
> Had to impose ...
> (*Paradise Lost* 1 547–67)

The Mantineans arrived when the battle was all over, and when they found out that they were too late to fight they declared they

---

[1] The *aulos* 'pipe' actually gave a strident, reedy sound, but Milton can be forgiven this minor error.

should pay a price for this terrible failure. When they learned that the Medes with Artabazus were making their escape, they wanted to pursue them as far as Thessaly, but the Lacedaemonians would not allow them to go off in pursuit. On their return home, the Mantineans exiled the commanders of their army. The Eleans arrived later and went away as distressed as the Mantineans and they too banished their leaders. That's how it was according to the Eleans and Mantineans. (9.77)

Herodotus has already mentioned latecomers joining the Hellene army in the course of the confrontation but not named them, and it is a reasonable assumption that they joined up with national contingents already there. The Mantineans had previously shown their commitment by sending 500 hoplites to Thermopylae, a number exceeded only by the Tegeans and the Arcadians. However, the Eleans' only recorded previous involvement was helping with the building of the wall at the Isthmus, possible evidence of reluctance to campaign outside the Peloponnese. Nonetheless, they are listed on the Serpent Column, but the Mantineans are not.

Herodotus presents Pausanias as a noble victor in two stories. In the first he has an encounter with a Hellene woman who had been captured by the Persians and made a concubine, and he treats her with great gallantry. In the second, a leading Aeginetan called Lampon congratulates him fulsomely on his 'outstandingly great and glorious achievement' and urges him to treat Mardonius' corpse in the same way as Xerxes treated Leonidas'. Pausanias is not persuaded:

'First you praise me, my fatherland and my achievement to the skies, but then you belittle me by suggesting that I defile a corpse and by telling me that I shall be praised even more highly for doing this. That would be a normal act for a Barbarian but not for a Hellene, and we despise Barbarians for doing such things.[1] As for your demand that I avenge Leonidas in this way, I say that he has been mightily avenged. The price has been paid for him and all the others who fell at Thermopylae in the numberless souls of those slain in

---

[1] Impalement and dismemberment of the dead and the living was common practice in ancient Persia as punishment for crimes such as treason.

this place. As for you, do not ever come near me again to make such a suggestion or to try and give me any advice; just be grateful that no harm has been done to you!' On hearing this Lampon took himself off.

Pausanias had the heralds proclaim that no one should touch any of the spoils and ordered the Helots to gather everything together in one place. When this had been done, the Hellenes put a tenth aside for dedication to the god of Delphi; with this they set up the golden tripod resting on the bronze triple-headed serpent[1] that stands next to the altar. A tenth they put aside for dedication to the god of Olympia, and with this they set up a figure of Zeus cast in bronze and 10 cubits [4.5m] tall. And they put aside a tenth of the spoils for the god of the Isthmus, with which they set up a bronze figure of Poseidon 7 cubits tall. When they had set aside these amounts, they divided up what remained, and all received their due share of the Persians' women, gold and silver, and all the rest of the spoils, and also the draught animals. There is no record of the share allocated to those who had fought best at Plataea, but I think that they would have been rewarded.[2] Indeed, Pausanias received a tenfold share of the women, horses, bullion, camels and all the rest.

It is said that Xerxes left behind all his campaign gear with Mardonius when he fled from Greece. The story goes that when Pausanias saw Mardonius' quarters decked out with gold and silver and brightly coloured fabrics, he ordered the pastrycooks and the chefs to prepare a dinner just as they would for Mardonius. They did as they were told and Pausanias was astonished by the sight of the gold and silver couches with their rich coverings and the gold and silver tables, and by the sheer magnificence of the banquet and all the good things set before him. So, as a joke, he ordered his own servants to prepare a Laconian dinner. When that very different banquet was served, Pausanias burst out laughing and sent for the Hellene commanders. When they had gathered, Pausanias pointed to the two dinners laid out before them and said, 'Men of Hellas, I have called you together because I want to show you the folly of the Medes'

---

[1] The Serpent Column.
[2] Perhaps the dead heroes' shares went to their families.

leader. This was the style in which he lived, yet he came here to rob us of our pitiful rations.' This is what Pausanias said to the Hellene commanders, so that story goes. (9.79–82)

It is well documented that the Great Kings went on campaign with all the immense luxuries of home and that their commanders and elite troops did not travel light. The size and richness of the monuments made from the tenth shares set aside for the three gods are evidence of the massive value of the spoils won by the Hellenes, and also of their piety. This is not invention on the part of Herodotus or his sources to highlight the contrast between Hellene and Barbarian ways of life and values. However, the double feast probably is. Even if the supplies, furnishings and kitchen equipment were intact after the looting of the camp, it is even less likely that the cooks and other staff were still at their posts. But it is an excellent story. Months later as Pausanias began his rapid fall from grace, Thucydides remarks that, amongst other Barbarian behaviours, 'he dined in the Persian way', and Herodotus' audiences probably enjoyed that irony as much as he did himself.

When the Hellenes had divided the spoils at Plataea, each contingent buried its dead in a separate place. The Lacedaemonians made three tombs: in the first they buried the Spartans,[1] including Posidonius, Amompharetus, Philocyon, and Callicrates. In the second they buried the rest of the Lacedaemonians[2] and in the third they buried the Helots;[3] that is how the Lacedaemonians buried their dead. The Tegeans dug a separate mass grave. So did the Athenians, and also the Megarians and Phleiasians for those who had been killed by the cavalry. There were bodies in all of these tombs but, as far as I know, the rest of the tombs that can be seen at Plataea are just empty mounds built for the benefit of

---

[1] All the manuscripts have the word *eiren* here, a word otherwise found in much later sources and thought to mean a young Spartiate aged 20–29. But there must have been casualties older than this, the high-ranking Amompharetus for one.

[2] All the manuscripts have 'the rest of the Spartans', but 'Lacedaemonians' or indeed '*perioikoi*' makes better sense and the resulting arrangement reflects Lacedaemonian hierarchy well.

[3] This is the best evidence that the Helots fought. Camp-followers on the winning side seldom suffer casualties.

future generations by people who were ashamed that they took no part in the battle. Indeed, there is one known as the tomb of the Aeginetans, which, I am told, was built as much as ten years after the battle at their request by their Plataean representative, Cleades son of Autodicus. (9.85)

It is hard to deny that there is some prejudice here. On the last day, several, even a majority of the Hellene contingents, may have had no contact with the enemy, except perhaps in the final looting of their camp, and taken no casualties, but it is unlikely that any contingent went through the battle without some loss. However, the Aeginetans are the most misrepresented. Herodotus records their involvement in three of the war's battles, Artemisium, Salamis and Plataea and details their exceptional contribution to the victory at Salamis, but he belittles them here, in the story about Lampon and with an allegation that they made themselves wealthy by cheating the Helots who had collected up the spoils at Plataea. However, the Aeginetans were enemies of Athens before and after the Persian War and Herodotus' attitude to them would have played well with Athenian audiences. There is nothing on the burial of the Barbarian dead beyond speculation about what happened to the trophy corpse:

Mardonius' body disappeared the day after the battle, but I am quite unable to say who took it, though I've been told of many places in which he may have been buried, and of many people who might have done this. (9.84)

Pausanias' travel guide has only a few lines on the battlefield:

On the right of the highway there is a memorial[1] which is said to be for Mardonius, but it is generally agreed that his body went missing immediately after the battle and there is no agreement as to who actually buried it ... The graves of those who fought against the Persians are near the point where the road enters Plataean territory. The Hellenes other than the Lacedaemonians and the Athenians have a shared memorial. The Lacedaemonians and Athenians who

---

[1] The word used here, *mnema*, can mean 'monument' or 'burial mound'.

fell have their own graves on which are inscribed elegiac verses by Simonides. Not far from the communal tomb of the Hellenes there is an altar of Zeus, God of Freedom. Even now[1] they hold the Freedom Games there every four years. Great prizes are offered for running and the competitors race in armour before the altar. The trophy which the Hellenes set up for the battle of Plataea stands about 15 *stades* [3km] from the city. (*Guide to Greece* 9.2)

Pausanias appears to have been considerably less interested in this battlefield than he was in Marathon. But by his time, many of the graves and memorials would have faded into the landscape. The greatest pity is that he could not be more informative about the location of the Hellene trophy because, if he had identified it correctly, that could have pinpointed the climax of this history-making engagement somewhere in the rolling foothills of Cithaeron.

There was still some unfinished business:

As soon as they had buried their dead, the Hellenes conferred and decided to march against Thebes and demand that those responsible for the city's medism be handed over. Most of all they wanted Timagenides and Attaginus,[2] who had been the ringleaders amongst their foremost citizens. If these men were not given up, they said they would not abandon the siege until they had taken the city. Having made their decision, they came to Thebes ten days after the battle and laid siege to it, and demanded the surrender of these men. When the Thebans refused to give them up, the Hellenes laid waste their land and attacked their walls and carried on harassing them. When almost three weeks[3] had passed, Timagenides made this speech to the Thebans: 'Citizens of Thebes, since the Hellenes have made up their minds not to raise the siege till our city is taken or we are handed over to them, do not let the land of Boeotia suffer any more on our account. If it is actually money they want and their demand for our surrender is just a cover for this, let us give them cash from

---

[1] In the 2nd century AD.

[2] Herodotus credits Timagenides earlier with advising Mardonius to cut off the Hellenes' supplies and Attaginus welcomed Mardonius to Boeotia with a great banquet.

[3] Probably including the ten days between the battle and the start of the siege.

public funds, because the decision to medize was a collective one, not our decision alone.[1] However, if the Hellenes are besieging the city because they really want us, then we will give ourselves up to face their charges.'

This seemed a most welcome and timely suggestion to the Thebans and they immediately sent a herald to Pausanias with an offer to hand over the men, and agreement was reached on these terms. However, Attaginus managed to escape from the town. His sons were brought before Pausanias, but he acquitted them of the charge, declaring that they had no responsibility for the city's medism. As for the rest of the individuals that the Thebans handed over, they expected to be given a chance to defend themselves and were confident that they could buy their release. Pausanias suspected as much and, when they had been handed over to him, he disbanded the whole allied army, took the men to Corinth and put them to death there.

So that is what happened at Plataea and Thebes. (9.86–88)

Thebes was a large and powerful city, clearly more strongly fortified than the Barbarian camp and the Thebans were well able to defend themselves despite their setback at the hands of the Athenians. Moreover, the Hellene Alliance probably did not have much enthusiasm for further fighting, especially against brother Hellenes. Wasting the city's farms, fields, orchards and vineyards was a much lower-risk strategy and proved to be just as effective. Pausanias' moderation is again displayed in his magnanimity towards Attaginus' sons, but there is more than a hint of autocratic behaviour in his disposal of the prisoners after disbanding the army. A year later he was to be ousted as commander-in-chief because he had begun 'acting more like a tyrant than a general', and in two decades' time Thebes was fighting on the side of the Spartans against Athens and her allies.

Aeschylus supplies a powerful postscript. The Chorus in the *Persae* laments Xerxes' folly in 'causing the destruction of his people

---

[1] The decision may have been collectively taken, but the commitment of Theban troops to the defence of Thermopylae indicates that it was not unanimous or even a majority vote, and Herodotus indicates that it was driven through undemocratically by a powerful few, whether or not they were a formal oligarchy. In the end the Thebans seemed quite pleased to hand these 'ringleaders' over.

by senseless and ruinous wars' and calls up the ghost of his father Darius, 'who was named Divine Counsellor ... since he guided his people well'. Darius emerges from his tomb and his first reaction is to ask, 'did some mental sickness possess my son?' Then, overlooking Marathon and the near-disaster of his Scythian expedition, he declares 'I never brought such calamity on this city'. The Chorus seeks his advice:

Chorus After this, what can the Persian people do for the best?
Darius Best not to go to war on Hellenes in their land,
Not even if the Median army outnumbers theirs.
The very land becomes their ally.
Chorus What do you mean? How can the land be their ally?
Darius It starves to death an over-mighty army.
Chorus But we have sent a well-equipped and hand-picked force.
Darius There will be no safe homecoming for those men.
Not even that army left behind in the land of Hellas!
Chorus How can you say that? Surely the whole Barbarian army
Will cross Helle's channel out of Europe?
Darius There will be scant survivors from so many,
If we are to believe in what the gods ordain
When we consider these events. It will all happen.
And if this is so, vain hopes drove Xerxes
To leave those chosen troops behind.
They are now waiting on the plain watered by Asopus' stream,
That generous feeder of Boeotia's soil.
There, utter disaster lies in wait for them,
Payment of the price of their impiety and godless thoughts.
For, when they reached the land of Hellas,
Without shame they ravaged sacred images and set temples ablaze.
Altars were smashed, holy shrines ripped from their foundations
And tumbled into shambles of shattered stone.
Such evil have they done, so great will be their suffering.
And more will follow; their river of pain is not dry, still it gushes.

> The Dorian spear[1] will make Plataea's soil a bloody swamp
> And heaped-up corpses will send to mortal men,
> Even the next three generations, this unvoiced message:
> You are mortal, do not think over-mighty thoughts.
> For, when *hubris*[2] has blossomed and ripened on the bough,
> It yields a bitter harvest of delusion.[3]
> (*Persae* 788–822)

Darius encapsulates the warnings given to Xerxes and Mardonius by Artabanus and Demaratus against underestimating the challenges to be faced by an army invading Greece, presented both by the nature of the terrain and by the quality of its hoplite defenders, especially the 'Dorian' Spartans. Then, in a few devastating lines, he explains how Xerxes and the Persians have brought upon themselves the tragic fate of all who offend the gods, a theme that comes to the surface of Herodotus' narrative from time to time and is seldom far beneath it.

Aeschylus' contemporary Simonides wrote about the war extensively and fragments survive of a grand elegy on the battle of Plataea. Opening lines liken its Hellene heroes, Pausanias 'the best' of them, to the epic heroes of the siege of Troy. Tantalizingly, there are a few words that suggest the Spartans set off on their march to the Isthmus with more public ceremony than recounted by Herodotus. And there are some lines that celebrate a more significant and glorious contribution on the part of the Corinthians, supporting Plutarch's argument that they are short-changed in the *Historia*. In spite of Herodotus' likely close familiarity with Simonides as a source and as a highly important figure in 5th-century literature, these were probably not the only points of historical detail over which the great lyric poet and 'the father of

---

[1] As wielded by the 'Dorian' Spartans above all. In later lines the naval victory is credited to the Ionian seamen and ships, meaning the Athenians above all.

[2] No one English word can embrace, as this Greek word does, the 'impiety and godless thoughts', the 'shameless' desecration of holy things and places, and the thinking of 'over-mighty thoughts' in defiance of the gods and fate that all combined to bring this disaster upon Persia.

[3] *Ate*: delusion leading to irrational behaviour, often thought to be caused by the gods. This 'mental sickness' was personified as Ate, a daughter of Zeus exiled from Olympus to punish mankind.

history' disagreed. But for both, Plataea was 'the most glorious victory ever known'. Without Thermopylae, Artemisium and Salamis and even, arguably, Marathon, this victory could not have been won. But, if it had been lost, Mardonius would have secured Hellas for the Great King and set the future on a different course. Plato recognizes the importance of the battle in his last dialogue, completed in 348, the year before he died:

Cretan It was the sea-battle at Salamis, fought by the Hellenes against the Barbarians that saved Hellas.

Athenian Yes, that is what most Hellenes and Barbarians say. But we say it was the land-battles at Marathon and Plataea that were the salvation of Hellas, the former setting it in train, the latter completing it. (*Laws* 707)

Freedom first and foremost

Mycale and Afterwards

Now on the very same day the Persians met with disaster at Plataea, it chanced that something very similar happened at Mycale in Ionia. When the Hellenes who had sailed with Leotychidas the Lacedaemonian had made their base at Delos, envoys arrived from Samos. The Samians had kept this mission secret from the Persians and from Theomestor son of Androdamas, whom the Persians had made tyrant of Samos. When they came before the generals, Hegesistratus son of Aristagoras,[1] one of these envoys, made a lengthy and tortuous speech. He said that the Ionians only needed sight of the Hellenes to be persuaded to defect from the Persians and that then the Barbarians would immediately abandon Ionia, but that, if the Barbarians stayed there, the Hellenes could find no easier prey. He begged them in the name of the gods they shared to deliver their fellow Hellenes from slavery and drive the Barbarians away, arguing that this could easily be brought about because the Persians' ships were in poor condition[2] and would be no match for the Hellenes'. He added that, if the Hellenes had any suspicion that the Samian envoys were luring them into a trap, they were quite prepared to be taken hostage and held on board their ships.

---

[1] Otherwise unknown, and not Aristagoras of Miletus.

[2] In need of drying out and maintenance after an extended period at sea and therefore 'heavy' and 'slow-sailing'. It is more likely that both Hellenes and Barbarians had dried out their ships over the winter.

In the middle of all this pleading, Leotychidas, either seeking some words of prophecy or perhaps even divinely inspired,[1] asked, 'What is your name, Samian stranger?' 'Hegesistratus,' he replied. Then Leotychidas cut short whatever else the man was launching into and said: 'I accept the good omen of your name,[2] Samian stranger. Before you, you must pledge Samian commitment to our alliance.' So he spoke and put them under oath, and the Samians gave their pledge and swore an oath that they would be allies of the Hellenes. Then they sailed off, but Leotychidas commanded Hegesistratus to stay with the Hellenes by reason of his auspicious name. The Hellenes remained where they were for the rest of that day and, next day, the omens from their sacrifices were good. (9.90–92)

The Samians succeeded where the Chians (and, two decades before, Aristagoras of Miletus) had failed, in spite of the meal Hegesistratus clearly made of their appeal. Leotychidas, persuaded by the intelligence of the condition of the Barbarians' ships and by the Samians' credible assurance of their own and other Ionians' readiness to revolt, saw his opportunity to eliminate the Persian fleet. His confidence was reinforced by the good omens, but not to the extent that he was willing to let Hegesistratus out of his sight.

Herodotus does not detail the Hellene order of battle. As at Salamis, Athens presumably supplied the largest element, perhaps up to half of the total of 110; in any case, the Athenian contingent alone had sufficient manpower to besiege and eventually take Sestos at the end of the year's campaigning. Sparta was unlikely to have supplied more than 16 ships, the number it had at Salamis. The Corinthians, the Sicyonians and the Troezenians are also named as taking part in the campaign, and it is probable that there was a unit from Aegina, where the fleet had assembled. The total of around 25,000 men, including not more than 300–400 hoplites, was probably considered to be all that could be safely detached from the land army that was to face Mardonius or from any reserve that was held at the Isthmus.

[1] Or because he had heard quite enough.
[2] 'Army leader'.

The omens were good and the Hellenes sailed from Delos and headed for Samos. When they reached Calami on Samos, they moored near the temple of Hera there and made their preparations for battle. But when the Persians found out that they were on the way, they put to sea themselves and made for the mainland with all their ships, except they detached the Phoenicians and sent them away. They had decided not to give battle at sea because they did not feel they were a match for the Hellenes. So, they headed for the mainland and the protection of the land force at Mycale which had been left behind under orders from Xerxes to secure Ionia. This force was 60,000 strong and Tigranes,[1] who surpassed all other Persians in looks and stature, was in command. The Persian fleet commanders' plan was to run to this army for shelter, beach their ships and build a palisade around them to protect them and to serve them as a stronghold. This was their plan as they put to sea and sailed past the sanctuary of the Potniae[2] at Mycale and as far as Scolopoeis on the River Gaeson and the nearby shrine of Eleusinian Demeter.[3] They dragged their ships up the beach there and built a wall of timber and stones around them, and cut down fruit trees and set sharpened stakes into the ramparts. They were ready to endure a siege or to win victory, having made their preparations with these alternatives in mind. (9.96–97)

The Persians' decision not to take on the Hellenes at sea is likely to have preceded the decision to detach the Phoenician squadron, the best and, most likely, largest element of their fleet. They may not have been prepared to risk its loss, if they were anticipating defeat because of the poor condition of their ships and concerns about the effectiveness or reliability of other contingents, in spite of their likely numerical advantage. Alternatively, there may have been greater need for the

---

[1] Tigranes was an Achaemenid, a member of the Persian royal family, and commander of the Median division, possibly a 10,000-strong unit, in the previous year's invasion.

[2] 'The Mistresses', Demeter and her daughter, Persephone, goddesses of agriculture, and fertility and growth. This holy place was somewhere towards the western end of Cape Mycale.

[3] The exact location of these three landmarks is also unknown. The first may have been a settlement renamed after the Persian stockade (*scolopes* means 'pointed stakes'); the second is generally thought to be the name of a river or stream; the third was the cape's second shrine dedicated to Demeter and probably about half-way along its south side.

Phoenicians' services to protect the Great King's interests elsewhere in the eastern Mediterranean. What was then left could indeed have been less than a match for Leotychidas' fleet and may have consisted mainly of contingents of subject Hellenes from up and down the eastern seaboard of the Aegean. These could not now be relied upon, even if they were stiffened up, as in the previous year, with Barbarian deck-fighters. Tigranes' force was probably a few thousand, but certainly not 60,000 strong. Assuming the Persian fleet included the same complements of Barbarian deck-fighters as in the previous year's naval campaign (30 Persians, Medians or Sacae per ship) its arrival might have added around 4,000–5,000 trustworthy troops.

When the Hellenes found out that the Barbarians had sailed to the mainland, they were not pleased to know that their enemy had escaped them, and they could not make up their minds whether to go home or to head off to the Hellespont. In the end they decided to do neither of these things, but to sail to the mainland. So, they got the gangplanks[1] ready with everything else that they needed for a sea-battle and set course for Mycale, but they could see nobody pulling out to meet them as they approached the enemy encampment. However, they could see the ships hauled up within the walls and a large force drawn up along the beach. Then Leotychidas brought his ship in as close to the shore as he could and used a herald to give this message to the Ionians: 'Men of Ionia, if you can hear me, listen carefully to what I say, and don't worry about the Persians: they won't be able to understand any of it. When we join battle, you must each think of freedom first and foremost, and then remember the password "Hebe".[2] If you can hear this, pass it on to those who cannot.' Leotychidas' purpose was the same as Themistocles' at Artemisium. Either the Barbarians would not be aware of the message and it would inspire the Ionians, or, if the Barbarians did find out about it, then it would make them distrust their Hellene allies.

---

[1] For boarding enemy ships after ramming or closing alongside.

[2] The goddess Hebe personified the vigour of youth and was associated with Heracles and seems an appropriate choice for a password to be used in battle. However, it is unclear why a password might be needed: Ionians were easily distinguishable from Persians or other Barbarians.

Next, after Leotychidas had given the Ionians this message, the Hellenes beached their ships, disembarked and formed up on the shore. When the Persians observed the Hellenes preparing for battle and had become aware of the appeal they had made to the Ionians, they disarmed the Samians. They suspected that they would support the Hellenes in some way, and, indeed, the Samians had released some of their prisoners. These were Athenians left behind in Attica who had been taken prisoner by Xerxes' men and brought over in the Barbarian fleet.[1] The Samians had set them all free and sent them back to Athens with everything they needed for their passage, so they were already under suspicion because, by this act, they had released 500 of Xerxes' enemies. Additionally, the Persians tasked the Milesians with guarding the tracks that led up to the heights of Mycale, ostensibly because they knew the area best, though the true purpose was to get them out of the camp. In this way the Barbarians thought to protect themselves from any mischief these Ionians might do, if they found an opportunity. This done, they set up their shield wall. (9.98–99)

The Hellenes were still expecting to fight the Persians at sea and prepared to use boarding tactics as well as, or instead of, ramming tactics. The larger complements of hoplites required for the former would have strengthened Leotychidas' task force for land operations. The Persians' decision not to offer battle at sea was wise. Equally wise was the Hellenes' decision not to attempt an opposed landing. Triremes were beached stern first and the troops had the option of disembarking down one or two gangplanks in single file, or of gathering as near the stern as possible to jump down, a drop of 2m or more made more awkward by the weight of shield, spear and armour. Either way, they would have had no chance to form an effective battle line in the face of concentrated Barbarian archery, and withdrawal under attack would have proved very difficult, if not impossible. So Leotychidas elected to sail further on after calling on the Ionians to defect and increasing the Persians' distrust of them (the message would have been quickly

---

[1] There is no mention of any prisoners being taken in the previous year's capture of the Acropolis but perhaps other Athenians stayed behind in the city or outside it for similar reasons rather than evacuating to Salamis.

translated for those who did not understand Greek). In spite of their earlier pledge given to Leotychidas, which the Persians may not have known about, and their release of the Athenian prisoners, the Samians had still been under arms on the Persian side. In any case, as it finally turned out, Leotychidas was more successful than Themistocles had been after Artemisium with his appeal to the Hellenes on the Persian side to defect.

Leotychidas took his ships 3,000–4,000m further along the coast beyond the Persian camp at a pace fast enough to outrun any pursuit along the shore by footsoldiers, and Tigranes had no cavalry. This bought enough time to make an unopposed landing, probably in a bay just to the west of the city of Priene. The Persians' plan was to meet the Hellenes outside their fortifications and, if they could not defeat them in battle, to fall back into their camp and settle for a siege. They were probably better provisioned than the Hellenes and may have expected reinforcements to arrive from Sardis fairly soon.

Cape Mycale can be conveniently included in a couple of days of a tour of the west coast of Turkey taking in Priene, Miletus and Ephesus, all superb sites. It lies on the north side of what used to be a large, shallow bay. The River Maeander flows into it 50km to the east of the cape's westernmost point and has filled it with sediment over the centuries. As at Thermopylae, the sea is now some distance from the battlefield, but the high ridge of the cape must be little changed and it is easy to visualize the strip of shore and level ground that the Athenians and the Hellene left advanced over, while the ridges that the Spartans and the right had to negotiate are plain to see. The site of the Persian camp and the precise location of the battlefield are unknown, but the modern village of Atburgaz is a likely spot and fruit trees still grow there. Samos is in view close to the tip of the cape and Miletus and the island of Lade (now landlocked) are 10km to the south, directly across the bay. It is not surprising that the Persians suspected the loyalty of the Samians and Milesians so close to home.

When the Hellenes were ready they began to advance on the Barbarians and, as they went, a herald's staff was seen lying at the

Mycale, 479

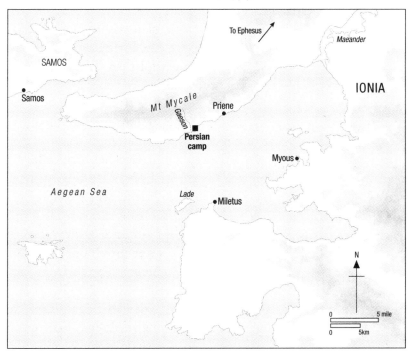

water's edge and rumour[1] flew through the ranks that the Hellenes facing Mardonius' army in Boeotia had been victorious. Now, there is a great deal of evidence for the involvement of the gods in the affairs of men, as in this case, when that rumour was conveyed to the Hellenes on the very same day that disaster befell the Persians at Plataea and was about to befall them at Mycale. Anyway, it certainly boosted the men's morale and put them in good heart as they prepared to go into harm's way. There also happened to be plots of land dedicated to Eleusinian Demeter on each battlefield, for, as I have already said, the fighting at Plataea took place near the precinct of Demeter there, and the same thing was about to happen

---

[1] Rumour (*Pheme*) was personified as a goddess and was also credited with bringing the news to Athens of the Delian League's great victory over the Persians on the River Eurymedon in 467/6. That news was said to have arrived on the day of the battle, having travelled a considerably greater distance than Plataea to Mycale. The herald's staff (perhaps a piece of driftwood in the rough shape of one) might have been associated with Pheme.

at Mycale. And then, the rumour of a victory won by the Hellenes
with Pausanias turned out to be true, and, in fact, victory at Plataea
was won while it was still morning while victory at Mycale came in
the afternoon. Not long afterwards, careful investigation established
that these two events did indeed take place on the same day of the
same month. Actually, before rumour came amongst them, the
Hellenes had been full of trepidation, not so much for themselves as
for their comrades with Pausanias, and fearful that Hellas would be
overcome by Mardonius. But when those words of good omen flew
amongst them, they increased the pace of their advance. So, Hellenes
and Barbarians alike were eager to fight for the prize set before them,
control of the islands and the Hellespont. (9.100–01)

Herodotus presents the stories of the herald's staff and the rumour
of victory at Plataea and the nice coincidence of the two precincts of
Demeter in a tone that suggests he does accept that these are indeed
pieces of 'evidence for the involvement of the gods in the affairs of men'.
On the day of the battle the Hellenes at Mycale could have known that
the Hellene land army was confronting the Persians in Boeotia and quite
possibly even that the fighting had begun, but there was no possibility
of their receiving word of the final victory on the same day. However,
there is a slight shrug in Herodotus' 'anyway', perhaps allowing for the
possibility of pre-battle speeches or gossip holding out the prospect of
simultaneous victories. Diodorus reflects on this usefully:

While the Hellenes were making their preparations[1] for battle, a
rumour came to them of the victory over the Persians at Plataea.
Acting on this, Leotychidas and his commanders gathered their
troops together to inspire them for the fight, and in amongst the rest
of the things they had to say, they announced the victory at Plataea
in the most dramatic manner, reckoning that this would boost the
men's confidence as they were about to go into battle. And there was
a wonderful outcome since it transpired that the two battles, the one
at Mycale and the one at Plataea, were fought and won on the same
day. This suggests that Leotychidas and his commanders did not yet

---

[1] Presumably including the customary sacrifices, if the auspicious results obtained before leaving
Delos were not considered sufficient.

know about the victory, but that they fabricated the good news as part of their strategy. The great distance involved is proof that this message could not actually have been communicated.[1] (*Library of History* 11.35)

The battle of Mycale may have been fought on the same day as Plataea was won, and even in the afternoon of that day. But the exact timing of these events may never have been known and could not possibly have been established in later years or centuries. Plutarch advises caution in the matter of dating events in the history of 5th-century Hellas:

This battle[2] was fought on the fourth of the month Boedromion, according to the Athenians, but four days before the end of the month Panemus according to the Boeotians. On the latter date even now, the congress of the Hellenes assembles in Plataea and the Plataeans offer sacrifices to Zeus Deliverer to give thanks for the victory. We should not be surprised at the discrepancy between these dates; even now, when astronomy is a more precise science, different peoples begin and end their months on different days.[3] (*Aristides* 19.4–7)

Herodotus continues with the Hellenes in battle order advancing from the east with the Spartans on the right flank and the Athenians on the left. The Persians were waiting for them outside their fort, drawn up behind their palisade of shields:

The Athenians and those who were positioned next to them,[4] about half the total force, were moving along the shore and over level ground, but the Lacedaemonians and those next to them had to make their way across a gully and some ridges. So, while the Lacedaemonians

---

[1] It has been suggested that the news of victory at Plataea could have been transmitted by fire signals. But it is unlikely that all sources would have omitted this detail, and there would have been real practical difficulties in setting up a chain of beacons that maintained connection with the fleet as it island-hopped from Delos to Samos and then sailed into the bay under the shelter of Cape Mycale, blocking line of sight to Samos.

[2] The last day at Plataea.

[3] About 150 years before Plutarch wrote this, Julius Caesar had sorted out the Roman calendar, which by then had drifted out to three months ahead of the lunar calendar.

[4] Taken as meaning they advanced in line rather than column.

were still working their way over this ground, the other division had already gone into battle. So long as their wicker shields remained standing, the Persians put up a strong defence and held their own in the fighting. But when the Athenians and the contingents with them increased the pressure, urging each other on to finish the job and deny the Lacedaemonians credit for it, then the situation changed. Breaking through the shield wall, they fell on the Persians, sweeping forward in a mass.

The Persians absorbed the charge and held out for quite a while but finally fell back on their stockade. The Athenians, Corinthians, Sicyonians and Troezenians (the order in which they were positioned in the line) hotly pursued them to the stockade and poured in behind them. With their defences breached, the Barbarians put up no more resistance and tried their best to escape, all except for the Persians, who fought on in small groups with the Hellenes as they continued to stream in. Two of the Persian commanders managed to escape and two were killed: Artayntes and Ithamitres, from the fleet, were the two that got away; Mardontes and Tigranes, the commander-in-chief of the land force, died fighting.

The Persians were still fighting when the Lacedaemonians and the contingents with them arrived, and they helped finish them off. But there were many Hellene casualties as well, amongst the Sicyonians in particular and including their commander Perilaus. The Samians who had been serving in the Median army until they were disarmed could see right from the start that the battle could go either way and they did whatever they could to assist the Hellenes.[1] The rest of the Ionians followed the Samians' lead, changed sides and also attacked the Barbarians. The Persians had detached the Milesians to guard the passes and to be ready to guide them to safety over the heights of Mycale; they had taken this precaution in case they suffered such a setback as actually befell them. This was why the Milesians were given that task, but the Persians' purpose was also to remove them from the army to prevent them doing anything to sabotage it. But the Milesians did exactly the opposite of what they were tasked to do and led the fleeing Persians down paths that took them into the midst of their enemies. In the end the Milesians themselves killed

---

[1] Probably not much without weapons.

them and proved themselves the fiercest of the Barbarians' foes. This was how Ionia revolted from the Persians a second time.

In this battle the Athenians fought best of all the Hellenes, and the best of the Athenians was Hermolycus son of Euthoenus. He was a champion *pankration*[1] fighter who later met his death in battle at Cyrnus in Carystus during a war between Athens and Carystus.[2] After the Athenians, the Corinthians, Troezenians and Sicyonians fought best. When the Hellenes had dealt with most of the Barbarians, either fighting or in flight, they laid the spoils out on the beach and found chests full of treasure amongst them. Then, after burning the ships and all the fortifications, they put to sea. (9.102–06)

In comparison to Plataea this was a small-scale battle and, unfortunately, Herodotus gives little more space to the actual fighting (9.102–04) than to the various elements of the tradition that Plataea and Mycale were fought on the same day (9.100–01). The neat parallels with the final day's action at Plataea and the balancing emphasis on the decisive contribution of the Athenians arouse suspicions of biased creativity on the part of Herodotus or his sources. However, there are also important contrasts, for example, Tigranes' lack of cavalry and his well-founded distrust of his Hellene levies, and the reversal of the situation at the beginning of the day at Plataea when it was the Hellenes who were on the defensive and the Persians who were taking the initiative. Leotychidas' and Xanthippus' aggressive and high-tempo generalship was admirable, and Tigranes had very limited options in the position in which he found himself and, without the Ionians, may well have been outnumbered. Finally, the nature of the fighting as described by Herodotus is consistent with what is known about other clashes between Hellenes and Barbarians, and with the make-up of the opposing forces and also with the probable strength of each at Mycale.

Assuming an average of 30 per trireme, Leotychidas had 3,300 hoplites at his disposal and would have deployed all of them in the

---

[1] A ferocious and potentially lethal combination of fist-fighting and all-in wrestling. In Athens, anything was allowed except biting and gouging.

[2] This war, briefly mentioned by Thucydides, was fought towards the end of the decade as Athens steadily tightened her grip on the Delian League.

attack on the Persian camp. It is probable that the hoplites had the support of a significantly larger numbers of *psiloi*, drawn from the fleet's rowing and deck crews, which would have totalled about 20,000; a few of the oarsmen may even have doubled as hoplites. The Athenian force that landed on the island of Sphacteria in 425 during the Peloponnesian War included 'all of the crews except for the *thalamioi* (oarsmen from the lowest tier, 54 per trireme) of over 70 ships with whatever weapons they had with them' (Thucydides, *History of the Peloponnesian War* 4.32). In the battle that followed, the Athenian *psiloi* outnumbered their hoplite comrades by a factor of at least ten and swamped the 420 Lacedaemonians trapped on the island. An arrangement such as this may have given Leotychidas numerical superiority over Tigranes and Mardontes and their Asian troops; because the Hellene ships were all beached or moored behind their advancing battle line, most of the crewmen would have been available to fight and only a few needed to stay with their ships. If each trireme also carried a group of four archers, as was customary later in the century, Leotychidas had a useful, if modest counter to Persian archery firepower and there would have been a few slingers and javelin-throwers amongst his light-armed forces.

Assuming the right and left divisions were about equal in size, the battle in front of the camp was initiated by a Hellene force that could have been several thousand strong and spearheaded by 1,500–1,700 hoplites. Diodorus states that Tigranes had assembled an army of 100,000 men (and equips Leotychidas with 250 triremes). On Herodotus' count of 60,000, the Persian force, more heavily armed than the *psiloi* and much more numerous than the hoplites, would have been more than a match for the Hellenes and unlikely to have been troubled by turncoat Ionians. However, though significantly smaller than this, his force must have been large enough to give Tigranes the confidence to stand and fight outside his fortifications and perhaps he took that decision when he saw the size of the enemy force advancing along the shore. But he may not have seen the right division, concealed as it was by the broken ground it had to cross. This reference to the terrain and its effect is one detail in Herodotus' narrative that stands out from the stock phrases which are found in various combinations in all his descriptions of land-battles, and it is something that could have been part of the collective memory of Mycale. This is not to say that the stock phrases, as far as they go, are untrue, but they tell us little more than that the battle took the same general course as many other battles of this era. However, it does seem that there was no stand-off, which had been a feature of Marathon, Thermopylae and, at more than one stage over its several days, Plataea. This may have taken the Persians by surprise.

A second distinctive feature, the left division was first into the attack. The Athenians' motivation to 'deny the Lacedaemonians credit' is believable since they had been the victors of Marathon and were, as at Salamis, the largest contingent, albeit under Spartan command. There would have been Marathon veterans in the ranks and it is easy to imagine them closing with the Persians in a running charge through the arrow storm, as they had done 11 years before. Indeed, there are features of Mycale that closely match features of Marathon and it is a little surprising that Herodotus does not draw attention to these parallels. The victory over the Persians on the River Eurymedon in 467/6, also on Asian soil, under the leadership of Cimon, might also have been brought to mind. But Herodotus chose not to upstage the decisive main event in Boeotia and the Spartans' universally acclaimed and decisive role in it. Nonetheless, his Athenian sources may have spiced things up a little.

It is unlikely that a break would have been allowed to open up at any point in the advancing line between the Spartan right and the Athenian left, it being a fundamental rule of hoplite combat that each man stuck close to his surrounding comrades, above all the one on his right. But, at Mycale, the further the line advanced the more it would have bent as the more difficult terrain slowed the right flank elements. The consequence was that the Athenians and those nearest to them, the Corinthians, the Sicyonians and the Troezenians, who had been able to advance more quickly over the level ground along the shore engaged with the Persian line as one, whilst the units further to their right attacked in echelon, the Spartans arriving last, though possibly after less delay than Herodotus implies. Once the hoplites had broken the Persian line, the *psiloi* joined in the rout and it appears that the Barbarian camp's defences, which may have been less elaborate than those at Plataea, were easily breached. This can, of course, only be based on the argument that Herodotus would have included his stock siege-combat language if he felt his information justified it.

Diodorus Siculus sees the battle a little differently:

When both sides had drawn up their troops in battle order and were advancing upon each other, the Persians saw how few the Hellenes were. They reckoned they did not amount to anything and bore down on them with loud yells. Now, the Samians and Milesians had unanimously agreed beforehand to support the Hellene cause and were moving up all together at the double. But, although the Ionians thought this would encourage the Hellenes, it had exactly the opposite effect when the Hellene army caught sight of them approaching. Leotychidas' troops thought that Xerxes had arrived from Sardis in full strength and was now advancing upon them, and they were seized with fear. They argued amongst themselves and could not reach agreement on what action to take; some were for retreating to their ships and leaving the place as quickly as possible, others for staying where they were and resolutely holding their position. While they were still in this state of confusion, the Persians came into sight, terrifying to look at in all their gear and charging at them with loud war-cries.

The Hellenes, given no time to think about it, had no option but to receive the Barbarians' attack. Initially both sides fought resolutely and the battle could have gone either way. Great numbers fell in each army. But when the Samians and Milesians appeared on the scene, the Hellenes became more determined, while the Barbarians were stricken with terror and broke and ran. There was great slaughter as Leotychidas' and Xanthippus' men drove into the beaten Barbarians and chased them back to their camp. The Aeolians took part in the battle, once the outcome was certain, along with many other Hellenes of Asia, because a fierce longing for liberty had seized the hearts of the people who lived in the Hellene cities of Asia. (*Library of History* 11.36)

The Samians and Milesians are presented as playing a more central part than in Herodotus' account, unambiguously committed to the cause from the start. However, the Aeolians and 'other Hellenes of Asia' are then shown up as hedging their bets initially, and it would be intriguing to know if this was a detail Diodorus incorporated from his source, the Aeolian Ephorus. From Herodotus' account it seems that 'the rest of the Ionians' at least began the battle on the Persian side. They were, presumably, fully armed and, when and if they actively changed sides, could have had more impact than the Samians, who joined the fight as *psiloi*, at best, with whatever weapons they could pick up or improvise.

In Herodotus' account, the fighting satisfactorily concludes with the Milesians taking their revenge on the Persians, 15 years after the destruction and enslavement of their city. And 'Ionia revolted from the Persians a second time'.

On arriving at Samos from Mycale, the Hellenes held a conference and considered the evacuation of all Hellenes from Ionia, and discussed which might be the most appropriate Hellene-controlled territories to settle them in. The feeling was that they should leave the whole region to the Barbarians because of the impossibility of maintaining a presence that would protect the Ionians from the enemy for all time; without such protection, there could be no hope that the Persians would let the Ionians get away with what they had done. The Peloponnesian delegates, who favoured evacuation, proposed that Hellenes who had medized be relocated from their centres of commerce and that the Ionians be resettled in them in their place. But the Athenians did not at all like the idea of uprooting the Ionians and allowing the Peloponnesians to decide on the fate of settlements that Athens had established. They opposed it strongly and the Peloponnesians gave way. And so they brought into their alliance the Samians, Chians and Lesbians, and all the other islanders who had served with them, and bound them with pledges of loyalty and oaths that they would not defect. After these oaths had been sworn, the Hellenes sailed off to break the bridges, thinking they were still in place. So, they set sail for the Hellespont. The Barbarians who escaped, and there were not many of them, gathered on the heights of Mycale and got away to safety in Sardis. (9.106–07)

Xerxes' bridges of boats had been destroyed by an autumn storm or were dismantled in 480. Satisfied that the bridges were no longer there, Leotychidas took the Peloponnesian contingent home. However, Xanthippus and the Athenians decided to stay and 'make an attempt on the Chersonese', which commanded the vital sea-lane from the Black Sea. The area had previously been colonized by Athens until Miltiades, the hero of Marathon, had been driven out by the Phoenicians in 492. The Athenians laid siege to Sestos, the strongest city on the peninsula, and, late in the autumn, eventually starved the defenders out. The Persian garrison made an unsuccessful attempt to escape and the city was taken. It quickly became one of Athens' most important overseas naval bases. The massive cables for the Persian bridges had been stored there, presumably for possible reuse, and the Athenians took them home as trophies. Herodotus' *Historia* ends at this point.

Thucydides picks up the narrative with a summary of the 50-year period in which the power of Athens grew and the Peloponnesian War became inevitable (1.88–118). This long digression is prefaced by the briefest statement of what he considered to be the main underlying cause of the Peloponnesian War:

> In arriving at their decision to go to war, the Lacedaemonians were influenced, not so much by the arguments of their allies, as by their fear of the growing power of the Athenians, because they could see that they already controlled much of Hellas. (*History of the Peloponnesian War* 1.88)

From the brink of hostilities in 431, Thucydides jumps back to autumn 479:

> After the departure of the Barbarians from their country, the Athenian people immediately set about bringing back their children and wives, and what possessions they had left, from the places where they had sent them, and prepared to rebuild their city and their fortifications. (*History of the Peloponnesian War* 1.89)

The Spartans and their allies, already nervous of Athens' newly acquired strength, tried to persuade the Athenians to leave their city unfortified. They argued, somewhat speciously, that all Hellene cities outside the Peloponnese should be left open to prevent the Persians using them as bases as they had used Thebes, if they invaded again. For the Spartans, of course, it was a matter of pride and principle that their city was not walled. Themistocles, clearly back in the centre of things whatever the reason for his apparent absence from the year's campaigns, advised the Athenians to send the Spartan embassy home with the promise that an Athenian delegation would soon come after them to discuss the issue in Sparta. He then asked to be sent ahead alone and instructed the rest of the delegates to follow only when the walls had reached a defensible height.

Themistocles was able to play for time, trading on the personal friendship and respect he had built in the previous year, and then resorting to blatant disinformation. At his suggestion the Spartans sent a new delegation to check whether the rumours of intense building activity were true. This was, in effect, held hostage until the Athenians were ready to send the rest of their delegation to Sparta. Themistocles was then able to formally announce that the city was fortified. He accompanied this with a lecture on the Athenians' right to self-determination, emphasizing their proven ability to identify what was both in their own best interest and in the best interest of Hellas. He closed with the assertion that either all members of the alliance should do without city walls, or they should all have them. However, 'the Spartans did not make any show of anger with the Athenians ... but were privately annoyed at failing to achieve their purpose.' The Athenians went on to fortify the port of Piraeus in the following year under Themistocles' direction, completing the work he had set in train 15 years before and thus 'laying the foundations of empire'.

Very little is known about Themistocles' career over the next few years, but he remained active enough in Athenian politics to suffer ostracism towards the end of the decade, finally on the losing side in that uniquely Athenian democratic process which had previously worked to his benefit on more than one occasion. According to an anecdote recorded by Plutarch, he had been warned. Recalling the comparison to a scrapped trireme, Themistocles might have appreciated the irony:

In an attempt to persuade him not to pursue a career in public service, Themistocles' father pointed out the old triremes, beached, abandoned and scrapped and declared that the people treated their leaders in exactly the same way when they decided they were no longer of any use to them. (*Themistocles* 2)

The victories of 479 did not bring the war to an end. Thucydides continues:

> Pausanias son of Cleombrotus was dispatched from Lacedaemon as commander of the Hellenes with 20 triremes from the Peloponnese. The Athenians with 30 ships and a larger number of other allies sailed with him. They attacked Cyprus and subdued most of the island and then moved on to Byzantium, which was in the hands of the Medes, and took possession of it after a siege. These things were done while Pausanias was in command.
>
> But by now the Hellenes, particularly the Ionians and others who had recently been liberated from the Great King's rule, were finding Pausanias' behaviour intolerably overbearing. These people approached the Athenians and called upon them as kinsfolk to become their leaders and rescue them from his violent ways. The Athenians agreed to this; they were not prepared to tolerate such behaviour themselves and also determined to direct operations with their own best interests in mind. At the same time, the Lacedaemonians recalled Pausanias to face an investigation into the reports they had been receiving. A number of accusations of serious wrongdoing had been levelled against him in Sparta by Hellene visitors. He did indeed seem to be acting more like a tyrant than a general and, as it happened, this summons arrived just at the time when the ill feeling that he inspired caused the allies, all except for the troops from the Peloponnese, to place themselves under Athenian command.
>
> On his arrival in Lacedaemon, Pausanias was reprimanded for the wrongs he had personally done to individuals but cleared of the most serious charges. Medism was foremost amongst these and there seemed to be strong evidence of it. Anyway, the Lacedaemonians did not reinstate him in his command and Dorcis[1] and others were sent out with a small force to replace him. But the allies would no longer accept Spartan leadership and, acknowledging this, they went home. The Lacedaemonians did not send out anyone else because they were afraid that whoever they sent would be corrupted in the same way as Pausanias. Besides, they wanted nothing more to do with the

---

[1] Otherwise unheard of.

Median War, but had confidence in the Athenians' ability to lead the alliance and in their present goodwill towards them. (*History of the Peloponnesian War* 1.94–95)

The expedition to Cyprus was more likely to have been a display of support for the powerful cities that had seceded from Persian rule during the Ionian Revolt to encourage them to align themselves with Hellas once again. It would have taken a far larger force and probably much more than one season's campaigning to 'subdue most of the island' if the Cypriots were resistant to the idea. In any case the island was to be fought over for the next 30 years until Persia regained full control of it. It was a long haul from Cyprus to Byzantium but the capture of the city was of more immediate practical use than the establishment of what was probably no more than a loose alliance with Cyprus. Like the capture of Sestos on the Hellespont the previous autumn, it secured the important, grain-bearing shipping route from the Black Sea to the Aegean.

Herodotus mentions Pausanias' alleged 'un-Hellene' activities in a brief aside in his account of the Ionian Revolt:

Darius put his cousin Megabates, a Persian of the Achaemenid clan, in command of the attack on Naxos. If the story is true, it was his daughter that Pausanias the Lacedaemonian, son of Cleombrotus, later proposed to marry in his great desire to become tyrant[1] of Hellas. (5.32)

Thucydides has more to say on the subject. He has Pausanias corresponding with Xerxes and seeking his favour with an offer to marry his daughter and an undertaking to deliver Sparta and the rest of Hellas to him as subjects. He also describes his behaviour in more detail:

On receiving the Great King's response, Pausanias, already feted by the Hellenes for his leadership at Plataea, became even more carried away. He was no longer satisfied with a normal lifestyle. He put on Median garb, went on excursions from Byzantium into Thrace with

---

[1] *Tyrannos.* Mardonius entertained the same ambition, to be made satrap of Hellas.

a retinue of Median and Egyptian spearmen, and dined in Persian style. He was quite unable to contain himself and these small pieces of evidence clearly revealed his ambition to go on to grander things. (*History of the Peloponnesian War* 1.130)

The Athenians were quick to assert their leadership and take control of the alliance's administration:

> The Athenians, having taken over as leaders with the full agreement of the allies because of their profound dislike of Pausanias, then decided which cities were to contribute money for the war against the Barbarian and which were to contribute ships. Their declared purpose was to ravage the Great King's lands to avenge the harm he had done to them. It was at this time that the office of Treasurers of Hellas[1] was created by the Athenians. Their role was to take in the *phoros*, as the financial contributions were called. The contributions were set to bring in a total of 460 talents. The alliance's treasury was at Delos and the Hellenes held their meetings in the temple there. (*History of the Peloponnesian War* 1.96)

Phoros seems an unfortunate term to use for members' contributions with its connotations of tribute paid to foreign powers (including in very recent memory Persia) and as Hellene Alliance mutated into Athenian Empire and the decades passed, it aroused similar resentment. It is not known whether the 460 talents represented a target or a total actually collected, nor whether it reflected the value of contributions in kind (ships and men) alongside cash contributions. However, this amount would have provided the alliance with the means to build in the region of 200 triremes and fund a navy of that size for several months of campaigning. Delos (hence Delian League, the modern name given to the alliance) was chosen for its status as a cult centre venerated by all Hellenes and for its geographical position midway between Greece and the west coast of Asia. But it was associated more strongly with the Ionian ethnic grouping, which included Athens, than the Dorian, which included Sparta.

---

[1] *Hellenotamiai.*

Thucydides moves quickly on to the subsequent evolution of the alliance and the swing of the balance of power towards Athens:

At first the allies kept their independence under Athenian leadership and acted on decisions taken in communal meetings. Between the Median war and the present conflict,[1] the Athenians made war or took other measures against Barbarians, against their own allies when they tried to abandon the alliance, and against the Peloponnesians in various confrontations. I am writing about these events and making this digression here because it is a period of history that has been overlooked by all my predecessors, who have instead concentrated on the history of Hellas before the Median war, or on that war itself. In any case, these events illustrate how it was that the Athenian Empire came into being.

First the Athenians laid siege to Eion on the Strymon and took it from the Medes, and they sold the inhabitants into slavery. Their commander was Cimon son of Miltiades. Next, they made slaves of the people of Scyros, the island in the Aegean that was a Dolopian[2] settlement, and planted a settlement of their own. This was followed by a campaign against Carystus. The rest of Euboea stayed neutral, and after a while the Carystians agreed terms. Then the Naxians defected and the Athenians went to war with them, forcing them to rejoin the alliance after a siege. This was the first instance of the subjugation of an allied city, an action contrary to the principles of the alliance and one that was to befall other members in similar circumstances.

Shortfalls in tribute payments or quotas of ships, or withdrawal of manpower were the main reasons for defection. For the Athenians were demanding leaders and caused great resentment by the pressure they applied to peoples who were unused to hard work and, indeed, unwilling to engage in it. For other reasons, the Athenians were no longer as popular as leaders as they had been, and if they did more than their share of campaigning, that made it easy for them to deal with any defectors. The allies had only themselves to blame for this. In their reluctance to go on campaign, most of them arranged to

---

[1] The Peloponnesian War.

[2] The Dolopians were a Thessalian people and were presumably being punished here for medizing in 480.

make their assessed contributions in cash rather than supply ships and so avoided having to leave home. Consequently, the Athenians were able to use the funds contributed to enlarge their own navy and, as for the allies, if ever they considered defection, they found themselves neither equipped for war nor in training for it. (*History of the Peloponnesian War* 1.97–100)

Through the 470s, the growing antagonism between the Athenians and the Spartans and other Peloponnesians remained an undercurrent, but the alliance remained focused on its mission to protect Hellas from the Persian Empire. Plutarch fleshes out Thucydides' compact account of this decade a little. His sharper characterization of the increasingly reluctant, even indolent allies, unwittingly yielding their sovereignty to Athens, recalls Dionysius the Phocaean's experience as he attempted to train up his command at Lade. The Athenians, on the other hand, are shown as displaying the same energy, ambition and effectiveness as Herodotus admires in them in the decade immediately following Cleisthenes' democratic reforms. Cimon son of Miltiades was in the ascendant from 478, though he was to suffer ostracism in 461:

The allies continued to pay tribute, but no longer supplied their agreed quotas of men or ships. They now had an aversion to military service and no longer had any desire for war, and just wanted to work their land and live a quiet life. The Barbarians were gone and no longer worried them, so they neither manned their ships nor sent any troops. The rest of the Athenian generals tried to compel them to do these things and made their leadership a grievous burden with their impeachments and the penalties they imposed. But Cimon's behaviour as general was quite different. He put no pressure on any of the Hellenes but accepted cash or ships without crews from those who did not wish to go on campaign. So, he allowed the allies to give in to the attractions of a life of ease and to spend their time at home farming and trading, warriors turned into civilians by their foolish love of comfort. On the other hand, Cimon manned the ships with large numbers of Athenians, who took it in turns to serve, and he built up their experience of campaigning. So, before very long, he had used the funds raised to make the Athenians masters of the allies who had contributed them. Those who did no military service grew to fear and be servile towards those who were continually at sea and forever under arms, physically fit and well trained, and so they failed to see that they were changing from allies into tribute-paying subjects. (*Cimon* 11–12)

After his acquittal, Pausanias returned to Byzantium, possibly in some official capacity. He aroused new suspicions of medism and was ejected by the Athenians after a siege. He then settled in the Troad but was recalled to Sparta around the end of the decade to stand trial on the same charge as before. Once again, he was acquitted for lack of firm evidence, according to Thucydides who seems to be quite sure of his guilt. In any case Pausanias was then accused of plotting a Helot revolt, a crime probably more heinous than medism in Spartan eyes. He sought sanctuary in a temple to avoid arrest but the ephors had him walled in and he starved to death. Thucydides brings Themistocles back into his narrative at this point:

> Going back to the medism of Pausanias, the Lacedaemonians sent envoys to Athens to demand that Themistocles receive the same punishment as Pausanias on the grounds that evidence that implicated him had been found in the course of their investigation. The Athenians agreed to this. But, of course, Themistocles had been ostracized and was living in Argos and travelling from there to other parts of the Peloponnese. So, they sent men with orders to arrest him wherever they found him and the Lacedaemonians readily joined them in the hunt. But Themistocles found out about this and was able to escape ... (*History of the Peloponnesian War* 1.135)

Always keeping ahead of his pursuers, Themistocles went first to Corcyra, then travelled overland via Molossia to Pydna in Macedonia and sailed east from there in a merchant ship. Bad weather took his ship to Naxos, which the Athenians were besieging at the time, but he avoided detection and finally reached Ephesus, Asia and safety. Thucydides describes this odyssey in enough detail to show that it could not have been accomplished by anyone lacking Themistocles' wealth, connections and famous wiliness. He has nothing to say about any evidence of treason brought against him, and there may well not have been any. But his residence in Argos and travels around the rest of Peloponnese would have caused the Spartans to suspect and even fear him. Argos was a historic enemy of Sparta and Themistocles probably did take any opportunity available to him in a private capacity to promote Athenian interests in the Peloponnese. Ironically, political enmities at home and a desire for appeasement may have provoked Athenian agreement to the judgement passed on him by the Spartans. In any case, the Athenians no longer needed him; they had Cimon.

According to Thucydides, Themistocles wasted no time in offering his services to the Great King. If the letter he is said to have sent existed and was written on his arrival in Asia, it would have been addressed to Xerxes. Artaxerxes had succeeded his father after his assassination four or five years later in 465.

Themistocles sent a letter to Artaxerxes, Xerxes' son, who had recently come to the throne. This is what he said in the letter: 'I, Themistocles, am coming over to you. I am the man who did your royal house more harm than any other Hellene in the period when I had no choice but to defend myself against your father's invasion. But then, when I was safe and he was retreating and in danger, the good I did for him far outweighed that harm, so now you owe me a favour in return. (Themistocles is referring here to the information he had sent to Xerxes from Salamis that the Hellenes were holding back and that the bridges were still intact, for which he falsely claimed credit.) The Hellenes have laid charges against me because of my friendship with you and here I am, ready to do you great service.'

The Great King was delighted with Themistocles' proposal. Accordingly, he stayed in Ephesus for a year and learned as much as he was able of the Persian language and of the customs of the land. At the end of the year he presented himself to the King and was received with greater honour than any other Hellene before him. This was partly due to his established reputation and there was always the expectation that he might assist in the subjugation of Hellas, but, most of all, it was because he regularly displayed his great wisdom. (*History of the Peloponnesian War* 1.137–38)

Themistocles' position at court was much the same as that occupied by Histiaeus, Hippias, Demaratus and many other non-Barbarians who had held positions of honour, retained as advisers for their connections and knowledge of their home nations, and potential usefulness as vassal rulers in the event of invasion and conquest. Evidence of past service was not necessarily required.

> Themistocles' life was ended by sickness, though some say he killed himself by taking poison because he found himself unable to carry out the promises he had made to the Great King. Today there is a memorial to him in the marketplace of Magnesia in Asia. He was made governor of the region and the King gave him Magnesia for his bread, which brought him in an annual income of 50 talents, Lampsacus, thought to be the most productive region of all at that time, for his wine, and Myous for his meat.[1] Themistocles' relatives say that his bones were brought home at his request and buried in Attica but that this was done in secret because exiles charged with treason were not allowed burial in Attic soil.
>
> So end the tales of the two most famous Hellenes of their age, Pausanias the Lacedaemonian and Themistocles the Athenian.
> (*History of the Peloponnesian War* 1.138)

Themistocles is thought to have died in 459 when he would have been into his 60s and would have been well able to talk himself out of trouble as long as he lived. Old age or disease were more likely to have caused his death than suicide or indeed assassination. Thucydides, having earlier given Themistocles the full credit due to him for the Hellene victory at Salamis, the battle that had to be fought and won to defeat the Persian fleet and enable Hellas to unite on land in sufficient force to destroy the occupying army in the following year, supplies a fitting epitaph:

> Themistocles very clearly displayed immense natural ability that was more worthy of admiration than in any other man. Applying his native intelligence, without any prior research or subsequent study,

---

[1] There is evidence that both Myous and Lampsacus were members of the Hellene Alliance so their produce may not have been in the Great King's gift. On the other hand, compliance might have been seen as a worthwhile price to pay for Persian goodwill; they were a long way from Athens.

he could find highly effective solutions to immediately pressing problems after giving them the briefest consideration, and he was also brilliant at visualizing developments far off in the future. He was good at explaining whatever task he had in hand, and if it was something outside his experience, this did not impair the soundness of his judgment. He could look into the unknown and clearly foresee the good or evil that might come out of it. In sum, through the power of his intellect and the speed with which he applied it, this man was superbly equipped to decide on the spot what needed to be done. (*History of the Peloponnesian War* 1.138)

Pausanias begins his *Guide to Greece* at Piraeus and offers evidence that Themistocles was properly recognized once again by the Athenians and forgiven and, in effect, recalled from exile after his death:

When Themistocles became archon, he made Piraeus the Athenian port since he considered it most suitable as a base for the navy with its three harbours as against one at Phalerum. Even up to my time there were ship-sheds there, and Themistocles' tomb is near the largest of the harbours. For it is said that the Athenians regretted their treatment of him, and that members of his family were able to retrieve his bones and bring them home from Magnesia. Moreover, his children returned to Athens and set up a painting in the Parthenon, in which Themistocles is depicted. (*Guide to Greece* 1.1.2)

Themistocles did more than any other individual Hellene to secure the future of Hellas and with it the 5th-century flowering of Hellene culture and its enduring glittering legacy.

Returning to Hellene and increasingly Athenian operations against the Persians, Thucydides picks up his compressed and chronologically vague narrative with just two sentences on the greatest victory over the Barbarians since Salamis and Plataea:

Next, the Athenians and their allies fought land and sea-battles against the Medes on the River Eurymedon in Pamphylia. The Athenians under the command of Cimon son of Miltiades won both battles on the same day, and they captured 200 Phoenician triremes and destroyed them all. (*History of the Peloponnesian War* 1.100)

This was the culmination around 467 (the exact date is not known) of ten years of successful campaigning on the western and south-western fringes of the Persian Empire and gave the Delian League control of the eastern Aegean and cities spread along the western coastal strip of Asia. It is likely that the Persian mission in Pamphylia was to prevent the Hellenes advancing further eastward and, ideally, to push them back. But it was more important to hold Cyprus, which was considerably more valuable in strategic terms. The island was to be contested for the next 15 years and was once more firmly under Persian control by 450, so the defeat on the Eurymedon changed nothing in that respect, and the Hellenes did not subsequently mount any significant campaign further to the east. But it was a costly setback for the Persians who from then on seem to have been even less inclined to take the war back into Hellas.

Xerxes was assassinated in 465 and was succeeded as Great King by his son, Artaxerxes. Five or six years later there was, yet again, a major revolt against Persian rule in Egypt and the Athenians sent a large fleet and army to support it. Artaxerxes first tried to bribe the Spartans to invade Attica to make the Athenians leave Egypt. He was unsuccessful in this, but then subdued the revolt by direct force and eventually defeated the Athenians and their allies after a long siege on an island somewhere in the Nile delta. In 454 the treasury of the Delian League was moved to Athens and around this time its members began to be referred to as 'the cities that Athens controls' and were treated as such; their freedom from imperial rule won in 479 had lasted for just 25 years. By the end of this decade hostilities between Greece and Persia seem to have come to an end. There is uncertainty as to whether a formal treaty (the so-called Peace of Callias) was actually agreed.

A few years earlier, increasing friction between Athens, and Sparta and her Peloponnesian allies had culminated in the first major clash between the two sides at Tanagra in Boeotia, and conflict closer to home became the overriding strategic priority. In the decades that followed, Persia interfered from time to time in Hellene affairs on their western borders. Artaxerxes was still attempting to open negotiations with Sparta when he died in 424. He was succeeded by Darius II, who began to take more interest in Ionia after the disastrous Athenian failure in Sicily in 413. He succeeded in forming an alliance with Sparta the following year with the purpose of winning back the Empire's former subjects.

Persia's financial support was not as consistent or whole-hearted, nor the relationship as close as initially envisaged at the signing of the treaty, but it contributed significantly to Sparta's final victory in 404.

In 386, in the reign of Artaxerxes II, the King's Peace guaranteed the autonomy of Greece that had 'hung on a razor's edge' in 480 and 479. The main condition was that the Hellene cities of Asia, the coastal islands and Cyprus be recognised as Persian possessions: full circle from the Ionian Revolt, which had been 'the beginning of evil events for Hellenes and Barbarians alike'.

Bibliography and Further Reading

The books I list fall into one or both of two categories: those I found myself referring to most often, and those I particularly enjoyed for their broader overviews or different perspectives, or for their deeper investigation of individual topics and their web of footnotes and references. Unfortunately, some are hard to lay hands on outside university libraries but tracking them down is well worth the effort.

THE ANCIENT VOICES

There are several translations of the *Historia* and I list three below. Aubrey de Selincourt's *Penguin Classic* has been a standard-bearer for the series for 65 years and is now in its second revised edition. Tom Holland presents Herodotus as 'the most entertaining of historians' in the first line of his preface, and his version lives up to this, capturing as it does the voice of a master storyteller. Thirdly, *The Landmark Herodotus* (Strassler) has been a close companion for more than ten years and my copy is almost worn out. The introduction and 21 appendices contributed by a stellar conference line-up of scholars, expert in as many different facets of Herodotus and the Persian War, together fill 160 of its 1,000 plus pages; the 100-page index is a meal in itself. The *Cambridge Greek and Latin Classics* 'green and yellow' editions of Herodotus *Book 8* (Bowie) and *Book 9* (Flower & Marincola) proved themselves 'essential for exploring the meaning (or range of possible meanings)' of the text, to quote slightly out of context from the latter's back cover. Working on the earlier books of Herodotus, I made extensive use of the commentaries of Macan and How & Wells, accessible online alongside the venerable *Loeb Classical Library* parallel text and translation. I also list editions of *Aeschylus Persae* (Garvie) and *Timotheus* (Jansson). Nearly all the primary sources I have used can be accessed in the original language and in translation via Tuft University's *Perseus Digital Library* (http://www.perseus. tufts.edu). Heartfelt thanks to Professor Gregory Crane and his Perseus Project team for creating and maintaining this invaluable and immense resource.

Bowie, A.M., *Herodotus Histories Book VIII*, Cambridge: Cambridge University Press, 2007

de Selincourt, Aubrey (trans.), Marincola J. (rev.) *Herodotus the Histories*, London: Penguin Classics, 1972

Flower, Michael A. and Marincola, John, *Herodotus Histories Book IX*, Cambridge: Cambridge University Press, 2002

Garvie, A.F., *Aeschylus Persae*, Oxford: Oxford University Press, 2009

Green, Peter, *Diodorus Siculus, Books 11–12.37.1: Greek History, 480–431 BC – The Alternative Version*, Austin: University of Texas Press, 2010

Holland, Tom, *Herodotus the Histories*, London: Penguin Classics, 2013

Jansson, T.H., *Timotheus Persae, a Commentary*, Amsterdam: Hakkert, 1984

Mynott, Jeremy, *Thucydides the War of the Peloponnesians and the Athenians*, Cambridge: Cambridge University Press, 2013

Scott-Kilvert, Ian, *Plutarch the Rise and Fall of Athens: Nine Greek Lives*, London: Penguin Classics, 1960

Sommerstein, Alan H. (trans.), *Aeschylus The Persians and Other Plays*, London: Penguin Classics, 2010

Strassler, Robert B. (ed.) and Purvis, Andrea L. (trans.), *The Landmark Herodotus*, New York: Pantheon, 2007

HISTORICAL OVERVIEW AND BACKGROUND

At the reference end of the spectrum, the two editions of *Cambridge Ancient History* Volume IV, in close to 1,700 pages, authoritatively present the Persian War in the context of all the major cultural and political developments in the Mediterranean and Near Eastern world of the time. The *Barrington Atlas* (Talbert) is unequalled in quality and scale, and in price. I list seven comprehensive histories of the war, all valuable and illustrative of the different architectures that can be applied to Professor Sabin's 'inverted pyramid'. *Persian Fire* (Holland), the most recently published, stands out as the essential introduction and overview. *The Classical World* (Lane Fox) places the Persian War in the broad sweep of history over the nine centuries from the beginnings of the Archaic era in Greece to Hadrian's Rome. Of the remaining ten titles, five focus on central characters, Herodotus, Themistocles and Xerxes, five on the war's two main adversaries: Hellenes and Barbarians. The list concludes with Noah Whatley's wise and comprehensive advice on how to do Ancient Military History, first publicly delivered almost 100 years ago and not diminished by age in any way.

Boardman, John, Hammond, N.G.L., Lewis, D.M. and Ostwald, M., *Cambridge Ancient History*, Vol. IV (2nd edition): *Persia, Greece and the Western Mediterranean c.525–479 BC*, Cambridge: Cambridge University Press, 1988

Bridges, Emma, *Imagining Xerxes*, London: Bloomsbury, 2015

Burn, A.R., *Persia and the Greeks: The Defense of the West 546–478 BC*, Stanford: Stanford University Press, 1962

Bury, J.B., Cook, S.A. and Adcock, F.E., *Cambridge Ancient History*, Vol. IV: *The Persian Empire and the West*, Cambridge: Cambridge University Press, 1926

Cartledge, Paul, *Ancient Greece: A Very Short Introduction*, Oxford: Oxford University Press, 2009

Cawkwell, George, *The Greek Wars: The Failure of Persia*, Oxford: Oxford University Press, 2011

Cook, J.M., *The Persian Empire*, London: Dent, 1983

Garland, Robert, *Athens Burning: The Persian Invasion of Greece and the Evacuation of Attica*, Baltimore: Johns Hopkins University Press, 2017

Green, Peter, *The Greco-Persian Wars*, Berkeley: University of California Press, 1996

Grundy, G.B., *The Great Persian War and its Preliminaries*, London: John Murray, 1901

Hall, Edith, *Introducing the Ancient Greeks*, London: Bodley Head, 2015

Hart, John, *Herodotus and Greek History*, London: Croom Helm, 1993

Hignett, C., *Xerxes' Invasion of Greece*, Oxford: Oxford University Press, 1963

Holland, Tom, *Persian Fire: The First World Empire and the Battle for the West*, London: Little, Brown, 2005

Lane Fox, Robin, *The Classical World: An Epic History of Greece and Rome*, London: Allen Lane, 2005

Lazenby, J.F., *The Defence of Greece, 490–479 BC*, Warminster: Aris & Phillips, 1993

Podlecki, A.J., *The Life of Themistocles: A Critical Survey of the Literary and Archaeological Evidence*, Montreal: McGill-Queen's University Press, 1975

Roberts, Jennifer T., *Herodotus: A Very Short Introduction*, Oxford: Oxford
    University Press, 2011
Stoneman, Richard, *Xerxes: A Persian Life*, New Haven: Yale University
    Press, 2015
Talbert, Richard J.A., *Barrington Atlas of the Greek and Roman World*,
    Princeton: Princeton University Press, 2000
Vlassopoulos, Kostas, *Greeks and Barbarians*, Cambridge: Cambridge
    University Press, 2013
Waters, Matt, *Ancient Persia: A Concise History of the Achaemenid Empire
    550–330 BCE*, Cambridge: Cambridge University Press, 2014
Whatley, N., 'On the Possibility of Reconstructing Marathon and Other
    Ancient Battles', *Journal of Hellenic Studies* 84, 1964; also in Wheeler,
    Everett, *The Armies of Classical Greece*, London: Routledge, 2007

HOPLITE WARFARE

The Persian War was a brief and very distinct episode during the long evolution of the hoplite way of war over the best part of four centuries and the fuller evidence for later battles and campaigns cannot be assumed to apply to this earlier, less well-documented conflict. The valuable insights gained through re-enactment (Matthew), gaming (Sabin) and scientific experimentation with replica weapons and defensive materials (Gabriel) have their limitations. Re-enactors do not mass in thousands and try to kill each other; however elaborate the simulation of a battle, it will still be a very simplified model of a much more complex reality; and the laboratory is as far removed as re-enactment and gaming are from the bloody dust of 'the dancing floor of Ares'.

Moreover, the Hellene warriors of the Persian War were responding to probably unique sets of circumstances in ways that did not fit in with any established tactical doctrine. But the diverse schools of thought on the hoplite way of war and its evolution are certainly worth exploring with this in mind, and are well represented below. *Men of Bronze* (Kagan), probably the best place to start, reviews the state of play in the perennial debate around 'the hoplite question' and moves it forward.

Campbell, Brian and Tritle, Lawrence A., *The Oxford Handbook of Warfare in
    the Classical World*, Oxford: Oxford University Press, 2013
Connolly, Peter, *Greece and Rome at War*, London: Greenhill Books, 2006
Gabriel, Richard A. and Metz, Karen S., *From Sumer to Rome: The Military
    Capabilities of Ancient Armies*, Westport: Greenwood Press, 1991
Hanson, Victor Davis, *The Western Way of War: Infantry Battle in Classical
    Greece* (2nd edition), Berkeley: University of California Press, 2009

Kagan, Donald and Viggiano, Gregory F., *Men of Bronze: Hoplite Warfare in Ancient Greece*, Princeton: Princeton University Press, 2013

Lazenby, J.F., *The Spartan Army* (reissue), Barnsley: Pen & Sword, 2015

Lissarrague, Francois, *L'autre guerrier: archers, peltastes, cavaliers dans l'imagerie Attique*, Paris: Editions de la Découverte, 1990

Matthew, Christopher, *A Storm of Spears*, Barnsley: Pen & Sword, 2012

Pritchett, W.K., *Studies in Ancient Greek Topography* (vols I–V), Berkeley: University of California Press, 1965–85

Pritchett, W.K., *The Greek State at War* (vols I–V), Berkeley: University of California Press, 1971–91

Sabin, Philip, van Wees, Hans and Whitby, Michael, *Cambridge History of Greek and Roman Warfare I: Greece, the Hellenistic World and the Rise of Rome*, Cambridge: Cambridge University Press, 2007

Sabin, Philip, *Lost Battles: Reconstructing the Great Clashes of the Ancient World*, London: Hambledon Continuum, 2007

Schwartz, Adam, *Reinstating the Hoplite: Arms, Armour and Phalanx Fighting in Archaic and Classical Greece*, Stuttgart: Franz Steiner Verlag, 2010

Sidebottom, Harry, *Ancient Warfare: A Very Short Introduction*, Oxford: Oxford University Press, 2004

Sekunda, Nicholas, *The Persian Army 560–330 BC*, Oxford: Osprey Publishing, 1992

Sekunda, Nicholas, *Greek Hoplite 480–323 BC*, Oxford: Osprey Publishing, 2000

Snodgrass, A.M., *Arms and Armor of the Greeks*, Baltimore: Johns Hopkins University Press, 1999

van Wees, Hans, *Greek Warfare: Myths and Realities*, London: Duckworth, 2004

THE TRIREME AND NAVAL WARFARE

The construction and sea trials of *Olympias* answered all the main questions and resolved the long debate about the construction and operation of this complex and sophisticated warship. *The Athenian Trireme* (Morrison et al., 2000) is a fascinating account of the whole experiment.

Casson, Lionel, *Ships and Seamanship in the Ancient World*, Baltimore: Johns Hopkins University Press, 1995

Custance, Rear Admiral Sir Reginald N., *War at Sea, Modern Theory and Ancient Practice*, London: William Blackwood and Sons, 1919; reissued London: Conway Maritime Press, 1970

Hale, John R., *Lords of the Sea: The Epic Story of the Athenian Navy and the Birth of Democracy*, London: Penguin Books, 2010

Morrison, J.S. and Williams, R.T., *Greek Oared Ships, 900–322 BC*, Cambridge: Cambridge University Press, 1968

Morrison, J.S., Coates, J.F. and Rankov, N.B., *The Athenian Trireme: The History and Reconstruction of an Ancient Greek Warship*, Cambridge: Cambridge University Press (2nd edition), 2000

Rankov, Boris, *Trireme Olympias the Final Report: Sea Trials 1992–4 Conference Papers*, Oxford: Oxbow Books, 2012

Shaw, Timothy, *The Trireme Project: Operational Experience 1987–90, Lessons Learnt*, Oxford: Oxbow Books, 1993

MARATHON, THERMOPYLAE, SALAMIS AND PLATAEA

Which was the most important battle: *Marathon: How One Battle Changed Western Civilization*; *Thermopylae: The Battle that Changed the World*; *Salamis: The Naval Encounter that Saved Greece – and Western Civilization*? But Herodotus had it right. To him, Plataea was 'the most glorious victory ever seen', although it scarcely features in the numerous compilations listing 'the greatest battles of history', whereas Marathon, Thermopylae and Salamis are very well represented. There are no books solely dedicated to the battles of Artemisium and Mycale. The sources pay less attention to them than to the other four battles, largely because each was overshadowed by a more celebrated battle fought on or around the same days.

Marathon, Thermopylae, Salamis and *Plataea* are respectively volumes 108, 188, 222 and 239 in Osprey's unique Campaign series in which a compact but detailed narrative is supported by meticulously researched battlescene artwork, three-dimensional 'birds-eye-views' maps and numerous photographs; *Salamis* and *Plataea* (Shepherd) respectively include sections on Artemisium and Mycale. Visual representation does not add authority to the verbal narrative, but it adds discipline to the process of reconstruction by reducing ambiguity and by illuminating the choices made from amongst the options offered by the evidence; in short, it concentrates the mind.

Marathon's 2,500th anniversary was marked by the publication of three books within months of each other in 2010–11 (Billows, Lacy, Krentz), just three of the 400 items dating from the 1850s to 2012 in Fink's comprehensive bibliography.

Billows, Richard A., *Marathon: How One Battle Changed Western Civilization*, London: Overlook Duckworth, 2010

Fink, Dennis L., *The Battle of Marathon in Scholarship: Research, Theories and Controversies Since 1850*, Jefferson: McFarland, 2014

Krentz, Peter, *The Battle of Marathon*, New Haven: Yale University Press, 2010

Lacey, Jim, *The First Clash: The Miraculous Greek Victory at Marathon and its Impact on Western Civilization*, New York: Bantam Books, 2011

Lagos, Constantinos and Karianos, Fotis; Carr, John (trans.), *Who Really Won the Battle of Marathon? A Bold Re-appraisal of One of History's Most Famous Battles*, Barnsley: Pen & Sword, 2019

Sekunda, Nicholas, *Marathon 490 BC: The First Persian Invasion of Greece* (Campaign 108), Oxford: Osprey Publishing, 2002

Thermopylae is level with the battle of Marathon in terms of popular recognition and exceeds it in mythic status. 'Thermopylae: Herodotus versus the Legend' (van Wees) examines the immediate reasons for this, demonstrating that it was founded on a 'Spartan version' of what took place. Paul Cartledge explores the battle's historical context and its afterlife as inspiration, legend and symbol through antiquity to the modern era. Stephen Pressfield and Frank Miller extend the legend into fiction, the former respectably historical and a gripping read, the latter through a best-selling graphic novel, outrageously unhistorical and laced with toxic ideology, but compelling in its way (and then there's the movie...).

Cartledge, Paul, *Thermopylae: The Battle that Changed the World*, London: Macmillan, 2006

Fields, Nic, *Thermopylae 480 BC: Last Stand of the 300* (Campaign 188), Oxford: Osprey Publishing, 2007

Golding, William, *The Hot Gates and other occasional pieces*, London: Faber & Faber, 1965

Matthew, Christopher & Trundle, Matthew, *Beyond the Gates of Fire: New Perspectives on the Battle of Thermopylae*, Barnsley: Pen & Sword, 2013

Miller, Frank, *300*, Milwaukee: Dark Horse, 2000

Pressfield, Steven, *Gates of Fire: An Epic Novel of the Battle of Thermopylae*, London, Doubleday, 1998

Van Wees, H., 'Thermopylae: Herodotus versus the Legend', in van Gils, L., de Jong, I. and Kroon, C. (eds), *Textual Strategies in Ancient War Narrative Thermopylae, Cannae and Beyond*, Leiden: Brill, 2018

Salamis: *La Bataille de Salamine* (Rados) is, like *War at Sea, Modern Theory and Ancient Practice* (Custance, above), of more than antiquarian interest. Rados was a Greek scholar and naval historian who naturally associated Salamis with Lepanto. Custance was an admiral in the Royal Navy when Britannia could still claim to rule the waves. Both offer intriguing insights but are also reminders of Whatley's caution against superimposing the terminology and doctrines of later wars on the evidence of the ancient past.

Garland, Robert, *Athens Burning: The Persian Invasion of Greece and the Evacuation of Attica*, Baltimore: Johns Hopkins University Press, 2017
Rados, Constantin N., *La bataille de Salamine*, Paris: Fontemoing et Cie, 1915
Shepherd, William, *Salamis 480 BC: The Naval Campaign that Saved Greece* (Campaign 222), Oxford: Osprey Publishing, 2010
Strauss, Barry, *The Battle of Salamis: The Naval Encounter that Saved Greece – and Western Civilization*, New York: Simon & Schuster, 2004

Plataea: When I began work on my contributions to the Osprey Campaign series, searches for books with Plataea in the title threw up nothing but Wright's 1904 survey of the literary sources and Grundy's scholarly study of the battlefield's topography published in 1894, when the landscape could have matched its 5th-century form considerably more closely than it does today. I was quite excited by the prospect of remedying what I saw as more than a century of neglect. Then two books appeared in quick succession, *La bataille de Platées* (Corvisier) and *After Thermopylae* (Cartledge). The former is similar in scope to an Osprey Campaign but a less visual treatment. In the latter, as in the author's *Thermopylae*, a concise account of the fighting lies at the heart of an examination of the Oath of Plataea and that battle's afterlife in competing Hellene memories of their victory, particularly in the context of the Peloponnesian War.

Cartledge, Paul, *After Thermopylae: The Oath of Plataea and the End of the Graeco-Persian Wars*, Oxford: Oxford University Press, 2013
Corvisier, Jean-Nicolas, *La bataille de Platées, 479 av. J.-C.*, Clermont-Ferrand: Les Editions Maison, 2010
Grundy, G.B., *The Battle of Plataea*, London: John Murray, 1894
Shepherd, William, *Plataea 479 BC: The Most Glorious Victory Ever Seen* (Campaign 239), Oxford, Osprey Publishing, 2012
Wright, Henry Burt, *The Campaign of Plataea*, New Haven: Tuttle, Morehouse & Taylor, 1904

Index